1817–2011

The Official Catholic Directory®
Anno Domini 2011
Part II

The Official Catholic Directory, Part II 2011

Published by P.J. Kenedy & Sons in association with National Register Publishing

Chief Executive Officer	Fred Marks
Chief Financial Officer	Vincent Papa
Chief Technology Officer	Ariel Spivakovsky

PUBLISHERS

Co-Publisher	Robert Docherty
Co-Publisher	Jeanne LoGiurato Hanline

EDITORIAL

Managing Editor	Eileen Fanning
Content Manager	Sara Morgenroth
Content Editors	Linda Hummer
	Elizabeth Melillo
	Mary J. Whitehouse

EDITORIAL SERVICES

Production Manager	David Lubanski

MARKETING

Creative Services Manager	Kathleen F. Stein

BOOK SALES

Director of Sales	Kelli MacKinnon
Wholesale Account Representative	Gina Marie Delia

ADVERTISING/SALES

Account Executive	Anne Collins

INFORMATION TECHNOLOGY

Composition Programmer	Tom Haggerty

Published by P.J. Kenedy & Sons in association with National Register Publishing

Printed and bound in the United States of America

International Standard Book Number: 978-0-87217-011-7
International Standard Serial Number: 0078-3854
Library of Congress Catalog Card Number: 81-30961

God Hears Every Prayer
Expand the power of prayer by joining with parishioners around the world.

Ordination Class of 2011

Diocese of Albany
Rev. Jay Atherton

Diocese of Amarillo
Rev. Haider Quintero

Diocese of Arlington
Rev. Luke Dundon

Archdiocese of Atlanta
Rev. Joshua Allen
Rev. Charles Okeke
Rev. Juan Jose Sanchez Teran

Diocese of Austin
Rev. John Paul Hudson

Archdiocese of Baltimore
Rev. Warren Tanghe

Diocese of Baton Rouge
Rev. Christopher Todd Lloyd
Rev. P. Brent Maher

Diocese of Belleville
Rev. Anthony O. Onyango

Diocese of Birmingham
Rev. Vincent Bresowar

Diocese of Bismarck
Rev. William Ruelle
Rev. Jason Signalness

Diocese of Biloxi
Rev. Ryan McCoy

Archdiocese of Boston
Rev. Michael Farrell
Rev. Sean Patrick Hurley, F.P.O.

Diocese of Brooklyn
Rev. Rodnev Lapommeray
Rev. Daniel Rajski

Diocese of Brownsville
Rev. Manuel-Alfredo Razo Canales
Rev. Marco Reynoso
Rev. Joaquin Zermeno

Diocese of Buffalo
Rev. Steven Jekielek
Rev. Daniel Serbicki

Diocese of Burlington
Rev. James Dodson
Rev. Mark Murphy

Diocese of Charleston
Rev. David Nerbun

Archdiocese of Chicago
Rev. Lorenzo Gamboa Cadena
Rev. Heman Cuevas
Rev. Elliott Richard Dees
Rev. Orlando Flores
Rev. John G. Hetland
Rev. Joel Medina, S.J.
Rev. Filbert Ngwila
Rev. Collins Kisaka Nyache
Rev. Phillip T. Owen
Rev. Wojciech Jan Oleksy
Rev. Gosbertus Rwezahura

Archdiocese of Cincinnati
Rev. Daniel K. Hess
Rev. Adam D. Puntel
Rev. C. Scott Wright

Diocese of Cleveland
Rev. Charles Butkowski
Rev. Franz Dool
Rev. John Schneider
Rev. Joseph Seebauer
Rev. Christopher Zerucha

Diocese of Colorado Springs
Rev. Charles Dygert

Diocese of Columbus
Rev. Ryan Schmit
Rev. Tyron Tomson

Diocese of Corpus Christi
Rev. Joseph Thang Nguyen

Diocese of Covington
Rev. Nicholas Rottman

Diocese of Dallas
Rev. Alan McDonald
Rev. James Yamauchi

Archdiocese of Denver
Rev. Brian Larkin
Rev. Braden Wagner
Rev. Michael Wagner
Rev. Grzegorz Wojcik

Diocese of Des Moines
Rev. Guthrie Dolan

Archdiocese of Detroit
Rev. Eric Fedewa
Rev. Rafal Ligenza
Rev. Stephen Pullis

Diocese of Dodge City
Rev. Donald Bedore

Archdiocese of Dubuque
Rev. Noah J. Diehm
Rev. Anthony J. Kruse

Diocese of Duluth
Rev. Anthony Craig

Diocese of Erie
Rev. Jason R. Feigh

Diocese of El Paso
Rev. Mariano Lopez

Diocese of Fargo
Rev. Christopher Markman
Rev. Neil Pfeife

Diocese of Fort Wayne-South Bend
Rev. Matthew Coonan
Rev. Terrence Coonan, Jr.

Diocese of Fort Worth
Rev. Philip Petta

Archdiocese of Galveston-Houston
Rev. Jude Ezuma
Rev. Eurel Manzano
Rev. Victor Perez

Diocese of Grand Island
Rev. Neal Hock

Diocese of Grand Rapids
Rev. Luis F. Garcia

Diocese of Green Bay
Rev. William J. Brunner
Rev. Luke A. Ferris

Diocese of Harrisburg
Rev. Brian J. Wayne

Archdiocese of Hartford
Rev. Cidouane Joseph, O.F.M.
Rev. Diego Alejandro Jimenez Olaya
Rev. George Mukuka

Diocese of Helena
Rev. David Severson

Diocese of Houma-Thibodaux
Rev. Andre Melancon

Archdiocese of Indianapolis
Rev. Dustin Boehm

Diocese of Jefferson City, MO
Rev. Nicholas Reid

Diocese of Joliet
Rev. Steven Borello

Diocese of Kalamazoo
Rev. Ted Martin

Archdiocese of Kansas City, KS
Rev. Barry Clayton
Rev. Michael Peterson

Diocese of Lafayette, LA
Rev. Joshua Bennett
Rev. Nathan Comeaux
Rev. David Hebert
Rev. Garrett McIntyre
Rev. Johnathan Janise
Rev. Sean Pogue
Rev. Anthony Rowland

Diocese of Lafayette in Indiana
Rev. Matt Arbuckle

Diocese of Lake Charles
Rev. Scott Conner
Rev. John Huckaby
Rev. Jeffrey Starkovich

Diocese of Lansing
Rev. Jonathan Perrotta
Rev. David Rosenberg

Diocese of Laredo
Rev. Joel Perez

Diocese of Lexington
Rev. Jeffrey Estacio
Rev. Richard Watson

Diocese of Lincoln
Rev. Matthew Zimmer

Archdiocese of Los Angeles
Rev. Augustine Chang
Rev. David Genders
Rev. Jose Martinez
Rev. Michael Perucho
Rev. Patrick Sheridan

Archdiocese of Louisville
Rev. Matthew Hardesty

Diocese of Madison
Rev. Jorge Miramontes-Medina
Rev. Timothy Renz

Diocese of Manchester
Rev. Kyle Stanton

Diocese of Marquette
Rev. Nicholas Thompson

Diocese of Metuchen
Rev. Heherson Balabbo, C.M.F.
Rev. Lukasz Blicharski
Rev. Martin Espinoza
Rev. Leopoldo S. Salvania

Archdiocese of Miami
Rev. Jose Vanegas

Archdiocese of Milwaukee
Rev. Hugo Armando Londoño Gallego
Rev. Christopher Klusman

Archdiocese of Mobile
Rev. Travis J. Burnett
Rev. Stephen G. Vrazel

Diocese of Nashville
Rev. Leon Gerald Strange

Archdiocese of New Orleans
Rev. Chris DeLerno
Rev. Bryan Howard
Rev. Jeffrey C. Johnson, S.J.
Rev. Dominic Pham
Rev. Aaron Pidel
Rev. Frank Zero

Diocese of New Ulm
Rev. Zachary Peterson

Archdiocese of New York
Rev. Erick Lopez
Rev. Adaly Rosado
Rev. Jeremiah Shryock
Rev. Giuseppe Maria Siniscalchi
Rev. Daniel Williamson

Archdiocese of Newark
Rev. Eduardo A. Bustamante
Rev. Hong-Ray Peter Cho
Rev. John C. DeSousa
Rev. Frank J. Fano
Rev. Paul C. Houlis
Rev. John R. Job
Rev. Yeongmin Kim
Rev. Zbigniew Kukielka
Rev. Robert P. McLaughlin
Rev. Juan P. Morales
Rev. Marco Pacciana
Rev. Alfie A. Pangilinan
Rev. Janusz Pigan
Rev. Roy B. Regaspi
Rev. Mayhel A. Velasquez
Rev. Pedro E. Vilchez
Rev. Kevin G. Waymel
Rev. Rolando Rosendo DeGracia Yadao

Diocese of Norwich
Rev. Luis Henry Agudelo

Diocese of Oakland
Rev. Alexander Castillo
Rev. Edilberto Castanas
Rev. Rafal Duda
Rev. Mark Francis Manzano
Rev. Tammylee Ngo
Rev. Gerald Pedrera
Rev. Jojo Puthussery, M.F.

Archdiocese of Omaha
Rev. Andrew Syring
Rev. Kevin Vogel

Diocese of Orange, CA
Rev. Nicolas Nguyen
Rev. Daniel Reader
Rev. Quan Tran

Diocese of Palm Beach
Rev. Dominic Toan Thien Thanh Tran

Diocese of Paterson
Rev. Roberto Amador
Rev. Pawel Bala
Rev. Jared J. Brogan
Rev. Michael Lee
Rev. Jose Lopez
Rev. Leonardo Lopez
Rev. Marcin Michalowski
Rev. Ricardo Ortega
Rev. Raimundo Rivera

Diocese of Pensacola-Tallahassee
Rev. Thomas Dillon
Rev. Timothy Holeda
Rev. Matthew Worthen

Archdiocese of Philadelphia
Rev. Kenneth Brabazon, Jr
Rev. David Friel
Rev. Christopher Landis
Rev. James McCabe

Diocese of Pittsburgh
Rev. Christopher Donley
Rev. Michael Roche

Archdiocese of Portland in Oregon
Rev. Mark Gikenyi
Rev. Bryce McProud

Diocese of Providence
Rev. Stephen Dandeneau

Diocese of Pueblo
Rev. Michael Chrisman

Diocese of Raleigh
Rev. Brendan K. Buckler

Diocese of Rapid City
Rev. Nathan Sparks

Diocese of Richmond
Rev. Eric Ayers

Diocese of Rochester
Rev. Scott Caton

Diocese of Rockford
Rev. Michael Chernetzk
Rev. Christopher DiTomo
Rev. Joseph Jaskierny
Rev. Joel Lopez
Rev. Johnson Lopez
Rev. Keith Romke
Rev. Adalberto Sanchez Mejia

Diocese of Rockville Centre
Rev. Richard John Mary Mastrogiacomo
Rev. Dennis Anthony Suglia

Diocese of Sacramento
Rev. Jeffrey Henry
Rev. Brian Soliven

Diocese of Saginaw
Rev. Edwin Dwyer
Rev. J. Marcel Portelli
Rev. Nathan Harburg
Rev. Robert P. Schikora

Diocese of Salina
Rev. Charles Awotwi

Diocese of San Angelo
Rev. Joseph Prem Sunil Thumma

Diocese of San Bernardino
Rev. Peter Phan

Diocese of San Jose
Rev. Angelo David
Rev. Steve Kim

Diocese of Savannah
Rev. Dawid Kwiatkowski

Archdiocese of Seattle
Rev. Paul Brunet
Rev. Brad Hagelin
Rev. Bryan Ochs

Diocese of Sioux Falls
Rev. Kristopher Cowles

Diocese of Spokane
Rev. Jeffrey Core
Rev. Jason Hiner
Rev. Jeffrey Lewis
Rev. Tyler Smedley

Diocese of Springfield, IL
Rev. Brian Alford

Diocese of Springfield, MA
Rev. Raymond Cordani
Rev. Ryan Rooney
Rev. Michael James Wood, Jr.

Diocese of St. Cloud
Rev. Matthew Crane
Rev. John Knopik

Archdiocese of St. Louis
Rev. Timothy Foy
Rev. Joseph Grilliot
Rev. Joseph Minuth

Archdiocese of St. Paul and Minneapolis
Rev. Jonathan Kelly
Rev. Cole Kracke
Rev. James Lannan
Rev. Nathan LaLiberte
Rev. Anthony O'Neill

Diocese of Steubenville
Rev. Michael Gossett

Diocese of Stockton
Rev. Jeffrey Wilson

Diocese of Syracuse
Rev. James A. Schultz

Diocese of Toledo
Rev. Jerome "Jerry" Schetter
Rev. Philip Smith

Diocese of Trenton
Rev. Todd Carter
Rev. Fernando Lopez

Diocese of Tulsa
Rev. Jorge Gomez
Rev. Michael Pratt

Diocese of Tyler
Rev. Brandon Bernhard
Rev. Hank Lanik

Archdiocese of Washington
Rev. R. Alejandro Diaz-Caceres
Rev. Michael Okechukwu
Rev. Michael Paris

Diocese of Wichita
Rev. Marco A. de Loera
Rev. Daniel J. Duling
Rev. Jeremy S. Huser
Rev. John P. Fogliasso

Diocese of Wilmington
Rev. Joseph McQuaide, IV
Rev. John Solomon

Diocese of Worcester
Rev. Guillermo J. Ochoa

Diocese of Youngstown
Rev. Michael Marcelli
Rev. Ernesto Rodriguez
Rev. Jeffrey Stealey
Rev. Stephen Zeigler

Holy Protection of Mary Byzantine Catholic Eparchy
Rev. Diodoro Mendoza

Eparchy of St. Thomas the Apostle (Chaldean), MI
Rev. Pierre Konja

Religious Order Priests
Rev. John Britto Antony, C.S.C.
Rev. Hyacinth Marie Cordell, O.P.
Rev. Angelo Casimiro, M.I.C.
Rev. J Patrick Hough, S.J.

Rev. Austin Litke, O.P.
Rev. Dominic McManus, O.P.
Rev. Cassian Sama, O.P.
Rev. Paul M. Ybarra, C.S.C.

Diocese of Ordination not known at time of publication

Rev. Anthony Bui
Rev. Nicholas Blaha
Rev. Tom Cannon
Rev. Brian W. Capuano
Rev. Gregorio Congote
Rev. Hugo Esparza-Perez
Rev. Ryan Ford
Rev. Joseph Grilliot
Rev. Iain Highet
Rev. Dominic Huynh
Rev. Radmar Jao
Rev. John Lee
Rev. Michael Leschinsky
Rev. Hugo Londono
Rev. Manny B. Lopez
Rev. James Lowe
Rev. Juan Medina
Rev. Leonar Mejia
Rev. Anton Miranda
Rev. Jose Alexander Gaitan Montes
Rev. George Sombe Mukuka
Rev. Dat Nguyen
Rev. Joseph Minh Nguyen
Rev. Rheo Ofalsa
Rev. James Phan
Rev. Nelson Rivera
Rev. Michael Roemmele
Rev. Benjamin Romero
Rev. Alejandro Orlando Augustinus Saenz
Rev. Rodolfo Salinas
Rev. Cory Stanley
Rev. Anthony J. Stoeppel
Rev. Dariusz Strzelecki
Rev. Carlos D. Suarez
Rev. Michal Tomaszawski
Rev. Bao Trung Tran
Rev. Robert LaMar Turner, II
Rev. Peter Tynan
Rev. Rodrigo Ulloa-Chavarry
Rev. Anthony Joseph Urban
Rev. Adam Verona
Rev. Stephen Vrazel
Rev. James Weeder
Rev. Riley Williams

2011 Newly Ordained Priests List courtesy of The United States Conference of Catholic Bishops (USCCB); list supplemented with data from The Official Catholic Directory; 299 of the 467 newly ordained priests (Source: Center for Applied Research in the Apostolate; CARA) are listed above. For more information about the Ordination Class of 2011, including a report prepared by CARA, visit http://www.usccb.org/beliefs-and-teachings/vocations/ordination-class/class-of-2011/index.cfm.

The Official Catholic Directory®

P.J. Kenedy & Sons, Publishers

Since 1817

FOREWORD

Throughout our long history of publishing, the primary goal of **The Official Catholic Directory®** has always been to provide a detailed and thorough portrait of the Roman Catholic Church in the United States.

As in years past, we have provided the very useful Archdioceses and Dioceses of the World listings. In this section, with permission granted by the publishers of the Annuario Pontificio, we have an alphabetical list of all the Archdioceses and Dioceses of the world. Listings contain the ordinary of the (arch)diocese, telephone, fax, email and website which are useful in securing sacramental records and facilitating communication.

The second area of **Part II** is the new and updated (arch)diocesan information not appearing in the main volume.

As with the main volume of **The Official Catholic Directory 2011**, it is with pleasure that we present **The Official Catholic Directory 2011 Part II**.

Sincerely,

Jeanne LoGiurato Hanline
Co-Publisher

Table of Contents

Archdioceses & Dioceses of the World 1

Archdioceses & Dioceses of the World—Geographic Index 77

Alphabetical List of the Cardinals, Archbishops, Bishops, Archabbots and Abbots of the United States 87

Archdioceses and Dioceses in the United States and U.S. Territories 95

The Official Catholic Directory® 2011

Archdioceses & Dioceses of the World

As foreign organizations, these entities are not included in the United States Conference of Catholic Bishops Group Ruling tax exemption ruling.

P.J. Kenedy & Sons
in association with National Register Publishing.
300 Connell Drive, Suite 2000, Berkeley Heights, NJ 07922

Archdioceses & Dioceses of the World

Permission granted by the Vatican Secretariat of State, Vatican Perss-Libreria Editrice Vaticana-Annuario Pontificio, in using the 2011 edition of the Annuario Pontificio as the principal source for information regarding Archdioceses and Dioceses of the World

A

Aachen—Most Rev. Heinrich Mussinghoff; Klosterplatz 7, Aachen, D-52062, Germany.
Tel: 49-0241-45-20 ***Fax:*** 49-0241-45-24-96
Email: bistum-aachen@bistum-aachen.de

Aba—Most Rev. Vincent Valentine Egwuchukwu Ezeonyia, C.S.Sp.; Bishop's Office P.O. Box 7526, Aba, Abia State, Nigeria.
Tel: 080-331-11-464
Email: regis@skannet.com

Abaetetuba—Most Rev. Flavio Giovenale, S.D.B.; C.P. 10, Rua Padre Luíz Varela 1636, Abaetetuba, PA 68440-000, Brazil.
Tel: 55-091-3751-1088 ***Fax:*** 55-091-3751-1883
Email: abaete.diocese@uol.com.br

Abakaliki—Most Rev. Michael Nnachi Okoro; Bishop's House, St. Teresa's Cathedral P.O. Box 90, Abakaliki, Ebonyi State, Nigeria.
Tel: 080-379-57-411; 080-347-41-496
Email: cdapastcom@yahoo.com

Abancay—Most Rev. Gilber Gomez Gonzalez; Apartado 42, Plaza de Armas s/n, Abancay, Apurímac, Peru.
Tel: 51-83-32-11-36 ***Fax:*** 51-83-32-16-50
Email: obispadoabancay@speedy.com.pe

Abengourou—Most Rev. Gbaya Boniface Ziri; Evêché, B.P. 92, Abengourou, Ivory Coast.
Tel: 225-35-913-078 ***Fax:*** 225-35-913-078
Email: dioceseabeng@yahoo.fr

Abeokuta—Most Rev. Alfred Adewale Martins; Bishop's House P.O. Box 206, Ibara-Abeokuta, Ogun State, Nigeria.
Tel: 0803-322-2081
Email: cdabk@hotmail.com

Aberdeen—Most Rev. Hugh (Edward) Gilbert, O.S.B.; Bishop's House, 3 Queen's Cross, Aberdeen, AB15 4XU, Scotland.
Tel: 44-01224-31-9154 ***Fax:*** 44-01224-32-9154
Email: joyce@rcd-abdn.org

ABIDJAN—Most Rev. Jean-Pierre Kutwa; Archevêché, av. Jean Paul II, 01 B.P. 1287, Abidjan, 01, Ivory Coast.
Tel: 225-20-21-23-08/9 ***Fax:*** 225-20-21-40-22
Email: archevecheabidjan@aviso.ci

Abomey—Most Rev. Eugène Cyrille Houndékon; Evêché, B.P. 18, Abomey Zou, Benin.
Tel: 22-50-00-46 ***Fax:*** 22-50-00-47
Email: eveche_abomey@yahoo.fr

ABUJA—Most Rev. John Olorunfemi Onaiyekan; Archbishop's House-Area 3-Section 2 P.O. Box 286, Garki, Abuja, Federal Capital Territory, Nigeria.
Tel: 0803-451-1635

ACAPULCO—Most Rev. Carlos Garfias Merlos; Arzobispado, Quebrada 16, Acapulco, Geurrero, 39300, Mexico.
Tel: 52-74448-3-05-63 ***Fax:*** 52-74448-2-07-63
Email: tribunalecleac@hotmail.com

Acarigua-Araure—Most Rev. Joaquin José Morón Hidalgo; Avenida 38 con Calle 26, Barrio Paraguay, Acarigua 3101, Edo. Portuguesa, Venezuela.
Tel: 0255-622-64-43 ***Fax:*** 0255-622-29-96

ACCRA—Most Rev. Gabriel Charles Palmer-Buckle; Chancery Office P.O. Box GP 247, Accra, Ghana.
Tel: 030-22-22-728 ***Fax:*** 030-22-31-619

ACERENZA—Most Rev. Giovanni Ricchiuti; Curia Arcivescovile, Largo Consigliere Gala 14, Acerenza, Potenza, 85011, Italy.
Tel: 39-0971-749-221 ***Fax:*** 39-0971-741-921
Email: curia.acerenza@tiscali.it

Acerra—Most Rev. Salvatore Giovanni Rinaldi; Vescovado, Piazza Duomo 6, Acerra, Napoli, 80011, Italy.
Tel: 39-081-520-6717 ***Fax:*** 39-081-520-6717
Email: curia@diocesidiacerra.it

Achonry—Most Rev. Brendan Kelly; Bishop's House, St. Nathy's, Ballaghaderreen, Co. Roscommon, Ireland.
Tel: 094-98-60-021 ***Fax:*** 094-98-60-921
Email: bishop@achonrydiocese.org

Acireale—Most Rev. Antonino Raspanti; Vescovado, Largo Giovanni XXIII 3, Acireale, Catania, 95024, Italy.
Tel: 39-095-60-11-02 ***Fax:*** 39-095-763-10-00
Email: curia.acireale@tiscali.it

Acqui—Most Rev. Pier Giorgio Micchiardi; Vescovado, Piazza Duomo 9, Acqui Terme, Alessandria, 15011, Italy.
Tel: 39-0144-32-20-78 ***Fax:*** 39-0144-35-24-49
Email: curiavescovile@acquiterme.it

ADDIS ABEBA—Most Rev. Berhaneyesus Demerew Souraphiel, C.M.; Catholic Archbishop's House P.O. Box 21903, Addis Ababa, Ethiopia.
Tel: 251-011-111-16-67 ***Fax:*** 252-011-155-13-48
Email: ecs@ethionet.et

ADELAIDE—Most Rev. Philip Edward Wilson; G.P.O. Box 1364, Adelaide, S.A., 5001, Australia.
Tel: 61-08-8210-8108 ***Fax:*** 61-08-8223-2307
Email: vg@adelaide.catholic.org.au
Catholic Diocesan Centre 39 Wakefield St, Adelaide, S.A., 5000, Australia.

Adigrat—Most Rev. Tesfaselassie Medhin; P.O. Box 8, Adigrat, (Tigray), Ethiopia.
Tel: 203-034-445-43-94 ***Fax:*** 203-034-445-43-94
Email: aevg@ethionet.et

Adilabad—Most Rev. Joseph Kunnath, C.M.I.; S.H. Church, Near R.D.O. Office, P.O., Mancherial, Adilabad Dt., A.P., 504208, India.
Tel: 08736-258-262

Adria-Rovigo—Most Rev. Lucio Soravito de Franceschi; Via Giacomo Sichirollo 18, Rovigo, 45100, Italy.
Tel: 39-0425-2096-19 ***Fax:*** 39-0425-2096-13
Email: diocesi.adriarovigo@tin.it

Afogados da Ingazeira—Most Rev. Egidio Bisol; Residência Episcopal, Rua Dr. Roberto Nogueira Lima 366, Afogados da Ingazeira, PE, 56800-000, Brazil.
Tel: 55-087-3838-1201 ***Fax:*** 55-087-3838-1582
Email: diocafog@planetacyber.com.br

AGAÑA—Most Rev. Anthony Sablan Apuron, O.F.M.Cap., D.D. (AGN); Chancery Office - 196B, Cuesta San Ramon, Agaña, Guam, 96910, Oceania.
Tel: 671-472-6116 ***Fax:*** 671-477-3519

Agartala—Most Rev. Lumen Monteiro, C.S.C.; Jeevajyothi Diocesan Centre Airport Road, P.O. Durjoynagar, Agartala, Tripura, 799009, India.
Tel: 0381-234-24-01 ***Fax:*** 0381-234-29-69

Agats—Most Rev. Aloysius Murwito, O.F.M.; Keuskupan Agats, Kotak Pos 14, Timika, Papua, 99910, Indonesia.
Tel: 0902-31-056 ***Fax:*** 0902-31-058
Email: uskupagats@gmail.com

Agboville—Most Rev. Alexis Touabli Youlo; B.P. 122, Quartier Sambregnan, Agboville, Ivory Coast.
Tel: 225-23-56-62-74 ***Fax:*** 23-54-67-45
Email: evecheagboville@yahoo.fr

Agen—Most Rev. Hubert Herbreteau; Evêché, 5 rue Roger Johan, Agen, 47000, France.
Tel: 5-53-66-10-23 ***Fax:*** 5-53-47-14-88
Email: eveche.agen@catholique-agen.cef.fr

AGRA—Most Rev. Albert D'Souza; Archbishop's House, Wazirpura Rd., Agra, U.P., -282003, India.
Tel: 0562-2526-397; 0562-2851-318
Email: archdagra@yahoo.co.in

AGRIGENTO—Most Rev. Francesco Montenegro; Arcivescovado, Via Duomo 96, Agrigento, 92100, Italy.
Tel: 39-0922-49-0011 ***Fax:*** 39-0922-49-0024
Email: curia@diocesiag.it

Aguascalientes—Most Rev. José Maria De la Torre Martin; Obispado, Apartado 167, Venustiano Carranza 106, Aguascalientes, Ags., 20000, Mexico.
Tel: 52-449-915-32-61 ***Fax:*** 52-449-916-33-12

Ahiara—Vacant; Bishop's House P.M.B. 205, Ogbe, Ahiara, Ahiara Mbaise L.G.A., Imo State, Nigeria.
Tel: 0806-604-4235
Email: takwalo2000@yahoo.com

Ahmedabad—Most Rev. Thomas Ignatius Macwan; Bishop's House, Dr. Tankaria Rd., Mirzapur, Ahmedabad, Gujarat, 380001, India.
Tel: 079-2562-4105 ***Fax:*** 079-2563-1942

AHWAZ—Most Rev. Hanna Zora; Archbishop's House, Suleiman Farsi St., Bldg. 334, Ahwaz, Iran.
Tel: 98-061-222-4980

Aire et Dax—Most Rev. Philippe Jean Louis Breton; Evêché, B.P. 224, 40105 CEDEX, Dax, France.
100 avenue Francis Planté, Dax, 40100, France.
Tel: 5-58-56-59-90 ***Fax:*** 5-58-56-59-93

Aitape—Most Rev. Otto Separy; Bishop's House P.O. Box 179, Aitape, Sandaun Province, P.N.G. 553, Papua New Guinea.
Tel: 675-857-20-46/7 ***Fax:*** 675-857-20-56
Email: kdla@global.net.pg

AIX—Most Rev. Christophe Dufour; 7 Cours de la Trinité, Aix-en-Provence CEDEX 01, 13625, France.
Tel: 4-42-17-58-00 ***Fax:*** 4-42-17-58-12
Email: secretariat.archeveque@aixarles.cef.fr

Aizawl—Most Rev. Stephen Rotluanga, C.S.C.; Catholic Bishop's House, Ramthar Veng P.O. Box 45, Aizawl, Mizoram, 796001, India.
Tel: 0389-234-71-99 ***Fax:*** 0389-234-22-57
Email: mzbhouse@rediffmail.com

Ajaccio—Vacant; Evêché, 8 Blvd. Sylvestre Marcaggi, B.P. 306, Ajaccio, CEDEX, -20181, France.
Tel: 4-95-51-75-50 ***Fax:*** 4-95-51-75-60
Email: eveche-ajaccio@wanadoo.fr

Ajmer—Most Rev. Ignatius Menezes; Bishop's House Kaiserganj, Ajmer, Rajasthan, -305001, India.
Tel: 0145-2460-074
Email: aubertcar@hotmail.com

AKKA, SAN GIOVANNI D'ACRI, TOLEMAIDE—Most Rev. Elias Chacour; Archevêché, Grec-Catholique, B.P. 9450, rue Hagefen 33, Haifa, 31094, Israel.
Tel: 972-04-8508-105 ***Fax:*** 972-04-8508-106
Email: office@melkitegalilee.org

Alagoinhas—Most Rev. Paulo Romeu Dantas Bastos; Rua Dr. Manoel Vitorino 368, Alagoinhas, BA, 48005-500, Brazil.
Tel: 55-075-3421-1842 ***Fax:*** 55-075-3422-3209

Alajuela—Most Rev. Angel San Casimiro Fernández; Casa Episcopal, Dulce Nombre, La Garita, Apartado 943, Alajuela, 4050, Costa Rica.
Tel: 506-2433-60-05 ***Fax:*** 506-2433-60-05
Email: alajuela1921@racsa.co.cr

Alaminos—Most Rev. Marlo M. Peralta; Bishop's Residence, Alaminos, Pangasinan, 2404, Philippines.
Tel: 63-075-552-7062 ***Fax:*** 63-075-654-0043
Email: curia@dioceseofalaminos.org

Alba—Most Rev. Giacomo Lanzetti; Curia Vescovile, Piazza Mons. Grassi 9, Alba, Cuneo, 12051, Italy.
Tel: 39-0173-44-03-50 ***Fax:*** 39-0173-44-03-50
Email: curia@alba.chiesacattolica.it

ALBA IULIA—Most Rev. György-Miklós Jakubínyi; Arhiepiscopia Romano-Catolica, Str. Mihai Viteazul 21, Alba Iulia, RO-510010, Romania.
Tel: 40-0258-811-689 ***Fax:*** 40-0258-811-454
Email: ersekseg@romkat.ro

Albacete—Most Rev. Ciriaco Benavente Mateos; Obispado, Calle Salamanca 10, Albacete, 02001, Spain.
Tel: 34-967-21-44-78 ***Fax:*** 34-967-52-23-39
Email: obalbacete@planalfa.es

Albano—Most Rev. Marcello Semeraro; Curia Vescovile, Piazza della Rotonda 11, Albano Laziale, Roma, 00041, Italy.
Tel: 39-06-932-68-401 ***Fax:*** 39-06-932-38-44
Email: curia@diocesidialbano.it

Albany—Most Rev. Howard James Hubbard, D.D. (ALB); Chancery Office: Pastoral Center, 40 N. Main Ave., Albany, NY, 12203-1422.
Tel: 518-453-6600 ***Fax:*** 518-453-6795
Email: chancery@rcda.org

Albenga-Imperia—Most Rev. Mario Oliveri; Via Episcopio 5, Albenga, Savona, 17031, Italy.
Tel: 39-0182-50-288 ***Fax:*** 39-0182-51-440
Email: cancellarius.albingaunensis@gmail.com

ALBI—Most Rev. Jean Marie Henri Legrez, O.P.; 12 rue de la République, CEDEX 9, Albi, 81012, France.
Tel: 5-63-48-18-20 ***Fax:*** 5-63-48-18-21
Email: diocesealbi.accueil@wanadoo.fr

Alcalá de Henares—Most Rev. Juan Antonio Reig Pla; Obispado, Plaza de Palacio 1, Alcalá de Henares, 28801, Spain.
Tel: 34-91-888-27-00 ***Fax:*** 34-91-888-62-94
Email: diocesis@obispadoalcala.org

ALEP, BEROEA, HALAB—Most Rev. Jean-Clément Jeanbart; Archdiocese for Greek Catholics, 9 Place Farhat, B.P. 146, Alep, Syria.
Tel: 963-021-211-93-04/6 ***Fax:*** 963-021-211-93-08
Email: gr.melkcath@mail.sy

Alep, Beroea, Halab—Most Rev. Antoine Audo, S.J.; Eveche Chaldeen Catholique, 1 rue Patriarche Elias IV Mouawwad, Soulemaniye, B.P. 4643, Alep, Syria.
Tel: 963-021-444-16-60 ***Fax:*** 963-021-460-08-00

Alep, Beroea, Halab (Armenian)—Most Rev. Boutros Marayati; Archeveche Armenien-Catholique B.P. 97, 33 rue Tillel, Alep, -Syria.
Tel: 021-212-39-46 ***Fax:*** 021-211-66-37
Email: armen.cath@mail.sy

Alep, Beroea, Halab (Maronite)—Most Rev. Youssef Anis Abi-Aad; Archeveche Maronite 57 rue Fares-el-Khoury, B.P. 203, Alep, Syria.
Tel: 021-211-80-48 ***Fax:*** 021-212-30-48
Email: maronite-aleppo@net.sy

Alep, Beroea, Halab (Syrian)—Most Rev. Denys Antoine Chahda; Archeveche Syrien Catholique Place Mere Teresa de Calcutta, Azizie, Alep, Syria.
Tel: 021-212-67-50 ***Fax:*** 021-212-67-52

Ales-Terralba—Most Rev. Giovanni Dettori; Vescovado, Via Episcopio 7, Ales Oristano, 09091, Italy.
Tel: 39-0783-91-760 ***Fax:*** 39-0783-99-80-15
Email: curia@ales-terralba.chiesacattolica.it

Alessandria—Most Rev. Giuseppe Versaldi; Via del Vescovado 1, Alessandria, 15121, Italy.
Tel: 39-0131-51-22-11 ***Fax:*** 39-0131-44-48-97
Email: segreteriacuria@interfree.it

Alessandria of Copti—His Eminence S.B. Antonios Cardinal Naguib; Patriarcat Coptic Catholic, B.P. 69, 34 Rue Ibn Sandar, Saray El Koubbeh, Cairo, 11712, Egypt.
Tel: 02-2257-1740 ***Fax:*** 02-2454-5766
Email: residence50@gmail.com

Alexandria—Most Rev. Ronald Paul Herzog; P.O. Box 7417, Alexandria, LA, 71306-0417.
Tel: 318-445-2401 ***Fax:*** 318-448-6121
Email: msgrrhoppe@diocesealex.org
4400 Coliseum Blvd, Alexandria, LA, 71303.

Alexandria-Cornwall—Vacant; Centre diocésain, 220 Chemin Montreal, C.P. 1388, Cornwall, ON, K6H 5V4, Canada.
Tel: 613-933-1138 ***Fax:*** 613-937-4931
Email: diocese@alexandria-cornwall.ca

ALGER—Most Rev. Ghaleb Moussa Abdalla Bader; Archevêché, 13 rue Khelifa-Boukhalfa, Alger-Gare, 16000, Algeria.
Tel: 021-63-35-62 ***Fax:*** 021-63-38-42
Email: evechealger@yahoo.fr

Alghero-Bosa—Most Rev. Mauro Maria Morfino, S.D.B.; Vescovado, Via Principe Umberto 15, Alghero, Sassari, 07041, Italy.
Tel: 39-079-97-52-09 ***Fax:*** 39-079-97-52-09
Email: curiaalgherobosa@tiscali.it

Alife-Caiazzo—Most Rev. Valentino Di Cerbo; Curia Vescovile, Via Angelo Scorciarini Coppola 230/B, Piedimonte Matese, Caserta, 81016, Italy.
Tel: 39-0823-54-36-18 ***Fax:*** 39-0823-54-35-15

Alindao—Most Rev. Peter Marzinkowski, C.S.Sp.; Eveche de Alindao, c/o Maison Saint Charles, B.P. 780, Bangui, Central African Republic.
Email: vicaire-general@diocese-alindao.org

Aliwal—Most Rev. Michael Wüstenberg; 24 Young Street, P.O. Box 27, Aliwal North, C.P., 9750, South Africa.
Tel: 27-051-61-10-026 ***Fax:*** 27-051-63-33-078
Email: jkizito@hotmail.com

Allahabad—Most Rev. Isidore Fernandes; Bishop's House, 32 Thornhill Rd., Allahabad, 211001, India.
Tel: 91-0532-240-74-51; 91-0532-240-83-70

Allentown—Most Rev. John O. Barres, S.T.D., J.C.L., D.D. (ALN); Chancery Office 4029 W. Tilghman St., P.O. Box F, Allentown, PA, 18105.
Tel: 610-437-0755 ***Fax:*** 610-433-7822
Email: aschlert@allentowndiocese.org

Alleppey—Most Rev. Stephen Athipozhiyil; Bishop's House P.O. Box 4804, Alleppey, Kerala State, 688012, India.
Tel: 91-0477-2244-488 ***Fax:*** 91-0477-2243-362
Email: fr.therath@gmail.com

Almenara—Most Rev. Hugo Maria van Steekelenburg, O.F.M.; Rua João Pessoa 187, Almenara, MG, 39900-000, Brazil.
Tel: 55-033-3721-1517 ***Fax:*** 55-033-3721-1661
Email: avilo@ipw.com.br

Almería—Most Rev. Adolfo Gonzalez Montes; Obispado, Plaza de la Catedral 1, Almería, 04001, Spain.
Tel: 34-950-23-26-00 ***Fax:*** 34-950-88-51-63
Email: canciller@diocesisalmeria.es

Alotau-Sideia—Most Rev. Rolando Santos, C.M.; Bishop's House P.O. Box 105, Alotau, Milne Bay Province, 211, Papua New Guinea.
Tel: 641-10-91 ***Fax:*** 641-13-25

Alquoch—Most Rev. Mikha Pola Maqdassi; Evêché Chaldéen, Ninewah, Alquoch, Iraq.
Tel: 060-64-1212

Altamura-Gravina-Acquaviva delle Fonti—Most Rev. Mario Paciello; Curia Vescovile, Arco Duomo, 1, Altamura, Bari, 70022, Italy.
Tel: 39-080-311-70-24 *Fax:* 39-080-316-05-47
Email: curiadiocesana@libero.it

Alto Paraná - See Ciudad del Este—

Alto Solimes—Most Rev. Evangelista Alcimar Caldas Magalhães, O.F.M.Cap.; Rua Pedro Teixeira 540, Centro, Tabatinga, AM, 69640-000, Brazil.
Tel: 55-097-3412-2514 *Fax:* 55-097-3412-3320
Email: curiadas@yahoo.com.br

Alto Valle del Río Negro—Most Rev. Marcelo Alejandro Cuenca Revuelta; Obispado, Coronel Rodhe 433, General Roca, Río Negro, R8332AXI, Argentina.
Tel: 02941-430-860 *Fax:* 02941-433-530
Email: obaltovalle@speedy.com.ar

Altoona-Johnstown—Most Rev. Mark L. Bartchak; 927 S. Logan Blvd., Hollidaysburg, PA, 16648.
Tel: 814-695-5579 *Fax:* 814-695-8894
Email: tdegol@dioceseaj.org

Amadiyah, Amadia—Most Rev. Rabban Al-Qas; Evêché Chaldéen, Duhok, Iraq.

AMALFI-CAVA DE' TIRRENI—Most Rev. Orazio Soricelli; Curia Arcivescovile, Salita Episcopio, Amalfi, Salerno, 84011, Italy.
Tel: 39-089-871-324 *Fax:* 39-089-873-460
Email: curiaamalfi@diocesiamalficava.it

Amargosa—Most Rev. João Nílton dos Santos Souza; Cúria Diocesana, Avenida Lomanto Júnior 11, Amargosa, BA, 45300-000, Brazil.
Tel: 075-3634-11-76 *Fax:* 075-3634-11-76

Amarillo—Most Rev. Patrick James Zurek (AMA); Chancery Office 1800 N. Spring St., P.O. Box 5644, Amarillo, TX, 79117.
Tel: 806-383-2243 *Fax:* 806-383-8452
Email: vgamarillodiocese@yahoo.com

Ambanja—Most Rev. Rosario Saro Vella, S.D.B.; Evêché, B.P. 1, Ambanja, 203, Madagascar.
Tel: 020-86-501-80

Ambato—Most Rev. German Trajano Pavón Puente; Obispado Calle Bolívar 17-33, Apartado 18, Ambato, 01-0124, Ecuador.
Tel: 593-03-2826-132 *Fax:* 593-03-2823-650
Email: diocesisambato@yahoo.es

Ambatondrazaka—Most Rev. Antoine Scopelliti, O.SS.T.; Evêché, B.P. 33, Ambatondrazaka, 503, Madagascar.
Tel: 056-020-54-813-84

Ambikapur—Most Rev. Patras Minj, S.J.; Bishop's House Ambikapur, Surguja Dt., Chhattisgarh, 497001, India.
Tel: 07774-230-063 *Fax:* 07774-230-063; 07774-230-973
Email: lakragyan@yahoo.com

Amboina—Most Rev. Petrus Canisius Mandagi, M.S.C.; Keuskupan, Jl. Pattimura 26, Ambon, Maluku, 97124, Indonesia.
Tel: 62-0911-344-231 *Fax:* 62-0911-352-556

Ambositra—Most Rev. Fidelis Rakotonarivo, S.J.; Evêché, Ekar Andrefantsena, B.P. 127, Ambositra, 306, Madagascar.
Tel: 020-47-710-38

Amiens—Most Rev. Jean-Luc Bouilleret; Evêché, 21 rue François Génin B.P. 43008, Amiens CEDEX I, 80030, France.
Tel: 3-22-71-46-12 *Fax:* 3-22-72-05-17
Email: secretariat-eveque@diocese-amiens.com

Amos—Most Rev. Gilles Lemay; Evêché, 450 rue Principale Nord, Amos, QC, J9T 2M1, Canada.
Tel: 819-732-6515 *Fax:* 819-732-7994
Email: diocese-amos@cableamos.com

Amparo—Most Rev. Pedro Carlos Cipolini; Rua Conde de Parnaíba 294, C.P. 248, Ribeirao Amparo, S.P., 13900-970, Brazil.
Tel: 019-3817-3434 *Fax:* 019-3807-3192
Email: diamparo@uol.com.br

Amravati—Vacant; Bishop's House Amravati Camp P.O., Amravati, Maharashtra State, 444602, India.
Tel: 0721-2663-171 *Fax:* 0721-2666-403
Email: bishopshouseamt@dataone.in

Anagni-Alatri—Most Rev. Lorenzo Loppa; Curia Vescovile, Via Leone XIII 2, Anagni, Frosinone, 03012, Italy.
Tel: 39-0775-51-42-14 *Fax:* 39-0775-54-71-05
Email: cancelleria@diocesianagnialatri.it

Anápolis—Most Rev. João Wilk, O.F.M.Conv.; Praça Bom Jesus s/n, C.P. 178, Anápolis, GO, 75001-970, Brazil.
Tel: 55-062-3321-2280 *Fax:* 55-062-3321-2280
Email: dioceans@turboseg.com.br

Añatuya—Most Rev. Adolfo Armando Uriona, F.D.P.; Obispado, Avda. España 150, Añatuya, Santiago del Estero, G3760ASO, Argentina.
Tel: 54-03844-421-172 *Fax:* 54-03844-421-769
Email: obituya@gmail.com

ANCHORAGE—Most Rev. Roger Lawrence Schwietz, O.M.I. (ANC); Chancery Office 225 Cordova St., Anchorage, AK, 99501.
Tel: 907-297-7700 *Fax:* 907-279-3885
Email: mail@caa-ak.org

ANCONA-OSIMO—Most Rev. Edoardo Menichelli; Piazza del Senato 7, Ancona, 60121, Italy.
Tel: 39-071-207-47-03; 39-071-20-23-40 *Fax:* 39-071-20-85-822
Email: curia@diocesi.ancona.it

Andong—Most Rev. John Chrysostom Kwon Hyok-ju; Diocesan Office, Andong-shi, Anmak-Dong 136, Andong, Kyongbuk, 760-340, Korea, South.
Tel: 82-054-858-3111 *Fax:* 82-054-858-3116
Email: sa3111@hanafos.com

Andria—Most Rev. Raffaele Calabro; Vescovado, Piazza Vittorio Emanuele II 23, Andria, Bari, 70031, Italy.
Tel: 39-0883-59-30-32 *Fax:* 39-0883-59-30-32
Email: curia@diocesiandria.it

Anécho—Most Rev. Isaac Jogues Agbémenya Gaglo; Evêché, B.P. 113, Anécho, Togo.
Tel: 331-02-60 *Fax:* 331-02-61
Email: eveche_aneho@yahoo.fr

Angers—Most Rev. Emmanuel Delmas; Eveche, 8 Place Mgr. Rumeau, B.P. 90246, Angers CEDEX 01, 49002, France.
Tel: 2-41-88-07-00 *Fax:* 2-41-88-60-91
Email: dblanchet@diocese49.org

Angoulême—Most Rev. Claude Dagens; Maison Diocésaine, 226 rue de Bordeaux, Angoulême CEDEX, 16021, France.
Tel: 5-45-91-34-44 *Fax:* 5-45-91-96-05
Email: secretariatdio16@orange.fr

Angra—Most Rev. António de Sousa Braga, S.C.I.; Câmara Eclesiástica, rua dos Canos Verdes 127, Apartado 55, Angra do Heroísmo CODEX, Açores, 9701-901, Portugal.
Tel: 39-295-213-495 *Fax:* 39-295-216-661
Email: diocese.angra@iol.pt

ANKING (ANQING), HUAI-NING—Catholic Mission, Archbishop's House, Anqing, Anhui, China.

Ankwo (Anguo)—Catholic Mission, Si-Kuan, Anguo, Hebei, China.

Annecy—Most Rev. Yves Boivineau; Evêché, B.P. 41, 5 bis avenue de la Visitation, Annecy CEDEX, 74001, France.
Tel: 4-50-52-37-00 *Fax:* 4-50-45-63-64
Email: eveche@diocese-annecy.fr

Anse-à-Veau et Miragoâne—Most Rev. Pierre-André Dumas; Rue Goin 1, Anse-a-Veau, B.P. 3202 Miragoane, Haiti.
Tel: 3635-5654

ANTANANARIVO—Most Rev. Odon Marie Arsène Razanakolona; Archevêché, Andohalo B.P. 3030, Antananarivo, 101, Madagascar.
Tel: 020-222-07-26 *Fax:* 020-226-41-81
Email: didih@blueline.mg

ANTÉLIAS—Most Rev. Youssef Béchara; Archevêché Maronite, B.P. 70400, Antélias, Lebanon.
Tel: 04-41-00-20 *Fax:* 04-41-58-72

ANTEQUERA, OAXACA—Most Rev. José Luis Chávez Botello; Av. Independencia 700, Apartado 31, Oaxaca, 68000, Mexico.
Tel: 52-951-516-4822 *Fax:* 52-951-516-4822
Email: arzobispadodeantequera@hotmail.com

Antigonish—Most Rev. Brian Joseph Dunn; Bishop's House 168 Hawthorne St., P.O. Box 1330, Antigonish, NS, B2G 2L7, Canada.
Tel: 902-863-3335 *Fax:* 902-863-0037
Email: chancery.ant@ns.sympatico.ca

Antipolo—Most Rev. Gabriel V. Reyes; Diocesan Curia Fairmount Hills Subdivision, Daang Bakal Rd., Antipolo City, 1870, Philippines.
Tel: 0632-02-994-8368 *Fax:* 0632-02-696-2828
Email: antipolo_chancery_2005@yahoo.com

ANTOFAGASTA—Most Rev. Pablo Lizama Riquelme; Arzobispado, San Martín 2634, Antofagasta, Chile.
Tel: 055-556-782 *Fax:* 055-556-788
Email: secretaria.antofagasta@iglesia.cl

Antsirabé—Most Rev. Phillippe Ranaivomanana; Evêché, B.P. 100, Antsirabé, 110, Madagascar.
Tel: 020-44-48-005 *Fax:* 020-44-490-05

ANTSIRANANA—Most Rev. Michel Malo; Archevêché, 5 Boulevard Le Myre de Villers, B.P. 415, Antsiranana, 201, Madagascar.
Tel: 020-82-21-605; 032-04-748-23
Email: perevenance@blueline.mg

Antwerpen, Anvers—Most Rev. Johan Jozef Bonny; Bisdom, Schoenmarkt 2, Antwerpen, B-2000, Belgium.
Tel: 03-202-84-30 *Fax:* 03-202-84-31
Email: secretariaat.bisdom.antwerpen@kerknet.be

Anuradhapura—Most Rev. Norbert Marshall Andradi, O.M.I.; Bishop's House Church Rd., Anuradhapura, Sri Lanka.
Tel: 94-025-22-22-503 *Fax:* 94-025-22-34-901
Email: bandradi@sltnet.lk

Aosta—Most Rev. Giuseppe Anfossi; Vescovado, Via Mgr. de Sales 3/A, Aosta, 11100, Italy.
Tel: 39-0165-23-85-15/6 *Fax:* 39-0165-23-85-17
Email: vicario@diocesiaosta.it

APARECIDA—His Eminence Raymundo Cardinal Damasceno Assis; Cúria Metropolitana, Rua Barao do Rio Branco 412, C.P. 82, Aparecida, SP, 12570-000, Brazil.
Tel: 012-3104-2707; 012-3104-5500 *Fax:* 012-3104-2733
Email: curia@arquidioceseaparecida.org.br

Apartadó—Most Rev. Luis Adriano Piedrahita Sandoval; Curia Episcopal, Carrera 99N. 102-52, Barrio La Chinita, Apartadó (Antioquia), Colombia.
Tel: 57-41-828-03-57; 41-828-52-57; 41-828-67-97 *Fax:* 57-41-829-00-72
Email: apartadodioc@cec.org.co

Apatzingán—Most Rev. Miguel Patiño Velázquez, M.S.F.; Apartado 100, Calle Esteban Baca Calderón 1, Apatzingán, Mich., 60600, Mexico.
Tel: 52-453-53-41-787 *Fax:* 52-453-53-42-226
Email: diocesis-apatzingan@hotmail.com

Apucarana—Most Rev. Celso Antonio Marchiori; Cúria Diocesana, C.P. 203, Rua Prof. Joao Cândido Ferreira 14, Apucarana, 86800-070, Brazil.
Tel: 55-043-3423-1428 *Fax:* 55-043-3423-1428
Email: diocese@diocesedeapucarana.com.br

Aqra, Akra—Vacant; Mala Brwan, Aqra, Iraq.
Tel: 062-781-34-66
Email: aqradiocese@yahoo.com

ARACAJU—Most Rev. José Palmeira Lessa; Cúria Metropolitana, Praça Mons. Olímpio de Campos 228, Aracaju, SE, 49010-040, Brazil.
Tel: 55-079-3216-3000; 3214-0058 *Fax:* 55-079-3216-3010
Email: chancelaria@arquidiocesedearacaju.org

Araçatuba—Most Rev. Sérgio Krzywy; Rua Brig. Luiz Antonio 342, C.P. 71, Araçatuba, SP, 16001-970, Brazil.
Tel: 018-3624-3561 *Fax:* 018-3624-3561
Email: diocesearacatuba@ig.com.br

Araçuaí—Vacant; Cúria Diocesana, Rua Goiás 339, Araçuaí, MG, 39600-000, Brazil.
Tel: 55-033-3731-3159 *Fax:* 55-033-3731-1498

Arauca—Most Rev. Jaime Munoz Pedroza; Casa Episcopal, Calle 21 N. 19-23, Arauca, Intendencia de Arauca, Colombia.
Tel: 79-7-885-20-90; 885-20-82 *Fax:* 79-7-885-68-69

ARBIL, ERBIL—Most Rev. Bashar Warda, C.SS.R.; Archevêché Catholique Chaldéen, Ainkawa, Arbil, Iraq.
Tel: 964-0665-449-90-26

Ardagh—Most Rev. Colm O'Reilly; Bishop's House St. Michael's, Longford, Co. Longford, Ireland.
Tel: 043-33-46-432 *Fax:* 043-33-46-833
Email: ardaghdi@iol.ie

Arecibo—Most Rev. Daniel Fernandez Torres; 206 Dr. Salas St., P.O. Box 616, Arecibo, 00613, Puerto Rico.
Tel: 787-878-3180 *Fax:* 787-880-2661

AREQUIPA—Most Rev. Javier Augusto del Río Alba; Arzobispado, Apdo 149, Moral San Francisco 118, Arequipa, Peru.
Tel: 51-54-23-40-94 *Fax:* 51-54-24-27-21
Email: arzaqp@arzobispadoarequipa.org.pe

Arezzo-Cortona-Sansepolcro—Most Rev. Riccardo Fontana; Piazza del Duomo 3, Arezzo, 52100, Italy.
Tel: 39-0575-40-27-226 *Fax:* 39-0575-35-02-63
Email: cancelleria@diocesi.arezzo.it

Argyll and The Isles—Most Rev. Joseph Anthony Toal; Bishop's House, Corran Esplanade, Oban, Argyll, PA34 5AB, Scotland.
Tel: 44-01631-567-436 *Fax:* 44-01631-564-986
Email: rcd.argyll@btconnect.com

Ariano Irpino-Lacedonia—Most Rev. Giovanni D'Alise; Vescovado, Piazza Plebiscito 13, Ariano Irpino, Avellino, 83031, Italy.
Tel: 39-0825-87-11-39 *Fax:* 39-0825-87-11-39
Email: curia@diocesiarianolacedonia.it

Arica—Most Rev. Héctor Eduardo Vargas Bastidas, S.D.B.; 21 de Mayo 912, Casilla 147, San Marcos 260, Arica, Chile.
Tel: 56-058-251-393 *Fax:* 56-058-251-393
Email: arica@episcopado.cl

Arlington—Most Rev. Paul S. Loverde, D.D., S.T.L., J.C.L. (ARL); The Chancery 200 N. Glebe Rd., Ste. 914, Arlington, VA, 22203.
Tel: 703-841-2500 *Fax:* 703-524-5028

ARMAGH—His Eminence Sean Baptist Brady; Archbishop's House, Ara Coeli, Cathedral Road, Armagh, BT61 7QY, Ireland.
Tel: 44-28-3752-2045 *Fax:* 44-28-3752-6182
Email: admin@aracoeli.com

Armenia—Most Rev. Fabio Duque Jaramillo, O.F.M.; Obispado, Calle 23 N. 12-26 Centro de Servicios Diocesanos, Armenia, Quindio, Colombia.
Tel: 57-67-741-4171 *Fax:* 57-67-741-4171
Email: diocesisarm@telesat.com.co

Armidale—Most Rev. Luc Julian Matthys; Chancery Office P.O. Box 93, Armidale, N.S.W., 2350, Australia.
Tel: 61-02-6772-4971 *Fax:* 61-02-6771-1772
Email: chancery@arm.catholic.edu.au

Arras—Most Rev. Jean-Paul Jaeger; Evêché, 4 Rue des Fours, B.P. 137, Arras CEDEX, 62003, France.
Tel: 3-21-23-7507 *Fax:* 3-21-23-7374
Email: vicaire.general@arras.catholique.fr

Arua—Most Rev. Sabino Ocan Odoki; Bishop's House P.O. Box 135, Arua, Uganda.
Tel: 0772-868-837
Email: diocesearua@yahoo.com

Arundel and Brighton—Most Rev. Kieran Thomas Conry; Bishop's House The Upper Drive, Hove, East Sussex, BN3 6NB, England.
Tel: 44-01273-506-387 *Fax:* 44-01273-501-527
Email: vg@dabnet.org.uk

ARUSHA—Most Rev. Josaphat Louis Lebulu; Archbishop's House P.O. Box 3044, Arusha, Tanzania.
Tel: 255-027-254-4361 *Fax:* 255-027-254-8004
Email: angelo.arusha@habari.co.tz

Asansol—Most Rev. Cyprian Monis; Sacred Heart Presbytery, G.T. Road West, Asansol-713301, Burdwan Dt., West Bengal, India.
Tel: 0341-2282-836
Email: asndio@hotmail.com

Ascoli Piceno—Most Rev. Silvano Montevecchi; Vescovado, Piazza Arringo 10/C, Ascoli Piceno, 63100, Italy.
Tel: 39-0736-25-99-01 *Fax:* 39-0736-24-55-04
Email: curia@ap.chiesacattolica.it

Asmara—Most Rev. Menghisteab Tesfamariam, M.C.C.I.; Gonder St. 19, P.O. Box 244, Asmara, Eritrea.
Tel: 01-120-206 *Fax:* 01-126-519
Email: kimehret@gemel.com.er

Assis—Most Rev. Jose Benedito Simao; Cúria Diocesana, C.P. 809 Rua Dom José Lázaro Neves 414, Assis, SP, 19814-970, Brazil.
Tel: 018-3322-2279 *Fax:* 018-3322-2279
Email: curiadeassis@superig.com.br

Assisi-Nocera Umbra-Gualdo Tadino—Most Rev. Domenico Sorrentino; Piazza del Vescovado 3, Assisi, Perugia, 06081, Italy.
Tel: 39-075-81-24-83 *Fax:* 39-075-81-98-805
Email: curiadiocesana@assisi.chiesacattolica.it

Assiut, Lycopolis—Most Rev. Kyrillos William; Evêché Copte Catholique, B.P. 32, 140 rue As-Saoura, Assiut, 71511, Egypt.
Tel: 20-088-232-79-01; 20-088-232-10-60; 20-088-232-26-91 *Fax:* 20-088-231-44-66

Asti—Most Rev. Francesco Guido Ravinale; Via Carducci 50, Asti, 14100, Italy.
Tel: 39-0141-59-21-76 *Fax:* 39-0141-32-69-41
Email: cancelleria2@diocesidiasti.it

Astorga—Most Rev. Camilo Lorenzo Iglesias; Obispado, Calle el Carmen 4, Astorga, León, 24700, Spain.
Tel: 34-987-61-53-50 *Fax:* 34-987-61-91-51
Email: obastorga@planalfa.es

ASUNCIÓN—Most Rev. Eustaquio Pastor Cuquejo Verga, C.Ss.R.; Arzobispado, C.C. 654, Mariscal López 130, esq. Independencia Nacional, Asunción, Paraguay.
Tel: 595-021-44-5551; 021-595-44-3187 *Fax:* 595-021-44-7510
Email: cancilleria@arzobispado.org.py

Atakpamé—Most Rev. Nicodéme Anani Barrigah-Bénissan; Evêché, B.P. 11, Atakpamé, Togo.
Tel: 228-440-10-71 *Fax:* 228-440-11-13
Email: evatakpame@diocese-atakpame.org

Atambua—Most Rev. Dominikus Saku; Keuskupan, Jl. Nela Raya 17, Lalian Tolu, Atambua, 85702, Timor, Indonesia.
Tel: 62-0389-23-25-741 *Fax:* 62-0389-23-25-741
Email: uskatab@yahoo.co.id

ATHENS—Most Rev. Nikolaos Foskolos; Odos Homirou 9, 106 72, Athens, Greece.
Tel: 30-210-362-43-11 *Fax:* 30-210-361-86-32

Atlacomulco—Most Rev. Odilon Martinez Garcia; Hildago Sur 1, Atlacomulco, 50450, Mexico.
Tel: 52-712-122-05-53 *Fax:* 52-712-122-02-54
Email: diocesisatlacomulco@prodigy.net.mx

ATLANTA—Most Rev. Wilton D. Gregory; Catholic Center 2401 Lake Park Dr., Smyrna, GA, 30080-8862.
Tel: 404-885-7214 *Fax:* 404-885-7230
Email: jcorbett@archatl.com

AUCH—Most Rev. Maurice Gardès; Secrétariat de l'Archevêché, B.P. 80082, 13 rue du Docteur-Samalens, Auch CEDEX, 32002, France.
Tel: 33-5-62-61-91-55 *Fax:* 33-5-62-61-85-01

Auchi—Most Rev. Gabriel Ghieakhomo Dunia; Catholic Diocese of Auchi 3 Bishop's Court Rd., Off Old Igarra, P.O. Box 425, Auchi, Edo State, Nigeria.
Tel: 080-339-38-873

Auckland—Most Rev. Patrick James Dunn; Pompallier Diocesan Centre, 30 New St., Ponsonby, Private Bag 47904, Auckland, 1144, New Zealand.
Tel: 64-09-378-4380 *Fax:* 64-09-376-2829
Email: bishop@cda.org.nz

Augsburg—Most Rev. Konrad Zdarsa; Fronhof 4, D-86152, Augsburg, Germany.
Tel: 49-0821-3166-0 *Fax:* 49-0821-3166-209
Email: generalvikariat@bistum-augsburg.de

Auki—Most Rev. Christopher Cardone, O.P.; Bishop's House P.O. Box A 13, Auki, Malaita, Solomon Islands.
Tel: 677-40-130
Email: doauki@solomon.com.sb

Aurangabad—Most Rev. Edwin Colaço; Bishop's House, 34, Cantonment, Aurangabad Cantt., 431002, Maharashtra, India.
Tel: 0240-2370-576/545

Austin—Most Rev. Joe Steve Vasquez; 6225 E. Hwy. 290, Austin, TX, 78723.
Tel: 512-949-2400 *Fax:* 512-949-2520

Autlán—Most Rev. Gonzalo Galván Castillo; Obispado, Apartado 8, Hildago 78, Autlán, Jalisco, 48900, Mexico.
Tel: 52-317-382-41-55/12-28 *Fax:* 52-317-382-22-61
Email: obispadodeautlan@yahoo.com.mx

Autun—Most Rev. Benoît Rivière; Evêché, 1 Place Cardinal Perraud, Autun CEDEX, 71407, France.
Tel: 3-85-86-97-30 *Fax:* 3-85-86-97-31

Aveiro—Most Rev. António Francisco dos Santos; Cúrio Diocesana, rua de Cândido dos Reis 130, Apartado 541, Aveiro CODEX, 3801-901, Portugal.
Tel: 351-234-404-900 *Fax:* 351-234-404-901
Email: diocese.aveiro@diocaveiro.net

Avellaneda-Lanús—Most Rev. Rubén Oscar Frassia; Ameghino 907, BI870CVS, Avellaneda-Buenos Aires, 1870, Argentina.
Tel: 011-4222-4381 ; 011-4222-5184
Email: obispadoavelan@infovia.com.ar

Avellino—Most Rev. Francesco Marino; Palazzo Vescovile, Piazza della Libertá 19, Avellino, 83100, Italy.
Tel: 39-0825-74-595
Email: cancelliere@diocesi.avellino.it

Aversa—Most Rev. Angelo Spinillo; Strada S. Maria a Piazza 49, Aversa, Caserta, 81031, Italy.
Tel: 39-081-890-17-64 ; 39-081-503-76-26 *Fax:* 39-081-504-55-97
Email: segreteriadiocesiaversa@virgilio.it

Avezzano—Most Rev. Pietro Santoro; Vescovado, Corso della Libertà 54, Avezzano, L'Aquila, 67051, Italy.
Tel: 39-0863-41-38-27 *Fax:* 39-0863-41-27-25
Email: curiamarsi@libero.it

AVIGNON—Most Rev. Jean-Pierre Cattenoz; Archevêché, 31 rue Paul Manivet, B.P. 40050, Cedex 01, Avignon, 84005, France.
Tel: 4-90-27-26-00 *Fax:* 4-90-27-07-58
Email: archeveche@diocese-avignon.fr

Avila—Most Rev. Jesús García Burillo; Obispado, Plaza de Teniente Arévalo 5, Avila, 05001, Spain.
Tel: 34-920-35-3900 *Fax:* 34-920-21-10-73
Email: info@obav.es

Awgu—Most Rev. John Ifeanyichukwu Okoye; Diocesan Secretariat P.O. Box 256, Enugu State, Awgu, Nigeria.
Tel: 080-370-80-052
Email: awgudiocese@yahoo.com

Awka—Most Rev. Paulinus Chukwuemeka Ezeokafor; Bishop's House P.M.B. 5021, Awka, Anambra State, Nigeria.
Tel: 080-665-22-207

AYACUCHO O HUAMANGA—Most Rev. Salvador Pineiro Garcia-Calderon; Arzobispado, Apartado 30, Jr. 28 de Julio 148, Ayacucho, Peru.
Tel: 66-31-23-67 *Fax:* 66-31-23-67
Email: arzaya.secretaria@gmail.com

Azogues—Most Rev. Carlos Aníbal Altamirano Argüello; Apartado 03-01-0759, Calle Solano 2-20 y Matovelle, Azogues, Cañar, Ecuador.
Tel: 593-07-2240-051; 593-07-2243-421 *Fax:* 593-07-2240-417
Email: dioceazog@hotmail.com

Azul—Most Rev. Hugo Manuel Salaberry Goyeneche, S.J.; Obispado, Colón 695, B7300IAM, Azul, Buenos Aires, Argentina.
Tel: 02281-424-155 *Fax:* 02281-431-443
Email: obispado@diocesisdeazul.org.ar

B

Ba Ria—Most Rev. Thomas Nguyên Van Trâm; Tóa Giám Muc, 227 Cách Mang Tháng Tám, Phuóng Phuóc Hiêp, Tx. Bà Ria, Bà Ria, Vung Tàu, Vietnam.
Tel: 064-3551-284
Email: vptgmbr@yahoo.com

BAALBEK, BA'LBEK, ELIOPOLI—Most Rev. Elias Youssef Rahal; Archevêché Grec-Catholique Baalbek, Lebanon.
Tel: 08-370-200 *Fax:* 08-373-986

Baalbek - Deir El-Ahmar—Most Rev. Simon Atallah, O.A.M.; Evêché Maronite, Deir El-Ahmar, Lebanon.
Tel: 08-32-04-32 *Fax:* 08-32-04-31
Email: hannarahme@yahoo.fr

Babahoyo—Vacant; Calle Cinco de Junio 1000 y Rocafuerte, Babahoyo, Los Rios, Ecuador.
Tel: 05-2732-691 *Fax:* 05-2730-030
Email: dlbabahoyo@yahoo.es

Bac Ninh—Most Rev. Cosme Hoàng Van Dat, S.J.; Tóa Giám Muc, Tx. Bac Ninh, Tinh Bac Ninh, Vietnam.
Tel: 0241-3821-438 *Fax:* 0241-3824-843
Email: tgmbn@yahoo.com

Bacabal—Most Rev. Armando Martin Gutiérrez, F.A.M.; Rua Teixeira Mendes 45, C.P. 01, Bacabal, MA, 65700-000, Brazil.
Tel: 55-099-3621-1280 *Fax:* 55-099-3621-1000
Email: diocesebacabal@bol.com.br

Bacolod—Most Rev. Vicente M. Navarra; Bishop's Residence Rizal St., P.O. Box 141, Bacolod City, 6100, Philippines.
Tel: 63-034-432-1984; 63-034-432-2181 *Fax:* 63-034-434-5916
Email: bacolodchancery@yahoo.com.ph

Badulla—Most Rev. Julian Winston Sebastian Fernando, S.S.S.; Bishop's House, Rockhill, Spring Valley Road, Badulla, 90000, Sri Lanka.
Tel: 055-222-2079 *Fax:* 055-222-9241
Email: bphsbd@sltnet.lk

Bafatá—Most Rev. Carlos Pedro Zilli, P.I.M.E.; C.P. 385, Bissau, Bafatá, Guinea-Bissau.
Tel: 661-27-42

Bafia—Most Rev. Jean-Marie Benoît Bala; Evêché, B.P. 70, Bafia, Cameroon.
Tel: 2228-52-91 *Fax:* 2228-52-68
Email: mbam_catho@yahoo.fr

Bafoussam—Most Rev. Dieudonné Watio; Evêché, B.P. 263, Bafoussam, Cameroon.
Tel: 237-344-18-66 *Fax:* 237-344-18-66
Email: eveche.bafoussam@yahoo.fr

Bagdogra—Most Rev. Thomas D'Souza; Bishop's House P.O. Pradhan, Nagar, Siliguri, West Bengal, 734003, India.
Tel: 0353-2511-182 ***Fax:*** 0353-2518-153
Email: bishbagdogra@satyam.net.in

Bagé—Most Rev. Gílio Felício; C.P. 270, Rua Marcílio Dias 1586, Bagé, RS, 96400-200, Brazil.
Tel: 55-053-32-42-4772 ***Fax:*** 55-053-32-42-4772
Email: curiadebage@bol.com.br

BAGHDAD (BABILONIA)—His Eminence S.B. Emmanuel Delly III; Patriarcat Chaldéen Catholique P.O. Box 6112, Al-Mansour, Baghdad, Iraq.
Tel: 01-537-9164 ***Fax:*** 01-537-8556
Email: info@st-addayyahoo.com

BAGHDAD (BABILONIA) (ARMENIAN)—Most Rev. Emmanuel Dabbaghian; Archevêché Arménien Catholique Karrada Sharkia, Section 903, rue 27, B.P. 2344, Baghdad, Iraq.
Tel: 01-719-24-61; 01-719-18-27 ***Fax:*** 01-719-40-34

BAGHDAD (BABILONIA) (LATIN)—Most Rev. Jean Benjamin Sleiman, O.C.D.; Archevêché Latin Hay Al-Wahda, Mahallat 904, rue 8, Imm. 44, P.O. Box 35130, Baghdad, 12906, Iraq.
Tel: 07-807-40-01
Email: moutrania@gmail.com

BAGHDAD (BABILONIA) (SYRIAN)—Most Rev. Yousif Abba; Archevêché Syrien Catholique Baghdad, 90321, Iraq.
Tel: 01-719-18-50/69-48 ***Fax:*** 01-719-01-66

Baguio—Most Rev. Carlito J. Cenzon, C.I.C.M.; Bishop's Residence 72 Father Carlu Loop, P.O. Box 55, Baguio City, 2600, Philippines.
Tel: 074-442-3756 ***Fax:*** 074-442-5748
Email: baguiochancery@yahoo.com.ph

BAHÍA BLANCA—Most Rev. Guillermo José Garlatti; Arzobispado, Avenida Colón 164, Bahía Blanca, Buenos Aires, B8000FTO, Argentina.
Tel: 54-0291-455-0707 ***Fax:*** 54-0291-455-0707
Email: arzobis@arzobispadobahia.org.ar

Baie-Comeau—Most Rev. Jean-Pierre Blais; Evêché, 639 rue de Bretagne, Baie-Comeau, Quebec, G5C 1X2, Canada.
Tel: 418-589-5744 ***Fax:*** 418-295-3145
Email: diocese.bcomeau@cgocable.ca

Bairut, Beirut—Most Rev. Michel Kassarji; Evêché Chaldéen de Beyrouth, B.P. 373, Baadba, Brazilia, Beyrouth, Lebanon.
Tel: (05) 457-732; (05) 459-088 ***Fax:*** (05) 457-731
Email: chaldepiscopus@hotmail.com

BAIRUT, BEIRUT ARMENIAN—Most Rev. S.B. Nerses Bedros XIX Tarmouni; Patriarch Arménian Catholique rue de L'Hopital Orthodoxe Beirut, Jeitaoui, Beyrouth, 2078 5605, Lebanon.
Tel: 01-570-555/6/7 ***Fax:*** 01-570-562

BAIRUT, BEIRUT-JBEIL—Most Rev. Cyrille Salim Bustros, S.M.S.P.; Archevêché Grec-Melkite Catholique, 655 rue de Damas, B.P. 11-901, Beyrouth, Lebanon.
Tel: 961-01-61-61-04/5/6 ***Fax:*** 961-01-61-61-09
Email: agmcb@terra.net.lb

BAIRUT, BEIRUT (MARONITE)—Most Rev. Paul Youssef Matar; Archevêché Maronite 10 rue Collège de la Sagesse, Achrafieh, Beyrouth, 5545, Lebanon.
Tel: 01-561-980-1/2 ***Fax:*** 01-561-930

Bairut, Beirut (Syrian)—Most Rev. S.B. Ignance Pierre Abdel-Ahad VIII; Patriarcat Syrien Catholique Rue de Damas, B.P. 116-5087, Beyrouth, 1106-2010, Lebanon.
Tel: 01-615-892 ***Fax:*** 01-616-573
Email: psc_lb@yahoo.com

Baker—Vacant; P.O. Box 5999, Bend, OR, 97708.
Tel: 541-388-4004 ***Fax:*** 541-388-2566
Email: chancellor@dioceseofbaker.org
911 S.E. Armour St., Bend, OR, 97702.

Balanga—Most Rev. Ruperto Cruz Santos; Bishop's Residence Aguirre St., Balanga, Bataan, 2100, Philippines.
Tel: 047-237-3226 ***Fax:*** 047-237-3226

Balasore—Most Rev. Thomas Thiruthalil, C.M.; Bishop's House, Baleshwar, Orissa, 756001, India.
Tel: 91-06782-262-056
Email: blsbishop@yahoo.co.in

Ballarat—Most Rev. Peter Joseph Connors; 5 Lyons St. S., Ballarat, Vic., 3350, Australia.
Tel: 61-0353-377-121 ***Fax:*** 61-0353-321-122
Email: bishop@ballarat.catholic.org.au

Balsas—Most Rev. Énemesio Ângelo Lazzaris, F.D.P.; Cúria Diocesana, C.P. 18, Praça Getúlio Vargas 149, Centro, Balsas, MA, 65800-000, Brazil.
Tel: 55-099-3541-2483 ***Fax:*** 55-099-3541-2566
Email: diocese@suprisul1.com.br

BALTIMORE—Most Rev. Edwin F. O'Brien, S.T.D., D.D. (BAL); Catholic Center 320 Cathedral St., Baltimore, MD, 21201.
Tel: 410-547-5446 ***Fax:*** 410-727-8234
Email: chancery@archbalt.org

BAMAKO—Most Rev. Jean Zerbo; Archevêché, B.P. 298, Bamako, Mali.
Tel: 223-20-22-58-42 ***Fax:*** 223-20-22-78-50

Bambari—Most Rev. Edouard Mathos; Evêché de Bambari B.P. 944, Bambari, Central African Republic.
Tel: 236-75-50-17-22
Email: dio.debambari@yahoo.fr

BAMBERG—Most Rev. Ludwig Schick; Erzbishöfliches Ordinariat, Domplatz 3, Bamberg, D-96049, Germany.
Tel: 49-0951-502-0 ***Fax:*** 49-0951-502-250

BAMENDA—Most Rev. Cornelius Fontem Esua; Archbishop's House P.O. Box 82, Bamenda, North-West Province, Cameroon.
Tel: 237-3303-5745 ***Fax:*** 237-3303-5746
Email: archbishopshouse@yahoo.com

Ban Mê Thuôt—Most Rev. Vincent Nguyen Van Ban; Toà Giám Muc, 104 Phan Chu Trinh, Tp., Ban Mê Thuôt, Dak Lak, Vietnam.
Tel: 050-3852-756 ***Fax:*** 050-3840-087
Email: tgmbmt@yahoo.com

Bandung—Most Rev. Johannes Maria Trilaksyanta Pujasumarta; Keuskupan, Jl. Jawa 26, Bandung, Jawa, 40113, Indonesia.
Tel: 62-022-420-4537 ***Fax:*** 62-022-421-3992
Email: stefanus@bdg.centrin.net.id

Banfora—Most Rev. Lucas Kalfa Sanou; Evêché B.P. 52, Banfora, Burkina Faso.
Tel: 20-91-00-71 ***Fax:*** 20-91-03-96

BANGALORE—Most Rev. Bernard Blasius Moras; Archbishop's House, P.B. 2, 75 Miller Rd., Bangalore, 560046, India.
Tel: 91-080-2333-04-38; 91-080-2333-08-38 ***Fax:*** 91-080-2353-16-00
Email: vicargeneral@bangalorearchdiocese.com

Bangassou—Most Rev. Juan José Aguirre Muñoz, M.C.C.I.; Evêché, B.P. 84, Bangassou, Central African Republic.

BANGKOK—Most Rev. Francis Xavier Kriengsak Kovithavanij; 51 Catholic Mission, Charoenkrung Rd. 40, Bangrak, Bangkok, 10500, Thailand.
Tel: 02-237-10-31; 02-233-87-12 ***Fax:*** 02-237-10-33
Email: arcdibkk@catholic.or.th

Bangued—Most Rev. Leopoldo C. Jaucian, S.V.D.; Chancery Office, Bangued, Abra, 2800, Philippines.
Tel: 63-074-752-8040 ***Fax:*** 63-074-752-8028
Email: rcbbabra@hotmail.com

BANGUI—Vacant; Archevêché, B.P. 1518, Bangui, Central African Republic.
Tel: 236-21-61-08-98 ***Fax:*** 236-21-61-46-92
Email: archibangui@yahoo.fr

Baní—Most Rev. Freddy Antonio de Jesús Bretón Martínez; Obispado, Apartado 25, Calle Sánchez s/n, Baní, Peravia, Dominican Republic.
Tel: 809-522-5892 ***Fax:*** 809-522-5916
Email: obispado@diocesisdebani.org

BANIYAS, CESAREA DI FILIPPO, PANEADE—Most Rev. Georges Nicolas Haddad; Archevêché de Panéas, Jdeidet Marjeyoun, Lebanon.
Tel: 07-830-007 ***Fax:*** 07-830-007

Banja Luka—Most Rev. Franjo Komarica; Biskupski Ordinarijat, Kralja Petra 1 80, Banja Luka, BiH-78000, Bosnia-Herzegovina.
Tel: 387-051-305-984 ***Fax:*** 387-051-304-993
Email: ordinar@inecco.net

Banjarmasin—Most Rev. Petrus Boddeng Timang; Jl. Parit Mas 15, Pelaihari, Tanah Laut, Kalimantan Selatan, 70814, Indonesia.
Tel: 62-0512-21-159

Banjul—Most Rev. Robert Patrick Ellison, C.S.Sp.; Bishop's House P.O. Box 165, Banjul, Gambia.
Tel: 220-4390-767 ***Fax:*** 220-4377-607
Email: catholicsec@qanet.gm

Banmaw—Most Rev. Raymond Sumlut Gam; St. Patrick's Cathedral Kokko Taw, Banmaw, 01131, Myanmar.
Tel: 95-074-50-453
Email: frlaumun@gmail.com

Banská Bystrica, Neosolio—Vacant; Biskupsky úrad, post. schránka 107, Banská Bystrica, Námestie SNP 19, SK-975 90, Slovakia.
Tel: 42-048-4125-726; 42-048-4720-800 ***Fax:*** 42-048-4720-827
Email: bystrica@kbs.sk

BAR (ANTIVARI)—Most Rev. Zef Gashi, S.D.B.; Nadbiskupski Ordinarijat, Popovici 98, Bar, Crna Gora, 85000, Montenegro.
Tel: 381-085-344-236 ***Fax:*** 381-085-344-233
Email: zega_bar@t-com.me

Barahona—Most Rev. Rafael Leónidas Felipe y Núñez; Obispado, Apartado 170, c/Colón esq. Av, Luperón, Barahona, Dominican Republic.
Tel: 809-524-2876 ***Fax:*** 809-524-4211
Email: obispbarahona@codetel.net.do

Barbastro-Monzón—Most Rev. Alfonso Milián Sorribas; Obispado, Juan de Lanuza 6, Barbastro, Huesca, 22300, Spain.
Tel: 34-974-31-06-97 ***Fax:*** 34-974-31-49-75
Email: obbarbastromonzon@planalfa.es

BARCELONA—His Eminence Lluis Martinez Sistach; Arzobispado, Carrer del Bisbe 5, Barcelona, 08002, Spain.
Tel: 34-93-270-10-12 ***Fax:*** 34-93-270-13-03
Email: secgral@arqbcn.cat

Barcelona—Most Rev. César Ramón Ortega Herrera; Obispado, Apartado 67, Avda., Country Club con c/San Carlos, Urb. Urdaneta, Edo. Anzoátegui, Barcelona, 6001-A, Venezuela.
Tel: 0281-2774-889 ***Fax:*** 0281-2764-993

Bareilly—Most Rev. Anthony Fernandes; Bishop's House, 63 Cantt., Bareilly, U.P., 243001, India.
Tel: 91-0581-2511-181 ***Fax:*** 91-0581-2510-598
Email: bareillydiocese1989@yahoo.in

Barentu—Most Rev. Thomas Osman, O.F.M.Cap.; Catholic Eparchy P.O. Box 9, Barentu, Gash Barka, Eritrea.
Tel: 01-18-46-98 ***Fax:*** 01-18-46-98

BARI-BITONTO—Most Rev. Francesco Cacucci; Corso A. De Gasperi 274/a, Bari, 70125, Italy.
Tel: 39-080-528-81-11 ***Fax:*** 39-080-569-03-14
Email: curia@odegitria.bari.it

Barinas—Most Rev. Ramón Antonio Linares Sandoval; Palacio Episcopal, Av., Briceño Méndez, Frente Plaza Bolivar, Barinas, Venezuela.
Tel: 58-0273-552-23-15 ***Fax:*** 58-0273-552-23-15
Email: diocesisbarinas@hotmail.com

Baroda—Most Rev. Godfrey de Rozario, S.J.; Bishop's House, 71 Alkapuri Society, Vadodara, Gujarat, 390007, India.
Tel: 0265-231-18-37 ***Fax:*** 0265-233-94-80
Email: barodadiocese@gmail.com

BARQUISIMETO—Most Rev. Antonio José López Castillo; Arzobispado, Avenida Venezuela con Calle 30 Av. Simón Rodriguez, Sotano de Catedral, Edo. Lara, Barquisimeto, 3001, Venezuela.
Tel: 58-0251-231-34-46 ***Fax:*** 58-0251-231-37-24
Email: curia_arbqto@hotmail.com

Barra—Most Rev. Luiz Flávio Cappio, O.F.M.; Rua Dr. Augusto Torres 02, C.P. 12, Barra, BA, 47100-000, Brazil.
Tel: 55-074-3662-2014 ***Fax:*** 55-074-3662-2014

Barra do Garças—Most Rev. Protógenes José Luft, S.C.; Rue Carlos Gomes 567, C.P. 337, Barro do Garças, MT, 78600-000, Brazil.
Tel: 066-3401-9025 ***Fax:*** 066-3401-5105
Email: mitradiocesanabg@yahoo.com.br

Barra do Piraí-Volta Redonda—Most Rev. Francesco Biasin; Rua 25/b 44, Vila Santa Cecilia, Volta Redonda, RJ, 27260-330, Brazil.
Tel: 55-024-3340-2801 ***Fax:*** 55-024-3340-2801
Email: diocese.vr@quick.com.br

Barrancabermeja—Most Rev. Camilo Fernando Castrellón Pizano, S.D.B.; Residencia Episcopal, Carrera 16 N. 48-19, Barrancabermeja, Santander, Colombia.
Tel: 57-76-22-34-99 ***Fax:*** 57-76-22-48-58
Email: diocesisbarrancabermeja@hotmail.com

BARRANQUILLA—Most Rev. Jairo Jaramillo Monsalve; Curia Arzobispal, Calle 75B N., Barranquilla, 42F-83, Colombia.
Tel: 5-36-90-769 ***Fax:*** 5-36-90-767

Barreiras—Most Rev. Josafa Menezes da Silva; Cúria Diocesana, Rua 26 de Maio 427, Barreiras, BA, 47804-090, Brazil.
Tel: 55-077-3611-5926 ***Fax:*** 55-077-3611-5926
Email: diocesebarreiras@hotmail.com

Barretos—Most Rev. Edmilson Amador Caetano, O.Cist; Rua 20 N. 01600, Barretos, SP, 14787-279, Brazil.
Tel: 55-017-3323-7400; 55-017-3324-2982; 55-017-3322-3565 ***Fax:*** 55-017-3322-3565
Email: mitrabarretos@terra.com.br

Baruipur—Most Rev. Salvadore Lobo; Bishop's House 24 - Parganas South, Baruipur, W.B., 700144, India.
Tel: 91-033-2433-8299
Email: baruipurdiocese@rediffmail.com

Basankusu—Most Rev. Joseph Mokobe Ndjoku; Evêché de Basankusu c/o Procure des Missions - Sainte Anne, B.P. 1800, Kinshasa 1, Democratic Republic of Congo.
Tel: (092) 29-13-90
Email: evechebasankusu@yahoo.fr

Basel, Bâle, Basilea—Most Rev. Felix Gmur; Bischöfliches Ordinariat, Postfach 216, Baselstrasse 58, Solothurn, CH-4501, Switzerland.
Tel: 41-032-625-58-25/41 ***Fax:*** 41-032-625-58-45
Email: kanzlei@bistum-basel.ch

Basse-Terre—Vacant; Maison Diocesaine, B.P. 369, Place Saint-François, Basse-Terre, 97100, Guadeloupe.
Tel: 590-81-3669 ***Fax:*** 590-81-9823

BASSORAH, BASRA—Vacant; Archevêché Chaldéen P.O. Box 217, Ashar-Basrah, Iraq.
Tel: 964-040-61-3427
Email: efather2006@yahoo.com

Bata—Most Rev. Juan Matogo Oyana, C.M.F.; Obispado, Apdo 82, Bata, Litoral, Equatorial Guinea.
Tel: 08-2759 ***Fax:*** 08-2759

Bathurst—Most Rev. Michael Joseph McKenna; Bishop's House 84 George St., P.O. Box 246, Bathurst, N.S.W., 2795, Australia.
Tel: 02-6334-6400 ***Fax:*** 02-6331-4869
Email: reception@bathurst.catholic.org.au

Bathurst (in Canada)—Most Rev. Valéry Vienneau; Evêché 645 Avenue Murray, Bathurst, C.P. 460, Bathurst, NB, E2A 3Z4, Canada.
Tel: 506-546-1420 ***Fax:*** 506-546-1423
Email: diocesedebathurst@nb.aibn.com

Baton Rouge—Most Rev. Robert William Muench, D.D. (BR); Chancery Office: Catholic Life Center 1800 S. Acadian Thruway, P.O. Box 2028, Baton Rouge, LA, 70821-2028.
Tel: 225-387-0561 ***Fax:*** 225-336-8789
Email: chancery@diobr.org

Batouri—Most Rev. Faustin Ambassa Ndjodo, C.I.C.M.; Evêché, B.P. 56, Batouri, Kadei, Cameroon.
Tel: 2226-24-24 ***Fax:*** 2226-25-37
Email: diocesebri2005@yahoo.fr

Batrun—Most Rev. Paul-Emile Saadé; Evêché Maronite, Kfarhay, Batrun, 4001, Lebanon.
Tel: 06-642-259 ***Fax:*** 06-744-337
Email: mestfan@diocesebatroun.org

Battery (Syro-Malankaras)—Most Rev. Joseph Thomas Konnath; Catholic Bishop's House, P.B. 7, Sulthan Bathery, Wayanad Dt., Kerala, 673592, India.
Tel: 04936-220-207 ***Fax:*** 04936-221-287
Email: bybathery@gmail.com

Baucau—Most Rev. Basílio do Nascimento; Largo da Catedral, Baucau, 88810, East Timor.

Bauchi—Most Rev. Malachy John Goltok; Bishop's House, St. John's Catholic Cathedral Yandoka Rd., P.O. Box 17, Bauchi, Nigeria.
Tel: 077-54-14-75

Bauru—Most Rev. Caetano Ferrari, O.F.M; Avenida Rodrigues Alves 10-35, Bauru, SP, 17015-002, Brazil.
Tel: 55-014-3879-8706 ***Fax:*** 55-014-3879-8706
Email: bispadobauru@bispadobauru.org.br
C.P. 550, Bauru, SP, 17015-970, Brazil.

Bayeux—Most Rev. Jean-Claude Boulanger; Evêché, 7 Impasse Glatigny, B.P. 62250, Bayeux CEDEX, 14406, France.
Tel: 2-31-51-16-51 ***Fax:*** 2-31-51-28-79
Email: chancellerie@bayeuxlisieux.catholique.fr

Bayombong—Most Rev. Ramon B. Villena; Domus Mariae Reginae Apostolorum, Bayombong, Nueva Vizcaya, 3700, Philippines.
Tel: 63-078-805-3689; 63-078-321-2170 ***Fax:*** 63-078-321-2170
Email: bayombongchancery@hotmail.com

Bayonne—Most Rev. Marc Aillet; Evêché, 16 Place Mgr. Vansteenberghe, Bayonne CEDEX, 64115, France.
Tel: 5-59-59-16-88 ***Fax:*** 5-59-59-67-90
Email: secretariat.general@eveche-bayonne.org

Beaumont—Most Rev. Curtis John Guillory, S.V.D.; Diocesan Pastoral Office 710 Archie St., P.O. Box 3948, Beaumont, TX, 77704-3948.
Tel: 409-924-4300 *Fax:* 409-838-4511
Email: vicargeneral@dioceseofbmt.org

Beauvais—Most Rev. Jacques Benoit-Gonnin; Evêché, 15 Rue Jeanne Hachette, B.P. 20636, Beauvais CEDEX, 60026, France.
Tel: 3-44-06-28-25 *Fax:* 3-44-06-28-26
Email: diocese.beauvais@catho6o.cef.fr

BEIRA—Most Rev. Jaime Pedro Gonçalves; Cúria Arquiepiscopal, Rua Correia de Brito 613, C.P. 544, Beira, Mozambique.
Tel: 258-23-322-313 *Fax:* 258-23-327-639
Email: arquidbeira@teledata.mz

Beja—Most Rev. António Vitalino Fernandes Dantas, O.Carm.; Bispado, Rua D. Afonso Henriques 1A, Apartado 94, 7800-902, Beja CODEX, 7800-049, Portugal.
Tel: 351-284-323-159 *Fax:* 351-284-323-250
Email: curia@diocese-beja.pt

BELÉM DO PARÁ—Most Rev. Alberto Taveira Corrêa; Cúria Metropolitana Av. Governador, José Malcher 915, Belém, PA, 66055-260, Brazil.
Tel: 55-091-3215-7002 *Fax:* 55-091-3215-7001
Email: secretaria@arquidiocesedebelem.com.br

Belfort-Montbéliard—Most Rev. Claude Schockert; Evêché, 25 Place de la République, B.P. 60067, Belfort CEDEX, 90020, France.
Tel: 3-84-46-62-20 *Fax:* 3-84-58-12-05
Email: secretariat@diocesebm.fr

Belgaum—Most Rev. Peter Machado; Bishop's House, B.C. 69, Belgaum, Karnataka State, 590001, India.
Tel: 0831-2420-587 *Fax:* 0831-2424-226
Email: chancellorbelgaum@gmail.com

Belize City-Belmopan—Most Rev. Dorick McGowan Wright; Bishop's House 144 N. Front St., P.O. Box 616, Belize City, Belize.
Tel: 011-227-2122
Email: cathpres@gmail.com

Bellary—Most Rev. Henry D'Souza; Bishop's House, 57 Munro Rd., Bellary, Karnataka, 583104, India.
Tel: 91-08392-240-315/177
Email: bphousebly@hotmail.com

Belleville—Most Rev. Edward K. Braxton; The Chancery 222 S. Third St., Belleville, IL, 62220.
Tel: 618-277-8181 *Fax:* 618-277-0387
Email: jmcevilly@diobelle.org

Belley-Ars—Most Rev. Guy Bagnard; 31 rue Docteur-Victor-Nodet, B.P 154, Bourg-en-Bresse, 01004, France.
Tel: 4-74-32-86-32 *Fax:* 4-74-32-86-31
Email: sdpco1@gmail.com

Belluno-Feltre—Most Rev. Giuseppe Andrich; Curia Vescovile, Piazza Duomo 3, C.P. 193, Belluno, 32100, Italy.
Tel: 39-0437-94-08-96 *Fax:* 39-0437-94-27-46
Email: curia@diocesi.it

BELO HORIZONTE—Most Rev. Walmor Oliveira de Azevedo; Cúria Metropolitana, Av. Brazil 2079, Belo Horizonte, MG, 30140-002, Brazil.
Tel: 55-031-3269-3103 *Fax:* 55-031-3269-3149
Email: mitra.doc@arquidiocesebh.org.br

Belthangady—Most Rev. Lawrence Mukkuzhy; Bishop's House P.O. Box 13, P.O. Belthangady, Dhakshina Kannada Dt., Karnataka, 574214, India.
Tel: 08256-233-975 *Fax:* 08256-233-056
Email: frjosephvf@gmail.com

BENEVENTO—Most Rev. Andrea Mugione; Palazzo Arcivescovile, Piazza Orsini 27, Benevento, 82100, Italy.
Tel: 39-0824-32-33-24 *Fax:* 39-0824-32-33-78

Benguela—Most Rev. Eugenio Dal Corso, P.S.D.P.; Bispado, C.P. 670, Rua Gago Coutinho 11, Benguela, Angola.
Tel: 02722-33-871 *Fax:* 02722-35-127

BENIN CITY—Most Rev. Augustine Obiora Akubeze; Chancery Office 30 Airport Rd., P.O. Box 35, Benin City, Edo State, Nigeria.
Tel: 234-052-253-787 *Fax:* 234-052-255-763
Email: beninarchdiocese@yahoo.co.uk

Benjamín Aceval—Most Rev. Candido Cárdenas Villalba; Obispado, Carlos Antonio Lopéz y General José Eduvigis Diaz, Benjamín Aceval, Chaco, 9800, Paraguay.
Tel: 595-0271-27-22-11 *Fax:* 595-0271-27-22-11

BEOGRAD—Most Rev. Stanislav Hocevar, S.D.B.; Nadbiskupski Ordinarijat, Svetozara Markovica 20, Belgrade, 11000, Serbia.
Tel: 381-011-303-2246 *Fax:* 381-011-303-2248
Email: nadbiskupija@kc.org.rs

Berbérati—Evêché, B.P. 22, Berbérati, Central African Republic.
Tel: 00871-762-698-686 *Fax:* 00871-762-698-688
Email: diocesedeberberati@yahoo.fr

Bereina—Most Rev. Rochus Josef Tatamai, M.S.C.; Bishop's House Boroko, N.C.D. 111, P.O. Box 300, Bereina, Papua New Guinea.
Tel: 32-56-102 *Fax:* 32-56-103
Email: chancery@dioceseofbereina.org.pg

Bergamo—Most Rev. Francesco Beschi; Piazza Duomo 5, Bergamo, 24129, Italy.
Tel: 39-035-278-111 *Fax:* 39-035-278-250
Email: diocesi@diocesi.bergamo.it

Berhampur—Most Rev. Sarat Chandra Nayak; Bishop's House, P.B. 27, Brahampur, Ganjam Dt., Orissa, 760001, India.
Tel: 91-0680-645-04-42 *Fax:* 91-0680-240-43-37
Email: bishopofberhampur@gmail.com

BERLIN—Most Rev. Rainer Maria Woelki; Niederwallstr. 8-9, Berlin-Bundesrepublik, D-10117, Germany.
Tel: 49-030-32-68-40 *Fax:* 49-030-32-68-42-76

BERTOUA—Most Rev. Joseph Atanga, S.J.; Archevêché, B.P. 40, Bertoua, Cameroon.
Tel: 237-2224-17-48 *Fax:* 237-2224-25-85

BESANÇON—Most Rev. André Lacrampe; Archevêché, 3 rue de la Convention, Besançon CEDEX, 25041, France.
Tel: 3-81-82-60-20 *Fax:* 3-81-82-6035
Email: archeveche-besancon.accueil@wanadoo.fr

Bethlehem—Most Rev. Jan de Groef; Bishop's House 218 Cambridge St., P.O. Box 366, Bethlehem, O.F.S., 9700, South Africa.
Tel: 27-058-303-53-51 *Fax:* 27-058-303-53-52
Email: diocese@bhm.dorea.co.za

Bettiah—Most Rev. Victor Henry Thakur; Bishop's House, Bettiah, West Champaran, Bihar, 845438, India.
Tel: 06254-243-955 *Fax:* 06254-243-590

Bhadravathi—Most Rev. Joseph Arumachadath, M.C.B.S.; Bishop's House, St. Joseph's Church Sagar Rd., Shimoga Karnataka, 577204, India.
Tel: 08182-256-549 *Fax:* 08182-256-549
Email: bhadravathidiocese@rediffmail.com

Bhagalpur—Most Rev. Kurien Valiakandathil; Chancery Office Nawab Colony, P.B. 61, Bhagalpur, Bihar, 812001, India.
Tel: 91-0641-2400-878
Email: chan_bpa@yahoo.co.in

BHOPAL—Most Rev. Leo Cornelio, S.V.D.; Archbishop's House, 33 Ahmedabad Palace Rd., Bhopal, M.P., 462001, India.
Tel: 91-0755-254-08-29 *Fax:* 91-0755-254-47-37
Email: archdiocebpl@gmail.com

BIALYSTOK—Most Rev. Edward Ozorowski; Kuria Metropolitalna, Pl., Bialystok, ul. Koscielna I, 15-087, Poland.
Tel: 48-085-665-24-00 *Fax:* 48-085-665-24-31
Email: sekretariat@bialystok.opoka.org.pl

Biella—Most Rev. Gabriele Mana; Via Vescovado 10, Biella, Vercelli, 13900, Italy.
Tel: 39-015-252-22-74 *Fax:* 39-015-22-721
Email: cancelleria@diocesi.biella.it

Bielsko-Zywiec—Most Rev. Tadeusz Rakoczy; Zeromskiego 5-7, Bielsko-Biala, 43-300, Poland.
Tel: 033-819-0601 *Fax:* 033-819-1202
Email: kuria@diecezja.bielsko.pl

Bijnor—Most Rev. John Vadakel, C.M.I.; Bishop's House, Padampur Sukhro, Kotdwar, Pauri Garhwal Dt., U.P., 246149, India.
Tel: 91-01382-222-231 *Fax:* 91-01382-222-511
Email: bijnordiocese@yahoo.com

Bilbao—Most Rev. Mario Iceta Gavicagogeascoa; Virgen de Begoña 38, Bilbao, 48006, Spain.
Tel: 34-94-466-7979 *Fax:* 34-94-466-7971
Email: idazkaria@bizkeliza.org

Biloxi—Most Rev. Roger P. Morin; Chancery Office 1790 Popps Ferry Rd., Biloxi, MS, 39532-2118.
Tel: 228-702-2112 *Fax:* 228-702-2125
Email: dfullam@biloxidiocese.org

BIRMINGHAM—Most Rev. Bernard Longley; Cathedral House, St. Chad's Queenway;, Birmingham, B4 6EX, England.
Tel: 44-0121-230-6237 *Fax:* 44-0121-233-2699
Email: john.moran@rc-birmingham.org

Birmingham (in Alabama)—Most Rev. Robert Joseph Baker (BIR); Chancery Office 2121 3rd Ave. N, Birmingham, AL, 35203-3314.
Tel: 205-838-8322 *Fax:* 205-836-1910
Email: gnabors@bhmdiocese.org

Bismarck—Most Rev. Paul Albert Zipfel; Chancery Office 420 Raymond St., P.O. Box 1575, Bismarck, ND, 58502-1575.
Tel: 701-223-1347 *Fax:* 701-223-3693
Email: jguthrie@bismarckdiocese.com

Bissau—Most Rev. José Câmnate na Bissign; C.P. 20, Av. 14 de Novembro, Bissau Codex, 1001, Guinea-Bissau.
Tel: 245-25-10-57 *Fax:* 245-25-10-58
Email: diocesebissau@yahoo.it

Bjelovar-Krizevci—Most Rev. Vjekoslav Huzjak; Bjelovar-Krizevci, Croatia.
Tel: 043-638-635 *Fax:* 638-637
Email: ordinarijat@biskupija-bk.hr

BLANTYRE—Most Rev. Tarcisius Gervazio Ziyaye; Archbishop's House P.O. Box 385, Blantyre, Malawi.
Tel: 265-163-79-05 *Fax:* 265-163-79-05
Email: archdblantyre@africa-online.net

BLOEMFONTEIN—Most Rev. Jabulani Nxumalo, O.M.I.; Archbishop's House 7/a White's Rd., P.O. Box 362, Bloemfontein, 9300, South Africa.
Tel: 27-051-448-1658 *Fax:* 27-051-447-2420
Email: bfnarch@mweb.co.za

Blois—Most Rev. Maurice Le Bègue de Germiny; Evêché, 2 rue Porte Clos Haut, Blois, 41000, France.
Tel: 2-54-56-40-60 *Fax:* 2-54-56-01-94
Email: vicaire.general@catholique-blois.net

Blumenau—Most Rev. Giuseppe "Jose" Negri, P.I.M.E.; C.P. 222, Blumenau, SC, 89010-970, Brazil.
Rua XV de Novembro s/n, Blumenau, SC, 89010-003, Brazil.
Tel: 047-3322-4435 *Fax:* 047-3322-4435

Bo—Most Rev. Charles Allieu Matthew Campbell; Sierra Leone.

Boac—Most Rev. Reynaldo G. Evangelista; Sacred Heart Pastoral Center, Boac, Marinduque, 4900, Philippines.
Tel: 042-332-1014 *Fax:* 042-332-1278
Email: dioceseofboac@yahoo.com

BOBO-DIOULASSO—Most Rev. Paul Yemboaro Ouedraogo; Archevêché, Lafiaso, 01 B.P. 312, Bobo-Dioulasso, Burkina Faso.
Tel: 226-20-97-04-35 *Fax:* 20-97-19-50
Email: lafiaso@fasonet.bf

Bogor—Most Rev. Cosmas Michael Angkur, O.F.M.; Keuskupan, Jl. Kapten Muslihat 22, Bogor, Jawa Barat, 16122, Indonesia.
Tel: 62-0251-8313-997 *Fax:* 62-0251-8359-102
Email: uskup@keuskupanbogor.org

BOGOTÁ—Most Rev. Jesus Rubén Salazar Gómez; Arzobispado, Carrera 7a N. 10-20, Bogotá, D.C. 1, Colombia.
Tel: 1-350-55-11 *Fax:* 1-350-72-90
Email: cancilleria@arquidiocesisbogota.org.co

Boise—Most Rev. Michael Patrick Driscoll; 1501 Federal Way, Boise, ID, 83705-5925.
Tel: 208-342-1311 *Fax:* 208-342-0224

Bokungu-Ikela—Most Rev. Fridolin Ambongo Besungu, O.F.M.Cap.; Mission Catholique, par Boende, Bokungu, Equateur, Democratic Republic of Congo.
Tel: 081-837-1268
Email: bokunguikela@yahoo.fr

BOLOGNA—His Eminence Carlo Caffarra; Arcivescovado, Via Altabella 6, Bologna, 40126, Italy.
Tel: 39-051-648-06-11 *Fax:* 39-051-648-07-34
Email: canc@bologna.chiesacattolica.it

Bolzano-Bressanone, Bozen-Brixen—Most Rev. Ivo Muser; Vescovado, Piazza Duomo 2, Bolzano, 39100, Italy.
Tel: 39-0471-30-62-00 *Fax:* 39-0471-30-63-60
Email: vicario.generale@bz-bx.net

Bom Jesus da Lapa—Most Rev. Jose Valmor Cesar Teixeira, S.D.B.; Cúria Diocesana, Av. São Vicente de Paulo s/n, C.P. 20, Bom Jesus da Lapa, BA, 47600-000, Brazil.
Tel: 55-077-3481-2086/4522 *Fax:* 55-077-3481-2086/4522

Bom Jesus do Gurguéia—Most Rev. Ramón López Carrozas, O.deM.; Cúria Diocesana, Av. Getúlio Vargas 600, C.P. 05, Bom Jesus, PI, 64900-000, Brazil.
Tel: 55-089-3562-1134 *Fax:* 55-089-3562-1134
Email: diocesebj@bol.com.br

Boma—Most Rev. Cyprien Mbuka, C.I.C.M.; Evêché, B.P. 72, Boma, Bas-Congo, Democratic Republic of Congo.
Tel: 099-840-60-69 *Fax:* 00871-762-601-621
Email: evecheboma@hotmail.com

BOMBAY—His Eminence Oswald Gracias; Archbishop's House, 21 Nathalal Parekh Marg, Bombay, 400001, India.
Tel: 91-022-2202-10-93/11-93 *Fax:* 91-022-2285-38-72
Email: diocesebombay@gmail.com

Bondo—Most Rev. Etienne Ung'eyowun; Evêché, B.P. 21, c/o B.P. 505, Bondo, Uélé, Eveché de Kisangani, Democratic Republic of Congo.
Email: diocesebondo@yahoo.fr

Bondoukou—Most Rev. Félix Kouadjo; Evêché, B.P. 444, Bondoukou, Ivory Coast.
Tel: 35-91-53-22
Email: evechbkou@aviso.ci

Bonfim—Most Rev. Francisco Canindé Palhano; Rue Conego Hugo 96, Senhor do Bonfim, BA, 48970-000, Brazil.
Tel: 55-074-3541-1652 *Fax:* 55-074-3541-1652
Email: diocesedebonfim@yahoo.com.br

Bongaigaon—Most Rev. Thomas Pulloppillil; Bishop's House B.P. 10, Bongaigaon, Assam, 783380, India.
Tel: 03664-241-650 *Fax:* 03664-242-184
Email: bpbongai1@sancharnet.in

BORDEAUX—His Eminence Jean-Pierre Ricard; Archvêché, 183 cours de la Somme, Bordeaux CEDEX, 33077, France.
Tel: 5-56-91-81-82 *Fax:* 5-56-92-12-98
Email: accueil@bordeaux.catholique.fr

Borongan—Most Rev. Crispin B. Varquez; Bishop's Residence Borongan, Eastern Samar, 6800, Philippines.
Tel: 055-560-93-25

BOSRA E HAURAN—Most Rev. Boulos Nassif Borkhoche; Archevêché Grec-Melkite-Catholique, Khabab, Hauran, Syria.
Tel: 015-85-50-12

Bossangoa—Vacant; Evêché, B.P. 1728, Bossangoa, Central African Republic.
Tel: 70-90-40-02
Email: eveche_bgoa@yahoo.fr

BOSTON—His Eminence Sean P. O'Malley, O.F.M.Cap.; 66 Brooks Dr., Braintree, MA, 02184-3839.
Tel: 617-254-0100 *Fax:* 617-779-4571
Email: vicar_general@rcab.org

BOTUCATU—Most Rev. Maurício Grotto de Camargo; Cúria Metropolitana, Rua Dr. Costa Leite 668, C.P. 33, Botucatu, SP, 18600-010, Brazil.
Tel: 55-014-3882-0909 *Fax:* 55-014-3882-0535
Email: curiabotucatu@hotmail.com

BOUAKÉ—Most Rev. Paul-Siméon Ahouanan Djro, O.F.M.; 01 B.P. 649, Bouaké, Ivory Coast.
Tel: 31-63-24-59 *Fax:* 31-63-24-06
Email: archevbke@aviso.ci

Bouar—Most Rev. Armando Umberto Gianni, O.F.M.Cap.; Evêché, B.P. 23, Bouar, Central African Republic.
Tel: 0236-31-40-43 *Fax:* 0236-31-40-43

Bougainville—Most Rev. Bernard Unabali; P.O. Box 85, Buka, North Solomons Province, Papua New Guinea.
Tel: 675-973-9044 *Fax:* 675-973-9043

BOURGES—Most Rev. Armand Maillard; Archevêché, 4 Avenue du 95ème-de-Ligne, B.P. 95, Bourges CEDEX, 18020, France.
Tel: 2-48-23-12-90 *Fax:* 2-48-24-37-44

BRAGA—Most Rev. Jorge Ferreira da Costa Ortiga; Rua São Domingos 94B, Braga CODEX, 4710-435, Portugal.
Tel: 351-253-20-31-80 *Fax:* 351-253-20-31-90
Email: diocese@diocese-braga.pt

Bragança do Pará—Most Rev. Luigi Ferrando; Cúria Diocesana, C.P. 013, Praça da Catedral 368, Bragança, PA, 68600-000, Brazil.
Tel: 55-091-3425-1108 *Fax:* 55-091-3425-2018

Bragança-Miranda—Most Rev. Jose Manuel Garcia Cordeiro; Cúria Diocesana, Rua Emídio Navarro 2, Bragança, 5300-210, Portugal.
Tel: 351-273-300-360 *Fax:* 351-273-300-361

Bragança Paulista—Most Rev. Sérgio Aparecido Colombo; Cúria Diocesana, Rua Coronel Assis Gonçalves 521, Bragança Paulista, SP, 12900-480, Brazil.
Tel: 55-011-4033-0858 *Fax:* 55-011-4033-0858
Email: curia@vivax.com.br

BRASÍLIA—Most Rev. Sérgio da Rocha; Cúria Metropolitana, Esplanada dos Ministérios, Emi Lote 12, Brasília, DF, 70050-000, Brazil.
Tel: 55-061-3213-3333 ***Fax:*** 55-061-3213-3331
Email: mab.chanceler@terra.com.br

BRATISLAVA—Most Rev. Stanislav Zvolenský; Arcibiskupsky úrad, Špitálska 7, Bratislava, SK-814 92, Slovakia.
Tel: 02-572-00-611 ***Fax:*** 02-572-00-612
Email: vikar@abuba.sk

Bratislava (Byzantine)—Most Rev. Peter Rusnák; Gréckokatolicka cirkev, ul. 29 Augusta 7, Bratislava, SK-81108, Slovakia.
Tel: 02-526-22-081 ***Fax:*** 02-526-22-081
Email: eparchia@grkatba.sk

BRAZZAVILLE—Most Rev. Anatole Milandou; Archevêché, B.P. 2301, Brazzaville, Republic of the Congo.
Tel: 05-535-00-42; 06-978-44-70
Email: archibrazza@yahoo.fr

Breda—Vacant; P.B. 90189, Breda, 4800 RN, The Netherlands.
Tel: 31-076-522-34-44 ***Fax:*** 31-076-521-62-44
Email: secretariaat@bisdombreda.nl
Veemarkstraat 46, Breda, 4811 ZG, The Netherlands.

Brejo—Most Rev. Jose Valdeci Santos Mendes; Residência Episcopal, Praça Benedito Leite 166, Brejo, MA, 65520-000, Brazil.
Tel: 55-098-3472-1151 ***Fax:*** 55-098-3472-1304
Email: diocesedebrejo@hotmail.com

Brentwood—Most Rev. Thomas McMahon; Cathedral House, 28 Ingrave Rd., Brentwood, Essex, CM15 8AT, England.
Tel: 44-01277-23-22-66 ***Fax:*** 44-01277-26-1152
Email: bishopthomas@dioceseofbrentwood.org

Brescia—Most Rev. Luciano Monari; Vescovada, Via Trieste 13, Brescia, 25121, Italy.
Tel: 39-030-37-221 ***Fax:*** 39-030-37-22-265
Email: diocesi@brescia.chiesacattolica.it

Bridgeport—Most Rev. William E. Lori; Chancery-The Catholic Center 238 Jewett Ave., Bridgeport, CT, 06606-2892.
Tel: 203-372-4301 ***Fax:*** 203-371-8698
Email: bishopsoffice@diobpt.org

Bridgetown—Most Rev. Charles Jason Gordon; Bishop's House Ladymeade Gardens, St. Michael, P.O. Box 1223, Bridgetown, Barbados, West Indies.
Tel: 246-426-3510 ***Fax:*** 246-429-6198

BRINDISI-OSTUNI—Most Rev. Rocco Talucci; Arcivescovado, Piazza Duomo 12, Brindisi, 72100, Italy.
Tel: 39-0831-523-053 ***Fax:*** 39-0831-528-315
Email: curia@diocesibrindisiostuni.it

BRISBANE—Most Rev. John Alexius Bathersby; Wynberg, 790 Brunswick Street, P.O. Box 936, New Farm, QLD, 4005, Australia.
Tel: 61-07-3131-5500 ***Fax:*** 61-07-3358-1357
Email: archbishop@bne.catholic.net.au

Brno—Most Rev. Vojtech Cikrle; Biskupství brnenské, Petrov 8, Brno 1, 601 43, Czech Republic.
Tel: 420-54-32-35-030 ***Fax:*** 420-54-32-37-042
Email: brno@biskupstvi.cz

Broken Bay—Most Rev. David Louis Walker; P.O. Box 340, Pennant Hills, NSW, 1715, Australia.
Tel: 61-02-9847-0230 ***Fax:*** 61-02-9847-0501

Brooklyn—Most Rev. Nicholas A. DiMarzio; Chancery Office 310 Prospect Park W., Brooklyn, NY, 11215.
Tel: 718-399-5990 ***Fax:*** 718-399-5934
Email: curia@diobrook.org

Broome—Most Rev. Christopher Alan Saunders; Bishop's House P.O. Box 76, 13 Barker St., Broome, W.A., 6725, Australia.
Tel: 61-0891-921-060 ***Fax:*** 61-0891-922-136
Email: secretary@broomediocese.org

Brownsville—Most Rev. Daniel E. Flores; 1910 University Blvd., Brownsville, TX, 78520.
Tel: 956-542-2501 ***Fax:*** 956-542-6751
Web: www.cdob.org
Email: cdob@cdob.org

Brugge, Bruges—Most Rev. Josef De Kesel; Bisdom, Heilige-Geeststraat 4, Brugge, B-8000, Belgium.
Tel: 32-050-33-59-05 ***Fax:*** 32-050-34-14-32
Email: secretariaat.bisdom.brugge@kerknet.be

Bubanza—Most Rev. Jean Ntagwarara; Evêché de Bubanza, D.S. 213, Bujumbura, Burundi.
Tel: 257-22-26-11-09/89 ***Fax:*** 257-22-26-11-51
Email: jntagwa@yahoo.fr

BUCARAMANGA—Most Rev. Ismael Rueda Sierra; Arzobispado, Calle 33 N. 21-16, Bucaramanga, Santander, Colombia.
Tel: 57-7-6424-387/6425-132 ***Fax:*** 57-7-6421-361
Email: prensacuria@gmail.com

Buchach—Most Rev. Dmytro (Bohdan) Hryhorak, O.S.B.M.; Monastryrska I, Ternopilska oblast, Chortkiv, 48500, Ukraine.
Tel: 03552-223-17 ***Fax:*** 03552-227-91
Email: buchacheparchy@ukr.net

BUCURESTI, BUCAREST—Most Rev. Ioan Robu; Arhiepiscopia Romano-Catolica, Str. Gen. Berthelot, 19, Bucuresti, RO-010164, Romania.
Tel: 40-021-315-49-55; 201-54-80 ***Fax:*** 40-021-312-12-07
Email: secretariat@arcb.ro

Budjala—Most Rev. Philibert Tembo Nlandu, C.I.C.M.; Diocèse de Budjala, B.P. 1800, Kinshasa, Democratic Republic of Congo.
Tel: 099-791-01-47
Email: jbzabusu@yahoo.fr

Buéa—Most Rev. Immanuel Bushu; Bishop's House P.O. Box 64, Soppo, S.W. Province, Buéa, Fako Division, Cameroon.
Tel: 237-3332-2241 ***Fax:*** 237-3322-2671
Email: dioceseofbuea@yahoo.com

Buenaventura—Most Rev. Hector Epalza Quintero, P.S.S.; Apartado Aéreo 637, Calle 3B N. 8-47, Buenaventura, Valle, Colombia.
Tel: 092-2-241-17-38 ***Fax:*** 092-2-242-25-60
Email: buenaventuradioc@cec.org.co

BUENOS AIRES—His Eminence Cardinal Jorge Mario Bergoglio, S.J.; Arzobispado, Rivadavia 415, Buenos Aires, C1002AAC, Argentina.
Tel: 54-011-4343-0812 ***Fax:*** 54-011-4334-8373; 54-011-4342-9238
Email: arzobispado@arzbaires.org.ar

Buffalo—Most Rev. Edward U. Kmiec, D.D., S.T.L. (BUF); Chancery Office 795 Main St., Buffalo, NY, 14203-1250.
Tel: 716-847-5500 ***Fax:*** 716-847-5557
Web: www.buffalodiocese.org
Email: dob@buffalodiocese.org

Buga—Most Rev. Hernan Giraldo Jaramillo; Curia Episcopal, Carrera 14 N. 4-83, Buga, Valle, Colombia.
Tel: 57-22-227-1812/66 ***Fax:*** 57-22-236-63-36
Email: diocebuga@hotmail.com

Bùi Chu—Most Rev. Joseph Hoang Van Tiem, S.D.B.; Toà Giám Muc, Xuân Ngoc, Xuân Truong, Nam Dinh, Vietnam.
Tel: 0350-3887-142 ***Fax:*** 0350-3887-521
Email: tgmbc@hn.vnn.vn

BUJUMBURA—Most Rev. Evariste Ngoyagoye; Evêché, B.P. 690, Bujumbura, Burundi.
Tel: 257-22-23-14-76 ***Fax:*** 257-22-23-11-65
Email: dicabu@cni.cbinf.com

BUKAVU—Most Rev. François Xavier Maroy Rusengo; Archevêché, Avenue Mbaki 18, B.P. 3324, Bukavu, Kivu, Democratic Republic of Congo.
Tel: 081-31-80-621
Email: archevechebk@yahoo.fr

Bukoba—Most Rev. Nestorius Timanywa; Bishop's House P.O. Private Bag, Bukoba, Tanzania.
Tel: 255-028-2220-189/96 ***Fax:*** 255-028-2222-113
Email: b.officebk@yahoo.com

BULAWAYO—Most Rev. Alex Thomas Kaliyanil, S.V.D.; Bishop's House Lobenguela St., 108A 9th Ave., P.O. Box 837, Bulawayo, Zimbabwe.
Tel: 263-09-63-590 ***Fax:*** 263-09-60-359
Email: archdbyo@netconnect.co.zw

Bunbury—Most Rev. Gerard Joseph Holohan; Chancery Office, St. Patrick's Cathedral 18 Parkfield St., P.O. Box 2005, Bunbury, W.A., 6231, Australia.
Tel: 61-08-9721-0500 ***Fax:*** 61-08-9721-3216
Email: tonyc@bunburycatholic.org.au

Bunda—Most Rev. Renatus Leonard Nkwande; Tanzania.

Bungoma—Most Rev. Norman King'oo Wambua; P.O. Box 617, Bungoma, 50200, Kenya.
Tel: 055-30-456 ***Fax:*** 055-30-403
Email: catdibgm@yahoo.com

Bunia—Most Rev. Dieudonné Uringi Uuci; Eveche B.P. 19, Bunia, Haut-Congo, Democratic Republic of Congo.
Tel: 099-401-01-12
Email: evechebunia@yahoo.fr

BURGOS—Most Rev. Francisco Gil Hellin; Arzobispado, Calle Eduardo Martínez del Campo 18, Burgos, 09003, Spain.
Tel: 34-947-20-84-40 ***Fax:*** 34-947-27-56-36
Email: arzburgos@planalfa.es

Burlington—Most Rev. Salvatore R. Matano, D.D., S.T.L., J.C.D. (BUR); Chancery Office 55 Joy Dr., South Burlington, VT, 05403.
Tel: 802-658-6110 *Fax:* 802-658-0436
Email: chancery@vermontcatholic.org

Bururi—Most Rev. Venant Bacinoni; Evêché de Bururi, D.S. 140, Bujumbura, Burundi.
Tel: 257-50-2327
Email: firminiy@yahoo.fr

Buta—Most Rev. Joseph Banga Bane; Evêché, B.P. 105, Buta, Democratic Republic of Congo.
Tel: 081-852-24-02
Email: butaeveche@yahoo.fr

Butare—Most Rev. Philippe Rukamba; Evêché, B.P. 69, Butare, Rwanda.
Tel: 32-076-530-129 *Fax:* 32-076-530-652
Email: evechebutare@yahoo.fr

Butembo-Beni—Most Rev. Melchisedec Sikuli Paluku; B.P. 63, Butembo, Nord-Kivu, Democratic Republic of Congo.
Tel: 099-838-68-26
Email: evebube@yahoo.fr

Butuan—Most Rev. Juan de Dios Pueblos; Bishop's Residence P.O. Box 54, Ampayon, Butuan City, 8600, Philippines.
Tel: 085-342-37-47/9 *Fax:* 085-815-9251
Email: lospadresbxu_chancery@yahoo.com

Buxar—Most Rev. Sebastian Kallupura; Bishop's House Nayi Bazaar, Bihar, Buxar, 802101, India.
Tel: 0183-226-717
Email: bpbuxar@gmail.com

Bydgoszcz—Most Rev. Jan Tyrawa; Kuria Diecezjalna, ul. Ks. Malczewskiego 1, 85-104 Bydgoszcz, Poland.
Tel: 052-366-98-00 *Fax:* 052-366-98-20
Email: kuria@byd.pl

Byumba—Most Rev. Servilien Nzakamwita; Evêche B.P. 5, Byumba, Rwanda.
Tel: 252-564-562 *Fax:* 252-564-096
Email: diocabyumba@yahoo.fr

C

Caacupé—Most Rev. Catalino Claudio Giménez Medina; Obispado, Calle Eligio Ayala 1549, Caacupé, Paraguay.
Tel: 595-0511-242-276 *Fax:* 595-0511-242-276
Email: obispadocaacupe@gmail.com

Cabanatuan—Most Rev. Sofronio A. Bancud, S.S.S.; Bishop's Office C.I.C. Building, Del Pilar St., Cabanatuan City, 3100, Philippines.
Tel: 63-044-463-3849 *Fax:* 63-044-463-7695
Email: dioceseofcabanatuan@yahoo.com

Cabimas—Most Rev. William Enrique Delgado Silva; Obispado, Apartado 27, Avenida Universidad 1, Esquina Carretera H, Cabimas, Edo. Zulia, 4013, Venezuela.
Tel: 58-0264-241-27-65 *Fax:* 58-0264-241-10-63
Email: diocabi@hotmail.com

Cabinda—Most Rev. Filomeno do Nascimento Vieira Dias; Bispado, Rua Gago Countinho, Cabinda, Angola.
Tel: 02312-22-237
Email: milanzednicek@yahoo.com.br

Caçador—Most Rev. Severino Clasen, O.F.M.; C.P. 227, Rua Mafra 235, Caçador, SC, 89500-000, Brazil.
Tel: 55-049-3563-2045 *Fax:* 55-049-3563-2045
Email: mitradiocesana@diocesedecacador.org.br

CACERES—Most Rev. Leonardo Z. Legaspi, O.P.; Archbishop's House Elias Angeles St., P.O. Box 6085, Naga City, 4400, Philippines.
Tel: 63-054-473-8483 *Fax:* 63-054-473-83-83
Email: chancerynaga@yahoo.com

Cachoeira do Sul—Most Rev. Irineu Silvio Wilges, O.F.M.; Cúria Diocesana, Rua Moron 1007, Cachoeira do Sul, RS, 96508-031, Brazil.
Tel: 55-051-3722-1875 *Fax:* 55-051-3722-1875
Email: diocese@diocesenet.com.br

Cachoeiro de Itapemirim—Most Rev. Dario Campos, O.F.M.; Cúria Diocesana, Rua Costa Pereira 39, Cachoeiro de Itapemirim, ES, 29300-090, Brazil.
Tel: 55-028-2101-7604 *Fax:* 55-028-2101-7602
Email: diocese@dci.org.br

Cádiz y Ceuta—Most Rev. Rafael Zornoza Boy; Casa de la Iglesia, Calle Hospital de Mujeres 26 dupl., Cádiz, 11001, Spain.
Tel: 34-956-80-70-18 *Fax:* 34-956-80-71-42
Email: secretariac@obispadodecadizyceuta.org
Plaza de Nuestra Señora de Africa, Ceuta 11701, Spain.
Tel: 34-956-51-77-32

Caetité—Most Rev. Guerrino Riccardo Brusati; Cúria Diocesana, C.P. 06, Rua Barão de Caetite 22, Caetité, BA, 46400-970, Brazil.
Tel: 55-077-3454-4405 *Fax:* 55-077-3454-1094
Email: bispocte@gbi.com.br

CAGAYAN DE ORO—Most Rev. Antonio J. Ledesma, S.J.; Archbishop's Residence Fernandez St., Brgy. 1, Cagayon de Oro City, 9000, Philippines.
Tel: 63-08822-722-375 *Fax:* 63-08822-726-304
Email: acdo_chancery@yahoo.com

CAGLIARI—Most Rev. Giuseppe Mani; Arcivescovado, Via Mons. Cogoni 9, Cagliari, 09121, Italy.
Tel: 39-070-528-43-204 *Fax:* 39-070-528-43-305
Email: cancelleria@diocesidicagliari.it

Caguas—Most Rev. Rubén Antonio González Medina, C.M.F.; Apartado 8698, Caguas, PR, 00726, Puerto Rico.
Tel: 787-747-5885 *Fax:* 787-747-5616
Email: diocesisdecaguas@hotmail.com

Cahors—Most Rev. Norbert José Henri Turini; 134 rue Frederic Suisse, Cahors, 46000, France.
Tel: 5-65-35-40-43
Email: secretariat.eveche.cahors@wanadoo.fr

Caicó—Most Rev. Manoel Delson Pedreira da Cruz, O.F.M. Cap.; C.P. 31, Largo Dom Manuel Tavares s/n, Bairro Paraíba, Caicó, RN, 59300-000, Brazil.
Tel: 55-084-3421-2125 *Fax:* 55-084-3417-2732
Email: pe.edson@gmail.com

Cairns—Most Rev. James Foley; Chancery Office 183 Abbott St., P.O. Box 625, Cairns, QLD, 4870, Australia.
Tel: 61-0740-512-071 *Fax:* 61-0740-314-625
Email: bishop@cairns.catholic.org.au

Cajamarca—Most Rev. José Carmelo Martínez Lázaro, O.A.R.; Obispado, Apartado 34, Jr. del Batán 109, Cajamarca, Peru.
Tel: 51-76-36-26-15 *Fax:* 51-76-36-27-99; 51-76-36-26-15
Email: obispadocajamarca@speedy.com.pe

Cajazeiras—Most Rev. José González Alonso; Cúria Diocesana, Rua Padre Rolim 571, C.P. 13, Cajazeiras, PB, 58900-000, Brazil.
Tel: 55-083-3531-1335 *Fax:* 55-083-3531-1335
Email: diocajaz@uol.com.br

CALABAR—Most Rev. Joseph Edra Ukpo; Catholic Secretariat, 1 Bishop Moynagh Ave., P.M.B. 1044, Calabar, Cross River State, Nigeria.
Tel: 234-087-231-666; 0803-607-0707
Email: archdical@yahoo.com

CALABOZO—Most Rev. Manuel Felipe Díaz Sánchez; Arzobispado, Carrera 4 entre carrera 12 N. 11-82, Calabozo, Edo. Guárico, 2312, Venezuela.
Tel: 58-0246-871-0483 *Fax:* 58-0246-871-2097
Email: arquicalabozocc@gmail.com

Calahorra y La Calzada-Logroño—Most Rev. Juan José Omella Omella; Obispo Fidel García 1, Logroño, La Rioja, 26004, Spain.
Tel: 34-941-27-00-08 *Fax:* 34-941-27-10-98
Email: secretariogeneral@iglesiaenlarioja.org

Calbayog—Most Rev. Isabello C. Abarquez; Bishop's House J.D. Avelino St., P.O. Box 2, Calbayog City, Western Samar, 6710, Philippines.
Tel: 055-20-91-372 *Fax:* 055-20-93-012
Email: calbchancery@yahoo.com

CALCUTTA—Most Rev. Lucas Sirkar, S.D.B.; Archbishop's House 32 Mother Teresa Sarani, Kolkata, West Bengal, 700016, India.
Tel: 033-2287-19-60; 033-2287-93-38 *Fax:* 033-2287-62-50

Caldas—Most Rev. José Soleibe Arbeláez; Curia Epsicopal, Calle 130 Sur 49-43, Caldas, Antioquia, Colombia.
Tel: 57-94-278-55-06 *Fax:* 57-94-303-16-39
Email: diocaldas@une.net.co

Calgary—Most Rev. Frederick Bernard Henry; Catholic Pastoral Centre Room 290 The Iona Bldg., 120-17th Ave. S.W., Calgary, AB, T2S 2T2, Canada.
Tel: 403-218-5500 *Fax:* 403-264-0272
Email: modcuria@rcdiocese-calgary.ab.ca

CALI—Most Rev. Dario de Jesus Monsalve Mejia; Curia Arzobispal, Carrera 4 N. 7-17, Cali, Colombia.
Tel: 57-2-889-05-62 *Fax:* 57-2-883-79-80
Email: arquicali@arquidiocesiscali.org

Calicut—Most Rev. Joseph Kalathiparambil; Bishop's House Malaparamba, Kozhikode, Kerala, 673009, India.
Tel: 91-0495-237-23-10; 91-0495-237-03-13 ***Fax:*** 91-0495-237-70-13
Email: calicut_diocese@yahoo.com

Callao—Most Rev. Miguel Irízar Campos, C.P.; Jr. Bolognesi 283, Bellavista, Callao, 02, Peru.
Tel: 51-1-429-4918; 51-1-465-3575; 51-1-429-1918 ***Fax:*** 51-1-465-4040
Email: obcall@rcp.net.pe

Caltagirone—Most Rev. Calogero Peri, O.F.M.Cap.; Vescovado, Piazza S. Francesco d'Assisi 11, Caltagirone, Catania, 95041, Italy.
Tel: 39-0933-36-86-45 ***Fax:*** 39-0933-36-86-44
Email: curia@diocesidicaltagirone.it

Caltanissetta—Most Rev. Mario Russotto; Vescovado, Via Cairoli 8, Caltanissetta, 93100, Italy.
Tel: 39-0934-21-446 ***Fax:*** 39-0934-543-449
Email: curia@diocesicaltanissetta.it

CAMAGÜEY—Most Rev. Juan García Rodríguez; Calle Luaces 55, Apartado 105, Camagüey, 70100, Cuba.
Tel: 032-2853-33 ***Fax:*** 032-2871.43

Camaçari—Most Rev. Joao Carlos Petrini; Brazil.

CAMBRAI—Most Rev. François Garnier; Archevêché, 11 rue du Grand Séminaire, B.P. 149, Cambrai CEDEX, 59403, France.
Tel: 3-27-81-34-96 ***Fax:*** 3-27-81-34-91
Email: diocesedecambrai@nordnet.fr

Camden—Most Rev. Joseph Anthony Galante, D.D., J.C.D. (CAM); Chancery Office: Camden Diocesan Center 631 Market St., Camden, NJ, 08102.
Tel: 856-756-7900 ***Fax:*** 856-963-2655

CAMERINO-SAN SEVERINO MARCHE—Most Rev. Francesco Giovanni Brugnaro; Arcivescovado, Piazza Cavour 7, Camerino, Macerata, 62032, Italy.
Tel: 39-0737-63-04-00 ***Fax:*** 39-0737-63-14-20
Email: curia@arcidiocesicamerino.it

Campanha—Most Rev. Diamantino Prata de Carvalho, O.F.M.; Cúria Diocesana, Rua João Luiz Alves 106, C.P. 14, Campanha, MG, 37400-000, Brazil.
Tel: 55-035-3261-1217 ***Fax:*** 55-035-3261-1956
Email: curiadiocesanadecampanha@yahoo.com.br

Campeche—Most Rev. Ramón Castro Castro; Obispado, Calle 53 N. 1-B, entre 8 y 10, Apartado 127, Campeche, Camp., 24000, Mexico.
Tel: 52-981-81-662-48 ***Fax:*** 52-981-81-603-39
Email: diocesis_campeche@hotmail.com

Campina Grande—Most Rev. Jaime Vieira Rocha; Cúria Diocesana, Rua Afonso Campos 251, Campina Grande, PB, 58400-235, Brazil.
Tel: 55-083-3321-4199 ***Fax:*** 55-083-3321-0492
Email: diocese@gmail.com

CAMPINAS—Vacant; Cúria Metropolitana, Rua Irmã Serafina 88, C.P. 98, 13012-970, Campinas, SP, 13026-066, Brazil.
Tel: 55-019-3232-2327; 55-019-3231-7122; 55-019-3231-7374 ***Fax:*** 55-019-3232-3285

CAMPO GRANDE—Most Rev. Dimas Lara Barbosa; Cúria Metropolitana, Rua Amando de Oliveria 448, B. Amamabaí, Campo Grande, MS, 79008-010, Brazil.
Tel: 55-067-3320-2800 ***Fax:*** 55-067-3317-4955
Email: arqcgr@terra.com.br

Campo Limpo—Most Rev. Luiz Antônio Guedes; Cúria Diocesana, Rua Lira Paulista 30, Jardim Bom Refúgio, C.P. 60757, Campo Limpo, São Paulo, SP, 05788-320, Brazil.
Tel: 55-011-3584-9000 ***Fax:*** 55-011-3584-9027; 55-011-3584-9000
Email: curia@diocesedecampolimpo.org.br

Campo Maior—Most Rev. Eduardo Zielski; Cúria Diocesana, C.P. 31, Praça Bona Primo 428, Campo Maior, PI, 64280-000, Brazil.
Tel: 55-086-3252-1132 ***Fax:*** 55-086-3252-2192
Email: diocese@ig.com.br

Campo Mourão—Most Rev. Francisco Javier Del Valle Paredes; Rua Harrison José Borges 811, Campo Mourão, PR, 87300-380, Brazil.
Tel: 55-044-3525-1824 ***Fax:*** 55-044-3525-1147
Email: curiacampomourao@brturbo.com.br

CAMPOBASSO-BOIANO—Most Rev. Giancarlo Maria Bregantini, C.S.S.; Arcivescovado, Via Mazzini 76, Campobasso, 86100, Italy.
Tel: 39-0874-60-694 ***Fax:*** 39-0874-60-149
Email: archdiocesi@aliseo.it

Campos—Most Rev. Roberto Francisco Ferreria Paz; Cúria Diocesana, Av. 7 de Setembro 247, Campos dos Goytacazes, RJ, 28013-330, Brazil.
Tel: 55-022-2734-0750; 55-022-2722-7750 ***Fax:*** 55-022-2722-7750
Email: mitracampos@censanet.com.br

Cân Tho—Most Rev. Stephanus Tri Buu Thien; Toà Giám Muc, 12 Nguyên Trai, Tp. Cân Tho, Hau Giang, Vietnam.
Tel: 0710-381-36-55

CANBERRA-GOULBURN—Most Rev. Mark Benedict Coleridge; G.P.O. Box 89, Canberra, A.C.T., 2601, Australia.
Tel: 61-02-6201-9811 ***Fax:*** 61-02-6248-0287
Email: archbishop@cg.catholic.org.au

Candia, Creta, La Canea—Vacant; Katholiki Ekklisia, Patrós Antoniou 2, Iraklion, 71202, Greece.

Canelones—Most Rev. Alberto Francisco Maria Sanguinetti Montero; José Batlle y Ordóñez 579, Canelones, 90000, Uruguay.
Tel: 598-0332-2568 ***Fax:*** 598-0332-3587
Email: curiacan@adinet.com.uy

CANTON (GUANGZHOU)—Vacant; Catholic Mission She-Se, Guangzhou, Guangdong, China.

CAP-HAÏTIEN—Most Rev. Louis Kébreau, S.D.B.; Archevêché, B.P. 22, rue 19-20 H, Cap-Haïtien, W.I., Haiti.
Tel: 509-03-2262-0071; 509-03-2262-1365; 509-03-2262-1278 ***Fax:*** 509-03-2262-1278
Email: georgevincent@yahoo.fr

CAPE COAST—Most Rev. Matthias Kobena Nketsiah; Archdiocesan Secretariat P.O. Box 112, Cape Coast, Ghana.
Tel: 233-042-33-471/2 ***Fax:*** 233-042-33-473
Email: archcape@ghanacbc.org

Cape Palmas—Most Rev. Andrew Jagaye Karnley; Catholic Mission P.O. Box 11, Harper, Cape Palmas, Liberia.
Tel: 00874-231-47-16-232c/o Mission Catholique, B.P. 354, San Pedro, Ivory Coast.
Tel: 682-8220
Email: nyantigayemelvin@yahoo.com

CAPE TOWN, KAAPSTAD—Most Rev. Stephen Brislin; Cathedral Place, 12 Bouquet St., Cape Town, 8001, South Africa.
Tel: 27-021-462-2417 ***Fax:*** 27-021-461-9330
Email: info@catholic-ct.org.za

CAPIZ—Most Rev. Onesimo C. Gordoncillo; Chancery Office P.O. Box 44, Roxas City, Capiz, 5800, Philippines.
Tel: 036-6215-595 ***Fax:*** 036-6211-053

CAPUA—Most Rev. Bruno Schettino; Palazzo Arcivescovile, Piazza Landolfo 1, Capua, Caserta, 81043, Italy.
Tel: 39-0823-96-14-44 ***Fax:*** 0823-62-14-10

Carabayllo—Most Rev. Lino Mario Panizza Richero, O.F.M.Cap; Jirón Mecurio 7598, Urb. Sol de Oro, Los Olivos, Lima, 39, Peru.
Tel: 01-533-5753; 01-533-0616 ***Fax:*** 01-533-5016
Email: secretaria@obispadocarabayllo.org.pe

CARACAS, SANTIAGO DE VENEZUELA—His Eminence Jorge Liberato Urosa Savino; Arzobispado, Apartado 954, Monjas a Gradillas, Plaza Bolívar, Caracas, 1010-A, Venezuela.
Tel: 58-0212-542-17-55; 58-0212-542-19-44 ***Fax:*** 58-0212-542-02-97; 58-0212-542-07-90
Email: arzobispado@cantv.net

Caraguatatuba—Most Rev. Antonio Carlos Altieri, S.D.B; C.P. 215, rua Santos Dumont 100, Caraguatatuba, SP, 11660-970, Brazil.
Tel: 012-3883-4888; 012-3883-6668 ***Fax:*** 012-3883-4888; 012-3883-6668
Email: curia@diocesecaraguatatuba.com.br

Carapeguá—Most Rev. Joaquin Hermes Robledo Romero; Cap. Rogelio Santacruz 834, Carapeguá, Paraguay.
Tel: 595-0532-212-241 ***Fax:*** 595-0532-212-352
Email: obiscar@hotmail.es

Caratinga—Most Rev. Emanuel Messias de Oliveira; Cúria Diocesana, Praça Cesário Alvim 172, C.P. 13, 35300-970, Caratinga, MG, 35300-036, Brazil.
Tel: 55-033-3321-4600 ***Fax:*** 55-033-3321-4600
Email: curiadiocesanacaratinga@hotmail.com

Carcassonne et Narbonne—Most Rev. Alain Planet; Evêché, 89 rue Jean Bringer, B.P. 103, Carcassonne CEDEX, 11003, France.
Tel: 4-68-47-0531 ***Fax:*** 4-68-47-7681
Email: vicaire@eglisecatho-aude.cef.fr

CARDIFF—Most Rev. George Stack; Archbishop's House 41-43 Cathedral Rd., Cardiff, South Glamorgan, Wales, CF11 9HD, England.
Tel: 44-029-20-379-494 ***Fax:*** 44-029-20-379-036

Carolina—Most Rev. José Soares Filho, O.F.M. Cap.; Cúria Diocesana, C.P. 15, Av. Getúlio Vargas 23, Carolina, MA, 65980-000, Brazil.
Tel: 55-099-3531-2292

Caroline Islands—Most Rev. Armando Samo; Bishop's House P.O. Box 939, Chuuk, Caroline Islands, FM, 96942.
Tel: 691-330-2399
Email: diocese@mail.fm

Carora—Vacant; Obispado, Calle Lara 3-12, Carora, Edo. Lara, 3040, Venezuela.
Tel: 58-0252-421-62-67 ***Fax:*** 58-0252-421-33-74
Email: curiadecarora@cantv.net

Carpi—Most Rev. Elio Tinti; Vescovado, Corso M. Fanti 13, Carpi, Modena, 41012, Italy.
Tel: 39-059-68-60-48 ***Fax:*** 39-059-632-65-30
Email: douglasregattieri@libero.it

CARTAGENA—Most Rev. Jorge Enrique Jiménez Carvajal, C.I.M.; Casa Arzobispal, Carrera del Arzobispado 5 N. 34-55, Apdo 400, Cartagena, Colombia.
Tel: 05-664-53-08; 05-664-40-02 ***Fax:*** 05-664-49-74

Cartagena (in Spain)—Most Rev. José Manuel Lorca Planes; Palacio Episcopal, Plaza del Cardenal Belluga 1, Murcia, 30001, Spain.
Tel: 968-22-13-71 ***Fax:*** 968-21-21-72
Email: secretariageneral@diocesisdecartagena.org

Cartago—Most Rev. José Francisco Ulloa Rojas; Costado Norte de la Catedral, Parroquia Nuestra Señora del Carmen, Apartado 1221, Cartago, 7050, Costa Rica.
Tel: 2553-30-50; 2552-90-82 ***Fax:*** 2553-29-69
Email: curiacartago@ice.co.cr

Cartago—Most Rev. Jose Alejandro Castano Arbelaez, O.A.R.; Residencia Episcopal, Carrera 5, N. 13-87, Cartago, Valle, Colombia.
Tel: 57-092-212-3746 ***Fax:*** 57-092-211-3568
Email: diocesisctgo@uniweb.com

Caruaru—Most Rev. Bernardino Marchió; Cúria Diocesana, Avenida Oswaldo Cruz 207, Maurício de Nassau, Caruaru, PE, 55012-040, Brazil.
Tel: 55-081-3721-1510 ***Fax:*** 55-081-3721-0273
Email: curiadiocesanacaruaru@gmail.com

Carúpano—Most Rev. Jaime Villarroel Rodriguez; Callejón Santa Rosa 3, Carúpano, Edo. Sucre, 6124, Venezuela.
Tel: 0294-332-24-79 ***Fax:*** 0294-332-24-79
Email: diocesiscarupano@cantv.net

Casale Monferrato—Most Rev. Alceste Catella; Vescovado, Via Liutprando 1, Casale Monferrato, Alessandria, 15033, Italy.
Tel: 39-0142-45-22-19 ***Fax:*** 39-0142-45-58-20
Email: diocesi@diocesidicasale.191.it

CASCAVEL—Most Rev. Mauro Aparecido dos Santos; Cúria Metropolitana, Rua Maranhão 1595, Cascavel, PR, 85801-051, Brazil.
Tel: 55-045-3225-2324 ***Fax:*** 55-045-3225-2324
Email: curiacvl@terra.com.br
C.P. 432, Cascavel, PR, 85802-970, Brazil.

Caserta—Most Rev. Pietro Farina; Piazza Duomo 11, Caserta, 81100, Italy.
Tel: 39-0823-21-45-44 ***Fax:*** 39-0823-21-4543
Email: vescovo@diocesicaserta.it

CASHEL—Most Rev. Dermott Clifford; Archbishop's House Thurles, Co. Tipperary, Ireland.
Tel: 353-0504-21512 ***Fax:*** 353-0504-22680
Email: office@cashel-emly.ie

Cassano all'Jonio—Vacant; Vescovado, Piazza S. Eusebio 1, Cassano all'Jonio, Cosenza, 87011, Italy.
Tel: 39-0981-71-048 ***Fax:*** 39-0981-782-250
Email: info@diocesicassanoalloionio.it

Castanhal—Most Rev. Carlo Verzeletti; Rua Major Wilson 481, Bairro Nova Olinda, Castanhal, PA, 68741-320, Brazil.
Tel: 091-3711-3390 ***Fax:*** 091-3711-3390

Castellaneta—Most Rev. Pietro Maria Fragnelli; Vescovado, Via Maria Immacolata 4, Castellaneta, Taranto, 74011, Italy.
Tel: 39-099-8441-421 ***Fax:*** 39-099-8435-099
Email: curia@castellaneta.chiesacattolica.it

CASTRIES—Most Rev. Robert Rivas, O.P.; Chancery Offices Battery Road, Vigie, P.O. Box 267, Castries, Saint Lucia, West Indies.
Tel: 758-452-2416 ***Fax:*** 758-452-3697
Email: archbishop@candw.lc

Catamarca—Most Rev. Luis Urbanc; Obispado, Calle San Martin 655, San Fernando del Valle de Catamarca, K4700BOM, Argentina.
Tel: 54-3833-422-003 ***Fax:*** 3833-431-201
Email: obispadocatamarca@cedeconet.com.ar

Catanduva—Most Rev. Otacilio Luziano Da Silva; Praça da Independência 123, Barrio Higienópolis, Catanduva, SP, 15804-015, Brazil.
Tel: 017-3521-6501 ***Fax:*** 017-3521-6504
Email: diocese@catanduva.com.br

CATANIA—Most Rev. Salvatore Gristina; Arcivescovado, Via Vittorio Emanuele 159, Catania, 95131, Italy.
Tel: 39-095-715-90-62; 39-095-25-04-311 ***Fax:*** 39-095-25-04-358
Email: curia@diocesi.catania.it

CATANZARO-SQUILLACE—Most Rev. Vincenzo Bertolone, S.d.P.; Via dell'Arcivescovado 13, Catanzaro, 88100, Italy.
Tel: 39-0961-72-13-35 ***Fax:*** 39-0961-72-13-35
Email: curiaczsq@email.it

Catarman—Most Rev. Emmanuel C. Trance; Diocesan Catholic Center Catarman, Northern Samar, 6400, Philippines.
Tel: 055-251-8174 ***Fax:*** 055-251-8173
Email: catarmandiocese@yahoo.com

Caxias do Maranhão—Most Rev. Vilson Basso, S.C.I.; Cúria Diocesana, Praça Magalhaes de Almeida 744, Caxias, MA, 65606-060, Brazil.
C.P. 54, Caxias, MA, 65606-970, Brazil.
Tel: 099-3521-1658 ***Fax:*** 099-3521-1658
Email: diocesedecaxias@bol.com.br

Caxias do Sul—Most Rev. Alessandro Carmelo Ruffinoni, C.S.; Cúria Diocesana, Rua Os 18 do Forte 1771, C.P. 59, 95001-970, Caxias do Sul, RS, 95020-472, Brazil.
Tel: 55-054-3214-5388 ***Fax:*** 55-054-3214-5388
Email: mitra@diocesedecaxias.org.br

Caxito—Most Rev. Antonio Francisco Jaca, S.V.D.; Rua Direita de Caxito s/n, C.P. 3579, Caxito, Angola.
Tel: 0234-290-176 ***Fax:*** 0234-281-119
Email: diocesecaxito@yahoo.com

Cayenne—Most Rev. Emmanuel Lafont; Evêche, 24 rue Madame Payé, Cayenne, 97300, French Guiana.
Tel: 594-28-98-48 ***Fax:*** 594-30-20-33

CEBU—Most Rev. Jose S. Palma; Chancery, Cardinal Rosales Pastoral Center Cor. P.Gomez and P. Burgos St., P.O. Box 52, Cebu City, 6000, Philippines.
Tel: 032-254-1861; 032-253-0123 ***Fax:*** 032-253-0123

Cefalù—Most Rev. Vincenzo Manzella; Vescovado, Piazza Duomo 12, Cefalù, Palermo, 90015, Italy.
Tel: 39-0921-92-63-60 ***Fax:*** 39-0921-92-63-63

Celaya—Most Rev. Benjamín Castillo Plascencia; Curia Diocesana, Apartado 207, Manuel Doblado 110, Celaya, Guanajuato, 38000, Mexico.
Tel: 52-461-612-48-35 ***Fax:*** 52-461-612-43-98

Celje—Most Rev. Stanislav Lipovsek; Škofijski ordinariat, Prešernova ulica 23, Celje, 3000, Slovenia.
Tel: 386-059-080-600 ***Fax:*** 386-059-080-609
Email: ordinariat@skofija-celje.si

Cerignola-Ascoli Satriano—Most Rev. Felice di Molfetta; Piazza Duomo 42, Cerignola, Foggia, 71042, Italy.
Tel: 39-0885-421-572 ***Fax:*** 39-0885-429-490
Email: vinovincenzo@libero.it

Cerreto Sannita-Telese-Sant'Agata de' Goti—Most Rev. Michele De Rosa; Curia Vescovile, Via Vescovile I, Cerreto Sannita, Benevento, 82032, Italy.
Tel: 39-0824-861-115 ***Fax:*** 39-0824-861-115
Email: curiacerreto@tin.it

Cesena-Sarsina—Most Rev. Douglas Regattieri; Vescovado, Via Giovanni XXIII 13, Cesana, Forlì, 47521, Italy.
Tel: 39-0547-22-501 ***Fax:*** 39-0547-61-37-15
Email: cancelleria@cesena-sarsina.chiesacattolica.it

Ceské Budejovice—Most Rev. Jiri Padour, O.F.M.Cap.; Biskupství Ordinariát, Biskupská 4, Post Schranka 14, Ceské Budejovice, 370 21, Czech Republic.
Tel: 380-42-03-11 ***Fax:*** 380-42-03-00
Email: kurie@bcb.cz

Chachapoyas—Most Rev. Emiliano Antonio Cisneros Martínez, O.A.R.; Obispado, Jr. Ayacucho 1008, Apartado 69, Chachapoyas, Peru.
Tel: 51-41-47-77-94 ***Fax:*** 51-41-47-70-04
Email: ecisner@terra.com.pe

Chalan Kanoa—Vacant; Bishop's House P.O. Box 500745, Chalan Kanoa, Saipan, MP, 96950.
Tel: 670-234-3000 ***Fax:*** 670-235-3002
Email: laling@cnmicatholic.org

Chalatenango—Most Rev. Luis Morao Andreazza; Casa Episcopal, Calle San Martin 4, Barrio El Centro, Chalatenango, El Salvador.
Tel: 503-2301-0211/0209 ***Fax:*** 503-2335-2520
Email: curiachalatenango@hotmail.com

Châlons—Most Rev. Gilbert Louis; Evêché, 20 rue de l'Abbé Gillet, Châlons-en-Champagne CEDEX, 51038, France.
Tel: 3-26-68-07-03 ***Fax:*** 3-26-68-98-70
Email: assdiocchalons.secretariat@wanadoo.fr

CHAMBÉRY—Most Rev. Philippe Gabriel Marie Augustin Ballot; Maison diocésaine, 2 place Cardinal Garrone, CS 10107, Chambéry CEDEX, 73001, France.
Tel: 4-79-33-21-46 ***Fax:*** 4-79-33-26-95
Email: dioceses.savoie@wanadoo.fr

Chanda—Most Rev. Vijay Anand Nedumpuram, C.M.I.; Bishop's House Balharshah, Ballarpur, Chandrapur Dt., Maharashtra, 442701, India.
Tel: 07172-240-537; 07172-242-729 ***Fax:*** 07172-242-729
Email: bishopch_cha@sancharnet.in

CHANGANACHERRY—Most Rev. Joseph Perumthottam; Metropolitan Curia P.B.. 20, Changanassery, Kerala, 686101, India.
Tel: 91-0481-2420-040 ***Fax:*** 91-0481-2427-372

CHANGSHA (CHANGSHA)—Catholic Mission, Archbishop's House Changsha, Hunan, China.

Changteh (Changde)—Bishop's House Changde, Hunan, China.

Chanthaburi—Most Rev. Silvio Siripong Charatsri; Chanthaburi Diocesan Center 21/3, M. 1, Tambol Surasak, Sriracha, Chonburi, 20110, Thailand.
Tel: 66-038-312-708 ***Fax:*** 66-038-323-577
Email: vicargeneral@hotmail.com

Chaohsien (Zhaoxian)—Pien-Tsun, Catholic Mission, Kao-y, Hebei, China.

Chapecó—Most Rev. Manoel João Francisco; Residência Episcopal, Av. Getúlio Vargas 121-S, C.P. 726, 89801-970, Chapecó, SC, 89801-001, Brazil.
Tel: 55-049-3322-3362 ***Fax:*** 55-049-3322-3362
Email: diocese@diocesechapeco.org.br

Charleston—Most Rev. Robert E. Guglielmone; Chancery Office 119 Broad St., P.O. Box 818, Charleston, SC, 29402.
Tel: 843-853-2130 ***Fax:*** 843-724-6387
Web: www.catholic-doc.org

Charlotte—Most Rev. Peter J. Jugis (CHL); Chancery Office 1123 South Church Street, P.O. Box 36776, Charlotte, NC, 28203.
Tel: 704-370-6299 ***Fax:*** 704-370-3379
Web: charlottediocese.org
Email: chancery@charlottediocese.org

Charlottetown—Most Rev. Richard J. Grecco; Bishop's House 350 N. River Rd., P.O. Box 907, Charlottetown, PE, C1A 7L9, Canada.
Tel: 902-368-8005 ***Fax:*** 902-892-1253
Email: chancellor@dioceseofcharlottetown.com

Chartres—Most Rev. Michel Pansard; 1 rue Saint-Eman, Chartres CEDEX, 28000, France.
Tel: 2-37-88-00-09 ***Fax:*** 2-37-91-14-91

Chascomús—Most Rev. Carlos Humberto Malfa; Avda. Mitre 73, Chascomús, Buenos Aires, B7130DQA, Argentina.
Tel: 54-02241-425-429 ***Fax:*** 54-02241-425-429
Email: obispadochascomus@speedy.com.ar

Cheju—Most Rev. Peter Kang U-il; Diocesan Office 3-do 2-dong 114, P.O. Box 50, Jeju City, 690-600, Korea, South.
Tel: 82-064-751-0145/6/7; 82-064-753-7672 ***Fax:*** 82-064-756-5531
Email: catholic-cheju@hanmail.net

Chengchow (Zhengzhou)—Catholic Mission, Bishop's House Min-Kun-Kiao, Zhengzhou, Henan, China.

Chengting (Zhengding)—Catholic Mission, Bishop's House, Zhengding, Hebei, China.

Chengtu (Chengdu)—Catholic Mission, Pingankiao, 29, Chengdu, Sichuan, China.

Cheongju—Most Rev. Gabriel Chang Bong-hun; 29-8 Sacheon-dong, Sangdang-gu, Cheongju-si, Chungbuk, 360-220, Korea, South.
Tel: 82-043-210-1710 ***Fax:*** 82-043-210-1799
Email: cjsamu@hanmail.net

Cheyenne—Most Rev. Paul D. Etienne; Chancery Office 2121 Capitol Ave., P.O. Box 1468, Cheyenne, WY, 82003-1468.
Tel: 307-638-1530 ***Fax:*** 307-637-7936
Web: www.dioceseofcheyenne.org
Email: dmcintyre@dioceseofcheyenne.org

Chiang Mai—Most Rev. Francis Xavier Vira Arpondratana; Catholic Mission 5/3 Charoen Prathet Rd. 12, Chiang Mai, 50100, Thailand.
Tel: 66-053-821-064 ***Fax:*** 66-053-821-067
Email: mission@loxinfo.co.th

Chiavari—Most Rev. Alberto Tanasini; Vescovado, C.P. 137, Piazza Nostra Signora dell'Orto 7, Chiavari, Genova, 16043, Italy.
Tel: 39-0185-59-051 ***Fax:*** 39-0185-32-41-73
Email: curia@chiavari.chiesacattolica.it

CHICAGO—His Eminence Francis Cardinal George, O.M.I., Ph.D., S.T.D. (CHI); Archbishop Quigley Center & Cardinal Meyer Center P.O. Box 1979, Chicago, IL, 60690-1979.
Tel: 312-534-8200
Email: archbishop@archchicago.org

Chiclayo—Most Rev. Jesús Moliné Labarta; Obispado, Apartado 700, Elías Aguirre 850, Chiclayo, Peru.
Tel: 51-74-233-554 ***Fax:*** 51-74-234-972

Chicoutimi—Most Rev. André Rivest; Evêché 602 rue Racine Est, Chicoutimi, QC, G7H 1V1, Canada.
Tel: 418-543-0783 ***Fax:*** 418-543-2141
Email: diocese.chicoutimi@videotron.net

CHIETI-VASTO—Most Rev. Bruno Forte; Piazza G. G. Valignani 4, Chieti, 66100, Italy.
Tel: 39-0871-35-911 ***Fax:*** 39-0871-33-05-15
Email: arcidiocesi@diocesichieti.it

Chihfeng (Chifeng)—Catholic Mission Bishop's House, Chifeng, Ulanhad, China.

CHIHUAHUA—Most Rev. Constancio Miranda Weckmann; Arzobispado, Av. Cuauhtémoc 1828, Chihuahua, Chih., 31020, Mexico.
Tel: 52-614-410-32-02/3 ***Fax:*** 52-614-410-56-21

Chikmagalur—Most Rev. Anthony Swamy Thomasappa; Bishop's Office Jyothinagar, Chikmagalur, Karnataka, 577102, India.
Tel: 91-08262-220-389 ***Fax:*** 91-08262-220-389
Email: bishopckm@yahoo.co.in

Chikwawa—Most Rev. Peter Martin Musikuwa; Bishop's House P.O. Box 135, Chikwawa, Malawi.
Tel: 265-1-42-02-68 ***Fax:*** 265-1-42-02-29
Email: ckcdiocese@malawi.net

Chilaw—Most Rev. Warnakulasurya Wadumestrige Devasritha Valence Mendis; Bishop's House, Chilaw, 6100, Sri Lanka.
Tel: 032-2222-332 ***Fax:*** 032-2223-233

Chillán—Most Rev. Carlos Eduardo Pellegrín Barrera, S.V.D; Avda. Libertad 640, Casilla 117, Chillán, Chile.
Tel: 56-042-22-23-37 ***Fax:*** 56-042-22-72-40
Email: chillan@episcopado.cl

Chilpancingo-Chilapa—Most Rev. Alejo Zavala Castro; Obispado, Abasolo Esquino con Hidalgo 3, Col. Centro, Chilpancingo, Guerrero, 39000, Mexico.
Tel: 52-747-471-05-92; 52-747-471-06-12 ***Fax:*** 52-747-491-64-12
Email: curia@chilpancingo.com.mx

Chimbote—Most Rev. Ángel Francisco Simón Piorno; Apartado 59, Jr. Ladislao Espinar 456, Chimbote, Peru.
Tel: 51-43-32-41-71; 51-43-32-23-96 ***Fax:*** 51-43-32-19-66
Email: correo@obispadodechimbote.org

Chimoio—Most Rev. Francisco João Silota, M.Afr.; Bispado, C.P. 461, Chimoio, Mozambique.
Tel: 258-251-23-347 ***Fax:*** 258-251-22-022

Chingleput—Most Rev. Anthonisamy Neethinathan; Bishop's House, Kancheepuram Road, Thimmavaram, Chingleput, Tamil Nadu, 603101, India.
Tel: 044-2742-6649 ***Fax:*** 044-2743-1784
Email: ambrosep66@gmail.com

Chinhoyi—Most Rev. Dieter Scholz, S.J.; Bishop's House 26 Robson Manyika Drive, Chinhoyi, Zimbabwe.
Tel: 263-067-22562 ***Fax:*** 263-067-22217
Email: diochin@mango.zw

Chioggia—Most Rev. Adriano Tessarollo; Vescovado, C.P. 213, Rione Duomo 1006, Chioggia, Venezia, 30015, Italy.
Tel: 39-041-400-513 ***Fax:*** 39-041-401-321
Email: curia@chioggia.chiesacattolica.it

Chios—Vacant; Iustiniani 4, Chios, 82100, Greece.
Tel: 30-22830-22-382 ***Fax:*** 30-22830-24-769; 30-22830-22-382

Chipata—Most Rev. George Cosmas Zumaire Lungu; Bishop's House P.O. Box 510103, Chipata, Zambia.
Tel: 260-2162-21-375 ***Fax:*** 260-2162-21-551

Chiquinquirá—Most Rev. Luis Felipe Sánchez Aponte; Curia Episcopal, Calle 16 N. 10-50, Chiquinquirá Boyacá, Colombia.
Tel: 57-87-26-20-43; 57-87-26-20-17 ***Fax:*** 57-87-26-20-43; 57-87-26-20-17
Email: curia@diocesisdechiquinquira.org

Chisinau—Most Rev. Anton Cosa; Str. Mitropolit Dosoftei 85, Chisinau, 2012, Moldova.
Tel: 022-223-470 ***Fax:*** 022-225-210
Email: episcopia@starnet.md

Chitré—Most Rev. Fernando Torres Durán; Obispado, Apartado 49, Calle Melitón Martín, Chitré, Panama.
Tel: 996-7285 ***Fax:*** 996-7284

Chittagong—Most Rev. Moses Costa, C.S.C.; Bishop's House Bandel Road, P.O. Box 152, Patharghata, Chittagong, 4000, Bangladesh.
Tel: 880-031-61-46-50
Email: bhctgl@gmail.com

Choluteca—Most Rev. Guido Plante, P.M.E.; Casa Episcopal, Apartado 40, Choluteca, D.D, 060101, Honduras.
Tel: 504-782-0582 ***Fax:*** 504-782-2301
Email: secretariado@diocesisdecholuteca.org

Chosica—Most Rev. Norbert Klemens Strotman Hoppe, M.S.C.; Obispado Apartado Postal 08-001, Jr. Fray Martín s/n Lotización, El Descanso, Huaycán - Ate. Vitarte, Lote 12 y 13, Lima, 03, Peru.
Tel: 1-359-4141 ***Fax:*** 1-359-4074
Email: obispadochosica@speedy.com.pe

Chowchich (Zhouzhi)—Catholic Mission Bishop's House, Zhouzhi, Shaanxi, China.

Chowtsun (Zhoucun)—Catholic Mission Bishop's House, Zhoucun, Shandong, China.

Christchurch—Most Rev. Barry Philip Jones; Cathedral House 122 Barbadoes St., P.O. Box 4544, Christchurch, 8011, New Zealand.
Tel: 64-03-3669-869 ***Fax:*** 64-03-3749-619

Chulucanas—Most Rev. Daniel T. Turley Murphy, O.S.A.; Obispado, Calle Cuzco 381, Chulucanas, Depto. de Piura, Peru.
Tel: 51-73-37-85-69 ***Fax:*** 51-73-37-81-62
Email: casafrat@speedy.com.pe

Chumatien (Zhumadian)—Catholic Mission Nan-Da-Yuan, Zhumadian, Henan, China.

Ch'unch'on—Most Rev. Lucas Kim Woon-hoe; Diocesan Office Ch'unch'on-shi Hyoja 2-dong 400, Kang-won, 200-948, Korea, South.
Tel: 033-240-6040 ***Fax:*** 033-240-6045
Email: ccsamou@catholic.or.kr

CHUNGKING (CHONGQING)—Catholic Mission Chongqing, Sichuan, China.

Chur—Most Rev. Vitus Huonder; Bischöfliches Ordinariat, Hof 19, Chur, CH-7000, Switzerland.
Tel: 41-081-258-6000 ***Fax:*** 41-081-258-6001
Email: ordinariat@bistum-chur.ch

Churchill-Baie d'Hudson—Most Rev. Reynald Rouleau, O.M.I.; C.P. 10, 242 La Verendrye, Churchill, MB, R0B 0E0, Canada.
Tel: 204-675-2252 ***Fax:*** 204-675-2140

Ciego de Avila—Most Rev. Mario Eusebio Mestril Vega; Obispado, Joaquín de Agüero 52 Este, Ciego de Avila, 65100, Cuba.
Tel: 033-266-374 ***Fax:*** 033-266-373

Cienfuegos—Most Rev. Domingo Oropesa Lorente; Obispado, Calle 37 N. 5602, e/56 y 58, Cienfuegos, 55100, Cuba.
Tel: 043-51-30-19 ***Fax:*** 043-55-16-79

CINCINNATI—Most Rev. Dennis M. Schnurr, J.C.D., D.D. (CIN); Archdiocesan Offices 100 E. Eighth St, Cincinnati, OH, 45202-2129.
Tel: 513-421-3131 ***Fax:*** 513-421-6225
Web: www.catholiccincinnati.org
Email: communications@catholiccincinnati.org

CIPRO—Most Rev. Joseph Soueif; The Maronite Church 8 Ayios Maronas Str., P.O. Box 22249, Nicosia, Cyprus.
Tel: 357-022-42-79-66; 357-022-31-49-19
Email: betmorounincyprus@cytanet.com.cy

Città di Castello—Most Rev. Domenico Cancian, F.A.M.; Vescovado, Piazza V. Gabriotti 10, Città di Castello, Perugia, 06012, Italy.
Tel: 39-075-855-30-30 ***Fax:*** 39-075-855-33-59
Email: cancelleriadiocesi@tiscali.it

CIUDAD ALTAMIRANO—Most Rev. Maximino Martínez Miranda; Benito Juárez 205 Oriente, Ciudad Altamirano, Guerrero, 40660, Mexico.
Tel: 52-767-672-0037; 52-767-672-1774 ***Fax:*** 52-767-672-0037; 52-767-672-1774

CIUDAD BOLÍVAR—Most Rev. Ulises Antonio Gutiérrez Reyes, O.de.M.; Arzobispado, Apartado 43, Avda. Andrés Eloy Blanco con Avda. Naiguatá, Ciudad Bolívar, Edo. Bolívar, 8001, Venezuela.
Tel: 58-0285-654-49-60 ***Fax:*** 58-0285-654-08-21
Email: arz_cb@cantv.net.ve

Ciudad del Este—Most Rev. Rogelio Ricardo Livieres Plano; Pamplìega 415, Ciudad del Este, Alto Paraná, Paraguay.
Tel: 061-512-318 ***Fax:*** 061-511-390
Email: obispado@diocesiscde.org

Ciudad Guayana—Most Rev. Mariano José Parra Sandoval; Curia Diocesana, Urbanización Villa Alianza I, Senda Sula 93-94, Puerto Ordaz, Ciudad Guayana, Edo. Bolívar, 8015-A, Venezuela.
Tel: 58-0286-922-14-29 ***Fax:*** 58-0286-922-16-38

Ciudad Guzmán—Most Rev. Braulio Rafael León Villegas; Ramón Corona 26, Apartado 26, Ciudad Guzmán, Jalisco, 49000, Mexico.
Tel: 52-341-412-15-44; 52-341-412-05-28 ***Fax:*** 52-341-412-05-28
Email: diocesiscdguzman@hotmail.com

Ciudad Juárez—Most Rev. Renato Ascensio León; Casa de Gobierno Eclesiástico, Calles Mejía y Perú, Ciudad Juárez, Chihuahua, 32030, Mexico.
Tel: 52-656-615-09-22; 52-656-615-09-82 ***Fax:*** 52-656-615-00-24
Email: info@diocesisdeciudadjuarez.org

Ciudad Lázaro Cárdenas—Most Rev. Fabio Martínez Castilla; Obispado, Av. Autonomia Universitaria 15, 20 Sector de Fideicomisso, Apartado 199, Ciudad Lázaro Cárenas, Michoacan, 60950, Mexico.
Tel: 52-753-541-64-07 ***Fax:*** 52-753-541-64-01
Email: dioclac@prodigy.net.mx

Ciudad Obregón—Most Rev. Felipe Padilla Cardona; Sonora 166 Norte, Ciudad Obregón, Sonora, 85000, Mexico.
Tel: 52-644-413-20-98 ***Fax:*** 52-644-414-99-94
Email: diocesisobrego@prodigy.net.mx

Ciudad Quesada—Most Rev. Oswaldo Brenes Álvarez; Apdo. 212 San Carlos, Ciudad Quesada, 4400, Costa Rica.
Tel: 2460-5811 ***Fax:*** 2460-5154
Email: juancastro99@yahoo.com

Ciudad Real—Most Rev. Antonio Ángel Algora Hernando; Obispado, Calle Caballeros 5, Ciudad Real, 13001, Spain.
Tel: 34-926-25-02-50 ***Fax:*** 34-926-25-12-58
Email: obcreal@planalfa.es

Ciudad Rodrigo—Most Rev. Cecilio Raul Berzosa Martinez; Obispado, Díez de Taravilla 15, Ciudad Rodrigo, Salamanca, 37500, Spain.
Tel: 34-923-460-843 ***Fax:*** 34-923-463-028
Email: obcrodrigo@planalfa.es

Ciudad Valles—Most Rev. Roberto Octavio Balmori Cinta, M.J.; Calle 16 de Septiembre 726, Apartado 170, Ciudad Valles, San Luis Potosí, 79000, Mexico.
Tel: 52-481-382-25-97 ***Fax:*** 52-481-382-47-96
Email: obispad@prodigy.net.mx

Ciudad Victoria—Most Rev. Antonio González Sánchez; Apartado 335, Morelos 1046-A Ote. Zona Centro, Ciudad Victoria, Tamaulipas, 87000, Mexico.
Tel: 52-834-312-87-16 ***Fax:*** 52-834-312-87-16

Civita Castellana—Most Rev. Romano Rossi; Curia Diocesana, Piazza Matteotti 27, Civita Castellana, Viterbo, 01033, Italy.
Tel: 39-0761-51-51-52 ***Fax:*** 39-0761-59-92-13
Email: diocesicivitacastellana@albaclick.com

Civitavecchia-Tarquinia—Most Rev. Luigi Marrucci; Piazza Calamatta 1, Civitavecchia, Roma, 00053, Italy.
Tel: 39-0766-23-320 ***Fax:*** 39-0766-50-17-96
Email: curia@civitavecchia.chiesacattolica.it
Via Roma 11, Tarquinia, Viterbo, 01016, Italy.
Tel: 39-0766-84-08-43; 39-0766-85-60-43

CLERMONT—Most Rev. Hippolyte Simon; Archevêché, 9 rue d'Ambert, Clermont-Ferrand, 63000, France.
Tel: 4-73-98-01-40 ***Fax:*** 4-73-98-01-49
Email: eveche63@wanadoo.fr

Cleveland—Most Rev. Richard G. Lennon, D.D., M.A., M.Th. (CLV); Cathedral Square Plaza 1404 E. Ninth St., Cleveland, OH, 44114.
Tel: 216-696-6525 ***Fax:*** 216-621-7332
Email: chancellor@dioceseofcleveland.org

Clifton—Most Rev. Declan Ronan Lang; Alexander House 160 Pennywell Rd, Bristol, BS5 0BX, England.
Tel: 44-0117-902-5591 ***Fax:*** 44-0117-902-5520
Email: finance.office@cliftondiocese.com

Clogher—Most Rev. Liam Sean MacDaid; Bishop's House Tigh an Easpaig, Monaghan, Co. Monaghan, Ireland.
Tel: 353-047-81019 ***Fax:*** 353-047-84773
Email: diocesanoffice@clogherdiocese.ie

Clonfert—Most Rev. John Kirby; Bishop's House St. Brendan's, Coorheen, Loughrea, Co. Galway, Ireland.
Tel: 353-091-841-560 ***Fax:*** 353-091-841-818
Email: clonfert@iol.ie

Cloyne—Vacant; Cloyne Diocesan Center Cobh, Co. Cork, Ireland.
Tel: 353-021-4811-430 *Fax:* 353-021-4811-026
Email: cloyne@indigo.ie

Cluj-Gherla, Claudiopoli-Armenopoli—Most Rev. Florentin Crihalmeanu; Calea Motilor 26, Cluj-Napoca, RO-400001, Romania.
Tel: 0264-439-018 *Fax:* 0264-431-964

Coatzacoalcos—Most Rev. Rutilo Muñoz Zamora; Apartado 395 y 396, Aldama 502, Coatzacoalcos, Veracruz, 96400, Mexico.
Tel: 52-921-212-23-99/59-03 *Fax:* 52-921-212-95-00
Email: dicoatza@prodigy.net.mx

COCHABAMBA—Most Rev. Tito Solari Capellari, S.D.B.; Arzobispado, Casilla 129, Av. Heroínas, esquina Zenteno Anaya, Cochabamba, 0152, Bolivia.
Tel: 591-04-425-6562/3 *Fax:* 591-04-425-0522
Email: cancilleriacbba@gmail.com

Cochin—Most Rev. Joseph Kariyil; Bishop's House Fort Cochin, Kochi, Kerala, 682001, India.
Tel: 91-0484-6513-116 *Fax:* 91-0484-2215-404

Coimbatore—Most Rev. Thomas Aquinas Lephonse; Bishop's House P.B. 6, Coimbatore, Tamil Nadu, 641001, India.
Tel: 91-0422-2382-806 *Fax:* 91-0422-2394-530
Email: coimbatorediocese@gmail.com

Coimbra—Most Rev. Virgilio do Nascimento Antunes; Cúria Diocesana, Rua do Brazil, Ap. 3069, Coimbra CODEX, 3001-401, Portugal.
Tel: 351-239-70-83-20 *Fax:* 351-239-70-83-21
Email: casaepiscopal@diocesedecoimbra.pt

Colatina—Most Rev. Décio Zandonade, S.D.B.; Cúria Diocesana, Rua Santa Maria 350, Colatina, ES, 29700-200, Brazil.
Tel: 55-027-2102-5000 *Fax:* 55-027-2102-5015
Email: curia@diocesedecolatina.org.br

Colima—Most Rev. José Luis Amezcua Melgoza; Palacio Episcopal, Hildago 135, Apdo. 1, Colima, Col., 28000, Mexico.
Tel: 52-312-312-02-62; 52-312-312-43-44 *Fax:* 52-312-312-43-44
Email: obispado@diocesisdecolima.org

COLOMBO—His Eminence Albert Malcolm Ranjith Cardinal Patabendige Don; Archbishop's House 976 Gnanartha Pradeepaya Mawatha, Columbo, 08, Sri Lanka.
Tel: 94-011-2695-471/2/3 *Fax:* 94-011-2692-009

Colón Kuna Yala—Most Rev. Audilio Aguilar Aguilar; Calle 5, Ave. Herrera, Cristóbal Colón, Panama.
Tel: 507-441-8466 *Fax:* 507-441-8805
Email: diocesiscolon@gmail.com

Colorado Springs—Most Rev. Michael J. Sheridan, S.Th.D. (COS); Diocesan Office 228 N. Cascade Ave., Colorado Springs, CO, 80903-1498.
Tel: 719-636-2345 *Fax:* 719-636-1216

Columbus—Most Rev. Frederick F. Campbell, Ph.D., D.D.; Chancery Office 198 E. Broad St., Columbus, OH, 43215.
Tel: 614-224-2251 *Fax:* 614-224-6306
Email: smoloney@colsdioc.org

Comayagua—Most Rev. Roberto Camilleri Azzopardi, O.F.M.; Obispado, Calle de la Catedral, Apartado 41, Comayaga, 12101, Honduras.
Tel: 504-772-0169 *Fax:* 504-772-4138

Como—Most Rev. Diego Coletti; Vescovado, Piazza Grimoldi 5, Como, 22100, Italy.
Tel: 39-031-33-12-211 *Fax:* 39-031-30-43-54
Email: cancelliere@diocesidicomo.it

Comodoro Rivadavia—Most Rev. Joaquin Gimeno Lahoz; Obispado, Rivadavia 750, Comodoro Rivadavia, Chubut, U9000AKW, Argentina.
Tel: 54-0297-447-26-47 *Fax:* 54-0297-447-66-62
Email: obcrivad@speedy.com.ar

CONAKRY, KONAKRY—Most Rev. Vincent Coulibaly; Archevêché, B.P. 2016, Conakry, Guinea.
Tel: 64-45-58-97; 64-42-37-74
Email: conakriensis@yahoo.fr

CONCEPCIÓN—Most Rev. Fernando Natalio Chomali Garib; Calle Barros Arana 544, Casilla 65-C, Concepción, Chile.
Tel: 56-041-262-61-13 *Fax:* 56-041-223-28-44
Email: concepcion@episcopado.cl

Concepción en Paraguay—Most Rev. Zacarías Ortiz Rolón, S.D.B.; Obispado, Nuestra Señora de la Concepción y Mariscal Estigarribia, Concepción, Paraguay.
Tel: 0331-242-357 *Fax:* 0331-242-827

Concepción (in Argentina)—Most Rev. Armando José Maria Rossi, O.P.; Obispado, Calle España 1525, Concepción, Tucumán, T4146CCG, Argentina.
Tel: 03865-421-376 *Fax:* 03865-424-220
Email: obispadoconcepcion@arnet.com.ar

Concordia—Most Rev. Luis Armando Collazuol; Obispado, Calle Pellegrini 800, Concordia, Entre Ríos, E3200AMN, Argentina.
Tel: 54-0345-421-1253 *Fax:* 54-0345-421-1253
Email: obispado@concordia.com.ar

Concordia-Pordenone—Most Rev. Giuseppe Pellegrini; Curia Vescovile, C.P. 337, Via Revedole 1, Pordenone, 33170, Italy.
Tel: 39-0434-22-11-11 *Fax:* 39-0434-27-213
Email: diocesi@diocesi.concordia-pordenone.it

Constantine—Most Rev. Paul Desfarges, S.J.; Evêché, 32 Bd. Belouïzdad, Constantine, 25002, Algeria.
Tel: 213-031-92-33-67 *Fax:* 213-031-92-32-21
Email: eveche.constant@gmail.com

Conversano-Monopoli—Most Rev. Domenico Padovano; Vescovado, Via S. Benedetto 1, Conversano, Bari, 70014, Italy.
Tel: 39-080-495-14-28; 39-080-742-211 *Fax:* 39-080-742-211
Email: curia@conversano.chiesacattolica.it

Copiapó—Most Rev. Gaspar Francisco Quintana Jorquera, C.M.F.; Calle Chacabuco 441, Copiapó, Chile.
Tel: 56-052-35-23-20 *Fax:* 56-052-35-23-24
Email: copiapo@episcopado.cl

CÓRDOBA—Most Rev. Carlos José Ñáñez; Arzobispado, Avda. Hipólito Yrigoyen 98, Córdoba, X5000JHN, Argentina.
Tel: 54-0351-425-50-82 *Fax:* 54-0351-422-10-15
Email: scanciller@arzobispadocba.org.ar

Córdoba (in Mexico)—Most Rev. Eduardo Porfirio Patiño Leal; Avenida 3 Esquina Calle 5 N. 303, Zona Centro, Córdoba, Ver., 94500, Mexico.
Tel: 271-714-05-74 *Fax:* 271-714-91-56

Córdoba (in Spain)—Most Rev. Demetrio Fernández González; Torrijos 12, Córdoba, 14003, Spain.
Tel: 957-49-6474 *Fax:* 957-49-6475
Email: obispado@diocesisdecordoba.com

CORFÙ - ZANTE, CEFALONIA—Most Rev. Ioannis Spiteris, O.F.M.Cap.; Archevêché Catholique, Montsenigou 3, Kérkyra, 49100, Greece.
Tel: 30-026610-30-277 *Fax:* 30-026610-31-675
Email: cathepco@otenet.gr

Coria-Cáceres—Most Rev. Francisco Cerro Chaves; Obispado, Plaza de Santa María 1, Cáceres, 10003, Spain.
Tel: 34-927-24-52-50 *Fax:* 34-927-21-40-24
Email: obcoriacaceres@planalfa.es

Cork and Ross—Most Rev. John Buckley; Diocesan Office Redemption Rd., Cork, Ireland.
Tel: 353-021-430-17-17 *Fax:* 353-021-430-15-57
Email: secretary@corkandross.org

Cornélio Procópio—Most Rev. Getúlio Teixeira Guimarães, S.V.D.; C.P. 381, Av. Alberto Carazzai 1080, Cornélio Procópio, PR, 86300-000, Brazil.
Tel: 55-043-3524-1942 *Fax:* 55-043-3524-1942
Email: mitraprocopense@uol.com.br

Corner Brook and Labrador—Most Rev. Peter Joseph Hundt; St. Mary's on the Humber 469 Curling Street, Corner Brook, NF, A2H 3K8, Canada.
Tel: 709-639-7073 *Fax:* 709-639-8662
Email: diocese@nf.aibn.com

CORO—Most Rev. Roberto Lückert León; Arzobispado, Apartado 7342, Calle Federación Esquina Calle Palmasola, Coro, Edo. Falcón, Venezuela.
Tel: 58-0268-251-79-30; 0268-251-70-24 *Fax:* 251-88-68
Email: arquidioscoro@hotmail.com

Coroatá—Most Rev. Sebastiao Bandeira Coelho; Travessa Oscar Jansen 158, C.P. 6, Coroatá, MA, 65415-000, Brazil.
Tel: 55-099-3641-1425 *Fax:* 55-099-3641-1425
Email: dcoroata@coroatanet.com.br

Coroico—Most Rev. Juan Vargas Aruquipa; Calle Felipe López 339, Villa Fatima, Coroico, Nor Yungas, Bolivia.
Tel: 02-010-2213-492 *Fax:* 02-010-2213-492
Email: diocesisdecoroico@gmail.com

Coronel Oviedo—Most Rev. Juan Bautista Gavilán Velásquez; Residencia Obispal, Mariscal Estigarribia 115, Coronel Oviedo, Paraguay.
Tel: 595-0521-20-2229 *Fax:* 595-0521-20-2199
Email: diocesis_coroneloviedo@hotmail.com

Corpus Christi—Most Rev. William M. Mulvey; Chancery Office 620 Lipan St., Corpus Christi, TX, 78401.
Tel: 361-882-6191 ***Fax:*** 361-882-1018
Email: chancery@diocesecc.org
P.O. Box 2620, Corpus Christi, TX, 78403-2620.

CORRIENTES—Most Rev. Andrés Stanovnik, O.F.M.Cap.; Arzobispado, Calle Nueve de Julio 1543, Corrientes, W3400AZA, Argentina.
Tel: 54-03783-42-2436 ***Fax:*** 54-03783-42-2436
Email: arzctes@arnet.gov.ar

Corumbá—Most Rev. Segismundo Martínez Álvarez, S.D.B.; Cúria Diocesana, Rua Masor Gama 1332, C.P. 12, Corumbá, MS, 79332-040, Brazil.
Tel: 55-067-3231-4416 ***Fax:*** 55-067-3232-8668
Email: curiacorumba@terra.com.br

COSENZA-BISIGNANO—Most Rev. Salvatore Nunnari; Arcivescovado, Piazza A. G. Parrasio 16, Cosenza, 87100, Italy.
Tel: 39-0984-68-77-16; 39-0984-24-819 ***Fax:*** 39-0984-25-883

COTABATO—Most Rev. Orlando B. Quevedo, O.M.I.; Archbishop's Residence 141 Sinsuat Ave., P.O. Box 186, Cotabato City, 9600, Philippines.
Tel: 064-421-29-18 ***Fax:*** 064-421-14-46

COTONOU—Most Rev. Antoine Ganyé; Archevêché, 01 B.P. 491, Cotonou, Benin.
Tel: 229-21-30-01-45 ***Fax:*** 229-21-30-07-07
Email: archeveche.cotonou@ifrance.com

Coutances—Most Rev. Stanislas Lalanne, France; Evêché, 6-8 rue du Perthuis Trouard, B.P. 129, Coutances CEDEX, 50201, France.
Tel: 2-33-45-1806 ***Fax:*** 2-33-45-4787
Email: diocese.coutances@wanadoo.fr

Covington—Most Rev. Roger Joseph Foys (COV); 401 E. 20th St., Fl. 3, P.O. Box 15550, Covington, KY, 41015-0550.
Tel: 859-392-1510 ***Fax:*** 859-392-1508
Email: swagner@covingtondiocese.org

Coxim—Most Rev. Antonino Migliore; Cúria Diocesana, C.P. 60, Av. Viriato Bandeira 834, Coxim, MS, 79400-000, Brazil.
Tel: 067-3291-1928 ***Fax:*** 067-3291-1928

Crateús—Most Rev. Jacinto Furtado de Brito Sobrinho; Cúria Diocesana, Rua Firmino Rosa 1064, Crateús, CE, 63700-000, Brazil.
Tel: 55-088-3691-2366 ***Fax:*** 55-088-3691-2366
Email: diocrateus@ig.com.br

Crato—Most Rev. Fernando Panico, M.S.C.; Cúria Diocesana, Rua Teófilo Siqueira 631, Crato, CE, 63100-010, Brazil.
Tel: 55-088-3521-1110 ***Fax:*** 55-088-3521-1110
Email: curia@diocesedecrato.org.br

Crema—Most Rev. Oscar Cantoni; Piazza Duomo 27, Crema, Cremona, 26013, Italy.
Tel: 39-0373-25-62-74 ***Fax:*** 39-0373-85-312
Email: amministrazione@diocesidicrema.it

Cremona—Most Rev. Dante Lafranconi; Palazzo Vescovile, Piazza S. Antonio M. Zaccaria 5, Cremona, 26100, Italy.
Tel: 39-0372-495-011 ***Fax:*** 39-0372-495-017
Email: curiavescovile@diocesidicremona.it

Créteil—Most Rev. Michel Santier; 2 av. Pasteur-Vallery-Radot, Créteil, 94000, France.
Tel: 1-45-17-24-38 ***Fax:*** 1-45-17-24-49
Email: chancellerie@eveche-creteil.cef.fr

Criciúma—Most Rev. Jacinto Inacio Flach; C.P. 94, 88801-970, Rua João Pessoa 16, Criciúma, SC, 88801-530, Brazil.
Tel: 048-3433-6313 ***Fax:*** 048-3433-6313
Email: diocri@diocesecriciuma.com.br

Crookston—Most Rev. Michael J. Hoeppner, D.D. (CR); 1200 Memorial Drive, Crookston, MN, 56716.
Tel: 218-281-4533 ***Fax:*** 218-281-3328
Email: dbaumgartner@crookston.org

CROTONE-SANTA SEVERINA—Most Rev. Domenico Graziani; Arcivescovado, Piazza Duomo 19, Crotone, 88900, Italy.
Tel: 39-0962-21-520 ***Fax:*** 39-0962-25-674
Email: don.giovanni@gmail.com

Cruz Alta—Most Rev. Frederico Heimler, S.D.B.; Cúria Diocesana, Rua Duque de Caxias 729, C.P. 54, Cruz Alta, RS, 98005-200, Brazil.
Tel: 055-3322-6920 ***Fax:*** 055-3322-5751
Email: diocese@comnet.com.br

Cruz del Eje—Most Rev. Santiago Olivera; Residencia Episcopal, Calle España 421, Cruz del Eje, Córdoba, X5280HNI, Argentina.
Tel: 54-03549-422-435 ***Fax:*** 54-03549-422-435
Email: obispado_cde@yahoo.com.ar

Cruzeiro do Sul—Most Rev. Mosé Joâo Pontelo, C.S.Sp.; Residência Episcopal, Praça da Glória 185, Cruzeiro do Sul, AC, 69980-000, Brazil.
Tel: 55-068-3322-8931 ***Fax:*** 55-068-3322-2480
Email: dioceseczs@yahoo.com.br

Cuauhtémoc-Madera—Most Rev. Juan Guillermo López Soto; Hidalgo 404, Cuauhtémoc, Chih., 31500, Mexico.
Tel: 091-625-581-57-22 ***Fax:*** 091-625-581-57-22

Cuautitlán—Most Rev. Guillermo Rodrigo Teodoro Ortiz Mondragón; Apartado 29, Sor Juana Inés de la Cruz 208, Cuautitlán de Romero Rubio, Méx., 54800, Mexico.
Tel: 55-5872-27-86 ***Fax:*** 55-5872-30-04
Email: curiacuautitlan@gmail.com

Cubao—Most Rev. Honesto F. Ongtioco; Bishop's House 41 Lantana St., Cubao, 1111 Quezon City, Philippines.
Tel: 02-723-51-13/5 ***Fax:*** 02-723-78-47
Email: chancery@dioceseofcubao.org

Cúcuta—Most Rev. Julio César Vidal Ortiz; Curia Episcopal, Avenida 1a, N. 27-121, Barrio San Rafael, Cúcuta, Colombia.
Tel: 57-572-73-93; 57-572-20-76 ***Fax:*** 57-572-20-76
Email: diocesisdecucuta@gmail.com

Cuddapah—Most Rev. Prasad Gallela; Bishop's House Mariapuram, Kadapa, A.P., 516003, India.
Tel: 91-08562-241-148 ***Fax:*** 91-08562-249-534
Email: dkadapa@yahoo.com

CUENCA—Most Rev. Luis Cabrera Herrera, O.F.M.; Apartado 46, Bolívar 7-64 y Luis Cordero, Cuenca, Ecuador.
Tel: 593-07-284-72-34; 593-07-283-16-51 ***Fax:*** 593-07-284-44-36
Email: iglesia@arquidiocesisdecuenca.org.ec

Cuenca (in Spain)—Most Rev. José María Yanguas Sanz; Obispado, Calle Obispo Valero 1, Cuenca, 16001, Spain.
Tel: 969-24-19-00 ***Fax:*** 969-24-19-01
Email: vicariageneral@eacsl.com

Cuernavaca—Most Rev. Alfonso Cortes Contreras; Calle Hildago 17, Anexo Catedral, Col. Centro, Cuernavaca, Mor., 62000, Mexico.
Tel: 52-777-318-45-90 ***Fax:*** 52-777-318-63-18
Email: diocesiscuernavaca@yahoo.com.mx

CUIABÁ—Most Rev. Mílton Antônio dos Santos, S.D.B.; Cúria Metropolitana, C.P. 22, Praça do Seminário 489, Cuiabá, MT, 78005-970, Brazil.
Tel: 55-065-3321-3631 ***Fax:*** 55-065-3322-8893
Email: curia.secretaria@terra.com.br

Culiacán—Most Rev. Jonas Guerrero Corona; Blvd. Juan Pablo II 26, Ote. Col. Lomas de Guadalupe, 80220, Apartado 666, Culiacán, Sinaloa, 80000, Mexico.
Tel: 52-667-712-32-72 ***Fax:*** 52-667-712-14-97
Email: obispado@cln.megared.net.mx

CUMANÁ—Most Rev. Diego Rafael Padrón Sánchez; Arzobispado, Calle Bolívar 34, Cumaná, Edo. Sucre, 6101-A, Venezuela.
Tel: 58-0293-431-25-25 ***Fax:*** 58-0293-433-34-14

Cuneo—Most Rev. Giuseppe Cavallotto; Via Roma 7, Cuneo, 12100, Italy.
Tel: 39-0171-69-35-23 ***Fax:*** 39-0171-60-25-65
Email: curia@diocesicuneo.it

CURITIBA—Most Rev. Moacyr José Vitti, C.S.S.; Cúria Metropolitana, Av. Jaime Reis 369, Curitiba, PR, 80510-010, Brazil.
Tel: 55-041-2105-6302 ***Fax:*** 55-041-3225-1014
Email: lia@arquidiocesecwb.org.br

CUTTACK-BHUBANESWAR—Most Rev. John Barwa, S.V.D.; Archbishop's House 9/16 Satya Nagar, Bhubaneswar, Orissa, 751007, India.
Tel: 91-0674-257-52-25; 91-0674-257-05-14 ***Fax:*** 91-0674-253-40-97

CUZCO—Most Rev. Juan Antonio Ugarte Pérez; Arzobispado, Apartado 148, Hatun Rumiyoc s/n, Cusco, Peru.
Tel: 51-84-22-52-11 ***Fax:*** 51-84-22-27-81
Email: seccusco@speedy.com.pe

Cyangugu—Most Rev. Jean Damascène Bimenyimana; Evêché, B.P. 5, Cyangugu, Rwanda.
Tel: 252-537-216 ***Fax:*** 252-537-216
Email: diocyangugu@yahoo.fr

CZESTOCHOWA—Most Rev. Stanislaw Nowak; Kuria Metropolitalna, al. Najswietszej Maryi Panny 54, Czestochowa, 42-200, Poland.
Tel: 48-034-324-10-44; 48-034-324-9628 ***Fax:*** 48-034-365-11-82
Email: kuria@czestochowa.opoka.org.pl

D

Dà Lat—Most Rev. Antoine Vu Huy Chuong; Tóa Giám Muc, 9 Nguyên Thái Hoc, Tp. Da Lat, Vietnam.
Tel: 84-063-3822-415 ***Fax:*** 84-063-3830-112
Email: tgmdalat@gmail.com

Dà Nang—Most Rev. Joseph Chau Ngoc Tri; Tóa Giám Muc, 156 Trân-Phú, B.P. 143, Tp. Dà Nang, Vietnam.
Tel: 0511-3826-628 ***Fax:*** 0511-3871-856
Email: tgmdng@gmail.com

DAEGU—Most Rev. Thaddeus Cho Hwan-Kil; Diocesan Office, Jung-gu Namsan 3-dong 225-1, Daegu, 700-804, Korea, South.
Tel: 82-053-250-3000 ***Fax:*** 82-053-250-3018
Email: daegu@dgca.or.kr

Daejeon—Most Rev. Lazzaro You Heung-sik; Diocesan Office, Tong-gu Yongjon-dong 15-1, Taejeon-shi, 300-824, Korea, South.
Tel: 82-042-630-7780 ***Fax:*** 82-042-630-7706
Email: tjsamu@hanmail.net

Daet—Most Rev. Gilbert A. Garcera; Diocesan House Gahonon, P.O. Box 38, Daet, Camarines Norte, 4600, Philippines.
Tel: 054-721-1625; 054-721-1431 ***Fax:*** 054-440-1471
Email: daetchancery@yahoo.com

DAKAR—His Eminence Theodore-Adrien Sarr; Archêvché B.P. 1908, Avenue Jean XXIII, Dakar, Senegal.
Tel: 33-889-06-00 ***Fax:*** 33-823-48-75
Email: archevechedkr@orange.sn

Dakovo-Osijek—Most Rev. Marin Srakic; Nadbiskupski Ordinarijat Strossmayerov trg 6, Dakovo, 31400, Croatia.
Tel: 385-031-802-200 ***Fax:*** 385-031-812-310
Email: biskupski-ordinarijat-djakovo@os.t-com.hr

Dallas—Most Rev. Kevin Joseph Farrell, D.D. (DAL); Chancery Office 3725 Blackburn St., P.O. Box 190507, Dallas, TX, 75219.
Tel: 214-528-2240 ***Fax:*** 214-526-1743
Web: www.cathdal.org
Email: kfarrell@cathdal.org

Daloa—Most Rev. Maurice Konan Kouassi; Evêché B.P. 710, Daloa, Ivory Coast.
Tel: 225-32-78-32-31 ***Fax:*** 225-32-78-32-31
Email: dddaloa@yahoo.fr

Daltonganj—Most Rev. Gabriel Kujur, S.J.; Bishop's House Station Rd., Daltonganj, Palamau Dt., Jharkhand, 822101, India.
Tel: 91-06562-222-643

DAMAS, AS-SAM, DAMASCO, DIMASQ—Most Rev. Gregorios Elias Tabé; Archevêché Syrien Catholique B.P. 2129, rue Al-Mustaqeem 157, Bab Charki, Damas, Syria.
Tel: 963-011-544-53-43

DAMAS, AS-SAM, DAMASCO, DIMASQ - GREEK MELKITE—Most Rev. S.B. Gregorios III Laham; Patriarcat Grec-Melkite Catholique B.P. 22249, avenue Az-Zeitoun 12, Bab Charki, Damas, Syria.
Tel: 963-011-544-10-30; 963-011-544-65-29 ***Fax:*** 963-011-541-79-00
Email: pat.melk@scs-net.org

DAMAS, AS-SAM, DAMASCO, DIMASQ - MARONITE—Most Rev. Samir Nassar; Archevêché Maronite, Bab Touma, B.P. 2179, Damas, Syria.
Tel: 963-011-543-60-01; 963-011-541-28-88 ***Fax:*** 963-011-543-60-02

Damongo—Most Rev. Peter Paul Yelezuome Angkyier; Bishop's House P.O. Box 67, Damongo, Ghana.
Tel: 037-23-22-000 ***Fax:*** 0717-22-069
Email: damongobishop@yahoo.com

Dapaong—Most Rev. Jacques Nyimbusède Tukumbé Anyilunda; Evêché B.P. 61, Dapaong, Togo.
Tel: 228-770-85-35 ***Fax:*** 228-770-80-37
Email: eveche-dapaong@ids.tg

DAR-ES-SALAAM—His Eminence Cardinal Polycarp Pengo; Archbishop's House P.O. Box 167, Dar-es-Salaam, Tanzania.
Tel: 255-022-211-3223 ***Fax:*** 255-022-212-5751
Email: nyumba@cats-net.com

Darjeeling—Most Rev. Stephen Lepcha; Bishop's House 13 Dr. Yen Singh Rd., Darjiling, West Bengal, 734101, India.
Tel: 91-0354-2254-929 ***Fax:*** 91-0354-2254-929
Email: bishopdj@sify.com

Daru-Kiunga—Most Rev. Gilles Côté, S.M.M.; Bishop's House P.O. Box 42, Kiunga, W.P. 335, Papua New Guinea.
Tel: 675-6491-078 ***Fax:*** 675-6491-050

Darwin—Most Rev. Daniel Eugene Hurley; Bishop's Office 2 St. John's Court, The Gardens, G.P.O Box 476, 0801, Darwin, N.T., 0820, Australia.
Tel: 61-08-8942-6000 ***Fax:*** 61-08-8942-6060
Email: diocadmin@darwin.catholic.org.au

Dassa-Zoumé—Vacant; Evêche B.P. 106, Dassa-Zoumé, Benin.
Tel: 229-22-53-01-80; 229-94-90-09-02 ***Fax:*** 229-22-53-04-77
Email: diocese.dassa@laposte.net

DAVAO—Most Rev. Fernando R. Capalla; Archbishop's Residence 247 Fr. Torres St., Davao City, Philippines.
Tel: 63-082-22-75-992/11-234 ***Fax:*** 63-082-22-79-771
Email: bishopdavao@yahoo.com

Davenport—Most Rev. Martin J. Amos, D.D. (DAV); ***Chancery:*** Diocesan Pastoral Center 780 W. Central Park Ave., Davenport, IA, 52804-1901.
Tel: 563-324-1911 ***Fax:*** 563-324-5842
Email: communications@davenportdiocese.org

David—Most Rev. José Luis Lacunza Maestrojuán, O.A.R.; Obispado Apartado 0426-00109, David, Chiriqui, Panama.
Tel: 507-775-2916 ***Fax:*** 507-774-3920
Email: irunako@cwpanama.net

De Aar—Most Rev. Adam Leszek Musialek, S.C.I.; 1 Van Riebeeck Str., P.O. Box 73, De Aar, 7000, South Africa.
Tel: 27-053-631-1149 ***Fax:*** 27-053-631-1043

Debrecen-Nyíregyháza—Most Rev. Nándor Bosák; Varga u. 4, Pf. 240, Debrecen, H-4002, Hungary.
Tel: 52-431-631; 52-530-451 ***Fax:*** 52-431-632
Email: debreceb.nyiregyhaza@t-online.hu

Dédougou—Most Rev. Judes Bicaba; Evêché B.P. 35, Dédougou, Burkina Faso.
Tel: 20-52-00-37 ***Fax:*** 20-52-00-37
Email: eveche.ddg@fasonet.bf

Dedza—Most Rev. Emmanuel Kanyama; Bishop's House P.O. Box 80, Dedza, Malawi.
Tel: 265-1-223-103 ***Fax:*** 265-1-223-246

DELHI—Most Rev. Vincent Michael Concessao; Archbishop's House 1 Ashok Place, New Delhi, 110001, India.
Tel: 91-011-2334-3457 ***Fax:*** 91-011-2374-6575
Email: archbishopdelhi@yahoo.co.in

Denpasar—Most Rev. Silvester San; Jl. Rambutan 27, Kotak pos 3081, Denpasar, Bali, 80030, Indonesia.
Tel: 62-0361-222-020 ***Fax:*** 62-0361-261-407
Email: sekret_kdps@yahoo.com

DENVER—Vacant; Pastoral Center 1300 S. Steele St., Denver, CO, 80210.
Tel: 303-722-4687 ***Fax:*** 303-715-2041
Web: www.archden.org

Derry—Most Rev. Séamus Hegarty; Bishop's House St. Eugene's Cathedral, P.O. Box 227, Derry, BT48 9YG, Ireland.
Tel: 44-28-7126-2302 ***Fax:*** 44-28-7137-1960
Email: office@derrydiocese.org

Des Moines—Most Rev. Richard Pates (DM); Chancery 601 Grand Ave., Des Moines, IA, 50309.
Tel: 515-243-7653 ***Fax:*** 515-237-5071
Email: bishop@dmdiocese.org

DETROIT—Most Rev. Allen H. Vigneron; ***Archbishop's Office:*** 1234 Washington Blvd., Detroit, MI, 48226.
Tel: 313-237-5816 ***Fax:*** 313-237-4642

DHAKA—Most Rev. Paulinus Costa; Archbishop's House G.P.O. Box 3, 1 Kakrail Rd., Ramna, Dhaka, 1000, Bangladesh.
Tel: 880-02-935-8247; 880-02-835-18-71

Dharmapuri—Most Rev. Joseph Anthony Irudayaraj, S.D.B; Bishop's House Nethaji By-pass Road, P.B. 32, Dharmapuri, Tamil Nadu, 636701, India.
Tel: 04342-264-403 ***Fax:*** 04342-212-200

DIAMANTINA—Most Rev. João Bosco Oliver de Faria; Cúria Metropolitana Rua do Contrato 104, Diamantina, MG, 39100-000, Brazil.
Tel: 55-038-3531-1094 ***Fax:*** 55-038-3531-1094
Email: mitra@arquidiamantina.org.br

Diamantino—Vacant; C.P. 02, Rua das Camélias 75, Bairro Jardim Eldorado, Diamantino, MT, 78400-000, Brazil.
Tel: 55-065-336-1213 ***Fax:*** 55-065-336-1213
Email: diocesedtno@uol.com.br

DIARBEKIR, AMIDA—Vacant; Archevêché Chaldéen Hamalbasi Caddesi 48, Galatasaray, Beyoglu, Istanbul, 80070, Turkey.
Tel: 0212-252-34-49 ***Fax:*** 0212-252-34-49
Email: prfyakan@hotmail.fr

Dibrugarh—Most Rev. Joseph Aind, S.D.B.; Bishop's House, P.O. Box 50, Dibrugarh, Assam, 786001, India.
Tel: 91-0373-2324-436; 91-0373-2321-496 ***Fax:*** 91-0373-2321-496

Diébougou—Most Rev. Der Raphaël Dabiré Kusiélé; Evêché B.P. 35, Diébougou, Burkina Faso.
Tel: 226-20-90-53-85 ***Fax:*** 226-20-90-53-22
Email: evedieb@fasonet.bf

Digne—Most Rev. Francois-Xavier Loizeau; Evêché, 13 Avenue Paul Martin, B.P. 67, Digne-les-Bains CEDEX, 04002, France.
Tel: 4-92-31-32-90 ***Fax:*** 4-92-32-21-13
Email: digne.eveche@free.fr

Digos—Most Rev. Guillermo V. Afable; Home of the Clergy Doña Aurora St., Digos, Davao del Sur, 8002, Philippines.
Tel: 082-553-2012 ***Fax:*** 082-553-5852
Email: athoc_dod@yahoo.com

DIJON—Most Rev. Roland Minnerath; Archevêché 20 rue du Petit-Potet, B.P. 57989, Dijon, 21079, France.
Tel: 3-80-63-16-63 ***Fax:*** 3-80-63-16-79
Email: vicaire.general@eveche-dijon.com

Díli—Most Rev. Alberto Ricardo da Silva; Câmara Eclesiástica, Av. Direitos Humanos, P.O. Box 50, Bidau Lecidere, Díli, 88010, East Timor.
Tel: 0390-332-28-50 ***Fax:*** 0390-332-23-93

Dinajpur—Vacant; Bishop's House P.O. Box 5, Dinajpur, 5200, Bangladesh.
Tel: 880-0531-65-669
Email: marandy-79@hotmail.com

Dindigul—Most Rev. Antony Pappusamy; Bishop's House P.O. Box 6, Mullipadi P.O., B.K. Pudur SO, Dindigul, Tamil Nadu, 624005, India.
Tel: 0451-241-15-51
Email: dgldiocese@yahoo.co.in

Diphu—Most Rev. John Moolachira; Bishop's House Diphu, Karbi Anglong Dt., P.B. 18, Assam, 782460, India.
Tel: 91-03671-2724-42/2725-52 ***Fax:*** 91-03671-2725-51
Email: bishopdiphu@gmail.com

Dipolog—Most Rev. Jose R. Manguiran; Millennium Bldg., P. Ramon St., Estaka, Dipolog City, 7100, Philippines.
Tel: 065-212-2879 ***Fax:*** 065-212-2879
Email: dio_dipolog@yahoo.com

Divinópolis—Most Rev. Tarcisio Nascentes dos Santos; Cúria Diocesana Rua Mato Grosso 503, Divinópolis, MG, 35500-027, Brazil.
Tel: 55-037-3214-3925 ***Fax:*** 55-037-3221-3066
Email: curiadiodiv@ig.com.br

Djibouti—Most Rev. Giorgio Bertin, O.F.M.; Evêché Boulevard de la République, B.P. 94, Djitbouti, Djibouti.
Tel: 253-35-01-40 ***Fax:*** 253-35-48-31
Email: evechcat@intnet.dj

Djougou—Most Rev. Paul Kouassivi Vieira; Evêché B.P. 125, Djougou, Benin.
Tel: 23-80-01-96 ***Fax:*** 23-80-00-66

Doba—Most Rev. Michele Russo, M.C.C.I.; Evêché B.P. 22, Doba, Chad.
Tel: 625-63-33

Dodge City—Most Rev. John B. Brungardt; Catholic Church Offices 910 Central Ave., Dodge City, KS, 67801.
Tel: 620-227-1500 ***Fax:*** 620-227-1570
Web: www.dcdiocese.org

Dodoma—Most Rev. Gervas John Mwasikwabhila Nyaisonga; Bishop's House P.O. Box 922, Dodoma, Tanzania.
Tel: 255-026-239-4462 ***Fax:*** 255-026-239-4513
Email: bishops_house@yahoo.com

Dori—Most Rev. Joachim Ouédraogo; Evêché, B.P. 139, Manga, Burkina Faso.
Tel: 226-40-46-04-08

Doruma-Dungu—Most Rev. Richard Domba Mady; Evêché B.P. 20, Dungu par Isiro, Haut-Congo, Democratic Republic of Congo.
Tel: 242-081-699-21-08
Email: secdiocesain@yahoo.fr

DOUALA—Most Rev. Samuel Kleda; Archevêché B.P. 179, Douala, Cameroon.
Tel: 237-3342-3714 ***Fax:*** 237-3343-1837
Email: mukjp2004@yahoo.fr

Doumé-Abong' Mbang—Most Rev. Jan Ozga; Evêché B.P. 42, Doumé, Cameroon.
Tel: 7528-21-66

Dourados—Most Rev. Redovino Rizzardo, C.S.; Cúria Diocesana C.P. 493, Rua João Cândido da Câmara 400, Dourados, MS, 79804-970, Brazil.
Tel: 55-067-3422-6910 ***Fax:*** 55-067-3422-6911
Email: diocesedourados@terra.com.br

Down and Connor—Most Rev. Noël Treanor; Bishop's House Lisbreen, 73 Somerton Rd., Belfast, BT15 4DE, Ireland.
Tel: 44-28-9077-6185 ***Fax:*** 44-28-9077-3977
Email: dccuria@downandconnor.org

Dresden-Meissen—Most Rev. Joachim Friedrich Reinelt; Bischöfliches Ordinariat Käthe-Kollwitz-Ufer 84, Dresden, D-01309, Germany.
Tel: 37-0351-33-646-00 ***Fax:*** 37-0351-33-647-91
Email: stephan.thuge@ordinariat-dresden.de

Drohiczyn—Most Rev. Antoni Pacyfik Dydycz, O.F.M.Cap.; Kuria Diecezjalna ul. Koscielna 10, Drohiczyn, 17-312, Poland.
Tel: 48-085-655-78-08/70-01 ***Fax:*** 48-085-655-80-04
Email: kuria@drohiczyn.opoka.org.pl

Dromore—Most Rev. John McAreavey; Bishop's House 44 Armagh Rd., Newry, Co. Down, BT35 6PN, Ireland.
Tel: +44-28302-62-444 ***Fax:*** +44-28302-60-496

DUBLIN—Most Rev. Diarmuid Martin; Archbishop's House Drumcondra, Dublin, 9, Ireland.
Tel: 353-01-837-37-32 ***Fax:*** 353-01-836-97-96
Email: archbishop@abhouse.org

Dubrovnik, Ragusa—Most Rev. Mate Uzinic; Biskupski Ordinarijat p.p. 85, Poljana Paska Milicevica 4, Dubrovnik, 20001, Croatia.
Tel: 385-020-324-911 ***Fax:*** 385-020-324-912
Email: biskupija@du.t-com.hr

DUBUQUE—Most Rev. Jerome G. Hanus, O.S.B.; Chancery, Archdiocesan Center 1229 Mount Loretta Ave., Dubuque, IA, 52003-7826.
Tel: 563-556-2580 ***Fax:*** 563-556-5464
Email: dbqcco@arch.pvt.k12.ia.us

Duitama-Sogamoso—Most Rev. Carlos Prada Sanmiguel; Obispado, Calle 13 N. 15-34, Duitama, Boyacá, Colombia.
Tel: 57-87-760-2811; 57-87-760-23-31 ***Fax:*** 57-87-760-2812
Email: diocesisduitama@hotmail.com

Duluth—Most Rev. Paul D. Sirba; Pastoral Center 2830 E. Fourth St, Duluth, MN, 55812.
Tel: 218-724-9111 ***Fax:*** 218-724-1056

Dumaguete—Most Rev. John F. Du; Diocesan Chancery Office P.O. Box 85, Dumaguete City, 6200, Philippines.
Tel: 035-225-0612; 035-422-7764; 035-422-9059 ***Fax:*** 035-225-4614
Email: chancerydgte@yahoo.com

Dumka—Most Rev. Julius Marandi; Bishop's House Dudhani, Bhagalpur Rd., Dumka, Dumka Dt., Jharkhand, 814101, India.
Tel: 91-06434-222-413 ***Fax:*** 91-06434-223-377
Email: bspdumka@yahoo.co.in

Dundee—Most Rev. Thomas Graham Rose; Postnet Suite 95, P.O. Box x6603, New Castle, 2940, South Africa.
Tel: 27-034-312-65-91 ***Fax:*** 27-034-312-65-92
Email: dundeediocese@gmail.com

Dundo—Vacant; C.P. 73, Dundo, Lunda Norte, Angola.
Tel: 254-2522-64-474 ***Fax:*** 254-2522-64-474

Dunedin—Most Rev. Colin David Campbell; Catholic Pastoral Centre 300 Rattray St., Private Bag 1941, Dunedin, 9054, New Zealand.
Tel: 64-03-474-5750 ***Fax:*** 64-03-474-5758
Email: johnharr@xtra.co.nz

Dunkeld—Most Rev. Vincent Logan; Bishop's House 24-28 Lawside Road, Dundee, DD3 6XY, Scotland.
Tel: 44-01382-22-54-53 ***Fax:*** 44-01382-20-45-85

Duque de Caxias—Most Rev. José Francisco Rezende Dias; C.P. 4, Avenida Presidente Kennedy 1861, Duque de Caxias, RJ, 25010-009, Brazil.
Tel: 55-021-3552-9901 ***Fax:*** 55-021-3552-9902
Email: mitraduquedecaxias@veloxmail.com.br

DURANGO—Most Rev. Héctor González Martínez; Arzobispado, Apartado 116, 20 de Noviembre 306 Poniente, Durango, Dgo., 34000, Mexico.
Tel: 52-618-811-42-42; 52-618-811-62-33 ***Fax:*** 52-618-812-88-81
Email: arqdgo@prodigy.net.mx

DURBAN—His Eminence Cardinal Wilfrid Fox Napier, O.F.M.; Archbishop's House 154 Gordon Rd., Durban, KwaZulu-Natal, 4001, South Africa.
Tel: 27-031-303-1417 ***Fax:*** 27-031-312-1848
Email: vg@catholic-dbn.org.za
P.O. Box 47489, Greyville, 4023, South Africa.

E

East Anglia—Vacant; The White House 21 Upgate, Poringland, Norwich, Norfolk, NR14 7SH, England.
Tel: 44-01508-49-22-02 ***Fax:*** 44-01508-49-53-58
Email: office@east-angliadiocese.org.uk

Ebebiyin—Most Rev. Juan Nsue Edjang May; Obispado, Apartado 117, Ebibeyin, Kie Ntem, Equatorial Guinea.
Tel: 222-07-2246
Email: asumo_aa@hotmail.com

Ebolowa—Most Rev. Jean Mbarga; Evêché, B.P. 910, Ebolowa, Ntem, Cameroon.
Tel: 2207-6880
Email: abephrembb@yahoo.com

Ecatepec—Most Rev. Onésimo Cepeda Silva; Obispado, Plaza Principal s/n, San Cristóbal Centro Apartado 95, Ecatepec de Morelos, Méx., 55000, Mexico.
Tel: 55-5770-1404/5116-0976

Edéa—Most Rev. Jean-Bosco Ntep; Evêché, B.P. 244, Edéa, Cameroon.
Tel: 3303-34-17 ***Fax:*** 3302-87-66

EDMONTON—Most Rev. Richard William Smith; Catholic Pastoral Centre 8421-101st Ave., Edmonton, AB, T6A 0L1, Canada.
Tel: 780-469-1010 ***Fax:*** 780-465-3003
Email: chancery@caedm.ca

Edmonton (Ukrainian)—Most Rev. David Montiuk; Eparch's Chancery 9645-108 Ave., Edmonton, AB, T5H 1A3, Canada.
Tel: 780-424-5496 ***Fax:*** 780-425-2330
Email: chancery@edmontoneparchy.com

Edmundston—Most Rev. Claude Champagne, O.M.I.; Centre diocésain 60 rue Bouchard, Edmundston, NB, E3V 3K1, Canada.
Tel: 506-735-5578 ***Fax:*** 506-735-4271
Email: diocese@nbnet.nb.ca

EGER—Most Rev. Csaba Ternyák; Széchenyi u. 1, Pf. 80, Eger, H-3301, Hungary.
Tel: 36-517-589; 36-517-750 ***Fax:*** 36-517-751

Eichstätt—Most Rev. Gregor Maria Hanke, O.S.B; Bischöfliches Ordinariat Postfach 1354, Luitpoldstr. 2, Eichstätt, D-85067, Germany.
Tel: 49-08421-500 ***Fax:*** 49-08421-50-209
Email: generalvikariat@bistum-eichstaett.de

Eisenstadt—Most Rev. Agidius Zsifkovics; St. Rochusstrasse 21, Eisenstadt, A-7000, Austria.
Tel: 43-02682-77-70 ***Fax:*** 43-02682-777-252
Email: office@martinus.at

Ekiti—Most Rev. Felilx Femi Ajakaye; Catholic Secretariat P.O. Box 136, Ado-Ekiti, Ekiti State, Nigeria.
Tel: 081-256-74-455
Email: ekiticatholicdiocese@yahoo.com

El Alto—Most Rev. Jesús Juárez Párraga, S.D.B.; Zona Ferropetrol, Plaza Boris Banzer 19, El Alto, Bolivia.
Tel: 02-2844-307; 02-2844-257 ***Fax:*** 02-2844-257
Email: dcelalto@ceibo.entelnet.bo

El Banco—Most Rev. Jaime Enrique Duque Correa, M.X.Y; Carrera 9 N. 3-18, El Banco (Magdalena), Colombia.
Tel: 5-429-30-73 ***Fax:*** 5-429-29-87
Email: diocelbanco@yahoo.es

El Obeid—Most Rev. Macram Max Gassis, M.C.C.I.; Catholic Church P.O. Box 386, El Obeid, Sudan.
Tel: 611-822-653; 611-822-820 ***Fax:*** 611-822-820
Email: antmen@hotmail.com

El Paso—Most Rev. Armando X. Ochoa, D.D. (ELP); Chancery Office 499 St. Matthews St., El Paso, TX, 79907.
Tel: 915-872-8407 ***Fax:*** 915-872-8413
Email: jstowe@elpasodiocese.org

El Vigía - San Carlos del Zulia—Most Rev. José Luis Azuaje Ayala; Av. 1 Calle 8-101, Urbanización Buenos Aires, El Vigía, Edo. Mérida, Venezuela.
Tel: 0275-881-7021 ***Fax:*** 0275-881-4473
Email: elvigiasancarlos@yahoo.es

Elblag—Most Rev. Jan Styrna; Kuria Diecezjalna ul. Sw. Ducha 11, Elblag, 82-300, Poland.
Tel: 48-055-232-73-70 ***Fax:*** 48-055-232-54-09
Email: kuria@elblag.opoka.org.pl

Eldoret—Most Rev. Cornelius Kipng'eno Arap Korir; Nyerere Rd., P.O. Box 842, Eldoret, 30100, Kenya.
Tel: 254-053-2063-981; 254-053-2031-867 ***Fax:*** 254-053-2062-004
Email: catdioce@africaonline.co.ke

Elk—Most Rev. Jerzy Mazur, S.V.D.; Kuria Diecezjalna, Pl. Katedralny 1, Elk, 19-300, Poland.
Tel: 087-621-6802/4 ***Fax:*** 087-621-6803
Email: kuria@diecezja.elk.pl

Elphin—Most Rev. Christopher Jones; Bishop's House St. Mary's, Sligo, Ireland.
Tel: 353-071-9162-670 ***Fax:*** 353-071-9162-414
Email: elphindo@eircom.net

Eluru—Vacant; Bishop's House Xavier Nagar, Eluru, West Godavary Dr., A.P., 534007, India.
Tel: 91-08812-230-707 ***Fax:*** 91-08812-237-407
Email: bjmelr@rediffmail.com

Embu—Most Rev. Paul Kariuki Njiru; Bishop's House P.O. Box 1499, Embu, 60100, Kenya.
Tel: 254-068-31-531/31-522; 254-020-21-72-864 ***Fax:*** 254-068-31-531/31-522; 254-020-21-72-864
Email: doe.clergy@gmail.com

Emdeber—Most Rev. Musie Ghebreghiorghis, O.F.M.Cap.; Catholic Eparchy of Emdember P.O. Box 23, Emdibir, Guraghe Zone, Ethiopia.
Tel: 011-331-01-65 ***Fax:*** 011-331-00-37

Encarnación—Most Rev. Ignacio Gogorza Izaguirre, S.C.I; Calle Gral. Cabañas 305, C.C. 81, Encarnación, Paraguay.
Tel: 595-071-20-3305 ***Fax:*** 595-071-20-3777
Email: diocesisenc@click.com.py

ENDE—Most Rev. Vincentius Sensi; Keuskupan Agung, Tromol Pos 210, Jl. Katedral 5, Ndona-Ende, Flores, 86312, Indonesia.
Tel: 0381-21-176 ***Fax:*** 0381-22-873

Engativá—Most Rev. Héctor Luis Gutiérrez Pabón; Transversal 70C, bis.N. 77-60, Barrio Bonanza, Engativá, Bogotá, D.C., Colombia.
Tel: 1-437-05-81 ***Fax:*** 1-540-49-98
Email: diocesisengativa@etb.net.co

Ensenada—Most Rev. Sigifredo Noriega Barceló; Av. Guadalupe 565, Col. Obrera, Ensenada, B.C., 22830, Mexico.
Tel: 646-176-37-40 ***Fax:*** 646-176-37-40
Email: diocesisensenada@gmail.com

Enugu—Most Rev. Callilstus Valentine Onaga; Bishop's House P.O. Box 302, Ogui, Enugu, Enugu State, Nigeria.
Tel: 0803-33-75-672
Email: cathsen1@yahoo.com

Erexim—Most Rev. Girônimo Zanandréa; Cúria Diocesana C.P. 795, Av. 7 de Setembro 1251, Erexim, RS, 99700-000, Brazil.
Tel: 55-054-3522-3611 ***Fax:*** 55-054-3522-3611
Email: pe.balestrin@diocesedeerexim.org.br

Erfurt—Most Rev. Joachim Wanke; Bischöfliches Ordinariat Herrmannsplatz 9, Erfurt, D-99084, Germany.
Tel: 0361-65720 ***Fax:*** 0361-6572-444
Email: ordinariat@bistum-erfurt.de

Erie—Most Rev. Donald W. Trautman, S.T.D., S.S.L. (E); Chancery: St. Mark's Catholic Center 429 E. Grandview Blvd., P.O. Box 10397, Erie, PA, 16514-0397.
Tel: 814-824-1111 ***Fax:*** 814-824-1128
Email: chancery@eriercd.org

ERNAKULAM-ANGAMALY—Most Rev. George Alencherry; Archbishop's House P.O. Box 2580, Kochi, Kerala, 682031, India.
Tel: 91-0484-235-2629; 91-0484-235-2906 ***Fax:*** 91-0484-235-5010
Email: cardinal@ernakulamarchdiocese.org

Escuintla—Most Rev. Víctor Hugo Palma Paúl; Obispado, 3a Calle A 2-36, Zona 1, Escuintla, Guatemala.
Tel: 09-7888-02-76 ***Fax:*** 09-7888-05-78
Email: sudbistum@turbonett.com

Eséka—Most Rev. Dieudonné Bogmis; Evêché, B.P. 35, Eséka, Cameroon.

Eshowe—Most Rev. Xolelo Thaddaeus Kumalo; Bishop's House P.O. Box 553, Eshowe, Zululand, 3815, South Africa.
Tel: 27-035-474-4151 ***Fax:*** 27-035-474-4644
Email: dioofesh@mweb.co.za

Espinal—Most Rev. Pablo Emiro Salas Anteliz; Casa Episcopal Carrera 7A N. 10-14, El Espinal, Tolima, Colombia.
Tel: 57-8-2484-328; 57-8-2486-650 ***Fax:*** 57-8-2483-614
Email: resoreriadiocesisdelespinal@hotmail.com

Essen—Most Rev. Franz-Josef Overbeck; Bischöfliches Generalvikariat Zwölfling 16, Essen, D-45127, Germany.
Postfach 100464, Essen, D-45004, Germany.
Tel: 0201-2204-1 ***Fax:*** 0201-2204-570
Email: generalvikariat@bistum-essen.de

Estância—Most Rev. Marco Eugênio Galrão Leite de Almeida; Cúria Diocesana C.P. 141, Praça Jackson de Figueiredo 13, Estância, SE, 49200-000, Brazil.
Tel: 55-079-3522-1083 ***Fax:*** 55-079-3522-1083

Estelí—Most Rev. Juan Abelardo Mata Guevara, S.D.B.; Obispado, Apartado 16, Estelí, Nicaragua.
Tel: 505-713-5939 *Fax:* 505-713-5939
Email: celiana22@cablenet.com.ni

ESZTERGOM-BUDAPEST—His Eminence Péter Erdö; Primási és Érseki Hivatal, Uri utca 62, Pf.1, Budapest, H-1250, Hungary.
Tel: 1-225-2590 *Fax:* 1-202-5458Primási és Érseki Hivatal, Mindszenty hercegprímás tére 2, Pf. 25, H-2501, Esztergom, Hungary.
Tel: 33-510-120 *Fax:* 33-411-085
Email: egombp@katolikus.hu

Eunápolis—Most Rev. José Edson Santana de Oliveira; Bispado, Praça Frei Calixto s/n, C.P. 2, Eunápolis, BA, 45820-970, Brazil.
Tel: 073-3281-4851 *Fax:* 073-3281-4851
Email: curiadioceseeunapolis@veloxmail.com.br

Evansville—Most Rev. Charles C. Thompson; Catholic Center 4200 N. Kentucky Ave., Evansville, IN, 47711.
Tel: 812-424-5536 *Fax:* 812-421-1334

ÉVORA—Most Rev. José Francisco Sanches Alves; Cúria Arquiepiscopal Largo Marquês de Marialva 6, Évora, 7000-809, Portugal.
Tel: 351-266-748-854 *Fax:* 351-266-748-851
Email: pastoral@diocese-evora.pt

Evreux—Most Rev. Christian Nourrichard; Evêché, B.P. 165, 11B rue Jean Bart, Evreux CEDEX, 27001, France.
Tel: 2-32-62-82-20 *Fax:* 2-32-62-40-66
Email: accueildiocesainstjean@orange.fr

Evry-Corbeil-Essonnes—Most Rev. Michel Dubost, C.I.M.; Maison diocésaine B.P. 170, 21 Cours Mgr. Romero, Evry CEDEX, 91000, France.
Tel: 33-1-60-91-17-00 *Fax:* 33-1-69-91-1714
Email: diocese@eveche-evry.com

F

Fabriano-Matelica—Most Rev. Giancarlo Vecerrica; Vescovado, Piazza Papa Giovanni Paolo II 2, Fabriano, Ancona, 60044, Italy.
Tel: 39-0732-3049 *Fax:* 30-0732-22142
Email: curia@fabriano-matgelica.chiesacattolica.it

Facatativá—Most Rev. Luis Antonio Nova Rocha; Casa Episcopal Calle 5 N. 2-10, Facatativá, Cund., Colombia.
Tel: 57-1-842-30-04/27-14 *Fax:* 57-1-842-31-47/24-18
Email: cancilleriafacatativa@gmail.com

Fada N'Gourma—Vacant; Evêché, B.P. 12, Fada N'Gourma, Burkina Faso.
Tel: 226-40-77-01-33 *Fax:* 226-40-77-04-96
Email: eveche.fada@fasonet.bf

Faenza-Modigliana—Most Rev. Claudio Stagni; Vescovado, Piazza XI Febbraio 10, Faenza, Ravenna, 48018, Italy.
Tel: 39-0546-21-642 *Fax:* 39-0546-69-30-63
Email: curia@faenza.chiesacattolica.it

FAGARAS SI ALBA IULIA—Most Rev. Lucian Muresan; Str. Petru Pavel Aron 2, Blaj, AB, RO-515400, Romania.
Tel: 40-0258-71-08-55/71-20-57 *Fax:* 40-0258-71-36-02
Email: mitropolia@bru.ro

Fairbanks—Most Rev. Donald J. Kettler (FBK); Chancery Office 1316 Peger Road, Fairbanks, AK, 99709.
Tel: 907-374-9500 *Fax:* 907-374-9580
Web: www.cbna.info

Faisalabad—Most Rev. Joseph Coutts; Bishop's House Railway Rd., P.O. Box 87, Faisalabad, 38000, Pakistan.
Tel: 92-041-262-48-78 *Fax:* 92-041-261-68-54
Email: harmony@fsd.comsats.net.pk

Fajardo-Humacao—Most Rev. Eusebio Ramos Morales; Carretera 987 Km. 02, Fajardo, 00738, Puerto Rico.
Tel: 787-801-5700 *Fax:* 787-801-2600
Email: diocesisfajardohumacao@gmail.com

Fall River—Most Rev. George W. Coleman (FR); Chancery Office 450 Highland Ave., P.O. Box 2577, Fall River, MA, 02722-2577.
Tel: 508-675-1311 *Fax:* 508-730-2447
Email: chancery@dioc-fr.org

Fano-Fossombrone-Cagli-Pergola—Most Rev. Armando Trasarti; Vescovado, Via Rainerio 5, Fano, Pesaro, 61032, Italy.
Tel: 39-0721-80-37-37 *Fax:* 39-0721-82-55-95
Email: curia@fanodiocesi.it

Farafangana—Most Rev. Benjamin Marc Ramaroson, C.M.; Evêché, B.P. 24, Farafangana 309, Madagascar.
Tel: 261-032-42-903-42
Email: klemen.stolcar@yahoo.fr

Fargo—Most Rev. Samuel J. Aquila, D.D. (FAR); Chancery Office 5201 Bishops Blvd., Ste. A, Fargo, ND, 58104-7605.
Tel: 701-356-7900 *Fax:* 701-356-7999
Web: www.fargodiocese.org

Faro—Most Rev. Manuel Neto Quintas, S.C.I.; Cúria Diocesana Largo da Sé 20, Faro, 8000-138, Portugal.
Tel: 351-289-829-206/807-590 *Fax:* 351-289-805-400
Email: chancelaria@diocese-algarve.pt

FEIRA DE SANTANA—Most Rev. Itamar Vian, O.F.M.Cap.; C.P. 276, Feira de Santana, BA, 44001-970, Brazil.
Tel: 55-075-3623-2875 *Fax:* 55-075-3623-2875
Email: secretaria@arquidiocese-fsa.org.br
Cúria Metropolitana Av. Getúlio Vargas 394, Feira de Santana, 44025-010, Brazil.

Feldkirch—Most Rev. Elmar Fischer; Bischöfliches Ordinariat Bahnhofstrasse 13, Feldkirch, A-6800, Austria.
Tel: 43-05522-3485-308 *Fax:* 43-05522-3485-322
Email: ordinariat@kath-kirche-vorarlberg.at

Fengsiang (Fengxiang)—Catholic Mission Bishop's House, Si-kie, Fengxiang, Shaanxi, China.

Fenoarivo Atsinanana—Most Rev. Marcellin Randriamamonjy; Evêché, B.P. 22, Sahavola, Fenerive-Est 509, Madagascar.
Tel: 034-39-58-395; 033-25-02-038
Email: peredahymarc@yahoo.fr

Fenyang (Fenyang)—Catholic Mission Bishop's House, Fenyang, Shanxi, China.

FERMO—Most Rev. Luigi Conti; Arcivescovado Via Sisto V 11, Fermo, Ascoli Piceno, 63023, Italy.
Tel: 39-0734-22-90-05 *Fax:* 39-0734-22-03-85
Email: curia@fermo.chiesacattolica.it

Ferns—Most Rev. Dennis Brennan; Bishop's House Summerhill, Wexford, Ireland.
Tel: 353-053-91-22-177 *Fax:* 353-053-91-23-436
Email: adm@ferns.ie

FERRARA-COMACCHIO—Most Rev. Paolo Rabitti; Arcivescovado Corso Martiri della Libertà 77, Ferrara, 44121, Italy.
Tel: 39-0532-20-26-57 *Fax:* 39-0532-24-89-64
Email: curia@diocesiferrara.it

FIANARANTSOA—Most Rev. Fulgence Rabemahafaly; Archevêché B.P. 1440, Ecar Ambozontany, Fianarantsoa, 301, Madagascar.
Tel: 020-75-933-43 *Fax:* 020-75-514-36
Email: ecardiofianar@mel.moov.mg

Fidenza—Most Rev. Carlo Mazza; Curia Vescovile Piazza A. Grandi 16, Fidenza, Parma, 43036, Italy.
Tel: 39-0524-51-26-00 *Fax:* 39-0524-84-152
Email: curia@diocesifidenza.it

Fiesole—Most Rev. Mario Meini; Vescovado, Piazza della Cattedrale 1, Fiesole, Firenze, 50014, Italy.
Tel: 39-055-59-242 *Fax:* 39-055-59-95-87
Email: cancelliere@curiafiesole.191.it

FIRENZE—Most Rev. Giuseppe Betori; Arcivescovado Piazza S. Giovanni 3, Firenze, 50129, Italy.
Tel: 39-055-27-63-71 *Fax:* 39-055-27-63-741
Email: info@diocesifirenze.it

Florencia—Vacant; Curia Diocesana Carrera 14 N. 13-35, Parque San Francisco, Florencia, Caquetá, Colombia.
Tel: 57-8-435-8650 *Fax:* 57-8-435-2528; 57-8-435-8650

Floresta—Most Rev. Adriano Ciocca Vasino; Cúria Diocesana Praça Antônio Ferraz, Boiadeiro 01, Floresta, PE, 56400-000, Brazil.
Tel: 55-087-3877-1149 *Fax:* 55-087-3877-1258
Email: diocesefloresta@gmail.com

Floriano—Most Rev. Valdemir Ferreira dos Santos; Curia Diocesana Av. Euripedes de Aguiar 633, C.P. 44, Floriano, 64800-000, Brazil.
Tel: 089-3522-1762 *Fax:* 089-3522-1772
Email: diocese@florianonet.com.br

FLORIANÓPOLIS—Most Rev. Wilson Tadeu Jonck, S.C.I.; Cúria Metropolitana Rua Esteves Júnior 447, Florianópolis, SC, 88015-130, Brazil.
Tel: 55-048-3224-4799 *Fax:* 55-048-3224-4799
Email: arquifln@arquifln.org.br

Florida—Most Rev. Martin Pablo Pérez Scremini; Obispado, Calle Alejandro Gallinal 532, Florida, 94000, Uruguay.
Tel: 598-035-22164 *Fax:* 598-035-22863
Email: ceuflodu@montevideo.com.uy

FOGGIA-BOVINO—Most Rev. Francesco Pio Tamburrino, O.S.B.; Arcivescovado, Via Oberdan 13, Foggia, 71100, Italy.
Tel: 39-0881-76-61-11 *Fax:* 39-0881-72-32-71
Email: info@diocesifoggiabovino.it

Foligno—Most Rev. Gualtiero Sigismondi; Piazza Mons. Faloci Pulignani 3, Foligno, Perugia, 06034, Italy.
Tel: 39-0742-35-04-73 *Fax:* 39-0742-34-90-21
Email: info@diocesidifoligno.it

Fontibón—Most Rev. Enrique Sarmiento Angulo; Carrera 98 N. 17A-81, Fontibón, Colombia.
Tel: 011-1-418-1036 *Fax:* 011-1-418-1042
Email: diocesisdefontibon@yahoo.com

FOOCHOW (FUZHOU), MIN-HOU—Catholic Mission Archbishop's House, Fuzhou, Fujian, China.

Forlì-Bertinoro—Most Rev. Lino Pizzi; Vescovado, Piazza Dante 1, Forlì, 47100, Italy.
Tel: 39-0543-28-240 *Fax:* 39-0543-24-303
Email: diocefo@tin.it

Formosa—Most Rev. José Vicente Conejero Gallego; Obispado, Calle España 975, Formosa, P 3600, Argentina.
Tel: 54-03717-430-814 *Fax:* 54-03717-430-343
Email: obispado@obispadoformosa.org.ar

Formosa (in Brazil)—Most Rev. Paulo Roberto Beloto; Cúria Diocesana Rua Olímpio Jacinto 560, Formosa, GO, 73801-400, Brazil.
Tel: 061-3631-0131 *Fax:* 061-3631-8837
Email: curiadiocesanaformosa@hotmail.com

FORT-DE-FRANCE—Most Rev. Michel Méranville; Archevêché B.P. 586, 5-7 rue du Révérend Père Pinchon, Fort-de-France CEDEX, 97207, Martinique.
Tel: 596-63-70-70 *Fax:* 595-72-45-30
Email: archeveche-martinique@wanadoo.fr

Fort-Liberté—Vacant; Evêché, 87 Rue Sténio Vincent, B.P. 237, Fort Liberté, Cap-Haïtien, Haiti.
Tel: 509-0509-2262-2026; 509-0509-2453-1723 *Fax:* 553-0822
Email: diocesef_liberte@yahoo.fr

Fort Portal—Most Rev. Robert Muhiirwa; Bishop's House P.O. Box 214, Fort Portal, Uganda.
Tel: 256-0483-427-332 *Fax:* 256-0483-422-072

Fort Wayne South Bend—Most Rev. Kevin C. Rhoades; Archbishop Noll Catholic Center 915 S. Clinton St., P.O. Box 390, Fort Wayne, IN, 46801.
Tel: 260-422-4611 *Fax:* 260-969-9145
Web: www.diocesefwsb.org
Email: dlewandowski@fw.diocesefwsb.org

Fort Worth—Most Rev. Kevin William Vann; The Catholic Center 800 West Loop 820 S., Fort Worth, TX, 76108.
Tel: 817-560-3300 *Fax:* 817-244-8839
Web: www.fwdioc.org
Email: sberg@fwdioc.org

FORTALEZA—Most Rev. José Antônio Aparecido Tosi Marques; Cúria Metropolitana Av. Dom Manoel 3, Fortaleza, CE, 60060-090, Brazil.
Tel: 55-085-4005-7850 *Fax:* 085-4005-7856
Email: contabilidadc@arquidiocesedefortaleza.org.br

Fossano—Most Rev. Giuseppe Cavallotto; Via Vescovado 8, Fossano, Cuneo, 12045, Italy.
Tel: 39-0172-60-071 *Fax:* 39-0172-63-7691
Email: cancelleria@diocesifossano.it

Foz do Iguaçu—Most Rev. Dirceu Vegini; Cúria Diocesana Rua Venânti Otremba 585, Foz do Iguaçu, PR, 85852-020, Brazil.
Tel: 55-045-3574-5811 *Fax:* 55-045-3574-5811
Email: mitra@compubras.com.br

Franca—Most Rev. Pedro Luiz Stringhini; Cúria Diocesana C.P. 220, Rua Major Claudiano 1545, Franca, SP, 14400-970, Brazil.
Tel: 55-016-3721-2294 *Fax:* 55-016-3721-2294
Email: curia@diocesefranca.org.br

Franceville—Most Rev. Timothée Modibo-Nzockena; Evêché, B.P. 230, Franceville, Gabon.
Tel: 06-67-91-02
Email: diocese_fcv@yahoo.fr

Frascati—Most Rev. Raffaello Martinelli; Curia Vescovile Piazza Paolo III 10, Frascati, Roma, 00044, Italy.
Tel: 39-06-942-04-67 *Fax:* 39-06-940-10-201

Frederico Westphalen—Most Rev. Antônio Carlos Rossi Keller; Cúria Diocesana Rua do Comércio 672, Frederico Westphalen, RS, 98400-000, Brazil.
Tel: 55-055-3744-2789 *Fax:* 55-055-3744-3782
Email: curia@diocesefw.com.br

FREETOWN—Most Rev. Edward Tamba Charles; Santanno House 10 Howe. St., P.O. Box 98, Freetown, Sierra Leone.
Tel: 022-224-590 *Fax:* 022-224-075
Email: metroadfb@yahoo.com

FREIBURG IM BREISGAU—Most Rev. Robert Zollitsch; Erzbischöfliches Ordinariat, Schoferstr. 2, Freiburg im Breisgau, D-79098, Germany.
Tel: 49-0761-2188-201 *Fax:* 49-0761-2188-505
Email: info@ordinariat-freiburg.de

Fréjus-Toulon—Most Rev. Dominique Rey; Evêché, B.P. 518, 68 Impasse Beaulieu, Toulon, CEDEX 9, 83041, France.
Tel: +4-94-27-9270 *Fax:* +4-94-27-9275

Fresno—Vacant; ***Chancery Office:*** 1550 N. Fresno St., Fresno, CA, 93703-3788.
Tel: 559-488-7400 *Fax:* 559-488-7464
Email: msgrmyron@dioceseoffresno.org

Frosinone-Veroli-Ferentino—Most Rev. Ambrogio Spreafico; Via dei Monti Lepini 73, Frosinone, 03100, Italy.
Tel: 39-0775-29-09-73 *Fax:* 39-0775-20-23-16
Email: segr-vescovospreafico@diocesifrosinone.com

Fukuoka—Most Rev. Dominic Ryoji Miyahara; 6-28 Josui-dori, Chuo-ku, Fukuoka-shi, 810-0028, Japan.
Tel: 81-092-522-5139 *Fax:* 81-092-523-2152
Email: cdf-curia01@mbe.nifty.com

Fulda—Most Rev. Heinz Josef Algermissen; Paulustor 5, Fulda, D-36037, Germany.
Tel: 49-0661-870 *Fax:* 49-0661-87-578
Email: bgv@bistum-fulda.de

Funchal—Most Rev. António José Cavaco Carrilho; Câmara Eclesiástica, C.P. 4550, Largo Visconde Ribeiro Real 49, Funchal CODEX, Ilha da Madeira, 9001-801, Portugal.
Tel: 351-291-74-1337 *Fax:* 351-291-74-1357
Email: diocesefunchal@mail.telepac.pt

Funíng (Xiapu)—Catholic Mission Santuao, Xiapu, Fujian, China.

Fushun (Fushun)—Catholic Mission Bishop's House, Fushun, Liaoning, China.

G

Gaborone—Most Rev. Valentine Tsamma Seane; Bishop's House Plot 162, Queens Rd., P.O. Box 218, Gaborone, Botswana.
Tel: 267-391-29-58 *Fax:* 267-395-69-70
Email: gabs.diocese@botsnet.bw

GAETA—Most Rev. Fabio Bernardo D'Onorio; Arcivescovado Piazza Episcopio 2, Gaeta, Latina, 04024, Italy.
Tel: 39-0771-45-30-207 *Fax:* 39-0771-45-30-219
Email: arcivescovo@arcidiocesigaeta.it

GAGNOA—Most Rev. Joseph Aké Yapo; Archevêché B.P. 527, Gagnoa, Ivory Coast.
Tel: 225-32-772-568 *Fax:* 225-32-772-568
Email: evechegagnoa@aviso.ci

Galle—Most Rev. Raymond Kingsley Wickramasinghe; Bishop's House Kaluwella, Galle, Sri Lanka.
Tel: 94-091-2234-256 *Fax:* 94-091-4385-602
Email: bishopsecri@gmail.com

Galloway—Most Rev. John Cunningham; Bishop's House Candida Casa, 8 Corsehill Road, Ayr, KA7 2ST, Scotland.
Tel: 44-01292-266-750 *Fax:* 44-01292-289-888
Email: administration@gallowaydiocese.org.uk

Gallup—Most Rev. James S. Wall; Chancery 711 S. Puerco Dr., P.O. Box 1338, Gallup, NM, 87305-1338.
Tel: 505-863-4406 *Fax:* 505-722-9131
Email: officeofbishop@gmail.com

GALVESTON-HOUSTON—His Eminence Daniel Cardinal DiNardo (GAL); Chancery Office 1700 San Jacinto St., P.O. Box 907, Houston, TX, 77001-0907.
Tel: 713-659-5461 *Fax:* 713-759-9151

Galway and Kilmacduagh—Most Rev. Martin Drennan; Diocesan Office The Cathedral, Galway, Ireland.
Tel: 353-091-563-566 *Fax:* 353-091-568-333
Email: galwaydiocese@eircom.net

GANDHINAGAR—Most Rev. Stanislaus Fernandes, S.J.; Archbishop's House Sector 8, Gandhinagar, Gujarat, 382008, India.
Tel: 079-2322-7541 ***Fax:*** 079-2322-1912

Gap—Most Rev. Jean-Michel di Falco Leandri; Maison Diocesaine 9 rue Capitaine de Bresson, B.P. 76, Gap CEDEX, 05003, France.
Tel: 4-92-40-02-75 ***Fax:*** 4-92-40-02-73
Email: accueil@diocesedegap.com

Garagoa—Most Rev. José Vicente Huertas Vargas; Calle 14 N. 10-28, Garagoa, Boyacá, Colombia.
Tel: 57-87-500-085 ***Fax:*** 57-87-500-026
Email: curiagaragoa@hotmail.com

Garanhuns—Most Rev. Fernando José Monteiro Guimarães; Cúria Diocesana Av. Santo Antônio 61, C.P. 54, 55293-970, Garanhuns, PE, 55290-000, Brazil.
Tel: 55-087-3761-0805 ***Fax:*** 55-087-3761-0805
Email: curia@diocesegaranhuns.org.br

Garissa—Most Rev. Paul Darmanin, O.F.M.Cap.; P.O. Box 7, Garissa, 70100, Kenya.
Tel: 254-046-210-2102 ***Fax:*** 254-046-210-3462

GAROUA—Most Rev. Antoine Ntalou; Archevêché B.P. 272, Garoua, Cameroon.
Tel: 237-2227-1353 ***Fax:*** 237-2227-2942
Email: archigaroua@yahoo.fr

Gary—Most Rev. Dale Joseph Melczek; Chancery Office 9292 Broadway, Merrillville, IN, 46410.
Tel: 219-769-9292 ***Fax:*** 219-738-9034

Garzón—Vacant; Obispado Calle 6a N. 7-14, Garzón, Huila, Colombia.
Tel: 57-82-8332-194; 57-82-8332-438; 57-82-8332-257 ***Fax:*** 57-82-8332-439
Email: obgarzon@gmail.com

Gaspé—Most Rev. Jean Gagnon; Evêché 172 rue Jacques Cartier, C.P. 440, Gaspé, QC, G4X 1M9, Canada.
Tel: 418-368-2274 ***Fax:*** 418-368-3772
Email: diogaspe@globetrotter.net

GATINEAU—Most Rev. Paul-Andre Durocher; Centre Diocésain 180 boul. Mont-Bleu, Gatineau, QC, J8Z 3J5, Canada.
Tel: 819-771-8391 ***Fax:*** 819-778-8969
Email: gormanl@diocesegatineau.org

Gaylord—Most Rev. Bernard A. Hebda; Diocesan Pastoral Center 611 W. North St., Gaylord, MI, 49735-8349.
Tel: 989-732-5147 ***Fax:*** 989-705-3589
Email: vlooker@dioceseofgaylord.org

Gbarnga—Most Rev. Anthony Fallah Borwah; Diocese of Gbarnga P.O. Box 5297/RS, Monrovia, Liberia.
Tel: 231-6-515-968
Email: rcbcdg@gmail.com

GDANSK—Most Rev. Slawoj Leszek Glódz; Kuria Metropolitalna ul. Biskupa Edmunda Nowickiego 1, Gdansk-Oliwa, 80-330, Poland.
Tel: 48-058-552-00-51 ***Fax:*** 48-058-552-27-75
Email: kuria@diecezja.gda.pl

Geita—Most Rev. Damian Dallu; P.O. Box 120, Geita, Tanzania.
Tel: 028-2520-120; 028-2520-208 ***Fax:*** 028-2520-208

GENOVA—His Eminence Angelo Bagnasco; Arcivescovado Piazza Matteotti 4, Genova, 16123, Italy.
Tel: 39-010-27-001 ***Fax:*** 39-010-27-00-220

Gent, Gand—Most Rev. Lucas Van Looy, S.D.B.; Bisdomplein 1, Gent, B-9000, Belgium.
Tel: 32-09-225-16-26 ***Fax:*** 32-09-223-39-59
Email: ludo.collin@kerknet.be

Georgetown—Most Rev. Francis Alleyne, O.S.B.; Bishop's House 27 Brickdam, P.O. Box 101488, Georgetown, Guyana.
Tel: 592-226-4469 ***Fax:*** 592-225-8519
Email: rcbishopgy@gmail.com

Geraldton—Most Rev. Justin Joseph Bianchini; Bishop's House 7 Maitland St., P.O. Box 46, Geraldton, W.A., 6530, Australia.
Tel: 61-08-9921-3221 ***Fax:*** 61-08-9964-1097
Email: dioger@diocese-geraldton.org

Getafe—Most Rev. Joaquín María López de Andújar y Cánovas del Castillo; Obispado Almendro 4, Getafe, 28901, Spain.
Tel: 34-91-696-17-65 ***Fax:*** 34-91-683-87-62
Email: obsipado@diocesisgetafe.es

Gibraltar—Most Rev. Ralph Heskett, C.SS.R.; 215 Main St., Gibraltar.
Tel: 200-76-688 ***Fax:*** 200-43-112
Email: cathedral@gibtelecom.net

Gikongoro—Most Rev. Augustin Misago; Secrérariat de l'Evêché B.P. 77, Gikongoro, Rwanda.
Tel: 252-535-077
Email: evechegik@yahoo.fr

Girardot—Most Rev. Héctor Julio López Hurtado, S.D.B.; Obispado Calle 19 N. 11-65, Girardot, Cundinamarca, Colombia.
Tel: 57-1-833-2706; 57-1-833-4940; 57-1-833-4116 ***Fax:*** 57-1-830-9510
Email: diocesisdegirardot@yahoo.es

Girardota—Most Rev. Guillermo Orozco Montoya; Curia Episcopal Calle 7 N. 14-27, Girardota, Antioquia, Colombia.
Tel: 57-4-289-08-82 ***Fax:*** 57-4-289-06-80

Girona—Most Rev. Francesc Pardo Artigas; Bisbat Plaça del Vi 2, Girona, 17004, Spain.
Tel: 34-972-41-27-20 ***Fax:*** 34-972-41-28-72
Email: bisbatgirona@bisbatgirona.cat

GITEGA—Most Rev. Simon Ntamwana; Archevêché B.P. 118, Gitega, Burundi.
Tel: 22-40-2160 ***Fax:*** 22-40-2620

Gizo—Most Rev. Luciano Capelli, S.D.B.; Bishop's House P.O. Box 22, Gizo, Solomon Islands.
Tel: 677-60-130 ***Fax:*** 677-60-121
Email: dogizo@solomon.com.sb

GLASGOW—Most Rev. Mario Joseph Conti; Curial Offices 196 Clyde St., Glasgow, G1 4JY, Scotland.
Tel: 44-0141-226-5898 ***Fax:*** 44-0141-225-2600
Email: curia@rcag.org.uk

Gliwice—Most Rev. Jan Walenty Wieczorek; Kuria Diecezjalna ul. Luzycka 1, Gliwice, 44-101, Poland.
Tel: 48-032-230-71-42 ***Fax:*** 48-032-230-78-88
Email: info@kuria.gliwice.pl

GNIEZNO—Most Rev. Jozef Kowalczyk; ul. Prymasa Jana Laskiego 7, Gniezno, 62-200, Poland.
Tel: 48-061-426-21-02 ***Fax:*** 48-061-426-21-05
Email: kuria@gniezno.opoka.org.pl

GOA E DAMAO—Most Rev. Filipe Neri António Sebastiao do Rosário Ferrao; Paço Patriarcal P.O. Box 216, Altinho, Panjim, Goa, 403001, India.
Tel: 0832-2223-353; 0832-2225-291 ***Fax:*** 0832-2224-139
Email: archbpgoa@gmail.com

Goaso—Most Rev. Peter Kwaku Athuahene; P.O. Box 28, Goaso, Ghana.
Tel: 035-20-91-809
Email: cathsecgoaso@yahoo.com

GOIÂNIA—Most Rev. Washington Cruz, C.P.; Cúria Metropolitana Praça Dom Emanuel s/n, Goiânia, GO, 74030-140, Brazil.
Tel: 55-062-3223-0759 ***Fax:*** 55-062-3223-8532
Email: curia@arquidiocesedegoiania.org.br
C.P. 174, Goiânia, GO, 74001-970, Brazil.

Goiás—Most Rev. Eugène Lambert Adrian Rixen; Cúria Diocesana Rua Dr. Joaquim Rodrigues s/n, C.P. 05, Goiás, GO, 76600-000, Brazil.
Tel: 55-062-3371-1206 ***Fax:*** 55-062-3371-2380
Email: diocesedegoias@cultura.com.br

Gokwe—Most Rev. Angel Floro Martinez, I.E.M.E.; Bishop's House P.O. Box 90, Gokwe, Zimbabwe.
Tel: 263-059-23-96 ***Fax:*** 263-059-23-82
Email: diogokwe@adtech.co.zw

Goma—Most Rev. Theophile Kaboy Ruboneka; Evêché B.P. 50, Goma, Nord-Kivu, Democratic Republic of Congo.
Email: chancelleriegoma@yahoo.fr

Gómez Palacio—Most Rev. José Guadalupe Torres Campos; Independence 105, 35000, Gómez Palacio, Dgo., Mexico.
Tel: 871-723-79-66 ***Fax:*** 871-723-79-66

Gorakhpur—Most Rev. Thomas Thuruthimattam, C.S.T; Bishop's House Civil Lines, University P.O., Gorakhpur, U.P., 273009, India.
Tel: 91-0551-2332-723 ***Fax:*** 91-0551-2342-357

Goré—Most Rev. Rosario Pio Ramolo, O.F.M.Cap.; Eveché B.P. 61, Moundou-Goré, Chad.
Tel: 00871-762-602-289 ***Fax:*** 00871-762-602-291; 00871-762-602-289
Email: gore@sat.signis.net

GORIZIA—Most Rev. Dino De Anonti; Via Arcivescovado 2, Gorizia, 34170, Italy.
Tel: 39-0481-59-76-02 ***Fax:*** 39-0481-59-76-66
Email: cancelleria@arcidiocesi.gorizia.it

Görlitz—Most Rev. Wolfgang Ipolt; Carl-von-Ossietzky-Strasse 41/43, Görlitz, D-02826, Germany.
Tel: 03581-47-820 ***Fax:*** 03581-478-212
Email: ordinariat@bistum-goerlitz.de
Postfach 300943, Görlitz, D-02814, Germany.

Goroka—Most Rev. Francesco Sarego, S.V.D.; Bishop's House P.O. Box 109, Goroka E.H.P., Papua New Guinea.
Tel: 675-532-1525 ***Fax:*** 675-732-1799

Gospic-Senj—Most Rev. Mile Bogovic; Biskupski Ordinarijat ul. Senjskih Zrtava 36, Gospic, 53000, Croatia.
Tel: 053-746-400 ***Fax:*** 053-746-402
Email: biskupija-gospic@inet.hr

Governador Valadares—Most Rev. Werner Franz Siebenbrock, S.V.D.; Cúria Diocesana Av. Brazil 2770, Governador Valadares, MG, 35010-020, Brazil.
Tel: 55-033-3271-6056 ***Fax:*** 55-033-3271-2968
Email: secretaria@diocesegv.org.br

Goya—Most Rev. Ricardo Oscar Faifer; Mariano I. Loza 592, Casilla 40, Goya, Corrientes, W3450BXL, Argentina.
Tel: 54-03777-422-314 ***Fax:*** 54-03777-421-578
Email: obispado@goyanet.com.ar

Gozo—Most Rev. Mario Grech; Bishops Curia Triq Ir-Republika, Victoria, P.O. Box 1, Gozo, VCT 1000, Malta.
Tel: 21-556-661; 21-551-211 ***Fax:*** 21-551-278
Email: gozocuria@onvol.net

Grajaú—Most Rev. Franco Cuter, O.F.M.Cap.; Cúria Diocesana C.P. 13, Praça Dom Roberto Colombo s/n, Grajaú, MA, 65940-000, Brazil.
Tel: 55-099-3532-6180 ***Fax:*** 55-099-3532-6405
Email: curia@diocesegrajau.org.br

GRANADA—Most Rev. Francisco Javier Martínez Fernández; Plaza Alonso Cano, Granada, 18001, Spain.
Tel: 34-958-21-63-23 ***Fax:*** 34-958-22-97-25
Email: arzgranada@planalfa.es

Granada (in Colombia)—Most Rev. José Figueroa Gómez; Carrera 13 N. 23-71, Granada, Meta, Colombia.
Tel: 8-658-01-10 ***Fax:*** 8-658-00-08

Granada (in Nicaragua)—Most Rev. Jorge Solórzano Pérez; Obispado Plaza Independencia 1, Granada, Nicaragua.
Tel: 2552-2142; 2552-3086 ***Fax:*** 2552-7236
Email: odg@turbonett.com.ni

Grand-Bassam—Most Rev. Raymond Ahoua, F.D.P.; Evêché B.P. 57, Grand-Bassam, Ivory Coast.
Tel: 21-30-15-22 ***Fax:*** 21-30-15-22
Email: evechgb@aviso.ci

Grand Falls—Most Rev. Robert A. Daniels; Chancery Office 8 A Church St., P.O. Box 397, Grand Falls-Windsor, NL, A2A 2J8, Canada.
Tel: 709-489-4019 ***Fax:*** 709-489-6393
Email: pcarey@rcdiocesegrandfalls.ca

Grand Island—Most Rev. William J. Dendinger; Chancery Office 2708 Old Fair Rd., Grand Island, NE, 68803.
Tel: 308-382-6565 ***Fax:*** 308-382-6569

Grand Rapids—Most Rev. Walter Allison Hurley (GR); Administrative Office 360 Division Ave. S., Grand Rapids, MI, 49503-4539.
Tel: 616-243-0491 ***Fax:*** 616-243-4910
Email: wduncan@dioceseofgrandrapids.org

Graz-Seckau—Most Rev. Egon Kapellari; Bischöfliches Ordinariat Bischofplatz 4, Graz, A-8010, Austria.
Tel: 43-0316-80-410 ***Fax:*** 43-0316-80-41-303
Email: ordinariat@graz-seckau.at

Great Falls-Billings—Most Rev. Michael William Warfel; Chancery Office 121 23rd St. S., P.O. Box 1399, Great Falls, MT, 59403-1399.
Tel: 406-727-6683 ***Fax:*** 406-454-3480
Web: www.dioceseofgfb.org
Email: chancery@dioceseofgfb.org

Green Bay—Most Rev. David L. Ricken, D.D., J.C.L. (GB); Chancery 1825 Riverside Dr., P.O. Box 23825, Green Bay, WI, 54305-3825.
Tel: 920-437-7531 ***Fax:*** 920-435-1330
Email: jdoerfler@gbdioc.org

Greensburg—Most Rev. Lawrence E. Brandt; Pastoral Center 723 E. Pittsburgh St., Greensburg, PA, 15601.
Tel: 724-837-0901 ***Fax:*** 724-837-0857

Gregorio de Laferrere—Most Rev. Juan Horacio Suárez; Obispado, Ricardo Gutiérrez 6037, Gregorio de Laferrere, Buenos Aires, B1757DHJ, Argentina.
Tel: 54-011-4457-4844 ***Fax:*** 54-011-4457-4844
Email: obispadodelaferrere@yahoo.com.ar

Grenoble-Vienne—Most Rev. Guy de Kerimel; Evêché 12 Place Lavalette, Grenoble CEDEX 1, 38028, France.
Tel: 4-38-38-00-38 ***Fax:*** 4-38-38-00-39
Email: secretariateveque@diocese-grenoble-vienne.fr

Grodno—Most Rev. Aleksander Kaszkiewicz; ul. K. Marksa 4, Grodno, 230025, Belarus.
Tel: 0152-74-00-73 ***Fax:*** 0152-75-64-55
Email: kuria-grodno@catholic.by

Groningen-Leeuwarden—Most Rev. Gerard Johannes Nicolaus de Korte; Bisdom, Ubbo Emmiussingel 79, Groningen, 9711 BG, The Netherlands.
Tel: 31-050-406-58-88 ***Fax:*** 31-050-314-12-40
Email: info@bisdomgroningenleeuwarden.nl

Grosseto—Most Rev. Franco Agostinelli; Vescovado Corso G. Carducci 11, Grosseto, 58100, Italy.
Tel: 39-0564-29-044 ***Fax:*** 39-0564-20-116
Email: curia@grosseto.chiesacattolica.it

GROUARD-MCLENNAN—Most Rev. Gerard Pettipas, C.SS.R; Archevêché 210 Ière rue ouest, C.P. 388, McLennan, AB, T0H 2L0, Canada.
Tel: 780-324-3002 ***Fax:*** 780-324-3952
Email: clavoie@serbernet.com

GUADALAJARA—His Eminence Cardinal Juan Sandoval Íñiguez; Alfredo R. Plascencia 995, Col. Chapultepec Country, Apartado 61-33, Guadalajara, Jal., 44620, Mexico.
Tel: 33-36-14-55-04 ***Fax:*** 33-36-58-23-00
Email: arzgdl@arquidiocesisgdl.org

Guadix—Most Rev. Gines Ramon Garcia Beltran; Obispado Santa María del Buen Aire 4, Guadix, Granada, 18500, Spain.
Tel: 34-958-66-08-00/4 ***Fax:*** 34-958-66-29-19
Email: canciller@diocesisdeguadixbaza.org

Guajará-Mirim—Most Rev. Geraldo Verdier; Cúria Diocesana Av. Costa Marques 571, C.P. 55, Guajará-Mirim, RO, 76850-000, Brazil.
Tel: 55-069-3541-2275 ***Fax:*** 55-069-3541-1525

Gualeguaychú—Most Rev. Jorge Eduardo Lozano; Obispado Calle Mons. Chalup 30, Gualeguaychú, Entre Ríos, E2820EZB, Argentina.
Tel: 54-03446-426-336 ***Fax:*** 54-03446-433-884
Email: obispo@diocesisgchu.org.ar

Guanare—Most Rev. José de la Trinidad Valera Angulo; Obispado Calle 15 N. 4-49, Guanare, Edo. Portuguesa, Venezuela.
Tel: 58-0257-251-68-25 ***Fax:*** 58-0257-251-69-40
Email: diocesisguanare@hotmail.com

Guanhães—Most Rev. Emanuel Messias de Oliveira; Bispado Rua Amàvel Nunes 55, Guanhães, MG, 39740-000, Brazil.
Tel: 55-033-3421-1586 ***Fax:*** 55-033-3421-1586
Email: mitra@ghnet.com.br

Guantánamo-Baracoa—Most Rev. Wilfredo Pino Estévez; Obispado Paseo N. 812, entre San Gregorio y Cuartel, Guantánamo, 95100, Cuba.
Tel: 021-32-35-04/5/6 ***Fax:*** 021-35-5228

Guarabira—Most Rev. Francisco De Assis Dantas de Lucena; Cúria Diocesana C.P. 17, Dr. Sales 42, Guarabira, PB, 58200-000, Brazil.
Tel: 55-083-3271-4242 ***Fax:*** 55-083-3271-3271
Email: diocgba@hotmail.com

Guaranda—Most Rev. Ángel Polivio Sánchez Loaiza; Obispado Calle 10 de Agosto 617 y 7 de Mayo, Guaranda, Bolívar, Ecuador.
Tel: 03-298-16-39 ***Fax:*** 03-2981-323
Email: dguaranda@hotmail.com

Guarapuava—Most Rev. Antônio Wagner da Silva, S.C.I.; Cúria Diocesana Rua Vicente Machado 1129, 85010-260, C.P. 304, Guarapuava, PR, 85100-970, Brazil.
Tel: 55-042-3623-5984 ***Fax:*** 55-042-3623-5984

Guarda—Most Rev. Manuel da Rocha Felício; Antigo Colegio de Sao Jose Rua do Encontro 33, Guarda, 6300-704, Portugal.
Tel: 351-271-212-959 ***Fax:*** 351-271-223-769
Email: dioceseguarda@gmail.com

Guarenas—Most Rev. Gustavo García Naranjo; Calle Comercio 06-02, Guarenas 1220, Edo. Miranda, Venezuela.
Tel: 0212-363-77-34; 0212-363-84-81 ***Fax:*** 0212-362-00-18
Email: diocesisguarenas@cantv.net

Guarulhos—Most Rev. Luiz Gonzaga Bergonzini; Rua Gilberto Dini 519, Bom Clima, Guarulhos, SP, 07122-210, Brazil.
Tel: 55-011-2408-0403 ***Fax:*** 55-011-2440-0177
Email: curia@diocesedeguarulhos.org.br

GUATEMALA—Most Rev. Oscar Julio Vian Morales, S.D.B.; Arzobispado 7a Avenida 6-21, Zona 1, Ciudad de Guatemala, 01001, Guatemala.
Tel: 502-223-29-707; 502-223-29-601 ***Fax:*** 502-225-15-068
Email: curiaarzobispal@itelgua.com

Guaxupé—Most Rev. José Lanza Neto; Cúria Doicesana Rua Francisco Ribeiro do Valle 242, Guaxupé, MG, 37800-000, Brazil.
Tel: 55-035-3551-1013 ***Fax:*** 55-035-3551-1013
Email: curia@guaxupe.org.br

GUAYAQUIL—Most Rev. Antonio Arregui Yarza; Arzobispado Apartado 09-01-254, Calle Clemente Ballén 501 y Chimborazo, Guayaquil, Ecuador.
Tel: 593-04-2322-778; 593-04-2328-872 ***Fax:*** 593-04-2329-695

Gubbio—Most Rev. Mario Ceccobelli; Largo Vescovado 1, Gubbio, Perugia, 06024, Italy.
Tel: 39-075-927-39-80 ***Fax:*** 39-075-927-39-80
Email: diocesigubbio@tiscali.it

Guiratinga—Most Rev. Derek John Christopher Byrne, S.P.S.; Av. Marechal Rondon 878, C.P. 114, Guiratinga, MT, 78760-000, Brazil.
Tel: 55-066-3431-1474 ***Fax:*** 55-066-3431-1246
Email: dio.guira@terra.com.br

Guizeh—Most Rev. Antonios Aziz Mina; Evêché Copte Catholique, 8 Quartier, Rue 4, Parcelle 30B, Ville de 6 Octobre, Egypt.
Tel: 20-02-383-65-258 ***Fax:*** 20-02-383-78-929

Gulbarga—Most Rev. Robert Miranda; Kripalaya, Bishop's House Kotnoor-D Village, Nandikur Post, Gulbarga, Karnataka, 585102, India.
Tel: 20-08472-272-705
Email: gulbargadiocese@gmail.com

GULU—Most Rev. John Baptist Odama; Archbishop's House P.O. Box 200, Gulu, Uganda.
Tel: 256-0471-432-026 ***Fax:*** 256-0471-432-860
Email: metrog@archdioceseofgulu.org

Gumaca—Most Rev. Buenaventura M. Famadico; Bishop's House Brgy. Rosario, Gen. Luna St., Gumaca, Quezon, 4307, Philippines.
Tel: 042-317-6214 ***Fax:*** 042-317-7620
Email: gumacadiocese@yahoo.com

Gumla—Most Rev. Paul Alois Lakra; Bishop's House, Gumla, Jharkhand, 835207, India.
Tel: 06524-223-228
Email: amxalxo@yahoo.com

Guntur—Most Rev. Bali Gali; Bishop's House Chandramouli Nagar, Guntur, A.P., 522007, India.
Tel: 0863-2350-720 ***Fax:*** 0863-2351-234

Gurk—Most Rev. Alois Schwarz; Bischöfliches Ordinariat Mariannengasse 2, Klagenfurt, A-9021, Austria.
Tel: 43-0463-57-770 ***Fax:*** 43-0463-57-770-10-29
Email: generalvikariat@kath-kirche-kaernten.at

Gurué—Most Rev. Francisco Lerma Martinez, I.M.C.; Bispado C.P. 116, Gurué, Zambézia, Mozambique.
Tel: 24-91-0028 ***Fax:*** 24-91-0028

GUWAHATI—Most Rev. Thomas Menamparampil, S.D.B; Archbishop's House P.O. Box 100, Guwahati, Assam, 781001, India.
Tel: 91-0361-2547-664 ***Fax:*** 91-0361-2515-588

Gwalior—Most Rev. Joseph Kaithathara; Bishop's House Diocesan Center, Jonagar, Kheriya Modi, Morar, Gwalior, M.P., 474006, India.
Tel: 0751-256-93-45 ***Fax:*** 0751-256-93-00

Gweru—Most Rev. Martin Munyanyi; Bishop's House 77 Kopje Rd., P.O. Box 622, Gweru, Zimbabwe.
Tel: 263-054-223-565 ***Fax:*** 263-054-223-381

Györ—Most Rev. Lajos Pápai; Egyházmegyei Hatóság, Káptalandomb 5/a, Gyor, H-9021, Hungary.
Tel: 36-96-550-740 ***Fax:*** 36-96-550-741
Email: ehivatal@gyor.egyhazmegye.hu

H

HÀ NÔI—Most Rev. Pierre Nguyên Van Nhon; Toà Tông Giám Muc, 40 Phô Nhà Chung, Ha Nôi, Vietnam.
Tel: 04-38-25-44-24 ***Fax:*** 04-39-28-50-73
Email: ttgmhn@gmail.com

Haarlem-Amsterdam—Most Rev. Joseph Maria Punt; Nieuwe Gracht 80, Haarlem, 2011 NJ, The Netherlands.
Tel: 31-023-511-2600 ***Fax:*** 31-023-511-2629
Email: efennis@bisdomhaarlem-amsterdam.nl

Hai Phóng—Most Rev. Joseph Vu Van Thiên; Tóa Giám Muc, 46 Hoang Van Thu, Hai Phóng, Vietnam.
Tel: 031-3745-387 ***Fax:*** 031-3745-765
Email: antninh61@yahoo.com

HAIFA - TERRA SANTA—Vacant; Roubin St. 5, P.O. Box 1442, Haifa, 31000, Israel.
Tel: 04-864-34-27 ***Fax:*** 04-864-34-27

Haimen (Haimen)—Catholic Mission Bishop's House, Haimen, Jiangsu, China.

Hajdúdorog—Most Rev. Peter Fulop Kocsis; Hajdúdorogi Püspöki Hivatal, Pf. 60, Bethlen Gábor u. 5, Nyíregyháza, H-4401, Hungary.
Tel: 36-42-415-901; 36-42-508-540 ***Fax:*** 36-42-415-911
Email: eparchia@gorogkatolikus.hu

Hakha—Most Rev. Nicholas Mang Thang; Bishop's Residence Zethit Quarter, Hakha Myo, Chin State, -Myanmar.
Tel: 070-21-186
Email: cathhakhadio@myanmar.com.mm

HALIFAX-YARMOUTH—Most Rev. Anthony Mancini; Chancery Office 1531 Grafton St., P.O. Box 1527, Halifax, NS, B3J 2X3, Canada.
Tel: 902-429-9800 ***Fax:*** 902-423-5201
Email: chancery@catholichalifax.org

Hallam—Most Rev. John Anthony Rawsthrone; Diocesan Centre St. Charles' St., Sheffield, Yorkshire, S9 3WU, England.
Tel: 44-0114-256-64-53 ***Fax:*** 44-0114-256-26-73
Email: tribunal@hallam-diocese.com

HAMBURG—Most Rev. Werner Thissen; Erzbischöfliches Generalvikariat, Danzigerstr. 52 A, Hamburg, D-20099, Germany.
Tel: 040-248-770 ***Fax:*** 040-248-77-233
Email: egv@egv-erzbistum-hh.de

Hamhung—Catholic Mission, Hamhung, Korea, North.

Hamilton—Most Rev. David Douglas Crosby, O.M.I.; Chancery Office 700 King St. W., Hamilton, ON, L8P 1C7, Canada.
Tel: 905-528-7988 ***Fax:*** 905-528-1088
Email: wdunn@hamiltondiocese.com

Hamilton (in Bermuda)—Most Rev. Robert J. Kurtz, C.R.; St. Theresa's Cathedral P.O Box HM 1191, Hamilton, HM EX, Bermuda.
Tel: 441-232-4414 ***Fax:*** 441-232-44472 Astwood Rd, Hamilton, Paget, DV 04, Bermuda.

Hamilton (in New Zealand)—Most Rev. Denis George Browne; Chanel Centre 51 Grey St., P.O. Box 4353, Hamilton East, 3247, New Zealand.
Tel: 64-07-856-6989 ***Fax:*** 64-07-856-1215

Hanchung (Hanzhong)—Catholic Mission Ming-Teh-kie, Hanzhong, Shaanxi, China.

HANGCHOW (HANGZHOU)—Catholic Mission Archbishop's House, Hangzhou, Zhejiang, China.

HANKOW (HANKOU)—Catholic Mission 16 Shangai Rd., Hankou, Hubei, China.

Hanyang (Hanyang)—Catholic Mission Bishop's House, Hanyang, Hubei, China.

HARARE—Most Rev. Robert Christopher Ndlovu; Archbishop's House 66 Fifth St., P.O. Box CY 330, Causeway, Harare, Zimbabwe.
Tel: 263-04-764-403
Email: hrearch@zol.co.zw

Harrisburg—Most Rev. Joseph P. McFadden (HBG); Chancery Office 4800 Union Deposit Rd., Harrisburg, PA, 17111-3710.
Tel: 717-657-4804 ***Fax:*** 717-657-2453
Email: general@hbgdiocese.org

HARTFORD—Most Rev. Henry Joseph Mansell; Chancery Office 134 Farmington Ave., Hartford, CT, 06105-3784.
Tel: 860-541-6491 ***Fax:*** 860-541-6293
Email: abhartford@aohct.org

HASSAKÉ-NISIBI—Most Rev. Jacques Behnan Hindo; Archevêché Syrien Catholique, B.P. 6, Hassaké, Syria.
Tel: 963-052-320-812 ***Fax:*** 963-052-316-340

Hasselt—Most Rev. Patrick Hoogmartens; Bisdom, Vrijwilligersplein 14, Hasselt, B-3500, Belgium.
Tel: 32-011-28-84-40 ***Fax:*** 32-011-28-84-78
Email: secretariaat@bisdomhasselt.be

Hazaribag—Most Rev. Charles Soreng, S.J.; Bishop's House Catholic Ashram, Hazaribag, Jharkhand, 825301, India.
Tel: 06546-222-340 ***Fax:*** 06546-226-820
Email: hzb-hcdhaz@sancharnet.in

Hearst—Most Rev. Vincent Cadieux, O.M.I.; Evêché, C.P. 1330, 76 Septième rue, Hearst, ON, P0L 1N0, Canada.
Tel: 705-362-4903 ***Fax:*** 705-362-4421
Email: eveche@ntl.sympatico.ca

Helena—Most Rev. George L. Thomas (HEL); Chancery Office 515 North Ewing St., P.O. Box 1729, Helena, MT, 59624.
Tel: 406-442-5820 ***Fax:*** 406-442-5191
Email: chancery@diocesehelena.org

Helsinki—Most Rev. Teemu Jyrki Juhani Sippo, S.C.I.; Rehbinderintie 21, FIN-00150, Helsinki, Suomi, Finland.
Tel: 358-09-6877-460 ***Fax:*** 358-09-639-820
Email: curia@catholic.fi

Hengchow (Hengyang)—Catholic Mission Pei-Men, Hengyang, Hunan, China.

HERMOSILLO—Most Rev. José Ulises Macías Salcedo; Arzobispado, Dr. Paliza 81, Hermosillo, Son., 83260, Mexico.
Tel: 52-662-213-21-38; 52-662-217-23-39 ***Fax:*** 52-662-213-13-27
Email: arzohmo2@gmail.com

Hexham and Newcastle—Most Rev. Seamus Cunningham; Bishop's House East Denton Hall, 800 West Road, Newcastle upon Tyne, NE5 2BJ, England.
Tel: 44-0191-228-0003 ***Fax:*** 44-0191-274-0432
Email: office@rcdhn.org.uk

Hildesheim—Most Rev. Norbert Trelle; Domhof 18/21, Hildesheim, 31134, Germany.
Tel: 49-05121-3070 ***Fax:*** 49-05121-307-488
Email: generalvikar@bistum-hildesheim.de

Hinche—Most Rev. Simon-Pierre Saint-Hillien; Evêché de Hinche, 6 rue des Lattes, Hinche, Haïti, West Indies.
Tel: 2453-6928 ***Fax:*** 2277-0288
Email: diocesehinche@hotmail.com

Hiroshima—Most Rev. Thomas Aquino Manyo Maeda; Bishop's House 4-42, Nobori-cho, Naka-ku, Hiroshima-shi, 730-0016, Japan.
Tel: 81-082-221-6017 ***Fax:*** 81-082-221-6019
Email: info@hiroshima.catholic.jp

Ho—Most Rev. Francis Anani Kofi Lodonu; Diocesan Secretariat P.O. Box 350, Ho, V.R., Ghana.
Tel: 091-26-548/27-643 ***Fax:*** 091-27-720
Email: akornu@yahoo.com

HOBART—Most Rev. Adrian Leo Doyle; Archbishop's Office G.P.O. Box 62, Hobart, Tas., 7001, Australia.
Tel: 61-03-6208-6222 ***Fax:*** 61-03-6208-6293
Email: vicar.general@aohtas.org.au

Hoima—Most Rev. Deogratias Muganwa Byabazaire; Bishop's House P.O. Box 34, Hoima, Uganda.
Tel: 0465-440-061 ***Fax:*** 0465-440-694
Email: hoimadiocese@yahoo.co

Holguín—Most Rev. Emilio Aranguren Echeverría; Calle Martí 136, Holguín, 80100, Cuba.
Tel: 07-024-4232-34 ***Fax:*** 07-024-4680-79
Email: obiholguin@cocc.co.cu

Homa Bay—Most Rev. Philip Anyolo; P.O. Box 326, Homa Bay, 40300, Kenya.
Tel: 059-21-408 ***Fax:*** 059-22-123
Email: catholicdioceseofhomabay@yahoo.com

HOMS EMESA—Most Rev. Théophile George Kassab; Archevêché Syrien Catholique B.P. 368, rue Hamidié, Homs, Syria.
Tel: 031-2221-575 ***Fax:*** 031-2224-350

HOMS EMESA - Greek Melkite—Vacant; Archevêché Grec-Catholique rue El-Mo'tazila, Boustan-el-Diwane, B.P 1525, Homs, Syria.
Tel: 963-031-24-82-587 ***Fax:*** 963-031-24-64-587
Email: melkite.homs@gmail.com

Hong Kong (Xianggang)—Most Rev. John Tong Hon; Catholic Diocese Centre 12 F, 16 Caine Rd., Hong Kong, China.
Tel: 28-43-46-79 ***Fax:*** 28-73-15-45
Email: bishophk@pacific.net.nk

HONIARA—Most Rev. Adrian Thomas Smith, S.M.; Holy Cross G.P.O. Box 237, Honiara, Solomon Islands.
Tel: 677-21-943 ***Fax:*** 677-26-426
Email: honiarachancery@gmail.com

Honolulu—Most Rev. Clarence Silva; Chancery Office 1184 Bishop St., Honolulu, HI, 96813.
Tel: 808-585-3345 ***Fax:*** 808-537-1869
Email: malexander@rcchawaii.org

Houma-Thibodaux—Most Rev. Sam Gallip Jacobs; 2779 Highway 311, P.O. Box 505, Schriever, LA, 70395.
Tel: 985-868-7720 ***Fax:*** 985-868-7727
Email: jbaker@htdiocese.org

Hpa-an—Most Rev. Justin Saw Min Thide; Bishop's House Thukamein Rd., Hpa-an, Keyen State, Myanmar.
Tel: 058-21-52
Email: hpandiocese@gmail.com

Hradec Králové—Most Rev. Jan Vokal; Biskupství královéhradecké, Velké nám. 35, Hradec Králové, 500 01, Czech Republic.
Tel: 49-50-63-606 ***Fax:*** 49-55-12-850
Email: konzistor@diecezehk.cz

Hsíamen (Xiamen), Amoy—Catholic Mission Kulangsu, Xiamen, Fujian, China.

Hsinchu—Most Rev. John Baptist Lee Keh-mien; 156-1 Chungcheng Rd., Hsinchu, 30051, Taiwan.
Tel: 886-035-25-41-98; 886-035-25-42-19 ***Fax:*** 886-035-26-47-86
Email: hcd@hcd.org.tw

Huacho—Most Rev. Antonio Santarsiero Rosa, O.S.I.; Obispado, Apartado 104, Plaza de Armas s/n, Huacho, Peru.
Tel: 51-034-1239-3011 ***Fax:*** 51-034-1239-5121
Email: vicariogeneralh@yahoo.com

Huajuapan de León—Most Rev. Teodoro Enrique Pino Miranda; Apartado 43, Madero 8, Huajuapan de León, Oaxaca, 69000, Mexico.
Tel: 52-953-532-0797 ***Fax:*** 52-953-532-0797
Email: sagmitra@yahoo.com.mx

HUAMBO—Most Rev. José de Queirós Alves, C.SS.R.; Arcebispado C.P. 10, Huambo, Angola.
Tel: 244-2412-20-133 ***Fax:*** 244-2412-20-853
Email: bispado.huambo@sat.signis.net

Huancavelica—Most Rev. Isidro Barrio Barrio; Av. da Andres Avelino Caceres 790, Huancavelica, Peru.
Tel: 67-45-29-01 ***Fax:*** 67-45-29-01

HUANCAYO—Most Rev. Pedro Ricardo Barreto Jimeno, S.J.; Arzobispado Jr. Puno 430, Huancayo, Peru.
Tel: 51-64-234-952/232-774 ***Fax:*** 51-64-239-189
Email: arzohyo@hotmail.com

Huánuco—Most Rev. Jaime Rodríguez Salazar, M.C.C.I.; Obispado, Jr. Dámaso Beraún 741, Huánuco, Peru.
Tel: 51-062-51-29-87 ***Fax:*** 51-062-51-19-85
Email: diocesis.hco@speedy.com.pe

Huaraz—Most Rev. José Eduardo Velásquez Tarazona; Obispado, Parque Santa Rosa de Lima 378, Huaraz, Ancash, Peru.
Tel: 51-043-422-007 ***Fax:*** 51-043-422-007
Email: obispadohzsecretaria@yahoo.es

Huari—Most Rev. Ivo Baldi Gaburri; Jr. Manuel Alvarez 680, Huari, Ancash, Peru.
Tel: 43-45-30-66 ***Fax:*** 43-45-30-66
Email: diocesishuari@davide.it

HUÊ—Most Rev. Etienne Nguyên Nhu Thê; Toà Tông Giám Muc, 6 Nguyên Truóng Tô, Tp., Huê, Vietnam.
Tel: 84-054-3824-937 ***Fax:*** 84-054-3833-656
Email: tgmhue@gmail.com

Huehuetenango—Most Rev. Rodolfo Francisco Bobadilla Mata, C.M.; Apartado 12, Huehuetenango, 13901, Guatemala.
Tel: 502-07-76-41-302 ***Fax:*** 502-07-76-41-302
Email: dihuehue@intelnett.com

Huejutla—Most Rev. Salvador Rangel Mendoza, O.F.M.; Obispado Apartado 8, Ave. Corona del Rosal s/n, Huejutla, Hgo, 43000, Mexico.
Tel: 789-89-6-0185 ***Fax:*** 789-89-6-0185
Email: diocesisdehuejutla@yahoo.com.mx

Huelva—Most Rev. José Vilaplana Blasco; Obispado, Apartado 144, Av. Manuel Siurot 31, Huelva, 21080, Spain.
Tel: 34-959-25-21-00 ***Fax:*** 34-959-54-0639
Email: cancilleria@diocesisdehuelva.es

Huesca—Most Rev. Julian Ruiz Martorell; Obispado Plaza de la Catedral 8, Huesca, 22002, Spain.
Tel: 34-974-221-027 ***Fax:*** 34-974-220-679
Email: info@diocesisdehuesca.org

Humaitá—Most Rev. Franz Josef Meinrad Merkel, C.S.Sp.; Cúria Diocesana Praça da Matriz s/n, Humaitá, AM, 69800-000, Brazil.
Tel: 55-097-3373-1356 ***Fax:*** 55-097-3373-2055
Email: diocesedehumaita@gmail.com

Hung Hoá—Most Rev. Jean Marie Vu Tat; Toà Giám Muc Hung Hoá, 5 Le Loi, Tx. Son Tây, Hung Hóa, Hà Tây, Vietnam.
Tel: 043-3832-453 ***Fax:*** 043-3834-461
Email: tgmsontay@gmail.com

Hungtung (Hongdong)—Catholic Mission Bishop's House, Hongdong, Shanxi, China.

Hvar—Most Rev. Slobodan Štambuk; Biskupski Ordinarijat, p.p. 68, Hvar, 21450, Croatia.
Tel: 385-021-741-152 ***Fax:*** 385-021-743-107
Email: biskupski.ordinarijat.hvar@st.t-com.hr

Hwalien—Most Rev. Philip Huang Chao-ming; Bishop's House 168 Chung-mei Rd., Minli Li, Hualien, 970, Taiwan.
Tel: 886-03-822-7670 ***Fax:*** 886-03-823-7920
Email: huacuria@ms6.hinet.net

Hwange—Most Rev. Joseph Albert Serrano Antón; Bishop's House 6 Old Bulawayo Rd., P.O. Box 25, Hwange, Zimbabwe.
Tel: 263-081-22325 ***Fax:*** 263-081-22260
Email: bishouse@comone.co.zw

HYDERABAD—Most Rev. Thumma Bala; Archbishop's House 9-1-17/1 Sardar Patel Road, Secunderabad, A.P., 500003, India.
Tel: 91-040-2780-5545/2780-5418 ***Fax:*** 91-040-2780-0709
Email: abphydmjoji@rediffmail.com

Hyderabad (in Pakistan)—Most Rev. Max John Rodrigues; Bishop's House G.P.O Box 60, A-37, G.O.R. Colony, Hyderabad, 71000, Pakistan.
Tel: 92-022-263-07-13 ***Fax:*** 92-022-278-37-30
Email: cdhhyd_pak@cyber.net.pk

I

Iasi—Most Rev. Petru Gherghel; Episcopia Romano-Catolica Bul. Stefan-cel-Mare 26, Iasi, RO, 700064, Romania.
Tel: 40-0232-212-003/4 ***Fax:*** 40-0232-212-006
Email: ercis@mail.dntis.ro

Iba—Most Rev. Florentino Galang Lavarias; Chancery Office, Iba, Zambales, 2201, Philippines.
Tel: 047-811-1214 ***Fax:*** 047-811-1214
Email: diofiba@hotmail.com

IBADAN—Most Rev. Felix Alaba Adeosin Job; Archbishop's House P.M.B. 5057, 8 Bale Latosa Rd., Onireke, Ibadan, Oyo State, Nigeria.
Tel: 00805-30-84-992

IBAGUÉ—Most Rev. Flavio Calle Zapata; Curia Arzobispal Calle 10 N. 2-58, Ibagué, Tolima, Colombia.
Tel: 57-82-2611-680; 57-82-2636-918 ***Fax:*** 57-82-2632-681
Email: arquibague@hotmail.com

Ibarra—Most Rev. Valter Dario Maggi; Obispado, Calle García Moreno 548, Casilla 10-01-004, Ibarra, Ecuador.
Tel: 593-06-295-5773/295-5683 ***Fax:*** 593-06-264-1897
Email: dioibarra@andinanet.net

Ibiza—Most Rev. Vicente Juan Segura; Obispado, Calle Pedro Francés 12-2a, Ibiza, Baleares, 07800, Spain.
Tel: 34-971-31-27-76 ***Fax:*** 34-971-31-27-76
Email: obibiza@obispadodeibiza.es

Ica—Most Rev. Héctor Eduardo Vera Colona; Obispado, Cajamarca 246, Apartado 95, Ica, Peru.
Tel: 51-056-23-15-11 ***Fax:*** 51-056-23-26-42
Email: obispadoica@usat.edu.pe

Ichang (Yichang)—Catholic Mission Bishop's House, Yichang, Hubei, China.

Ichow (Linyi)—Catholic Mission Bishop's House, Linyi, Shandong, China.

Idah—Most Rev. Anthony Ademu Adaji, M.S.P.; P.O. Box 55, Idah, Kogi State, Nigeria.
Tel: 0805-44-47-111

Idiofa—Most Rev. Jose Moko Ekanga, P.S.S.; Evêché, B.P. 1, Idiofa o B.P. 8251, Kinshasa 1, Democratic Republic of Congo.
Tel: 080-690-11-32

Idukki—Most Rev. Mathew Anikuzhikattil; Bishop's House Karimpan, Manippara P.O., Idukki, Kerala, 685602, India.
Tel: 04862-230-204 ***Fax:*** 04862-230-151

Iglesias—Most Rev. Giovanni Paolo Zedda; Curia Vescovile, Piazza Municipio 1, Iglesias, Cagliari, 09016, Italy.
Tel: 39-0781-22411 ***Fax:*** 39-0781-23150
Email: curia_iglesias@libero.it

Iguatu—Most Rev. Joao Jose da Costa, O.Carm.; Cúria Diocesana Rua Eduardo Lavor 475, Iguatu, CE, 63500-000, Brazil.
Tel: 55-088-3581-0731

Ihosy—Most Rev. Fulgence Razakarivony, M.S.; Eglise Catholique B.P. 36, Ihosy, 313, Madagascar.
Tel: 50-20-758-0050
Email: imprecar@moov.mg

Ijebu-Ode—Most Rev. Albert Ayinde Fasina; Bishop's House Idomila Rd., P.O. Box 32, Ijebu-Ode, Ogun State, 120001, Nigeria.
Tel: 0806-021-7112
Email: ijodecathdio@yahoo.com

Ikot Ekpene—Most Rev. Camillus Raymond Umoh; Diocesan Secretariat Cardinal Ekandem Ave., P.O. Box 870, Ikot Ekpene, Akwa Ibom State, Nigeria.
Tel: 234-080-240-86-166

Ilagan—Most Rev. Joseph A Nacua, O.F.M.Cap.; Bishop's Residence, Ilagan, Isabela, 3300, Philippines.
Tel: 078-622-2594 ***Fax:*** 078-622-2594
Email: angovsky@yahoo.com

Ilhéus—Most Rev. Mauro Montagnoli, C.S.S.; Cúria Diocesana Rua Dom Valfredo Tepe 21, Ilhéus, BA, 45650-000, Brazil.
Tel: 55-073-3231-3368 ***Fax:*** 55-073-3231-3368
Email: curiailheus@gmail.com

Iligan—Most Rev. Elenito R. Galido; Diocesan Curia Isabel Village, Pala-o, Illigan City, Lanao del Norte, 9200, Philippines.
Tel: 063-221-23-55 ***Fax:*** 063-221-6487

Ilorin—Most Rev. Ayo-Maria Atoyebi, O.P.; Bishop's House 16 Umar Audi Rd., Tanke Junction, P.O. Box 686, Ilorin, Kwara State, Nigeria.
Tel: 080-3356-0751; 080-5218-1859

Imola—Most Rev. Tommaso Ghirelli; Vescovado Piazza Duomo 1, Imola, Bologna, 40026, Italy.
Tel: 39-0542-25-000 ***Fax:*** 39-0542-34-672
Email: cancelleria@imola.chiesacattolica.it

Imperatriz—Most Rev. Gilberto Pastana de Oliveira; Avenida Dorgival Pinheiro de Sousa 396, C.P. 142, Imperatriz, MA, 65903-970, Brazil.
Tel: 55-099-3524-8665 ***Fax:*** 55-099-3525-4344
Email: dioceseimp@jupiter.com.br

Impfondo—Most Rev. Jean Charles Emile Gardin; c/o de la Maison Libermann, B.P. 1524, Brazzaville, Republic of the Congo.
B.P. 30, impfondo, Republic of the Congo.
Tel: 05-526-09-21

IMPHAL—Most Rev. Dominic Lumon; Archbishop's House P.O. Box 35, Imphal, Manipur, 795001, India.
Tel: 91-0385-242-76-36 ***Fax:*** 91-0385-242-76-36
Email: frkdjoy@yahoo.co.in

Imus—Vacant; Bishop's Residence, Imus, Cavite, 4103, Philippines.
Tel: 63-046-471-2786 ***Fax:*** 63-046-471-2786
Email: doi.chancery@gmail.com

Incheon—Most Rev. Boniface Choi Ki-san; Diocesan Office Jung-gu Dap-dong 3, Incheon, 400-090, Korea, South.
Tel: 82-032-765-6961 ***Fax:*** 82-032-765-6987
Email: samoo@caincheon.or.kr

INDIANAPOLIS—Most Rev. Daniel M. Buechlein, O.S.B., D.D. (IND); 1400 N. Meridian St., P.O. Box 1410, Indianapolis, IN, 46206.
Tel: 317-236-1405 ***Fax:*** 317-236-1406
Web: www.archindy.org
Email: chancery@archindy.org

Indore—Most Rev. Chacko Thottumarickal, S.V.D.; Bishop's House 10 Old Sehore Road, P.O. Box 168, Indore, M.P., 452001, India.
Tel: 91-0731-2492-203 ***Fax:*** 91-0731-2494-630
Email: indorediocese@gmail.com

Inhambane—Most Rev. Adriano Langa, O.F.M.; Bispado Caixa Postal 178, Rua Comandante Matos s/n, Inhambane, 20100, Mozambique.
Tel: 293-20-942 ***Fax:*** 293-20-869
Email: diocesecuriabane@yahoo.com.br

Innsbruck—Most Rev. Manfred Scheuer; Bischöfliches Ordinariat Riedgasse 9-11, Innsbruck, A-6020, Austria.
Tel: 43-0512-22-30 ***Fax:*** 43-0512-22-30-21-99
Email: generalvikariat@dibk.at

Inongo—Most Rev. Philippe Nkiere Kena, C.I.C.M.; Evêché, B.P. 12, Inongo, Democratic Republic of Congo.
Tel: 081-238-10-69
Email: eveche_inongo@yahoo.fr
B.P. 1800, Kinshasa I, Democratic Republic of Congo.

Ipameri—Most Rev. Guilherme Antônio Werlang, M.S.F.; Cúria Diocesana Av. Brabão do Rio Branco 1, Ipameri, GO, 75780-000, Brazil.
Tel: 55-064-3491-1634 ***Fax:*** 55-064-3491-1634
Email: diocesedeipameri@g8net.com.br

Ipiales—Most Rev. Arturo de Jesús Correa Toro; Carrera 7 N. 7-12, Ipiales, Nariño, Colombia.
Tel: 57-27-73-2812 ***Fax:*** 57-27-73-3562

Ipil—Most Rev. Julius Sullan Tonel; Chancery Office Villafuerte St., Zamboanga del Sur, Ipil, 7001, Philippines.
Tel: 062-333-22-66 ***Fax:*** 062-333-25-74
Email: prelatureipil@yahoo.co

Iquique—Most Rev. Marco Antonio Órdenes Fernández; Casilla 18D, Calle Bolívar 588, Iquique, Chile.
Tel: 057-418-391 ***Fax:*** 057-425-984
Email: iquique@episcopado.cl

Irapuato—Most Rev. José de Jesús Martínez Zepeda; Juárez 138-407, Irapuato, Gto., 36500, Mexico.
Tel: 462-622-35-47/22-95 ***Fax:*** 462-622-36-72
Email: diocesisdeirapuato@prodigy.net.mx

Irecê—Most Rev. Tommaso Cascianelli, C.P.; Praca Goes Calmon s/n, C.P. 14, Irecê, BA, 44900-000, Brazil.
Tel: 55-074-3641-3835 ***Fax:*** 55-074-3641-3848
Email: dioceseirece@holistica.com.br

Iringa—Most Rev. Tarcisius Ngalalekumtwa; Bishop's Residence P.O. Box 133, Iringa, Tanzania.
Tel: 255-026-2702-772; 255-026-2700-635 ***Fax:*** 255-026-2700-650
Email: dioceseofir@hotmail.com

Irinjalakuda—Most Rev. Pauly Kannookadan; Catholic Bishop's House P.O. Box 59, Irinjalakuda, Kerala, 680121, India.
Tel: 0480-2826-830; 0480-2826-820 ***Fax:*** 0480-2825-050
Email: bphijk@irinjalakudadiocese.com

Isangi—Vacant; Mission Catholique, B.P. 43, Isangi, par Kisangani, Democratic Republic of Congo.

Ischia—Most Rev. Filippo Strofaldi; Vescovado, Via Seminario 26, Ischia, Napoli, 80077, Italy.
Tel: 39-081-991-706 ***Fax:*** 39-081-991-706
Email: diocesischia@metis.it

Isernia-Venafro—Most Rev. Salvatore Visco; Vescovado, Piazza Andrea d'Isernia 2, Isernia, 86170, Italy.
Tel: 39-0865-50-849 ***Fax:*** 39-0865-41-53-37
Email: diocesiiserniavenafro@virgilio.it

Isiro-Niangara—Most Rev. Julien Andavo Mbia; Evêché, B.P. 320, Isiro, Haut-Congo, Democratic Republic of Congo.
Tel: 081-0001-662
Email: isirosecretariat@yahoo.fr

Iskanderiya, Alessandria—Most Rev. Kirkor-Okosdinos Coussa; Patriarcat Arménien Catholique 36 Rue Mohamed Sabri Abou Alam, Le Caire, 11121, Egypt.
Tel: 20-02-2393-8429 ***Fax:*** 20-02-2393-2025
Email: pacal.eg@gmail.com

Islamabad-Rawalpindi—Most Rev. Rufin Anthony; Bishop's House Tameezuddin Rd., Lalkurthi, Rawalpindi Cantt., 46000, Pakistan.
Tel: 92-051-558-16-16 ***Fax:*** 92-051-556-40-82

Islas Canarias—Most Rev. Francisco Cases Andreu; Obispado, Plaza de Santa Ana 12, Las Palmas de Gran Canaria, 35001, Spain.
Tel: 34-928-31-36-00 ***Fax:*** 34-928-33-22-14
Email: info@diocesisdecanarias.org

Ismayliah—Most Rev. Makarios Tewfik; Evéché Copte Catholique, B.P. 127, 15 rue Orabi, Ismayliah, Egypt.
Tel: 20-064-391-91-91 ***Fax:*** 20-064-392-33-00

ISPAHAN—Most Rev. Ignazio Bedini, S.D.B.; Consolata Church 70 Neauphle le Chateau Ave., P.O. Box 11155-445, Teheran, Iran.
Tel: 98-021-6670-3210 ***Fax:*** 98-021-6672-4749
Email: latin.diocese@gmail.com

Ispahan, Esfáan—Vacant; Armenian Catholic Bishopric Ave. Hafez Ghazali 29, Teheran, Iran.
Tel: 98-021-667-07-204 ***Fax:*** 98-021-667-27-533

Issele-Uku—Most Rev. Michael Odogwu Elue; Bishop's House P.O. Box 63, Issele-Uku, Delta State, Nigeria.
Tel: 234-080-3714-23-69
Email: bpmyke@yahoo.com

ISTANBUL, COSTANTINOPOLI—Most Rev. Hovhannes Tcholakian; Sakizagaci Caddesi 31, P.K. 183, Beyoglu, Istanbul, 34435, Turkey.
Tel: 90-212-244-12-58 ***Fax:*** 90-212-243-23-64

Istmina - Tadó—Most Rev. Julio Hernando Garcia Pelaez; Despacho Episcopal Calle 8a N. 20A-01, Istmina, Chocó, Colombia.
Tel: 4-670-30-95 ***Fax:*** 4-670-01-12; 4-670-30-95
Email: diteduca@telecom.com.co

Itabira-Fabriciano—Most Rev. Odilon Guimarães Moreira; Cúria Diocesana Rua Coronel Linhares Guerra 100, Itabira, MG, 35900-020, Brazil.
Tel: 55-031-3831-3614 ***Fax:*** 55-031-3831-3675
Email: dioceseitabira@veloxmail.com.br

Itabuna—Most Rev. Czeslaw Stanula, C.Ss.R.; Rua das Naçoes Unidas 400, C.P. 71, 45600-606, Itabuna, BA, 45600-605, Brazil.
Tel: 55-073-3211-3520 ***Fax:*** 55-073-3211-3520

Itaguaí—Most Rev. José Ubiratan Lopes, O.F.M.Cap.; Rua Coronel Freitas 45, Itaguaí, RJ, 23815-260, Brazil.
Tel: 55-021-2688-3292 ***Fax:*** 55-021-2688-1315
Email: diocese@dioceseitaguai.org.br

Itanagar—Most Rev. John Thomas Kattrukudiyil; Bishop's House Mowb-II, P.O. Box 141, Itanagar, Papumpare Dt., Arunachal Pradesh, 79111, India.
Tel: 0360-2292-074 ***Fax:*** 0360-2290-605
Email: itanagardiocese@yahoo.co.in

Itapetininga—Most Rev. Gorgônio Alves da Encarnaçao Neto, C.R.; Curia Diocesana Rua General Carniero 409, Itapetininga, SP, 18200-800, Brazil.
Tel: 015-3272-8557; 015-3271-2350 ***Fax:*** 015-3271-2350
Email: curiadiocesanaitape@terra.com.br

Itapeva—Most Rev. José Moreira de Melo; Rua Coronel Crescêncio 311, Itapeva, SP, 18400-140, Brazil.
Tel: 015-3522-0015 ***Fax:*** 015-3522-2710
Email: mitra.itapeva@terra.com.br

Itapipoca—Most Rev. Antônio Roberto Cavuto, O.F.M.Cap.; Cúria Diocesana Av. Duque de Caxias 1125, Itapipoca, CE, 62500-000, Brazil.
Tel: 55-088-3631-2022 ***Fax:*** 55-088-3631-2022
Email: diocitapipoca@hotmail.com

Ituiutaba—Most Rev. Francisco Carlos da Silva; Rua 20 N. 541, Ituiutaba, MG, 38300-074, Brazil.
Tel: 55-034-3262-0610 ***Fax:*** 55-034-3262-0610
Email: curiaituiutaba@terra.com.br
C.P. 195, Ituiutaba, MG, 38300-970, Brazil.

Itumbiara—Most Rev. Antônio Lino da Silva Dinis; Cúria Diocesana Rua Paranaíba 160, C.P. 93,75503-970, Itumbiara, GO, 75503-040, Brazil.
Tel: 55-064-3431-7867 ***Fax:*** 55-064-3431-2754
Email: diocese.iub@netsite.com.br

Ivano-Frankivsk, Stanislaviv—Most Rev. Volodymyr Viytyshyn; vul. Knjahynyn 15, Ivano-Frankivsk, 76005, Ukraine.
Tel: 0342-78-5376 ***Fax:*** 0342-40-084

Ivrea—Most Rev. Arrigo Miglio; Vescovado, Piazza Castello 3, Ivrea, Torino, 10015, Italy.
Tel: 39-0125-64-11-38 ***Fax:*** 39-0125-43-682
Email: curiauffici@diocesivrea.it

IZMIR—Most Rev. Ruggero Franceschini, O.F.M.Cap.; Necati Bey Bulvari 2, P.K. 267, Izmir, 35210, Turkey.
Tel: 90-0232-484-0531 ***Fax:*** 90-0232-484-5358
Email: curiaves@gmail.com

J

Jabalpur—Most Rev. Gerald Almeida; Bishop's House 599 South Civil Lines, Jabalpur, M.P., 482001, India.
Tel: 91-0761-401-8322; 91-0761-262-24-13 ***Fax:*** 91-0761-262-43-60
Email: snehsadan@rediffmail.com

Jaboticabal—Most Rev. Antônio Fernando Brochini, C.S.S.; Cúria Diocesana C.P. 48, Jaboticabal, SP, 14870-970, Brazil.
Tel: 55-016-3202-0390 ***Fax:*** 55-016-3202-0390
Email: curia@diocesejaboticabal.org.br
Rua Rui Barbosa 546, Jaboticabal, 14870-300, Brazil.

Jaca—Most Rev. Julian Ruiz Martorell; Obispado Calle del Obispo 5, Jaca, Huesca, 22700, Spain.
Tel: 34-974-36-10-17 ***Fax:*** 34-974-35-52-80
Email: objaca@planalfa.es

Jacarezinho—Most Rev. Antonio Braz Benevente; Cúria Diocesana Av. Getúlio Vargas 262, Jacarezinho, PR, 86400-000, Brazil.
Tel: 043-3525-0707 ***Fax:*** 043-3525-0707
Email: curia@diocesedejacarezinho.com.br

Jackson—Most Rev. Joseph Latino; Chancery Office 237 E. Amite St., P.O. Box 2248, Jackson, MS, 39225-2248.
Tel: 601-969-1880 ***Fax:*** 601-960-8455
Web: www.jacksondiocese.org
Email: chancery@jacksondiocese.org

Jacmel—Most Rev. Launay Saturne; B.P. 74, Route de Lamandou, Jacmel, 9110, Haiti.
Tel: 509-2288-2162/3 ***Fax:*** 509-2288-2163

Jaén—Most Rev. Ramón del Hoyo López; Obispado Plaza de Santa María 2, Jaén, 23002, Spain.
Tel: 34-953-230-036 ***Fax:*** 34-953-230-039
Email: obispado@diocesisdejaen.es

Jaffna—Most Rev. Thomas Savundaranayagam; Bishop's House P.O. Box 2, Jaffna, Sri Lanka.
Tel: 94-021-222-85-18 ***Fax:*** 94-021-222-99-53
Email: frjustin@e-mnet.com

Jagdalpur—Most Rev. Simon Stock Palathara, C.M.I.; Bishop's House P.O., Lal-Bagh, Jagdalpur, Bastar Dt., Chhattisgarh, 494001, India.
Tel: 91-07782-228-283 ***Fax:*** 91-07782-228-307
Email: jagdalpurbishop@gmail.com

Jaipur—Most Rev. Oswald Lewis; Bishop's House Ghat-Gate, Jaipur, Rajasthan, 302003, India.
Tel: 0141-260-0743 ***Fax:*** 0141-260-0743
Email: cathbishjaipur@hotmail.com

JAKARTA—Most Rev. Ignatius Suharyo Hardjoatmodjo; Keuskupan Agung Jl. Katedral 7, Jakarta, 10710, Indonesia.
Tel: 62-021-381-33-45; 62-021-381-43-22 ***Fax:*** 62-021-385-56-81
Email: kaj_sekretariat@yahoo.co.id

JALAPA—Most Rev. Hipólito Reyes Larios; Arzobispado Av. Manuel Avila Camacho 73, Apartado 359, Xalapa, Veracruz, 91000, Mexico.
Tel: 52-228-812-05-79; 52-228-817-29-35 ***Fax:*** 52-228-817-55-78
Email: arzobispadoxal@prodigy.net.mx

Jalapa (in Guatemala)—Most Rev. Julio Edgar Cabrera Ovalle; Obispado 7a Avenida 0-42, Jalapa, Zone 1, 21001, Guatemala.
Tel: 7922-3742 ***Fax:*** 7922-4254
Email: diocesisjalapa@hotmail.com

Jales—Most Rev. Luiz Demétrio Valentini; Cúria Diocesana C.P. 109, Rua Vinte 3016, Jales, SP, 15700-000, Brazil.
Tel: 55-01736-32-1370 ***Fax:*** 55-01736-32-1370
Email: curia@melfinet.com.br

Jalingo—Most Rev. Charles Hammawa; Bishop's House P.O. Box 110, Jalingo, Taraba State, Nigeria.
Tel: 079-223-574 ***Fax:*** 079-223-600
Email: catsecdiojalingo@yahoo.co.uk

Jalpaiguri—Most Rev. Clement Tirkey; Bishop's House P.O. Mohitnagar, Jalpaiguri, Jalpaiguri Dt., West Bengal, 735101, India.
Tel: 91-03561-255-371 ***Fax:*** 91-03561-255-370
Email: bishjal@yahoo.co.uk

Jammu-Srinagar—Most Rev. Peter Celestine Elampassery, O.F.M.Cap.; Bishop's House Jammu Cantt., Jammu and Kashmir, 180003, India.
Tel: 0191-2430-083 ***Fax:*** 0191-2454-325
Email: bishopjammu@gmail.com

Jamshedpur—Most Rev. Felix Toppo, S.J.; Bishop's House Golmuri P.O., Jamshedpur, Jharkhand, 831003, India.
Tel: 0657-2340-299 ***Fax:*** 0657-2341-279
Email: crprabhu1939@hotmail.com

Janaúba—Most Rev. José Ronaldo Ribeiro; Curia Diocesana Praca Dr. Mauricio Azevedo 66, Janauba, MG, 39440-000, Brazil.
Tel: 038-3821-6851 ***Fax:*** 038-3821-6851
Email: catedral@nortecnet.com.br

Januária—Most Rev. José Moreira da Silva; C.P. 96, Rua Gualberto de Almeida 116, Januária, MG, 39480-000, Brazil.
Tel: 55-038-3621-1342 ***Fax:*** 55-038-3621-5182
Email: mitrajanuaria@comnt.hotmail.com

Jardim—Most Rev. Jorge Alves Bezerra, S.S.S.; C.P. 104, Rua Campo Grande 869, Jardim, MS, 79240-000, Brazil.
Tel: 55-067-3251-1101 ***Fax:*** 55-067-3251-1002
Email: diocesedejardim@yahoo.com.br

JARO—Most Rev. Angel N. Lagdameo; Archbishop's House, Jaro, Iloilo City, 5000, Philippines.
Tel: 63-033-329-4442 ***Fax:*** 63-033-329-3197
Email: abpjaro@yahoo.com

Jashpur—Most Rev. Emmanuel Kerketta; Bishop's House P.O. Kunkuri, Jashpur Dt., Chhattisgarh, 496225, India.
Tel: 07764-250-224; 07764-250-704
Email: secjashpur@yahoo.in

Jasikan—Most Rev. Gabriel Akwasi Ababio Mante; Bishop's House P.O. Box JA 64, Jasikan, Ghana.
Tel: 028.91-01-550

Jataí—Most Rev. Jose Luiz Majella Delgado, C.SS.R.; Cúria Diocesana C.P. 02, Av. Joaquim Cândido de Carvalho 56, Jataí, GO, 75800-035, Brazil.
Tel: 55-064-3631-1820 ***Fax:*** 55-064-3631-2423
Email: diocese@jatainet.com.br

Jayapura—Most Rev. Leo Laba Ladjar, O.F.M.; Keuskupan Kotak Pos 1379, Jl. Kesehatan 4, Dok II, Jayapura, Irian Jaya, 99112, Indonesia.
Tel: 62-0967-536411; 62-0967-533092 ***Fax:*** 62-0967-536427
Email: bas-dar@yahoo.co.id

Jbeil, Byblos—Most Rev. Béchara Raï, O.M.M.; Evêché Maronite Rue Dr. Chahid El-Khoury, Amchit, Jbeil, Lebanon.
Tel: 09-621-056 ***Fax:*** 09-621-449

Jefferson City—Most Rev. John Raymong Gaydos; Chancery 2207 W. Main St., P.O. Box 104900, Jefferson City, MO, 65110-4900.
Tel: 573-635-9127 ***Fax:*** 573-635-0386
Web: www.diojeffcity.org
Email: vicargeneral@diojeffcity.org

Jehol (Jinzhou)—Catholic Mission Bishop's House, Jinzhou, Chaoyang, Liaoning, China.

Jelgava—Most Rev. Eduards Pavlovskis; Katolu iela 11, Jelgava, LV-3001, Latvia.
Tel: 630-21-550 ***Fax:*** 630-21-550

Jeonju—Most Rev. Vincent Ri Pyung-ho; Diocesan Office Wansan-gu Namnosong-dong 18-3, Jeonju-si, Jeonbuk, 560-110, Korea, South.
Tel: 063-230-1004 ***Fax:*** 063-285-0119
Email: 19691215@hanmail.net

Jequié—Most Rev. Cristiano Jakob Krapf; Cúria Diocesana Rua 10 de Julho 31, Jequié, BA, 45202-350, Brazil.
Tel: 55-073-3525-6770 ***Fax:*** 55-073-3525-6770
Email: diocesejequie@ig.com.br

Jérémie—Most Rev. Joseph Gontrand Decoste, S.J.; Evêché 38 rue Brouette, Jérémie, 7110, Haiti.
Tel: 509-2284-5167 ***Fax:*** 509-2284-6096

Jerez de la Frontera—Most Rev. Jose Mazuelos Perez; Plaza del Arroyo 50, Jerez de la Frontera, Cádiz, 11403, Spain.
Tel: 34-956-33-88-00 ***Fax:*** 34-956-33-85-61
Email: obispado@diocesisdejerez.org

Jericó—Most Rev. José Roberto López Londoño; Obispado Calle 6 N. 2-43, Jericó, Antioquia, Colombia.
Tel: 4-8523-555 ***Fax:*** 4-8524-046
Email: comunicaciones@jerico.diocesis.ws

Jesi—Most Rev. Gerardo Rocconi; Vescovado Piazza Federico II 6, Jesi, Ancona, 60035, Italy.
Tel: 39-0731-22-67-42 ***Fax:*** 39-0731-22-67-43
Email: cancelleria@jesi.chiesacattolica.it

Jhabua—Most Rev. Devprasad John Ganawa, S.V.D.; Bishop's House Meghnagar P.O., Dt., Jhabua, M.P., 457779, India.
Tel: 07390-284-829; 07390-284-830 ***Fax:*** 07390-284-831
Email: catholicdio@bsnl.in

Jhansi—Most Rev. Frederick D'Souza; Bishop's House 64 Cantt., Jhansi, U.P., 284001, India.
Tel: 0510-2471-391; 0510-2471-594 ***Fax:*** 0510-2471-594
Email: cdoj2009@yahoo.com

Ji-Paraná—Most Rev. Bruno Pedron, S.D.B.; Rua Marechal Rondon 400, Ji-Paraná, RO, 76900-027, Brazil.
Tel: 55-069-3416-4203/4 ***Fax:*** 55-069-3416-4223

Jinja—Most Rev. Charles Martin Wamika; Bishop's House P.O. Box 673, Jinja, Uganda.
Tel: 256-043-4122-347 ***Fax:*** 256-043-4123-143

Jinotega—Most Rev. Carlos Enrique Herrera Gutiérrez, O.F.M.; Obispado Farmacia San Juan 1/2 C. al este, Jinotega, Nicaragua.
Tel: 2782-2753 ***Fax:*** 2782-4237

Joaçaba—Most Rev. Mario Marquez, O.F.M.Cap.; Cúria Diocesana C.P. 101, Av. Santa Teresinha, s/n, Joaçaba, SC, 89600-000, Brazil.
Tel: 55-049-3522-0848 ***Fax:*** 55-049-3522-0848
Email: dijoacaba@softline.com.br

JOHANNESBURG—Most Rev. Buti Joseph Tlhagale, O.M.I.; Archbishop's House P.M.B. X10, Doornfontein, 2028, South Africa.
Tel: 27-011-402-6400 ***Fax:*** 27-011-402-6406
Email: catholic@icon.co.za

Joinville—Most Rev. Irineu Roque Scherer; Cúria Diocesana Rua Jagnaruna 147, 89201-450, Joinville, Brazil.
Tel: 55-047-3451-3707/8 ***Fax:*** 55-047-3451-3724
Email: scuria@diocesejlle.com.br
C.P. 284, 89201-974, Joinville, SC, -Brazil.

Joliet (in Illinois)—Most Rev. R. Daniel Conlon; Chancery Office 425 Summit St., Joliet, IL, 60435.
Tel: 815-722-6606 ***Fax:*** 815-722-6602
Web: www.dioceseofjoliet.org
Email: jdavies@dioceseofjoliet.org

Joliette—Most Rev. Gilles Lussier; Evêché 2 rue Saint-Charles-Borromée Nord, C.P. 470, Joliette, QC, J6E 6H6, Canada.
Tel: 450-753-7596 ***Fax:*** 450-759-0929
Email: chancel@diocesedejoliette.org

JOS—Most Rev. Ignatius Ayau Kaigama; Archbishop's House 20 Joseph D. Gomwalk Rd., Riyom Dr., P.O. Box 494, Jos, Plateau State, -930001, Nigeria.
Tel: 234-073-45-28-78 ***Fax:*** 234-073-45-15-47
Email: josarch@hisen.org

Joubbé, Sarba and Jounieh—His Eminence Cardinal Nasrallah Pierre Sfeir; Patriarcat Maronite, Bkerké, Lebanon.
Tel: 09-915-441 ***Fax:*** 09-938-844
Email: jtawk@bkerke.org.lb

Jowai—Vacant; Bishop's House Jowai, Jaintia Hills, Meghalaya, -793150, India.
Tel: 03652-221-585

Juazeiro—Most Rev. José Geraldo da Cruz, A.A.; Cúria Diocesana C.P. 192, Av. Dr. Adolfo Viana 08, Juazeiro, BA, 48903-970, Brazil.
Tel: 55-074-3611-7378 ***Fax:*** 55-074-3611-7825

JUBA—Most Rev. Paulino Lukudu Loro, M.C.C.I.; Catholic Church P.O. Box 32, Juba, Equatoria Province, Sudan.
Tel: 811-820-303 ***Fax:*** 811-820-755
Email: archbishopofjuba@hotmail.com

Juigalpa—Most Rev. René Sócrates Sándigo Jirón; Residencia Episcopal, Juigalpa, Nicaragua.
Tel: 505-2512-0343 ***Fax:*** 505-2512-2442
Email: jobemo11@yahoo.es

Juína—Most Rev. Neri José Tondello; Cúria Diocesana Rua Bispo Dom Franco Dalla Valle 187, C.P. 201, Juina, MT, 78320-000, Brazil.
Tel: 066-3566-2928 ***Fax:*** 066-3566-2379
Email: diocese@juina-fox.com.br

JUIZ DE FORA—Most Rev. Gil Antônio Moreira; Arcebispado Rua Henrique Surerus 30, Juiz de Fora, MG, 36010-030, Brazil.
Tel: 55-032-3229-5450
Email: contato@arquidiocesejuizdefora.org.br

Jujuy—Vacant; Sarmiento 246, Casilla 6, San Salvador de Jujuy, Y4600DYF, Argentina.
Tel: 54-0388-4226-569; 0388-4234-777 ***Fax:*** 54-0388-4234-196
Email: sec-obispadojujuy@arnet.com.ar

Jullundur—Most Rev. Anil Joseph Thomas Couto; Bishop's House Civil Lines, Jalandhar City, Punjab, 144001, India.
Tel: 91-0181-2223-987
Email: diojal5ab@gmail.com

Jundiaí—Most Rev. Vicente Costa; Cúria Diocesana Rua Eng. Roberto Mange 400, Jundiaí, S.P., -13200-240, Brazil.
Tel: 011-4583-7474 ***Fax:*** 011-4583-7475
Email: secretariacuria@diocesedejundiai.org.br
C.P. 21, Jundiai, S.P., -13200-970, Brazil.

Juneau—Most Rev. Edward J. Burns; Chancery 415 Sixth St., Ste. 300, Juneau, AK, 99801.
Tel: 907-586-2227 ***Fax:*** 907-463-3237
Web: www.dioceseofjuneau.org
Email: junodio@gci.net

Juticalpa—Most Rev. Tomás Andrés Mauro Muldoon, O.F.M.; Apartado 2, Juticalpa, Olancho, 16101, Honduras.
Tel: 504-2785-2011 ***Fax:*** 504-2785-2787

K

Kabale—Most Rev. Callistus Rubaramira; Bishop's House P.O. Box 56, Kabale, Uganda.
Email: kabaletrustees@utlonline.co.ug

Kabankalan—Most Rev. Patricio A. Buzon, S.D.B.; Diocesan Curia Office 611 Negros Occidental, Kabankalan City, 6111, Philippines.
Tel: 63-034-4712-163 ***Fax:*** 63-034-4712-163
Email: dio_kab@hotmail.com

Kabgayi—Most Rev. Smaragde Mbonyintege; Evêché B.P. 66, Gitarama, Rwanda.
Tel: 252-562-865 ***Fax:*** 252-562-101
Email: dkabgayi@rwanda1.com

Kabinda—Most Rev. Valentin Masengo Nkinda; Evêché B.P. 1000, Mbuji-Mayi, Kasayi Oriental, Democratic Republic of Congo.
c/o Cooperation Technique Miba, B.P. 1000, Brussels, Belgium.

KADUNA—Most Rev. Matthew Man-Oso Ndagoso; Archbishop's House P.O. Box 248, 71 Tafawa Balewa Way, Kaduna, Nigeria.
Tel: 080-734-82-374 ***Fax:*** 062-240-026
Email: catholickaduna@yahoo.com

Kafanchan—Most Rev. Joseph Danlami Bagobiri; Bishop's House P.O. Box 85, Kafanchan, Kaduna State, 801101, Nigeria.
Tel: 080-556-27-619; 081-266-55-330
Email: cathdiokaf@yahoo.co.uk

Kaga-Bandoro—Most Rev. Albert Vanbuel, S.D.B.; Evêché B.P. 07, Bangui, Central African Republic.

Kagoshima—Most Rev. Paul Kenjiro Koriyama; 13-42 Terukuni-cho, Kagoshima-shi 892-0841, Japan.
Tel: 81-099-226-5100 ***Fax:*** 81-099-225-0440
Email: kagoxavi@po5.synapse.ne.jp

Kahama—Most Rev. Ludovic Minde, O.S.S.; Bishop's House P.O. Box 400, Kahama, Tanzania.
Tel: 028-27-10-177

KAIFENG (KAIFENG)—Catholic Mission Archbishop's House, Kaifeng, Henan, China.

Kaišiadorys—Most Rev. Juozas Matulaitis; Vyskupijos Kurija Kestucio 44, Kaisiadorys, 56124, Lithuania.
Tel: 346-53-950 ***Fax:*** 346-60-036
Email: kurija@ks.lcn.lt

Kakamega—Most Rev. Philip Sulumeti; Bishop's House P.O. Box 150, Kakamega, 50100, Kenya.
Tel: 056-41-190 ***Fax:*** 056-41-346
Email: dioceseofkakamega@africaonline.co.ke

Kalamazoo—Most Rev. Paul J. Bradley; Chancery 215 N. Westnedge Ave., Kalamazoo, MI, 49007-3760.
Tel: 269-349-8714 ***Fax:*** 269-349-6440

Kalay—Most Rev. Felix Lian Khen Thang; Bishop's Residence Thazin St. 4/5, Thuriya Rd., Kalaymyo, Sagaing Division, -Myanmar.
Tel: 073-21-880 ***Fax:*** 073-21-534

Kalemie-Kirungu—Vacant; Evêché B.P. 475, Kalemie, Shaba, Democratic Republic of Congo.

Kalibo—Most Rev. Jose Corazon T. Tala-oc; Bishop's House, Kalibo, Aklan, 5600, Philippines.
Tel: 06-036-26-85-145 ***Fax:*** 06-036-26-85-145
Email: dioceseofkalibo@yahoo.com

Kalisz—Most Rev. Stanislaw Napierala; Kuria Diecezjalna ul. Widok 80/82, Kalisz, 62-800, Poland.
Tel: 48-062-766-7855 ***Fax:*** 48-062-766-7860
Email: kuria@kalisz.opoka.org.pl

KALOCSA-KECSKEMÉT—Most Rev. Balázs Bábel; Érseki Hatóság Szentháromság tér 1, Pf. 29, Kalocsa, H-6301, Hungary.
Tel: 011-36-78-462-166 ***Fax:*** 011-36-78-462-130
Email: hivatal@asztrik.hu

Kalookan—Most Rev. Deogracias S. Iñiguez; San Roque Cathedral Compound 10th Ave. cor. A. Mabini St., Kalookan City, Philippines.
Tel: 02-287-0380/288-9116 ***Fax:*** 02-287-9035
Email: rcbk822@yahoo.com

Kalyan—Most Rev. Thomas Elavanal, M.C.B.S.; Bishop's House Plot B/38, I.I.T., Market Gate, Post Bag 8434, P.O. Powai, Mumbai, 400076, India.
Tel: 022-2578-2385/5515 ***Fax:*** 022-2577-6100
Email: kalyanbp@mtnl.net.in

Kamichlié—Vacant; Evêché Arménien Catholique B.P. 17, Kamichlié, Syria.
Email: armen.cath@mail.sy

Kamina—Most Rev. Jean-Anatole Kalala Kaseba; Evêché B.P. 309, Kamina-Ville, Democratic Republic of Congo.

Kamloops—Most Rev. David John James Monroe; Bishop's House 635 A Tranquille Road, Kamloops, BC, V2B 3H5, Canada.
Tel: 250-376-3351 ***Fax:*** 250-376-3363
Email: rcbk@telus.net

KAMPALA—Most Rev. Cyprian Kizito Lwanga; Archbishop's House P.O. Box 14125, Mengo-Kampala, Uganda.
Tel: 0414-27-01-83/4 ***Fax:*** 041-4345-441
Email: klarchdioc@infocom.co.ug

Kamyanets-Podilskyi—Most Rev. Leonid Maksymilian Dubrawski, O.F.M.; vul. Frantyskanska 2, Kamyanets-Podilskyi, 32301, Ukraine.
Tel: 7-03849-9-11-57 ***Fax:*** 7-03849-9-11-57
Email: curiapodole@gmail.com

KANANGA—Most Rev. Marcel Madila Basanguka; Archevêché B.P. 70, Kananga, Democratic Republic of Congo.
Email: archidiocesekananga@yahoo.fr

Kanchow (Ganzhou)—Catholic Mission Bishop's House, Ganzhou, Jiangxi, China.

Kandi—Most Rev. Clet Feliho; Evêché B.P. 65, Kandi, Benin.
Tel: 23-63-53-10; 95-35-72-11
Email: evechekandi@yahoo.fr

Kandy—Most Rev. Joseph Vianney Fernando; Bishop's House 873 Peradeniya Rd., Kandy, 20000, Sri Lanka.
Tel: 94-081-447-16-01/2 ***Fax:*** 94-081-223-27-92

Kangtíng (Kangding)—Catholic Mission Bishop's House, Kangding, Sichuan, China.

Kanjirapally—Most Rev. Mathew Arackal; Pastoral Centre P.O. Box 22, Kanjirapally, Kottayam Dt., Kerala, -686507, India.
Tel: 91-04828-20-26-65; 91-04828-20-20-95 ***Fax:*** 91-04828-20-52-00
Email: mpaikatt@gmail.com

Kankan—Most Rev. Emmanuel Félémou; Evêché B.P. 208, Kankan, Guinea.
Tel: 62-97-81-23

Kannur—Most Rev. Varghese Chakkalakal; Bishop's House Chovva P.O., Kannur, Kerala, 670006, India.
Tel: 91-0497-272-9977/9988 ***Fax:*** 91-0497-272-9955
Email: cnn_diocese@sancharnet.in

Kano—Most Rev. John Namaza Niyiring, O.S.A.; Bishop's House 19 Race Course Road, P.O. Box 11115, Kano, 700001, Nigeria.
Tel: 234-064-648-152; 803-743-3244
Email: bishop@kanocathdiocese.org

KANSAS CITY (IN KANSAS)—Most Rev. Joseph F. Naumann; Catholic Chancery Office 12615 Parallel Parkway, Kansas City, KS, 66109.
Tel: 913-721-1570 ***Fax:*** 913-721-1577
Web: www.archkck.org
Email: archkck@archkck.org

Kansas City-St. Joseph—Most Rev. Robert W. Finn (KC); PO Box 419037, Kansas City, MO, 64141-6037.
Tel: 816-756-1850 ***Fax:*** 816-756-0878
Web: www.diocese-kcsj.org
Email: bishopsoffice@diocesekcsj.org
Chancery 20 W. 9th St., Kansas City, MO, 64105.

Kaohsiung—Most Rev. Peter Liu Cheng-chung; Bishop's House 125 Sze-wei 3rd Road, Lingya District, Kaohsiung, 80250, Taiwan.
Tel: 886-07-331-0169 ***Fax:*** 886-07-333-4583
Email: khs.dioc@msa.hinet.net

Kaolack—Most Rev. Benjamin Ndiaye; Evêché B.P. 58, route de Fatick, Kaolack, Senegal.
Tel: 221-33-941-1374 ***Fax:*** 221-33-941-5294
Email: evekao@orange.sn

Kaposvár—Most Rev. Béla Balás; Egyhazmegyei Hatosag Zárda u. 4, Kaposvár, H-7400, Hungary.
Tel: 36-82-511-718 ***Fax:*** 36-82-511-718

Kara—Most Rev. Jacques Danka Longa; Evêché B.P. 45, Kara, Togo.
Tel: 228-660-02-18 ***Fax:*** 228-660-15-50
Email: evechekara@yahoo.fr

KARACHI—Most Rev. Evarist Pinto; St. Patrick's Cathedral Saddar, Karachi, 74400, Pakistan.
Tel: 92-021-278-15-33 ***Fax:*** 92-021-278-15-32
Email: cck@cyber.net.pk

Karaganda—Most Rev. Janusz Kaleta; Oktyabrskaya 25, Karaganda, 100029, Kazakhstan.
Tel: 7-7212-22-1472 ***Fax:*** 7-7212-22-1472
Email: diocesekaraganda@gmail.com

Karonga—Most Rev. Martin Anwel Mtumbuka; Bishop's House P.O. Box 140, Karonga, Malawi.
Tel: 088-885-43-05; 099-589-25-82

Karwar—Most Rev. Derek Fernandes; Bishop's Office Puneeth Sadan, Shirwad, Karwar, Uttara Kannada, Karnataka, 581306, India.
Tel: 91-08382-282-364 ***Fax:*** 91-08382-282-452
Email: diocese_kwr@vbsnl.in

KASAMA—Vacant; Archbishop's House P.O. Box 410143, Kasama, Zambia.
Tel: 260-214-22-12-48 ***Fax:*** 260-214-22-22-02
Email: archkasama@hotmail.com

Kasana-Luweero—Most Rev. Paul Ssemogerere; P.O. Box 303, Luweero, Uganda.
Tel: 256-392-700-762
Email: kdl@africaonline.co.ug

Kasese—Most Rev. Egidio Nkaijanabwo; Bishop's House P.O. Box 75, Kasese, Uganda.
Tel: 256-0483-444-881 ***Fax:*** 256-0483-444-877
Email: kasedio@utlonline.co.ug

Kasongo—Vacant; Evêché B.P. 39 Kasongo, par Kindu, Manyema, Democratic Republic of Congo.
Tel: 081-1709-385Evêché de Kasongo c/o Missionnaires d'Afrique, B.P. 333, Cyangugu, Rwanda.

Katiola—Most Rev. Ignace Bessi Dogbo; B.P. 596, Yamoussoukro, Ivory Coast. Evêché B.P. 110, Katiola, Ivory Coast.
Tel: 225-3166-0435 ***Fax:*** 225-3166-0435
Email: evechekatiola@yahoo.fr

KATOWICE—Most Rev. Damian Zimon; Kuria Metropolitalna ul. Jordana 39, Katowice, 40-056, Poland.
Tel: 48-032-2512-160 ***Fax:*** 48-032-2514-830
Email: kancelaria@kuria.katowice.pl

KAUNAS—Most Rev. Sigitas Tamkevicius, S.J.; Rotuses 14/a, Kaunas, 44279, Lithuania.
Tel: 07-37-409-026 ***Fax:*** 07-37-320-090
Email: kurija@kn.lcn.lt

Kavieng—Most Rev. Ambrose Kiapseni, M.S.C.; Bishop's House P.O. Box 49, Kavieng, New Ireland Province, 631, Papua New Guinea.
Tel: 675-98-42-055 ***Fax:*** 675-98-41-279
Email: diokvg@global.net.pg

Kaya—Most Rev. Thomas Kaboré; Evêché B.P. 169, Kaya, Burkina Faso.
Tel: 226-40-45-32-79 ***Fax:*** 226-40-45-32-46

Kayanga—Most Rev. Almachius Vincent Rweyongeza; Catholic Diocese P.O. Box 500, Kayanga, Tanzania.
Tel: 028-222-71-13; 7681-65-804 ***Fax:*** 028-222-71-13

Kayes—Vacant; Evêché B.P. 91, Kayes, Mali.
Tel: 223-21-52-1899 ***Fax:*** 223-21-52-1999

Kayíng (Meixian), Kíayíng—Catholic Mission via Shantou, Meixian, Guangdong, China.

Keetmanshoop—Most Rev. Phillip Pöllitzer, O.M.I.; 88 Cathedral St., P.O. Box 88, Keetmanshoop, 9000, Namibia.
Tel: 063-222-007 ***Fax:*** 063-222-692
Email: khpdioc@iway.na

KEEWATIN-LE PAS—Most Rev. Sylvain Lavoie, O.M.I.; Chancery Office 76 First Street West, P.O. Box 270, The Pas, MB, R9A 1K4, Canada.
Tel: 204-623-6152 ***Fax:*** 204-623-6121

Keimoes-Upington—Most Rev. Edward Gabriel Risi, O.M.I.; P.O. Box 323, 4 Main St., Keimoes, 8860, South Africa.
Tel: 27-054-461-1846 ***Fax:*** 27-054-461-1846
Email: omikeimoes@telkomsa.net

Kenema—Most Rev. Patrick Daniel Koroma; Bishop's House Dama Road, P.O. Box 200, Kenema, Sierra Leone.
Tel: 232-033-867-051; 232-076-639-352/652-206
Email: dio71ken@sierratel.sl

Kenge—Most Rev. Jean Gaspard Mudiso Mund'la, S.V.D.; Diocèse de Kenge B.P. 8631, Kinshasa 1, Democratic Republic of Congo.
Tel: 242-081-051-75-63
Email: evechekenge@yahoo.fr

Keningau—Most Rev. Cornelius Piong; Bishop's House P.O. Box 256, Keningau, Sabah, 89008, Malaysia.
Tel: 60-087-33-29-35 ***Fax:*** 60-087-33-14-11

Kengtung—Most Rev. Peter Louis Cakü; Catholic Church, Kyaingtong, 06231, Myanmar.
Tel: 95-084-22-018

Kerema—Most Rev. Patrick Taval, M.S.C.; Catholic Church P.O. Box 90, Kerema, Gulf Province, 311, Papua New Guinea.
Tel: 675-64-81-012 ***Fax:*** 675-64-81-088
Email: taval@datec.net.pg

Keren—Most Rev. Kidane Yebio; P.O. Box 460, Keren, Eritrea.
Tel: 291-01-401-907 ***Fax:*** 291-01-401-604
Email: cek@tse.com.er

Kericho—Most Rev. Emmanuel Okombo Wandera; P.O. Box 1500, Kericho, 20200, Kenya.
Tel: 254-052-30-485 ***Fax:*** 254-052-30-491

KERKUK—Most Rev. Louis Sako; Archevêché Chaldeén B.P. 490, Kerkuk, Iraq.
Tel: 964-050-22-08-22

Kerry—Most Rev. William Murphy; Bishop's House Cathedral Walk, Killarney, Co. Kerry, Ireland.
Tel: 353-064-6631-168 ***Fax:*** 353-064-6631-364
Email: bishopshouse@eircom.net

Keta-Akatsi—Most Rev. Anthony Kwami Adanuty; Bishop's House P.O. Box 90, Volta Region, Akatsi, Ghana.
Tel: 036-26-94-028

Ketapang—Most Rev. Blasius Pujaraharja; Keuskupan, Jl. A. Yani 74, Ketapang, Kalimantan Barat, 78811, Indonesia.
Tel: 62-0534-32-181 ***Fax:*** 62-0534-31-008
Email: uskup_ktp@yahoo.com

Khammam—Most Rev. Paul Maipan; Bishop's House Naidupet, Khammam, A.P., 507003, India.
Tel: 91-08742-2224-59 ***Fax:*** 91-08742-2230-83
Email: bppaulkmm@rediffmail.com

Khandwa—Most Rev. Alangaram Arockia Sebastian Durairaj, S.V.D.; Bishop's House, Khandwa, M.P., 450001, India.
Tel: 91-0733-22-22-935 ***Fax:*** 91-0733-22-24-038
Email: kandwadiocese@gmail.com

Kharkiv-Zaporizhia—Most Rev. Marian Buczek; Vul Gogola +, Kharkiv, 61057, Ukraine.
Tel: 380-057-706-17-66 ***Fax:*** 380-057-706-17-66
Email: rku.kharkiv@ukrpost.ua

KHARTOUM—His Eminence Gabriel Zubeir Wako; Catholic Church P.O. Box 49, Khartoum, Sudan.
Tel: 011-183-782-174 ***Fax:*** 011-183-783-518
Email: okeny72@yahoo.com

Khulna—Vacant; Bishop's House Main Road, Sonadanga, Khulna, 9000, Bangladesh.
Tel: 880-041-73-05-69 ***Fax:*** 880-041-81-38-78

Khunti—Most Rev. Stephen M. Tiru; Bishop's House St. Michael's Church, P.O. Khunti, Jharkhand, 835210, India.
Tel: 91-06528-220-389

Kí-an (Jí'an)—Catholic Mission Bishop's House, Jí'an, Jiangxi, China.

Kíatíng (Leshan)—Catholic Mission Bishop's House, Leshan, Sichuan, China.

Kiayi—Most Rev. Thomas Chung An-zu; Bishop's House 502 Taya Road sect. 2, Chiayi, 600, Taiwan.
Tel: 886-05-276-6371 ***Fax:*** 886-05-275-2487
Email: kiacuria@ms4.hinet.net

Kibungo—Vacant; Evêché B.P. 30, Kibungo, Rwanda.
Tel: 252-566-185 ***Fax:*** 252-566-185
Email: diokib@yahoo.fr

Kichow (Qichun)—China.

Kidapawan—Most Rev. Romulo T. de la Cruz; Bishop's House Balindog, P.O. Box 107, Kidapawan City, Cotabato, 9400, Philippines.
Tel: 064-288-1774/5 ***Fax:*** 064-288-1776
Email: diokidpl@yahoo.com

Kielce—Most Rev. Kazimierz Ryczan; Kuria Diecezjalna ul. Jana Pawla II 3, Kielce, 25-013, Poland.
Tel: 48-041-34-45-425 ***Fax:*** 48-041-34-15-656
Email: kuriakie@kielce.opoka.org.pl

KIGALI—Most Rev. Thaddée Ntihinyurwa; Archevêché B.P. 715, Kigali, Rwanda.
Tel: 252-575-769 ***Fax:*** 252-572-274
Email: kigarchi@yahoo.fr

Kigoma—Most Rev. Protase Rugambwa; Bishop's House P.O. Box 71, Kigoma, Tanzania.
Tel: 028-280-3115 ***Fax:*** 028-280-2043
Email: diocesekigoma@yahoo.co.uk

Kikwit—Most Rev. Edouard Mununu Kasiala, O.C.S.O.; Evêché B.P. 7245, Kinshasa 1, Democratic Republic of Congo.
Tel: 00871-099-8464-968
Email: eveche_kikwit@yahoo.fr

Kildare and Leighlin—Vacant; Bishop's House, Old Dublin Road, Carlow, Ireland.
Tel: 059-91-76-725 ***Fax:*** 059-91-76-850
Email: bishopshouse@kandle.ie

Killala—Most Rev. John Fleming; St. Muredach's Sligo Rd., Ballina, Co. Mayo, Ireland.
Tel: 353-096-21518 ***Fax:*** 353-096-70344
Email: deocilala@eircom.net

Killaloe—Most Rev. Kieran O'Reilly, S.M.A.; Westbourne, Ennis, Co. Clare, Ireland.
Tel: 353-065-682-8638 ***Fax:*** 353-065-684-2538
Email: office@killaloediocese.ie

Kilmore—Most Rev. Philip Leo O'Reilly; Bishop's House, Cullies, Cavan, Ireland.
Tel: 353-049-433-1496; 353-049437-3872 ***Fax:*** 353-049-436-1796
Email: bishop@kilmorediocese.ie

Kilwa-Kasenga—Most Rev. Fulgence Muteba Mugalu; Evêché B.P. 74, Kilwa, par Lubumbashi, Democratic Republic of Congo.
Tel: 099-82-66-297; 081-15-44-640
Email: dkilwakasenga@yahoo.fr
c/o Procure de Missions Don Bosco Wespeelaarseban 250, 3190 Boortmeerbek, Democratic Republic of Congo.

Kimbe—Most Rev. William Fey, O.F.M.Cap.; Bishop's House P.O. Box 182, Kimbe, West New Britain Province, 621, Papua New Guinea.
Tel: 983-49-25; 983-50-87 ***Fax:*** 983-50-87; 983-42-94

Kimberley—Most Rev. Abel Gabuza; Bishop's House 20 Dalham Road, P.O. Box 309, Kimberley, 8300, South Africa.
Tel: 27-053-831-18-61/2 ***Fax:*** 27-053-831-18-63

Kindu—Most Rev. Willy Ngumbi Ngengele; Evêché B.P. 18, Kindu, Democratic Republic of Congo.

Kinghsien (Jingxian)—Catholic Mission Bishop's House, Jingxian, Hebei, China.

KINGSTON—Most Rev. Brendan Michael O'Brien; Catholic Diocesan Centre 390 Palace Road, Kingston, ON, K7L 4T3, Canada.
Tel: 613-548-4461 ***Fax:*** 613-548-4744
Email: chancery@romancatholic.kingston.on.ca

KINGSTON (IN JAMAICA)—Most Rev. Charles Henry Dufour; Archbishop's Residence 21 Hopefield Ave., P.O. Box 43, Kingston 6, Jamaica.
Tel: 876-927-9915; 876-978-6567 ***Fax:*** 876-927-4487
Email: rcabkgn@cwjamaica.com

Kingstown—Most Rev. Charles Jason Gordon; Bishop's Office P.O. Box 862, Kingstown, St. Vincent & the Grenadines, West Indies.
Tel: 784-457-2363 ***Fax:*** 784-457-1903
Email: redok@vincysurf.com

Kinkala—Most Rev. Louis Portella Mbuyu; Evêché B.P. 200 Brazzaville, Kinkala, Republic of the Congo.
Tel: 06-626-27-19; 05-547-38-36
Email: diocesekinkala@yahoo.fr

KINSHASA—His Eminence Laurent Cardinal Monsengwo Pasinya; Archevêché Avenue de l'Université, B.P. 8431, Kinshasa 1, Democratic Republic of Congo.
Tel: 012-3723-546
Email: archikin@ic.cd

Kírín (Jilin)—Catholic Mission, Bishop's House Kiang-Yen-Chien, Jilin, China.

KISANGANI—Most Rev. Marcel Utembi Tapa; Archevêché Av. Mpolo 10/b, B.P. 505, Kisangani, Democratic Republic of Congo.
Tel: 085-135-60-59; 099-425-13-82
Email: chkisangani@yahoo.fr

Kisantu—Most Rev. Fidèle Nsielele Zi Mputu; Evêché B.P. 25, Inkisi, Bas-Congo, Democratic Republic of Congo.
Tel: 304-099-102-54-50

Kisii—Most Rev. Joseph Mairura Okemwa; Bishop's House P.O. Box 331, Kisii, 40200, Kenya.
Tel: 254-058-31-050 ***Fax:*** 254-058-31-050
Email: nobanyi@hotmail.com

KISUMU—Most Rev. Zacchaeus Okoth; P.O. Box 1728, Kisumu, 40100, Kenya.
Tel: 254-057-202-07-25 ***Fax:*** 254-057-202-22-03
Email: archdiocese-ksm@net2000ke.com

Kitale—Most Rev. Maurice Anthony Crowley, S.P.S.; Bishop's Office P.O. Box 4656, Kitale, 30200, Kenya.
Tel: 054-30-899 ***Fax:*** 054-31-485; 054-30-118
Email: kitalecd@wananchi.com

Kitui—Most Rev. Anthony Muheria; Bishop's House P.O. Box 119, Kitui, 90200, Kenya.
Tel: 254-044-22-844 ***Fax:*** 254-044-22-675
Email: cdokpastoral@dioceseofkitui.org

Kiyinda-Mityana—Most Rev. Joseph Anthony Zziwa; P.O. Box 175, Mityana, Uganda.
Tel: 256-046-444-2175 ***Fax:*** 256-046-444-2175
Email: kmd@utlonline.co.ug

Klerksdorp—Most Rev. Zithulele Patrick Mvemve; 14 Convent Lane, Elandsheuwel, Klerksdrop 2571, P.O. Box 3071, Freemanville, 2573, South Africa.
Tel: 27-018-462-2261 ***Fax:*** 27-018-462-9168
Email: klddio@gds.co.za

Knoxville—Most Rev. Richard F. Stika; The Chancery 805 Northshore Dr., S.W., Knoxville, TN, 37919.
Tel: 865-584-3307 ***Fax:*** 865-584-7538
Email: fxm@dioceseofknoxville.org

Kobenhavn, Copenhagen—Most Rev. Czeslaw Kozon; Katolsk Bispekontor Gl. Kongevej 15, Kobenhavn V, DK-1610, Denmark.
Tel: 43-33-55-60-80 ***Fax:*** 45-33-55-60-86
Email: bispekontor@katolsk.dk

Koforidua—Most Rev. Joseph Kwaku Afrifah-Agyekum; Bishop's House P.O. Box KF 625, Koforidua, Ghana.
Tel: 233-22-22-536 ***Fax:*** 233-20-22-728
Email: kofidir@yahoo.com

Kohima—Most Rev. James Thoppil; Bishop's House P.O. Box 519, Kohima, Nagaland, 797001, India.
Tel: 0370-2800-978 ***Fax:*** 0370-2228-452

Kokstad—Most Rev. William Slattery, O.F.M.; Bishop's House 107 Hope St., P.O. Box 65, Kokstad, Natal, 4700, South Africa.
Tel: 27-039-727-2239 ***Fax:*** 27-039-727-1151
Email: slatteryws@telkomsa.net

Kolda—Most Rev. Jean-Pierre Bassène; Evêché B.P. 4, Kolda, Senegal.
Tel: 33-996-19-30 ***Fax:*** 33-996-15-04
Email: diocesekolda@sentoo.sn

Kole—Vacant; Evêché de Kole B.P. 1800, Kinshasa, Democratic Republic of Congo.

KÖLN—His Eminence Cardinal Joachim Meisner; Erzbischöfliches Generalvikariat Marzellenstr. 32, Köln, D-50668, Germany.
Tel: 49-0221-16-420 ***Fax:*** 49-0221-1642-1700
Email: generalvikar@erzbistum-koeln.de

Kolomyia-Chernivtsi—Most Rev. Mykola Simkaylo; vul. Ivan Franko 29, Kolomyia, 78200, Ukraine.
Tel: 03433-21-670 ***Fax:*** 03433-24-476
Email: katedra-2005@ukr.net

Kolwezi—Most Rev. Nestor Ngoy Katahwa; Evêché B.P. 900, Kolwezi, Shaba, Democratic Republic of Congo.
Tel: 023-21-736 ***Fax:*** 023-21-736
Email: evkolwezi@gmail.com

Kondoa—Most Rev. Bernardin Francis Mfumbusa; Tanzania.

Kongmoon (Jiangmen)—Catholic Mission Bishop's House, Jiangmen, Guangdong, China.

Kongolo—Most Rev. Oscar Ngoy wa Mpanga, C.S.Sp; Evêché B.P. 274, Katanga, Kongolo, Democratic Republic of Congo.
Tel: 081-253-04-36
Email: eveche.kongolo57@yahoo.com

Konongo-Mampong—Most Rev. Joseph Osei-Bonsu; Bishop's House P.O. Box 382, Mampong, Ashanti, Ghana.
Tel: 032-22-91-776 ***Fax:*** 032-22-22-101
Email: bishop@kmdiocese.org

Kontum—Most Rev. Michel Hoang Dúc Oanh; Tóa Giám Muc 56 Trân Hung Dao, Tx. Kontum, Vietnam.
Tel: 060-3862-372 ***Fax:*** 060-3862-372
Email: tgmktum@yahoo.ca

Koper—Most Rev. Metod Pirih; Trg Brolo 11, Koper, 6000, Slovenia.
Tel: 05-6117-200 ***Fax:*** 05-6271-059
Email: skofija.koper@rkc.si

KORHOGO—Most Rev. Marie-Daniel Dadiet; B.P. 1581, Yamoussoukro, Ivory Coast.
Tel: 225-3686-01-18 ***Fax:*** 225-3685-16-29
Email: archevechekgo@yahoo.fr

Koszalin-Kolobrzeg—Most Rev. Edward Dajczak; Kuria Biskupia ul. Ksiedza Kardynala Stefana Wyszynskiego 25, Skr. p. 167, Koszalin, 75-062, Poland.
Tel: 094-343-8710 ***Fax:*** 094-343-8739
Email: kuria@koszalin.opoka.org.pl

KOTA KINABALU—Most Rev. John Lee Hiong Fun-Yit Yaw; Archbishop's House P.O. Box 10289, Kota Kinabalu, Sabah, 88803, Malaysia.
Tel: 60-088-712-297 ***Fax:*** 60-088-711-954
Email: diosec@gmail.com

Kothamangalam—Most Rev. George Punnakottil; Bishop's House P.B. 6, Kothamangalam, Kerala, 686691, India.
Tel: 91-0485-2862-236; 91-0485-2862-237; 91-0485-2861-555 ***Fax:*** 91-0485-2861-555
Email: mkochupura@vsnl.net

Kotido—Most Rev. Giuseppe Filippi, M.C.C.I.; P.O. Box 55, Kotido, Uganda.
Email: kotidodiocese2005@yahoo.co.uk

Kotor—Most Rev. Ilija Janjic; Biskupski Ordinarijat Trg Sv. Tripuna 336, Kotor, Crna Gora, 85330, Montenegro.
Tel: 381-082-322-315 ***Fax:*** 381-082-322-175; 381-082-322-315
Email: info@kotorskabiskupija.net

Kottapuram—Most Rev. Joseph Karikkassery; Bishop's House, Kottapuram, Kerala, 680667, India.
Tel: 91-0480-2802-165 ***Fax:*** 91-0480-2802-865
Email: skunnathur@rediffmail.com

Kottar—Most Rev. Peter Remigius; Catholic Bishop's House Nagercoil, Kanyakumari Dt., P.O. Box 17, Tamil Nadu, 629001, India.
Tel: 91-04652-278-343; 91-04652-279-152 ***Fax:*** 91-04652-278-570
Email: kottardiocese@yahoo.co.in

KOTTAYAM—Most Rev. Mathew Moolakkatt, O.S.B.; Catholic Metropolitan's House P.O. Box 71, Kottayam, Kerala, 686001, India.
Tel: 91-0481-256-3527/3812 ***Fax:*** 91-0481-256-3327
Email: cbhktym@hotmail.com

Koudougou—Vacant; Evêché B.P. 34, Koudougou, Burkina Faso.
Tel: 50-44-00-70 ***Fax:*** 50-44-01-78
Email: vchkdg@yahoo.fr

KOUPÉLA—Most Rev. Séraphin François Rouamba; Archevêché B.P. 51, Koupéla, Burkina Faso.
Tel: 40-70-00-30 ***Fax:*** 40-70-02-65
Email: ardiokou@fasonet.bf

KOŠICE—Most Rev. Bernard Bober; Arcibiskupský úrad Hlavná ulica 28, Košice, SK-041 83, Slovakia.
Tel: 42-055-68-28-101 ***Fax:*** 42-055-62-21-034
Email: abukosice@kbs.sk

Košice (Byzantine)—Most Rev. Milan Chautur, C.S.S.R.; Gréckokatolícka Eparchia Dominikánske nám. 2/a, pošt. schránka G-13, Košice, SK-043 43, Slovakia.
Tel: 055-72-71-911 ***Fax:*** 055-62-27-453
Email: sekretariat@grkatke.sk

Kpalimé—Most Rev. Benoît Comlan Messan Alowonou; Evêché B.P. 83, Kpalimé, Togo.
Tel: 441-03-45 ***Fax:*** 441-05-76
Email: kpalimeveche@yahoo.fr

KRAKÓW—His Eminence Stanislaw Dziwisz; Kuria Metropolitalna ul. Franciszkanska 3, Kraków, 31-004, Poland.
Tel: 48-012-628-8100 ***Fax:*** 48-012-429-4617
Email: kuria@diecezja.krakow.pl

Kribi—Most Rev. Joseph Befe Ateba; B.P. 301, Kribi, Cameroon.
Tel: 237-9617-5560; 237-9948-0539
Email: diocesedekribi@gmail.com

Krishnagar—Most Rev. Joseph Suren Gomes, S.D.B.; Bishop's House Nadia Dt., Krishnanagar, West Bengal, 741101, India.
Tel: 91-03472-252-554; 91-03472-252-664 ***Fax:*** 91-03472-252-664

Krizevci, Crisio—Most Rev. Nikola Nino Kekic; Ordinarijat Krizevacke Eparhije Kaptol 20, Zagreb, 10000, Croatia.
Tel: 385-01-48-11-872 ***Fax:*** 385-01-48-11-873
Email: krizevacki.biskup@gmail.com

Krk, Veglia—Most Rev. Valter Zupan; Biskupski Ordinarijat Ul. Biskupa Antuna Mahnica 18, Krk, 51500, Croatia.
Tel: 385-051-221-018 ***Fax:*** 385-051-221-483
Email: bisk.ordinarijat.krk@ri.t-com.hr

Kroonstad—Most Rev. Peter Holiday; Bishop's House, The Peak P.O. Box 129, Kroonstad, 9500, South Africa.
Tel: 27-056-212-6639 ***Fax:*** 27-056-212-7705
Email: bishop.krd@xsinet.co.za

KUALA LUMPUR—Most Rev. Murphy Nicholas Xavier Pakiam; Rumah Uskup Agung 528 Jalan Bukit Nanas, Kuala Lumpur, 50250, Malaysia.
Tel: 60-03-207-85-089 *Fax:* 60-03-203-13-815
Email: frantrcakl@yahoo.com

KUCHING—Most Rev. John Ha Tiong Hock; Archbishop's Office 118 Jalan Tun Abang Haji Openg, Kuching, Sarawak, 93700, Malaysia.
Tel: 60-082-242-634 *Fax:* 60-082-425-724
Email: abcofkuc@po.jaring.my
P.O. Box 940, Kuching, 93718, Malaysia.

KUMASI—Most Rev. Thomas Kwaku Mensah; Archbishop's House P.O. Box KS 99, Kumasi, Ghana.
Tel: 233-051-24-012 *Fax:* 233-051-27-684
Email: cadiokum@ghana.com

Kumbakonam—Most Rev. Antonisamy Francis; Bishop's House P.O. Box 3, Kumbakonam, Thanjavur Dt., Tamil Nadu, 612001, India.
Tel: 91-0435-2432-232 *Fax:* 91-0435-2423-679
Email: kumbakonamdiocese@gmail.com

Kumbo—Most Rev. George Nkuo; Bishop's House P.O. Box 115, Kumbo, N.W. Province, Cameroon.
Tel: 237-3348-1149 *Fax:* 237-3348-1307
Email: diocesiskumboensis@gmail.com

Kundiawa—Most Rev. Anton Bal; Bishop's House P.O. Box 177, Kundiawa, Simbu Province, 461, Papua New Guinea.
Tel: 675-53-51-007 *Fax:* 675-53-51-007
Email: cdkundiawa@datec.net.pg

KUNMING (KUNMING)—Catholic Mission Tuo-Tuwg Rd., Kunming, Yunnan, China.

KUPANG—Most Rev. Peter Turang; Keuskupan Agung Jl. Thamrin, Oepoi, Kupang, Timor, 85111, Indonesia.
Tel: 62-0380-826-199; 62-0380-833-331 *Fax:* 62-0380-833-331

Kurnool—Most Rev. Anthony Poola; Bishop's House B Camp, Kurnool, A.P., 518002, India.
Tel: 91-08518-270-393 *Fax:* 91-08518-270-313

Kurunegala—Most Rev. Harold Anthony Perera; Catholic Bishop's House 409 Negombo Rd., Kurunegala, 60000, Sri Lanka.
Tel: 94-037-2222-854; 94-037-2224-935 *Fax:* 94-037-2224-935
Email: biskuru@sltnet.lk

KWANGJU—Most Rev. Hyginus Kim Hee-jong; Diocesan Office 997-1 Sangmu 2 Dong, Seo-Gu, Kwangju, 502-855, Korea, South.
Tel: 82-062-380-2801 *Fax:* 82-062-380-2806
Email: chongmu@kjcatholic.or.kr

Kweiteh (Shangqui)—Catholic Mission Bishop's House, Shangqiu, Henan, China.

KWEYANG (GUIYANG)—Catholic Mission Archbishop's House, Guiyang, Guizhou, China.

Kwito-Bié—Most Rev. José Nambi; Cúria Diocesana C.P. 16, Kwito-Bié, Angola.
Tel: 244-923-725-775
Email: diocese-kuito@hotmail.com

KYIV-VYSHHOROD—Most Rev. Sviatoslav Shevchuk; vul. Riznytcka 11-B/28-29, Kyiv, 01011, Ukraine.
Tel: 044-254-56-10 *Fax:* 044-254-56-10
Email: kyiv@ugcc.org.ua

Kyiv-Zhytomyr—Most Rev. Petro Herkulan Malchuk, O.F.M.; vul. Basejna 9, Zhytomyr, 10014, Ukraine.
Tel: 0412-47-49-28 *Fax:* 0412-47-49-28
Email: curia@ukr.net

Kyoto—Most Rev. Paul Yoshinao Otsuka; 423 Shimomaruya-cho, Kawaramachi Sanjo Agaru, Nakagyo-ku, Kyoto-fu, 604-8006, Japan.
Tel: 075-211-3025 *Fax:* 075-211-3041
Email: honbu@kyoto.catholic.jp

L

L'AQUILA—Most Rev. Guiseppe Molinari; Zona Industriale Campo di Pile, L'Aquila, 67100, Italy.
Tel: 39-0862-33-23-01 *Fax:* 39-0862-33-23-21
Email: arcidiocesi@laquila.chiesacattolica.it

La Crosse—Most Rev. William P. Callahan, O.F.M.Conv.; Chancery Office 3710 East Ave. S., 54601, P.O. Box 4004, La Crosse, WI, 54602-4004.
Tel: 608-788-7700 *Fax:* 608-788-8413
Web: www.dioceseoflacrosse.com
Email: mailbox@dioceseoflacrosse.com

La Dorada-Guaduas—Most Rev. Oscar Aníbal Salazar Gómez; Carrera 3 N. 15-35, La Dorada, Caldas, Colombia.
Tel: 57-6-857-48-00; 57-6-8573-026 *Fax:* 57-6-8573-026
Email: doradadioc@ccc.org.co

La Guaira—Vacant; Obispado, Apartado 266, Av. La Playa 05-01, Macuto, Edo. Vargas, 1164, Venezuela.
Tel: 58-0212-5168-498 *Fax:* 58-0212-3310-774

LA PAZ—Most Rev. Edmundo Luis Flavio Abastoflor Montero; Calle Ballivián 1277, Casilla 259, La Paz, Bolivia.
Tel: 591-02-2203-690/840 *Fax:* 591-02-2203-672
Email: arzobispadodelapaz@yahoo.es

La Paz en la Baja California Sur—Most Rev. Miguel Angel Alba Díaz; Apartado 25, Revolución y 5 de Mayo, La Paz, Baja California Sur, 23000, Mexico.
Tel: 52-612-122-2596 *Fax:* 52-612-122-8272
Email: obispadolapaz@hotmail.com

LA PLATA—Most Rev. Héctor Rubén Aguer; Arzobispado Calle 14 N. 1009, C.C. 102, La Plata, Buenos Aires, B1900DVQ, Argentina.
Tel: 54-0221-425-1656/8269; 54-0221-483-76-27
Email: arzolap@satlink.com.ar

La Rioja—Most Rev. Roberto Rodríguez; Obispado, San Nicolás de Bari 560 Oeste, La Rioja, F5300AAS, Argentina.
Tel: 54-03822-433-942; 54-03822-434-255 *Fax:* 54-03822-434-255; 54-03822-433-942
Email: obispadolr@ciudad.com.ar

La Rochelle—Most Rev. Bernard Housset; 7 Place Foch, B.P. 1088, La Rochelle CEDEX 02, 17087, France.
Tel: 5-46-41-40-06 *Fax:* 5-46-41-41-64
Email: diocese@diocese17.fr

LA SERENA—Most Rev. Manuel Gerardo Donoso Donoso, SS.CC.; Calle Los Carrera 450, La Serena, Chile.
Tel: 56-051-54-58-60 *Fax:* 56-051-54-65-36
Email: laserena@episcopado.cl

La Spezia-Sarzana-Brugnato—Most Rev. Francesco Moraglia; Vescovado, Via Don Giovanni Minzoni 64, C.P. 215, La Spezia, 19121, Italy.
Tel: 39-0187-73-44-24/45-03 *Fax:* 39-0187-73-21-87
Email: curia.vescovile@castagna.it

La Vega—Most Rev. Antonio Camilo González; Calle Leoncio Ramos, Esq. Sanchez, La Vega, Dominican Republic.
Tel: 809-573-2201/2601 *Fax:* 809-573-6303
Email: obispado.lavega@yahoo.es

Lae—Most Rev. Christian Blouin, C.M.M.; Bishop's House P.O. Box 3, Lae, Morobe Province, 411, Papua New Guinea.
Tel: 472-5130 *Fax:* 479-0076

Lafayette—Most Rev. Michael Jarrell, D.D. (LAF); Administrative Offices: Diocesan Office 1408 Carmel Drive, Lafayette, LA, 70501.
Tel: 337-261-5500 *Fax:* 337-261-5635
Web: www.diolaf.org
Email: rstevenson@diolaf.org

Lafayette (in Indiana)—Most Rev. Timothy L. Doherty; Bishop's Office 610 Lingle Ave., P.O. Box 260, Lafayette, IN, 47902-0260.
Tel: 765-742-0275 *Fax:* 765-742-7513
Web: www.dioceseoflafayette.org

Lafia—Most Rev. Matthew Ishaya Audu; Catholic Diocese P.O. Box 84, Lafia, Nasarawa State, Nigeria.
Tel: 070-12-71-972
Email: diocesanchancerylafia@gmail.com

Lages—Most Rev. Irineu Andreassa, O.F.M.; Cúria Diocesana C.P. 20, Rua Correia Pinto 247, Lages, SC, 88502-970, Brazil.
Tel: 55-049-3222-1520 *Fax:* 55-049-3222-1520
Email: mitral@gesabol.com.br

Laghouat—Most Rev. Claude Rault, M. Afr.; Evêché, B.P. 62, Ghardaïa, 47008, Algeria.
Tel: 213-029-88-19-66 *Fax:* 213-029-88-17-96
Email: evghardaia@yahoo.fr

LAGOS—His Eminence Cardinal Anthony Olubunmi Okogie; Archdiocesan Secretariat 19 Catholic Mission St., P.O. Box 8, Lagos, Nigeria.
Tel: 080-340-70-770
Email: arclagos@yahoo.com

LAHORE—Vacant; Archdiocesan Curia 1 Lawrence Rd., P.O. Box 909, Lahore, 54000, Pakistan.
Tel: 042-36366-137 *Fax:* 042-36368-336
Email: abishop@lhr.comsats.net.pk

Lai—Most Rev. Miguel Angel Sebastián Martínez, M.C.C.I.; Evêché, B.P. 7, Lai, Tandjilé, Chad.
Tel: 6627-16-69

Lake Charles—Most Rev. Glen John Provost (LKC); Chancery Office 414 Iris St., P.O. Box 3223, Lake Charles, LA, 70602.
Tel: 337-439-7400 *Fax:* 337-439-7413
Web: lcdiocese.laol.net
Email: lcdiocese@laol.net

Lamego—Most Rev. Jacinto Tomás de Carvalho Botelho; Cúria Diocesana Rua das Cortes 2, Lamego, 5100-132, Portugal.
Tel: 351-254-612-147 *Fax:* 351-254-619-387
Email: geral@diocese-lamego.pt

Lamezia Terme—Most Rev. Luigi Antonio Cantafora; Vescovado, Via Lissania 2, Lamezia Terme, Catanzaro, 88046, Italy.
Tel: 39-0968-21-923 *Fax:* 39-0968-44-2071
Email: curialamezia@libero.it

Lancaster—Most Rev. Michael Gregory Campbell, O.S.A.; Bishop's Apartment Cathedral House, Balmoral Road, Lancaster, LA1 3BT, England.
Tel: 44-01524-59-60-50 *Fax:* 44-01524-59-60-53

LANCHOW (LANZHOU), KAO-LAN—Catholic Mission Archbishop's House, Lanzhou, Gansu, China.

LANCIANO-ORTONA—Most Rev. Emidio Cipollone; Arcivescovado C.P. 223, Via Gennaro Finamore 32, Lanciano, Chieti, 66034, Italy.
Tel: 39-0872-71-26-48 *Fax:* 39-0872-71-59-03
Email: dioclaor@webzone.it

Lang Són et Cao Bang—Most Rev. Joseph Dang Dúc Ngân; Tóa Giám Muc, 2 Van Miêu, Phúong Chi Lâng, Tx. Lang Són, Vietnam.
Tel: 025-3810-367 *Fax:* 025-3810-632
Email: tgmlscb@giaophanlangson.org

Langres—Most Rev. Philippe Gueneley; Evêché, 11 rue des Platanes, B.P. 1036, Chaumont CEDEX, 52008, France.
Tel: 3-25-01-1818 *Fax:* 3-25-32-5688
Email: secretariat@catholique-hautemarne.cef.fr

Lanlung (Anlong)—Catholic Mission Hing-I-Fu, Anlong, Guizhou, China.

Lansing—Most Rev. Earl Alfred Boyea (LAN); Chancery 228 N. Walnut St., Lansing, MI, 48933.
Tel: 517-342-2440 *Fax:* 517-342-2519

Lanusei—Most Rev. Antioco Piseddu; Curia Vescovile Via Roma 102, Lanusei, Nuoro, 08045, Italy.
Tel: 39-0782-42-634 *Fax:* 39-0782-48-02-61
Email: info@diocesilanusei.it

Laoag—Vacant; Bishop's Residence P. Gomez St., P.O. Box 12, Laoag City, Ilocos Norte, 2900, Philippines.
Tel: 077-770-52-10 *Fax:* 077-772-18-05
Email: dioceseoflaoag@yahoo.com

Laohokow (Laohekou)—Catholic Mission Bishop's House, Laohekow, Hubei, China.

Larantuka—Most Rev. Franciscus Kopong Kung; Keuskupan, Jl. Miguel Rangel 1-2, San Domingo,, Larantuka, Flores Timur, 86213, Indonesia.
Tel: 62-0383-21-170 *Fax:* 62-0383-21-443
Email: sandokl@plasa.com

Laredo—Most Rev. James Anthony Tamayo, D.D. (LAR); Chancery Office 1901 Corpus Christi St., Laredo, TX, 78043.
Tel: 956-727-2140 *Fax:* 956-727-2777
Email: vicargeneral@dioceseoflaredo.org

Las Cruces—Most Rev. Ricardo Ramírez, C.S.B., D.D. (LSC); The Pastoral Center 1280 Med Park Dr., Las Cruces, NM, 88005.
Tel: 575-523-7577 *Fax:* 575-524-3874
Web: www.dioceseoflascruces.org
Email: pastoralcenter@dioceseoflascruces.org

Las Vegas—Most Rev. Joseph Anthony Pepe, D.D., J.C.D. (LAV); Chancery Office 336 Cathedral Way, Las Vegas, NV, 89109.
Tel: 702-735-3500 *Fax:* 702-735-8941
Email: mcauliffe@dioceseoflasvegas.org

Lashio—Most Rev. Philip Lasap Za Hawng; Bishop's House San Kaung Road, Lashio, N.S.S., 06301, Myanmar.
Tel: 082-22-603
Email: cathdio_lso@gmail.com

Latacunga—Most Rev. José Victoriano Naranjo Tovar; Curia Episcopal Calle Sánchez de Orellana 70-63, Latacunga, Ecuador.
Tel: 593-03-2810-269 *Fax:* 593-03-2810-283
Email: diocesis_ltg@andinanet.net

Latina-Terracina-Sezze-Priverno—Most Rev. Giuseppe Petrocchi; Vescovado, Via Sezze 16, Latina, 04100, Italy.
Tel: 39-0773-69-42-61; 39-0773-48-01-11 *Fax:* 39-0773-66-81-60
Email: pastorale@diocesi.latina.it

LATTAQUIÉ—Most Rev. Nicolas Sawaf; Archevêché Grec-Catholique, Rue Al-Moutanabi, B.P. 151, Lattaquié, Syria.
Tel: 963-041-46-07-77 *Fax:* 964-041-47-60-02

Lattaquié, Laodicea, Lattaqiya—Most Rev. Youssef-Massoud Massoud; Evêché Maronite, B.P. 161, rue Hamrat, Tartous, Syria.
Tel: 963-031-222-32-11 *Fax:* 963-031-2461-461
Email: mgr.antoine@hotmail.com

Lausanne, Genève et Fribourg (Freiburg)—Vacant; C.P. 512, 86 rue de Lausanne, Fribourg, CH-1701, Switzerland.
Tel: 41-026-347-4850 *Fax:* 41-026-347-4851
Email: chancellerie@diocese-lgf.ch

Laval—Most Rev. Thierry Scherrer; 27 rue du Cardinal Suhard, B.P. 31225, Laval CEDEX, 53012, France.
Tel: 2-43-69-2421 *Fax:* 2-43-66-8746
Email: chancellerie@eveche-laval.org

Le Caire—Most Rev. François Eid, O.M.M.; Evêché Maronite, 15 Rue Hamdi, Daher, Le Caire, 11271, Egypt.
Tel: 20-02-261-37-373 *Fax:* 20-02-259-39-610

Le Caire - Chaldean—Vacant; Evêché Chaldéen, Basilique N.D. de Fatima, 141 rue Nouzha, Héliopolis, Le Caire, 11361, Egypt.
Tel: 20-02-2635-5718 *Fax:* 20-02-2635-5718
Email: chaldean@libero.it

Le Caire - Syrian—Most Rev. Clément-Joseph Hannouche; Evêché Syrien Catholique, 46 Rue Daher, Le Caire, 11271, Egypt.
Tel: 20-02-2590-1234 *Fax:* 20-02-2592-3932

Le Havre—Most Rev. Jean-Luc Brunin; 22 rue Séry, B.P. 1029, Le Havre CEDEX, 76061, France.
Tel: 2-32-74-9720 *Fax:* 2-32-74-9721
Email: diocese.du.havre@wanadoo.fr

Le Mans—Most Rev. Jean-Yves Le Saux; Evêché 4 Place du Cardinal-Grente, Le Mans CEDEX 2, 72016, France.
Tel: 2-43-81-71-80 *Fax:* 2-43-81-77-26
Email: contact@eveche-lemans.org

Le Puy-en-Velay—Most Rev. Henri Brincard; Evêché, 2 Place du For, Le Puy-en-Velay, 43000, France.
Tel: 4-71-05-54-69 *Fax:* 4-71-05-87-92
Email: eveche.le-puy@wanaoo.fr

LECCE—Most Rev. Domenico Umberto D'Ambrosio; Palazzo Arcivescovile, Piazza Duomo 5, Lecce, 73100, Italy.
Tel: 39-0832-332-699 *Fax:* 39-0832-244-761
Email: curia@diocesilecce.org

Leeds—Most Rev. Arthur Roche; Diocesan Curial Offices, Hinsley Hall 62 Headingley Lane, Leeds, LS6 2BR, England.
Tel: 44-0113-261-8000 *Fax:* 44-0113-261-8035
Email: kheskin@googlemail.com

Legazpi—Most Rev. Joel Z. Baylon; Chancery Office 61 Sikatuna St., Legazpi City, 4500, Philippines.
Tel: 63-052-481-2178 *Fax:* 63-052-481-2178
Email: legazpichancery@yahoo.com

Legnica—Most Rev. Stefan Cichy; Kuria Diecezjalna, ul. Jana Pawla II 1, Legnica, 59-220, Poland.
Tel: 48-076-7244-100 *Fax:* 48-076-7244-101
Email: kuria@diecezja.legnica.pl

Leiria-Fátima—Most Rev. António Augusto dos Santos Marto; Largo Cónego Maia, Leiria, 2400-175, Portugal.
Tel: 351-244-832-539 *Fax:* 351-244-822-764

León—Most Rev. Julián López Martin; Obispado, Apartado 9, Plaza de la Regla 7, León, 24003, Spain.
Tel: 34-987-21-96-80 *Fax:* 34-987-26-06-65
Email: obleon@planalfa.es

LEON (IN MEXICO)—Most Rev. José Guadalupe Martin Rábago; Arzobispado, Pedro Moreno 312, Apartado 108, Leon, Gto., 37000, Mexico.
Tel: 477-713-2747 *Fax:* 477-713-12-86
Email: canciller@arquidiocesisdeleon.org

León (in Nicaragua)—Most Rev. César Bosco Vivas Robelo; Obispado, Costado sur de Catedral, Apartado 86, León, Nicaragua.
Tel: 2311-4820 *Fax:* 2311-1132

Leopoldina—Vacant; Cúria Diocesana C.P. 7, Praça Dom Helvécio 75, Leopoldina, MG, 36700-000, Brazil.
Tel: 55-032-3441-2008 *Fax:* 55-032-3441-2008
Email: recpcao@dioceseleopoldina.com

Leribe—Most Rev. Augustinus Tumaole Bane, O.M.I.; Bishop's House P.O. Box 1115, Saint Monica, 390, Lesotho.
Tel: 266-22-43-0285 *Fax:* 22-43-0310

Les Cayes—Most Rev. Chibly Langlois; Evêché, B.P. 43, 137 rue Antoine Simon, Les Cayes, 8110, Haiti.
Tel: 509-2286-0131
Email: dioceselescayes@yahoo.fr

Les Gonaïves—Most Rev. Yves-Marie Péan, C.S.C.; Evêché, Avenue des Dattes 89, Les Gonaïves, W.I., Haiti.

Lexington—Most Rev. Ronald William Gainer (LEX); The Catholic Center 1310 W. Main St., Lexington, KY, 40508-2048.
Tel: 859-253-1993 *Fax:* 859-254-6284
Email: kabbey@cdlex.org

Lezhë, Lesh—Most Rev. Ottavio Vitale, R.C.I.; Kuria Ipeshkvnore Rruga Varosh - Ish Dega Ushtarake, Lezhë, Albania.
Tel: 0224-215-249-21 *Fax:* 0224-215-249-21
Email: ipeshkvnia@tiscali.it

Líbano-Honda—Most Rev. José Miguel Gómez Rodríguez; Casa Episcopal, Carrera 6 N. 14-25, Líbano, Tolima, Colombia.
Tel: 57-8-2564-733 *Fax:* 57-8-2564-580
Email: diocesislibanohonda@yahoo.com

Libmanan—Most Rev. Jose Rojas Rojas Jr.; Bishop's House Station Church Site, Libmanan, Camarines Sur, 4407, Philippines.
Tel: 63-054-451-2875 *Fax:* 63-054-451-2876

LIBREVILLE—Most Rev. Basile Mvé Engone, S.D.B.; Archevêché, Sainte-Marie, B.P. 2146, Libreville, Gabon.
Tel: 241-722-073 *Fax:* 241-722-073

Lichinga—Most Rev. Elio Greselin, S.C.I.; C.P. 111, Lichinga, Niassa, Mozambique.
Tel: 271-20-238 *Fax:* 271-21-137

Liège, Luik, Lüttich—Most Rev. Aloysius Jousten; 25 rue de l'Evêché, Liège, B-4000, Belgium.
Tel: 32-04-230-31-50 *Fax:* 32-04-223-70-87
Email: vicariat.general@evechedeliege.be

Liepaja—Most Rev. Vilhelms Lapelis, O.P.; Peldu iela 15, Liepaja, LV-3401, Latvia.
Tel: 634-20-217 *Fax:* 634-20-217
Email: biskapss@inbox.lv

LILLE—Most Rev. Laurent Ulrich; Archeveche, 68 rue Royale, Lille CEDEX, 59042, France.
Tel: 3-20-55-2872 *Fax:* 3-20-74-2285
Email: diocese@catholique-lille.cef.fr

LILONGWE—Most Rev. Rémi Joseph Gustave Sainte-Marie, M.Afr.; Bishop's House P.O. Box 631, Lilongwe, Malawi.
Tel: 265-1-754-667 *Fax:* 265-1-751-426

LIMA—His Eminence Cardinal Juan Luis Cipriani Throne; Arzobispado Jr. Chancay 282, Apartado 1512, Lima I, 100, Peru.
Tel: 51-1-203-7700 *Fax:* 51-1-433-3740
Email: secretaria@arzobispadodelima.org

Limburg—Most Rev. Franz Peter Tebartz-van Elst; Bischöfliches Ordinariat Postfach 1355, Rossmarkt 4, Limburg, D-65549, Germany.
Tel: 49-06431-2950 *Fax:* 49-06431-29-54-76
Email: ordinariat@bistumlimburg.de

Limeira—Most Rev. Vilson Diaz de Oliveira, D.C.; Cúria Diocesana C.P. 333, Rua Barão de Cascalho 500, Limeira, SP, 13480-970, Brazil.
Tel: 55-019-3441-5329 *Fax:* 55-019-3441-5329
Email: curia@diocesedelimeira.org.br

Limerick—Vacant; Diocesan Offices Henry Street, Limerick, Ireland.
Tel: 353-061-31-58-56 *Fax:* 353-061-31-01-86
Email: office@ldo.ie

Limoeiro do Norte—Most Rev. José Haring, O.F.M.; Cúria Diocesana C.P. 27, Praça Padre Acelino 381, Limoeiro do Norte, CE, 62930-000, Brazil.
Tel: 55-088-3423-1171 *Fax:* 55-088-3423-1171
Email: dioceselimoeiro@brisanet.com.br

Limoges—Most Rev. Francois Michel Pierre Kalist; Evêché, 3 rue de la Cathédrale, B.P. 93, Limoges CEDEX 1, 87003, France.
Tel: 5-55-34-16-15 *Fax:* 5-55-32-73-37
Email: eveche.limoges@wanadoo.fr

Limón—Most Rev. José Rafael Quirós Quirós; Obispado, Apartado 1312, Limón, 7300, Costa Rica.
Tel: 580-2798-08-98 *Fax:* 580-2798-45-46
Email: curiadelimon@ice.co.cr

Linares—Most Rev. Tomislav Koljatic Maroevic; Obispado, Independencia 248, Linares, Chile.
Tel: 812-073-62-62-01 *Fax:* 812-073-62-72-20
Email: sjara@obispadodelinares.cl

Linares (in Mexico)—Most Rev. Ramón Calderón Batres; Obispado, Morelos y Antonio de Jesús Sacedón, Apartado 70, Linares, N.L., 67700, Mexico.
Tel: 821-212-18-12/05-52/63-10 *Fax:* 821-212-07-50
Email: obispado2@prodigy.net.mx

Lincoln—Most Rev. Fabian Wendelin Bruskewitz, D.D., S.T.D. (LIN); Chancery Office 3400 Sheridan Blvd., Lincoln, NE, 68506.
Tel: 402-488-0921 *Fax:* 402-488-3569
Email: fr.dan-rayer@lincolndiocese.org

Lindi—Most Rev. Bruno Pius Ngonyani; Bishop's House P.O. Box 1002, Lindi, Tanzania.
Tel: 255-023-220-2586/2490 *Fax:* 255-023-220-2274
Email: diolindi@yahoo.com

LINGAYEN-DAGUPAN—Most Rev. Socrates B. Villegas; Archbishop's House Jovellanos St., Dagupan City, Pangasinan, 2400, Philippines.
Tel: 63-075-523-5357 *Fax:* 63-075-522-1878

Lins—Most Rev. Irineu Danelon, S.D.B.; Cúria Diocesana Rua 9 de Julho 1010, Lins, SP, 16400-110, Brazil.
Tel: 55-014-3522-1622 *Fax:* 55-014-3522-1622
Email: diocese_lins@hotmail.com

Linz—Most Rev. Ludwig Schwarz, S.D.B.; Herrenstrasse 19, Postfach 251, Linz, A-4020, Austria.
Tel: 43-0732-772-676-1135 *Fax:* 43-0732-772-676-1137
Email: generalvikariat@dioezese-linz.at

LIPA—Most Rev. Ramon C. Argüelles; Archbishop's House St. Lorenzo Ruiz Dr., Lipa City, Batangas, 4217, Philippines.
Tel: 63-043-756-2572 *Fax:* 63-043-756-0005
Email: lipachancery@ymail.com

Lira—Most Rev. Giuseppe Franzelli, M.C.C.I.; Bishop's House P.O. Box 311, Lira, Uganda.
Tel: 256-0782-976-906 *Fax:* 256-0782-976-906
Email: liradiocese@gmail.com

Lisala—Most Rev. Louis Nkinga Bondala, C.I.C.M.; Evêché, c/o Procure Sainte Anne, B.P. 1800, Kinshasa 1, Democratic Republic of Congo.
Tel: 081-725-11-82
Email: dioceselisala@yahoo.fr

Lishui (Lishui)—Catholic Mission Bishop's House, Lishui, Zhejiang, China.

Lismore—Most Rev. Geoffrey Hilton Jarrett; Bishop's House 6 Keen St., P.O. Box 1, Lismore, N.S.W., 2480, Australia.
Tel: 61-02-6622-0407 *Fax:* 61-02-6621-9960
Email: chancery@lismore.catholic.org.au

Litomerice—Most Rev. Jan Baxant; Biskupský Ordinariát Dómské nám. 9, Litomerice, 412 88, Czech Republic.
Tel: 42-416-707-511 *Fax:* 42-416-707-524
Email: biskupstvi@dltm.cz

Little Rock—Most Rev. Anthony B. Taylor (LR); Chancery Office 2500 N. Tyler St., P.O. Box 7565, Little Rock, AR, 72217.
Tel: 501-664-0340 *Fax:* 501-664-6304
Email: bmcallister@dolr.org

LIVERPOOL—Most Rev. Patrick Altham Kelly; Centre for Evangelisation Croxteth Drive, Sefton Park, Liverpool, L17 1AA, England.
Tel: 44-0151-522-1012 *Fax:* 44-0151-522-1014
Email: j.davis@rcaol.co.uk

Livingstone—Most Rev. Raymond Mpezele; Bishop's House P.O. Box 60138, Livingstone, Zambia.
Tel: 260-213-321-667 *Fax:* 260-213-324-280
Email: seclivd@zamnet.zm

Livorno—Most Rev. Simone Giusti; Via del Seminario 61, Livorno, 57122, Italy.
Tel: 39-0586-27-62-11 *Fax:* 39-0586-27-62-43
Email: diocesi@livorno.chiesacattolica.it

Livramento de Nossa Senhora—Most Rev. Armando Bucciol; Rua Deoclides Alcantara 110, Livramento do Brumado, BA, 46140-000, Brazil.
Tel: 55-077-3444-2433

LJUBLJANA—Most Rev. Anton Stres, C.M.; Nadskofijski Ordinariat, Ciril-Metodov trg 4, p.p. 1990, Ljubljana, 1001, Slovenia.
Tel: 061-01-2342-600 *Fax:* 061-01-2314-169
Email: nadskofija.ljubljana@rkc.si

Lleida—Most Rev. Joan Piris Frigola; Palacio Episcopal, Calle del Bisbe 1, Lleida, 25002, Spain.
Tel: 34-973-26-9628 ***Fax:*** 34-973-27-2972
Email: cancalleria@bisbatlleida.org

Locri-Gerace—Most Rev. Giuseppe Fiorini Morosini, O.M.; Episcopio, Via Garibaldi 108, Locri, Reggio Calabria, 89044, Italy.
Tel: 39-0964-20-781 ***Fax:*** 39-0964-23-23-21
Email: curia@diocesilocri.it

Lodi—Most Rev. Giuseppe Merisi; Vescovado, Via Cavour 31, Lodi, 26900, Italy.
Tel: 39-0371-54-46-01 ***Fax:*** 39-0371-54-46-01
Email: cancelleria@diocesi.lodi.it

Lodwar—Most Rev. Dominic Kimengich; Bishop's House P.O. Box 101, Lodwar, 30500, Kenya.
Tel: 254-054-21-055 ***Fax:*** 254-054-21-417
Email: chancellor@dioceseoflodwar.com

LÓDZ—Most Rev. Wladyslaw Ziólek; Kuria Metropolitalna ul. Ks. Ignacego Skorupki 1, Lódz, 90-458, Poland.
Tel: 48-042-664-87-00 ***Fax:*** 48-042-664-87-96
Email: kuria@archidiecezja.lodz.pl

Loikaw—Most Rev. Sotero Phamo; Bishop's House, Loikaw, Kayah State, 09011, Myanmar.
Tel: 95-083-21-817/285 ***Fax:*** 95-083-21-285

Loja—Most Rev. Julio Parrilla Diaz; Casa Episcopal, Bernardo Valdivieso 07-50 y 10 de Agosto, Loja, Ecuador.
Tel: 593-07-2561-039 ***Fax:*** 593-07-2573-306

Lokoja—Most Rev. Martin Dada Abejide Olorunmolu; Bishop's House Maryville, P.O. Box 172, Lokoja, Kogi State, Nigeria.
Tel: 234-080-33-13-39-70; 234-080-55-97-21-57

Lokossa—Most Rev. Victor Agbanou; Evêché, B.P. 01, Lokossa, Benin.
Tel: 229-22-04-25-27
Email: eveche_lokossa@yahoo.fr

Lolo—Most Rev. Ferdinand Maemba Liwoke; Evêché de Lolo, B.P. 124, Bumba, Democratic Republic of Congo.

Lomas de Zamora—Most Rev. Jorge Rubén Lugones, S.J.; Obispado, Portela 433, Lomas de Zamora, Buenos Aires, B1832HX1, Argentina.
Tel: 54-011-4244-5253 ***Fax:*** 54-011-4292-6191
Email: obispadodelomas@ciudad.com.ar

LOMÉ—Most Rev. Denis Komivi Amuzu-Dzakpah; Archevêché, B.P. 348, 561 rue Aniko Palako, Lomé, Togo.
Tel: 228-222-26-10 ***Fax:*** 228-222-48-08
Email: archlom@yahoo.fr

Lomza—Most Rev. Stanislaw Stefanek, S.Chr.; Kuria Diecezjalna ul. Sadowa 3, Lomza, 18-400, Poland.
Tel: 48-086-473-46-11 ***Fax:*** 48-086-473-46-04
Email: kuria@lomza.opoka.org.pl

London—Most Rev. Ronald Peter Fabbro, C.S.B.; 1070 Waterloo St., London, ON, N6A 3Y2, Canada.
Tel: 519-433-0658 ***Fax:*** 519-433-0011
Email: info@rcec.london.on.ca

LONDRINA—Most Rev. Orlando Brandes; Rua Dom Bosco 145, Jardim Dom Bosco, C.P. 872,, Londrina, PR, 86060-340, Brazil.
Tel: 55-043-3371-3141 ***Fax:*** 55-043-3371-3141
Email: curialondrina@terra.com.br

Long Xuyên—Most Rev. Joseph Trân Xuân Tiéu; Toà Giám Muc, 80/1 Bui Van Danh, Tp. Long Xuyên, An Giang, Vietnam.
Tel: 84-076-3841-903 ***Fax:*** 84-076-3844-569
Email: tgmlx@gmail.com

Lorena—Most Rev. Benedito Beni dos Santos; Cúria Diocesana Rua Hepacaré 28, Lorena, SP, 12600-340, Brazil.
Tel: 55-012-3153-1256 ***Fax:*** 55-012-3153-1256
Email: curia@mitralorena.com.br

LOS ALTOS, QUETZALTENANGO-TOTONICAPÁN—Most Rev. Mario Alberto Molina Palma, O.A.R.; Arzobispado, Apartado 11, 11a Av. 6-27, Zona 1, Quetzaltenango, 09001, Guatemala.
Tel: 502-7761-2840 ***Fax:*** 502-7761-6049

LOS ANGELES—Most Rev. Jose H. Gomez; Archdiocesan Catholic Center Office 3424 Wilshire Blvd., Los Angeles, CA, 90010-2241.
Tel: 213-637-7000 ***Fax:*** 213-637-6000
Email: msgrrvadakin@la-archdiocese.org

Los Teques—Most Rev. Freddy Jesús Fuenmayor Suárez; Curia Diocesana Calle Guaicaipuro 115, 1201 Los Teques, Edo. Miranda, Venezuela.
Tel: 58-0212-321-96-92 ***Fax:*** 58-0212-322-33-01
Email: diocesisdelosteques@gmail.com

LOUISVILLE—Most Rev. Joseph E. Kurtz, D.D. (L); Chancery 212 E. College St., P.O. Box 1073, Louisville, KY, 40201.
Tel: 502-585-3291 ***Fax:*** 502-585-2466
Email: chancery@archlou.org

Lowicz—Most Rev. Andrzej Franciszek Dziuba; Stary Rynek 20, Lowicz, 99-400, Poland.
Tel: 48-046-837-4790 ***Fax:*** 48-046-837-43-49
Email: kuria@diecezja.lowicz.pl

Loyang (Luoyang)—Catholic Mission Bishop's House, Luoyang, Henan, China.

Lu An (Changzhi)—Catholic Mission Bishop's House, Changzhi, Shanxi, China.

LUANDA—Most Rev. Damião António Franklin; Arcebispado Largo do Palácio 9, C.P. 87, Luanda, 1230-C, Angola.
Tel: 0222-334-640 ***Fax:*** 0222-334-433
Email: spastoral@snet.com.ao

LUBANGO—Most Rev. Zacarias Kamwenho; Arcebispado C.P. 231, Lubango, Angola.
Tel: 02612-20-405; 0261-223-547 ***Fax:*** 0261-223-547
Email: arquidiocese.lubango@netangola.com

Lubbock—Most Rev. Plácido Rodríguez, C.M.F.; The Catholic Pastoral Center 4620 4th St., P.O. Box 98700, Lubbock, TX, 79499-8700.
Tel: 806-792-3943 ***Fax:*** 806-792-2953

LUBLIN—Most Rev. Stanislaw Budzik; Kuria Metropolitalna Skr. p. 198, ul. Ks. Prymasa Stefana Wyszynskiego 2, Lublin, 20-950, Poland.
Tel: 48-081-532-1058 ***Fax:*** 48-081-534-6141
Email: kanclerz@kuria.lublin.pl

LUBUMBASHI—Most Rev. Jean-Pierre Tafunga Mbayo, S.D.B.; Archevêché, 852 Av. Kapenda, Commune Lubumbashi, B.P. 72, Lubumbashi, Democratic Republic of Congo.
Tel: 099-70-31-991; 081-40-36-256 ***Fax:*** 023-48-601
Email: archidiolub@mwangaza.cd

LUCCA—Most Rev. Benvenuto Italo Castellani; Curia Arcivescovile Via Arcivescovato 45, Lucca, 55100, Italy.
Tel: 39-0583-430-91 ***Fax:*** 39-0583-430-944
Email: diocesi@diocesilucca.it

Lucena—Most Rev. Emilio Z. Marquez; Sentro Pastoral ng Diocesis P.O. Box 60, Isabang, Lucena City, 4301, Philippines.
Tel: 63-042-710-4585; 63-042-373-16-46 ***Fax:*** 63-042-710-4728
Email: dlucena2000@yahoo.com

Lucera-Troia—Most Rev. Domenico Cornacchia; Palazzo Vescovile, Piazza Duomo 13, Lucera, Foggia, 71036, Italy.
Tel: 39-0881-52-0882
Email: info@diocesiluceratroia.it

Lucknow—Most Rev. Gerald John Mathias; Bishop's House Hazratgunj, P.O. Box 70, Lucknow, U.P., 226001, India.
Tel: 91-0522-2615-644; 91-0522-2625-472 ***Fax:*** 91-0522-2624-885
Email: cbisluck@hotmail.com

Luçon—Most Rev. Alain Castet; Evêché, 30 Place Général-Leclerc, B.P. 219, Luçon CEDEX, 85402, France.
Tel: 2-51-28-5300 ***Fax:*** 2-51-28-5327
Email: chancelier@catho85.org

Luebo—Most Rev. Pierre-Célestin Tshitoko Mamba; Evêché de Luebo, B.P. 70, Kananga, Democratic Republic of Congo.
Tel: 081-814-4053
Email: luebodiocese@yahoo.fr

Lugano—Most Rev. Pier Giacomo Grampa; C.P. 5382, Borghetto 6, Lugano, CH-6901, Switzerland.
Tel: 41-091-913-8989 ***Fax:*** 41-091-913-8990
Email: curialugano@catt.ch

Lugazi—Most Rev. Matthias Ssekamanya; Bishop's House P.O. Box 87, Lugazi, Uganda.
Tel: 0752-695-146
Email: lugazi@africaonline.co.ug

Lugo—Most Rev. Alfonso Carrasco Rouco; Obispado, Apartado 12, Plaza de Santa María 1, Lugo, 27080, Spain.
Tel: 34-982-23-11-43 ***Fax:*** 34-982-28-41-38
Email: bispadodelugo@telefonica.net

Lugoj—Most Rev. Alexandru Mesian; Episcopia Români Unita, Str. Episcop Ioan Balan 6, Lugoj, RO-305500, Romania.
Tel: 40-0256-353-597 ***Fax:*** 40-0256-351-457
Email: episcopialugoj@bru.ro

Luiza—Most Rev. Léonard Kasanda Lumembu, C.I.C.M.; Evêché de Luiza, B.P. 70, Kananga, Democratic Republic of Congo.
Tel: 081-60-35-818; 099-45-33-140
Email: dioceseluiza@yahoo.fr

Lungro—Most Rev. Salvatore Nunnari, Apostolic Admin.; Vescovado, Corso Skanderbeg 54, Lungro, Cosenza, 87010, Italy.
Tel: 39-0981-94-72-34 ***Fax:*** 39-0981-94-72-34

Luqsor, Tebe—Most Rev. Youhannes Zakaria; Evêché Copte Catholique B.P. 23, Avenue El-Nil, Louxor, 85511, Egypt.
Tel: 20-095-237-2716 ***Fax:*** 20-095-237-4058

Lurín—Most Rev. Carlos Enrique García Camader; Obispado, Jr. Huàscar 328, Lurin, Lima, Peru.
Tel: 01-430-4121; 01-430-1134 ***Fax:*** 01-430-4121
Email: diolurin@speedy.com.pe

LUSAKA—Most Rev. Telesphore George Mpundu; Archdiocese 41 Wamulwa Rd., P.O. Box 32754, Lusaka, 10101, Zambia.
Tel: 211-255-973/4 ***Fax:*** 211-255-975/6
Email: adlseer@iconnect.zm

Lutsk—Most Rev. Markiyan Trofym'yak; Kuria Diecezjalna vul. Katedralna 17, Lutsk, 43016, Ukraine.
Tel: 0332-72-46-59 ***Fax:*** 0332-72-15-32
Email: luceoria@hotmail.com

LUXEMBOURG—Most Rev. Jean-Claude Hollerich, S.J; Archevêché, B.P. 419, 4 rue Génistre, L-2014, Luxembourg.
Tel: 352-02-46-20-23 ***Fax:*** 352-02-47-53-81
Email: archeveche@cathol.lu

Luz—Most Rev. Antônio Carlos Félix; Cúria Diocesana Rua Oito de Julho 153, Luz, MG, 35595-000, Brazil.
Tel: 55-037-3421-9000 ***Fax:*** 55-037-3421-9002
Email: mitraluz@catedralnet.com.br

Luziânia—Most Rev. Afonso Fioreze, C.P.; Bispado C.P. 122, Av. Claro Carneiro de Mendonça 199, Luziânia, GO, 72815-480, Brazil.
Tel: 55-061-3621-2022 ***Fax:*** 55-061-3621-2725
Email: mitradiocesanluziania@yahoo.com.br

LVIV—Most Rev. Mieczyslaw Mokrzycki; ul. Winniczenka 32, Lviv, 79008, Ukraine.
Tel: 0322-40-37-47 ***Fax:*** 0322-40-37-48
Email: rku@lviv.farlep.net

LVIV (UKRAINIAN)—Most Rev. Ihor Vozniak, C.Ss.R.; Ploscha Sviatoho Yura 5, Lviv, 79000, Ukraine.
Tel: 7-0322-61-08-94 ***Fax:*** 7-0322-61-08-94
Email: cerkvalviv@ugcc.org.ua

Lwena—Most Rev. Jesús Tirso Blanco, S.D.B; Cúria Diocesana C.P. 88, Lwena, Moxico, Angola.
Tel: 915-410-467
Email: dioceseluena@gmail.com

LYON—His Eminence Philippe Barbarin; Archevêché, 1 place de Fourvière, Lyon CEDEX 05, 69321, France.
Tel: 4-72-38-80-90 ***Fax:*** 4-78-36-06-00
Email: archeveche.de.lyon@wanadoo.fr

M

Maasin—Most Rev. Precioso D. Cantillas, S.D.B.; Chancery Office Maasin, Southern Leyte, 6600, Philippines.
Tel: 053-381-2033 ***Fax:*** 053-570-9215
Email: maasin_chancery@yahoo.com

Macapá—Most Rev. Pedro José Conti; Cúria Diocesana Rua São José 1790, Macapá, AP, 68906-110, Brazil.
Tel: 096-3222-0426 ***Fax:*** 096-3222-0087
Email: curiadiocesana@hotmail.com

Macau—Most Rev. José Lai Hung-seng; Paço Episcopal Largo da Sé, Macau, China.
Tel: 85-8397-5225 ***Fax:*** 85-2830-9861
Email: mdiocese@macau.ctm.net

MACEIÓ—Most Rev. Antônio Muniz Fernandes, O.Carm.; Cúria Metropolitana Av. D. Antônio Brandão 559/a, Maceió, AL, 57021-190, Brazil.
Tel: 55-082-3223-2732 ***Fax:*** 55-082-3372-7046
Email: curia@arquidiocesedemaceio.org.br

Macerata-Tolentino-Recanti-Cingoli-Treia—Most Rev. Claudio Giuliodori; Vescovado, Piazza S. Vincenzo Strambi 3, Macerata, 62100, Italy.
Tel: 39-0733-29-11-14 ***Fax:*** 39-0733-26-33-86
Email: segreteria@diocesimacerata.it

Machakos—Most Rev. Martin Musonde Kivuva; Bishop's Residence P.O. Box Box 344, Machakos, 90100, Kenya.
Tel: 044-21-554 ***Fax:*** 044-21-308
Email: bishopsomks@wananchi.com

Machala—Most Rev. Luis Antonio Sánchez Armijos, S.D.B.; Casilla 07-01-0707, Guayas 17-18, Machala, El Oro, Ecuador.
Tel: 593-07-293-2851 ***Fax:*** 593-07-293-7152
Email: diocesis_mach@hotmail.com

Machiques—Most Rev. Jesus Alfonso Guerrero Contreras, O.F.M.; Plaza Bolivar, 4021, Machiques, Est. Zulia, -Venezuela.
Tel: 063-73-0437; 063-73-4390 ***Fax:*** 063-73-4041

Mackenzie-Fort Smith—Most Rev. Murray Chatlain; Evêché 5117-52nd St., Yellowknife, NT, X1A 1T7, Canada.
Tel: 867-920-2129 ***Fax:*** 867-873-9021
Email: chancery.mackenzie@theedge.ca

MADANG—Most Rev. Stephen Joseph Reichert, O.F.M.Cap.; Archbishop's Residence P.O. Box 750, Madang, 511, Papua New Guinea.
Tel: 675-85-22-599 ***Fax:*** 675-85-22-596
Email: caom@global.net.pg

Madison—Most Rev. Robert Charles Morlino (MAD); Chancery Office 702 S. High Point Rd., P.O. Box 44983, Madison, WI, 53744-4983.
Tel: 608-821-3000 ***Fax:*** 608-821-3013
Email: diocese@madisondiocese.org

MADRAS AND MYLAPORE (MELIAPOR)—Most Rev. A. Malayappan Chinnappa, S.D.B.; Archbishop's House 41 San Thome High Road, Chennai, 600004, India.
Tel: 91-044-2464-1102/0833 ***Fax:*** 91-044-2464-1999
Email: archmsml@gmail.com

MADRE DI DIO A MOSCA—Most Rev. Paolo Pezzi, F.S.C.B; Malaya Gruzinskaya str. 27, Bldg. 2, Moskva, 123557, Russia.
Tel: 495-785-5434 ***Fax:*** 495-785-5470
Email: katmos@katmos.ru

MADRID—His Eminence Cardinal Antonio María Rouco Varela; Arzobispado, Bailén 8, Madrid, 28071, Spain.
Tel: 34-91-454-64-00 ***Fax:*** 34-91-542-79-06
Email: curiamadrid@planalfa.es

MADURAI—Most Rev. Peter Fernando; Archdiocesan Curia, Kosakulam Pudur, Madurai, 625007, India.
Tel: 91-0452-2566-198 ***Fax:*** 91-0452-2566-630
Email: secretaryab@yahoo.co.in

Magangué—Most Rev. Jorge Leonardo Gómez Serna, O.P.; Obispado, Calle 14A N. 3-28, Magangué, Bolívar, Colombia.
Tel: 57-952-5687-7686 ***Fax:*** 57-952-5687-8277; 57-952-5687-5711
Email: maganguedioc@cec.org.co

Magdeburg—Most Rev. Gerhard Feige; Bischöfliches Ordinariat Max-Josef-Metzger-Str. 1, Magdeburg, D-39104, Germany.
Tel: 0391-59-610 ***Fax:*** 0391-59-611-00
Email: ordinariat@bistum-magdeburg.de

Mahagi-Nioka—Most Rev. Sosthene Ayikuli Udjuwa; Evêché, B.P. 33, Mahagi, Ituri, Democratic Republic of Congo.
Tel: 081-500-99-63; 081-038-19-98
Email: ayiksosthene@yahoo.com

Mahajanga—Most Rev. Roger Victor Rakotondrajao; Evêché, rue Montee du Rova, B.P. 126, Mahajanga, 401, Madagascar.
Tel: 020-62-22-602 ***Fax:*** 020-62-23-103

Mahenge—Most Rev. Agapiti Ndorobo; Bishop's House, Kwiro P.O. Box 102, Mahenge, Tanzania.
Tel: 023-262-0342 ***Fax:*** 023-262-0319
Email: dmahenge@hotmail.com

Maiduguri—Most Rev. Oliver Dashe Doeme; Bishop's House P.O. Box 58, Maiduguri, Borno State, 600001, Nigeria.
Tel: 234-076-23-25-94 ***Fax:*** 234-076-34-22-46
Email: cathdiomaiduguri@yahoo.com

Mainz—His Eminence Cardinal Karl Lehmann; Bischöfliches Ordinariat Postfach 1560, D-55005, Bischofsplatz 2, Mainz, D-55116, Germany.
Tel: 49-06131-2530 ***Fax:*** 49-06131-253-401
Email: info@bistum-mainz.de

Maitland-Newcastle—Most Rev. William Joseph Wright; 841 Hunter St., Newcastle West, P.O. Box 780, Newcastle, N.S.W., 2300, Australia.
Tel: 02-4969-7677 ***Fax:*** 02-4969-7616
Email: chancery@mn.catholic.org.au

MAKASSAR—Most Rev. Johannes Liku Ada'; Keuskupan Agung, Jl. Thamrin 5-7, Makassar, Sulawesi Selatan, 90111, Indonesia.
Tel: 0411-315-744; 0411-312-706 ***Fax:*** 0411-326-674
Email: sekr_kams@yahoo.com

Makeni—Most Rev. George Biguzzi, S.X.; Bishop's House Teko Rd., P.O. Box 1, Makeni, Sierra Leone.
Tel: 076-696-961

Makurdi—Most Rev. Athanasius Atule Usuh; Bishop's House P.O. Box 21, 14 Kashim Ibrahim Road, Makurdi, Benue State, 970001, Nigeria.
Tel: 234-044-533-613 ***Fax:*** 234-044-532-919
Email: makurdiocese@yahoo.co.uk

MALABO—Most Rev. Ildefonso Obama Obono; Arzobispado, Apartado 106, Malabo, Bioko Norte, Equatorial Guinea.
Tel: 240-09-2909 ***Fax:*** 240-09-21-76
Email: arzobispadomalabo@hotmail.com

Málaga—Most Rev. Jesús Esteban Catalá Ibáñez; Calle Santa María 18, Málaga, 29015, Spain.
Tel: 34-952-22-43-86
Email: secretario-vicgen@diocesismalaga.es
Obispado, Apartado oficial 31, Malaga, 29071, Spain.

Málaga-Soatá—Most Rev. Victor Manuel Ochoa Cadavid; Obispado, Calle 13 N. 9-11, Málaga, Santander, Colombia.
Tel: 7-6608-512 ***Fax:*** 7-6607-734
Email: diocesismalagasoata@yahoo.es

Malakal—Vacant; Catholic Church P.O. Box 27, Malakal, U.N.S., Sudan.
Tel: 909-286-497

Malang—Most Rev. Herman Joseph Sahadat Pandoyoputro, O.Carm.; Jl. Guntur 2, Malang, Jawa, 65112, Indonesia.
Tel: 62-0341-362-524 ***Fax:*** 62-0341-323-744
Email: guntur_2@hotmail.com

MALANJE—Most Rev. Luis María Pérez de Onraita Aquirre; Bispado, C.P. 192, Malanje, Angola.
Email: malange.diocese@sat.signis.net

Malaybalay—Most Rev. Jose Araneta Cabantan; Bishop's Residence Datu Mampaalong St., P.O. Box 102, Malaybalay, Bukidnon, 8700, Philippines.
Tel: 088-813-3027 ***Fax:*** 088-813-3027
Email: malaybalaydiocese@yahoo.com

Maldonado-Punta del Este—Most Rev. Rodolfo Pedro Wirz Kraemer; Obispado, Calle José Dodera 820, Maldonado, 20000, Uruguay.
Tel: 598-042-222-325 ***Fax:*** 598-042-222-325
Email: ceumaldo@adinet.com.uy

Maliana—Most Rev. Norberto do Amaral; East Timor.

Malindi—Most Rev. Emmanuel Barbara, O.F.M.Cap.; P.O. Box 1573, Malindi, 80200, Kenya.
Tel: 042-21-30-767 ***Fax:*** 042-21-30-835
Email: malindidiocese@yahoo.com

Mallorca—Most Rev. Jesús Murgui Soriano; Obispado, Calle Seminari 4, Apartado 26, Palma de Mallorca, 07080, Spain.
Tel: 34-971-21-4370/3100 ***Fax:*** 34-971-72-5847
Email: bisbatmallorca@planalfa.es

Malolos—Most Rev. José F. Oliveros; Diocesan Center, Barasoain, Malolos, Bulacan, 3000, Philippines.
Tel: 044-791-0316; 044-662-7114 ***Fax:*** 044-791-2680
Email: diocese_of_malolos@yahoo.com

MALTA—Most Rev. Paul Cremona, O.P.; Archbishop's Curia P.O. Box 29, Valletta, VLT 1000, Malta.
Tel: 021-245-350 ***Fax:*** 021-242-971

Mamfe—Most Rev. Francis Teke Lysinge; P.O. Box 120, Mamfe, South West Province, Cameroon.
Tel: 7510-6513
Email: mamfediocese@gmal.com

Man—Most Rev. Gaspard Béby Gnéba; Evêché, B.P. 447, Man, Ivory Coast.
Tel: 225-3379-06-39 ***Fax:*** 225-3379-04-89
Email: evechman@aviso.ci

Manado—Most Rev. Joseph Theodorus Suwatan, M.S.C.; Jl. Sam Ratulangi 66, Kotak Pos 73, Manado, Sulawesi Utara, 95002, Indonesia.
Tel: 62-0431-864-225 ***Fax:*** 62-0431-861-543

MANAGUA—Most Rev. Leopoldo José Brenes Solórzano; Arzobispado, Sierritas de Santo Domingo, Apartado C-68, Managua, Nicaragua.
Tel: 505-02-276-0129/2436 ***Fax:*** 505-02-276-0130

Mananjary—Most Rev. José Alfredo Caires de Nobrega, S.C.I.; Evêché, Ampasimandrorona, B.P. 58, Mananjary, 317, Madagascar.
Tel: 034-16-47-305

Mananthavady—Most Rev. José Porunnedom; Bishop's House P.B. 1 Mananthavady, Wayanad Dt., Kerala, 670645, India.
Tel: 91-0493-5240-735; 91-0493-5240-745 ***Fax:*** 91-0493-5240-265
Email: bphmtdy@gmail.com

MANAUS—Most Rev. Luiz Soares Vieira; Cúria Metropolitana Av. Joaquim Nabuco 1023, Manaus, AM, 69020-030, Brazil.
Tel: 55-092-3212-9010 ***Fax:*** 55-092-3212-9011
Email: curia@arquimanaus.org.br

Manchester—Most Rev. John B. McCormack; Chancery Office 153 Ash St., P.O. Box 310, Manchester, NH, 03105-0310.
Tel: 603-669-3100 ***Fax:*** 603-669-0377
Email: webmaster@rcbm.org

MANDALAY—Most Rev. Paul Zinghtung Grawng; Archbishop's House 81st and 25th St., Mandalay, 06011, Myanmar.
Tel: 95-02-31-852 ***Fax:*** 95-02-39-531

Mandeville—Most Rev. Neil Tiedemann, C.P.; Catholic Pastoral Centre 59 Main St., Mandeville, Jamaica.
Tel: 876-962-1269 ***Fax:*** 876-962-1297
Email: diosofmville@gmail.com

Mandya (Syro-Malabarese)—Most Rev. George Njaralakatt; Bishop's House Jyothir Vikasa, Kalenahally, Mandya 571402, PB 5, Karnataka, 571401, India.
Tel: 08232-291-050; 08232-572-235
Email: mandyadiocese@gmail.com

MANFREDONIA - VIESTE-SAN GIOVANNI ROTONDO—Most Rev. Michele Castoro; Via Campanile 66, Manfredonia, Foggia, 71043, Italy.
Tel: 39-0884-58-18-44 ***Fax:*** 39-0884-51-6715
Email: curia@manfredonia.chiesacattolica.it

Manga—Most Rev. Gabriel Sayaogo; Evêché, B.P. 325, Manga, Burkina Faso.
Tel: 50-40-01-20/42 ***Fax:*** 50-40-01-72

Mangalore—Most Rev. Aloysius Paul D'Souza; Bishop's House Kodialbail, Mangalore, Dakshina Kannada, 575003, India.
Tel: 0824-244-0524

Mangochi—Most Rev. Alessandro Pagani, S.M.M.; Bishop's House P.O. Box 44, Mangochi, Malawi.
Tel: 1594-462 ***Fax:*** 1594-676
Email: mangochidiocese@malawi.net

MANILA—Most Rev. Luis Antonio G. Tagle; Arzobispado 121 Arzobispo St., Intramuros, Manila, 1099, Philippines.
Tel: 63-02-527-7631/6 ***Fax:*** 63-02-527-3956
Email: chancery@pldtsl.net

MANIZALES—Most Rev. Gonzalo Restrepo Restrepo; Arzobispado, Carrera 23 N., 19-22, Manizales, Caldas, Colombia.
Tel: 57-68-84-01-14; 57-68-84-33-44; 57-68-84-01-51 ***Fax:*** 57-68-82-18-53
Email: arquimanizales@hotmail.com

Mannar—Most Rev. Rayappu Joseph; Bishop's House, Pattim, Mannar, 41000, Sri Lanka.
Tel: 94-023-2222-710 ***Fax:*** 94-023-2222-709
Email: antonyvictorsosai@gmail.com

Manokwari-Sorong—Most Rev. Datus Hilarion Lega; Keuskupan, Jl. Jendral A. Yani 83, Kotak Pos 183, Sorong, Papua Barat, 98401, Indonesia.
Tel: 62-0951-321-201 ***Fax:*** 62-0951-321-201; 62-0951-323-794
Email: wiamapi@yahoo.co.uk

Manono—Most Rev. Vincent de Paul Kwanga Njubu; Evêché, B.P. 465, Manono, Katanga, Democratic Republic of Congo.
Tel: 0810-02-04-16; 099-591-40-30
Email: diocesemanono@yahoo.fr

Mansa—Vacant; Bishop's House P.O. Box 710036, Mansa, 710036, Zambia.
Tel: 212-82-13-73 ***Fax:*** 212-82-13-80; 212-82-18-87
Email: mansadiocese@zamtel.zm

Mantova—Most Rev. Roberto Busti; Palazzo Vescovile, Piazza Sordello 15, Mantova, 46100, Italy.
Tel: 39-0376-31-9511 ***Fax:*** 39-0376-22-4740
Email: info@diocesidimantova.it

Manzini—Most Rev. Louis Ncamiso Ndlovu, O.S.M.; Bishop's House Sandlane St., P.O. Box 19, Manzini M200, Swaziland.
Tel: 268-50-56-900 ***Fax:*** 268-50-56-762
Email: bishop@africaonline.co.sz

Mao-Monte Cristi—Most Rev. Diómedes Espinal de León; Casa Episcopal Apartado 37, Calle Trinitaria Esq. Maximo Cabral, Mao (Valverde), Dominican Republic.
Tel: 809-572-5022 ***Fax:*** 809-572-4962
Email: diocesismm@hotmail.com

MAPUTO—Most Rev. Francisco Chimoio, O.F.M.Cap.; Paço Arquiepiscopal, Avenida Eduardo Mondlane 1448, C.P. 258, Maputo, Mozambique.
Tel: 258-21-32-62-40 ***Fax:*** 258-21-32-18-73

Mar Addai of Toronto (Chaldean)—Most Rev. Hanna Zora; Canada.

Mar del Plata—Most Rev. Antonio Marino; Obispado, Pasaje Catedral 1750, Mar del Plata, Buenos Aires, B7600DQB, Argentina.
Tel: 54-0223-494-42-00 ***Fax:*** 54-0223-495-18-34
Email: omdp@iglesiamdp.org.ar

Marabá—Most Rev. José Foralosso, S.D.B.; Cúria Diocesana Trav. 13 de Maio 208, Marabá, PA, 68500-420, Brazil.
Tel: 55-094-3321-1339 ***Fax:*** 55-094-3321-1537
Email: diocese@skorpionet.com.br

MARACAIBO—Most Rev. Ubaldo Ramón Santana Sequera, F.M.I.; Arzobispado, Apartado 439, Calle 95 entre Avenidas 2y3, Maracaibo, Edo. Zulia, 4001, Venezuela.
Tel: 58-0261-7225-351 ***Fax:*** 58-0261-7211-730; 58-0261-7210-805
Email: arqui_maracaibo@yahoo.es

Maracay—Most Rev. Rafael Ramón Conde Alfonzo; Obispado, Av. Rótaria, Las Delicias, Maracay, Edo. Aragua, Venezuela.
Tel: 58-0243-2417-432; 58-0243-2417-065 ***Fax:*** 58-0243-2417-443
Email: dimarac@cantv.net

Maradi—Most Rev. Ambrose Ouédraogo; Evêché, B.P. 447, Maradi, 4000, Nigeria.
Tel: 20-410-330 ***Fax:*** 20-411-386
Email: evechemi@intnet.ne

Maralal—Most Rev. Virgilio Pante, I.M.C.; Bishops House P.O. Box 350, Maralal, 20600, Kenya.
Tel: 0656-2056 ***Fax:*** 0656-2056
Email: maralalcath@wananchi.com

Maramures—Most Rev. Vasile Bizau; Str. Vasile Lucaciu 50, Baia Mare, RO-430341, Romania.
Tel: 40-0262-213-398 ***Fax:*** 40-0362-814-531
Email: epgrcatmm@yahoo.com

Marbel—Most Rev. Dinualdo D. Gutierrez; Chancery Office P.O. Box 7869, Koronadal, South Cotabato, 9506, Philippines.
Tel: 083-228-2526 ***Fax:*** 083-228-2526

Margarita—Most Rev. Jorge Anibal Quintero Chacón; Calle Unión 11-20, Apartado 148, La Asunción, Edo, Nueva Esparta, 6301-A, Venezuela.
Tel: 58-0295-2422-740 ***Fax:*** 58-0295-2422-740
Email: diocmargarita@gmail.com

MARIA SANTISSIMA (IN ASTANA)—Most Rev. Tomash Peta; 3 Tashenova Str., P.O. Box 622, Astana, 010010, Kazakhstan.
Tel: 7172-37-29-35 ***Fax:*** 7172-37-29-27
Email: catholic_astana@mail.ru

MARIANA—Most Rev. Geraldo Lyrio Rocha; Arcebispado, Rua Direita 102, Mariana, MG, 35420-000, Brazil.
Tel: 55-031-3557-1237 ***Pager:*** 55-031-3557-1351 ***Fax:*** 55-031-3557-1364
Email: curiamariana@yahoo.com.br

Mariannhill—Most Rev. Pius Mlungisi Dlungwane; Bishop's House P.O. Box 11001, Mariannhill, Natal, 3624, South Africa.
Tel: 27-031-700-2704 ***Fax:*** 27-031-700-5600
Email: dom@telkomsa.net

Maribor—Most Rev. Marjan Turnsek; Nadškofijski Ordinariat, Slomškov trg 19, Maribor, 2000, Slovenia.
Tel: 059-080-100 ***Fax:*** 059-080-111
Email: ordinariat@nadskofija-maribor.si

Marília—Most Rev. Osvaldo Giuntini; Cúria Diocesana Av. Nelson Spielmann 531, C.P. 11, Marília, SP, 17500-970, Brazil.
Tel: 55-014-3433-9554 ***Fax:*** 55-014-3433-9554
Email: curia@diocesedemarilia.org.br

MARINGÁ—Most Rev. Anuar Battisti; Cúria Metropolitana Av. Tiradentes 740, Maringá, PR, 87012-360, Brazil.
C.P. 152, Maringa, PR, 87001-970, Brazil.
Tel: 55-044-3227-1706 ***Fax:*** 55-044-3226-1667
Email: curiamga@gmail.com

Maroua-Mokolo—Most Rev. Philippe Albert Joseph Stevens; Evêché, B.P. 49, Maroua, Diamaré, Cameroon.
Tel: 2215-28-35
Email: diocmm@yahoo.fr

Marquette—Most Rev. Alexander King Sample; Chancery Office 1004 Harbor Hills Dr., Marquette, MI, 49855.
Tel: 906-225-1141 ***Fax:*** 906-225-0437
Email bparis@dioceseofmarquette.org

Marsabit—Most Rev. Peter Kihara Kariuki; Bishop's House P.O. Box 6, Marsabit, 60500, Kenya.
Tel: 069-210-2025 ***Fax:*** 069-210-2023
Email: marsadio@wananchi.com

MARSEILLE—Most Rev. Georges Pontier; Archevêché, 14 Place du Colonel-Edon, Marseille CEDEX 07, 13007, France.
Tel: 4-91-52-38-23 ***Fax:*** 4-91-52-45-19
Email: archeveque-marseille@wanadoo.fr

Marthandom—Most Rev. Vincent Paulos Kulapuravilai; Bishop's House Christu Raja Puram, Marthandom, Kanyakumari Dt. Tamil Nadu, 629165, India.
Tel: 04651-270-180 ***Fax:*** 04651-272-910
Email: bpdiomar@vsnl.net

Masaka—Most Rev. Johh Baptist Kaggwa; Bishop's House, Kitovu P.O. Box 70, Masaka, Uganda.
Tel: 075-26-94-851 ***Fax:*** 256-0481-20-514

Masan—Most Rev. Francis Xavier Ahn Myonk-ok; Diocesan Office Masan-shi Happ'o-gu Odong-dong, 107-23, Kyongnam, Korea, 631-470, Korea, South.
Tel: 82-055-249-7015/7 ***Fax:*** 82-055-249-7018
Email: mssamu@hanmail.net
P.O. Box 23, Kyongnam, 631-600, Korea, South.

Masbate—Most Rev. Jose Salmorin Bantolo; Diocesan Pastoral Center, Masbate City, Masbate, 5400, Philippines.
Tel: 056-33-32-202 ***Fax:*** 056-33-32-202

MASERU—Most Rev. Gerard Tlali Lerotholi, O.M.I.; Archbishop's House 19 Orpen Rd., P.O. Box 267, Maseru, 100, Lesotho.
Tel: 22-31-25-65 ***Fax:*** 22-31-04-35

Massa Carrara-Pontremoli—Most Rev. Giovanni Santucci; Vescovado, Via Francesco M. Zoppi 14, Massa, 54100, Italy.
Tel: 39-0585-8990 ***Fax:*** 39-0585-81-02-87
Email: curia@massacarrara.chiesacattolica.it

Massa Marittima-Piombino—Most Rev. Carlo Ciattini; Vescovado, Piazza Garibaldi 1, Massa Marittima, Grosseto, 58024, Italy.
Tel: 39-0566-90-20-39 ***Fax:*** 39-0566-90-24-27

Masvingo—Most Rev. Michael Dixon Bhasera; Bishop's House P.O. Box 1400, Masvingo, Zimbabwe.
Tel: 039-263-465 ***Fax:*** 039-263-541
Email: bishopmd@zol.co.zw

Matadi—Most Rev. Daniel Nlandu Mayi; Evêché, B.P. 29, Matadi, Bas-Congo, Democratic Republic of Congo.
Tel: 099-89-23-646
Email: matadieclesia@yahoo.fr

Matagalpa—Most Rev. Rolando Jose Alvarez Lagos; Obispado, Calle de los Bancos, Apartado 53, Matagalpa, Nicaragua.
Tel: 2772-3730 ***Fax:*** 2772-3730

Matamoros—Most Rev. Ruy Rendon Leal; Apartado 70, Calle 5 entre Morelos y Gonzalez, Altos 37 s/n, Matamoros, Tamps., 87351, Mexico.
Tel: 52-868-813-55-11; 52-868-813-36-58 ***Fax:*** 52-868-816-06-08
Email: obispadodematamoros@hotmail.com

Matanzas—Most Rev. Manuel Hilario de Céspedes García Menocal; Calle 79 N. 30001, Matanzas, 40100, Cuba.
Tel: 53-045-245-120 ***Fax:*** 53-045-253-107

Matehuala—Most Rev. Lucas Martinez Lara; Calle Rayón 200, Matehuala, S.L.P., 78700, Mexico.
Tel: 488-88-266-02; 488-88-235-05 ***Fax:*** 488-88-235-05
Email: obispado@diocesisdematehuala.com

MATERA-IRSINA—Most Rev. Salvatore Ligorio; Arcivescovado, Piazza Duomo 7, Matera, 75100, Italy.
Tel: 39-0835-33-20-12; 39-0835-33-52-01 ***Fax:*** 39-0835-34-53-38
Email: arcidiocesimt@tin.it

Mati—Most Rev. Patricio H. Alo; St. John of the Cross Clergy House Compound Madang, Mati, Davao Oriental, 8200, Philippines.
Tel: 087-3883-707 ***Fax:*** 087-811-4190
Email: sjcmati@cbcpworld.com

Maturín—Most Rev. Enrique Pérez Lavado; Obispado, Calle Monagas 120, Maturín, Edo Monagas, Venezuela.
Tel: 0291-642-49-69; 0291-642-66-95 ***Fax:*** 0291-642-6695

Maumere—Most Rev. Gerulfus Kherubim Pareira, S.V.D.; Keuskupan J1. Mgr. Soegyapranoto 1, Maumere, Flores, 86113, Indonesia.
Tel: 0382-22-753 ***Fax:*** 0382-23-144
Email: keuskupan_maumere@yahoo.co.id

Mavelikara—Most Rev. Joshua Ignathios Kizhakeveettil; Catholic Bishop's House Punnamoodu, Mavelikara, Kerala, 690101, India.
Tel: 0479-2344-085 ***Fax:*** 0479-2344-083

Mawlamyine—Most Rev. Raymond Saw Po Ray; Upper Main Rd., Mayangone Quarter, Mawlamyine, Myanmar.
Tel: 057-24-018

Mayagüez—Most Rev. Alvaro Corrada del Rio, S.J.; Apartado 2272, Calle Obispado, Barrio Miradero, Mayagüez, 00681, Puerto Rico.
Tel: 787-833-5411; 787-833-5418 ***Fax:*** 787-265-7060

Mazara del Vallo—Most Rev. Domenico Mogavero; Vescovado, Piazza della Repubblica 6, Mazara del Vallo, Trapani, 91026, Italy.
Tel: 39-0923-90-27-12 ***Fax:*** 39-0923-90-27-12
Email: cancelliere@diocesimazara.it

Mazatlán—Most Rev. Mario Espinosa Contreras; Apartado 1, Canizalez y Benito Juárez, Mazatlán, Sin., 82000, Mexico.
Tel: 52-669-981-33-52 ***Fax:*** 52-669-981-0428
Email: obispadomazatlan2@yahoo.com.mx

Mbaïki—Most Rev. Guerrino Perin, M.C.C.I.; Evêché, B.P. 19, Mbaïki, Central African Republic.
Email: evechembaiki@yahoo.fr

Mbalmayo—Most Rev. Adalbert Ndzana; Evêché, B.P. 320, Mbalmayo, Cameroon.
Tel: 237-2228-1494 ***Fax:*** 237-2228-1494
Email: evechembalmayo@yahoo.fr

MBANDAKA-BIKORO—Most Rev. Joseph Kumuondala Mbimba; Archevêché, B.P. 1064, Mbandaka, Democratic Republic of Congo.
Tel: 081-596-70-59; 099-150-30-38
Email: mbandakabikoro@yahoo.fr

Mbanza Congo—Most Rev. Vicente Carlos Kiaziku, O.F.M.Cap.; Bispado de Mbanza Congo, C.P. 2, Luanda, Angola.
Email: diocesembanzacongo@gmail.com

MBARARA—Most Rev. Paul K. Bakyenga; Archbishop's Office P.O. Box 150, Nyamitanga, Mbarara, Uganda.
Tel: 256-0485-420-052 ***Fax:*** 256-0485-421-249
Email: mbarchd@utlonline.co.ug

Mbeya—Most Rev. Evaristo Marc Chengula, I.M.C.; Bishop's House P.O. Box 179, Mbeya, Tanzania.
Tel: 255-025-2503-138
Email: theoslaats1930@yahoo.com

Mbinga—Most Rev. John Chrisostom Ndimbo; Bishop's House P.O. Box 94, Mbinga, Peramiho, Tanzania.
Tel: 025-2640-307; 025-2640-070 ***Fax:*** 025-2640-070

Mbujimayi—Most Rev. Bernard Emmanuel Kasanda Mulenga; Evêché, B.P. 65, Kanshi, Mbujimayi, Kasaï Oriental, Democratic Republic of Congo.
Tel: 00243-081-5070-726
Email: chancelleriembujimayi@gmail.com

Mbulu—Most Rev. Beatus Kinyaiya, O.F.M.Cap; Bishop's House P.O. Box 49, Mbulu, Tanzania.
Tel: 027-253-3118 ***Fax:*** 029-253-3114
Email: mbuludiocese@Yahoo.com

Meath—Most Rev. Michael Smith; Bishop's House Dublin Rd., Mullingar,, Co. Westmeath, Ireland.
Tel: 353-044-93-48-841 ***Fax:*** 353-044-93-43-020
Email: secretary@dioceseofmeath.ie

Meaux—Most Rev. Albert-Marie de Monléon, O.P.; Evêché, 7 rue Notre Dame, B.P. 139, Meaux Cedex, 77107, France.
Tel: 33-1-64-36-4100 ***Fax:*** 33-1-60-44-0012
Email: diocese@eglisecatho-meaux.cef.fr

MECHELEN-BRUSSEL, MALINES-BRUXELLES—Most Rev. André-Joseph (Mutien) Leonard; Aartsbisdom, Wollemarkt 15, Mechelen, B-2800, Belgium.
Tel: 32-015-29-2628 ***Fax:*** 32-015-20-9485
Email: etienne.vanbilloen@skynet.be

MEDAN—Most Rev. Anicetus Bongsu Antonius Sinaga, O.F.M.Cap.; Jl. Imam Bonjol 39, Kotak Pos 1191, Medan, Sumatera Utara, 20152, Indonesia.
Tel: 62-061-451-6647/9768 ***Fax:*** 62-061-414-5745
Email: sekrkam@hotmail.com

MEDELLÍN—Most Rev. Ricardo Antonio Tobón Restrepo; Arzobispado, Calle 57 N. 49-44, Medellín, Colombia.
Tel: 57-4-251-7700; 57-4-251-83-06 ***Fax:*** 57-4-251-9395; 57-4-251-8306
Email: arquidiomed@une.net.co

Meerut—Most Rev. Francis Kalist; Bishop's House, 283 Roorkee Road, Meerut, Cantt., Uttar Pradesh, 250001, India.
Tel: 91-0121-2642-790 ***Fax:*** 91-0121-2630-091
Email: mrtdiocese@gmail.com

Melaka-Johor—Most Rev. Paul Tan Chee Ing, S.J.; 2101 Jalan Masai, Plentong, Johor, 81750, Malaysia.
Tel: 60-07-387-11-21 ***Fax:*** 60-07-387-24-98

MELBOURNE—Most Rev. Denis James Hart; James Goold House 228 Victoria Parade, P.O. Box 146, East Melbourne, Victoria, 8002, Australia.
Tel: 61-03-9926-5612 ***Fax:*** 61-03-9926-5613

Melfi-Rapolla-Venosa—Most Rev. Gianfranco Todisco, P.O.C.R.; Episcopio, Largo Duomo 12, Melfi, Potenza, 85025, Italy.
Tel: 39-0972-23-86-04 ***Fax:*** 39-0972-23-84-29
Email: curiamelfi@tiscali.it

Melipilla—Most Rev. Enrique Troncoso Troncoso; Obispado, Egana 399, Casilla 114, Melipilla, Chile.
Tel: 56-02-832-3456 ***Fax:*** 56-02-832-3456
Email: melipilla@episcopado.cl

Melo—Most Rev. Heriberto Andres Bodeant Fernandez; Obispado, Avda. Brazil 829, Melo, Dpto. de Cerro Largo, 37000, Uruguay.
Tel: 598-064-22-386
Email: obispadodemelo@hotmail.com

Memphis—Most Rev. James Terry Steib, S.V.D.; 5825 Shelby Oaks Dr., Memphis, TN, 38134-7316.
Tel: 901-373-1200 ***Fax:*** 901-373-1269

Mende—Most Rev. François Jacolin; Secrétariat de l'Evêché, 7 rue Mgr. de Ligonnès, Mende, 48000, France.
Tel: 4-66-65-61-93 ***Fax:*** 4-66-65-61-93
Email: chancelier_evechemende@yahoo.fr

Mendi—Vacant; Bishop's House P.O. Box 69, Mendi, Southern Highlands Province, 251, Papua New Guinea.
Tel: 675-54-91-102 ***Fax:*** 675-54-91-169
Email: dkaluza@datec.net.pg

MENDOZA—Most Rev. José María Arancibia; Arzobispado, Catamarca 98, Mendoza, M5500CKB, Argentina.
Tel: 54-0261-423-3862; 54-0261-425-09-16 ***Fax:*** 54-0261-423-3862
Email: cancilleria@arquimendoza.org.ar

Menevia—Most Rev. Thomas Matthew Burns, S.M.; 27 Convent Street, Greenhill, Swansea, W. Glam., Wales, SA1 2BX, England.
Tel: 44-01792-64-40-17 ***Fax:*** 44-01792-45-86-41
Email: pa@menevia.org

Menongue—Most Rev. Mário Lukunde; Bispado, C.P. 12, Menongue, Angola.
Tel: 049-280-095

Menorca—Most Rev. Salvador Gimenez Valls; Obispado, Ca'l Bisbe 8, Ciutadella de Menorca, Baleares, 07760, Spain.
Tel: 34-971-38-0343 ***Fax:*** 34-971-48-0796
Email: bisbatmenorca@planalfa.es

MERAUKE—Most Rev. Nicolaus Adi Seputra, M.S.C.; Keuskupan Agung, Jl. Raya, Mandala 30, Merauke, Irian Jaya, 99602, Indonesia.
Tel: 62-0971-326-210 ***Fax:*** 62-0971-326-574

Mercedes—Most Rev. Carlos María Collazzi Irazábal, S.D.B.; Obispado, Roosevelt 669, Mercedes, 75000, Uruguay.
Tel: 598-053-22-061 ***Fax:*** 598-053-22-061
Email: obismerc@adinet.com.uy

MERCEDES-LUJÁN—Most Rev. Agustín Roberto Radrizzani, S.D.B.; Arzobispado Calle 22 N. 745, Mercedes, Buenos Aires, B6600HDU, Argentina.
Tel: 54-02324-432-412; 54-02324-432-104; 54-02324-432-479 ***Fax:*** 54-02324-432-104
Email: arzomerce@yahoo.com

MÉRIDA—Most Rev. Baltazar Enrique Porras Cardozo; Arzobispado, Apartado 26, Avenida 4 Con Calle 23, Mérida, 5101-A, Venezuela.
Tel: 58-0274-252-57-86 ***Fax:*** 58-0274-252-12-38
Email: curiamer@gmail.com

MÉRIDA-BADAJOZ—Most Rev. Santiago García Aracil; Arzobispado Obispo San Juan de Ribera 2, Badajoz, 06002, Spain.
Tel: 34-924-22-28-47/8 ***Fax:*** 34-924-26-05-93
Email: cancilmeridaba@archimeridabadajoz.org

Merlo-Moreno—Most Rev. Fernando María Bargalló; Bernardino Rivadavia 694, Moreno, Buenos Aires, B1744BUN, Argentina.
Tel: 0237-4623-731; 0237-4636-225 ***Fax:*** 0237-4629-880
Email: obispadomm@gmail.com

Meru—Most Rev. Salesius Mugambi; Bishop's House P.O. Box 16, Meru, 60200, Kenya.
Tel: 254-064-32-261/317 ***Fax:*** 254-064-30-524

MESSINA-LIPARI-SANTA LUCIA DEL MELA—Most Rev. Calogero La Piana, S.D.B.; Arcivescovado, Via Garibaldi 67, Messina, 98122, Italy.
Tel: 39-090-66-841; 39-090-66-84-205 ***Fax:*** 39-090-66-84-206
Email: cancelleria@diocesimessina.it

Metuchen—Most Rev. Paul Gregory Bootkoski; 146 Metlars Ln., Piscataway, NJ, 08854.
Tel: 732-562-1990 ***Fax:*** 732-562-1399
Email: info@diometuchen.org
The Diocesan Center P.O. Box 191, Metuchen, NJ, 08840.

Metz—Most Rev. Pierre Raffin, O.P.; Evêché, 15 Place Sainte-Glossinde, B.P. 10690, Metz CEDEX 1, 57019, France.
Tel: 3-87-74-54-20 ***Fax:*** 3-87-37-00-62
Email: secretariat@eveche-metz.fr

Mexicali—Most Rev. José Isidro Guerrero Macías; Av. Morelos 192, Mexicali, B.C. Norte, 21100, Mexico.
Tel: 52-686-552-4009 ***Fax:*** 52-686-552-4596

MÉXICO—His Eminence Cardinal Norberto Rivera Carrera; Curia Arzobispal, Durango 90, Col. Roma, México, D.F., 06700, Mexico.
Tel: 55-5208-3200; 55-5208-2960 ***Fax:*** 55-5208-5350
Email: cancilleria@arprimex.org.mx

MIAMI—Most Rev. Thomas G. Wenski; The Chancery 9401 Biscayne Blvd., Miami Shores, FL, 33138.
Tel: 305-757-6241 ***Fax:*** 305-754-1897 (Chancery)
Email: information@theadom.org

Miao—Most Rev. George Palliparambil, S.D.B.; Bishop's House, Miao, Changlang Dt., Arunachal Pradesh, 792122, India.
Tel: 03807-222-975 ***Fax:*** 03807-223-229
Email: bpmiao@gmail.com

Miarinarivo—Most Rev. Jean Claude Randrianarisoa; Evêché, Miarinarivo-Itasy, 117, Madagascar.
Tel: 032-020-97-93
Email: diomiarinarivo@yahoo.fr

Middlesbrough—Most Rev. Terence Patrick Drainey; Diocesan Curia, 50A The Avenue, Linthorpe, Middlesbrough, Cleveland, TS5 6QT, England.
Tel: 44-01642-850-505 ***Fax:*** 44-01642-851-404
Email: bishopsecretary@dioceseofmiddlesbrough.co.uk

MILANO—His Eminence Angelo Cardinal Scola; Palazzo Arcivescovile, Piazza Fontana 2, Milano, 20122, Italy.
Tel: 39-02-85-561 ***Fax:*** 39-02-861-396
Email: cancelleria@diocesi.milano.it

Mileto-Nicotera-Tropea—Most Rev. Luigi Renzo; Via Episcopio 5, Mileto, Vibo Valentia, 89852, Italy.
Tel: 39-0963-33-8398; 39-0963-33-8397 ***Fax:*** 39-0963-33-8397
Email: curia@diocesimileto.it

Military Services, Archdiocese, U.S.A.—Most Rev. Timothy P. Broglio; Chancery P.O. Box 4469, Washington, DC, 20017-0469.
Tel: 202-719-3600 ***Fax:*** 202-269-9022
Web: www.milarch.org
Email: info@milarch.org

MILWAUKEE—Most Rev. Jerome E. Listecki; Chancery Office: Archbishop Cousins Catholic Center 3501 S. Lake Dr., P.O. Box 070912, Milwaukee, WI, 53207-0912.
Tel: 414-769-3300 ***Fax:*** 414-769-3408
Email: chancery@archmil.org

Minas—Most Rev. Jaime Rafael Fuentes; José Enrique Rodó 482, Minas, Lavalleja, 30000, Uruguay.
Tel: 598-044-223-77 ***Fax:*** 598-044-223-77

Mindelo—Most Rev. Ildo Augusto dos Santos Lopes Fortes; Cúria Diocesana C.P. 447, Mindelo, São Vicente, 2110, Cape Verde.
Tel: 231-88-70 ***Fax:*** 231-88-72
Email: diocesemindelo@cvtelecom.cv

Minna—Most Rev. Martin Igwemezie Uzoukwu; Bishop's House Ahmadu Bello Rd., P.O. Box 33, Minna, Niger State, Nigeria.
Tel: 234-066-221-046 ***Fax:*** 234-066-22-29-87
Email: cathsecminna@yahoo.com

MINSK - MOHILEV—Most Rev. Tadeusz Kondrusiewicz; ul. Revolutsionnaja 1/a, Minsk, 220030, Belarus.
Tel: 17-203-68-44 ***Fax:*** 17-226-90-92
Email: archdioces@catholic.by

Minya, Ermopoli Maggiore, Minieh—Most Rev. Ibrahim Isaac Sidrak; Evêché Copte-Catholique, B.P. 32, Minya, 61111, Egypt.
Tel: 20-086-362-007/343-904

Miracema do Tocantins—Most Rev. Philip Dickmans; Rua Dr. Francisco Aires 135, C.P. 10, Miracema do Tocantins TO, 77650-000, Brazil.
Tel: 55-063-9978-1120 ***Fax:*** 55-063-3363-1234
Email: diocesemirato@uol.com.br

Miri—Most Rev. Anthony Lee Kok Hin; Bishop's House P.O. Box 108, Tanjong Lobang, Miri, Sarawak, 98007, Malaysia.
Tel: 60-085-423-035; 60-085-439-870 ***Fax:*** 60-085-415-135

MOBILE—Most Rev. Thomas J. Rodi; Chancery Office 400 Government St., Mobile, AL, 36602.
Tel: 251-434-1585 ***Fax:*** 251-434-1588
Email: chancery@mobilearchdiocese.org

Mocoa-Sibundoy—Most Rev. Luis Alberto Parra Mora; Catedral San Miguel, Calle 7 N. 7-05, Mocoa, Colombia.
Tel: 57-8-429-5297 ***Fax:*** 57-8-429-5297
Email: leocafra@gmail.com

MODENA-NONANTOLA—Most Rev. Antonio Lanfranchi; Via Sant'Eufemia 13, Modena, 41121, Italy.
Tel: 39-059-213-3811 ***Fax:*** 39-059-213-3803
Email: curiaarcivescovile@modena.chiesacattolica.it

Mogadiscio—Vacant; C.P. 273, Ahmed Bin Idris, Mogadiscio, Somalia.
Tel: 252-01-20-184; 252-01-20-213c/o B.P. 94, Djibouti, Djibouti.
Tel: 253-35-01-40 ***Fax:*** 253-35-48-31
Email: evechcat@intnet.dj

Mogi das Cruzes—Most Rev. Airton José dos Santos; Cúria Diocesana, Rua Ipiranga 1469, Mogi das Cruzes, SP, 08730-000, Brazil.
Tel: 55-011-4724-9734 ***Fax:*** 55-011-4722-7745
Email: curiadiocesanamogi@uol.com.br

Mohale's Hoek—Most Rev. Sebastian Koto Khoarai, O.M.I.; St. Patrick's Cathedral P.O. Box 42, Mohale's Hoek, 800, Lesotho.
Tel: 266-22-785-342 ***Fax:*** 266-22-785-014
Email: diocesemhoek@leo.co.ls

Molegbe—Most Rev. Dominique Bulamatari; Evêché, B.P. 74, Procure Ste. Anne B.P. 1800, Gbado-Lite, Equateur, Democratic Republic of Congo.
Tel: 081-810-92-91

Molfetta-Ruvo-Giovinazzo-Terlizzi—Most Rev. Luigi Martella; Vescovado, Piazza Giovene 4, Molfetta, Bari, 70056, Italy.
Tel: 39-080-337-4235 ***Fax:*** 39-080-337-4231
Email: cancvescmolfetta@libero.it

MOMBASA—Most Rev. Boniface Lele; Catholic Secretariat Nyerere Ave., P.O. Box 84425, Mombasa, 80100, Kenya.
Tel: 254-041-231-18-01 ***Fax:*** 254-041-222-82-17
Email: catholicsecretariat@msarchdiocese.org

MONACO—Most Rev. Bernard Barsi; 6 rue des Fours, Monaco Ville, Principaute de Monaco, MC-98000, Monaco.
Tel: 33-93-30-77-86 ***Fax:*** 33-93-30-39-31
Email: chancellerie-mc@libello.com

MONCTON—Most Rev. André Richard, C.S.C.; 452 rue Amirault, Dieppe, NB, E1A 1G3, Canada.
Tel: 506-857-9531 ***Fax:*** 506-857-9533

Mondoñedo-Ferrol—Most Rev. Manuel Sánchez Monge; Obispado, Praza da Catedral 8, Mondoñedo, Lugo, -27740, Spain.
Tel: 34-982-52-1006 ***Fax:*** 34-982-52-1156Casa de la Iglesia Calle Miramar s/n, El Ferrol, A Coruna, 15401, Spain.
Tel: 981-35-32-95 ***Fax:*** 981-35-14-33
Email: obmondonedoferrol@planalfa.es

Mondovi—Most Rev. Luciano Pacomio; Vescovado, Via Vasco 17, Mondovi, Cuneo, 12084, Italy.
Tel: 39-0174-488-721 ***Fax:*** 39-0174-488-712
Email: cancelleria@diocesimondovi.it

Mongu—Most Rev. Evans Chinyama Chinyemba, O.M.I.; Bishop's Office P.O. Box 910449, Mongu, Western Province, Zambia.
Tel: 217-221-187 ***Fax:*** 217-221-984
Email: mongdioc@gmail.com

MONREALE—Most Rev. Salvatore Di Cristina; Palazzo Arcivescovile, Via Arcivescovado 8, Monreale, Palermo, 90046, Italy.
Tel: 39-091-640-24-24 ***Fax:*** 39-091-640-05-19
Email: curia@monreale.chiesacattolica.it

MONROVIA—Most Rev. Lewis Zeigler; Archbishop's Office 46 Ashmun St., P.O. Box 2078, Monrovia 10, 1000, Liberia.
Tel: 231-65-54-578
Email: archbishopofmonrovia@gmail.com

Mont-Laurier—Most Rev. Vital Massé; Evêché, 435 rue de la Madone, Mont-Laurier, Quebec, J9L 1S1, Canada.
Tel: 819-623-5530 ***Fax:*** 819-623-9523
Email: achalifoux@diocese-mont-laurier.org

Montauban—Most Rev. Bernard Ginoux; Secrétariat de l'Evêché, 6 Faubourg du Moustier, Montauban CEDEX, 82017, France.
Tel: 5-63-91-62-40 ***Fax:*** 5-63-91-62-44
Email: secretariat@catholique-montauban.cef.fr

Montego Bay—Vacant; Roman Catholic Chancery 1 Fort St., P.O. Box 197, Montego Bay, Saint James, Jamaica, West Indies.
Tel: 876-952-6678 ***Fax:*** 876-952-6679
Email: diosmbay@cwjamaica.com

Montelíbano—Vacant; Curia Diocesana Calle 17 N. 6-39, Montelíbano, Córdoba, Colombia.
Tel: 4-76-25-496 ***Fax:*** 4-76-25-496
Email: diomoneco@gmail.com

Montenegro—Most Rev. Paulo Antônio De Conto; C.P. 12, Rua Assis Brasil 1167, Montenegro, RS, -95780-000, Brazil.
Tel: 051-3632-3320 ***Fax:*** 051-3632-3320
Email: diocesemontenegro@diocesemontenegro.com.br

Montepulciano-Chiusi-Pienza—Most Rev. Rodolfo Cetoloni, O.F.M.; Vescovado, Via Fiorenzuola Vecchia 2, Montepulciano, Siena, 53045, Italy.
Tel: 39-0578-71-95-24 ***Fax:*** 39-0578-71-95-99
Email: diocesi@diocesimontepulciano.it

Monterey (in California)—Most Rev. Richard J. Garcia, D.D. (MRY); Pastoral Office 425 Church St., P.O. Box 2048, Monterey, CA, 93942-2048.
Tel: 831-373-4345 ***Fax:*** 831-373-1175
Email: diocese@dioceseofmonterey.org

Montería—Vacant; Obispado, Calle 27 N. 4-42, Montería, Córdoba, Colombia.
Tel: 57-4-782-31-22 ***Fax:*** 57-4-782-03-30
Email: curiaepiscopal@diocesisdemonteria.org

MONTERREY—His Eminence Francisco Robles Ortega; Aparatado 7, Zuazua 1100, Monterrey, Nuevo Leon, 64000, Mexico.
Tel: 81-1158-2450 ***Fax:*** 81-1158-2488
Email: cancilleria@arquidiocesismty.com

MONTES CLAROS—Most Rev. José Alberto Moura, C.S.S.; Cúria Metropolitana, Praca Dr. Chaves 52, Montes Claros, MG, 39400-005, Brazil.
Tel: 55-038-3221-8728 ***Fax:*** 55-038-3221-8728

MONTEVIDEO—Most Rev. Nicolás Cotugno Fanizzi, S.D.B.; Arzobispado, Calle Treinta y Tres 1368, C.C. 356, Montevideo, 11000, Uruguay.
Tel: 598-02-915-88-79 ***Fax:*** 598-02-915-89-26
Email: secretaria@arquidiocesis.net

MONTPELLIER—Most Rev. Pierre-Marie Joseph Carre; Villa Maguelonne, 31 ter ave. St. Lazare, CS 82137, Montpellier CEDEX 2, 34060, France.
Tel: 4-67-55-06-14 ***Fax:*** 4-67-55-85-01

MONTRÉAL—His Eminence Cardinal Jean-Claude Turcotte; Archevêché, 2000 rue Sherbrooke Ouest, Montréal, Quebec, H3H 1G4, Canada.
Tel: 514-931-7311 ***Fax:*** 514-931-3432
Email: chancellerie@diocesemontreal.org

Monze—Most Rev. Emilio Patriarca; Bishop's House Off Chivuna Rd., P.O. Box 660195, Monze, Zambia.
Tel: 260-213-250-316 ***Fax:*** 260-213-250-575
Email: secdiocese@gmail.com

Moosonee—Most Rev. Vincent Cadieux, O.M.I.; Evêché 2 Bay Rd., C.P. 40, Moosonee, ON, P0L 1Y0, Canada.
Tel: 705-336-2908 ***Fax:*** 705-336-2759
Email: rcdioceseofmoosonee@ontera.net

Mopti—Most Rev. Georges Fonghoro; Evêché, B.P. 45, Mopti, Mali.
Tel: 21-42-09-23 ***Fax:*** 21-43-00-56

Moramanga—Most Rev. Gaetano Di Pierro; Evêché, B.P. 24, Moramang 514, Madagascar.
Tel: 020-568-20-39

MORELIA—Most Rev. Alberto Suárez Inda; Arzobispado, Costado Catedral, Frente Ave. Madero Pte. s/n, Apartado 17, Morelia, Mich., 58000, Mexico.
Tel: 443-312-05-23; 443-312-37-37 ***Fax:*** 443-312-37-44
Email: arqmorelia@hotmail.com

Morogoro—Most Rev. Telesphore Mkude; Bishop's House P.O. Box 640, Morogoro, Tanzania.
Tel: 255-023-2603-340 ***Fax:*** 255-023-2613-341

Morombe—Most Rev. Zygmunt Robaszkiewicz, M.S.F.; Evêché, Morombe, 618, Madagascar.

Morón—Most Rev. Luis Guillermo Eichhorn; Obispado, Nuestra Señora del Buen Viaje 936, Morón, Buenos Aires, B1708ECR, Argentina.
Tel: 54-011-4629-3143 ***Fax:*** 54-011-4627-6892
Email: obmoron@speedy.com.ar

Morondava—Most Rev. Marie Fabien Raharilamboniaina, O.C.D.; Evêché, B.P. 132, Morondava, 619, Madagascar.
Tel: 020-95-923-45
Email: ekarmrdv@blueline.mg

Moroto—Most Rev. Henry Apaloryamam Ssentongo; Diocese of Moroto c/o Verona Fathers, P.O. Box 3872, Kampala, Uganda. P.O. Box 46, Moroto, Uganda.
Tel: 045-4470-086 ***Fax:*** 045-4470-086
Email: epimoroto@yahoo.com

Moshi—Most Rev. Isaac Amani Massawe; Chancery Office P.O. Box 3041, Moshi, Tanzania.
Tel: 255-027-2752-157 ***Fax:*** 255-027-2751-982
Email: bishophouse_moshi@yahoo.co.uk

Mossoró—Most Rev. Mariano Manzana; C.P. 16, Praça Coraçao de Jesus s/n, Mossoró, RN, 59600-970, Brazil.
Tel: 55-084-3314-7255 ***Fax:*** 55-084-3317-4785
Email: diocesedemossoro@uol.com.br

MOSSUL—Most Rev. Emil Shimoun Nona; Archevêché Chaldéen, Mayassa, B.P. 757, Mosul, Iraq.
Tel: 964-060-81-67-42 ***Fax:*** 964-060-81-67-42
Email: archdioceseofmossul@yahoo.com

MOSSUL (SYRIAN)—Most Rev. Boutros Moshe; Archevêché Syrien Catholique Hosh El-khan, Mosul, Iraq.
Tel: 0770-16-78-000
Email: khaddomouche1943@yahoo.com

Mostar-Duvno—Most Rev. Ratko Peric; Biskupski Ordinarijat, Nadbiskupa Cule BB, PP. 54, Mostar, 88000, Bosnia-Herzegovina.
Tel: 387-036-334-050 ***Fax:*** 387-036-334-080
Email: biskupija@cbismo.hr

Motherwell—Most Rev. Joseph Devine; Diocesan Centre, Coursington Rd., Lanarkshire, Motherwell, ML1 1PP, Scotland.
Tel: 44-01698-269-114 ***Fax:*** 44-01698-266-098
Email: chancellor@rcdom.org.uk

Mouila—Most Rev. Dominique Bonnet, C.S.Sp.; Evêché, B.P. 95, Mouila, Gabon.
Tel: 06-71-92-93; 07-82-52-03

Moulins—Most Rev. Pascal Roland; Maison Diocésaine Saint Paul 20 rue Colombeau, Moulins, CEDEX, 03000, France.
Tel: 4-70-35-1050 ***Fax:*** 4-70-35-1059

Moundou—Most Rev. Joachim Kouraleyo Tarounga; Evêché, B.P. 61, Moundou, Chad.
Tel: 235-269-13-70 ***Fax:*** 235-269-13-78
Email: evechemoundou@yahoo.fr

MOUNT HAGEN—Most Rev. Douglas Young, S.V.D.; Archbishop's Office P.O. Box 54, Mount Hagen, W.H.P 281, Papua New Guinea.
Tel: 54-21-285 ***Fax:*** 54-22-128
Email: santupol@online.net.pg

Mpanda—Most Rev. William Pascal Kikoti; P.O. Box 408, Mpanda, Tanzania.
Tel: 025-282-0127 ***Fax:*** 025-282-0138
Email: bishopmpanda@yahoo.com

Mpika—Most Rev. Ignatius Chama; Bishop's House P.O. Box 450007, Mpika, Zambia.
Tel: 214-370-438 ***Fax:*** 214-370-112

Mtwara—Most Rev. Gabriel Mmole; Bishop's House P.O. Box 526, Mtwara, Tanzania.
Tel: 255-023-2333-071 ***Fax:*** 255-023-2333-071
Email: diocese.mtwara@yahoo.com

Mukachevo—Vacant; pl. Andrea Bachinskoho 1, Uzhorod, 88000, Ukraine.
Tel: 380-0312-63-03-93 ***Fax:*** 380-0312-63-03-90
Email: eparchygc@utel.net.ua

Mukachevo (Latin)—Most Rev. Antal Majnek, O.F.M.; vul. Miru 15, 89600, Mukachevo, Ukraine.
Tel: 7-031-31-546-70 ***Fax:*** 7-031-31-546-70
Email: mrkp.titkar@gmail.com

MUKDEN (SHENYANG), FENGTIEN—Catholic Mission, Archbishop's House, Siao-Nan-Kuen, Shenyang, Liaoning, China.

Multan—Most Rev. Andrew Francis; Bishop's House 63 Aurangzeb Rd., P.O Box 133, Multan Cantt., 60000, Pakistan.
Tel: 92-061-451-2648 ***Fax:*** 92-061-458-6662
Email: catholicdiocese@gmail.com

MÜNCHEN UND FREISING—His Eminence Reinhard Cardinal Marx; Erzbischöfliches Ordinariat, Postfach 330360, Rochusstrasse 5, München, D-80063, Germany.
Tel: 49-089-213-70 ***Fax:*** 49-089-213-71-558
Email: generalvikariat@comuc.de

Münster—Most Rev. Felix Genn; Bischöfliches Generalvikariat, Domplatz 27, Münster, D-48143, Germany.
Tel: 49-0251-4950 ***Fax:*** 49-0251-495-285
Email: sekr.generalvikar@bistum-muenster.de

Muranga—Most Rev. James Maria Wainaina Kungu; P.O. Box 734, Murang'a, 10200, Kenya.
Tel: 020-261-51-67 ***Fax:*** 020-261-51-67
Email: cdmcath@yahoo.com

Murska Sobota—Most Rev. Peter Stumpf, S.D.B.; Skofijski ordinariat, Gregorciceva ulica 4, Murska Sobota, 9000, Slovenia.
Tel: 386-059-080-620 ***Fax:*** 386-059-080-622
Email: ordinariat@skofija-sobota.si

Musoma—Most Rev. Michael George Mabuga Msonganzila; Bishop's House P.O. Box 93, Musoma, Tanzania.
Tel: 068-028-2622-017 ***Fax:*** 068-028-2622-721
Email: abbamus@juasun.net

Mutare—Most Rev. Alexio Churu Muchabaiwa; Bishop's House Drumfrad, P.O. Box 47, Mutare, Zimbabwe.
Tel: 263-020-62347 ***Fax:*** 263-020-62347
Email: redomu@commone.co.zw

Muvattupuzha—Most Rev. Abraham Julios Kackanatt; St. Joseph's Church Mudavoor Post, Muvattupuzha, Vazhappilly, Kerala, -686669, India.
Tel: 0485-28-14-350; 0485-28-16-007

Muyinga—Most Rev. Joachim Ntahondereye; Evêché, B.P. 73, Muyinga, Burundi.
Tel: 22-30-67-19; 22-30-68-95 ***Fax:*** 22-30-68-95
Email: chancemuyi@yahoo.fr

Muzaffarpur—Most Rev. John Baptist Thakur, S.J.; Bishop's House Kalambagh Rd., Muzaffarpur, Muzaffarpur Dt., Bihar, 842001, India.
Tel: 91-0621-2243-225
Email: mdiocese@gmail.com

MWANZA—Most Rev. Jude Thaddaeus Ruwa'ichi, O.F.M.Cap.; Archbishop's House P.O. Box 1421, Mwanza, Tanzania.
Tel: 255-028-2501-029 ***Fax:*** 255-028-2501-029
Email: info@mwanzaarchdiocese.org

Mweka—Most Rev. Gérard Mulumba Kalemba; Evêché, B.P. 17, Mweka, Kasaï Occidental, Democratic Republic of Congo.

My Tho—Most Rev. Paul Bùi Van Doc; Tóa Giám Muc, 32 Hung Vuong, Phuong 7, Thanh-pho My Tho, Tiên Giang, Vietnam.
Tel: 84-073-3873-299 ***Fax:*** 84-073-3887-249
Email: vptgmmt@gmail.com

Myitkyina—Most Rev. Francis Daw Tang; Bishop's House, St. Columban's Cathedral Aungnan Yeiktha, Myitkyina, 01011, Myanmar.
Tel: 074-23-017; 074-23-016 ***Fax:*** 074-23-016
Email: myitkyinadioc@yahoo.com

Mymensingh—Most Rev. Paul Ponen Kubi, C.S.C.; Bishop's House Bhatikashor, P.O. Box 37, Mymensingh Town, 2200, Bangladesh.
Tel: 880-091-61-228/45-280

Mysore—Most Rev. Thomas Antony Vazhapilly; Bishop's House, Bangalore-Nilgiris Rd., P.B. 12, Mysore, Karnataka, 570001, India.
Tel: 91-0821-2448-395 ***Fax:*** 91-0821-2565-708
Email: bishmysore@rediffmail.com

Mzuzu—Most Rev. Joseph Mukasa Zuza; Bishop's House Katoto, P.O. Box 2, Mzuzu, Malawi.
Tel: 265-1-303-343 ***Fax:*** 265-1-303-470
Email: mzuzu-dio@malawi.net

N

N'Dali—Most Rev. Martin Adjou Moumouni; B.P. 45, N'Dali, Benin.
Tel: 23-62-09-41/42

Nacala—Most Rev. Germano Grachane, C.M.; C.P. 153, Nacala, Nampula, 78100, Mozambique.
Tel: 258-26-52-00-49 ***Fax:*** 258-26-52-00-48
Email: diocesencl@tdm.co.mz

NAGASAKI—Most Rev. Joseph Mitsuaki Takami, P.S.S.; Catholic Center 10-34 Ueno-machi, Nagasaki-shi, 852-8113, Japan.
Tel: 81-095-842-4450 ***Fax:*** 81-095-842-4460
Email: cnkn211@nagasaki.catholic.jp

Nagoya—Most Rev. Augustinus Jun-ichi Nomura; 2-6-35 Aoi, Higashi-ku, Nagoya-shi, 461-0004, Japan.
Tel: 81-052-935-2223 ***Fax:*** 81-052-935-2254
Email: curia@nagoya.catholic.or.jp

NAGPUR—Most Rev. Abraham Viruthakulangara; Archbishop's House 25 Kamptee Road, Mohan Nagar P.O., Nagpur, Maharashtra, 440001, India.
Tel: 91-0712-2533-765 ***Fax:*** 91-0712-2527-906
Email: jerome_p2006@yahoo.co.in

Naha—Most Rev. Berard Toshio Oshikawa, O.F.M.Conv.; Chancery Office 3 Chome 7-2, Asato, Naha-shi, Okinawa-ken, 902-0067, Japan.
Tel: 81-098-863-2020 ***Fax:*** 81-098-863-8474
Email: bishopnaha@aol.com

NAIROBI—His Eminence John Njue; Archbishop's House P.O. Box 14231, Nairobi, 00800, Kenya.
Tel: 254-020-2241-391 ***Fax:*** 254-020-4447-027
Email: arch-nbo@wananchi.com

Nakhon Ratchasima—Most Rev. Joseph Chusak Sirisut; Bishop's House 387 Suranari Rd., Nakhon Ratchasima, 30000, Thailand.
Tel: 66-044-274-535/256-268 ***Fax:*** 66-044-241-840
Email: diokorat@hotmail.com

Nakhon Sawan—Most Rev. Joseph Pibul Visitnondachai; Bishop's House 69/39 Daowadung Rd., Nakhon Sawan, 60000, Thailand.
Tel: 66-056-222-352; 66-056-312-893 ***Fax:*** 66-056-312-894
Email: nsdiocese@hotmail.com

Nakuru—Most Rev. Maurice Muhatia Makumba; Bishop's House P.O. Box 938, Nakuru, 20100, Kenya.
Tel: 254-051-2211-634 ***Fax:*** 254-037-2212-903
Email: cdnbshop@africaonline.co.ke

Nalgonda—Most Rev. Joji Govindu; Bishop's House Rashtrapathi Road, Nalgonda, A.P., 508001, India.
Tel: 91-08682-244-020 ***Fax:*** 91-08682-244-452
Email: bishopnlg@rediffmail.com

Namibe—Most Rev. Dionisio Hisiilenapo; Rua Che Guevara, C.P. 202, Namibe, Angola.
Tel: 02642-63-554 ***Fax:*** 02642-63-555
Email: diocesenamibe@gmail.com

NAMPULA—Most Rev. Tomé Makhweliha, S.C.J.; Paço Arquiepiscopal, C.P. 84, Nampula, 70100, Mozambique.
Tel: 258-26-21-30-24 ***Fax:*** 258-26-21-41-94
Email: info@arquidiocesenampula.net

Namur, Namen—Most Rev. Remy Victor Vancottem; Evêché, 1 rue de l'Evêché, Namur, B-5000, Belgium.
Tel: 32-081-25-10-80 ***Fax:*** 32-081-22-93-77
Email: secretariat.eveche.namur@skynet.be

NANCHANG (NANCHANG)—Catholic Mission Archbishop's House, Nanchang, Jiangxi, China.

Nancheng (Nancheng)—Catholic Mission Bishop's House, Nancheng, Jiangxi, China.

Nancy—Most Rev. Jean-Louis Papin; Evêché, 6 rue Girardet, B.P. 40260, Nancy CEDEX, 54005, France.
Tel: 3-83-17-2626 ***Fax:*** 3-83-17-2636
Email: evechedenancy.cn@wanadoo.fr

NANKING (NANJING)—China.

Nanning (Nanning)—Catholic Mission Archbishop's House, Nanning, Guanxi, China.

Nanterre—Most Rev. Gérard Daucourt; 85 rue de Suresnes, Nanterre CEDEX, 92022, France.
Tel: 33-1-41-38-12-30 ***Fax:*** 33-1-41-38-12-56
Email: vicaires@catholique-nanterre.cef.fr

Nantes—Most Rev. Jean-Paul James; B.P. 52204, 7 rue du Cardinal-Richard, Nantes CEDEX 3, 44322, France.
Tel: 2-40-76-22-00 ***Fax:*** 2-40-76-2226

Nanyang (Nanyang)—Catholic Mission Bishop's House, Kinkia Kang, Nanyang, Henan, China.

NAPOLI—His Eminence Crescenzio Sepe; Largo Donnaregina 22, Napoli, 80138, Italy.
Tel: 39-081-557-41-11 ***Fax:*** 39-081-45-17-97
Email: info@chiesadinapoli.it

Nardó-Gallipol—Most Rev. Domenico Caliandro; Vescovado, Piazza Pio XI 24, Nardó, Lecce, 73048, Italy.
Tel: 39-0833-87-16-59 ***Fax:*** 39-0833-87-46-51
Email: vescovo@diocesinardogallipoli.it

Nashik—Most Rev. Lourdes Daniel; Bishop's House Laxmibai St. Anne's Church, Jail Rd., Nashik Rd., Maharashtra, 422101, India.
Tel: 91-0253-2462-528 ***Fax:*** 91-0253-2451-550

Nashville—Most Rev. David R. Choby, D.D., J.C.L. (NSH); Chancery Office 2400 21st. Ave. S., Nashville, TN, 37212.
Tel: 615-383-6393 ***Fax:*** 615-292-8411

Nassau—Most Rev. Patrick Christopher Pinder; The Hermitage West St., P.O. Box N 8187, Nassau, W. I., Bahamas.
Tel: 242-322-8919 ***Fax:*** 242-322-2599; 242-322-7722
Email: rcchancery@batelnet.bs

NATAL—Most Rev. Matias Patrício de Macêdo; Cúria Metropolitana Av. Floriano Peixoto 674, C.P. 227, 59001-970, Natal, RN, 59020-500, Brazil.
Tel: 55-084-3615-2800 ***Fax:*** 55-084-3615-2800
Email: curia@arquidiocesedenatal.org.br

Natitingou—Vacant; Evêché, B.P. 102, Natitingou, Benin.
Tel: 229-23-82-12-04; 229-23-82-12-44 ***Fax:*** 229-23-82-12-44
Email: evechengou@yahoo.fr

Naval—Most Rev. Filomeno G. Bactol; Bishop's Office Burgos cor. Padre Inocentes St., Naval, Biliran Province, 6543, Philippines.
Tel: 053-500-9032 ***Fax:*** 053-500-9032

Navirai—Most Rev. Ettore Dottie; Brazil.

Navrongo-Bolgatanga—Most Rev. Alfred Agyenta; Diocesan Secretariat P.O. Box 351, Bolgatanga, U.E.R, Ghana.
Tel: 038-20-23-141; 038-20-22-273 ***Fax:*** 038-20-24-271

NAXOS, ANDROS, TINOS E MYKONOS—Most Rev. Nikolaos Printezis; Archevêché Catholique, Tinos, 84200, Greece.
Tel: 22830-22-382 ***Fax:*** 22830-24-769
Email: kamipai@cathecclesia.gr

Nazaré—Most Rev. Severino Batista de França, O.F.M.Cap.; Cúria Diocesana Praça Herculano Bandeira 35, C.P. 02, Nazaré da Mata, PE, 55800-000, Brazil.
Tel: 55-081-3633-1009 ***Fax:*** 55-081-3633-1302
Email: diocesedenazare@nazanet.com.br

Ndalatando—Most Rev. Almeida Kanda; Bispado, Rua da Missão C.P. 23, Ndalatando, Kuanza Norte, Angola.
Tel: 02352-801-73
Email: bispadondalatando@hotmail.com

N'DJAMÉNA—Most Rev. Matthias N'Gartéri Mayadi; Archevêché, B.P. 456, N'Djaména, Chad.
Tel: 235-2251-74-44 ***Fax:*** 235-2252-50-51
Email: archnja@intnet.td

Ndola—Most Rev. Alick Banda; Bishop's House 445 Evelyn Crescent, P.O. Box 70244, Ndola, Zambia.
Tel: 260-212-614-013; 260-212-612-241 ***Fax:*** 260-212-620-630
Email: diondola@zamnet.zm

Nebbi—Most Rev. Sanctus Lino Wanok; Bishop's House P.O. Box 88, Nebbi, Uganda.
Tel: 077-28-54-368

Neiva—Most Rev. Ramón Darío Molina Jaramillo, O.F.M; Calle 8 N. 5-58, Neiva, Huila, Colombia.
Tel: 57-88-871-74-54; 57-88-871-21-77 ***Fax:*** 57-88-871-30-11

Nellore—Most Rev. Moses Doraboina Prakasam; St. John's Minor Seminary, Subedarpet, Nellore, A.P., 524001, India.
Tel: 91-0861-2331-038 ***Fax:*** 91-0861-2323-950

Nelson—Most Rev. John Corriveau, O.F.M.Cap.; Chancery Office 402 West Richards St., Nelson, BC, V1L 3K3, Canada.
Tel: 250-352-6921 ***Fax:*** 250-352-1737
Email: nelson.diocese@telus.net

Netzahualcóyotl—Most Rev. Hector Luis Morales Sanchez; 4a Avenida con Bellas Artes, Col. Evolución, Ciudad, Netzahualcóyotl, Méx., 57700, Mexico.
Tel: 55-5797-61-32 ***Fax:*** 55-5792-45-61

Neuquén—Most Rev. Marcelo Angiolo Melani, S.D.B.; Opispado, Avda. Argentina 110, Neuquén, Q8300AYO, Argentina.
Tel: 54-0299-442-2866 ***Fax:*** 54-0299-442-2866
Email: obneuquen@speedy.com.ar

Nevers—Most Rev. Thierry Marie Jacques Brac de la Perriere; Evêché, 3 place du Palais, Nevers, 58000, France.
Tel: 3-86-61-02-89 ***Fax:*** 3-86-59-21-93
Email: philip.vivier@wanadoo.fr

NEW ORLEANS—Most Rev. Gregory M. Aymond (NO); 7887 Walmsley Ave., New Orleans, LA, 70125.
Tel: 504-861-6262 ***Fax:*** 504-866-2906

New Ulm—Most Rev. John M. LeVoir (NU); 1400 Sixth St., N., New Ulm, MN, 56073-2099.
Tel: 507-359-2966 ***Fax:*** 507-354-3667
Email: dnu@dnu.org

New Westminster—Most Rev. Kenneth Nowakowski; 502 5th Ave., New Westminster, BC, V3L 1S2, Canada.
Tel: 604-524-8824 ***Fax:*** 604-521-8015
Email: nweparchy@telus.net

NEW YORK—Most Rev. Timothy M. Dolan; 1011 First Ave., New York, NY, 10022-4134.
Tel: 212-371-1000 ***Fax:*** 646-794-3206
Email: silvana.usandivaras@archny.org

NEWARK—Most Rev. John J. Myers, D.D., J.C.D. (NEW); Chancery Office 171 Clifton Ave., P.O. Box 9500, Newark, NJ, 07104-9500.
Tel: 973-497-4000 ***Fax:*** 973-497-4018
Email: doranjoh@rcan.org

Newton (Melkite-Greek Catholic)—Most Rev. Nicholas J. Samra; The Chancery 3 Veterans of Foreign Wars Pkwy., Roslindale, MA, 02131.
Tel: 617-323-9922 ***Fax:*** 617-323-0944

Neyyattinkara—Most Rev. Vincent Samuel; Bishop's House, Neyyattinkara,, Aralummood P.O., Thiruvananthapuram, Kerala, 695123, India.
Tel: 0471-222-31-33 ***Fax:*** 0471-222-22-62
Email: ntabishopshouse@yahoo.co.in

Ngaoundéré—Most Rev. Joseph Djida, O.M.I.; Evêché, B.P. 513, Ngaoundéré, Cameroon.
Tel: 237-2225-20-89
Email: evqdiocndere@yahoo.fr

Ngong—Vacant; Diocese of Ngong P.O. Box 24801, Karen, 00502, Kenya.
Tel: 020-80-29-816 ***Fax:*** 020-80-29-816
Email: boffice@ngongdiocese.or.ke

Ngozi—Most Rev. Gervais Banshimiyubusa; Evêché, B.P. 2, Ngozi, Burundi.
Tel: 257-22-30-21-83 ***Fax:*** 257-22-30-21-50
Email: evechengozi@yahoo.fr

Nha Trang—Most Rev. Joseph Vo Duc Minh; Toà Giám Muc, 22 Tran Phu, B.P. 42, Nha Trang, Khánh Hoà, Vietnam.
Tel: 84-058-3523-842 ***Fax:*** 84-058-3522-494
Email: tgmnhatrang@gmail.com

NIAMEY—Most Rev. Michel Christian Cartatéguy, S.M.A.; Archevêché, B.P. 10270, Niamey, Niger.
Tel: 227-20-73-32-59 ***Fax:*** 227-20-73-80-01
Email: evecheny@intnet.ne

Nice—Most Rev. Louis Sankalé; Evêché, 23 av. Sévigné, Nice CEDEX 2, 06105, France.
Tel: 4-92-07-80-00 ***Fax:*** 4-92-07-80-25
Email: chancellerie@diocese06.fr

Nicolet—Most Rev. Andre Gazaille; Evêché 49 rue Mgr Brunault, Nicolet, QC, J3T 1X7, Canada.
Tel: 819-293-4696 ***Fax:*** 819-293-4653
Email: eveque@diocesenicolet.qc.ca

Nicopoli—Most Rev. Petko Jordanov Christov, O.F.M.Conv.; Evêché Catholique, 26/a Bratja Simeonovi str., Ruscuk, 7000, Bulgaria.
Tel: 082-835-245 ***Fax:*** 082-822-881
Email: diocesi_nicopoli@yahoo.com

Nicosia—Most Rev. Salvatore Muratore; Palazzo Vescovile, Largo Duomo 10, Nicosia, Enna, 94014, Italy.
Tel: 39-0935-64-60-40 ***Fax:*** 39-0935-64-60-40
Email: diocesi@nicosia.chiesacattolica.it

Niigata—Most Rev. Tarcisius Isao Kikuchi, S.V.D.; Bishop's House 656 Ichiban-cho, Higashi Ohata-dori, Niigata-shi, Niigata-ken, 951-8106, Japan.
Tel: 81-025-222-7457 ***Fax:*** 81-025-222-7467
Email: nig-cur@ecatv.home.ne.jp

Nîmes—Most Rev. Robert Wattebled; Evêché, B.P. 81455, 3 rue Guiran, Nîmes CEDEX 1, 30017, France.
Tel: 4-66-36-3350 ***Fax:*** 4-66-36-3356
Email: accueil@eveche30.fr

Níng Po (Ningbo), Ninghsien—Ciang-Pei-An, Catholic Mission, Ningbo, Zhejiang, China.

Ningsia (Yinchuan)—Catholic Mission Bishop's House, Yinchuan, Ningxia Hui, China.

Ningyüan (Xichang)—Catholic Mission Bishop's House, Xichang, Sichuan, China.

NITERÓI—Most Rev. Alano Maria Pena, O.P.; Cúria Metropolitana Rua Gavião Peixoto 250, Niterói, RJ, 24230-103, Brazil.
Tel: 55-021-3602-1700 ***Fax:*** 55-021-3602-1720
Email: gabinete.arquiepiscopal@arquidioceseniteroi.org.br

Nitra—Most Rev. Viliam Judák; Biskupský úrad, P.P. 46A, nam. Jana Pavla II 7, Nitra-Hrad, SK-950 50, Slovakia.
Tel: 42-037-772-1747 ***Fax:*** 42-037-772-1749
Email: nitra@kbs.sk

Njombe—Most Rev. Alfred Leonhard Maluma; Bishop's House P.O. Box 54, Njombe, Tanzania.
Tel: 026-278-2033 ***Fax:*** 026-278-2402
Email: njombe1@iwayafrica.com

Nkayi—Most Rev. Daniel Mizonzo; Evêché, B.P. 216, Nkayi, Republic of the Congo.
Tel: 06-670-87-36; 04-487-52-31
Email: kintuadi@yahoo.fr

Nkongsamba—Vacant; Evêché, B.P. 333, Nkongsamba, Cameroon.
Tel: 237-3349-1160 ***Fax:*** 237-3349-1160

Nnewi—Most Rev. Hilary Paul Odili Okeke; Diocesan Secretariat P.M.B. 5099, Nnewi, Nigeria.

Nocera Inferiore-Sarno—Most Rev. Giuseppe Giudice; Via Vescovado 4, Nocera Inferiore, Salerno, 84014, Italy.
Tel: 39-081-517-67-63 ***Fax:*** 39-081-92-04-52
Email: uff.informatico@diocesinocerasarno.org

Nola—Most Rev. Beniamino Depalma, C.M.; Vescovado, Via S. Felice 26, Nola, Napoli, 80035, Italy.
Tel: 39-081-512-3609 ***Fax:*** 39-081-512-1933
Email: curia@diocesinola.it

Nongstoin—Most Rev. Victor Lyngdoh; Bishop's House, Nongstoin, West Khasi Hills Dt., Meghalaya, 793119, India.
Tel: 09436-302-665

Northampton—Most Rev. Peter Doyle; Bishop's House Marriott St., Northampton, NN2 6AW, England.
Tel: 44-01604-715-635 ***Fax:*** 44-01604-792-186
Email: admin@northamptondiocese.com

Norwich—Most Rev. Michael Richard Cote, D.D. (NOR); 201 Broadway, Norwich, CT, 06360-0587.
Tel: 860-887-9294 ***Fax:*** 860-886-1670
Web: www.norwichdiocese.org

Nossa Senhora do Líbano em São Paulo—Most Rev. Edgar Madi; Cúria Eparquial Rua Tamandaré 355, Liberdade, São Paulo, SP, 01525-001, Brazil.
Tel: 011-3208-2904

Nossa Senhora do Paraíso em São Paulo—Most Rev. Fares Maakaroun; Cúria Eparquial Rua do Paraíso 21, Sao Paulo, SP, 04103-000, Brazil.
Tel: 55-011-3141-0639 ***Fax:*** 55-011-3171-3913
Email: monsenhorjoaquim@yahoo.br

Noto—Most Rev. Antonio Stagliano; Vescovado, Via Mons. Giovanni Blandini 6, Noto, Siracusa, 96017, Italy.
Tel: 39-0931-83-52-86 ***Fax:*** 39-0931-57-33-10

Nottingham—Most Rev. Malcolm Patrick McMahon, O.P.; Willson House 25 Derby Rd., Nottingham, NG1 5AW, England.
Tel: 44-0115-953-9800 ***Fax:*** 44-0115-953-9805
Email: bishop.chaplain@nrcdt.org.uk

Nouakchott—Most Rev. Martin Albert Happe, M.Afr.; Evêché, B.P. 5377, Nouakchott, Mauritania.
Tel: 02-52-50-427 ***Fax:*** 02-52-53-751

NOUMÉA—Most Rev. Michel-Marie-Bernard Calvet, S.M.; Archevêché, B.P. 3, rue Mgr-Fraysse, Nouméa, 98845, New Caledonia.
Tel: 687-26-53-53 ***Fax:*** 687-26-53-52
Email: archeveche@ddec.nc

Nouna—Most Rev. Joseph Sama; Evêché, Mission Catholique, B.P. 22, Nouna, Burkina Faso.
Tel: 20-537-005; 70-537-106
Email: econna@fasonet.bf

Nova Friburgo—Most Rev. Edney Gouvea Mattoso; Cúria Diocesana Rua Augusto Spinelli 41, C.P.96643, Nova Friburgo, RJ, 28610-190, Brazil.
Tel: 55-022-2522-2799; 55-022-2522-7332 ***Fax:*** 55-022-2533-1376
Email: mitranf@gigalink.com.br

Nova Iguaçu—Most Rev. Luciano Bergamin, C.R.L.; Cúria Diocesana Rua Dom Adriano Mandarino Hipolito 8, Nova Iguaçu, RJ, 26285-330, Brazil.
Tel: 55-021-2767-0472; 55-021-3767-7943 ***Fax:*** 55-021-2767-2876
Email: curia@mitrani.org.br

Novaliches—Most Rev. Antonio R. Tobias; Good Shepherd Cathedral Regalado Avenue Ext., Fairview Park 1, Quezon City, 1118, Philippines.
Tel: 02-461-50-51 ***Fax:*** 02-461-50-74
Email: novaliches_diocese@yahoo.com

Novara—Most Rev. Renato Corti; Vescovado, Via Puccini 11, Novara, 28100, Italy.
Tel: 39-0321-66-16-61 ***Fax:*** 39-0321-66-16-62
Email: curianovara@diocesinovara.org

Novo Hamburgo—Most Rev. Zeno Hastenteufel; Rua Joaquim Nabuco 543, Novo Hamburgo, RS, 93310-002, Brazil.
Tel: 55-051-3593-1755 ***Fax:*** 55-051-3594-6073
Email: mitranh@mitrnh.org.br

Novo Mesto—Most Rev. Andrej Glavan; Skofijski ordinariat, Kapiteljska ulica 1, p.p. 182, Novo Mesto, 8001, Slovenia.
Tel: 386-07-38-44-402 ***Fax:*** 386-07-38-44-416
Email: skofija.novo.mesto@rkc.si

Nsukka—Most Rev. Francis Emmanuel Ogbonna Okobo; Bishop's House P.O. Box 32, Nsukka, Enugu State, Nigeria.
Tel: 0803-746-48-38
Email: cathsec-nsk@yahoo.com

Nuestra Señora de la Altagracia en Higüey—Most Rev. Gregorio Nicanor Peña Rodríguez; Obispado, Apartado 1313, Ave. Dr. Vetilio Alfau Durán 12, Higüey, Dominican Republic.
Tel: 809-554-2431; 809-554-4120 ***Fax:*** 809-554-2827
Email: obispohiguey@codetel.net.do

Nuestra Señora de los Mártires del Líbano en México—Most Rev. Georges M. Saad Abi Younes, O.L.M.; Margaritas 382, Col. Florida, D.F., 01030, Mexico.
Tel: 55-5554-7014 ***Fax:*** 55-5554-0656

Nuestra Señora del Paraíso en México—Vacant; Obispado Greco-Melquita Católico Venustiano Carranza 107, México D.F., 06060, Mexico.
Tel: 55-5542-0225 ***Fax:*** 55-5559-4546

NUEVA PAMPLONA—Most Rev. Luis Madrid Merlano; Arzobispado Carrera 5 N. 4-87, Pamplona, Colombia.
Tel: 57-75-68-28-16 ***Fax:*** 57-75-68-4540
Email: pamplonaarq@cec.org.co

NUEVA SEGOVIA—Most Rev. Ernesto A. Salgado; Archbishop's House Vigan City, Ilocos Sur, 2700, Philippines.
Tel: 63-077-722-2018; 63-077-632-0783 ***Fax:*** 63-077-722-1591
Email: nschancery@yahoo.com.ph

Nueve de Julio—Most Rev. Martín de Elizalde, O.S.B.; Obispado, Edison 954, Nueve de Julio, Buenos Aires, B6500DRV, Argentina.
Tel: 54-02317-422-262 ***Fax:*** 54-02317-430-225
Email: cancilleria@internueve.com.ar

Nuevo Casas Grandes—Vacant; Av. Hidalgo 105, Nuevo Casas Grandes, Chih., 31700, Mexico.
Tel: 636-694-0520 ***Fax:*** 636-694-3615

Nuevo Laredo—Most Rev. Gustavo Rodriguez Vega; Veracruz 2426, Col. Madero, Nuevo Laredo, Tamps., 88270, Mexico.
Tel: 52-0867-711-2928 ***Fax:*** 52-0867-714-9135
Email: obispadonld@prodigy.net.mx

Nuoro—Most Rev. Mose Marcia; Curia Vescovile Piazza S. Maria della Neve 19, Nuoro, 08100, Italy.
Tel: 39-0784-230-416 ***Fax:*** 39-0784-208-359
Email: vicario@nuoro.chiesacattolica.it

Nyahururu—Most Rev. Luigi Paiaro; Catholic Diocese P.O. Box 842, Nyahururu, 20300, Kenya.
Tel: 020-239-22-69 ***Fax:*** 020-240-03-20
Email: cpnya@africaonline.co.ke

NYERI—Most Rev. Peter J. Kairo; Catholic Secretariat P.O. Box 288, Nyeri, 10100, Kenya.
Tel: 254-061-2030-446/7 ***Fax:*** 254-061-2030-435
Email: adn@wananchi.com

Nyundo—Most Rev. Alexis Habiyambere, S.J.; Evêché, B.P. 85, Gisenyi, Rwanda.
Tel: 07-883-05-255

N'ZÉRÉKORÉ—Most Rev. Raphaël Balla Guilavogui; Evêché, B.P. 45, N'Zérékoré, Guinea.
Tel: 66-26-42-42; 65-31-20-27

O

Oakland—Most Rev. Salvatore J. Cordileone; 2121 Harrison St., Oakland, CA, 94612-3788.
Tel: 510-893-4711 ***Fax:*** 510-893-0945
Email: chancellor@oakdiocese.org

Obala—Most Rev. Sosthene Leopold Bayemi Matjei; Evêché, B.P. 24, Obala, Lékié, Cameroon.
Tel: 237-2228-5623 ***Fax:*** 237-2228-5611

Oberá—Most Rev. Damian Santiago Bitar; Av. Libertad 75, Oberá, N336IDQA, Argentina.
Tel: 03755-405-320 ***Fax:*** 03755-405-320
Email: obispadooberа@hotmail.com

Obuasi—Most Rev. Gabriel Justice Yaw Anokye; Bishop's House P.O. Box 701, Obuasi, Ghana.
Tel: 032-25-40-480 *Fax:* 032-25-40-480

Ocaña—Most Rev. Jorge Enrique Lozano Zafra; Obispado, Carrera 13 N. 9-13, Ocaña, Norte de Santander, Colombia.
Tel: 57-74-5623-290 *Fax:* 57-74-5691-458
Email: diocesis.ocana@gmail.com

Odessa-Simferopol—Most Rev. Bronislaw Bernacki; vul. Katerininskaya 33, Odessa, 65045, Ukraine.
Tel: 048-728-64-75 *Fax:* 048-728-64-83
Email: kuria@catholic.od.ua

Odienné—Most Rev. Antoine Kone; Evêche, B.P. 162, Odienné, Ivory Coast.
Tel: 33-70-8806 *Fax:* 33-70-9968

Oeiras—Most Rev. Juarez Sousa da Silva; Cúria Diocesana Av. Prof. Rafael Farias 534, Oeiras, PI, -64500-000, Brazil.
Tel: 089-9984-1109; 089-3462-1710 *Fax:* 089-3462-1710
Email: dioceseoeiras@yahoo.com.br

Ogdensburg—Most Rev. Terry R. LaValley; Chancery Office 622 Washington St., P.O. Box 369, Ogdensburg, NY, 13669.
Tel: 315-393-2920 *Fax:* 866-314-7296
Email: vwoodard@dioogdensburg.org

Ogoja—Most Rev. John Ebebe Ayah; All Hallows Chancery P.O. Box 27, Ogoja, Cross River State, Nigeria.
Tel: 234-080-289-32-898
Email: ogojadiocese80@yahoo.com

Oita—Most Rev. Paul Sueo Hamaguchi; Bishop's House 3-7-30 Chuo-machi, Oita-shi, Oita-ken, 870-0035, Japan.
Tel: 81-0975-32-3397 *Fax:* 81-0975-38-6287

Okigwe—Most Rev. Solomon Amanchukwu Amatu; Catholic Secretariat P.O. Box 99, Villa Lourdes, Okigwe, Imo State, Nigeria.
Email: okigwecathdiocese@yahoo.com

OKLAHOMA CITY—Most Rev. Paul Coakley; Archdiocesan Curia 7501 Northwest Expressway, Oklahoma City, OK, 73132.
Tel: 405-721-5651 *Fax:* 405-721-5210
Email: eweisenburger@catharchdioceseokc.org

OLINDA E RECIFE—Most Rev. Fernando Antônio Saburido, O.S.B.; Av. Rui Barbosa 409, Gracas, Recife, PE, 52011-040, Brazil.
Tel: 55-081-3271-4270 *Fax:* 55-081-322-6536
Email: aorchance@ig.com.br

Oliveira—Most Rev. Miguel Ângelo Freitas Ribeiro; Cúria Diocesana C.P. 20, Praça Dona Manoelita Chagas 116, Oliveira, MG, 35540-000, Brazil.
Tel: 55-037-3331-1986 *Fax:* 55-037-3331-1986
Email: dioceseoliveira@yahoo.com.br

OLOMOUC—Most Rev. Jan Graubner; Arcibiskupský Ordinariát Biskupské náměstí 2, p. schr. 193, Olomouc, 771 01, Czech Republic.
Tel: 58-740-51-11 *Fax:* 58-522-22-44
Email: arcibol@arcibol.cz

OMAHA—Most Rev. George J. Lucas (OM); 100 N. 62nd St., Omaha, NE, 68132.
Tel: 402-558-3100 *Fax:* 402-558-3026
Web: www.archomaha.org

Ondjiva—Most Rev. Fernando Guimarães Kevanu; Bispado de Ondjiva, C.P. 20, Ondjiva-Kunene, Angola.
Tel: 02652-50-218 *Fax:* 02652-50-218
Email: secretaprocura@yahoo.com.br

Ondo—Most Rev. Jude Ayodeji Arogundade; Bishop's House P.O. Box 46, Akure, Ondo State, Nigeria.
Tel: 0803-842-8630

ONITSHA—Most Rev. Valerian Okeke; Archdiocesan Secretariat P.O. Box 411, Onitsha, Anambra State, Nigeria.
Tel: 234-046-41-3298
Email: secretariat@onitsha-archdiocese.org

Ootacamund—Most Rev. Amalraj Arulappan; Bishop's House Nilgiris Dt., Tamil Nadu, P.O. Box 5, Udhagamandalam, 643001, India.
Tel: 91-0423-2442-366 *Fax:* 91-0423-2447-996
Email: bishopooty@hotmail.com

Opole—Most Rev. Andrzej Czaja; Kuria Diecezjalna, ul. Ksiazat Opolskich 19, Opole, 45-005, Poland.
Tel: 48-077-454-3837 *Fax:* 48-077-453-7961
Email: kuria@diecezja.opole.pl

Oppido Mamertina-Palmi—Vacant; Via Rocco Pugliese 36, Palmi, Reggio Calabria, 89015, Italy.
Tel: 39-0966-419-811 *Fax:* 39-0966-419-823
Email: curia.op@i-2000net.it

Oradea Mare Gran Varadino—Most Rev. Virgil Bercea; Episcopia Română Unita Str. Mihai Pavel 4, apt. 15, Oradea, RO-410210, Romania.
Tel: 40-0259-436-492 *Fax:* 40-0259-430-509
Email: vicariat@egco.ro

Oradea Mare, Gran Varadino, Nagyvárad—Most Rev. László Böcskei; Episcopia Romano-Catolica Sirul Canonicilor 2, Cas. post. 14, Oradea, RO-410161, Romania.
Tel: 0259-41-11-80 *Fax:* 0259-41-11-80
Email: epiromca@rdsor.ro

Oran—Most Rev. Alphonse Georger; Evêché, 2 rue Saad Ben Rebbi, Oran El Maqqari, 31007, Algeria.
Tel: 213-041-28-3365 *Fax:* 213-041-28-2221
Email: evecheoran@yahoo.fr

Orán—Most Rev. Marcelo Daniel Colombo; Coronel Egües 720, A4530XBF San Ramón de la Nueva Orán, Salta, Argentina.
Tel: 54-03878-421-368 *Fax:* 54-03878-422-042
Email: obispadooran@arnet.com.ar

Orange (in California)—Most Rev. Tod David Brown, D.D. (ORG); 2811 E. Villa Real Dr., Orange, CA, 92867.
Tel: 714-282-3000 *Fax:* 714-282-3029
Email: info@rcbo.org

Orense—Vacant; Obispado Rua Progreso 26, Ourense, 32003, Spain.
Tel: 34-988-366-141 *Fax:* 34-988-366-142
Email: orcuria@obispadodeourense.com

Oria—Most Rev. Vincenzo Pisanello; Vescovado, Piazza Cattedrale 9, Oria, Brindisi, 72024, Italy.
Tel: 39-0831-84-50-93 *Fax:* 39-0831-84-98-44
Email: curia@oria.chiesacattolica.it

Orihuela-Alicante—Most Rev. Rafael Palmero Ramos; Calle Marco Oliver 5, Alicante, 03009, Spain.
Tel: 34-965-204-909; 34-965-204-822 *Fax:* 34-965-215-773
Email: obispado@diocesisoa.org

ORISTANO—Most Rev. Ignazio Sanna; Curia Arcivescovile Via Vittorio Emanuele 41, Oristano, 09170, Italy.
Tel: 39-0783-77-08-203 *Fax:* 39-0783-70-220
Email: vicariogenerale@oristano.chiesacattolica.it

Orizaba—Most Rev. Marcelino Hernández Rodriguez; Sur 9 N. 142 entre oriente 2 y 4, Orizaba, Ver., 94300, Mexico.
Tel: 272-724-48-75 *Fax:* 272-724-17-33
Email: dioriz@prodgy.net.mx

Orlando—Most Rev. John G. Noonan; Chancery Office 50 E. Robinson St., P.O. Box 1800, Orlando, FL, 32802-1800.
Tel: 407-246-4800 *Fax:* 407-246-4817
Web: www.orlandodiocese.org

Orléans—Most Rev. Jacques Andre Blaquart; Evêché, 14 Cloître Saint Aignan, Orléans CEDEX 1, 45057, France.
Tel: 2-38-78-86-00 *Fax:* 2-38-54-36-93
Email: vic.gen.orleans@club-internet.fr

Orlu—Most Rev. Augustine Tochukwu Ukwuoma; Bishop's House P.O. Box 430, Orlu, Imo State, Nigeria.
Tel: 0806-78-06-674
Email: orludiocesesec@yahoo.com

Oruro—Most Rev. Krzysztof Bialasik Wawrowska, S.V.D.; Obispado, Av. 6 de Octubre 6298, Casilla 368, Oruro, Bolivia.
Tel: 591-0252-57-922 *Fax:* 591-0252-57-922
Email: obis-or@coteor.net.bo

Orvieto-Todi—Vacant; Vescovado, Piazza Duomo 19, Orvieto, Terni, 05018, Italy.
Tel: 39-0763-341-264 *Fax:* 39-0763-395-008
Email: curiaorvieto@tiscali.it
Largo Mons. Antonio M. De Santis 4, Todi, Perugia, 06059, Italy.
Tel: 39-075-894-24-43

OSAKA—Most Rev. Leo Jun Ikenaga, S.J.; Tamatsukuri 2-24-22, Chuo-ku, Osaka-shi, 540-0004, Japan.
Tel: 81-06-6941-9700 *Fax:* 81-06-6946-1345
Email: curia@osaka.catholic.jp

Osasco—Most Rev. Ercílio Turco; Rua da Saudade 60, Osasco, SP, 06080-000, Brazil.
Tel: 011-3683-4522 *Fax:* 011-3683-7071
Email: curiaosasco@ig.com.br

Oslo—Most Rev. Markus Bernt Eidsvig, C.R.S.A.; Oslo Katolske Bispedomme Akersveien 5, Oslo, N-0177, Norway.
Tel: 47-2321-9506 *Fax:* 47-2321-9501
Email: arne.kirsebom@katolsk.no

Osma-Soria—Most Rev. Gerardo Melgar Viciosa; Obispado, Calle Mayor 52, El Burgo de Osma, Soria, 42300, Spain.
Tel: 975-34-09-62 ***Fax:*** 975-36-03-80Casa Diocesana, San Juan 5, Soria, 42003, Spain.
Tel: 975-21-21-76 ***Fax:*** 975-22-96-62
Email: cancilleria@osma-soria.org

Osnabrück—Most Rev. Franz-Josef Hermann Bode; Hasestrasse 40/A, Osnabrück, D-49074, Germany.
Tel: 49-0541-318-0 ***Fax:*** 49-0541-318-117
Email: generalvikariat@bistum-os.de

Osogbo—Most Rev. Gabriel 'Leke Abegunrin; Bishop's House P.O. Box 78, Oke-Ayepe, Osogbo, Osun State, Nigeria.
Tel: 035-24-10-84; 035-20-68-89 ***Fax:*** 035-24-22-84
Email: katolicdioceseosogbo@yahoo.co.uk

Osório—Most Rev. Jaime Pedro Kohl, P.S.D.P.; Cúria Diocesana Rua Dr. Mário Santo Dani 218, C.P. 21, Osório, RS, 95520-000, Brazil.
Tel: 051-3601-1443; 051-3663-4282 ***Fax:*** 051-3663-4282
Email: mitraoso@terra.com.br

Osorno—Most Rev. René Osvaldo Rebolledo Salinas; Calle Juan Mackenna 980, Osorno, Chile.
Tel: 56-064-55-76-10 ***Fax:*** 56-064-55-76-16
Email: osorno@episcopado.cl

Ossory—Most Rev. Séamus Freeman, S.A.C.; Sion House, Kilkenny, Ireland.
Tel: 056-7762-448 ***Fax:*** 056-7763-753
Email: admin@ossory.ie

Ostrava-Opava—Most Rev. František Václav Lobkowicz, O.Praem; Kostelní nám. 1, Ostrava 1, 728 02, Czech Republic.
Tel: 59-611-6522 ***Fax:*** 59-611-4819
Email: kurie@doo.cz

OTRANTO—Most Rev. Donato Negro; Piazza Basilica 1, Otranto, Lecce, 73028, Italy.
Tel: 39-0836-80-11-33 ***Fax:*** 39-0836-80-11-33
Email: curia@otranto.chiesacattolica.it

OTTAWA—Most Rev. Terrence Thomas Prendergast, S.J.; Archevêché, 1247 Kilborn place, Ottawa, ON, K1H 6K9, Canada.
Tel: 613-738-5025 ***Fax:*** 613-738-0130
Email: reception@archottawa.ca

Otukpo—Most Rev. Michael Ekwoy Apochi; Bishop's House P.O. Box 1400, Otukpo, Benue State, Nigeria.
Tel: 044-662-221 ***Fax:*** 044-662-220
Email: otcathdi@yahoo.com

OUAGADOUGOU—Most Rev. Philippe Ouédraogo; Archevêché, 01 B.P. 1472, Ouagadougou 01, Burkina Faso.
Tel: 226-50-30-67-04 ***Fax:*** 226-50-30-72-75

Ouahigouya—Most Rev. Justin Kientega; Evêché, B.P. 33, Ouahigouya, Burkina Faso.
Tel: 40-55-02-10 ***Fax:*** 40-55-03-49
Email: eveo@fasonet.bf

Oudtshoorn—Most Rev. Francisco Fortunato de Gouveia; Bishop's House 42 St. Saviours St., P.O. Box 97, Oudtshoorn, 6620, South Africa.
Tel: 044-279-1715 ***Fax:*** 044-272-8908
Email: bisdmodn@mweb.co.za

Ouesso—Most Rev. Yves Marie Monot, C.S.Sp.; Evêché, B.P. 81, Ouesso, Republic of the Congo.
Tel: 06-960-59-47; 06-650-19-46
Email: diocese_ouesso@yahoo.fr

Our Lady of Deliverance—Most Rev. Yousif B. Habash; 317 Avenue E, Bayonne, NJ, 07002-4678.
Tel: 201-455-8151 ***Fax:*** 201-455-8152
Email: marbarnaba@yahoo.com

Our Lady of Lebanon of Los Angeles—Most Rev. Robert Joseph Shaheen (OLL); 1021 S. 10th St., St. Louis, MO, 63104.
Tel: 314-231-1021 ***Fax:*** 314-231-1418
Email: stsharbel@sbcglobal.net

Our Lady of Nareg (in New York)—Most Rev. Mikael Antoine Mouradian, I.C.P.B.; 167 N. 6th St., Brooklyn, NY, 11211.
Tel: 718-388-4218 ***Fax:*** 718-486-0615

Ourinhos—Most Rev. Salvatore Paruzzo; Bispado, Rua Arlindo Luz 442, Ourinhos, SP, 19900-010, Brazil.
Tel: 014-3322-4929 ***Fax:*** 014-3322-4929

OVIEDO—Most Rev. Jesús Sanz Montes, O.F.M.; Arzobispado Corrada del Obispo 1, Oviedo, 33003, Spain.
Tel: 34-985-20-9728 ***Fax:*** 34-985-21-6428
Email: vicgeneral@iglesiadeasturias.org

Owando—Most Rev. Victor Abagna Mossa; Evêché, B.P. 06, Owando, Republic of the Congo.
Tel: 00870-509-50-20; 00870-636-53-80
Email: owandod@yahoo.fr

Owensboro—Most Rev. William F. Medley; Chancery Office 600 Locust St., Owensboro, KY, 42301-2130.
Tel: 270-683-1545 ***Fax:*** 270-683-6883

OWERRI—Most Rev. Anthony John Valentine Obinna; Villa Assumpta P.O. Box 85, Owerri, Imo State, Nigeria.
Tel: 234-080-606-84-482
Email: owcatsec@owerriarchdiocese.org

Oyem—Most Rev. Jean-Vincent Ondo Eyene; Evêché, B.P. 209, Oyem, Gabon.
Tel: 241-98-6011 ***Fax:*** 241-98-6320

Oyo—Most Rev. Emmanuel Adetoyese Badejo; Bishop's House Mariama Rd., P.O. Box 1480, Oyo, Nigeria.
Tel: 080-343-32-679
Email: oluzafrank@yahoo.com

OZAMIZ—Most Rev. Jesus A. Dosado, C.M.; Archbishop's House Rizal Avenue, Bañadero, P.O. Box 2760, Ozamiz City, 7200, Philippines.
Tel: 088-521-2771; 088-521-1574 ***Fax:*** 088-521-1574

Ozieri—Most Rev. Sergio Pintor; Piazza Episcopio 1, Ozieri, Sassari, 07014, Italy.
Tel: 39-079-78-72-10 ***Fax:*** 39-079-78-72-10
Email: dioc.oziericuria@tiscali.it

P

Padang—Most Rev. Martinus Dogma Situmorang, O.F.M.Cap.; Jl. Khairil Anwar 12, Padang, Sumbar, 25118, Indonesia.
Tel: 62-0751-32-816 ***Fax:*** 62-0751-20-743

PADERBORN—Most Rev. Hans-Josef Becker; Erzbischöfliches Generalvikariat Domplatz 3, Paderborn, D-33098, Germany.
Tel: 49-05251-1250 ***Fax:*** 49-05251-1251-470
Email: generalvikariat@erzbistum-paderborn.de

Padova—Most Rev. Antonio Mattiazzo; Via Dietro Duomo 15, Padova, 35139, Italy.
Tel: 39-049-822-61-11 ***Fax:*** 39-049-822-61-50
Email: diocesi@diocesipadova.it

Pagadian—Most Rev. Emmanuel T. Cabajar, C.Ss.R.; Bishop's Residence, Balangasan, P.O. Box 1400, Pagadian City, 7016, Philippines.
Tel: 63-062-215-15-33; 63-062-215-37-11

Paisley—Most Rev. Philip Tartaglia; Diocesan Offices Cathedral Precincts Incle St., Paisley, PA1 1HR, Scotland.
Tel: 0141-847-6130 ***Fax:*** 0141-847-6140
Email: curia@redop.org.uk

Pakhoi (Beihai)—Catholic Mission Bishop's House, Beihai, Guangdong, China.

Pala—Most Rev. Jean-Claude Bouchard, O.M.I.; Evêché B.P. 9, Pala, Chad.
Tel: 00871-762-698-714 ***Fax:*** 00871-762-698-716
Email: dioc.pala@sat.signis.net

Palai—Most Rev. Joseph Kallarangatt; Bishop's House Post Bag 18, Palai, Kerala, 686575, India.
Tel: 91-04822-221-22-16/7; 91-04822-221-4338 ***Fax:*** 91-04822-221-1379
Email: aramanapala@sancharnet.in

Palangkaraya—Most Rev. Aloysius Maryadi Sutrisnaatmaka, M.S.F.; Jl. Tjilik Riwut 6, Palangkaraya, Kalimantan Tengah, 73112, Indonesia.
Tel: 0536-323-15-13 ***Fax:*** 0536-323-15-12
Email: kepraya_uskup@yahoo.com

Palayamkottai—Most Rev. Arockiasamy Jude Gerald Paulraj; Catholic Bishop's House P.O. Box 108, Palayamkottai, Tirunelvely Dt., Tamil Nadu, 627002, India.
Tel: 0462-252-21-14 ***Fax:*** 0462-252-20-42
Email: rcdiopalayamkottai@yahoo.com

Palembang—Most Rev. Aloysius Sudarso, S.C.I.; Keuskupan Agung Jl. Tasik 18, Palembang, 30135, Indonesia.
Tel: 62-0711-350-417 ***Fax:*** 62-0711-314-776
Email: alva@mdp.net.id

Palencia—Most Rev. Esteban Escudero Torres; Obispado Calle Mayor Antigua 22, Palencia, 34005, Spain.
Tel: 34-979-70-69-13 ***Fax:*** 34-979-74-53-14
Email: obpalencia@planalfa.es

PALERMO—His Eminence Paolo Cardinal Romeo; Curia Arcivescovile Corso Vittorio Emanuele 461, Palermo, 90134, Italy.
Tel: 39-091-607-71-11 *Fax:* 39-091-611-36-42
Email: curia@diocesipa.it

Palestrina—Most Rev. Domenico Sigalini; Curia Vescovile Piazza Gregorio Pantanelli 8, Palestrina, Roma, 00036, Italy.
Tel: 39-06-953-44-28 *Fax:* 39-06-953-81-16
Email: curia@diocesipalestrina.it

Palghat—Most Rev. Jacob Manathodath; Bishop's House Vennakara, Noorani P.O., Palakkad, Kerala, 678004, India.
Tel: 91-0491-2515-277 *Fax:* 91-0491-2525-129
Email: palghat_diocese@dataone.in

Palm Beach—Most Rev. Gerald Michael Barbarito; Diocesan Pastoral Center 9995 North Military Tr., P.O. Box 109650, Palm Beach Gardens, FL, 33410-9650.
Tel: 561-775-9500 *Fax:* 561-775-9556
Email: info@diocesepb.org

Palmares—Most Rev. Genival Saraiva de França; C.P. 77, Rua da Conceição 1198, Palmares, PE, 55540-000, Brazil.
Tel: 55-081-3661-1320 *Fax:* 55-081-3661-0748
Email: diocese@onlife.com.br

PALMAS—Most Rev. Pedro Brito Guimaraes; Cúria Metropolitana 504 Sul, Alameda 04, Lote 62, Palmas, TO, 77021-690, Brazil.
Tel: 063-3218-8400 *Fax:* 063-3218-8401
Email: curiapalmas@gmail.com

Palmas-Francisco Beltrão—Most Rev. José Antônio Peruzzo; Cúria Diocesana Rua Bispo Dom Carlos 819, C.P. 50, Palmas, PR, 85555-000, Brazil.
Tel: 55-046-3263-1134 *Fax:* 55-046-3262-1511
Email: curiapalmas@proserv.com.br

Palmeira dos Índios—Most Rev. Dulcênio Fontes de Matos; Cúria Diocesana C.P. 81, Praça Mons. Macedo 190, Palmeira dos Índios, AL, 57600-520, Brazil.
Tel: 55-082-3421-3425 *Fax:* 55-082-3421-3425
Email: curia.palmeiradosindios@bol.com.br

Palmerston North—Most Rev. Peter James Cullinane; Bishop's Office 33 Amesbury St., P.O. Box 11012, Palmerston North, 5330, New Zealand.
Tel: 64-06-354-1780 *Fax:* 64-06-357-3624
Email: admin@pndiocese.org.nz

Palmira—Most Rev. Edgar de Jesus Garcia Gil; Obispado Calle 30 N. 29-79, Palmira, Valle, Colombia.
Tel: 92-2-272-28-72; 92-2-272-41-41 *Fax:* 92-2-272-41-41
Email: diocesisdepalmira@gmail.com

PALO—Vacant; Archdiocesan Chancery 6501 Palo, P.O. Box 173, Tacloban City, Leyte, 6500, Philippines.
Tel: 053-323-2213 *Fax:* 053-323-5607
Email: rcap_chancery@yahoo.com.ph

Pamiers—Most Rev. Philippe Mousset; Evêché 8 Cours Mercadal, B.P. 10122, Pamiers CEDEX, 09104, France.
Tel: 5-61-60-9390 *Fax:* 5-61-60-93-95
Email: eveche.pamiers@wanadoo.fr

PAMPLONA Y TUDELA—Most Rev. Francisco Pérez González; Arzobispado Plaza de Santa María la Real 1, Pamplona, Navarra, 31001, Spain.
Tel: 34-948-22-74-00 *Fax:* 34-948-21-04-40
Email: sec.arzobispo@iglesianavarra.org

PANAMÁ—Most Rev. Jose Domingo Ulloa Mendieta; Arzobispado Calle 1a sur Carrasquilla, Apartado 6386, Panamá 5, Panama.
Tel: 507-261-0002/0107 *Fax:* 507-261-0820

Panevezys—Most Rev. Jonas Kauneckas; Panavezio Vyskupijos Kurija Upytes 3, Panevezys, 35248, Lithuania.
Tel: 825-45-43-51-56 *Fax:* 825-45-50-04-07
Email: pkurija@takas.lt

Pangkal-Pinang—Most Rev. Hilarius Moa Nurak, S.V.D.; Keuskupan Jl. Batu Kadera 545A, Kelurahan Semabung Lama, Pangkalpinang, Bangka, 33147, Indonesia.
Tel: 62-0717-43-46-01 *Fax:* 62-0717-43-46-01
Email: sekretariatpkpinang@gmail.com

Paotíng (Baoding), Ching-Yüan—Catholic Mission Bishop's House, Baoding, Hebei, China.

Papantla—Most Rev. Lorenzo Cárdenas Aregullín; Apartado 27, Av. Benito Juárez 1102, Teziutlán, Pue., 73800, Mexico.
Tel: 52-231-313-2430 *Fax:* 52-231-313-3614
Email: dipa33614l@hotmail.com

PAPEETE—Vacant; Archevêché B.P. 94, Vallée de la Mission, Papeete, Iles Tahiti, 98713, French Polynesia.
Tel: 689-50-23-51 *Fax:* 689-42-40-32
Email: catholic@mail.pf

Paracatu—Most Rev. Leonardo de Miranda Pereira; Cúria Diocesana Rua Alexandre Silva 247, Paracatu, MG, 38600-000, Brazil.
Tel: 038-3671-7004 *Fax:* 038-3671-7004

PARAÍBA—Most Rev. Aldo di Cillo Pagotto, S.S.S.; Cúria Metropolitana Praça Dom Adauto, C.P. 13, João Pessoa, PB, 58001-970, Brazil.
Tel: 55-083-3241-3048 *Fax:* 55-083-3222-1629
Email: curia@arquidiocesepb.org.br

PARAKOU—Most Rev. Pascal N'Koué; Archevêché B.P. 75, Parakou, Benin.
Tel: 229-23-61-0254 *Fax:* 229-23-61-0109
Email: parcheveche@yahoo.fr

Paramaribo—Most Rev. Wilhelmus de Bekker; Bisschopshuis Henck Arronstraat 14, Paramaribo, Suriname.
Tel: 597-42-60-92 *Fax:* 597-42-67-82
Email: cabisdom@sr.net

PARANÁ—Most Rev. Juan Alberto Puiggari; Arzobispado Monte Caseros 77, Paraná, Entre Ríos, E3100ACA, Argentina.
Tel: 54-0343-422-0684; 54-0343-421-82-20; 54-0343-4311-440 *Fax:* 54-0343-4311-440; 54-0343-4230-372

Paranaguá—Most Rev. Joao Alves dos Santos, O.F.M.Cap.; Cúria Diocesana C.P. 531, Rua Conselheiro Sinimbú 498, Paranaguá, PR, 83203-970, Brazil.
Tel: 55-041-3422-8553 *Fax:* 55-041-3422-8553
Email: mitra-pgua@sul.com.br

Parañaque—Most Rev. Jesse E. Mercado; 34 Aguirre Ave., Cor. Fr. Cruz St., BF Homes, Phase III, Parañaque City, 1700, Philippines.
Tel: 02-807-16-62 *Fax:* 02-659-21-44
Email: chancerydop@gmail.com

Paranavaí—Most Rev. Geremias Steinmetz; Cúria Diocesana C.P. 453, Rua Francisco Vieira Borges 373, Paranavaí, PR, 87705-180, Brazil.
Tel: 55-044-3423-1045; 55-044-3423-7397 *Fax:* 55-044-3423-1045
Email: curiaparanavai@hotmail.com

Parintins—Most Rev. Giuliano Frigeni, P.I.M.E.; Avenida Amazonas 2139, Parintins, AM, 69151-000, Brazil.
Tel: 55-092-3533-2965 *Fax:* 55-092-3533-3459
Email: curiapin@jurupari.com.br

PARIS—His Eminence André Vingt-Trois; 7 Rue Saint Vincent, Paris, 75018, France.
Tel: 33-1-55-79-9595 *Fax:* 33-1-55-79-9585

Parma—Most Rev. Enrico Solmi; Piazza Duomo 1, Parma, 43121, Italy.
Tel: 39-0521-38-0508 *Fax:* 39-0521-23-0629
Email: cancelleria@diocesi.parma.it

Parma Byzantine—Most Rev. John M. Kudrick (PRM); Chancery Office 1900 Carlton Rd., Parma, OH, 44134-3129.
Tel: 216-741-8773 *Fax:* 216-741-9356

Parnaíba—Most Rev. Alfredo Schäffler; Cúria Diocesana C.P. 70, Rua Josias Morais 676, Parnaíba, PI, 64200-970, Brazil.
Tel: 55-086-3322-2358 *Fax:* 55-086-3322-2358

Parral—Most Rev. José Andrés Corral Arredondo; Calle Fray Bartolomé de las Casas 13, San José del Parral, Chihuahua, 33800, Mexico.
Tel: 52-627-525-3000; 52-627-522-0371 *Fax:* 52-627-522-0371
Email: diocesisdeparral@prodigy.net.mx

Parramatta—Most Rev. Anthony Colin Fisher, O.P.; 12 Victoria Rd., Parramatta, N.S.W., 2150, Australia.
Tel: 61-02-9683-6277 *Fax:* 61-02-9630-4813
Email: diocese@parra.catholic.org.au
P.O. Box 3066, Parramatta N.S.W., 1750, Australia.

Pasig—Most Rev. Mylo Hubert C. Vergara; Diocesan Curia Plaza Rizal, Brgy. Malinao, Pasig City, 1600, Philippines.
Tel: 02-643-93-25 *Fax:* 02-643-70-38
Email: chance461@yahoo.com

Passaic Byzantine—Most Rev. William Charles Skurla (PSC); Eparchial Center 445 Lackawanna Ave., Woodland Park, NJ, 07424.
Tel: 973-890-7777 *Fax:* 973-890-7175

Passau—Most Rev. Wilhelm Schraml; Bischöfliches Ordinariat Domplatz 7, Passau, D-94032, Germany.
Tel: 49-0851-393-1100 *Fax:* 49-0851-393-1109
Email: generalvikariat@bistum-passau.de

PASSO FUNDO—Most Rev. Pedro Ercílio Simon; Cúria Diocesana C.P. 230, Rua Coronel Chicuta 436, Passo Fundo, RS, 99001-970, Brazil.
Tel: 55-054-3045-9240 *Fax:* 55-054-3045-9222
Email: diocese@pastoral.com.br

Pasto—Most Rev. Julio Enrique Prado Bolaños; Obispado Carrera 24 N 17-70, Pasto, Nariño, Colombia.
Tel: 57-2-7232-228; 57-2-7233-226 *Fax:* 57-2-7235-055
Email: diocesisp@yahoo.com

Paterson—Most Rev. Arthur Joseph Serratelli, S.S.L., S.T.D., D.D.; Diocesan Center 777 Valley Rd., Clifton, NJ, 07013.
Tel: 973-777-8818 *Fax:* 973-777-8976
Web: www.patersondiocese.org
Email: aperro@patersondiocese.org

Pathanamthitta (Malankarese)—Most Rev. Yoohanon Chrysostom Kalloor; Catholic Bishop's House Pathanamthitta, Kerala, 689645, India.

Pathein—Most Rev. John Hsane Hgyi; St. Peter's Cathedral Tagaung Phaya Rd., Pathein, 10011, Myanmar.
Tel: 95-042-24-018
Email: mdaniel100@gmail.com

PATNA—Most Rev. William D'Souza, S.J.; Archbishop's House Bankipur P.O., Patna, Bihar, 800004, India.
Tel: 91-0612-230-1735 *Fax:* 91-0612-230-1816
Email: archbishop@satyam.net.in

Patos—Vacant; Rua Peregrino Filho 76, Patos, PB, 58700-450, Brazil.
Tel: 55-083-3421-2250 *Fax:* 55-083-3421-2619
Email: diocesedepatospb@uol.com.br

Patos de Minas—Most Rev. Cláudio Nori Sturm; Cúria Diocesana Rua Tiradentes 388, Patos de Minas, MG, 38700-134, Brazil.
Tel: 55-034-3821-3213 *Fax:* 55-034-3821-3184
Email: contato@diocesedepatosdeminas.org.br

Patti—Most Rev. Ignazio Zambito; Vescovado Via Cattedrale 7, Patti, Messina, 98066, Italy.
Tel: 39-0941-21-044 *Fax:* 39-0941-21-044
Email: curiapatti@diocesipatti.it

Paulo Afonso—Most Rev. Guido Zendron; Cúria Diocesana Av. Getúlio Vargas s/n, Paulo Afonso, BA, 48601-000, Brazil.
Tel: 55-075-3281-4268 *Fax:* 55-075-3281-3159

Pavia—Most Rev. Giovanni Giudici; Piazza Duomo 11, Pavia, 27100, Italy.
Tel: 39-0382-38-65-11 *Fax:* 39-0382-38-65-25
Email: servizigenerali@diocesi.pavia.it

Pécs—Most Rev. Gyorgy Udvardy; Pf. 113, Szent István-tér 23, Pécs, H-7624, Hungary.
Tel: 36-72-51-3030 *Fax:* 36-72-51-3031

Pekhon—Most Rev. Peter Hla; Bishop's House 06061 Pekhon, Southern Shan State, Myanmar.
Tel: 081-56-046
Email: daydereh@gmail.com

PEKING (BEIJING)—Catholic Mission Si-She-Ku, Beijing, Hebei, China.

PELOTAS—Most Rev. Jacinto Bergmann; Cúria Diocesana Praça José Bonifácio 104, Pelotas, RS, 96015-170, Brazil.
Tel: 55-053-3225-8055 *Fax:* 55-053-3222-5109
Email: mitrapel@terra.com.br

Pelplin—Most Rev. Jan Bernard Szlaga; Kuria Biskupia ul. Biskupa K. Dominika 11, Pelplin, 83-130, Poland.
Tel: 48-058-53-61-221/2 *Fax:* 48-058-53-61-699
Email: kuria@pelplin.opoka.org.pl

Pemba—Most Rev. Ernesto Maguengue; Paço Episcopal, C.P. 12, Rua 018 124, Pemba, Cabo Delgado, 80100, Mozambique.
Tel: 272-20-337 *Fax:* 272-20-335
Email: diocesepemba@yahoo.com

Pembroke—Most Rev. Michael Mulhall; Chancery Office 188 Renfrew St., P.O. Box 7, Pembroke, ON, K8A 6X1, Canada.
Tel: 613-732-7933 *Fax:* 613-732-1679
Email: chancellor@diocesepembroke.com

Penang—Most Rev. Antony Selvanayagam; Catholic Diocesan Centre 290 Jalan Macalister Rd., Penang, 10450, Malaysia.
Tel: 04-229-27-42 *Fax:* 04-228-56-71
Email: pgdioce@streamyx.com

Penedo—Most Rev. Valério Breda, S.D.B.; Cúria Diocesana C.P. 93, Rua Siqueira Campos 187, Penedo, AL, 57200-000, Brazil.
Tel: 55-082-3551-2227 *Fax:* 55-082-3551-4208

Pengpu (Bengbu), Peng-Fou—Catholic Mission Bishop's House, Bengbu, Anhui, China.

Penonomé—Most Rev. Uriah Ashley; Via Miraflores, Apartado 0229-0020, Coclé, Penonomé, Panama.
Tel: 997-7090 *Fax:* 997-8208
Email: obispen@cwpanama.net

Pensacola-Tallahassee—Vacant; 11 N. B St., P.O. Drawer 13284, Pensacola, FL, 32591.
Tel: 850-435-3500 *Fax:* 850-436-6424
Email: chancellor@ptdiocese.org

Peoria—Most Rev. Daniel Robert Jenky, C.S.C. (PEO); Chancery 419 N.E. Madison Ave., Peoria, IL, 61603.
Tel: 309-671-1550 *Fax:* 309-671-1576
Email: msgr-showalter@cdop.org

Pereira—Most Rev. Rigoberto Corredor Bermúdez; Obispado Calle 20, N. 7-40, Pereira, Risaralda, Colombia.
Tel: 57-6-32-48-484 *Fax:* 57-6-31-12-592
Email: diocesispereira@epm.net.co

Périgueux—Most Rev. Michel Mouïsse; Evêché 38 avenue Georges Pompidou, B.P. 5064, Périgueux CEDEX, 24005, France.
Tel: 33-553-08-0744 *Fax:* 33-553-54-0325
Email: eveche.de.perigueux@orange.fr

Perpignan-Elne—Most Rev. André Marceau; Evêché 8 rue de l'Académie, Perpignan CEDEX, 66027, France.
Tel: 4-68-35-20-65 *Fax:* 4-68-35-85-57
Email: eveque@catholique-perpignan.cef.fr

PERTH—Most Rev. Barry James Hickey; Catholic Church Office 21 Victoria Ave., Perth, W.A., 6000, Australia.
Tel: 61-08-9223-1351 *Fax:* 61-08-9221-1716
Email: archsec@perthcatholic.org.au

PERUGIA - CITTÁ DELLA PIEVE—Most Rev. Gualtiero Bassetti; Arcivescovado Piazza IV Novembre 6, Perugia, 06123, Italy.
Tel: 39-075-575-0350 *Fax:* 39-075-575-0325
Email: economato@diocesi.perugia.it

PESARO—Most Rev. Piero Coccia; Arcivescovado Via Rossini 62, Pesaro, 61100, Italy.
Tel: 39-0721-30-043
Email: segreteriavescovile@arcidiocesipesaro.it

PESCARA-PENNE—Most Rev. Tommaso Valentinetti; Piazza dello Spirito Santo 2, Pescara, 65121, Italy.
Tel: 39-085-422-25-71/2 *Fax:* 39-085-421-31-49
Email: curia@diocesipescara.it

Pescia—Most Rev. Giovanni De Vivo; Palazzo Vescovile Via G. Giusti 1, Pescia, Pistoia, 51017, Italy.
Tel: 39-0572-476-224 *Fax:* 39-0572-499-745
Email: diocesi_pescia@libero.it

Pesqueira—Vacant; Cúria Diocesana Rua Cardeal Arcoverde 23, Pesqueira, PE, 55200-000, Brazil.
Tel: 55-087-3835-1562 *Fax:* 55-087-3835-1562
Email: curia@diocesedepesqueira.org

Peterborough—Most Rev. Nicola De Angelis, C.F.I.C.; Bishop's House 350 Hunter St. W., P.O. Box 175, Peterborough, ON, K9J 6Y8, Canada.
Tel: 705-745-5123 *Fax:* 705-745-2555
Email: chancery@peterboroughdiocese.org

PETRA E FILADELFIA—Most Rev. Yasser Ayyach; Archevêché Grec-Melkite Catholique B.P. 2435, Jabal-Amman, Amman, 11181, Jordan.
Tel: 06-586-66-73 *Fax:* 06-586-66-73

Petrolina—Most Rev. Manoel dos Reis de Farias; Cúria Diocesana Praça Dom Antônio Malan 99, Petrolina, PE, 56302-330, Brazil.
Tel: 55-087-3861-2874 *Fax:* 55-087-3861-5929
Email: curia@diocesedepetrolina.org.br

Petrópolis—Most Rev. Filippo Santoro; Cúria Diocesana Rua Sao Pedro de Alcântara 12, Petrópolis, RJ, 25685-300, Brazil.
Tel: 55-024-2231-5212 *Fax:* 55-024-2231-5212
Email: mitra@diocesepetropolis.org.br

Phan Thiêt—Most Rev. Joseph Vu Duy Thong; Tóa Giám Muc 422 Trân Hung Dao, Tx., Phan Thiêt, Binh Thuân, Vietnam.
Tel: 84-062-3815-947 *Fax:* 84-062-3819-560

Phát Diêm—Most Rev. Joseph Nguyen Nang; Tóa Giám Muc 75 Phát Diêm Dong, Kim Son, Ninh Bình, Vietnam.
Tel: 030-386-2058 *Fax:* 030-386-2724
Email: tgmpdiem@gmail.com

PHILADELPHIA—Most Rev. Charles J. Chaput, O.F.M.Cap.; The Chancery 222 N. 17th St., Philadelphia, PA, 19103-1299.
Tel: 215-587-4538 *Fax:* 215-587-3907
Email: chancery@adphila.org

PHILADELPHIA - UKRAINIAN—Most Rev. Stefan Soroka, D.D., Ph.D. (PHU); Chancery Office 827 N. Franklin St., Philadelphia, PA, 19123-2097.
Tel: 215-627-0143 *Fax:* 215-627-0377
Email: ukrmet@catholic.org

Phoenix—Most Rev. Thomas James Olmsted; Diocesan Pastoral Center 400 E. Monroe St., Phoenix, AZ, 85004-2336.
Tel: 602-354-2480 *Fax:* 602-354-2427
Email: jdeck@diocesephoenix.org

Phoenix Byzantine—Most Rev. Gerald N. Dino; Pastoral Center 8105 N. 16th St., Phoenix, AZ, 85020.
Tel: 602-861-9778 ***Fax:*** 602-861-9796
Email: evnsecretary@qwestoffice.net

Phú Cuong—Most Rev. Pierre Trân Dinh Tu; Tòa Giám Muc 444 Cach Mang Tháng 8, Tx. Thu Dau Mot, Binh Duong, Vietnam.
Tel: 0650-3822-860 ***Fax:*** 0650-3821-266
Email: tgmphucuong@gmail.com

Piacenza-Bobbio—Most Rev. Gianni Ambrosio; Palazzo Vescovile Piazza Duomo 33, Piacenza, 29121, Italy.
Tel: 39-0523-30-83-11 ***Fax:*** 39-0523-30-83-25
Email: uffici@curia.pc.it

Piana degli Albanesi—Most Rev. Sotir Ferrara; Piazza San Nicola 1, Piana degli Albanesi, Palermo, 90037, Italy.
Tel: 39-091-85-71-029 ***Fax:*** 39-091-85-71-029

Piazza Armerina—Most Rev. Michele Pennisi; Via La Bella 3, Piazza Armerina, Enna, 94015, Italy.
Tel: 39-0935-68-01-13 ***Fax:*** 39-0935-68-74-58
Email: info@diocesiarmerina.it

Picos—Most Rev. Plínio José Luz da Silva; Cúria Diocesana Rua Padre Madeira 380, Picos, Pl, 64600-000, Brazil.
Tel: 55-089-3422-1961 ***Fax:*** 55-089-3422-1961
Email: curia@diocesedepicos.org.br

Piedras Negras—Most Rev. Alonso Gerardo Garza Treviño; Av. Obispado 107, Col. Tecnológico, 26080 Piedras Negras, Coah., Mexico.
Tel: 878-795-5610
Email: obispado@diocesispn.org

Pietersburg—Most Rev. Mogale Paul Nkhumishe; The Diocesan Office 8 Compensatie Str., Polokwane 0699, P.O. Box 166, Polokwane, 0700, South Africa.
Tel: 27-015-295-8156 ***Fax:*** 27-015-295-8152
Email: dioceseofpbg@metroweb.co.za

Pinar del Rio—Most Rev. Jorge Enrique Serpa Pérez; Calle Máximo Gómez 160 Este, Apartado 72, Pinar del Rio, 20100, Cuba.
Tel: 07-48-757-644 ***Fax:*** 07-48-778-362
Email: pjose@obipinar.co.cu

Pinerolo—Most Rev. Piergiorgio Debernardi; Via Vescovado 1, Pinerolo, Torino, 10064, Italy.
Tel: 39-0121-37-33-20 ***Fax:*** 39-0121-79-45-28
Email: cancelliere@diocesipinerolo.it

Pingliang (Pingliang)—Catholic Mission Bishop's House, Pingliang, Gansu, China.

Pinheiro—Most Rev. Ricardo Pedro Paglia, M.S.C.; Cúria Diocesana Av. Presidente Dutra 386, Pinheiro, MA, 65200-000, Brazil.
Tel: 55-098-3381-1278 ***Fax:*** 55-098-3381-1278
Email: diocesepinheiro@bol.com.br

Pinsk—Vacant; ul. Lenina 16, Pinsk, 225710, Belarus.
Tel: 0165-32-3157 ***Fax:*** 0165-32-3157
Email: pinsk_dioces@catholic.by

Piracicaba—Most Rev. Fernando Mason, O.F.M.Conv.; Cúria Diocesana Avenida Luciano Guidotti 166, Piracicaba, 13400-183, Brazil. C.P. 366, Piracicaba, SP, 13400-970, Brazil.
Tel: 55-019-2106-7575 ***Fax:*** 55-019-2106-7550
Email: curia@diocesedepiracicaba.org.br

PISA—Most Rev. Giovanni Paolo Benotto; Piazza Arcivescovado 18, Pisa, 56126, Italy.
Tel: 39-050-56-55-25/3 ***Fax:*** 39-050-55-06-00
Email: diocesi@pisa.chiesacattolica.it

Pistoia—Most Rev. Mansueto Bianchi; Vescovado Via Puccini 29, Pistoia, 51100, Italy.
Tel: 39-0573-97-61-33 ***Fax:*** 39-0573-97-65-28
Email: affarieconomici@diocesipistoia.it

Pitigliano-Sovana-Orbetello—Most Rev. Guglielmo Borghetti; Vescovado Piazza Fortezza Orsini 29, Pitigliano, Grosseto, 58017, Italy.
Tel: 39-0564-616-074 ***Fax:*** 39-0564-614-419
Email: cancelleria@email.it

Pittsburgh—Most Rev. David Allen Zubik, D.D. (PIT); Pastoral Center 111 Blvd. of the Allies, Pittsburgh, PA, 15222.
Tel: 412-456-3000 ***Fax:*** 412-456-3197
Email: communications@diopitt.org

PITTSBURGH - BYZANTINE—Vacant; Chancery Office 66 Riverview Ave., Pittsburgh, PA, 15214-2253.
Tel: 412-231-4000 ***Fax:*** 412-231-1697
Email: archpitt@aol.com

PIURA—Most Rev. José Antonio Eguren Anselmi, S.C.V.; Arzobispado Apartado 197, Libertad 1105, Piura, Peru.
Tel: 51-73-32-75-61; 51-73-31-37-95 ***Fax:*** 51-73-30-84-41
Email: secretarioarz@arzobispadodepiura.org

Plasencia—Most Rev. Amadeo Rodríguez Magro; Obispado Plaza de la Catedral s/n, Plasencia, Cáceres, 10600, Spain.
Tel: 34-927-41-16-12; 34-927-412-581; 34-927-41-31-62 ***Fax:*** 34-927-414-149
Email: vicariogeneral@diocesisplasencia.org

Plock—Most Rev. Piotr Libera; Kuria Diecezjalna ul. Tumska 3, Plock, 09-402, Poland.
Tel: 48-024-2622-640 ***Fax:*** 48-024-2626-716
Email: kuria@diecezjaplocka.pl

Plymouth—Most Rev. Hugh Christopher Budd; Bishop's House 31 Wyndham St., W., Plymouth, Devon, PL1 5RZ, England.
Tel: 44-01752-224-414 ***Fax:*** 44-01752-223-750
Email: bishop@plymouth-diocese.org.uk

Plzen—Most Rev. Frantisek Radkovský; Biskupství plzenské nám. Republiky 35, Plzen, 301 14, Czech Republic.
Tel: 42-377-22-31-12 ***Fax:*** 42-377-32-19-17
Email: bip@bip.cz

Pointe-Noire—Vacant; Evêché B.P. 659, Pointe-Noire, Republic of the Congo.
Tel: 294-16-36
Email: poulmel@yahoo.fr

POITIERS—Vacant; Archevêché 1-3 place Sainte-Croix, Poitiers CEDEX, 86035, France.
Tel: 33-549-50-12-04 ***Fax:*** 33-549-60-07-73
Email: gerard.mouchard@neuf.fr

Ponce—Most Rev. Félix Lázaro Martínez, Sch. P.; Obispado P.O. Box 32205, Estación 6, Ponce, PR, 00732-2205, Puerto Rico.
Tel: 787-848-5265 ***Fax:*** 787-841-1778
Email: obispado@diocesisdeponce.org

PONDICHERRY AND CUDDALORE—Most Rev. Antony Anandarayar; Archbishop's House 206 Cathedral St., P.O. Box 193, Puduchcheri, 605001, India.
Tel: 91-0413-233-4748/9911 ***Fax:*** 91-0413-420-1503
Email: dioceseofpondy@gmail.com

Ponta de Pedras—Most Rev. Alessio Saccardo, S.J.; Bispado de Ponta de Pedras Passagem Carneiro da Rocha 27/E, Belém, PA, 66020-010, Brazil.
Tel: 55-091-3225-1625 ***Fax:*** 55-091-3225-1625
Email: dioceseppedras@uol.com.br

Ponta Grossa—Most Rev. Sérgio Arthur Braschi; Cúria Diocesana Praça Marechal Floriano Peixoto 581, Ponta Grossa, PR, 84010-680, Brazil.
Tel: 55-042-3224-1140 ***Fax:*** 55-042-3224-1140
Email: curia@diocesepontagrossa.com.br

PONTIANAK—Most Rev. Hieronymus Herculanus Bumbun, O.F.M.Cap.; Keuskupan Agung Jl. A.R. Hakim 92 A, P.O. Box 1119, Pontianak, Kalimantan Barat, 78011, Indonesia.
Tel: 62-0561-732-382 ***Fax:*** 62-0561-738-785
Email: changjitmeuw@yahoo.com

Pontoise—Most Rev. Jean-Yves Riocreux; 16 Chemin de la Pelouse, Pontoise, 95300, France.
Tel: 33-1-30-38-3424 ***Fax:*** 33-1-30-73-8690
Email: d.ducasse@catholique95.fr

Poona—Most Rev. Thomas Dabre; Bishop's House 1-B Prince of Wales Dr., Pune, Maharashtra, 411001, India.
Tel: 91-020-2636-00-65/13-18 ***Fax:*** 91-020-2634-35-10
Email: punedioc@vsnl.com

POPAYÁN—Most Rev. Iván Antonio Marin López; Arzobispado Calle 5 N. 6-71, Popayán, Colombia.
Tel: 57-2-824-17-10/2 ***Fax:*** 57-2-824-01-01
Email: popayanarq@cec.org.co

Popokabaka—Most Rev. Louis Nzala Kianza; Evêché de Popokabaka B.P. 7245, Kinshasa 1, Democratic Republic of Congo.
Tel: 081-691-55-51; 099-831-17-56
Email: evechepopo@yahoo.fr

Porec i Pula—Most Rev. Ivan Milovan; Biskupski Ordinarijat Dobrilina 3, Porec, 52440, Croatia.
Tel: 385-052-42-90-32 ***Fax:*** 385-052-45-17-85
Email: biskupija-porec@pu.t-com.hr

PORT-AU-PRINCE—Most Rev. Guire Poulard; Archevêché B.P. 538, rue Dr. Aubry, Port-au-Prince, Haiti.
Tel: 3510-0653; 3513-2337
Email: archeveche-pap@globalsud.com

Port-Bergé—Most Rev. Armand Toasy; Evêché B.P. 5, Port-Bergé 419, Madagascar.
Tel: 032-473-06-10

Port Blair—Most Rev. Aleixo Das Neves Dias; Bishop's House Deeptidham, P.B. 466, P.O. Junglighat, Port Blair, Andaman Islands, 744103, India.
Tel: 91-03192-232-979 *Fax:* 91-03192-230-464
Email: portblaircathdiocese@gmail.com

Port-de-Paix—Most Rev. Pierre-Antoine Paulo, O.M.I.; Evêché rue de l'Hôpital, B.P. 61, Port-de-Paix, Haiti.
Tel: 509-04-2268-6134 *Fax:* 509-04-2268-6234

Port Elizabeth—Vacant; 10 Park Ln., Central, Port Elizabeth, 6001, South Africa.
Tel: 27-041-373-6735 *Fax:* 27-041-374-3921
Email: cathport@aerosat.co.za
P.O. Box 12194, Centrahil, Port Elizabeth, 6006, South Africa.

Port-Gentil—Most Rev. Mathieu Madega; Evêché B.P. 425, Port-Gentil, Gabon.
Tel: 241-55-11-25 *Fax:* 241-56-45-45

Port Harcourt—Most Rev. Camillus Archibong Etokudoh; Diocesan Chancery P.O. Box 1113, 1 Kaduna St., Port Harcourt, Rivers State, Nigeria.
Tel: 234-080-331-06-362; 234-080-560-52-041

Port-Louis—Most Rev. Maurice Piat, C.S.Sp.; Evêché 13 rue Mgr Gonin, Port-Louis, Mauritius.
Tel: 230-208-3068 *Fax:* 230-208-6607
Email: eveche@intnet.mu

PORT MORESBY—Most Rev. John Ribat, M.S.C.; Archbishop's House P.O. Box 1032, Boroko, National Capital District 111, Papua New Guinea.
Tel: 675-325-1192 *Fax:* 675-325-6731
Email: carchpom@datec.net.pg

PORT OF SPAIN—Most Rev. Edward Joseph Gilbert, C.Ss.R.; Archbishop's House 27 Maraval Road, Port of Spain, Trinidad and Tobago.
Tel: 868-622-1103 *Fax:* 868-622-1165
Email: abishop@carib-link.net

Port Pirie—Most Rev. Gregory O'Kelly, S.J.; 105 Gertrude St., Port Pirie, S.A., 5540, Australia.
Tel: 61-08-8632-0550 *Fax:* 61-08-8632-0599
Email: diocoffice@bigpond.com

Port Victoria o Seychelles—Most Rev. Denis Wiehe, C.S.Sp.; Bishop's House Olivier Maradan Str., P.O. Box 43, Port Victoria, Mahé, Seychelles.
Tel: 248-32-2152; 248-32-2652 *Fax:* 248-32-4045
Email: rcchurch@seychelles.net

Port-Vila—Most Rev. Jean (John) Bosco Baremes, S.M.; Evêché B.P. 59, Port-Vila, Vanuatu.
Tel: 678-22640 *Fax:* 678-25342
Email: catholik@vanuatu.com.vu

Portalegre - Castelo Branco—Most Rev. Antonino Eugenio Fernandes Dias; Bispado Apartado 20, Portalegre CODEX, 7301-901, Portugal.
Tel: 351-245-30-9480 *Fax:* 351-245-208-190
Email: curiadiocesana@portalegre-castelobranco.pt

Portland (in Maine)—Most Rev. Richard Joseph Malone, D.D., S.T.L., Th.D. (PRT); Chancery Office 510 Ocean Ave., P.O. Box 11559, Portland, ME, 04104.
Tel: 207-773-6471 *Fax:* 207-773-0182

PORTLAND (IN OREGON)—Most Rev. John G. Vlazny; Archdiocesan Pastoral Center 2838 E. Burnside, Portland, OR, 97214-1895.
Tel: 503-234-5334 *Fax:* 503-234-2545
Email: mtully@archdpdx.org

Porto—Most Rev. Manuel José Macário do Nascimento Clemente; Paço Episcopal Terreiro da Sé, Porto CODEX, 4050-573, Portugal.
Tel: 351-22-339-2330 *Fax:* 351-22-339-2348
Email: gabinf@diocese-porto.pt

PORTO ALEGRE—Most Rev. Dadeus Grings; Cúria Metropolitana Rua Espírito Santo 95, Porto Alegre, RS, 90010-370, Brazil.
Tel: 55-051-3228-6199 *Fax:* 55-051-3228-6199
Email: mitra.poa@terra.com.br

Porto Nacional—Most Rev. Romualdo Matias Kujawski; Cúria Diocesana Rua Dr. Francisco Aires 306, Porto Nacional, TO, 77500-000, Brazil.
Tel: 55-063-3363-1392 *Fax:* 55-063-3363-1392
Email: diocese@blznet.com.br

Porto Novo—Most Rev. Rene-Marie Ehuzu, C.I.M.; Evêché 01 B.P. 380, Porto-Novo, Benin.
Tel: 229-20-21-32-01 *Fax:* 229-20-21-49-83
Email: eveche.porto@intnet.bj

Porto-Santa Rufina—His Eminence Roger Etchegaray; Curia Vescovile Via del Cenacolo 53, Rome, 00123, Italy.
Tel: 39-06-30-89-38-48 *Fax:* 39-06-30-89-36-58
Email: curia@diocesiportosantarunfina.it

PORTO VELHO—Most Rev. Moacyr Grechi, O.S.M.; Cúria Metropolitana Rua Gonçalves Dias 288, C.P. 232, Porto Velho, RO, 78900-970, Brazil.
Tel: 55-069-3221-2270 *Fax:* 55-069-3224-1590
Email: dom@ronet.com.br

PORTOVIEJO—Most Rev. Lorenzo Voltolini Esti; Arzobispado Casilla 13-01-0024, Avda, Universitaria s/n, entre Alajuela y Ramos y Duarte, Portoviejo, Manabí, Ecuador.
Tel: 593-05-263-04-04/24-06 *Fax:* 593-05-263-44-28
Email: portoviejo.arq@gmail.com

Portsmouth—Most Rev. Roger Francis Crispian Hollis; St. Edmund House Edinburgh Rd., Portsmouth, Hants, -PO1 3QA, England.
Tel: 44-023-9282-5430 *Fax:* 44-023-9287-2424

Posadas—Most Rev. Juan Rubén Martínez; Obispado Félix de Azara 1604, Posadas, Misiones, N3300LQJ, Argentina.
Tel: 54-03752-423-221; 54-03752-439-249
Email: obispado@obposadas.org.ar

POTENZA-MURO LUCANO-MARSICO NUOVO—Most Rev. Agostino Superbo; Largo Duomo 5, Potenza, 85100, Italy.
Tel: 0971-26-426 *Fax:* 0971-26-535

Potosí—Most Rev. Ricardo Ernesto Centellas Guzman; Calle Ayacucho 18, Potosí, Bolivia.
Tel: 591-02-622-2770
Email: obispado@cedro.pts.entelnet.bo

POUSO ALEGRE—Most Rev. Ricardo Pedro Chaves Pinto Filho, O.Praem; Cúria Metropolitana Trav. Dr. Sylvio Fausto 33, Pouso Alegre, MG, 37550-000, Brazil.
Tel: 55-035-3421-1248 *Fax:* 55-035-3421-1248
Email: voniltonaugusto@yahoo.com.br

Pozega—Most Rev. Antun Skvorcevic; Trg Sv. Trojstva 18, Pozega, 34000, Croatia.
Tel: 034-290-300/310 *Fax:* 034-274-295
Email: biskupski-ordinarijat@po.t-com.hr

POZNAN—Most Rev. Stanislaw Gadecki; Kuria Metropolitalna ul. Ostrów Tumski 2, Poznan, 61-109, Poland.
Tel: 48-061-851-28-00 *Fax:* 48-061-851-28-14
Email: kuria@archpoznan.org.pl

Pozzuoli—Most Rev. Gennaro Pascarella; Via Campi Flegrei 12, Pozzuoli, Napoli, 80078, Italy.
Tel: 39-081-526-12-04 *Fax:* 39-081-526-30-68
Email: info@diocesipozzuoli.org

PRAHA—Most Rev. Dominik Duka, O.P.; Arcibiskupská Kurie Hradcanské nám. 56/16, Praha 1, 119 02, Czech Republic.
Tel: 42-220-39-21-23 *Fax:* 42-220-51-45-28
Email: apha@apha.cz

Prato—Most Rev. Gastone Simoni; Piazza Duomo 48, Prato, 59100, Italy.
Tel: 39-0574-499-722 *Fax:* 39-0574-499-732
Email: curia@diocesiprato.it

Presidente Prudente—Most Rev. Benedito Gonçalves dos Santos; Cúria Diocesana C.P. 276, Rua Padre João Goetz 400, Presidente Prudente, SP, 19061-460, Brazil.
Tel: 018-3918-5000 *Fax:* 018-3918-5002
Email: diocesepp@stetnet.com.br

Prešov—Most Rev. Ján Babjak, S.J.; Arcibiskupský úrad ul. Hlavná 1, pošt. schránka 135, Prešov, SK-081-35, Slovakia.
Tel: 42-051-7562-601; 42-051-7562-644 *Fax:* 42-051-7562-625
Email: abu@grkatpo.sk

PRETORIA—Most Rev. William Slattery, O.F.M.; Jolivet House 140 Visagie Street, P.O. Box 8149, Pretoria, 0001, South Africa.
Tel: 27-012-326-5311 *Fax:* 27-012-325-3994
Email: ptadiocese@absamail.co.za

Prince-Albert—Most Rev. Albert Thévenot; 1415-4th Ave., W., Prince Albert, SK, S6V 5H1, Canada.
Tel: 306-922-4747 *Fax:* 306-922-4754
Email: cecr@sasktel.net

Prince George—Most Rev. Gerald William Wiesner, O.M.I.; Chancery Office P.O. Box 7000, 6500 Southridge Ave., Prince George, BC, V2N 3Z2, Canada.
Tel: 250-964-4424 *Fax:* 250-964-2101
Email: bishop@netbistro.com

Propriá—Most Rev. Mário Rino Sivieri; Curia Diocesana Trav. Municipal 117, Propriá, SE, 49900-000, Brazil.
Tel: 55-079-3322-1757
Email: setorcom@bol.com.br

Providence—Most Rev. Thomas J. Tobin (PRO); Bishop's Office & Chancery Office One Cathedral Square, Providence, RI, 02903-3695.
Tel: 401-278-4500 ***Fax:*** 401-278-4621
Web: www.dioceseofprovidence.org

PRZEMYSL—Most Rev. Józef Michalik; Kuria Metropolitalna Pl. Katedralny 4/A, Przemysl, 37-700, Poland.
Tel: 48-016-678-66-94 ***Fax:*** 48-016-678-26-74
Email: kuria@przemyska.pl

PRZEMYSL-WARSZAWA—Most Rev. Jan Martyniak; ul. Basztowa 13, Przemysl, 37-700, Poland.
Tel: 016-678-78-68 ***Fax:*** 016-678-78-68
Email: kuria@przemyslgr.opoka.org.pl

Puchi (Puqi)—Catholic Mission Bishop's House, Puqi, Hubei, China.

PUEBLA DE LOS ANGELES, PUEBLA—Most Rev. Victor Sanchez Espinosa; Calle 16 de Septiembre 901, Puebla, Pue., 72000, Mexico.
Tel: 52-222-246-4005; 55-222-232-18-87 ***Fax:*** 55-222-246-2277
Email: arzobispadopuebla@prodigy.net.mx

Pueblo—Most Rev. Fernando Isern; Catholic Pastoral Center 101 N. Greenwood, Pueblo, CO, 81003.
Tel: 719-544-9861 ***Fax:*** 719-544-5202
Email: info@dioceseofpueblo.com

Puerto Cabello—Most Rev. Saul Figueroa Albornoz; Calle Bolivar 3-18, Zona Colonial, Puerto Cabello, Edo. Carabobo, Venezuela.
Tel: 0242-361-92-48 ***Fax:*** 0242-361-08-77
Email: igleptocabello@cantv.net

Puerto Escondido—Most Rev. Eduardo Cirilo Carmona Ortega; Felipe Merklin s/n, Col. Centro Puerto Escondido, Oax, 71980, Mexico.
Tel: 954-582-36-77 ***Fax:*** 954-582-36-57
Email: obispadopuertoescodido@hotmail.com

Puerto Iguazú—Most Rev. Marcelo Raúl Martorell; Guatambú 184, Puerto Iguazú, Misiones, N3370DPD, Argentina.
Tel: 54-03757-420-526 ***Fax:*** 54-03757-420-526
Email: obyguazu@yahoo.com.ar

PUERTO MONTT—Most Rev. Cristián Caro Cordero; Arzobispado Casilla 17, Calle Benavente 385, piso 2, Puerto Montt, Chile.
Tel: 065-25-22-15 ***Fax:*** 065-43-0849
Email: padretulio@surnet.cl

Puerto Plata—Most Rev. Julio César Corniel Amaro; Obispado Calle José del Carmen Ariza 36, Puerto Plata, Dominican Republic.
Tel: 809-586-2484 ***Fax:*** 809-586-2754
Email: obispadopp@yahoo.com

Punalur—Most Rev. Selvister Ponnumuthan; Bishop's House, P.B. 48, Kollam Dt., Punalur, Kerala, 691305, India.
Tel: 0475-222-70-78 ***Fax:*** 0475-222-54-19
Email: punalurdiocese@sancharnet.in

Puno—Most Rev. Jorge Pedro Carrión Pavlich; Obispado Apartado 93, Jr. Conde de Lemos 226, Puno, Peru.
Tel: 51-35-17-61 ***Fax:*** 51-35-34-81
Email: obispado.puno@terra.com.pe

Punta Arenas—Most Rev. Bernardo Miguel Bastres Florence; Obispado Casilla 35-D, Calle Monseñor Fagnano 630, Puntas Arenas, Chile.
Tel: 061-24-1739 ***Fax:*** 061-24-7839
Email: puntaaarenas@episcopado.cl

Puntarenas—Most Rev. Oscar Gerardo Fernández Guillén; Costado sur de la Catedral, Puntarenas, 5400, Costa Rica.
Tel: 2661-38-22 ***Fax:*** 2661-36-54
Email: pemiliocr@hotmail.com

Punto Fijo—Most Rev. Juan María Leonardi Villasmil; Obispado Calle Sucre, Plaza Jose Leonardo Chirinos, Punto Fijo, Edo. Falcón, Venezuela.
Tel: 0269-247-76-10 ***Fax:*** 0269-247-68-70
Email: diocesisdepuntofijo@intercable.net.ve

Purnea—Most Rev. Angelus Kujur, S.J.; Bishop's House Maharajaji Hata, P.O., Purnea, Bihar, 854301, India.
Tel: 06454-242-848 ***Fax:*** 06454-229-523
Email: bhpurnea@yahoo.co.in

Purwokerto—Most Rev. Julianus Kemo Sunarko, S.J.; Keuskupan Jl. Gereja 3, Purwokerto, Jawa-Tengah, 53115, Indonesia.
Tel: 62-0281-635-632 ***Fax:*** 62-0281-631-611
Email: kuria_kp@yahoogroups.com

Pusan—Most Rev. Paul Hwang Cheol-soo; Diocesan Office 70-4 Nam Cheon I Dong, Su Yeong-Gu, Pusan, 613-816, Korea, South.
Tel: 82-051-629-8711 ***Fax:*** 82-051-625-1765
Email: samu@catp.kr

Puthur (Malankarese)—Most Rev. Geevarghese Divannasios Ottathengil; Catholic Bishop's House Parladka P.O., Putter, Karnataka, -574203, India.

Pyay—Most Rev. Alexander Pyone Cho; Bishop's House Meegyaungyeh, Pyay, Myanmar.
Tel: 95-053-24-100

P'yong-yang—Most Rev. Francis Hong Yong-ho; Catholic Mission, P'yong-yang, Korea, South.

Q

Qacha's Nek—Vacant; Bishop's House P.O. Box 5, Qacha's Nek, 600, Lesotho.
Tel: 22-950-325

QUÉBEC—Most Rev. Gerald Cyprien Lacroix, I.S.P.X.; Chancellerie 1073 boul. René-Lévesque Ouest, Sillery, QC, G1S 4R5, Canada.
Tel: 418-688-1211 ***Fax:*** 418-688-2960
Email: diocese@ecdq.org

Queenstown—Most Rev. Dabula Anthony Mpako; 10-12 Grey St., P.O. Box 182, Queenstown, 5320, South Africa.
Tel: 27-045-839-7022 ***Fax:*** 27-045-838-2209
Email: qtdioces@telkomsa.net

Quelimane—Most Rev. Hilário Da Cruz Massinga, O.F.M.; C.P. 292, Quelimane, Mozambique.
Tel: 258-24-21-20-47 ***Fax:*** 258-24-21-33-99

Querétaro—Most Rev. Faustino Armendáriz Jiménez; Obispado Reforma 48, Apdo. 49, Querétaro, Qro., 76000, Mexico.
Tel: 52-442-224-0738; 52-442-212-1033 ***Fax:*** 52-442-212-1845
Email: cancilleria@diocesedequeretaro.org.mx

Quibdó—Vacant; Curia Episcopal Carrera 1 N. 26-91, Quibdó, Chocó, Colombia.
Tel: 4-671-17-46 ***Fax:*** 4-671-54-00

Quiché—Vacant; Residencia Episcopal 4a Calle 3-12, Zona 5, Santa Cruz del Quiche, 14901, Guatemala.
Tel: 775-51-111 ***Fax:*** 775-51-962

Quilmes—Most Rev. Carlos José Tissera; Obispado Carlos Pellegrini 3280, Quilmes Oeste Buenos Aires, BI879DLB, Argentina.
Tel: 54-011-4250-2323 ***Fax:*** 54-011-4250-1082
Email: obisquil@obisquil.org.ar

Quilon—Most Rev. Stanley Roman; Bishop's House Tangassery P.O., Kollam, 691007, Kerala, India.
Tel: 91-0474-2796-140 ***Fax:*** 91-0474-2791-850

Quimper, Cornouailles—Most Rev. Jean-Marie Le Vert; Evêché, 3 rue de Rosmadec, Quimper CEDEX, 29018, France.
Tel: 2-98-55-3447 ***Fax:*** 2-98-55-3177
Email: eveche@catholique-quimper.cef.fr

QUITO—Most Rev. Fausto Gabriel Trávez Trávez, O.F.M.; Arzobispado Apartado 17-01-00106, Calle Chile, Quito, 0E4-22, Ecuador.
Tel: 593-02-2284-429 ***Fax:*** 593-02-2580-973
Email: arzobispado_quito@andinanet.net

Quixadá—Most Rev. Angelo Pignoli; Cúria Diocesana Rua Eudásio Barroso 851, C.P. 34, Quixadá, CE, 63900-000, Brazil.
Tel: 55-088-3412-0548 ***Fax:*** 55-088-3412-0548
Email: curia@diocesequixada.org.br

Quy Nhon—Most Rev. Pierre Nguyên Soan; Toà Giám Muc, 116 Tran Hung Dao, Quy Nhon, Vietnam.
Tel: 056-3824-360 ***Fax:*** 056-3828-955
Email: vptgmqn@yahoo.com

R

RABAT—Most Rev. Vincent Landel, S.C.J.; Archevêché 1 rue Hadj Mohammed Riffai, B.P. 258 R.P., Rabat, 10001, Morocco.
Tel: 212-0537-709-239 ***Fax:*** 212-0537-706-282
Email: archev.rabat@wanadoo.net.ma

RABAUL—Most Rev. Francesco Panfilo, S.D.B.; Archbishop's House P.O. Box 357, Kokopo 613, East New Britain Province, Papua New Guinea.
Tel: 98-29-384 ***Fax:*** 98-28-404

Radom—Most Rev. Henryk Marian Tomasik; Kuria Diecezjalna ul. Malczewskiego 1, Radom, 26-600, Poland.
Tel: 048-340-6200 ***Fax:*** 048-340-6212
Email: kuria@radom.opoka.org.pl

Rafaela—Most Rev. Carlos María Franzini; Obispado Necochea 150, Rafaela, Santa Fe, S2300IED, Argentina.
Tel: 54-03492-424-637 ***Fax:*** 54-03492-501-819
Email: obispadoderafaela@wilnet.com.ar

Ragusa—Most Rev. Paolo Urso; Curia Diocesana Via Roma 105, Ragusa, 97100, Italy.
Tel: 39-0932-246-788 ***Fax:*** 39-0932-689-337
Email: curiadiragusa@tiscali.it

Raiganj—Most Rev. Alphonsus F. D'Souza, S.J.; Bishop's House Chotparua, P.O. Karnajora, Uttar Dinajpur Dt., West Bengal, 733130, India.
Tel: 07762-226-523 ***Fax:*** 07762-226-523

Raigarh—Most Rev. Paul Toppo; Bishop's House, St. Michael's Church Rambhata Raigarh, Chhatisgarh, 496001, India.
Tel: 07762-226-523 ***Fax:*** 07762-226-523
Email: frsudhirbara@yahoo.com

RAIPUR—Most Rev. Joseph Augustine Charanakunnel; Khristbandhu Niwas Byron Bazar, Raipur, Chhattisgarh, 492001, India.
Tel: 0771-2423-995 ***Fax:*** 0771-4052-429
Email: archdioceserpr@rediffmail.com

Rajkot—Most Rev. Jose Chittooparambil, C.M.I.; Bishop's House Kalawad Rd., P.O. Box 1501, Rajkot, Gujarat, 360005, India.
Tel: 91-0281-2563-891 ***Fax:*** 91-0281-2563-427
Email: bishoprajkot@sify.com

Rajshahi—Most Rev. Gervas Rozario; Bishop's House Omorpur, P.O. Sophura, Rajshahi, 6203, Bangladesh.
Tel: 880-0721-761-533
Email: rajdioc@bttb.net.bd

Raleigh—Most Rev. Michael F. Burbidge, D.D., Ed.D., V.G.; The Catholic Center 715 Nazareth St., Raleigh, NC, 27606-2187.
Tel: 919-821-9708 ***Fax:*** 919-821-9705
Web: www.dioceseofraleigh.org
Email: msgr.brockman@raldioc.org

Ramanathapuram (Syro-Malabarese)—Most Rev. Paul Alappatt; ***Bishop's House:*** Holy Trinity Cathedral Trichy Road, Ramanathapuram, Coimbatore, Tamil Nadu, -641045, India.
Tel: 0422-2317-366

Rancagua—Most Rev. Alejandro Goic Karmelic; Casilla 9-D, O'Carrol 535, Rancagua, Chile.
Tel: 56-072-24-35-27; 56-072-23-08-46 ***Fax:*** 56-072-23-08-46; 56-072-23-20-46
Email: rancagua@episcopado.cl

RANCHI—His Eminence Telesphore Placidus Toppo; Archbishop's House Purulia Road, P.O. Box 5, Ranchi, Jharkhand, 834001, India.
Tel: 91-0651-235-07-28 ***Fax:*** 91-0651-235-01-44

Raphoe—Most Rev. Philip Boyce, O.C.D.; Ard Adhamhnáin, Letterkenny, Co. Donegal, Ireland.
Tel: 074-91-21-208 ***Fax:*** 074-91-24-872
Email: raphoediocese@eircom.net

Rapid City—Most Rev. Robert D. Gruss; Chancery Office 606 Cathedral Dr., Rapid City, SD, 57701.
Tel: 605-343-3541 ***Fax:*** 605-348-7985
Email: chancery@diorc.org

Rarotonga—Most Rev. Paul Donoghue, S.M.; Catholic Mission P.O. Box 147, Avarua, Rarotonga, Cook Islands.
Tel: 682-20-817 ***Fax:*** 682-29-817

Ratchaburi—Most Rev. John Bosco Panya Kritcharoen; Bishop's House 31/2-4 Somboonkul Rd., Ratchaburi, 70000, Thailand.
Tel: 66-032-31-47-28 ***Fax:*** 66-032-32-31-84
Email: rbd_diocese@hotmail.com

Ratnapura—Most Rev. Cletus Chandrasiri Perera, O.S.B.; Bishop's House Madola, Avissawella, 10700, Sri Lanka.
Tel: 036-2232-368 ***Fax:*** 036-2232-369
Email: bisratnapura@gmail.com

RAVENNA-CERVIA—Most Rev. Guiseppe Verucchi; Curia Arcivescovile Piazza Arcivescovado 1, Ravenna, 48121, Italy.
Tel: 39-0544-54-1611 ***Fax:*** 39-0544-54-1699

Reconquista—Most Rev. Ramón Alfredo Dus; Obispado Chacabuco 841, Reconquista, Santa Fe, S3560BVQ, Argentina.
Tel: 54-03482-429-180 ***Fax:*** 54-03482-429-180
Email: cancilleria@obispadorqta.org.ar

Regensburg—Most Rev. Gerhard Ludwig Müller; Niedermünstergasse 1, Regensburg, Bundesrepublik, -D-93047, Germany.
Tel: 49-0941-597-01 ***Fax:*** 49-0941-597-1055
Email: info@bistum-regensburg.de

REGGIO CALABRIA-BOVA—Most Rev. Vittorio Luigi Mondello; Arcivescovado Via Tommaso Campanella 63, Reggio Calabria, 89127, Italy.
Tel: 39-0965-38-55-11 ***Fax:*** 39-0965-33-09-63
Email: curia@reggiocalabria.chiesacattolica.it

Reggio Emilia - Guastalla—Most Rev. Adriano Caprioli; Via Vittorio Veneto 8, Reggio Emilia, 42121, Italy.
Tel: 39-0522-43-26-54; 39-0522-43-66-26 ***Fax:*** 39-0522-40-22-07

REGINA—Most Rev. Daniel Joseph Bohan; 445 Broad St. N., Regina, SK, S4R 2X8, Canada.
Tel: 306-352-1651 ***Fax:*** 306-352-6313
Email: chancery@archregina.sk.ca

Registro—Most Rev. José Luíz Bertanha, S.V.D.; Cúria Diocesana Rua Nelson Brihi Badur 360, C.P. 302, Registro, SP, 11900-000, Brazil.
Tel: 55-013-3821-1595 ***Fax:*** 55-013-3821-3644
Email: curiargt@terra.com.br

REIMS—Most Rev. Thierry Jordan; Archevêché B.P. 2729, 3 rue du Cardinal-de-Lorraine, Reims CEDEX, 51058, France.
Tel: 3-26-47-05-33 ***Fax:*** 3-26-84-94-66
Email: eveche@catholique.reims.cef.fr

RENNES—Most Rev. Pierre d'Ornellas; Maison diocésaine 45 rue de Brest, Rennes CEDEX, 35042, France.
Tel: 2-99-14-35-35; 2-99-33-99-93

Reno—Most Rev. Randolph Roque Calvo, D.D., J.C.D. (RNO); Pastoral Center 290 S. Arlington St., Reno, NV, 89501-1713.
Tel: 775-329-9274 ***Fax:*** 775-348-8619
Web: www.dioceseofreno.org
Email: dioceseofreno@catholicreno.org

RESISTENCIA—Most Rev. Fabriciano Sigampa; Arzobispado Bartolomé Mitre 363, Resistencia, Chaco, H3500BLG, Argentina.
Tel: 54-03722-434-573 ***Fax:*** 54-03722-434-573
Email: arzobrcia@arnet.com.ar

Reykjavik—Most Rev. Pierre Bürcher; Biskupsstofa P.B. 490, Hávallagata 14, Reykjavik, IS-121, Iceland.
Tel: 354-1-552-53-88 ***Fax:*** 354-1-562-38-78
Email: catholica@catholica.is

Rezekne-Aglona—Most Rev. Janis Bulis; Latgales iela 88, Rezekne, LV-4601, Latvia.
Tel: 646-244-03 ***Fax:*** 646-244-03
Email: b.ordinarius@inbox.lv

RHODOS—Vacant; Archevêché Catholique Odos Ionos Dragoumi 5, Rhodos, Hellas, 85100, Greece.
Tel: 22410-21-845 ***Fax:*** 22410-26-688

RIBEIRÃO PRETO—Most Rev. Joviano de Lima Júnior, S.S.S.; Cúria Metropolitana C.P. 105, Rua Tibiriçá 879, Ribeirao Preto, SP, 14001-970, Brazil.
Tel: 55-016-3610-8477; 55-016-3610-1288
Email: arquidioceserp@netsite.com.br

Richmond—Most Rev. Francis Xavier DiLorenzo (RIC); The Chancery 7800 Carousel Ln., Richmond, VA, 23294.
Tel: 804-359-5661 ***Fax:*** 804-358-9159
Web: www.richmonddiocese.org
Email: tshreve@richmonddiocese.org

Rieti—Most Rev. Delio Lucarelli; Vescovado Via Cintia 83, Rieti, 02100, Italy.
Tel: 39-0746-25-361 ***Fax:*** 39-0746-20-02-28
Email: curia@rieti.chiesacattolica.it

RIGA—Most Rev. Zbignev Stankevics; Metropolijas Kurija Maza Pils iela 2/a, Riga, 1050, Latvia.
Tel: 672-24-314 ***Fax:*** 672-20-060
Email: sacerdos@inbox.lv

RIJEKA—Most Rev. Ivan Devcic; Nadbiskupski Ordinarijat Ivana Pavla II 1, Rijeka, 51000, Croatia.
Tel: 051-581-210 ***Fax:*** 051-581-215
Email: kancelarija@ri-nadbiskupija.hr

Rimini—Most Rev. Francesco Lambiasi; Vescovado Via IV Novembre 35, Rimini, 47900, Italy.
Tel: 0541-18-35-102 ***Fax:*** 0541-18-35-125
Email: vicario@diocesi.rimini.it

RIMOUSKI—Most Rev. Pierre-André Fournier; Archevêché 34 rue de l'Evêché Ouest, Rimouski, QC, G5L 4H5, Canada.
Tel: 418-723-3320 ***Fax:*** 418-722-8978
Email: diocriki@globetrotter.net

Rio Branco—Most Rev. Joaquín Pertíñez Fernández, O.A.R.; Praça da Catedral 4, Rio Branco, AC, 69908-970, Brazil.
Tel: 55-068-3223-2200 ***Fax:*** 55-068-3223-2101
Email: curiadiocesana@contilnet.com.br

Rio do Sul—Most Rev. Augustinho Petry; Cúria Diocesana Rua São Ludgero 79, Rio do Sul, SC, 89160-000, Brazil.
Tel: 55-047-3521-0315 ***Fax:*** 55-047-3521-2922
Email: diocesemitra@hotmail.com

Río Gallegos—Most Rev. Juan Carlos Romanin, S.D.B.; Obispado Errázuriz 53, Río Gallegos, Santa Cruz, Z9400HYA, Argentina.
Tel: 54-02966-422-325; 54-02966-422-616 ***Fax:*** 54-02966-426-183
Email: obispadorg@yahoo.com.ar

Rio Grande—Most Rev. José Mário Stroeher; Cúria Diocesana Rua João Alfreo 532, Rio Grande, RS, 96200-260, Brazil.
Tel: 55-053-3231-4066 ***Fax:*** 55-053-3232-4731
Email: diocrg@vetorial.net

Riobamba—Vacant; Obispado Apartado 06-01-36, Calle Espejo 2253, Riobamba, Ecuador.
Tel: 048-296-00-48/9 ***Fax:*** 048-296-98-34
Email: obriobamba@andianet.net

Riohacha—Most Rev. Héctor Salah Zuleta; Obispado Calle 13 N. 8-43, Riohacha, La Guajira, Colombia.
Tel: 57-728-06-62 ***Fax:*** 57-727-24-48
Email: diocrio@latinmail.com

Rochester—Most Rev. Matthew Harvey Clark, D.D. (ROC); 1150 Buffalo Rd., Rochester, NY, 14624-1890.
Tel: 585-328-3210 ***Fax:*** 585-328-3149
Web: www.dor.org

Rockford—Most Rev. Thomas George Doran, D.D., J.C.D. (RCK); Diocesan Chancery 555 Colman Center Dr., P.O. Box 7044, Rockford, IL, 61125.
Tel: 815-399-4300 ***Fax:*** 815-399-5266
Web: www.rockforddiocese.org

Rockhampton—Most Rev. Brian Heenan; Bishop's House 170 William Street, Rockhampton, 4700, Australia.
Tel: 61-07-4931-3620 ***Fax:*** 61-07-4931-3729
Email: vicgen@rok.catholic.net.au

Rockville Centre—Most Rev. William Francis Murphy, S.T.D., L.H.D. (RVC); Chancery Office 50 N. Park Ave., P.O. Box 9023, Rockville Centre, NY, 11571-9023.
Tel: 516-678-5800 ***Fax:*** 516-764-3316
Web: www.drvc.org
Email: chancellor@drvc.org

Rodez—Most Rev. Francois Fonlupt; Evêché, B.P. 821, 1 rue Frayssinous, Rodez CEDEX, 12008, France.
Tel: 5-65-68-06-28 ***Fax:*** 5-65-68-82-15
Email: asso.di@wanadoo.fr

Roermond—Most Rev. Franciscus Jozef Marie Wiertz; Paredisstraat 10, Roermond, 6041 JW, The Netherlands.
Tel: 31-0475-386-740 ***Fax:*** 31-0475-336-285
Email: g.smulders@bisdom-roermond.nl

Roma—Vatican City State, Rome, 00120, Italy.

Romblon—Vacant; Bishop's Residence Villa del Mar, Suwa, Lonos, Romblon City, Romblon, 5500, Philippines.
Tel: 0920-217-9718
Email: rcbr_3@hotmail.com

Rondonópolis—Most Rev. Juventino Kestering; Cúria Diocesana C.P. 150, Av. Frei Servácio 393, Rondonópolis, MT, 78700-970, Brazil.
Tel: 55-066-3426-6757 ***Fax:*** 55-066-3426-7606
Email: dioc.roo@terra.com.br

Roraima—Most Rev. Roque Paloschi; C.P. 163, Rua Bento Brasil 613, Boa Vista, RR, 69301-970, Brazil.
Tel: 55-095-3224-3741 ***Fax:*** 55-095-3224-2578
Email: curiarr@yahoo.com.br

ROSARIO—Most Rev. José Luis Mollaghan; Arzobispado Calle Córdoba 1677, Rosario, Santa Fe, S2000AWY, Argentina.
Tel: 54-0341-425-1298 ***Fax:*** 54-0341-425-1207
Email: arzobros@uolsinectis.com.ar

Roseau—Most Rev. Gabriel Malzaire; Bishop's House Turkey Ln., P.O. Box 790, Roseau, Dominica.
Tel: 767-448-2837; 767-488-8717 ***Fax:*** 767-448-3404
Email: bishop@cwdom.dm

ROSSANO-CARIATI—Most Rev. Santo Marcianó; Curia Arcivescovile Via Arcivescovado 5, Rossano Calabro, Cosenza, 87067, Italy.
Tel: 39-0983-52-02-82; 39-0983-52-15-27 ***Fax:*** 39-0983-52-17-50
Email: euria.rossan@email.it

Rottenburg-Stuttgart—Most Rev. Gebhard Fürst; Bischöfliches Ordinariat Saint-Claude-Str. 72, Rottenburg am Neckar, D-72108, Germany.
Tel: 49-07472-1690 ***Fax:*** 49-07472-169-561
Email: ordinariat@bo.drs.de

Rotterdam—Most Rev. Johannes Harmannes Jozeeus van den Hende; Bisdom, Koningin Emmaplein 3, Rotterdam, 3016 AA, The Netherlands.
Tel: 31-010-281-5171 ***Fax:*** 31-010-436-71-90
Email: a.d.jong@bisdomrotterdam.nl

ROUEN—Most Rev. Jean-Charles Descubes; Archevêché B.P. 886, 2 rue des Bonnetiers, Rouen CEDEX 01, 76001, France.
Tel: 2-35-71-20-52 ***Fax:*** 2-35-71-22-31
Email: diocese.rouen@wanadoo.fr

Rourkela—Vacant; Bishop's House Hamirpur, P.O., Rourkela, Sundargarh Dt., Orissa, 769003, India.
Tel: 91-0661-2640-702 ***Fax:*** 91-0661-2647-041

Rouyn-Noranda—Most Rev. Dorylas Moreau; 515 Ave. Cuddihy, Rouyn-Noranda, QC, J9X 4C5, Canada.
Tel: 819-764-4660 ***Fax:*** 819-764-3972
Email: dioceser-n@cablevision.qc.ca

Rožnava—Most Rev. Vladimír Filo; Biskupský úrad, nam. Baníkov 20, Post schranka 127, Roznava, SK-048 01, Slovakia.
Tel: 058-7877-201; 058-7877-226 ***Fax:*** 058-7877-210
Email: roznava@kbs.sk

Rrëshen—Most Rev. Cristoforo Palmieri, C.M.; Ipeshkëvia, Kishë Katedrale Katolike, Rruga Sh. Vinçenci de Paoli, Rrëshen, Albania.
Tel: 216-22-270 ***Fax:*** 216-22-270
Email: diocesirreshen@hotmail.com

Rubiataba-Mozarlândia—Most Rev. Adair José Guimarães; Cúria Diocesana C.P. 46, Rua Xixá 100, Rubiataba, GO, 76350-000, Brazil.
Tel: 55-062-3325-1211 ***Fax:*** 55-062-3325-1744
Email: dioceserumo@hotmail.com

Ruhengeri—Vacant; Curie Diocésaine de Ruhengeri Avenue Mikeno, B.P. 45, Ruhengeri, Rwanda.
Tel: 715-252-546-239 ***Fax:*** 715-252-546-930
Email: evecatholicruh@yahoo.fr

Rulenge-Ngara—Most Rev. Severine Niwemugizi; Bishop's House P.O. Box 135, Ngara, Tanzania.
Tel: 028-222-61-55 ***Fax:*** 028-222-61-55

Rumbek—Vacant; Rumbek Diocese c/o P.O. Box 21102, Nairobi, Kenya.
Tel: 020-38-75-345 ***Fax:*** 020-38-77-327
Email: bishopofrumbek@gmail.com

Rustenburg—Most Rev. Kevin Dowling, C.Ss.R.; Phokeng P.O. Box 45, Boshoek, North West Province, 0301, South Africa.
Tel: 27-014-573-3403 ***Fax:*** 27-014-573-3403
Email: diocrust@mweb.co.za

Rutana—Most Rev. Bonaventure Nahimana; B.P. 45, Rutana, Burundi.
Tel: 799-13-057

Ruteng—Most Rev. Hubertus Leteng; Keuskupan, Jln. A. Yani 10, Tromol pos 801, Ruteng, Flores, 86508, Indonesia.
Tel: 62-0385-21-214 ***Fax:*** 62-0385-21-065; 62-0385-22-256
Email: keuskupanruteng@yahoo.co.id

Ruy Barbosa—Most Rev. André de Witte; Rua Antônio Novais s/n, C.P. 2345, Ruy Barbosa, BA, 46800-000, Brazil.
Tel: 55-075-3252-1001 ***Fax:*** 55-075-3252-1001
Email: economodrb@yahoo.com.br

Ruyigi—Most Rev. Blaise Nzeyimana; Evêché de Ruyigi D.S. 119, Bujumbura, Burundi.
Tel: 257-22-40-61-40 ***Fax:*** 257-22-40-60-29

Rzeszów—Most Rev. Kazimierz Górny; Kuria Diecezjalna ul. Zamkowa 4, Rzeszów, 35-032, Poland.
Tel: 48-017-852-44-19 ***Fax:*** 48-017-852-17-83
Email: kuria@rzeszow.opoka.org.pl

S

Sabina-Poggio Mirteto—Most Rev. Ernesto Mandara; Vescovado Piazza Mario Dottori 14, Poggio Mirteto, Rieti, 02047, Italy.
Tel: 39-0765-24-755/019 ***Fax:*** 39-0765-44-10-19
Email: lucasanluca@libero.it

Sacramento—Most Rev. Jaime Soto, M.S.W. (SAC); Pastoral Center 2110 Broadway, Sacramento, CA, 95818-2541.
Tel: 916-733-0100 ***Fax:*** 916-733-0195
Web: www.diocese-sacramento.org

Sagar—Most Rev. Anthony Chirayath; Bishop's House P.O. Box 32, Saugor Cantt., M.P., 470001, India.
Tel: 91-07582-222-633 *Fax:* 91-07582-222-175
Email: sagardiocese@yahoo.com

Saginaw—Most Rev. Joseph R. Cistone (SAG); Chancery 5800 Weiss St., Saginaw, MI, 48603-2762.
Tel: 989-799-7910 *Fax:* 989-797-6670

SAÏDA, SAIDA, SIDONE—Most Rev. Elie Béchara Haddad, B.S.; Archevêché Grec-Melkite-Catholique, B.P. 247, Rue El-Moutran, Saïda, Lebanon.
Tel: 96-07-720-100 *Fax:* 96-07-722-055

SAINT ANDREWS AND EDINBURGH—His Eminence Cardinal Keith Michael Patrick O'Brien; Diocesan Offices Gillis Centre, 100 Strathearn Road, Edinburgh, EH9 1BB, Scotland.
Tel: 44-0131-623-8900 *Fax:* 44-0131-623-8899
Email: chancery@staned.org.uk

Saint Augustine—Most Rev. Felipe Jesus Estevez; Catholic Center 11625 Old St. Augustine Rd., Jacksonville, FL, 32258.
Tel: 904-262-3200 *Fax:* 904-262-0698
Web: www.dosafl.com
Email: bkelly@dosafl.com

SAINT-BONIFACE—Most Rev. Albert LeGatt; 151 Avenue de la Cathédrale, Saint-Boniface, MB, R2H OH6, Canada.
Tel: 204-237-9851 *Fax:* 204-231-2652

Saint-Brieuc—Most Rev. Denis Moutel; 10 rue Jean-Métairie, B.P. 4224, Saint-Brieuc CEDEX 02, 22042, France.
Tel: 2-96-68-12-70 *Fax:* 2-96-68-12-80
Email: gerard.nicole@diocese22.fr

Saint Catharines—Most Rev. Gerard Paul Bergie; Catholic Centre Saint Catharines, P.O. Box 875, ON, L2R 6Z4, Canada.
Tel: 905-684-0154 *Fax:* 905-684-7551
Email: chancery@vaxxine.com

Saint-Claude—Most Rev. Vincent Alexandre Edouard Elie Jordy; Evêché 1 rue Colonel-Mahon, B.P. 70, Lons-le-Saunier CEDEX, 39002, France.
Tel: 3-84-47-10-89 *Fax:* 3-84-24-86-32
Email: eveche@eglisejura.com

Saint Cloud—Most Rev. John Francis Kinney, D.D., J.C.D. (SCL); Diocesan Chancery 214 Third Ave. S., P.O. Box 1248, St. Cloud, MN, 56302-1248.
Tel: 320-251-2340 *Fax:* 320-251-0470
Web: www.stcdio.org
Email: rrolfes@gw.stcdio.org

Saint-Denis—Most Rev. Pascal Michel Ghislain Delannoy; Évêche, 16 blvd. Jules Guesde, Saint-Denis, 93200, France.
Tel: 33-1-48-20-35-01 *Fax:* 33-1-48-20-34-76
Email: evechesaintdenis@adsd.fr

Saint-Denis-de-La Réunion—Most Rev. Gilbert Aubry; Evêché 36 rue de Paris, B.P. 55, St.-Denis-de-La Réunion CEDEX, 97461, Reunion.
Tel: 262-94-8570 *Fax:* 262-94-8571
Email: eveche.lareunion@wanadoo.fr

Saint-Dié—Most Rev. Jean-Paul Mathieu; Evêché 7 rue de la Préfecture, Epinal CEDEX, 88025, France.
Tel: 3-29-82-21-63 *Fax:* 3-29-82-83-55

Saint-Etienne—Most Rev. Dominique Lebrun; Maison diocésaine 1 rue Hector-Berlioz, Saint-Etienne CEDEX 2, 42030, France.
Tel: 4-77-59-3000 *Fax:* 4-77-59-3001
Email: contact@diocese-saintetienne.fr

Saint-Flour—Most Rev. Bruno Grua; Evêché B.P. 20, 3 rue de la Frauze, Saint-Flour CEDEX, 15103, France.
Tel: 4-71-60-61-90 *Fax:* 4-71-60-02-49
Email: eveche@catholique-saint-flour.cef.fr

Saint George's in Canton (Romanian)—Most Rev. John Michael Botean, D.D. (ROM); *Chancery:* 1121 44th St., N.E., Canton, OH, 44714-1297.
Tel: 330-493-9958 *Fax:* 330-493-9963
Email: chancery@romaniancatholic.org

Saint George's (in Grenada)—Most Rev. Vincent Darius, O.P.; Bishop's House Morne Jaloux, P.O. Box 375, Saint George's, Grenada, West Indies.
Tel: 473-443-5299 *Fax:* 473-443-5758
Email: bishopgrenada@spiceisle.com

Saint-Hyacinthe—Most Rev. François Lapierre, P.M.E.; Evêché, C.P. 190, 1900 rue Girouard Ouest, Saint-Hyacinthe, QC, J2S 7B4, Canada.
Tel: 450-773-8581 *Fax:* 450-774-1895
Email: chancellerie@diocese-st-hyacinthe.qc.ca

Saint-Jean - Longueuil—Most Rev. Lionel Gendron, P.S.S.; Centre diocésain 740 boul. Sainte-Foy, Longueuil, QC, J4J 1Z3, Canada.
Tel: 450-679-1100 *Fax:* 450-679-1102
Email: everque@dsjl.org

Saint-Jérôme—Most Rev. Pierre Morissette; Evêché, 355 place du Curé-Labelle, Saint-Jérôme, QC, J7Z 5A9, Canada.
Tel: 450-432-9742 *Fax:* 450-432-8155

Saint John, New Brunswick—Most Rev. Robert Harris; Chancery Office 1 Bayard Dr., Saint John, NB, E2L 3L5, Canada.
Tel: 506-653-6800 *Fax:* 506-653-6812
Email: reception@dioceseofsaintjohn.org

Saint John's-Basseterre—Vacant; Chancery Offices P.O. Box 836, Saint John's, Antigua, West Indies.
Tel: 268-461-1135 *Fax:* 268-462-2383
Email: dsjb@candw.ag

SAINT JOHN'S, NEWFOUNDLAND—Most Rev. Martin William Currie; Chancery Office 200 Military Rd., St. John's, NF, A1C 2E8, Canada.
Tel: 709-726-3660 *Fax:* 709-726-3688
Email: fpuddister@nf.aibn.com

Saint Josaphat (Ukrainian) in Parma—Vacant; Chancery Office 5720 State Rd., P.O. Box 347180, Parma, OH, 44134-7180.
Tel: 440-888-1522 *Fax:* 440-888-3477
Email: josaphateparchy@cs.com

SAINT LOUIS—Most Rev. Robert James Carlson (STL); 20 Archbishop May Dr., St. Louis, MO, 63119-5738.
Tel: 314-792-7005 *Fax:* 314-792-7710
Web: www.archstl.org
Email: communication@archstl.org

Saint-Louis du Sénégal—Most Rev. Ernest Sambou; Evêché B.P. 260, Saint-Louis, Senegal.
Tel: 33-961-11-28 *Fax:* 33-961-26-57
Email: stlouiseveche@orange.sn

Saint-Maron de Montréal—Most Rev. Joseph Khoury; 12475 rue Grenet, Montreal, QC, H4J 2K4, Canada.
Tel: 514-331-2807 *Fax:* 514-334-5723
Email: beitmaron@videotron.ca

Saint Maron of Brooklyn—Most Rev. Gregory John Mansour; Maronite Chancery Office 109 Remsen St., Brooklyn, NY, 11201-4212.
Tel: 718-237-9913 *Fax:* 718-243-0444
Email: chancerystmaron@verizon.net

Saint Maron of Sydney—Most Rev. 'Ad Abikaram; Beit Maroun 105 The Boulevarde, P.O. Box 385, Strathfield, N.S.W., 2135, Australia.
Tel: 61-02-9642-0211 *Fax:* 61-02-9742-5290
Email: chancery@maronite.org.au

Saint Michael's of Sydney (Greek Melkites)—Most Rev. Robert Rabbat; Melkite-Greek Catholic Eparchy 80 Waterloo St., Greenacre, N.S.W., 2190, Australia.
Tel: 61-02-9758-0222 *Fax:* 61-02-9758-0233
Email: eparchy@melkite.org.au

Saint Nicholas (in Chicago)—Most Rev. Richard S. Seminack, D.D. (STN); Chancery Office 2245 W. Rice St., Chicago, IL, 60622.
Tel: 773-276-5080 *Fax:* 773-276-0314

SAINT PAUL AND MINNEAPOLIS—Most Rev. John C. Nienstedt; Chancery 226 Summit Ave., St. Paul, MN, 55102-2197.
Tel: 651-291-4406 *Fax:* 651-290-1629
Web: www.archspm.org
Email: chancery@archspm.org

Saint Paul (in Alberta)—Most Rev. Joseph Luc André Bouchard; Evêché, 4410 51ème avenue, Saint Paul, AB, T0A 3A2, Canada.
Tel: 780-645-3277 *Fax:* 780-645-6099
Email: diospaul@mcsnet.ca

Saint Peter the Apostle of San Diego—Most Rev. Sarhad Y. Jammo; Chaldean Eparchy 1627 Jamacha Way, El Cajon, CA, 92019.
Tel: 619-579-7997 *Fax:* 619-588-8281

Saint Petersburg—Most Rev. Robert N. Lynch (SP); Pastoral Center 6363 Ninth Ave. N., P.O. Box 40200, Saint Petersburg, FL, 33743-0200.
Tel: 727-344-1611 *Fax:* 727-345-3086
Web: www.dioceseofstpete.org
Email: rfm@dosp.org

Saint-Sauveur de Montréal—Most Rev. Ibrahim M. Ibrahim, B.S.; 10025 Boul. de l'Arcadie, Montreal, QC, H4N 2SI, Canada.
Tel: 514-272-6430 *Fax:* 514-272-2341
Email: eparchie.st-sauveur@bellnet.ca

Saint Thomas (in the Virgin Islands)—Most Rev. Herbert A. Bevard; Bishop's Residence 29A Princesse Gade, P.O. Box 301825, St. Thomas, VI, 00803-1825.
Tel: 340-774-3166 *Fax:* 340-774-5816
Email: chancery@islands.vi

Saint Thomas the Apostle of Chicago—Most Rev. Jacob Angadiath (SYM); Diocesan Office 372 S. Prairie Ave., Elmhurst, IL, 60126-4020.
Tel: 630-279-1383 *Fax:* 630-279-1479
Email: kaduppilroy@yahoo.com

Saint Thomas the Apostle of Detroit—Most Rev. Ibrahim N. Ibrahim, D.D., S.T.D. (EST); 25603 Berg Road, Southfield, MI, 48033.
Tel: 248-351-0440 *Fax:* 248-351-0443
Email: chaldeandiocese-detroit@comcast.net

Saint Thomas the Apostle of Sydney—Most Rev. Djibrail Kassab; 66-78 Quarry Rd., Bossley Park, NSW 2176, Australia.
P.O. Box 3120, Stockland Mall, Wetherill Park, NSW 2164, Australia.
Tel: 61-02-9823-1800 *Fax:* 61-02-9823-1266

Sainte-Anne-de-la-Pocatière—Most Rev. Yvon-Joseph Moreau, O.C.S.O.; Evêché 1200 4e avenue Painchaud, La Pocatière, QC, G0R 1Z0, Canada.
Tel: 418-856-1811 *Fax:* 418-856-5863
Email: diocese@diocese-ste-anne-net

Sainte-Croix-de-Paris—Most Rev. Grégoire Ghabroyan; 10 bis, rue Thouin, Paris, 75005, France.
Tel: 33-1-40-51-11-90 *Fax:* 33-1-40-51-11-99
Email: epaparis@wanadoo.fr

Saints Cyril and Methodius of Toronto—Most Rev. John Stephen Pazak, C.SS.R.; Eparchy of Saints Cyril & Methodius 223 Carlton Rd., Unionville, ON, L3R 3M2, Canada.
Tel: 905-477-4867 *Fax:* 905-479-9629
Email: byzslovakeparch@sympatico.ca

Saints Peter and Paul of Melbourne—Most Rev. Peter Stasiuk, C.SS.R.; Ukrainian Catholic Bishop's Chancery, 35 Canning Street, North Melbourne, Vic., 3051, Australia.
Tel: 61-03-9320-2560 *Fax:* 61-03-9320-2544
Email: eparchy@catholicukes.org.au

Saitama—Most Rev. Marcellino Daiji Tani; Bishop's Residence 6-4-12 Tokiwa, Urawa-ku,, Saitama-shi, 336-0001, Japan.
Tel: 81-048-831-3150 *Fax:* 81-048-824-3532
Email: saitama-kyoku@mbm.nifty.com

Sakania-Kipushi—Most Rev. Gaston Kashala Ruwezi, S.D.B.; Evêché, Kafubu-Kipushi, B.P. 521, Lubumbashi, Democratic Republic of Congo.
Tel: 243-099-70-20-409; 243-099-70-19-194
Email: diocsakaniakipushi@yahoo.fr

Salamanca—Most Rev. Carlos López Hernández; Obispado, Calle Rosario 18-28, Salamanca, 37001, Spain.
Tel: 34-923-12-89-00 *Fax:* 34-923-12-89-01
Email: secretaria@diocesisdesalamanca.com

Sale—Most Rev. Christopher Charles Prowse; Bishop's House 8 Pearson St., Sale, Victoria, -3850, Australia.
P.O. Box 183, Sale, Victoria, -3853, Australia.
Tel: 61-0351-44-6132 *Fax:* 61-0351-44-3855
Email: bishop@sale.catholic.org.au

Salem—Most Rev. Singaroyan Sebastianappan; Bishop's House P.B. 703, 2 Court Road, Maravaneri, Salem, Tamil Nadu, 636007, India.
Tel: 0427-241-56-41 *Fax:* 0427-241-15-17
Email: salemdiocese@gmail.com

SALERNO-CAMPAGNA-ACERNO—Most Rev. Luigi Moretti; Palazzo Arcivescovile, Via Roberto il Guiscardo 2, Salerno, 84121, Italy.
Tel: 39-089-25-83-052; 39-089-25-80-784 *Fax:* 39-089-25-81-241
Email: cancelleria@diocesisalerno.it

Salford—Most Rev. Terence John Brain; 3 Ford Street, Salford, M3 6DP, England.
Tel: 44-0161-817-2200 *Fax:* 44-0161-372-9993
Email: vicar.general@dioceseofsalford.org.uk

Salgueiro—Most Rev. Magnus Henrique Lopes, O.F.M.Cap.; Avenida Aurora de Carvalho Rose 2253, Salgueiro, 56000, Brazil.
Tel: 087-9607-9223

Salina—Vacant; Chancery Office 103 N. Ninth, P.O. Box 980, Salina, KS, 67402-0980.
Tel: 785-827-8746 *Fax:* 785-827-6133
Email: chancery@salinadiocese.org

Salmas, Shahpour—Most Rev. Thomas Meram; Khalifagari Kaldani Katholiq, P.O. 338, Urmia, 57135, Iran.
Tel: 98-0441-222-739 *Fax:* 98-0441-236-031
Email: thmeram@yahoo.com

Salt Lake City—Most Rev. John C. Wester (SLC); Diocesan Offices and Organizations 27 C. Street, Salt Lake City, UT, 84103.
Tel: 801-328-8641 *Fax:* 801-328-9680
Email: deacon.mayo@dioslc.org

SALTA—Most Rev. Mario Antonio Cargnello; Arzobispado, España 596, Salta, A4400ANL, Argentina.
Tel: 54-0387-4214-306 *Fax:* 54-0387-4213-101
Email: arzobispadosalta@arnet.com.ar

Saltillo—Most Rev. Josè Raúl Vera López, O.P.; Obispado, Hidalgo Sur 166, Apartado 25, Saltillo, Coah., 25000, Mexico.
Tel: 52-844-412-37-17 *Fax:* 52-844-414-92-67
Email: diocesiscommunication@diocesisdesaltillo.org.mx

Salto—Most Rev. Pablo Jaime Galimberti di Vietri; Obispado, 25 de Agosto 71, Salto, 50000, Uruguay.
Tel: 598-073-32-574 *Fax:* 598-073-28-056
Email: obispadodesalto@adinet.com.uy

Saluzzo—Most Rev. Giuseppe Guerrini; Corso Piemonte 56, Saluzzo, Cuneo, 12037, Italy.
Tel: 39-0175-24-88-60 *Fax:* 39-0175-24-88-55

SALZBURG—Most Rev. Alois Kothgasser, S.D.B.; Kapitelplatz 2, Postfach 62, Salzburg, A-5020, Austria.
Tel: 43-0662-80-47-1100 *Fax:* 43-0662-80-47-1100; 43-0662-80-47-1009
Email: salzburg@ordinariat.kirchin.net

Samarinda—Most Rev. Florentinus Sului Hajang Hau, M.S.F.; Keuskupan Agung Jl. D.I. Panjaitan 59A, Samarinda, Kalimantan Timur, 75010, Indonesia.
Tel: 62-0541-28-60-60; 62-0541-28-09-70
Email: komela@cbn.net.id

Sambalpur—Most Rev. Lucas Kerketta, S.V.D.; Bishop's House, Ainthapali, Sambalpur, Orissa, 768004, India.
Tel: 91-0663-2540-558 *Fax:* 91-0663-2541-656
Email: diogese@sancharnet.in

Sambir-Drohobych—Most Rev. Julian Voronovsky; vul. Stepana Bandery 19, Truskavets, 82200, Ukraine.
Tel: 03247-685-99 *Fax:* 03247-666-21
Email: sde@isa.org.ua

Same—Most Rev. Rogatus Kimaryo, C.S.Sp.; P.O. Box 8, Same, Tanzania.
Tel: 027-275-8029 *Fax:* 027-275-6080
Email: samediocese@yahoo.com

SAMOA-APIA—Most Rev. Alapati Lui Mata'eliga; Archbishop's House St. Joseph Building, P.O. Box 532, Apia, Samoa.
Tel: 685-20400 *Fax:* 685-20402
Email: archdiocese_chancellor@samoa.ws

Samoa-Pago Pago—Most Rev. John Quinn Weitzel, M.M.; Bishop's House P.O. Box 596, Fatuoaiga, Pago Pago, AS, 96799.
Tel: 699-1402 *Fax:* 699-1459

San—Most Rev. Jean-Gabriel Diarra; Evêché, B.P. 48, San, Mali.
Tel: 21-37-21-61 *Fax:* 21-37-24-64

San Andrés Tuxtla—Most Rev. José Trinidad Zapata Ortiz; Obispado, Constitución y Morelos s/n, San Andrés Tuxtla, Ver., 95700, Mexico.
Tel: 52-294-942-03-74 *Fax:* 52-294-942-03-74

San Angelo—Most Rev. Michael D. Pfeifer, O.M.I. (SAN); The Chancery 804 Ford, P.O. Box 1829, San Angelo, TX, 76902.
Tel: 325-651-7500 *Fax:* 325-651-6688
Email: ljdroll@aol.com

SAN ANTONIO—Most Rev. Gustavo Garcia-Siller, M.Sp.S.; Chancery Office 2718 W. Woodlawn Ave., P.O. Box 28410, San Antonio, TX, 78228.
Tel: 210-734-2620 *Fax:* 210-734-0231

San Benedetto del Tronto-Ripatransone-Montalto—Most Rev. Gervasio Gestori; Curia Diocesana, Piazza Sacconi 1, San Benedetto del Tronto, Ascoli Piceno, 63039, Italy.
Tel: 39-0735-58-18-55 *Fax:* 39-0735-57-94-73
Email: curia@diocesisbt.it

San Bernardino—Most Rev. Gerald R. Barnes, D.D. (SB); Diocesan Pastoral Center 1201 E. Higland Ave., San Bernardino, CA, 92404.
Tel: 909-475-5300 *Fax:* 909-475-5109

San Bernardo—Most Rev. Juan Ignacio González Errázuriz; Freire 516, piso 3, San Bernardo, Chile.
Tel: 56-02-85-91-137; 56-02-85-86-971; 56-02-85-98-163

San Carlos—Most Rev. Jose F. Advincula; Bishop's House, San Julio Subdivision, San Carlos City, Negros Occidental, 6127, Philippines.
Tel: 034-312-6272; 034-729-9349

San Carlos de Ancud—Most Rev. Juan Florindo Agurto Muñoz, O.S.M.; Casilla 407, Blanco Encalada 793, Ancud, Chile.
Tel: 56-065-62-23-25 *Fax:* 56-065-62-28-31
Email: obiancud@telsur.cl

San Carlos de Bariloche—Most Rev. Fernando Carlos Maletti; Obispado, Pasaje Gutiérrez 893, San Carlos de Bariloche, Río Negro, R8400GAC, Argentina.
Tel: 54-02944-423-142 ***Fax:*** 54-02944-423-142
Email: obispado@bariloche.com.ar

San Carlos de Venezuela—Most Rev. Tomás Jesús Zárraga Colmenares; Calle Carabobo 11-10, San Carlos, Edo. Cojedes, Venezuela.
Tel: 58-0258-4332-574 ***Fax:*** 58-0258-4337-666
Email: aadioce@cantv.net

San Charbel en Buenos Aires—Most Rev. Charbel Georges Merhi; Eparquía Maronita, Tronador 1464, C1427CSD, Buenos Aires, Argentina.
Tel: 54-011-4552-0380 ***Fax:*** 54-011-4552-0380

San Clemente a Saratov—Most Rev. Clemens Pickel; P.O. Box 1469, Saratov, 410012, Russia.
Tel: 8452-274-549 ***Fax:*** 8452-274-559

SAN CRISTÓBAL DE LA HABANA—His Eminence Cardinal Jaime Lucas Ortega y Alamino; Calle Habana 152, La Habana, 10100, Cuba.
Tel: 53-07-862-40-00/8/9 ***Fax:*** 53-07-866-8109
Email: arzhabana@arzhabana.co.cu

San Cristóbal de La Laguna, Tenerife—Most Rev. Bernardo Álvarez Afonso; Obispado, San Agustín 28, San Cristóbal de La Laguna, Santa Cruz de Tenerife, 38201, Spain.
Tel: 34-922-258-640 ***Fax:*** 34-922-256-362
Email: obispado@obispadodetenerife.es

San Cristóbal de las Casas—Most Rev. Felipe Arizmendi Esquivel; Calle 20 de Noviembre 1, San Cristóbal de las Casas, Chiapas, 29200, Mexico.
Tel: 52-967-678-0053 ***Fax:*** 52-967-678-3136
Email: diocesisancristobal@prodigy.net.mx

San Cristóbal de Venezuela—Most Rev. Mario del Valle Moronta Rodríguez; Obispado, Calle 3 con Carrera 3, San Cristóbal, Edo. Táchira, 5001, Venezuela.
Tel: 58-0276-343-7718 ***Fax:*** 58-0276-341-7318
Email: cmsb1@telcel.net.ve

San Diego—Most Rev. Robert H. Brom (SD); Pastoral Center 3888 Paducah Dr., P.O. Box 85728, San Diego, CA, 92186.
Tel: 858-490-8200 ***Fax:*** 858-490-8272
Email: scallaha@diocese-sdiego.org

San Felipe—Most Rev. Cristián Enrique Contreras Molina, O.de.M.; Merced 196, San Felipe, Chile.
Tel: 034-51-01-21 ***Fax:*** 034-51-34-72
Email: sanfelipe@episcopado.cl

San Felipe—Most Rev. Nelson Antonio Martínez Rust; Curia Diocesana Apartado 13, 8a Av. entre calle 9 y Av. Caracas, San Felipe, Edo. Yaracuy, 3201-A, Venezuela.
Tel: 56-0254-231-23-12; 56-0254-231-40-50
Email: curiasf@cantv.net

SAN FERNANDO—Most Rev. Paciano B. Aniceto; Chancery Office, San Jose, San Fernando, Pampanga, 2000, Philippines.
Tel: 63-045-961-28-19 ***Fax:*** 63-045-961-67-72

San Fernando de Apure—Most Rev. Víctor Manuel Pérez Rojas; Calle Bolívar 107, San Fernando de Apure, Edo. Apure, 7001, Venezuela.
Tel: 58-0247-342-1165 ***Fax:*** 58-0247-341-0582

San Fernando de la Union—Most Rev. Artemio L. Rillera, S.V.D.; Diocesan Center, P. Gomez St., San Fernando City, La Union, 2500, Philippines.
Tel: 63-072-888-23-53; 63-072-700-07-02 ***Fax:*** 63-072-888-23-53
Email: diocese_of_launion@yahoo.com

SAN FRANCISCO—Most Rev. George H. Niederauer, D.D., Ph.D. (SFR); The Chancery Office One Peter Yorke Way, San Francisco, CA, 94109.
Tel: 415-614-5500 ***Fax:*** 415-614-5555
Email: info@sfarchdiocese.org

San Francisco (Argentina)—Vacant; Obispado, Bulev. Sáenz Peña 1442, San Francisco, Córdoba, X2400BBO, Argentina.
Tel: 03564-426-114 ***Fax:*** 03564-420-514
Email: obisfco@arnet.com.ar

San Francisco de Macorís—Most Rev. Jesús María De Jesús Moya; Calle Santa Ana esq. Mella s/n, San Francisco de Macorís, Dominican Republic.
Tel: 809-588-2121 ***Fax:*** 809-588-4466
Email: diocesis.sfm@codetel.com

San Giusepe a Irkutsk—Most Rev. Cyryl Klimowicz; ul. Griboyedova 110, P.O. Box 4, Irkutsk, 664074, Russia.
Tel: 3952-41-03-10 ***Fax:*** 3952-41-01-14
Email: curiacat@curiacat.irk.ru

San Gregorio de Narek en Buenos Aires—Most Rev. Vartan Waldir Boghossian, S.D.B.; Charcas 3529, Buenos Aires, C1425BMU, Argentina.
Tel: 54-011-4824-1613; 54-011-4824-4518 ***Fax:*** 54-011-4827-1975
Email: exarmal@yahoo.com.ar

San Ignacio de Velasco—Most Rev. Carlos Stetter; Obispado, Plaza 31 de Julio, San Ignacio de Velasco, Dept. Santa Cruz, Bolivia.
Tel: 03-962-2011 ***Fax:*** 03-962-2010
Email: obispado@gmx.de

San Isidro—Most Rev. Alcides Jorge Pedro Casaretto; Obispado, Av. Libertador Gen. San Martín 16199, San Isidro, Buenos Aires, B1642CKI, Argentina.
Tel: 54-011-4743-1862 ***Fax:*** 54-011-4743-1862
Email: obispado@obispado-si.org.ar

San Isidro de El General—Most Rev. Guillermo Loría Garita; Casa Episcopal, San Isidro de El General, 8000, Costa Rica.
Tel: 2771-02-80 ***Fax:*** 2771-13-67
Email: diocsani@ice.co.cr

San Jacinto de Yaguachi—Most Rev. Anibal Nieto Guerra, O.C.D.; Calderón 505 y Lorenzo de Garaicoa, Yaguachi, Ecuador.
Tel: 04-2020-433

San Jose—Vacant; Chancery Office, Bonifacio St., San Jose City, Nueva Ecija, 3121, Philippines.
Tel: 044-511-13-71 ***Fax:*** 044-511-13-71
Email: chancerydiocese@yahoo.com

San Jose de Antique—Most Rev. Jose Romeo O. Lazo; Bishop's House Bantayan, San Jose de Buenavista, Antique, 5700, Philippines.
Tel: 036-540-8116 ***Fax:*** 036-540-9667
Email: sja_chancery@yahoo.com

SAN JOSÉ DE COSTA RICA—Most Rev. Hugo Barrantes Ureña; Arzobispado, Avenida Cuarta entre Calle Central y Calle Primera, Apartado 497, San José, 1000, Costa Rica.
Tel: 506-2258-1015 ***Fax:*** 506-2221-2427
Email: curiam@arquisanjose.org

San José de Mayo—Most Rev. Arturo Eduardo Fajardo Bustamente; Obispado, Calle Sarandí 371, San José de Mayo, 80000, Uruguay.
Tel: 598-034-22-124 ***Fax:*** 598-034-27-328
Email: ceusjose@adinet.com.uy

San Jose del Guaviare—Most Rev. Francisco Antonio Nieto Sua; Curia Episcopal, Carrera 24 N. 8-91, San Jose, Guaviare, Colombia.
Tel: 57-8-5840-023 ***Fax:*** 57-8-5840-023
Email: sanjosedelguaviaredioc@cec.org.co

San Jose (in California)—Most Rev. Patrick Joseph McGrath, D.D., J.C.D. (SJ); Diocese of San Jose 1150 N. First St., Ste. 100, San Jose, CA, 95112.
Tel: 408-983-0100 ***Fax:*** 408-983-0295
Email: chancellor@dsj.org

San Juan Bautista de Calama—Most Rev. Guillermo Patricio Vera Soto; Pasaje Mons. Juan Bautista Herrera, Calama, 1664, Chile.
Tel: 055-650-411; 055-650-400 ***Fax:*** 055-650-410; 055-650-406
Email: eoliveturu@hotmail.com

San Juan Bautista de las Misiones—Most Rev. Mario Melanio Medina Salinas; Av. Monseñor Gabino Rojas 807, San Juan Bautista de las Misiones, Paraguay.
Tel: 595-081-212-231
Email: curiasanjuba@yahoo.com

SAN JUAN DE CUYO—Most Rev. Alfonso Rogelio Delgado Evers; Arzobispado, Bartolomé Mitre 250 Oeste, San Juan, J5400CFX, Argentina.
Tel: 54-0264-422-2578 ***Fax:*** 54-0264-427-3530
Email: arzobispadosanjuan@infovia.com.ar

San Juan de la Maguana—Most Rev. José Dolores Grullón Estrella; Obispado, Apartado 99, Calle San Juan Bautista 42, San Juan de la Maguana, Dominican Republic.
Tel: 809-557-2898 ***Fax:*** 809-557-4823
Email: obispo.sjm@codetel.net.do

San Juan de los Lagos—Most Rev. Felipe Salazar Villagrana; Morelos 30, San Juan de los Lagos, Jal., 47000, Mexico.
Tel: 52-395-785-05-70 ***Fax:*** 52-395-785-29-71

SAN JUAN DE PUERTO RICO—Most Rev. Roberto Octavio González Nieves, O.F.M. (SJN); Arzobispado Calle San Jorge 201, Apartado 9021967, Santurce, San Juan, PR, 00902-1967, Puerto Rico.
Tel: 787-727-7373 ***Fax:*** 787-726-8280
Email: luciagu@arqsj.org

San Justo—Most Rev. Baldomero Carlos Martini; Dr. Ignacio Arieta 3065, San Justo, Buenos Aires, B1754AQA, Argentina.
Tel: 54-011-4650-3360 ***Fax:*** 54-011-4443-0091
Email: obsjusto@act.net.ar

San Lorenzo—Most Rev. Sebelio Peralta Alvarez; Cerro Corá 780, C.C. 22083, C/Saturio Ríos, San Lorenzo, Paraguay.
Tel: 21-576-021; 21-582-867 *Fax:* 21-582-867; 21-576-021
Email: obispado_sanlorenzo@yahoo.com

San Luis—Most Rev. Pedro Daniel Martinez Perea; Obispado, Avda. Presidente Illía 268, San Luis, D5700IEP, Argentina.
Tel: 54-02652-422-415 *Fax:* 54-02652-430-139
Email: obsanluis@infovia.com.ar

SAN LUIS POTOSÍ—Most Rev. Luis Morales Reyes; Arzobispado, Calle Francisco Madero 300, Apartado 1, San Luis Potosí, S.L.P., 78000, Mexico.
Tel: 52-444-812-4555 *Fax:* 52-444-812-7979
Email: arqsanluis@iglesiapotosina.org

San Marco Argentano - Scalea—Most Rev. Leonardo Antonio Paolo Bonanno; Via Vescovado 4, San Marco Argentano, Cosenza, 87018, Italy.
Tel: 39-0984-51-2059 *Fax:* 39-0984-51-3197
Email: cancelleria@diocesisanmarcoscalea.com

San Marcos—Most Rev. Alvaro Leonel Ramazzini Imeri; Obispado, 10a Avenida 6-28, Zona 4, San Marcos, 12001, Guatemala.
Tel: 502-7760-2315 *Fax:* 502-7760-2315

San Marino-Montefeltro—Most Rev. Luigi Negri; Curia Vescovile, P.le Giovanni Paolo II 1, Pennabilli, Pesaro, 61016, Italy.
Tel: 39-0541-91-37-14/5 *Fax:* 39-0541-91-37-35
Email: segreteriacuria@libero.it

San Martín—Most Rev. Guillermo Rodríguez-Melgarejo; Calle 91 N. 2416, San Martín, Buenos Aires, B1650BQH, Argentina.
Tel: 54-011-4755-2414/2950 *Fax:* 54-011-4755-2414/2950
Email: obsanmar@overnet.com.ar

San Miguel—Most Rev. Miguel Angel Morán Aquino; Obispado, 2a Avenida Nte. y Calle Siramà 101, Apdo. 33, San Miguel, El Salvador.
Tel: 503-2661-0962 *Fax:* 503-2661-1839
Email: obispadodesanmiguel@yahoo.com

San Miguel (in Argentina)—Most Rev. Sergio Alfredo Fenoy; Justo José de Urquiza 1769, San Miguel, Buenos Aires, B1663GXM, Argentina.
Tel: 011-4664-9207 *Fax:* 011-4664-9207
Email: curia@obsanmiguel.org

San Miniato—Most Rev. Fausto Tardelli; Vescovado, Piazza Duomo 2, San Miniato, Pisa, 56028, Italy.
Tel: 39-0571-41-80-71 *Fax:* 39-0571-40-00-92
Email: diocesi@diocesisanminiato.it

San Nicolás de los Arroyos—Most Rev. Héctor Sabatino Cardelli; Obispado, Calle Bartolomé Mitre 84, San Nicolás, Buenos Aires, B2900ACB, Argentina.
Tel: 54-03461-429-529; 54-03461-422-364 *Fax:* 54-03461-429-529
Email: obispado@obispadosn.com.ar

San Pablo—Most Rev. Leo M. Drona, S.D.B.; P.O. Box 8, San Pablo City, 4000, Philippines.
Tel: 049-562-83-01; 049-561-18-57 *Fax:* 049-561-18-57
Email: dioceseofsanpablo@yahoo.com

San Pedro—Most Rev. Adalberto Martínez Flores; Obispado, Mariscal Estigarribia y General Díaz 104, Villa de San Pedro, Paraguay.
Tel: 595-042-222-318 *Fax:* 595-042-222-318
Email: diocesisdesanpedroapostol@gmail.com

San Pedro de Macorís—Most Rev. Francisco Ozoria Acosta; Avda. General Duvergé 151, Apartado 175, San Pedro de Macorís, Dominican Republic.
Tel: 809-246-3800 *Fax:* 809-246-3506
Email: obispadospm@hotmail.com

San Pedro-en-Côte-d'Ivoire—Most Rev. Jean-Jacques Koffi Oi Koffi; Evêché, 01 B.P. 826, San Pedro 01, Ivory Coast.
Tel: 225-34-71-1826 *Fax:* 225-34-71-1826
Email: evechesp.ci@aviso.ci

San Pedro Sula—Most Rev. Angel Garachana Pérez, C.M.F.; Obispado, Apartado 207, 2a Avda. y Calle N.O. 2, San Pedro Sula, Honduras.
Tel: 504-553-52-53 *Fax:* 504-552-9424
Email: obispadosps@sulanet.net

San Rafael—Most Rev. Eduardo María Taussig; Obispado, Rivadavia 415, San Rafael, Mendoza, M5600FQA, Argentina.
Tel: 54-02627-422-815 *Fax:* 54-02627-422-815
Email: obispadosanrafael@speedy.com.ar

San Roque de Presidencia Roque Sáenz Peña—Most Rev. Hugo Nicolás Barbaro; General Martín de Güemes 260, Presidencia Roque Sáenz Peña, Chaco, H3700HJF, Argentina.
Tel: 54-03732-420-426 *Fax:* 54-03732-425-285
Email: obispadosanroque@arnet.com.ar

SAN SALVADOR—Most Rev. José Luis Escobar Alas; Arzobispado, Colonia Médica, Av. Dr. Emilio Alvarez y Av. Dr. Max Bloch, San Salvador, El Salvador.
Tel: 503-2234-5300 *Fax:* 503-2226-4979
Email: cancilleria_arz@yahoo.com

San Sebastián—Most Rev. José Ignacio Munilla Aguirre; Obispado, Calle Zabaleta 5, San Sebastián, 20002, Spain.
Tel: 34-943-28-50-00 *Fax:* 34-943-28-60-03
Email: idazkaritza@elizagipuzkoa.org

San Severo—Most Rev. Lucio Angelo Renna, O.Carm.; Vescovado, Via Soccorso 38, San Severo, Foggia, 71016, Italy.
Tel: 39-0882-33-10-44 *Fax:* 39-0882-33-66-58
Email: info@diocesisansevero.it

San Vicente—Most Rev. Jose Elias Rauda Gutierrez, O.F.M.; Obispado, 2a Avenida Norte 10, San Vicente, El Salvador.
Tel: 503-2393-0004 *Fax:* 503-2393-6802
Email: curiadesanvicente@gmail.com

Sandakan—Most Rev. Julius Dusin Gitom; Bishop's Office P.O. Box 2039, Sandakan, Sabah, -90723, Malaysia.
Tel: 089-22-46-23; 089-21-70-71 *Fax:* 089-21-86-23
Email: dospo1@gmail.com

Sandhurst—Vacant; Sacred Heart Cathedral Presbytery 172 McCrae St., P.O. Box 201, Bendigo, Vic., 3552, Australia.
Tel: 61-0354-41-2544 *Fax:* 61-0354-41-8278
Email: chancery@sand.catholic.org.au

Sandomierz—Most Rev. Krzysztof Nitkiewicz; ul. Mariacka 7, Sandomierz, 27-600, Poland.
Tel: 48-015-832-25-23; 48-015-832-25-38 *Fax:* 48-015-832-25-44
Email: kuria@sandomierz.opoka.org.pl

Sanggau—Most Rev. Giulio Mencuccini, C.P.; Keuskupan, Jl. Jenderal Sudirman 43, Sanggau Kapuas, Kalimantan Barat, 78512, Indonesia.
Tel: 62-0564-21223 *Fax:* 62-0564-21260
Email: kesa@telkom.net

Sangmélima—Most Rev. Christophe Zoa; Evêché, B.P. 239, Sangmélima, Cameroon.
Tel: 237-2228-8254 *Fax:* 237-2228-8254

Sankt Gallen—Most Rev. Markus Büchel; Bischöfliches Ordinariat, Klosterhof 6b, Postfach 263, Sankt Gallen, CH-9001, Switzerland.
Tel: 41-071-227-33-40 *Fax:* 41-071-227-33-41
Email: kanzlei@bistum-stgallen.ch

Sankt Pölten—Most Rev. Klaus Küng; Bischöfliches Ordinariat, Domplatz 1, Sankt Pölten, A-3100, Austria.
Tel: 43-02742-324 *Fax:* 43-02742-324-309
Email: bo.stpoelten@kirche.at

SANT'ANGELO DEI LOMBARDI-CONZA-NUSCO-BISACCIA—Most Rev. Francesco Alfano; Curia Arcivescovile, Via Belvedere 1, Sant'Angelo dei Lombardi, Avellino, 83054, Italy.
Tel: 39-0827-23-039 *Fax:* 39-0827-21-6114
Email: curia@diocesisantangelo.it

Sant Feliu de Llobregat—Most Rev. Agustín Cortés Soriano; Carrer d'Armenteres 35, Sant Feliu de Llobregat, Barcelona, 08980, Spain.
Tel: 93-632-76-30 *Fax:* 93-632-76-31
Email: secretaria@bisbatsantfeliu.org

Santa Ana—Most Rev. Romeo Tovar Astorga, O.F.M.; Casa Episcopal, 3a Av. Norte 3, Santa Ana, 02-102, El Salvador.
Tel: 503-2441-02-78 *Fax:* 503-2441-02-78
Email: diocesissta.ana@integra.com.sv

Santa Clara—Most Rev. Marcelo Arturo González Amador; Unión 51, entre Gloria y Buenviaje, Santa Clara, Villa Clara, 50100, Cuba.
Tel: 042-2006-80 *Fax:* 042-2080-32
Email: arnaldof37@obistclara.co.cu

SANTA CRUZ DE LA SIERRA—His Eminence Cardinal Julio Terrazas Sandoval; Arzobispado, Casilla 25, Calle Ingavi 49, Santa Cruz, Bolivia.
Tel: 591-03-3324-416; 591-03-3352-194 *Fax:* 591-03-3330-181
Email: cancilleria@cotas.com.bo

Santa Cruz do Sul—Most Rev. Canísio Klaus; Cúria Diocesana, Rua Ramiro Barcelos 717, Santa Cruz do Sul, RS, 96810-050, Brazil.
Tel: 55-051-3711-3668 *Fax:* 55-051-3713-1050
Email: curia@mitrascs.com.br

SANTA FE—Most Rev. Michael Jarboe Sheehan, S.T.L., J.C.D. (SFE); Catholic Center 4000 St. Joseph's Place N.W., Albuquerque, NM, 87120.
Tel: 505-831-8100 *Fax:* 505-831-8115
Email: chancellor@archdiosf.org

SANTA FE DE LA VERA CRUZ—Most Rev. José María Arancedo; Arzobispado, Avenida General López 2720, Santa Fe, S3000DCJ, Argentina.
Tel: 54-0342-459-5791 ***Fax:*** 54-0342-459-4491
Email: curia@arquisantafe.org.ar

SANTA FE DE ANTIOQUIA—Most Rev. Orlando Antonio Corrales García; Arzobispado, Plazuela Martínez Pardo 12-11, Santa Fe de Antioquia, Antioquia, Colombia.
Tel: 57-4-853-11-55 ***Fax:*** 57-4-853-11-44
Email: arquidiocesisantafel@edatel.net.co

SANTA MARIA—Most Rev. Hélio Adelar Rubert; Cúria Diocesana, Av. Rio Branco 793, 97010-492, C.P. 17, Santa Maria, RS, 97001-970, Brazil.
Tel: 55-055-3221-6060 ***Fax:*** 55-055-3223-8035
Email: bispado@terra.com.br

Santa Maria de Los Angeles (in Chile)—Most Rev. Pedro Felipe Bacarreza Rodríguez; Obispado, Lautaro 519, Los Angeles, Chile.
Tel: 043-32-91-80 ***Fax:*** 043-34-96-94
Email: losangeles@episcopado.cl

Santa María del Patrocinio en Buenos Aires—Vacant; Ramón L. Falcón 3960, Buenos Aires, C1407GSN, Argentina.
Tel: 54-011-4671-4192 ***Fax:*** 54-011-4671-7265
Email: pokrov@ciudad.com.ar

Santa Marta—Most Rev. Hugo Eugenio Puccini Banfi; Curia Episcopal, Carrera 4 N. 16-42, Santa Marta, Magdalena, Colombia.
Tel: 57-54-421-2643 ***Fax:*** 57-54-421-3661
Email: diocesissma@cdiocesano.edu.co

Santa Rosa—Most Rev. Mario Aurelio Poli; Obispado, Av. Bartolomé Mitre 140, Santa Rosa, La Pampa, L6300DSD, Argentina.
Tel: 54-02954-433-671 ***Fax:*** 54-02954-433-671
Email: obistar@speedy.com.ar

Santa Rosa de Copán—Most Rev. Luis Alfonso Santos Villeda, S.D.B.; Obispado 2a Calle N.E. 122, Santa Rosa de Copán, Honduras.
Tel: 504-2662-00-61 ***Fax:*** 504-2662-11-63

Santa Rosa de Lima—Most Rev. Bernabé de Jesús Sagastume Lemus, O.F.M.Cap.; Iglesia Catedral El Niño Dios, Cuilapa, Santa Rosa, 06001, Guatemala.
Tel: 7820-6073 ***Fax:*** 7886-5532
Email: obispadosrl@gmail.com

Santa Rosa de Osos—Most Rev. Jorge Alberto Ossa Soto; Obispado, Calle Real 28-72, Santa Rosa de Osos, Antioquia, Colombia.
Tel: 57-48-860-80-50 ***Fax:*** 57-48-860-80-96; 57-48-860-80-50
Email: info@dsro.org

Santa Rosa (in California)—Most Rev. Robert F. Vasa; Chancery Office 985 Ariway Ct., Santa Rosa, CA, 95403.
Tel: 707-545-7610 ***Fax:*** 707-542-9702
Web: www.srdiocese.org
Email: phawkins@srdiocese.org
P.O. Box 1297, Santa Rosa, CA, 95402.

Santander—Most Rev. Vicente Jiménez Zamora; Obispado, Plaza Obispo José Eguino Trecu 1, Santander, 39002, Spain.
Tel: 34-942-36-5657 ***Fax:*** 34-942-36-7400
Email: obisant@planalfa.es

Santarém—Most Rev. Manuel Pelino Domingues; Cúria Diocesana, Praça Sá da Bandeira, Edifício do Seminário, Santarém, 2000-135, Portugal.
Tel: 351-243-30-4060 ***Fax:*** 351-243-30-4067
Email: diocstr@sapo.pt

Santarém (in Brazil)—Most Rev. Esmeraldo Barreto de Farias; Cúria Diocesana, C.P. 133, Praça Mons. José Gregório 453, Santarém, PA, 68100-970, Brazil.
Tel: 093-3522-1668 ***Fax:*** 093-3522-6110
Email: curia.stm@gmail.com

Santiago de Cabo Verde—Most Rev. Arlindo Gomes Furtado; C.P. 46, Av. Amílcar Cabral, Largo 5 de Outubro, Praia, 7600, Cape Verde.
Tel: 261-11-19 ***Fax:*** 261-21-26
Email: diocesesantiagocv@gmail.com

SANTIAGO DE CHILE—Most Rev. Ricardo Ezzati Andrello, S.D.B; Erasmo Escala 1882, Santiago, Chile.
Tel: 56-02-787-56-00 ***Fax:*** 56-02-787-56-33
Email: cancilleriasantiago@iglesia.cl

SANTIAGO DE COMPOSTELA—Most Rev. Julián Barrio Barrio; Arzobispado, Plaza de la Inmaculada 1, Santiago de Compostela, A Coruña, 15704, Spain.
Tel: 34-981-57-23-00 ***Fax:*** 34-981-56-36-91
Email: arzsantiago@archicompostela.org

SANTIAGO DE CUBA—Most Rev. Dionisio Guillermo García Ibáñez; Arzobispado, Sánchez Hechavarría 607, Santiago de Cuba, 90100, Cuba.
Tel: 53-022-625-480 ***Fax:*** 53-022-686-186
Email: arzstgo@arzsantiago.co.cu

SANTIAGO DE LOS CABALLEROS—Most Rev. Ramón Benito de la Rosa y Carpio; Arzobispado, Calle Duvergé 14, Santiago de los Caballeros, Dominican Republic.
Tel: 809-582-2094 ***Fax:*** 809-581-3580
Email: arzobisp.stgo@codetel.net.do

Santiago de María—Most Rev. Rodrigo Orlando Cabrera Cuéllar; Obispado, 4a Av. Sur y Calle Bolívar, Santiago de María, Depto. de Usulután, El Salvador.
Tel: 503-2663-0282 ***Fax:*** 503-2663-0282

Santiago de Veraguas—Most Rev. Oscar Mario Brown Jimémez; Obispado, Apartado 48, Santiago de Veraguas, Panama.
Tel: 507-958-7085 ***Fax:*** 507-958-5117
Email: disantivera@cwp.net.pa

Santiago del Estero—Most Rev. Francisco Polti Santillán; Obispado, Avda. Belgrano Sur 450, Santiago del Estero, G4200AAR, Argentina.
Tel: 54-0385-421-1534; 54-0385-421-1260 ***Fax:*** 54-0385-421-1534
Email: cancilleria@obispadosgo.org.ar

Santísimo Salvador de Bayamo Y Manzanillo—Most Rev. Álvaro Julio Beyra Luarca; Obispado, Saco 52, Apartado 27, Bayamo, Granma, 85100, Cuba.
Tel: 023-42-71-27 ***Fax:*** 023-42-72-70
Email: info@obibayamo.co.cu

Santíssima Conceição do Araguaia—Most Rev. Dominique Marie Jean Denis You; Cúria Diocesana, Rua Maria Otavia 330, Conceição do Araguaia, PA, 68540-000, Brazil.
Tel: 55-094-3421-1307 ***Fax:*** 55-094-3421-1307
Email: curiaconceicao@gmail.com

Santissima Trinità (in Almaty)—Most Rev. Jose Luis Mumbiela Sierra; Kabanbai Batyra St. 77/16, Almaty, 050000, Kazakhstan.
Tel: 7-7272-72-62-40 ***Fax:*** 7-7272-616-776
Email: diocese-almaty@mail.ru

Santo Amaro—Most Rev. Fernando Antônio Figueiredo, O.F.M.; Cúria Diocesana, Av. Mascote 1171, São Paulo, SP, 04363-001, Brazil.
Tel: 55-011-5564-4829; 55-011-2821-8700; 55-011-2821-8711 ***Fax:*** 55-011-5564-4829
Email: secretariamitra@terra.com.br

Santo André—Most Rev. Nelson Westrupp, S.C.I.; Cúria Diocesana, Praça do Carmo 36, Santo André, SP, 09010-020, Brazil.
Tel: 55-011-4438-2077 ***Fax:*** 55-011-4438-2325
Email: dioc.santoandre@uol.com.br

Santo Ângelo—Most Rev. José Clemente Weber; Cúria Diocesana Rua Marquês do Herval 1113, C.P. 1100, Santo Ângelo, RS, 98800-971, Brazil.
Tel: 55-055-3313-5263 ***Fax:*** 55-055-3313-5263
Email: mitra@sol.psi.br

SANTO DOMINGO—His Eminence Cardinal Nicolás de Jesús López Rodríguez; Arzobispado, Apartado 186, Calle Isabel la Católica 55, Santo Domingo, Dominican Republic.
Tel: 809-685-3141/3 ***Fax:*** 809-688-7270; 809-685-8702
Email: tesoreria_arz@hotmail.com

Santo Domingo en Ecuador—Most Rev. Wilson Abraham Moncayo Jalil; Casa Bombolí, Calle Germán Maya 212, entre Mons. Shumacher y Jorge Iturralde, Urb. Las Palmas, Santo Domingo de los Colorados, Pichincha, Ecuador.
Tel: 02-2750-935; 02-2750-715 ***Fax:*** 02-2750-715
Email: diocesisdlc@andinanet.net

Santo Tomé—Most Rev. Hugo Norberto Santiago; Av. Bartolomé Mitre 930, Santo Tomé, Corrientes, W3340AMT, Argentina.
Tel: 54-03756-420-240 ***Fax:*** 54-03756-420-240
Email: obispado@obispadodesantotome.org.ar

Santorini, Thira—Most Rev. Franghískos Papamanólis, O.F.M.Cap.; Katholiki Episkopi, Thira, Hellas, 84700, Greece.

Santos—Most Rev. Jacyr Francisco Braido, C.S.; Av. Conselheiro Rodrigues Alves 254, Bairro Macuco, Santos, SP, 11015-200, Brazil.
Tel: 55-013-3228-8888 ***Fax:*** 55-013-3224-3101
Email: diocese@curiadesantos.com.br

Sanyüan (Sanyuan)—Catholic Mission, Bishop's House, Sanyuan, Shaanxi, China.

São Carlos—Most Rev. Paulo Sérgio Machado; Cúria Diocesana, Rua 9 de Julho 1515, São Carlos, SP, 13560-550, Brazil.
Tel: 55-016-3362-4480 ***Fax:*** 55-016-3362-4487

São Gabriel da Cachoeira—Most Rev. Edson Taschetto Damian; C.P. 61, Av. 7 de Setembro 205, São Gabriel da Cachoeira, AM, 69750-000, Brazil.
Tel: 55-097-3471-1367 *Fax:* 55-097-3471-1287
Email: edsondamian@gmail.com

São João Batista em Curitiba—Most Rev. Valdomiro Koubetch, O.S.B.M.; Cúria Eparquial, C.P. 8859, Rua Maranhão 1200, Bairro Água Verde, 80610-000, Curitiba, PR, 80611-970, Brazil.
Tel: 55-041-3329-7163
Email: eparquiasjbatist@uol.com.br

São João da Boa Vista—Most Rev. David Dias Pimentel; Av. Dr. Oscar Piraja Martins 268, Bairro Sto. Andre, São João da Boa Vista, SP, 13874-000, Brazil.
Tel: 55-019-3622-2245
Email: mitrasjbv@diocesesaojoao.org.br

São João del Rei—Most Rev. Célio de Oliveira Goulart, O.F.M.; Cúria Diocesana, Praça Frei Orlando 130, São João del Rei, MG, 36307-352, Brazil.
Tel: 55-032-3371-1011; 55-032-3371-4746 *Fax:* 55-032-3371-4746
Email: curiasjdr@mgconecta.com.br

São José do Rio Preto—Most Rev. Paulo Mendes Peixoto; Cúria Diocesana Av. da Constituiçao 1372, São José do Rio Preto, SP, 15025-120, Brazil.
Tel: 55-017-2136-8699 *Fax:* 55-017-2136-8694
Email: bispado@catolico.org.br

São José dos Campos—Most Rev. Moacir Silva; Cúria Diocesana, Praça Mons. Ascânio Brandão 1, São José dos Campos, SP, 12245-440, Brazil.
Tel: 55-012-3928-3911 *Fax:* 55-012-3928-3924
Email: mitra@diocesesjc.org.br

São José dos Pinhais—Most Rev. Ladislau Biernaski, C.M.; Rua Izabel Redentora 1372, São José do Pinhais, PR, 83005-010, Brazil.
Tel: 55-041-3035-9800 *Fax:* 55-041-3035-9812
Email: diocese@diocesesjp.org.br

São Luís de Montes Belos—Most Rev. Carmelo Scampa; Cúria Diocesana, Praça Dom Stanislao Van Melis s/n, São Luís de Montes Belos, GO, 76100-000, Brazil.
Tel: 55-064-3671-1690 *Fax:* 55-064-3671-1538
Email: curiasaoluiz@uol.com.br

SÃO LUÍS DO MARANHÃO—Most Rev. José Belisário da Silva, O.F.M.; Cúria Metropolitana, Avenida Dom Pedro II s/n, São Luís, MA, 65010-450, Brazil.
Tel: 55-098-3313-4160/7; 55-098-3313-4157 *Fax:* 55-098-3313-4158
Email: chancelaria_2004@yahoo.com.br
C.P. 11, São Luís, 65001-970, Brazil.

São Luiz de Cáceres—Most Rev. Antônio Emídio Vilar, S.D.B.; Cúria Diocesana, Praça Barão do Rio Branco 296, C.P. 250, Cáceres, MT, 78200-000, Brazil.
Tel: 55-065-3223-1788 *Fax:* 55-065-3223-1899
Email: dioccac@terra.com.br

São Mateus—Most Rev. Zanoni Demettino Castro; Cúria Diocesana, Av. João XXIII 410, C.P. 38, São Mateus, ES, 29930-420, Brazil.
Tel: 55-027-3763-1177 *Fax:* 55-027-3763-3140
Email: curia@diocesedesaomateus.org.br

São Miguel Paulista—Most Rev. Manuel Parrado Carral; Cúria Diocesana, Trav. Guilherme de Aguiar 40, Sao Miguel Paulista, São Paulo, SP, 08011-030, Brazil.
Tel: 55-011-2297-8611 *Fax:* 55-011-2297-3953
Email: diocesesaomiguel@terra.com.br

SÃO PAULO—His Eminence Odilo Pedro Scherer; Cúria Metropolitana, 01014-970, Av. Higienópolis 890, São Paulo, SP, -01238-000, Brazil.
Tel: 55-011-3826-0133 *Fax:* 55-011-3666-6425
Email: arquidiocesep.chancelaria@yahoo.com.br

São Raimundo Nonato—Most Rev. Pedro Brito Guimarães; Cúria Diocesana, Praça Comendador Piauilino 15, São Raimundo Nonato, PI, 64770-000, Brazil.
Tel: 55-089-3582-3632 *Fax:* 55-089-3582-3632

SÃO SALVADOR DA BAHIA—Most Rev. Murilo Sebastião Ramos Krieger, S.C.I.; Cúria Metropolitana, Av. Leovigildo Filgueiras 270, Garcia, Salvador, BA, 40100-000, Brazil.
Tel: 55-071-4009-6666/6600 *Fax:* 55-071-4009-6606; 55-071-4009-6635
Email: contato@arquidiocesesalvador.org.br

SÃO SEBASTIÃO DO RIO DE JANEIRO—Most Rev. Orani João Tempesta, O.Cist.; Cúria Metropolitana, Rua Benjamin Constant 23 Glória, Rio de Janeiro, RJ, 20241-150, Brazil.
Tel: 55-021-2292-3132 *Fax:* 55-021-2242-9295; 55-021-2252-1182
Email: curiarj@arquidiocese.org.br

São Tomé e Príncipe—Most Rev. Manuel António Mendes dos Santos, C.M.F.; Centro Diocesano, C.P. 104, Rua P. Pinto da Rocha I, São Tomé, São Tome and Príncipe.
Tel: 239-012-223-455 *Fax:* 239-012-227-348
Email: diocese@cstome.net

Sapë—Most Rev. Lucjan Avgustini; Kuria Dioqezane, Kisha Katolike, Sheshi Nënë Tereza, Vau Dejës, Shkodër, Albania.
Tel: 222-40-092 *Fax:* 222-40-092
Email: albarcadinoe@hotmail.com

Sapporo—Vacant; Catholic Bishop's Office, Higashi 6-chome 10, Kita 1-jo, Chûô-ku, Sapporo-shi, 060-0031, Japan.
Tel: 81-011-241-2785 *Fax:* 81-011-221-3668
Email: dio-office@csd.or.jp

Sarh—Most Rev. Edmond Djitangar; Evêché, B.P. 87, Sarh, Chad.
Tel: 2268-14-24 *Fax:* 2268-12-02
Email: diosarh@yahoo.fr

Saskatoon—Most Rev. Donald Bolen; 100-5th Avenue North, Saskatoon, SK, S7K 2N7, Canada.
Tel: 306-242-1500 *Fax:* 306-244-6010
Email: bishopoffice@saskatoonrcdiocese.com

Saskatoon (Ukrainian)—Most Rev. Bryan Bayda, C.SS.R.; 214 Avenue M. South, Saskatoonq, SK, -S7M 2K4, Canada.
Tel: 306-653-0138 *Fax:* 306-665-2569
Email: admin.skeparchy@sasktel.net

SASSARI—Most Rev. Paolo Mario Virgilio Atzei, O.F.M.Conv.; Via Arcivescovado 19, Sassari, 07100, Italy.
Tel: 39-079-20-21-810/1 *Fax:* 39-079-20-21-809
Email: curiadiocesana.ss@tiscali.it

Satna—Most Rev. Mathew Vaniakizhakkel, C.V.; Bishop's House Rewa Road, P.O. Box 22, Satna, M.P., -485001, India.
Tel: 91-07672-224-167 *Fax:* 91-07672-225-667

Satu Mare, Szatmár—Most Rev. Jeno Schönberger; Episcopia Romano-Catolica, Str. 1 Decembrie 1918 nr. 2, Satu Mare, RO-440010, Romania.
Tel: 40-0261-714-955; 40-0261-713-574 *Fax:* 40-0261-716-451
Email: puspokseg@szatmariegyhazmegye.ro

Sault Sainte Marie—Most Rev. Jean-Louis Plouffe; 30 Chemin Sainte-Anne, Sudbury, ON, P3C 5E1, Canada.
Tel: 705-674-2727; 705-674-6998
Email: chancery@diocesecentre.com

SAURIMO—Most Rev. José Manuel Imbamba; Bispado, Rua do Cemiterio, C.P. 52, Saurimo, Lunda, Angola.
Tel: 00871-0253-250-575 *Fax:* 00871-0253-250-575
Email: diocesesaurimo@ceastangola.org

Savannah—Most Rev. Gregory J. Hartmayer, O.F.M.Conv.; Catholic Pastoral Center 601 E. Liberty St., Savannah, GA, 31401-5196.
Tel: 912-201-4100 *Fax:* 912-201-4101
Web: www.dioceseofsavannah.org
Email: communications@diosav.org

Savona-Noli—Most Rev. Vittorio Lupi; Curia Vescovile, Piazza Vescovato 13, Savona, 17100, Italy.
Tel: 39-019-83-89-601 *Fax:* 39-019-83-89-642
Email: segreteria.curia@diocesisavona.it

Saïda, Saida, Sidone (Maronite)—Most Rev. Elias Nassar; Evêché Maronite Rue Riad El Solh, Saïda, Lebanon.
Tel: 07-721-133 *Fax:* 07-723-096
Email: diocesesaida@hotmail.com

Scranton—Most Rev. Joseph C. Bambera; Chancery Office 300 Wyoming Ave., Scranton, PA, 18503-1279.
Tel: 570-207-2216 *Fax:* 570-207-2236
Web: www.dioceseofscranton.org
Email: rev-brian-clarke@dioceseofscranton.org

SEATTLE—Most Rev. James Peter Sartain; Chancery Office 710 9th Ave., Seattle, WA, 98104.
Tel: 206-382-4560 *Fax:* 206-382-4840
Web: www.seattlearchdiocese.org
Email: info@seattlearch.org

Sées—Most Rev. Jacques Habert; Evêché, 29 rue Conté, B.P. 25, Sées, 61500, France.
Tel: 33-2-33-81-15-15 *Fax:* 33-2-33-81-15-11
Email: eveche-de-sees@diocesedeseez.org

Segorbe-Castellón de la Plana—Most Rev. Casimiro López Llorente; Obispado, Paseo Obispo Ahedo 2, Segorbe, Castellón, 12400, Spain.
Tel: 34-964-710-276Palacio Episcopal Gobernador Bermúdez de Castro 8, Castellón de la Plana, 12003, Spain.
Tel: 34-964-220-066 *Fax:* 34-964-225-882
Email: cancilleria@obsegorbecastellon.es

Ségou—Most Rev. Augustin Traoré; Evêché, B.P. 505, Ségou, Mali.

Segovia—Most Rev. Ángel Rubio Castro; Obispado, Seminario 4, Segovia, 40001, Spain.
Tel: 34-921-46-09-63; 34-921-46-62-36 *Fax:* 34-921-46-09-64
Email: obsegovia@planalfa.es

Sekondi-Takoradi—Most Rev. John Martin Darko; Bishop's Secreteriat East Windy Ridge, P.O. Box TD 236, Takoradi, Ghana.
Tel: 233-031-20-24-921; 233-031-20-21-185 *Fax:* 233-031-20-23-465

SEMARANG—Most Rev. Johannes Maria Trilaksyanta Pujasumarta; Kantor Palayanan Pastoral, Jl. Iman Bonjol 172, Semarang, Jawa, -50131, Indonesia.
Tel: 62-024-831-2276 *Fax:* 62-024-841-4741
Email: kuria@keuskupan-agung-smg.org

Sendai—Most Rev. Martin Tetsuo Hiraga; Chancery Office, Honcho 1-2-12, Aoba-ku, Sendai-shi, Miyagi-ken, 980-0014, Japan.
Tel: 81-022-222-7371 *Fax:* 81-022-222-7378
Email: curia_sendai@guitar.ocn.ne.jp

Senigallia—Most Rev. Giuseppe Orlandoni; Piazza Garibaldi 3, Senigallia, Ancona, 60019, Italy.
Tel: 39-071-65-92-45; 39-071-60-498 *Fax:* 39-071-60-094
Email: diocesi@senigallia.chiesacattolica.it

SENS—Most Rev. Yves Patenôtre; Achevêché, 7 rue Française, B.P. 287, Auxerre CEDEX, 89005, France.
Tel: 3-86-72-9393 *Fax:* 3-86-51-7513
Email: diocese89@wanadoo.fr

SEOUL—His Eminence Nicholas Cheong Jinsuk; Archbishop's House Chung-gu Myong-dong 2-ga, Seoul, Korea, 100-809, Korea, South.
Tel: 82-02-727-2021 *Fax:* 82-02-773-1947
Email: ao@seoul.catholic.or.kr

Serrinha—Most Rev. Ottorino Assolari, C.S.F.; Rua Pedro Tiago 383, Serrinha, BA, 48700-000, Brazil.
Tel: 075-3261-3687 *Fax:* 075-3261-3687
Email: dioceseserrinha@hotmail.com

Sessa Aurunca—Most Rev. Antonio Napoletano, C.Ss.R.; Via XXI Luglio 148, Sessa Aurunca, Caserta, 81037, Italy.
Tel: 39-0823-93-7167 *Fax:* 39-0823-93-71-67
Email: ucs@diocesisessa.it

Sete Lagoas—Most Rev. Guilherme Porto; Cúria Diocesana, Rua Major Campos 154, Sete Lagoas, MG, 35700-011, Brazil.
Tel: 55-031-3773-2270 *Fax:* 55-031-3773-2270
Email: diocese71@gmail.com

Setúbal—Most Rev. Gilberto Délio Gonçalves Canavarro dos Reis; Rua Frau Pacheco 109, Setúbal CODEX, 2900-376, Portugal.
Tel: 351-265-53-99-41 *Fax:* 351-265-53-99-43
Email: secretaria@diocese-setubal.pt

SEVILLA—Most Rev. Juan Jose Asenjo Pelegrina; Arzobispado, Plaza Virgen de los Reyes s/n, Sevilla, 41004, Spain.
Tel: 34-95-450-5505 *Fax:* 34-95-450-5506
Email: arzobispado@archisevilla.org

Shanghai (Shanghai)—St.-Joseph Church, Szechwan Road South, Shanghai, Jiangsu, China.

Shendam—Most Rev. James Naanman Daman, O.S.A.; Catholic Diocesan Chancery P.O. Box 12, Shendam, Plateau State, -940001, Nigeria.
Tel: 0803-586-8087; 0803-459-0747
Email: dioceseofshendam@yahoo.com

SHERBROOKE—Most Rev. Luc Cyr; Archevêché, 130 rue de la Cathédrale, Sherbrooke, QC, J1H 4M1, Canada.
Tel: 819-563-9934 *Fax:* 819-562-0125
Email: chancelier@diocesedesherbrooke.org

's-Hertogenbosch, Bois-le-Duc—Most Rev. Antonius Lambertus Maria Hurkmans; P.B. 1070, Parade 11, 5211 KL, 's-Hertogenbosch, 5200 BC, The Netherlands.
Tel: 31-073-612-54-88 *Fax:* 31-073-613-68-50
Email: bisdom@bisdomdenbosch.nl

Shíhnan (Enshi)—Catholic Mission, Bishop's House, Enshi, Hubei, China.

SHILLONG—Most Rev. Dominic Jala, S.D.B.; Archbishop's House, Shillong, Meghalaya, 793003, India.
Tel: 91-0364-222-3355
Email: archbishop@neline.com

Shimoga—Most Rev. Gerald Isaac Lobo; Bishop's House, Sagar Road, Shimoga, Karnataka, 577204, India.
Tel: 91-0818-2250-314
Email: malligemane@rediffmail.com

Shinyanga—Most Rev. Aloysius Balina; Bishop's House P.O. Box 47, Shinyanga, Tanzania.
Tel: 255-028-276-3040 *Fax:* 255-028-276-3040

Shiuchow (Shaoguan), Shao-Chou—Catholic Mission Bishop's House, Shaoguan, Guang-dong, China.

SHKODRË-PULT—Most Rev. Angelo Massafra, O.F.M.; Kryeipeshkëvi, Sheshi Gijon Pali II, Shkodër, Albania.
Tel: 022-427-44 *Fax:* 022-436-73
Email: curiashkoder@hotmail.com

Shohchow (Shuoxian)—Catholic Mission, Bishop's House, Shuoxian, Shanxi, China.

Shreveport—Most Rev. Michael Gerard Duca, J.C.L. (SHP); Chancery Office 3500 Fairfield Ave., Shreveport, LA, 71104.
Tel: 318-868-4441 *Fax:* 318-868-4469
Web: www.dioshpt.org
Email: drichter@dioshpt.org

Shrewsbury—Most Rev. Mark Davies; Curial Offices, 2 Park Road South, Prenton, Wirral, CH43 4UX, England.
Tel: 44-0151-652-9855 *Fax:* 44-0151-653-5172
Email: curia@dioceseofshrewsbury.org

Shunking (Nanchong)—Catholic Mission, Bishop's House, Nanchong, Sichuan, China.

Shunteh (Xingtai)—Catholic Mission, Pei-Men, Xingtai, Hebei, China.

SIAN (XI'AN), CHANG-AN—Catholic Mission, Tu-Ti-Miao, Xi'an, Shaanxi, China.

Siangyang (Xiangyang)—Catholic Mission, Bishop's House, Xiangyang, Hubei, China.

Šiauliai—Most Rev. Eugenijus Bartulis; Zveju skg. 2, Siauliai, 76294, Lithuania.
Tel: 41-52-1110 *Fax:* 41-52-1114
Email: s.kurija@takas.lt

Šibenik—Most Rev. Ante Ivas; Biskupski Ordinarijat, Biskupa Jeronima Milete 2a, Šibenik, 22000, Croatia.
Tel: 385-022-311-333 *Fax:* 385-022-312-620
Email: biskupski-ordinarijat-si@si.htnet.hr

Sibolga—Most Rev. Ludovikus Simanullang, O.F.M.Cap.; Jl. Ade Irma Suryani Nasution 27, Sibolga, Sumatera Utara, 22513, Indonesia.
Tel: 62-0631-21-291 *Fax:* 62-0631-21-045
Email: tana_tuan@yahoo.com

Sibu—Most Rev. Dominic Su Haw Chiu; Sacred Heart Catholic Church Lanang Rd., P.O. Box 495, Sibu, Sarawak, 96007, Malaysia.
Tel: 60-084-31-73-73 *Fax:* 60-084-32-12-99

Siedlce—Most Rev. Zbigniew Kiernikowski; Kuria Diecezjalna, ul. Pilsudskiego 62, Siedlce, 08-110, Poland.
Tel: 48-025-644-2195 *Fax:* 48-025-644-8744
Email: kuria@ks.internetdsl.pl

SIENA-COLLE DI VAL D'ELSA-MONTALCINO—Most Rev. Antonio Buoncristiani; Piazza Duomo 5, Siena, 53100, Italy.
Tel: 39-0577-42-020 *Fax:* 39-0577-28-18-40
Email: info@arcidiocesi.siena.it

Síenhsíen (Xianxian)—Catholic Mission, Chang-Kia-Chuang, Xianxian, Hebei, China.

Sigüenza-Guadalajara—Most Rev. Atilano Rodriguez Martinez; Obispado, Calle Josè de Villaviciosa 7, Sigüenza, Guadalajara, 19250, Spain.
Tel: 34-949-347-072 *Fax:* 34-949-391-911
Email: obsiguenza@planalfa.es

Sikasso—Most Rev. Jean-Baptiste Tiama; Evêché, B.P. 74, Sikasso, Mali.
Tel: 2162-0270 *Fax:* 2162-0520
Email: evechesik@yahoo.fr

Simdega—Most Rev. Vincent Barwa; Bishop's House P.O. Simdega 835223, Simdega, Dt. Jharkhand, India.
Tel: 06525-225-333

Simla and Chandigarh—Most Rev. Ignatius Loyola Mascarenhas; Bishop's Office Sector 19-A, P.O. Box 709, Chandigarh, 160019, India.
Tel: 91-0172-277-5777; 91-0172-277-3777 *Fax:* 91-0172-278-1630

Sincelejo—Most Rev. Nel Hedye Beltrán Santamaría; Obispado, Calle 27 N. 11-59, Barrio Rita de Arrázola Sincelejo, Sucre, Colombia.
Tel: 57-52-280-5275 *Fax:* 57-52-280-5605
Email: diocesin@yahoo.com

Sindhudurg—Most Rev. Anthony Alwyn Fernandes Barreto; Bishop's House Kankavli, Sindhudurg Dt., 416602, India.
Tel: 02367-232-061; 02367-232-661; 02367-230-033 ***Fax:*** 02367-230-033
Email: sindhudioc@rediffmail.com

SINGAPORE—Most Rev. Nicholas Chia Yeck Joo; Archbishop's House, 31 Victoria Street, 187 997, Singapore.
Tel: 65-6339-6715 ***Fax:*** 65-6333-4735

Singida—Most Rev. Desiderius Rwoma; P.O. Box 487, Singida, Tanzania.
Tel: 255-026-250-2299 ***Fax:*** 255-026-250-2534

Sinop—Most Rev. Gentil Delázari; Cúria Diocesana, Rua Coquerios 1257, Sinop, MT, 78556-080, Brazil.
Tel: 55-066-3531-3105 ***Fax:*** 55-066-3531-3105
Email: mitrasnp@terra.com.br

Sintang—Most Rev. Agustinus Agus; Keuskupan, JI. A. Yani 8, Sintang, Kalimantan Barat, 78611, Indonesia.
Tel: 62-0565-21213 ***Fax:*** 62-0565-21940
Email: skesi@telkom.net

Sínyang (Xinyang)—Catholic Mission, Bishop's House, Xinjang, Henan, China.

Sion, Sitten—Most Rev. Norbert Brunner; Evêché, C.P. 2124, rue de la Tour 12, CH-1950, Sion 2, Switzerland.
Tel: 027-32-91-818 ***Fax:*** 027-32-91-836
Email: diocese.sion@cath-vs.ch

Sioux City—Most Rev. R. Walker Nickless (SC); Chancery: Administrative Offices 1821 Jackson St., Sioux City, IA, 51105.
Tel: 712-255-7933 ***Fax:*** 712-233-7598
Email: markd@scdiocese.org

Sioux Falls—Most Rev. Paul Joseph Swain; Chancery Office 523 N. Duluth Ave., Sioux Falls, SD, 57104-2714.
Tel: 605-334-9861 ***Fax:*** 605-334-2092
Email: malthoff@sfcatholic.org

SIRACUSA—Most Rev. Salvatore Pappalardo; Arcivescovado, Piazza Duomo 5, Siracusa, 96100, Italy.
Tel: 39-0931-60-544 ***Fax:*** 39-0931-46-3776
Email: amministrazione@arcidiocesi.siracusa.it

Sisak—Most Rev. Vlado Kosic; Tgr. Bana Jelacical, Sisak, 44000, Croatia.
Tel: 044-544-555 ***Fax:*** 044-544-555
Email: biskupija@sk.t-com.hr

Sivagangai—Most Rev. Jebamalai Susaimanickam; Bishop's House, Britto Nagar, Melur Rd., Sivagangai, Tamil Nadu, 630561, India.
Tel: 04575-241-744 ***Fax:*** 04575-242-954
Email: svgbishop@gmail.com

Siwantze (Chongli-Xiwanzi)—Catholic Mission, Bishop's House, Chongli-Xiwanzi, Hohhot, China.

Skopje—Most Rev. Kiro Stojanov; Biskupski Ordinarijat, ul. Risto Šiškov 31, Skopje, 1000, Macedonia.
Tel: 389-02-3164-123 ***Fax:*** 389-02-3164-123
Email: katbiskupija@t-home.mk

Soacha—Most Rev. Daniel Caro Borda; Calle 5 N. 9-48, Leon XIII, Soacha, Colombia.
Tel: 1-719-10-87 ***Fax:*** 1-782-84-77
Email: cancilleriasoacha@hotmail.com

Sobral—Most Rev. Odelir Jose Magri, M.C.C.I.; Cúria Diocesana, Praça Quirino Rodrigues 76/4, Sobral, CE, 62011-260, Brazil.
Tel: 55-088-3611-0545 ***Fax:*** 55-088-3611-0545
Email: diocesedesobral@yahoo.com.br

Socorro y San Gil—Most Rev. Carlos Germán Mesa Ruiz; Obispado, Carrera 9 N. 12-42, San Gil, Santander, Colombia.
Tel: 57-77-724-3011; 57-77-724-22-05 ***Fax:*** 57-77-724-2204
Email: diocesissocorroysangil@yhoo.com

Sofia e Plovdiv—Most Rev. Gheorghi Ivanov Jovcev; bul. Maria Luisa 3, Plovdiv, 4000, Bulgaria.
Tel: 032-65-02-91 ***Fax:*** 032-62-15-22
Email: manolov@seznam.cz

Sohag—Most Rev. Youssef Aboul El Kher; Evêché Copte Catholique, B.P. 7, Sohag, Egypt.
Tel: 20-093-231-3599 ***Fax:*** 20-093-231-2986
Email: vescvcatsohag@yahoo.it

Soissons—Most Rev. Hervé Giraud; Evêché, 17 rue des Déportés et Fusillés, B.P. 166, Soissons CEDEX, 02204, France.
Tel: 3-23-53-0635 ***Fax:*** 3-23-53-4125

Sokal-Zhovkva—Most Rev. Mychajlo Koltun, C.Ss.R.; 7A vul. Lvivska str., Zhovkva, Lvivska Oblast, 80300, Ukraine.
Tel: 03252-6-13-36 ***Fax:*** 03252-6-13-35
Email: sokaleparchy@zhovkva.lviv.ua

Sokodé—Most Rev. Ambroise Kotamba Djoliba; Evêché, 300 B.P. 55, Sokodé, Togo.
Tel: 550-02-87 ***Fax:*** 550-04-13
Email: eveche_sokode@yahoo.fr

Sokoto—Most Rev. Matthew Hassan Kukah; Bishop's House 1 Aliyu Jodi Road, P.O. Box 2556, Sokoto State, Nigeria.
Tel: 060-23-22-28; 080-660-00-507
Email: sokdiocese@yahoo.com

Sololá-Chimaltenango—Most Rev. Gonzalo de Villa y Vásquez, S.J.; Obispado, Calle Santander 4-71, Zona 2, Panajachel, Sololá, 07001, Guatemala.
Tel: 7762-1215 ***Fax:*** 7762-1215
Email: curias_ch@yahoo.com

Solsona—Most Rev. Xavier Novell Goma; Casa del Bisbat, Pl. Palau 1, Solsona, Lleida, 25280, Spain.
Tel: 37-973-48-06-19 ***Fax:*** 34-973-48-09-51
Email: bisbatsolsona@bisbatsolsona.cat

Solwezi—Most Rev. Charles Joseph Sampa Kasonde; P.O. Box 110033, Solwezi, Zambia.
Tel: 218-821-312 ***Fax:*** 218-821-428
Email: diocsolwezi@yahoo.com

SONGEA—Most Rev. Norbert Wendelin Mtega; Archbishop's House P.O. Box 152, Songea, Tanzania.
Tel: 025-260-2004 ***Fax:*** 025-260-2354
Email: songea-archdiocese@yahoo.com

Sonsón-Rionegro—Most Rev. Fidel Leon Cadavid Marin; Obispado, Calle 51 N. 47-31, Rionegro, Antioquia, Colombia.
Tel: 57-4-531-52-52 ***Fax:*** 57-4-531-52-52
Email: diocesis@une.net.co

Sonsonate—Vacant; Av. Flavián Mucci, Costado Norte de Catedral, Apartado 52, Sonsonate, El Salvador.
Tel: 503-2451-5224 ***Fax:*** 503-2451-2546
Email: diocesissonsonate@hotmail.com

Soochow (Suzhou), Wuhsien—Catholic Mission, Bishop's House, Suzhou, Jiangsu, China.

Sora-Aquino-Pontecorvo—Most Rev. Filippo Iannone, O.Carm.; Vescovado, Via 11 Febbraio 1929, 3, Sora, Frosinone, 03039, Italy.
Tel: 39-0776-83-10-82 ***Fax:*** 39-0776-82-01-60
Email: cancelleria@diocesisora.191.it

SOROCABA—Most Rev. Eduardo Benes de Sales Rodrigues; Cúria Metropolitana, Av. Dr. Eugênio Salerno 60, Santa Terezinha, Sorocaba, SP, 18035-430, Brazil.
Tel: 55-015-3221-6880 ***Fax:*** 55-015-3221-6880
Email: curia@arquidiocesesorocaba.org.br

Soroti—Most Rev. Emmanuel Obbo; Bishop's House P.O. Box 650, Soroti, Uganda.
Tel: 045-44-61-506
Email: catholicbishopsrt@yahoo.co.uk

SORRENTO-CASTELLAMMARE DI STABIA—Most Rev. Felice Cece; Curia Arcivescovile, Via S. Anna 1, Castellammare di Stabia, Napoli, 80053, Italy.
Tel: 39-081-871-45-01; 39-081-878-12-44 ***Fax:*** 31-081-871-51-22
Email: segreteriacuria@diocesisorrentocmare.it

Sorsogon—Most Rev. Arturo M. Bastes, S.V.D.; Chancery Office P.O. Box 7, Padre Pedro Licup Hall, Sorsogon City, Sorsogon, 4700, Philippines.
Tel: 056-21-11-289 ***Fax:*** 056-21-11-842
Email: fr.rey_mabute@yahoo.com

Sosnowiec—Most Rev. Grzegorz Kaszak; ul. Wawel 19, Sosnowiec, 41-200, Poland.
Tel: 48-032-293-5151 ***Fax:*** 48-032-293-5188
Email: kuria@sosnowiec.opoka.org.pl

SOUTHWARK—Most Rev. Peter David Smith; Archbishop's House 150 St. George's Road, Southwark, London, SE1 6HX, England.
Tel: 44-020-7928-5592 ***Fax:*** 44-020-7401-7383
Email: chancery@rcsouthwark.co.uk

Speyer—Most Rev. Karl-Heinz Wiesemann; Bischöfliches Ordinariat, Kleine Pfaffengasse 16, Speyer, D-67346, Germany.
Tel: 49-06232-1020 ***Fax:*** 49-06232-102-300
Email: info@bistum-speyer.de

Spiš—Most Rev. Stefan Secka; Biskupský úrad, Spišské Kapitula 9, Spišské Podhradie, SK-053 04, Slovakia.
Tel: 42-053-454-1136 ***Fax:*** 42-053-450-2208
Email: biskupstvo@kapitula.sk

SPLIT-MAKARSKA—Most Rev. Marin Barišic; Nadbiskupski Ordinarijat Poljana kneza Trpimira 7, Split, 21000, Croatia.
Tel: 385-021-407-501 ***Fax:*** 385-021-407-538
Email: ivan.cubelic@st.t-com.hr

Spokane—Most Rev. Blase J. Cupich (SPK); Chancery Office W. 1023 Riverside Ave., P.O. Box 1453, Spokane, WA, 99210-1453.
Tel: 509-358-7300 ***Fax:*** 509-358-7302
Email: chancellor@dioceseofspokane.org

SPOLETO-NORCIA—Most Rev. Renato Boccardo; Archivescovado, Via Aurelio Saffi 13, Spoleto, Perugia, 06049, Italy.
Tel: 39-0743-23-101 ***Fax:*** 39-0743-231-036
Email: segreteria@spoletonorcia.it

Springfield-Cape Girardeau—Most Rev. James V. Johnston Jr., D.D., J.C.L. (SPC); The Catholic Centre 601 S. Jefferson Ave., Springfield, MO, 65806-3143.
Tel: 417-866-0841 ***Fax:*** 417-866-1140
Email: treidy@dioscg.org

Springfield (in Illinois)—Most Rev. Thomas J. Paprocki; Chancery Office 1615 W. Washington St., P.O. Box 3187, Springfield, IL, 62708-3187.
Tel: 217-698-8500 ***Fax:*** 217-698-0802
Email: ckemme@dio.org

Springfield (in Massachusetts)—Most Rev. Timothy Anthony McDonnell; Chancery Office 76 Elliot St., P.O. Box 1730, Springfield, MA, 01102-1730.
Tel: 413-732-3175 ***Fax:*** 413-737-2337
Email: c.connelly@diospringfield.org

Srijem—Most Rev. Duro Gasparovic; Biskupski Ordinarijat Strossmayerova 20, Petrovaradin, Srijem, 21131, Serbia.
Tel: 021-643-37-58 ***Fax:*** 021-643-25-44
Email: srijemska.biskupija@eunet.rs

Srikakulam—Most Rev. Innayya Chinna Addagatla; Bishop's House, Balaga Thope, Srikakulam, A.P., 532001, India.
Tel: 08942-223-265 ***Fax:*** 08942-222-940
Email: skldiocese@yahoo.com

Stamford (Ukrainian)—Most Rev. Paul P. Chomnycky, O.S.B.M. (STF); Chancery Office 14 Peveril Rd., Stamford, CT, 06902-3019.
Tel: 203-324-7698 ***Fax:*** 203-967-9948
Email: stamfordeparchy@optonline.net

Steubenville—Vacant; Chancery Office 422 Washington St., P.O. Box 969, Steubenville, OH, 43952-5969.
Tel: 740-282-3631 ***Fax:*** 740-282-3327
Email: kkemo@diosteub.org

Stockholm—Most Rev. Anders Arborelius, O.C.D.; Katolska Biskopsämbetet Götgatan 68, P.O. Box 4114, Stockholm, S-102 62, Sweden.
Tel: 46-08-462-66-00 ***Fax:*** 46-08-462-94-25
Email: sekretariat@katolskakyrkan.se

Stockton—Most Rev. Stephen E. Blaire, D.D. (STO); Chancery Office 212 N. San Joaquin St., Stockton, CA, 95202.
Tel: 209-466-0636 ***Fax:*** 209-941-9722
Email: rryan@stocktondiocese.org

STRASBOURG—Most Rev. Jean-Pierre Grallet, O.F.M.; Archevêché, 16 rue Brûlée, Strasbourg CEDEX, 67081, France.
Tel: 3-88-21-24-24 ***Fax:*** 3-88-21-24-36
Email: chancelier@archeveche-strasbourg.fr

Stryj—Most Rev. Taras Senkiv, O.M., Apostolic Admin.; vul. Shewchenko 80, Box 49, Stryj, 82400, Ukraine.
Tel: 03245-52-208 ***Fax:*** 03245-52-208
Email: rl.taras.stryj@gmail.com

Süanhwa (Xuanhua)—Catholic Mission Bishop's House, Xuanhua, Hebei, China.

Subotica—Most Rev. János Pénzes; Trg svete Terezije 3, Subotica, 24000, Serbia.
Tel: 381-024-553-610 ***Fax:*** 381-024-552-497
Email: subisk@tippnet.rs

Suchitepéquez-Retalhuleu—Most Rev. Pablo Vizcaíno Prado; Carretera antigua a Samayac, Mazatenango, Dep. Suchitepéquez, 0-170, Guatemala.
Tel: 7872-2929 ***Fax:*** 7872-2902

Süchow (Xuzhou)—Catholic Mission, Bishop's House, Xuzhou, Jiangsu, China.

SUCRE—Most Rev. Jesús Pérez Rodríguez, O.F.M.; Arzobispado, Casilla 205, Calle Bolívar 702, Sucre, Bolivia.
Tel: 04-6451-587 ***Fax:*** 04-6460-336
Email: arzsucre@entelnet.bo

Suifu (Yibin)—Catholic Mission, Bishop's House, Shungking, Szechwan, China.

SUIYÜAN (HOHOT), KUEI SUI—Catholic Mission, Archbishop's House, Hohot, China.

Sulaimaniya—Vacant; Kurdistan Nord, Sulaimaniya, Iraq.
Tel: 053-31-81-009

Sulmona-Valva—Most Rev. Angelo Spina; Vescovado, Viale Roosevelt 7, Sulmona, L'Aquila, 67039, Italy.
Tel: 39-0864-34065 ***Fax:*** 39-0864-33522
Email: curiasul@tin.it

Sumbawanga—Most Rev. Damian Kyaruzi; Bishop's House P.O. Box 34, Sumbawanga, Tanzania.
Tel: 025-2802-178

Sumbe—Most Rev. Benedito Roberto, C.S.Sp.; Bispado, C.P. 277, Rua do Soba Ulundo, Sumbe, Kwanza Sul, Angola.
Tel: 02362-30-120 ***Fax:*** 02362-30-120
Email: diocesedesumbe@yahoo.com.br

Sunyani—Most Rev. Matthew Kwasi Gyamfi; Bishop's House P.O. Box 450, Sunyani, Ghana.
Tel: 233-035-20-27379 ***Fax:*** 233-035-20-27093
Email: cdsunyani@gmail.com

Superior—Most Rev. Peter F. Christensen, M.A.S. (SUP); Chancery Office 1201 Hughitt Ave., Box 969, Superior, WI, 54880.
Tel: 715-392-2937 ***Fax:*** 715-392-2015

Surabaya—Most Rev. Vincentius Sutikno Wisaksono; Jl. Polisi Istimewa 17, Surbaya, Jawa, 60265, Indonesia.
Tel: 031-56-15-592; 031-56-77-796 ***Fax:*** 031-56-84-004
Email: sekrupsby@sby.dnet.net.id

Surat Thani—Most Rev. Joseph Prathan Sridarunsil, S.D.B.; Bishop's House 15 Moo 6 Chonkasem Road 41, Tambon Makhamtia, Muang, Surat Thani, 84000, Thailand.
Tel: 66-077-282-543/840 ***Fax:*** 66-077-218-348

Surigao—Most Rev. Antonieto D. Cabajog; Bishop's House Villa San Miguel, km. 2, Surigao City, 8400, Philippines.
Tel: 086-826-1316 ***Fax:*** 086-826-2433

Susa—Most Rev. Alfonso Bandini Confalonieri; Vescovado, Piazza S. Giusto 14, Susa, Torino, 10059, Italy.
Tel: 39-0122-62-21-94 ***Fax:*** 39-0122-62-21-94

SUVA—Most Rev. Petero Mataca; Archdiocesan Office Nicholas House, 25 Pratt St., P.O. Box 109, Suva, Fiji.
Tel: 679-330-19-55 ***Fax:*** 679-330-15-65

Suwon—Most Rev. Mathias Ri Iong-hoon; Diocesan Office Suwon-shi Chang-an-gu Chongja-dong 578, Kyonggi-do, 440-840, Korea, South.
Tel: 82-031-241-3720 ***Fax:*** 82-031-241-3991
Email: scgn@casuwon.or.kr

Swatow (Shantou)—Catholic Mission, Bishop's House, Shantou, Guangdong, China.

Swidnica—Most Rev. Ignacy Dec; Kuria Diecezjalna pl. Jana Pawla II 1, Swidnica, 58-100, Poland.
Tel: 074-856-44-00 ***Fax:*** 074-856-44-14
Email: kuria@diecezja.swidnica.pl

SYDNEY—His Eminence Cardinal George Pell; Level 16, Polding Centre, 133 Liverpool Street, Sydney, N.S.W., 2000, Australia.
Tel: 61-02-9390-5100 ***Fax:*** 61-02-9261-8312
Email: chancery@sydneycatholic.org

Sylhet—Most Rev. Bejoy Nicephorus D'Cruze, O.M.I.; Bangladesh.

Syracuse—Most Rev. Robert Joseph Cunningham; Chancery Office 240 E. Onondaga St., P.O. Box 511, Syracuse, NY, 13201-0511.
Tel: 315-422-7203 ***Fax:*** 315-478-4619

Syros—Most Rev. Franghískos Papamanólis, O.F.M.Cap.; Katholiki Episkopi, Odós Georgìou Papandreou 15, Hellas, Syros, 84100, Greece.
Tel: 30-22810-84-782 ***Fax:*** 30-22810-84-781
Email: syrensis@otenet.gr

SZCZECIN-KAMIEN—Most Rev. Andrzej Dziega; Kuria Metropolitalna ul. Papieza Pawla VI 4, Szczecin, 71-459, Poland.
Tel: 48-091-4542-292 ***Fax:*** 48-091-4536-908
Email: kuria@kuria.pl

Szeged-Csanád—Most Rev. László Kiss-Rigó; Aradi Vertanuk tere 2, Szeged, H-6720, Hungary.
Tel: 36-62-420-932 *Fax:* 36-62-312-947

Székesfehérvár—Most Rev. Antal Spányi; Városház tér 5, Pf 178, Székesfehérvár, H-8001, Hungary.
Tel: 36-22-510-691 *Fax:* 36-22-510-699
Email: tugrits@szfvar.katolikus.hu

Szepíngkai (Siping), Szepingchieh—Catholic Mission, Bishop's House, Siping Shi, Liao-Pei, China.

Szombathely—Most Rev. András Veres; Berzsenyi Dániel tér 3, Pf. 41, Szombathely, H-9701, Hungary.
Tel: 36-94-312-056 *Fax:* 36-94-318-538
Email: szombathely@katolikus.hu

T

Tabasco—Most Rev. Gerardo de Jesús Rojas López; Obispado, Doña Fidencia 502, Villahermosa, Tabasco, 86000, Mexico.
Tel: 52-993-312-1397 *Fax:* 52-993-312-1905

TABORA—Most Rev. Paul R. Ruzoka; Archbishop's House Private Bag, P.O. Tabora, Tanzania.
Tel: 255-026-2605-608 *Fax:* 255-026-2604-000
Email: archbishops_office@yahoo.co.uk

Tacámbaro—Most Rev. José Luis Castro Medellin, M.S.F.; Obisbado, Apartado 4, Profesor Enrique Aguilar 81, Tacámbaro, Mich., 61650, Mexico.
Tel: 52-459-596-0044 *Fax:* 52-459-596-0730
Email: obispadotac@prodigy.net.mx

Tacna y Moquegua—Most Rev. Marco Antonio Cortez Lara; Obispado, Apartado 426, Blondell 107, Tacna, Peru.
Tel: 51-52-243-178 *Fax:* 51-52-424-661

Tacuarembó—Most Rev. Julio César Bonino Bonino; Obispado, Calle Joaquín Suárez 235, Tacuarembó, 45000, Uruguay.
Tel: 598-063-23-529 *Fax:* 598-063-28-038

Tagbilaran—Most Rev. Leonardo Y. Medroso; Chancery Office P.O. Box 18, Tagbilaran City, Bohol, 6300, Philippines.
Tel: 038-41-13-487; 038-50-19-634 *Fax:* 038-41-15-653

Tagum—Most Rev. Wilfredo D. Manlapaz; Chancery Office Rizal St., Tagum City, Davao, 8100, Philippines.
Tel: 63-084-218-1402 *Fax:* 63-084-218-2878
Email: dioceseoftagum@yahoo.com

Taíchow (Linhai)—China.

Taichung—Most Rev. Martin Su Yao-wen; Bishop's House 368 Der Hwa Street, Taichung City, 40454, Taiwan.
Tel: 886-04-220-75-678 *Fax:* 886-04-220-68-722
Email: bishop.office@msa.hinet.net

Tainan—Most Rev. Bosco Lin Chi-nan; 15 Ch'ang Yung Lou-2, Tainan, 70127, Taiwan.
Tel: 886-06-237-5761 *Fax:* 886-06-274-9341

Taiohae o Tefenuaenata—Most Rev. Guy Chevalier, SS.CC.; Evêché, B.P. 10, Taiohae, Nuku-Hiva, Iles Marquises, 98742, French Polynesia.
Tel: 689-920-352 *Fax:* 689-920-288

TAIPEI—Most Rev. John Hung Shan-chuan, S.V.D.; Archbishop's House 94 Loli Road, Taipei, 10679, Taiwan.
Tel: 886-02-2737-1311 *Fax:* 885-02-2737-3710
Email: Taipei.archdiocese@gmail.com

TAIYUAN (TAIYUAN)—Catholic Mission Archbishop's House, Taiyuan, Shanxi, China.

Takamatsu—Most Rev. John Eijiro Suwa; Bishop's House, 1-8-9 Sakuramachi, Takamatsu-shi, Kagawa-ken, 760-0074, Japan.
Tel: 81-087-831-6659 *Fax:* 81-087-833-1484
Email: catholic-takamatsu@takamatsu.catholic.ne.jp

Talca—Most Rev. Horacio del Carmen Valenzuela Abarca; 4 Norte 851, Casilla 7, Talca, Chile.
Tel: 56-071-61-61-54 *Fax:* 56-071-61-61-54
Email: talca@episcopado.cl

Tali (Dali)—China.

Talibon—Most Rev. Christian Vicente F. Noel; Bishop's House, Talibon, Bohol, 6325, Philippines.
Tel: 038-515-5118 *Fax:* 038-515-0043; 038-515-5118
Email: chancerytalibon@yahoo.com

TAMALE—Most Rev. Philip Naameh; Archbishop's House Gumbehini Rd., P.O. Box TL 42, Tamale, N.R., Ghana.
Tel: 037-20-22-425 *Fax:* 037-20-22-425
Email: tamdio2@yahoo.co.uk

Tambacounda—Most Rev. Jean-Noël Diouf; Evêché, B.P. 68, Tambacounda, Senegal.
Tel: 221-33-981-10-45 *Fax:* 221-33-981-19-45
Email: evechetamba@yahoo.fr

Taming (Daming)—Catholic Mission Bishop's House, Daming, Hebei, China.

Tampico—Most Rev. José Luis Dibildox Martinez; Apartado 545, Calle Altamira 116 Oriente, Tampico, Tamps., 89000, Mexico.
Tel: 52-833-212-28-02/10 *Fax:* 52-833-212-67-81
Email: obispadotampico@prodigy.net.mx

Tandag—Most Rev. Nereo P. Odchimar; Diocesan Pastoral Center, Mabua, Tandag, Surigao del Sur, 8300, Philippines.
Tel: 63-086-211-3044 *Fax:* 63-086-211-4102
Email: joricorO6@yahoo.com

Tanga—Most Rev. Anthony Banzi; Bishop's House P.O. Box 1108, Tanga, Tanzania.
Tel: 255-027-2642-417 *Fax:* 255-027-2643-548

TANGER—Most Rev. Santiago Agrelo Martínez, O.F.M.; Sidi Bouabid 55, B.P. 2116, Socco, Tánger, 90000, Morocco.
Tel: 212-0539-932-762 *Fax:* 212-0539-949-117

Tanjore—Most Rev. Devadass Ambrose Mariadoss; Bishop's House P.O. Box 204, Thanjavur, Tamil Nadu, 613007, India.
Tel: 91-04362-231-252; 91-04362-234-123 *Fax:* 91-04362-234-123

Tanjung Selor—Most Rev. Justinus Harjosusanto, M.S.F.; Keuskupan Jl. Jelarai, P.O. Box 01, Tanjung Selor, Kaltim, 77212, Indonesia.
Tel: 0552-21-301 *Fax:* 0552-22-568
Email: keustansel@telkom.net

Tanjungkarang—Most Rev. Andreas Henrisusanta, S.C.I.; Pastoran Katolik, Jl. Way Lubuk 4, P.O. Box 93, Bandar Lampung, Sumatra, 35127, Indonesia.
Tel: 62-0721-252-531 *Fax:* 62-0721-260-358
Email: pietpr@gmail.com

Tapachula—Most Rev. Leopoldo González González; Av. Primera Sur 1, Apartado 70, Tapachula, Chiapas, 30700, Mexico.
Tel: 52-962-626-1503 *Fax:* 52-962-626-5024
Email: diotap@prodigy.net.mx

Tarahumara—Most Rev. Rafael Sandoval Sandoval, M.N.M.; Obispado, Cascada s/n, Col. Altavista, Apartado 11, Guachochi, Chih., 33180, Mexico.
Tel: 154-649-543-0710 *Fax:* 154-649-543-0882
Email: diocesisdetarahumara@hotmail.com

TARANTO—Most Rev. Benigno Luigi Papa, O.F.M.Cap.; Largo Arcivescovado 8, Taranto, 74121, Italy.
Tel: 39-099-47-09-611 *Fax:* 39-099-47-09-610
Email: infocuria@diocesi.taranto.it

Tarawa and Nauru—Most Rev. Paul Eusebius Mea Kaiuea, M.S.C.; Bishop's House P.O. Box 79, Bairiki, Tarawa, Kiribati.
Tel: 686-21-279 *Fax:* 686-21-401
Email: diocesetarawa@coconutwireless.ki

Tarazona—Most Rev. Eusebio Ignacio Hernandez Sola, O.A.R.; Obispado, Plaza de Palacio 1, Tarazona, Zaragoza, 50500, Spain.
Tel: 34-976-64-0800/0907 *Fax:* 34-976-64-2951
Email: obtarazona@planalfa.es

Tarbes et Lourdes—Most Rev. Jacques Perrier; Maison Diocesaine 51 rue de Traynès, Tarbes, 65000, France.
Tel: 5-62-440-970 *Fax:* 5-62-440-972
Email: administration.diocese.tarbes@wanadoo.fr

Tarija—Most Rev. Francisco Javier del Río Sendino; Obispado, Casilla 1192, Calle General Bernardo Trigo 769, Tarija, Bolivia.
Tel: 04-6643-793 *Fax:* 04-6113-593
Email: obistja@entelnet.bo

Tarlac—Most Rev. Florentino F. Cinense; Bishop's Residence, F. Tañedo St., Tarlac City, 2300, Philippines.
Tel: 63-045-982-1938 *Fax:* 63-045-982-1938

Tarma—Most Rev. Richard Daniel Alarcón Urrutia; Jr. Huancayo 347, Tarma, Junin, Peru.
Tel: 64-32-1966 *Fax:* 64-32-1966

Tarnów—Most Rev. Wiktor Skworc; Kuria Diecezjalna, ul. Legionów 30, Tarnów, 33-100, Poland.
Tel: 48-014-631-7300; 48-014-628-6423 *Fax:* 48-014-631-7309
Email: kuria@diecezja.tarnow.pl

TARRAGONA—Most Rev. Jaume Pujol Balcells; Arzobispado, Plà de Palau 2, Tarragona, 43003, Spain.
Tel: 34-977-23-34-12 ***Fax:*** 34-977-25-18-47
Email: arquebisbat@arquebisbattarragona.cat

Tatung (Datong)—Catholic Mission Bishop's House, Datong, Shanxi, China.

Taubaté—Most Rev. Carmo João Rhoden, S.C.I.; Cúria Diocesana, Praça Barão do Rio Branco 30, Taubaté, SP, 12010-090, Brazil.
Tel: 55-012-3632-2855 ***Fax:*** 55-012-3632-2855
Email: curiataubate@uol.com.br

Taunggyi—Most Rev. Matthias U Shwe; Archbishop's Office, L-198 Bayintnaung Rd., Taunggyi, 06011, Myanmar.
Tel: 95-081-21-689 ***Fax:*** 95-081-22-164

Taungngu—Most Rev. Isaac Danu; Catholic Church Compound, Khay Mar Street, Taungngu, 8101, Myanmar.
Tel: 95-054-24-297

Teano-Calvi—Most Rev. Arturo Aiello; Curia Vescovile, Piazza Duomo 1, Teano, Caserta, 81057, Italy.
Tel: 39-0823-87-54-28 ***Fax:*** 39-0823-65-70-63
Email: curiateanocalvi@alice.it

Techiman—Most Rev. Dominic Yeboah Nyarko; Catholic Diocese P.O. Box 251, Techiman, Brong Ahafo, Ghana.
Tel: 061-035-25-91-319

Teggiano-Policastro—Vacant; Episcopio, Piazza Mons. V. Vignone 1, Teggiano, Salerno, 84039, Italy.
Tel: 39-0975-79-053 ***Fax:*** 39-0975-79-053
Email: curia@diociteggiano.it

TEGUCIGALPA—His Eminence Cardinal Oscar Andrés Rodríguez Maradiaga, S.D.B.; Arzobispado, Apartado 106, Colonia Palcartagua, Tegucigalpa, 1113, Honduras.
Tel: 504-2236-2849 ***Fax:*** 504-2236-2967

TEHERAN—Most Rev. Ramzi Garmou; Enghelab Street, Shahid Abbas Moussavi St. 37, Teheran, 15819, Iran.
Tel: 98-021-88-82-3549 ***Fax:*** 98-021-88-30-87-14

Tehuacán—Most Rev. Rodrigo Aguilar Martínez; Agustín A. Cacho 113, Tehuacán, Pue., 75700, Mexico.
Tel: 52-238-383-2000 ***Fax:*** 52-238-383-1468
Email: obispadotehuacan@yahoo.com.mx

Tehuantepec—Most Rev. Oscar Campos Contreras; Obispado, Apartado 93, Mina s/n, Tehuantepec, Oax., 70760, Mexico.
Tel: 52-971-715-0060 ***Fax:*** 52-971-715-0060
Email: obispadodetehuantepec@hotmail.com.mx

Teixeira de Freitas-Caravelas—Most Rev. Carlos Alberto dos Santos; Cúria Diocesana, Rua Eurico Gaspar Dutra 38, Teixeira de Freitas, BA, 45995-112, Brazil.
Tel: 55-073-3291-1283 ***Fax:*** 55-073-3291-1283
Email: curiatx@uol.com.br

TELLICHERRY—Most Rev. George Valiamattam; Archbishop's House P.O. Box 70, Thalassery, Kerala, 670101, India.
Tel: 0490-234-1058 ***Fax:*** 0490-234-1412
Email: diocese@archdioceseoftellicherry.org

Telšiai—Most Rev. Jonas Boruta, S.J.; Katedros 5, Telšiai, 87131, Lithuania.
Tel: 444-60-636 ***Fax:*** 444-52-300
Email: tkurija@takas.lt

Tempio-Ampurias—Most Rev. Sebastiano Sanguinetti; Curia Vescovile, Via Episcopio 7, Tempio Pausania, Sassari, 07029, Italy.
Tel: 39-079-63-11-37 ***Fax:*** 39-079-63-11-37
Email: curia@diocesitempioampurias.it

Temuco—Most Rev. Manuel Camilo Vial Risopatrón; Casilla 40-D, Vicuna Mackenna 779, Temuco, Chile.
Tel: 56-045-29-76-02/3 ***Fax:*** 56-045-21-05-16
Email: vicgraltco@episcopado.cl

Tenancingo—Most Rev. Raul Gomez Gonzalez; Mexico.

Teófilo Otoni—Most Rev. Aloisio Jorge Pena Vitral; Cúria Diocesana, Rua Epaminondas Otoni 713, Teófilo Otoni, MG, 39800-013, Brazil.
Tel: 55-033-3522-2618 ***Fax:*** 55-033-3522-2618
Email: mitratotoni@veloxmail.com.br

Teotihuacan—Most Rev. Francisco Escobar Galicia; Prolongacion Cuauhtemoc s/n, Col. Centro, San Juan, Teotihuacan, 55800, Mexico.
Tel: 594-956-04-91 ***Fax:*** 594-956-04-91
Email: diocesisdeteotihaucan@hotmail.com

Tepic—Most Rev. Ricardo Watty Urquidi, M.Sp.S.; Obispado, Apartado 15, Tepic, Nay., 63000, Mexico.
Tel: 52-311-214-46-45/7 ***Fax:*** 52-311-213-2023
Email: diocesis@diocesisdetepic.org.mx
Av. de las Flores 10, Fraccione residencial La Loma, Tepic, Nay, 63137, Mexico.

Teramo-Atri—Most Rev. Michele Seccia; Vescovado, Piazza Martiri della Libertà 14, Teramo, 64100, Italy.
Tel: 39-0861-250-301 ***Fax:*** 39-0861-244-962
Email: curiateramo@libero.it

TERESINA—Vacant; Cúria Metropolitana, C.P. 70, Teresina PI, 64001-970, Brazil.
Tel: 55-086-3222-4350 ***Fax:*** 55-086-3221-2221
Email: curiathe@uol.com.br
Av. Frei Serafim 3200, Teresina, PI, 64001-500, Brazil.

Termoli-Larino—Most Rev. Gianfranco De Luca; Vescovado, Piazza S. Antonio 8, Termoli, Campobasso, 86039, Italy.
Tel: 39-0875-70-71-48 ***Fax:*** 39-0875-70-91-29
Email: curia@termolilarino.it

Terni - Narni - Amelia—Most Rev. Vincenzo Paglia; Vescovado, Piazza Duomo 11, Terni, 05100, Italy.
Tel: 39-0744-54-6511

Ternopil-Zboriv—Most Rev. Vasyl Semeniuk; vul. Sichovyh Striltziv 6/a, Ternopil, 46001, Ukraine.
Tel: 0352-23-50-09 ***Fax:*** 0352-52-04-73
Email: ugccternopil@yahoo.it

Terrassa—Most Rev. Josep Àngel Saiz Meneses; Carrer Església 16, 2o-3a, Terrassa, Barcelona, 08221, Spain.
Tel: 34-93-733-71-20 ***Fax:*** 34-93-733-70-95
Email: bisbatdeterrassa@bisbatdeterrassa.org

Teruel y Albarracín—Most Rev. Carlos Manuel Escribano Subias; Obispado, Apartado 12, Plaza Venerable Francés de Aranda 3, Teruel, 44001, Spain.
Tel: 34-978-619-950 ***Fax:*** 34-978-619-951
Email: tevicaria@planalfa.es

Tete—Most Rev. Inacio Saure, I.M.C.; C.P. 218, Tete, Mozambique.
Tel: 258-252-23-017/351 ***Fax:*** 258-252-23-091
Email: diocesedetete@tdm.co.mz

Texcoco—Most Rev. Juan Manuel Mancilla Sánchez; Obispado, Fray Pedro de Gante 2, Texcoco, Méx., 56100, Mexico.
Tel: 52-595-95-420-89 ***Fax:*** 52-595-95-420-89
Email: diocesisdetexcoco@diocesisdetexcoco.org

Tezpur—Most Rev. Michael Akasius Toppo; Bishop's House, Tezpur, Sonitpur, Assam, 784001, India.
Tel: 91-03712-220-193 ***Fax:*** 91-03712-230-181
Email: bhousetz@hotmail.com

Thái Bình—Most Rev. Pierre Nguyen Van De, S.D.B.; Toà Giám Muc, 06 Trân Hung Dao, Tx. Thái Bình, Vietnam.
Tel: 84-036-3640-650 ***Fax:*** 84-036-3836-580
Email: dvcthaibinh@yahoo.fr

Thamarasserry (Syro-Malabar)—Most Rev. Remigius Maria Paul Inchananiyil; Bishop's House P.O. Box 1, Kozhikode Dt., Tamarachery, Kerala, 673573, India.
Tel: 0495-222-33-76; 0495-222-25-69; 0495-222-30-19 ***Fax:*** 0495-222-30-19
Email: diocesetmy09@gmail.com

Thanh Hoá—Most Rev. Joseph Nguyên Chi Linh; Toà Giám Muc, 50 Nguyên Truóng Tố, Thanh Hóa, Vietnam.
Tel: 037-3853-138 ***Fax:*** 037-3713-599

THÀNH-PHÔ HÔ CHI MINH, HÔCHIMINH VILLE—His Eminence Cardinal Jean-Baptiste Pham Minh Mân; Toà Tông Giám Muc, 180 Nguyên Dinh Chiêu, Q. 3, Thành-Phô Hô Chi Minh, Vietnam.
Tel: 08-3930-3828 ***Fax:*** 08-3930-0598
Email: tgmsaigon@vnn.vn

THARE AND NONSENG—Most Rev. Louis Chamniern Santisukniran; Archbishop's House 362 Moo 2, Nongbuayai Rd., Thambon That Choengchum, Amphoe Muang, Sakon Nakhon, 47000, Thailand.
Tel: 66-042-71-1272 ***Fax:*** 66-042-71-2023
Email: tharedio@hotmail.com

Thiès—Vacant; Evêché, Place du Trésor, B.P. 3004, Thiès, Senegal.
Tel: 221-33-951-1341 ***Fax:*** 221-33-951-3783
Email: evethies@orange.sn

Thuckalay—Vacant; Bishop's House P.O. Box 12, Kanyakumari Dt., Thuckalay, Tamil Nadu, 629175, India.
Tel: 04651-250-633 ***Fax:*** 04651-253-167
Email: mystery_ngc@sancharnet.in

Thunder Bay—Most Rev. Frederick J. Colli; Bishop's House 1222 Reaume St., P.O. Box 10400, Thunder Bay, ON, P7B 6T8, Canada.
Tel: 807-343-9313 *Fax:* 807-343-9114
Email: chancery@dotb.ca

Tianguá—Most Rev. Francisco Javier Hernández Arnedo, O.A.R.; Av. Prefeito Jacques Nunes 1739, C.P. 51, Tianguá, CE, 62320-000, Brazil.
Tel: 55-088-3671-1180 *Fax:* 55-088-3671-1180
Email: diocesetiangua@yahoo.com.br

Tibú—Most Rev. Omar Alberto Sanchez Cubillos, O.P.; Calle 7 N. 4-40, Barrio El Carmen, Tibú, Norte de Santander, Colombia.
Tel: 7-566-32-89 *Fax:* 7-566-32-89
Email: diocesistibu@gmail.com

Tíentsín (Tianjin)—Catholic Mission, Laosikai, Tianjin, Hebei, China.

Tijuana—Most Rev. Rafael Romo Muñoz; Arzobispado, Calle Décima y Av. Ocampo, 8585, Tijuana, B.C.N., 22000, Mexico.
Tel: 52-664-684-8411 *Fax:* 52-664-684-7683
Email: obispado@iglesiatijuana.org

Tilarán—Most Rev. Vittorino Girardi Stellin, M.C.C.I.; Obispado, Guanacaste, Apartado 28, Tilarán, 5710, Costa Rica.
Tel: 2695-5016 *Fax:* 2695-5669
Email: obispadotilaran@gmail.com

Timika—Most Rev. John Philip Saklil; Keuskupan, Jl. Cendrawasih 12, Timika, Papua, 99910, Indonesia.
Tel: 0901-323-053 *Fax:* 0901-323-819
Email: bishopoftimika@yahoo.com

Timisoara—Most Rev. Martin Roos; Episcopia Romano-Catolica, Str. Augustin Pacha 4, Timisoara-Cetate, RO-300055, Romania.
Tel: 40-0256-490-081; 40-0256-433-061 *Fax:* 40-0256-497-201
Email: ep-rc-tm@lasting.ro

Timmins—Vacant; 65 Ave. Jubilee Est., Timmins, ON, P4N 5W4, Canada.
Tel: 705-267-6224 *Fax:* 705-267-6226
Email: dioctims@ntl.sympatico.ca

Tingchow (Changting)—Catholic Mission Bishop's House, Changting, Fujian, China.

TIRANË-DURRËS—Most Rev. Rrok K. Mirdita; Arqipeshkvia Bulevardi Zhan d'Ark, Tiranë, Albania.
Tel: 04-2232-082 *Fax:* 04-2230-727
Email: archtirana@yahoo.com

Tiruchirapalli—Most Rev. Antony Devotta; Bishop's House 12A Convent Rd., P.O. Box 14, Tiruchchirapalli, Tamil Nadu, 620001, India.
Tel: 91-0431-2415-635; 91-0431-2401-568 *Fax:* 91-0431-2417-502
Email: trichidio@eth.net

Tiruvalla—Most Rev. Thomas Koorilos Chakkalapadickal; Catholic Archbishop's House, P.B. 4, Marygiri, Thiruvalla, Kerala, 689101, India.
Tel: 0469-2701-319 *Fax:* 0469-2600-822
Email: archtvla@gmail.com

Tivoli—Most Rev. Mauro Parmeggiani; Curia Vescovile, Piazza Sant'Anna 2, Tivoli, Roma, 00019, Italy.
Tel: 39-0774-33-52-27; 39-0774-33-09-42/3 *Fax:* 39-0774-31-32-98
Email: curia@tivoli.chiesacattolica.it

TLALNEPANTLA—Most Rev. Carlos Aguiar Retes; Arzobispado, Apartado 268, Av. Juárez 42, Tlalnepantla, Méx, 54000, Mexico.
Tel: 55-5565-39-44 *Fax:* 55-5565-35-26

Tlapa—Most Rev. Oscar Roberto Domínguez Couttolenc, M.G.; Obispado, Calle Fonseca, Tlapa de Comonfort, Gro., 41304, Mexico.
Tel: 52-757-476-0835 *Fax:* 52-757-476-0835
Email: diocesistlapa@prodigy.net.mx

Tlaxcala—Most Rev. Francisco Moreno Barron; Obispado, Apartado 84, Lardizábal 45, Tlaxcala, Tlax., 90000, Mexico.
Tel: 52-246-462-3243 *Fax:* 52-246-462-0739
Email: obispadodetlaxcala@prodigy.net.mx

TOAMASINA—Most Rev. Désiré Tsarahazana; Evêché, 11 Rue du Commerce, B.P. 98, Toamasina, 501, Madagascar.
Tel: 020-53-321-28 *Fax:* 020-53-330-53
Email: ecartmt@wanadoo.mg

Tocantinópolis—Most Rev. Giovane Pereira de Melo; Cúria Diocesana, Rua XV de Novembro 245, Tocantinópolis, TO, 77900-000, Brazil.
Tel: 55-063-3471-1724 *Fax:* 55-063-3471-1724
Email: diotoc@msn.com

TOKYO—Most Rev. Peter Takeo Okada; Archbishop's House Sekiguchi 3-16-15, Bunkyo-ku, Tokyo, 112-0014, Japan.
Tel: 81-03-3943-2301 *Fax:* 81-03-3944-8511
Email: diocese@tokyo.catholic.jp

Tôlagnaro—Most Rev. Vincent Rakotozafy; Evêché, B.P. 47, Tôlagnaro, 614, Madagascar.
Tel: 020-92-210-18
Email: ecarev@mel.moov.mg

TOLEDO—Most Rev. Braulio Rodríguez Plaza; Arzobispado, Arco de Palacio 3, Toledo, 45002, Spain.
Tel: 34-925-224-100 *Fax:* 34-925-222-639
Email: arztoletan@planalfa.es

Toledo (in Brazil)—Most Rev. Francisco Carlos Bach; Cúria Diocesana, C.P. 220, Rua General Rondon 2006, Toledo, PR, 85900-970, Brazil.
Tel: 045-3252-1417 *Fax:* 045-3252-1417
Email: curia@diocesetoledo.org

Toledo (in Ohio)—Most Rev. Leonard P. Blair (TOL); Chancery Office 1933 Spielbusch Avenue, Toledo, OH, 43604-5360.
Tel: 419-244-6711 *Fax:* 419-244-4791
Web: www.toledodiocese.org
Email: chancery@toledodiocese.org

Toliara—Most Rev. Fulgence Rabeony, S.J.; Archevêché, B.P. 30, Toliara, 601, Madagascar.
Tel: 94-424-16 *Fax:* 94-424-16

Toluca—Most Rev. Francisco Javier Chavolla Ramos; Obispado, Apartado 82, Portal Reforma 104 Col. Centro, Toluca, Méx., 50000, Mexico.
Tel: 52-722-215-2535; 52-722-215-3959 *Fax:* 52-722-214-6955
Email: secre@diocesistoluca.org.mx

Tombura-Yambio—Most Rev. Edward Hiiboro Kussala; Bishop's Office Yambio P.O. Box 27114, Kampala, Uganda.
Tel: 256-249-91-66-89-897
Email: tydcuria@yahoo.co.uk

Tonga—Most Rev. Soane Patita Paini Mafi; Toutaimana Catholic Centre P.O. Box 1, Nuku'alofa, Tonga.
Tel: 676-23-822 *Fax:* 676-23-854
Email: cathbish@kalianet.to

Toowoomba—Most Rev. Brian V. Finnigan, Apostolic Admin.; Bishop's House 73 Margaret St., P.O. Box 756, Toowoomba, QLD, 4350, Australia.
Tel: 61-07-463-242-77 *Fax:* 61-07-463-922-51
Email: bishsec@twb.catholic.org.au

TORINO—Most Rev. Cesare Nosiglia; Via Val della Torre 3, Torino, 10149, Italy.
Tel: 011-515-6300 *Fax:* 011-515-6338
Email: vicariato@diocesi.torino.it

Torit—Most Rev. Akio Johnson Mutek; Regina Pacis House 6 Av. Parklands, P.O. Box 52802, Nairobi, Kenya.
Email: cdot.chancellor@gmail.com

TORONTO—Most Rev. Thomas Christopher Collins; Chancery Office 1155 Yonge St, Toronto, ON, M4T IW2, Canada.
Tel: 416-934-0606 *Fax:* 416-934-3433
Email: spiritual@archtoronto.org

Toronto (Ukrainian)—Most Rev. Stephen Victor Chmilar; 940 The East Mall 201, Toronto, ON, M9B 6J7, Canada.
Tel: 416-746-0154 *Fax:* 416-746-6003
Email: eparchto@bellnet.ca

TORORO—Most Rev. Denis Kiwanuka Lote; Archbishop's House P.O. Box 632, Tororo, Uganda.
Tel: 256-077-25-25-182 *Fax:* 256-045-44-45-255
Email: tororoad@africaonline.co.ug

Torreón—Most Rev. José Guadalupe Galván Galindo; Obispado, Av. Morelos 46 Poniente, Torreón, Coah., 27000, Mexico.
Tel: 871-712-5244; 871-712-30-43 *Fax:* 871-716-6810
Email: diocesistorr@prodigy.net.mx

Tortona—Most Rev. Martino Canessa; Vescovado, Piazza Duomo 12, Tortona, Alessandria, 15057, Italy.
Tel: 39-0131-81-6611 *Fax:* 39-0131-81-6607
Email: diocesitortona@libero.it

Tortosa—Most Rev. Javier Salinas Viñals; Palau Episcopal, Calle Cruera 5, Tortosa, Tarragona, 43500, Spain.
Tel: 977-44-07-00 *Fax:* 977-44-03-78
Email: bisbattortosa@planalfa.es

Torun—Most Rev. Andrzej Wojciech Suski; Kuria Diecezjalna ul. Lazienna 18, Torun, 87-100, Poland.
Tel: 48-056-622-3530 *Fax:* 48-056-621-0907
Email: kuria@diecezja.torun.pl

TOULOUSE—Most Rev. Robert Le Gall, O.S.B.; Archevêché, B.P. 7208, 24 rue Perchepinte, Toulouse CEDEX 07, 31073, France.
Tel: 5-61-14-82-70
Email: chancelier31@catholique-toulouse.cef.fr

Tournai, Doornik—Most Rev. Guy Harpigny; Evêché, 1 place de l'Evêché, Tournai, B-7500, Belgium.
Tel: 32-069-452-650 *Fax:* 32-069-211-535
Email: oliver.frolich@evechetournai.be

TOURS—Most Rev. Bernard-Nicolas Aubertin, O.Cist.; Archevêché, B.P. 41117, 27 rue Jules Simon, Tours CEDEX 1, 37011, France.
Tel: 2-47-70-41-41 *Fax:* 2-47-61-87-56
Email: chancellerie@catholique-tours.cef.fr

Townsville—Most Rev. Michael Ernest Putney; The Catholic Diocesan Centre 270 Stanley Street, P.O. Box 6149 MSO, QLD 4812, Townsville, QLD 4810, Australia.
Tel: 61-07-472-63200 *Fax:* 61-07-472-63211
Email: diocese@tsv.catholic.org.au

TRANI - BARLETTA - BISCEGLIE—Most Rev. Giovanni Battista Pichierri; Curia Arcivescovile, Via Beltrani 9, Trani, Bari, 70059, Italy.
Tel: 39-0883-494-203/4/5 *Fax:* 39-0883-494-248
Email: cancelleria@arctrani.it

Trapani—Most Rev. Francesco Micciché; Corso Vittorio Emanuele 38, Trapani, 91100, Italy.
Tel: 39-0923-432-111 *Fax:* 39-0923-432-227
Email: curiavescovile@diocesi.trapani.it

Trasfigurazione a Novosibirsk—Most Rev. Joseph Werth, S.J.; ul. Gorkogo 100, Novosibirsk, 630099, Russia.
Tel: 3832-18-1204 *Fax:* 3832-18-1153
Email: curiansk@rambler.ru

TRENTO—Most Rev. Luigi Bressan; Curia Arcivescovile, Piazza Fiera 2, C.P. 389, Trento, 38122, Italy.
Tel: 39-0461-89-11-11 *Fax:* 39-0461-89-11-99
Email: curia@diocesitn.it

Trenton—Most Rev. David M. O'Connell; Chancery Office 701 Lawrenceville Rd., Trenton, NJ, 08648.
Tel: 609-406-7400 *Fax:* 609-406-7412

Três Lagoas—Most Rev. Jose Moreira Bastos Neto; Cúria Diocesana, Rua Oscar Guimarães 1074, Três Lagoas, MS, 79600-000, Brazil.
Tel: 55-067-3521-3027 *Fax:* 55-067-3521-4401
Email: diocesetreslagoas@yahoo.com.br

Treviso—Most Rev. Gianfranco Agostino Gardin, O.F.M.Conv.; Curia Vescovile, Piazza Duomo 2, Treviso, 31100, Italy.
Tel: 39-0422-41-67-00 *Fax:* 39-0422-41-67-15
Email: cancelleria@diocesitv.it

Tricarico—Most Rev. Vincenzo Carmine Orofino; Episcopio, Piazza Mons. Raffaello delle Nocche 2, Tricarico, Matera, 75019, Italy.
Tel: 39-0835-723-052 *Fax:* 39-0835-723-052
Email: vicario@tricarico.chiesacattolica.it

TRICHUR—Most Rev. Andrews Thazhath; Catholic Archbishop's House, Thrissur, Kerala, 680005, India.
Tel: 91-0487-2333-325 *Fax:* 91-0487-2338-204
Email: curiatcr@yahoo.com

Trier—Most Rev. Stephan Ackermann; Bischöfliches Ordinariat, Hinter dem Dom 6, Trier, D-54290, Germany.
Tel: 49-0651-71-050 *Fax:* 49-0651-710-54-98
Email: bistum-trier@bistum-trier.de

Trieste—Most Rev. Giampaolo Crepaldi; Vescovado, Via Cavana 16, Trieste, 34124, Italy.
Tel: 39-040-318-54-11 *Fax:* 39-040-318-54-30
Email: diocesi@diocesi.trieste.it

Trincomalee-Batticaloa—Most Rev. Joseph Kingsley Swampillai; Bishop's House P.O. Box 43, Batticaloa, Sri Lanka.
Tel: 94-065-2222-723 *Fax:* 94-065-2224-667
Email: bptcobatti@yahoo.com

TRIPOLI DEL LIBANO, TARABULUS—Most Rev. Georges Bou-Jaoudé, C.M.; Archevêché Maronite, rue Al-Moutran, B.P. 104, Tripoli, Lebanon.
Tel: 06-62-43-24 *Fax:* 06-62-93-93
Email: rahmat@inco.com.lb

TRIPOLI DEL LIBANO, TARABULUS (GREEK MELKITE)—Most Rev. George Riashi, B.C.; Archevêché Grec-Catholique, rue Al-Kanaess, B.P. 72, Tripoli, Lebanon.
Tel: 06-43-16-02; 06-43-59-89 *Fax:* 06-44-17-16

TRIVANDRUM—Most Rev. Maria Callist Soosa Pakiam; Archbishop's House Vellayambalam, Thiruvananthapuram, Kerala, 695003, India.
Tel: 0471-2724-001 *Fax:* 0471-2725-001

TRIVANDRUM (SIRO MALANKAR)—Most Rev. S.B. Baselios Cleemis Thottunkal; Major Archbishop's House, Pattom, Thiruvananthapuram, Kerala, 695004, India.
Tel: 91-0471-2541-642/643 *Fax:* 91-0471-2541-635

Trivento—Most Rev. Domenico Angelo Scotti; Vescovado, Piazza Cattedrale 15, Trivento, Campobasso, 86029, Italy.
Tel: 39-0874-87-17-45 *Fax:* 39-0874-87-17-75
Email: cancelliere@diocesitrivento.it

TRNAVA—Most Rev. Róbert Bezák, C.SS.R; Arcibiskupsky urad, Jana Holleho ul. 10 Post. Schranka 78, Trnava 1, SK-917 66, Slovakia.
Tel: 033-59-12-111 *Fax:* 033-59-12-280

Trois-Rivières—Most Rev. Martin Veillette; Evêché, C.P. 879, 362 rue Bonaventure, Trois-Rivières, QC, G9A 5J9, Canada.
Tel: 819-379-1432 *Fax:* 819-375-6382
Email: chancellerie@evechetr.org

Troyes—Most Rev. Marc Stenger; Evêché, 3 rue du Cloître - Saint-Etienne, Troyes, 10000, France.
Tel: 3-25-80-58-30 *Fax:* 3-25-80-48-50
Email: eveche.troyes@catholique-troyes.cef.fr

TRUJILLO—Most Rev. Héctor Miguel Cabrejos Vidarte, O.F.M.; Arzobispado, Jr. Mariscal de Orbegoso 451, Trujillo, 3102, Peru.
Tel: 51-44-256-812; 51-44-201-961 *Fax:* 51-44-231-473
Email: arzobispado_tr@terra.com.pe

Trujillo (in Honduras)—Most Rev. Luis Solé Fa, C.M.; Obispado, Ave. Cristobal de Pedraza, Barrio el Centro, Trujillo, Dep. Colón, Honduras.
Tel: 434-4997 *Fax:* 434-4167
Email: diocesistrujillo2004@yahoo.com

Trujillo (in Venezuela)—Most Rev. Vicente Ramón Hernández Peña; Obispado, Avenida García de Paredes N. 10-52, Trujillo, Venezuela.
Tel: 0272-2366-904 *Fax:* 0272-2363-580
Email: diocesisdetrujillo@cantv.net

Tsaochow (Caozhou, Heze)—Catholic Mission Bishop's House, Heze, Shandong, China.

Tshumbe—Most Rev. Nicholas Djomo Lola; Evêché, B.P. 223, Tshumbe, via Lodja, Sankuru, Democratic Republic of Congo.
Tel: 081-215-37-73 *Fax:* 088-44-948
Email: tshumbevg@yahoo.fr

TSINAN (JINAN)—Catholic Mission, Kao-Tu-Sih-Hsiang, Jinan, Shandong, China.

Tsínchow (Tianshui)—Catholic Mission Bishop's House, Tianshui, Gansu, China.

Tsíngtao (Qingdao)—Catholic Mission Bishop's House, Qingdao, Shandong, China.

Tsíning (Jining)—Catholic Mission Mei-Kuei-Yin-Tze, Jining, Inner Mongolia, China.

Tsiroanomandidy—Most Rev. Gustavo Bombin Espino, O.SS.T.; Evêché, B.P. 30, Tsiroanomandidy, 119, Madagascar.
Tel: 048-830-88
Email: diotsiro_58@yahoo.fr

TUAM—Most Rev. Michael Neary; Archbishop's House, Saint Jarlath's, Tuam, Co. Galway, Ireland.
Tel: 353-093-24-166 *Fax:* 353-093-28-070
Email: archdiocesetuam@gmail.com

Tubarão—Vacant; Cúria Diocesana Rua Senador Gustavo Richard 90, C.P. 341, 88701-970, Tubarão, SC, 88701-220, Brazil.
Tel: 55-048-3622-1504 *Fax:* 55-048-3622-1504
Email: curiatb@hotmail.com

Tucson—Most Rev. Gerald Frederick Kicanas, D.D. (TUC); Chancery Office 111 S. Church Ave., Tucson, AZ, 85701-0031.
Tel: 520-838-2500
Web: www.diocesetucson.org
Email: diocese@diocesetucson.org

TUCUMÁN—Most Rev. Alfredo Horacio Zecca; Arzobispado, Av. Sarmiento 895, San Miguel de Tucumán, Tucumán, T4000GTI, Argentina.
Tel: 54-0381-431-0617; 54-0381-422-63-45 *Fax:* 54-0381-431-0617
Email: arztuc@arnet.com.ar

TUGUEGARAO—Most Rev. Sergio L. Utleg; Archbishop's House, Rizal Street, Tuguegarao City, Cagayan, 3500, Philippines.
Tel: 078-844-1663; 078-846-2822 *Fax:* 078-846-2822
Email: chanceryrcat@lycos.com

Tui-Vigo—Most Rev. Luis Quinteiro Fiuza; Obispado, Dr. Corbal 90, Vigo, 36207, Spain.
Tel: 34-986-37-51-53 *Fax:* 34-986-37-17-30
Email: bispado@diocesetuivigo.org

Tula—Most Rev. Juan Pedro Juárez Meléndez; Obispado, Apartado 31, 5 de Mayo N. 5, Tula de Allende, Hgo., 42800, Mexico.
Tel: 52-773-732-0275 *Fax:* 52-773-732-0275
Email: obispadotula@prodigy.net.mx

TULANCINGO—Most Rev. Domingo Diaz Martinez; Arzobispado, Apartado 14, Plaza de la Constitución, Tulancingo, Hgo., 43600, Mexico.
Tel: 55-775-75-33-091 ***Fax:*** 55-775-75-31-010
Email: sgamitra@prodigy.net.mx

Tulcán—Most Rev. Fausto Gaibor Garcia; Curia Diocesana, Apartado Aéreo 04-01-0023, Calle 10 de Agosto y Olmedo, Tulcán, Carchi, Ecuador.
Tel: 593-06-2982-699; 593-06-2987-955; 593-06-2980-680 ***Fax:*** 593-06-2980-680
Email: diocesisdetulcan@andinanet.net

Tulle—Most Rev. Bernard Charrier; Evêché, 19-21 av. de la Bastille, B.P. 79, Tulle CEDEX, 19002, France.
Tel: 5-55-26-22-16 ***Fax:*** 5-55-20-93-69
Email: evechetulle@wanadoo.fr

Tulsa—Most Rev. Edward James Slattery (TLS); P.O. Box 690240, Tulsa, OK, 74169-0240.
Tel: 918-294-1904 ***Fax:*** 918-252-1168
Email: bishop.office@dioceseoftulsa.org
12300 E. 91st St. South, Broken Arrow, OK, 74012.

Tumaco—Most Rev. Gustavo Girón Higuita, O.C.D.; Obispado, Apartado Aéreo 307, Calle Nueva Creación con Calle Popayán, Tumaco Nariño, Colombia.
Tel: 7-271-282 ***Fax:*** 7-271-278

Tunduru-Masasi—Most Rev. Castor Paul Msemwa; P.O. Box 240, Tunduru, Tanzania.
Tel: 075-736-63-98 ***Fax:*** 025-26-80-428

TUNIS—Most Rev. Maroun Elias Lahham; Archevêché, 4 rue d'Alger, Tunis, R.P., 1000, Tunisia.
Tel: 71-335-831 ***Fax:*** 71-335-831/2
Email: eveche.tunisie@evechetunisie.org

TUNJA—Most Rev. Luis Augusto Castro Quiroga, I.M.C.; Arzobisbado, Calle 17 N. 9-85, Tunja, Boyacá, Colombia.
Tel: 8-742-20-94 ***Fax:*** 8-742-31-30
Email: arquidiocol1@telecom.com.co

Tura—Most Rev. Andrew Marak; Bishop's House, P.B. 10, West Garo Hills Dt., Tura, Meghalaya, 794001, India.
Tel: 03651-222-370 ***Fax:*** 03651-221-318
Email: nokbishop@sancharnet.in

TURIN (SEE TORINO)—

Tursi-Lagonegro—Most Rev. Francescantonio Nolé, O.F.M.Conv.; Vescovado, Piazza Cattedrale 8, Tursi, Matera, 75028, Italy.
Tel: 39-0835-53-31-47 ***Fax:*** 39-0835-53-31-47
Email: curia.tursi@libero.it

Tuticorin—Most Rev. Yvon Ambroise; Bishop's House, Tuticorin, Tamil Nadu, 628001, India.
Tel: 0461-2320-035 ***Fax:*** 0461-2327-710
Email: vposwald@yahoo.com

Tuxpan—Most Rev. Juan Navarro Castellanos; Avda Independencia 56, Col. La Rivera, Tuxpan, Ver., 92870, Mexico.
Tel: 52-783-834-97-70; 52-783-834-16-36 ***Fax:*** 52-783-834-16-36
Email: curiatux@prodigy.net.mx

Tuxtepec—Most Rev. José Antonio Fernández Hurtado; Obispado, Apartado 9, Bonfil 597 entre Francisco Villa y Juárez, Tuxtepec, Oax., 68320, Mexico.
Tel: 52-287-875-4861 ***Fax:*** 52-287-875-4861
Email: obispadotux_2009@hotmail.com

TUXTLA GUTIERREZ—Most Rev. Rogelio Cabrera López; Uruguay 500/a Colonia El Retiro, Apartado 365, Tuxtla Gutiérrez, Chis., 29040, Mexico.
Tel: 52-961-60-406-44/5 ***Fax:*** 52-961-61-432-97
Email: diotuxtla@prodigy.net.mx

Tyler—Vacant; Chancery 1015 East S.E. Loop 323, Tyler, TX, 75701-9663.
Tel: 903-534-1077 ***Fax:*** 903-534-1370

TYR, TIRO, SUR—Most Rev. Georges Bacaouni; Archevêché Grec-Melkite-Catholique, B.P. 257, Tyr, Lebanon.
Tel: 07-740-015 ***Fax:*** 07-349-180

TYR, TIRO, SUR (MARONITE)—Most Rev. Chucrallah-Nabil Hage; Archevêché Maronite, Tyr, Lebanon.
Tel: 07-74-00-59 ***Fax:*** 07-34-48-91
Email: mgr.charbelabdallah@gmail.com

Tzaneen—Most Rev. Joao Noe Rodrigues; Bishop's House 31 Draai Road, Tzaneen, N. Transvaal, 0850, South Africa.
Tel: 27-015-307-5244 ***Fax:*** 27-015-307-3078
Email: tzndioc@mweb.co.za

U

UBERABA—Most Rev. Aloísio Roque Oppermann, S.C.I.; Cúria Metropolitana Praça Dom Eduardo 56, Uberaba, MG, 38060-280, Brazil.
Tel: 55-034-3312-9565 ***Fax:*** 55-034-3312-9565
Email: curia@arquidiocesedeuberaba.org.br

Uberlândia—Most Rev. Paulo Francisco Machado; Cúria Diocesana Praça Nossa Senhora Aparecida 130, Bairro Aparecida, Uberlândia, MG, 38400-726, Brazil.
C.P. 3006, Uberlândia, MG, 38400-900, Brazil.
Tel: 034-3235-0144 ***Fax:*** 034-3213-6310
Email: diocese@triang.com.br

Ubon Ratchathani—Most Rev. Philip Banchong Chaiyara, C.SS.R; Bishop's House 498 Chayangkun Road, P.O. Box 5, Ubon Ratchathani, 34000, Thailand.
Tel: 66-045-31-34-39 ***Fax:*** 66-045-28-36-94
Email: uboncatholic@hotmail.com

Udaipur—Most Rev. Joseph Pathalil; Bishop's House Khristanjali, 1-Alipura, Udaipur, Rajasthan, 313001, India.
Tel: 91-0294-252-4827 ***Fax:*** 91-0294-252-4827

UDINE—Most Rev. Andrea Bruno Mazzocato; Arcivescovado, Via Treppo 7, Udine, 33100, Italy.
Tel: 39-0432-414-511 ***Fax:*** 39-0432-200-889
Email: arcidiocesi@diocesiudine.it

Udon Thani—Most Rev. Joseph Luechai Thatwisai; Bishop's House P.O. Box 2, Udon Thani, 41002, Thailand.
Tel: 66-042-321-451/2 ***Fax:*** 66-042-243-990
Email: udondiocese@catholic.or.th

Ugento-Santa Maria di Leuca—Most Rev. Vito Angiuli; Vescovado, Piazza S. Vincenzo 21, Ugento, Lecce, 73059, Italy.
Tel: 39-0833-55-50-49 ***Fax:*** 39-0833-55-50-49
Email: diocesiugento@diocesiugento.org

Uíje—Most Rev. Emilio Sumbelelo; Cúria Diocesana C.P. 239, Uíje, Angola.
Tel: 0233-222-650
Email: bispadouije@hotmail.com

Uijongbu—Most Rev. Peter Lee Ki-heon; Diocesan Office 429-6 Uijeongbu 2-dong, Uijeongbu-si, Gyeonggi, 480-848, Korea, South.
Tel: 031-870-1703 ***Fax:*** 031-855-0900
Email: can@ujb.catholic.or.kr

Ujjain—Most Rev. Sebastian Vadakel, M.S.T.; Bishop's House B.P. 234, Dewas Road, Ujjain, M.P., 456010, India.
Tel: 91-0734-2515-970 ***Fax:*** 91-0734-2513-201

UJUNG PANDANG (SEE MAKASSAR)—Indonesia.

Umtata—Most Rev. Sithembele Anton Sipuka; Bishop's House 19 Craister Str., P.O. Box 85, Umtata, Eastern Cape, 5100, South Africa.
Tel: 27-047-532-2829 ***Fax:*** 27-047-532-2829
Email: kasuleh@goggaconnect.co.za

Umuahia—Most Rev. Lucius Iwejuru Ugorji; Bishop's House 57 Azikiwe Road, P.O. Box 99, Umuahia, Abia State, Nigeria.
Tel: 234-088-22-03-64 ***Fax:*** 234-088-22-27-30

Umuarama—Most Rev. Joao Mamede Filho, O.F.M.Conv.; Cúria Diocesana Av. Padre José Germano Neto Júnior 4260, Umuarama, PR, 87503-650, Brazil.
C.P. 191, Umuarama, PR, 87502-970, Brazil.
Tel: 044-3622-1301 ***Fax:*** 044-3622-1301
Email: pastoral@mdu.org.br

Umzimkulu—Most Rev. Stanislaw Jan Dziuba, O.S.P.P.E.; 19 Ballance St., P.O. Box 332, Harding, 4680, South Africa.
Tel: 27-039-433-1421 ***Fax:*** 27-039-433-1421

União da Vitória—Most Rev. João Bosco Barbosa de Sousa, O.F.M.; C.P. 237, Rua Manoel Estevão 275, União da Vitória, PR, 84600-000, Brazil.
Tel: 55-042-3522-3595 ***Fax:*** 55-042-3522-3595
Email: mitra@dioceseunivitoria.org.br

URBINO-URBANIA-SANT'ANGELO (IN VADO)—Most Rev. Giovanni Tani; Arcivescovado Piazza Pascoli 2, Urbino, Pesaro, 61029, Italy.
Tel: 39-0722-2850 ***Fax:*** 39-0722-2850
Email: arcidiocesiurbino@virgilio.it

Urdaneta—Most Rev. Jacinto A. Jose; Diocesan Curia Dr. Jose Areugo St., Urdaneta City, Pangasinan, 2428, Philippines.
Tel: 63-075-656-1165; 63-075-568-2670 ***Fax:*** 63-075-568-2670; 63-075-656-1165
Email: dioceseofurdaneta@yahoo.com

Urgell—Most Rev. Joan Enric Vives Sicilia; Obispado, Pati de Palau 1-5, La Seu d'Urgell, Lleida, 25700, Spain.
Tel: 34-973-350-054 ***Fax:*** 34-973-352-230
Email: secretariageneral@bisbaturgell.org

URMYA-URMIA, REZAYEH—Most Rev. Thomas Meram; Mendi Al Ghadam, Mirzaian St. 7, Urmia, 57138 55733, Iran.
Tel: 98-0441-2222-739 ***Fax:*** 98-0441-2236-031

Uromi—Vacant; Chancery Office P.M.B 7, Uromi, Edo State, Nigeria.
Tel: 080-548-48-205
Email: cathdiouromi@yahoo.com

Uruaçu—Most Rev. Messias Dos Reis Silveira; Cúria Diocesana C.P. 32, Rua Benedito Almeida Campos 21, Uruaça, GO, 76400-000, Brazil.
Tel: 55-062-3357-1230 ***Fax:*** 55-062-3357-1352
Email: dioceseuruacu@hotmail.com

Uruguaiana—Most Rev. Aloisio Alberto Dilli, O.F.M; Cúria Diocesana Rua Sant'Ana 2612, Uruguaiana, RS, 97510-490, Brazil.
Tel: 55-055-3412-1246 ***Fax:*** 55-055-3412-1486
Email: mitrauruguaiana@uol.com.br

UTRECHT—Most Rev. Willem Jacobus Eijk; Aartsbisdom Maliebaan 38-40, Utrecht, 3581 CR, The Netherlands.
PB 14019, Utrecht, 3508 SB, The Netherlands.
Tel: 030-233-80-30 ***Fax:*** 030-231-19-62
Email: secretariaat@aartsbisdom.nl

Uvira—Vacant; Evêché, Av Kivu 8, Nyamyanda, B.P. 18, Uvira, Democratic Republic of Congo.
c/o B.P. 645, Bujumbura, Burundi.
Tel: 081-36-03-699
Email: evecheuvira@hotmail.fr

Uyo—Most Rev. Joseph Effiong Ekuwem; Catholic Secretariat 5 Dominic Utuk Avenue, P.M.B. 1212, Uyo, Akwa-Ibom State, Nigeria.

V

Vác—Most Rev. Miklós Beer; Pf. 167, Vác, H-2601, Hungary.
Tel: 36-27-814-100 ***Fax:*** 36-27-814-101
Email: piroda@vaciegyhazmegye.hu
Egyházmegyei Hatóság, Migazzi Kristóf tér I, Vác, H-2600, Hungary.

Vacaria—Most Rev. Irineu Gassen, O.F.M.; Cúria Diocesana Rua Ramiro Barcelos 806, Vacaria, RS, 95200-000, Brazil.
Tel: 55-054-3231-1373 ***Fax:*** 55-054-3231-1373
Email: mitravacaria@m2net.com.br

VADUZ—Most Rev. Wolfgang Haas; Fürst-Franz-Josef-Str. 112, Postfach 103, Vaduz, FL-9490, Liechtenstein.
Tel: 233-23-11 ***Fax:*** 233-23-24
Email: erzbistum@powersurf.li

Valdivia—Most Rev. Ignacio Francisco Ducasse Medina; Obispado, Maipú 168, Casilla 520, Valdivia, Chile.
Tel: 56-063-21-3296 ***Fax:*** 56-063-21-5358
Email: valdivia@episcopado.cl

Valença—Most Rev. Elias James Manning, O.F.M.Conv.; Residência Episcopal C.P. 87332, Praça Visconde do Rio Preto 375, Valença, RJ, 27600-000, Brazil.
Tel: 55-024-2452-0207 ***Fax:*** 55-024-2452-0101
Email: curiadevalenca@uol.com.br

Valence—Most Rev. Jean-Christophe Lagleize; Maison Diocesaine du Bon Pasteur, 11 rue du Clos-Gaillard, B.P. 825, Valence CEDEX, 26008, France.
Tel: 4-75-81-77-07 ***Fax:*** 4-75-81-77-25
Email: vicaire.general@valence.cef.fr

VALENCIA—Most Rev. Carlos Osoro Sierra; Arzobispado, Palau 2, Valencia, 46003, Spain.
Tel: 34-96-382-97-00 ***Fax:*** 34-96-391-81-20
Email: archivalencia@archivalencia.org

VALENCIA EN VENEZUELA—Most Rev. Reinaldo Del Prette Lissot; Arzobispado Apartado 32, Av. Urdaneta 100-54, Valencia, Edo. Carabobo, 2001-A, Venezuela.
Tel: 58-0241-858-5865/9449 ***Fax:*** 58-0241-857-8061
Email: arqui_valencia@cantv.net

VALLADOLID—Most Rev. Ricardo Blázquez Pérez; Arzobispado San Juan de Dios 5, Valladolid, 47003, Spain.
Tel: 34-983-21-7929 ***Fax:*** 34-983-21-7930
Email: cancilleria@archivalladolid.org

Valle de Chalco—Most Rev. Luis Artemio Flores Calzada; Calle Alzate 10, Col. Centro, Chalco, Méx., 56600, Mexico.
Tel: 55-597-31-379 ***Fax:*** 55-597-31-381
Email: diochalco@hotmail.com

Valle de la Pascua—Most Rev. Ramón José Aponte Fernández; Calle España 1, Urb. Guamachal, Quinta "Villa de la Paz", Valle de la Pascua, Edo. Guárico, 2307, Venezuela.
Tel: 58-0235-3422-344 ***Fax:*** 58-0235-3422-411

Valledupar—Most Rev. Oscar José Vélez Isaza, C.M.F.; Curia Diocesana Carrera 7 N. 15-26, Valledupar, Cesar, Colombia.
Tel: 57-55-744-168; 57-55-743-167 ***Fax:*** 57-55-708-865
Email: josecrispin.clavij@telcom.com.co

Valleyfield—Vacant; Evêché, 11 rue de l'Eglise, Salaberry-de-Valleyfield, QC, J6T 1J5, Canada.
Tel: 450-373-8122 ***Fax:*** 450-371-0000
Email: info@diocesevalleyfield.org

Vallo della Lucania—Most Rev. Ciro Miniero; Vescovado, Piazza dei Martiri 2, Vallo della Lucania, Salerno, 84078, Italy.
Tel: 39-0974-4142 ***Fax:*** 39-0974-4142
Email: info@diocesivallodellalucania.it

Valparaíso—Most Rev. Gonzalo Duarte García de Cortázar, SS.CC.; Calle Carrera 430, Valparaíso, Chile.
Tel: 56-032-225-55-38 ***Fax:*** 56-032-274-90-37
Email: valparaiso@episcopado.cl

VANCOUVER—Most Rev. John Michael Miller, C.S.B.; Chancery Office 150 Robson St., Vancouver, BC, V6B 2A7, Canada.
Tel: 604-683-0281 ***Fax:*** 604-683-4288
Email: chancery@rcav.bc.ca

Vanimo—Most Rev. Cesare Bonivento, P.I.M.E.; Bishop's House P.O. Box 205, Vanimo, W.S.P., 551, Papua New Guinea.
Tel: 457-857-1031 ***Fax:*** 457-857-1105

Vannes—Most Rev. Raymond Centène; Evêché, 14 rue de l'Eveche, B.P. 3, Vannes CEDEX, 56001, France.
Tel: 2-97-68-30-60 ***Fax:*** 2-97-68-30-59
Email: secretariat.monseigneur@diocese-vannes.fr

Varanasi—Most Rev. Raphy Manjaly; Bishop's House 45 Varanasi Cantt., U.P., 221002, India.
Tel: 91-0542-250-27-61/42-35 ***Fax:*** 91-0542-250-27-67
Email: dovns@sify.com

Varazdin—Most Rev. Josip Mrzljak; Biskupski Ordinarijat Pavlinska 4, Varazdin, 42000, Croatia.
Tel: 042-321-408/9 ***Fax:*** 042-321-412
Email: biskupija@biskupija-varazdinska.hr

Vasai—Most Rev. Felix Anthony Machado; Bishop's House Barampur, Thane Dt., Maharashtra, Vasai, 401201, India.
Tel: 0250-238-1521; 0250-238-2964 ***Fax:*** 0250-2383-333
Email: vasaidiocese@gmail.com

Vélez—Most Rev. Luis Albeiro Cortés Rendón; Carrera 2 N. 9-28, Vélez, Santander, Colombia.
Tel: 57-7-756-48-40 ***Fax:*** 57-7-756-48-40
Email: diocesisdevelez@hotmail.com

Velletri-Segni—His Eminence Francis Arinze; Curia Vescovile Corso della Repubblica 343, Velletri, Roma, 00049, Italy.
Tel: 39-06-963-0051 ***Fax:*** 39-06-961-00596
Email: curia@diocesi.velletri-segni.it

Vellore—Most Rev. Soundaraj Periyanayagam, S.D.B.; Bishop's House 34 Officer's Line, P.B. 107, Vellore, Tamil Nadu, 632001, India.
Tel: 91-0416-2232-570 ***Fax:*** 91-0416-2226-977
Email: vellorediocesee@yahoo.com

Venado Tuerto—Most Rev. Gustavo Arturo Help; Curia Episcopal San Martín 82, Venado Tuerto, Santa Fe, S2600KUB, Argentina.
Tel: 54-03462-421-649; 54-03462-438-779 ***Fax:*** 54-03462-438-779
Email: obispventu@powervt.com.ar

Venice—Most Rev. Frank J. Dewane (VEN); Diocesan Center P.O. Box 2006, Venice, FL, 34284-2006.
Tel: 941-484-9543 ***Fax:*** 941-488-2561
Email: info@dioceseofvenice.org
1000 Pinebrook Rd, Venice, FL, 34285.

Ventimiglia-San Remo—Most Rev. Alberto Maria Careggio; Vescovado, Via Carlo Pisacane 2, San Remo, Imperia, 18038, Italy.
Tel: 39-0184-50-57-57 ***Fax:*** 39-0184-50-57-53
Email: curia.sanremo@sistel.it

Vera Paz, Cobán—Most Rev. Rodolfo Valenzuela Núñez; Obispado, 1a Avenida 1-31, Zona 3, Cobán, Alta Vera Paz, 16001, Guatemala.
Tel: 502-09-7952-1564 ***Fax:*** 502-09-7951-3080
Email: obispadoverapaz@gmail.com

Veracruz—Most Rev. Luis Felipe Gallardo Martín del Campo, S.D.B.; Insurgentes Veracruzanos 470, Veracruz, Ver., 91700, Mexico.
Tel: 52-229-931-2413 ***Fax:*** 52-229-932-2026

VERAPOLY—Most Rev. Francis Kallarakal; Latin Archbishop's House P.O. Box 2581, Kochi, Kerala, 682031, India.
Tel: 91-0484-2372-892 *Fax:* 91-0484-2360-911
Email: curia.verapoly@gmail.com

VERCELLI—Most Rev. Enrico Masseroni; Curia Arcivescovile Piazza S. Eusebio 10, Vercelli, 13100, Italy.
Tel: 39-0161-21-33-40 *Fax:* 39-0161-25-07-12
Email: curia.segreteria@arcidiocesi.vc.it

Verdun—Most Rev. François Maupu; Evêché, 27 rue de la Paix, B.P. 50090, Verdun CEDEX, 55103, France.
Tel: 33-3-29-86-0172 *Fax:* 33-3-29-86-3476
Email: lienhardt.eveche@orange.fr

Verona—Most Rev. Giuseppe Zenti; Curia Vescovile Piazza Vescovado 7, Verona, 37121, Italy.
Tel: 39-045-808-3711 *Fax:* 39-045-808-3782
Email: info@diocesiverona.it

Versailles—Most Rev. Eric Aumonier; Evêché, 16 rue Monseigneur Gibier, Versailles CEDEX, 78008, France.
Tel: 33-1-30-97-6760 *Fax:* 33-1-39-50-33-82
Email: diocese@catholique-yvelines.cef.fr

VESZPRÉM—Most Rev. Gyula Márfi; Foegyházmegyei Hatóság, Vár utca 18, Pf. 109, Veszprém, H-8201, Hungary.
Tel: 36-88-42-60-88 *Fax:* 36-88-42-62-87
Email: ersekseg@ersekseg.veszprem.hu

Viana—Most Rev. Sebastiao Lima Duarte; Cúria Diocesana Praça Mons. Arouche 132, C.P. 07, Viana, MA, 65215-000, Brazil.
Tel: 55-098-3653-2235 *Fax:* 55-098-3653-2235
Email: casadiocesana@yahoo.com.br

Viana—Most Rev. Joaquim Ferreira Lopes, O.F.M.Cap.; Ceast, C.P. 3579, Luanda, Angola.
Tel: 923-318-769; 915-200-011

Viana do Castelo—Most Rev. Anacleto Cordeiro Goncalves de Oliveira; Câmara Eclesiástica, Rua de Góis Pinto, Viana do Castelo, 4904-864, Portugal.
Tel: 351-258-824-567 *Fax:* 351-258-824-459
Email: curia@diocesedeviana.com

Vic—Most Rev. Román Casanova Casanova; Obispado, Calle Santa María 1, Vic, Barcelona, 08500, Spain.
Tel: 34-93-883-26-55 *Fax:* 34-93-889-43-89
Email: bisbatdevic@bisbatvic.com

Vicenza—Most Rev. Beniamino Pizziol; Vescovado, Piazza Duomo 10, Vicenza, 36100, Italy.
Tel: 39-0444-22-6300 *Fax:* 39-0444-32-6530
Email: diocesi@vicenza.chiesacattolica.it

Victoria—Most Rev. Richard Joseph Gagnon; Bishop's House 4044 Nelthorpe Street, Victoria, BC, V8X 2A1, Canada.
Tel: 250-479-1331 *Fax:* 250-479-5423
Email: chancery@rcdvictoria.org

Victoria (in Texas)—Most Rev. David Eugene Fellhauer (VIC); Chancery Office 1505 E. Mesquite Ln., P.O. Box 4070, Victoria, TX, 77903-4070.
Tel: 361-573-0828 *Fax:* 361-573-5725
Email: mbochat@victoriadiocese.org

Viedma—Most Rev. Esteban María Laxague, S.D.B.; Curia Diocesana Casilla Correo 32, Irigoyen 71, Viedma, Río Negro, R8500BCA, Argentina.
Tel: 54-02920-424-445 *Fax:* 54-02920-428-945
Email: obispadoviedma@speedy.com.ar

VIENNA—His Eminence Cardinal Christoph Schönborn, O.P.; Wollzeile 2, Vienna, A-1010, Austria.
Tel: 43-01-515-52-3229 *Fax:* 43-01-515-52-2760
Email: ordinariat.kanzlei@edw.or.at

Vigevano—Most Rev. Vincenzo Di Mauro; Curia Vescovile Piazza S. Ambrogio 14, Vigevano, Pavia, 27029, Italy.
Tel: 39-0381-69-13-89; 39-0381-69-24-42 *Fax:* 39-0381-69-13-89; 39-0381-69-67-67; 39-0381-69-24-42
Email: cancelleria@diocesivigevano.it

Vijayapuram—Most Rev. Sebastian Thekethecheril; Bishop's House, Good Shepherd P.O. Box 82, Kottayam, Kerala, 686001, India.
Tel: 91-0481-2304-346 *Fax:* 91-0481-2565-863
Email: josenavez@gmail.com

Vijayawada—Most Rev. Prakash Mallavarapu; Bishop's House 59 A-1-7 Ring Road, Patamata, Vijayawada, Krishna Dt., A.P., 520008, India.
Tel: 91-0866-2471-355 *Fax:* 91-0866-2478-629
Email: bishop_vja@sify.com

Vila Real—Most Rev. Amandio Jose Tomas; Cúria Episcopal Apartado 144, Rua Do Carmo, Vila Real de Trás-os-Montes CODEX, 5001-910, Portugal.
Tel: 351-259-323-448 *Fax:* 351-259-378-404
Email: vigario-geral@sapo.pt

Vilkaviškis—Most Rev. Rimantas Norvila; Vilkaviškio Vyskupijos Kurija, Kriauciuno 17, Marijampole, 68298, Lithuania.
Tel: 370-343-68-651 *Fax:* 370-343-53-231
Email: kurija@vk.lcn.lt

Villa de la Concepción del Río Cuarto—Most Rev. Eduardo Eliseo Martín; Obispado, Calle Buenos Aires 261, Río Cuarto, Córdoba, X5800DJE, Argentina.
Tel: 54-0358-4643-717; 54-0358-4631-859 *Fax:* 54-0358-4631-859; 54-0358-4643-717
Email: obisrio4@obispadoriocuarto.com.ar

Villa María—Most Rev. José Angel Rovai; Obispado, Manuel Belgrano 20, Villa María, Córdoba, X5901BGB, Argentina.
Tel: 54-0353-453-2026 *Fax:* 54-0353-453-2026
Email: obispadovm@multicanalbbt.com.ar

Villarrica—Most Rev. Francisco Javier Stegmeier Schmidlin; Casilla 276-V, Gerónimo de Alderete 939, Villarrica, Chile.
Tel: 045-41-11-89 *Fax:* 045-41-13-65
Email: diocesisvillarrica@gmail.com

Villarrica del Espíritu Santo—Most Rev. Ricardo Jorge Valenzuela Rios; Natalicio Talavera 720, Villarrica, Paraguay.
Tel: 595-0541-42687 *Fax:* 595-0541-42687

VILLAVICENCIO—Most Rev. Óscar Urbina Ortega; Carrera 39 N. 34-19, Villavicencio, Meta, Colombia.
Tel: 57-8-6630-337 *Fax:* 57-8-6653-200
Email: arquidiocesisdevillavicencio@hotmail.com

VILNIUS—His Eminence Cardinal Audrys Juozas Backis; Šventaragio 4, Vilnius, LT-01122, Lithuania.
Tel: 370-5-2627-098; 370-5-212-36-53 *Fax:* 370-5-212-2807
Email: curia@vilnensis.lt

Vinh—Most Rev. Paul Nguyen Thai Hop, O.P.; Tóa Giám Muc, Xã Doài, Nghi Diên, Nghi Lôc, Nghê An, Vietnam.
Tel: 038-3861-171 *Fax:* 038-3861-676
Email: tgmxadoai2004@yahoo.com

Vinh Long—Most Rev. Thomas Nguyên Van Tan; Tóa Giám Muc, 103 Duong 3 Thang 2, Tx., Vinh Long, Vinh Long, Vietnam.
Tel: 070-3824-016
Email: tgmvinhlong@gmail.com

Virac—Most Rev. Manolo A. de los Santos; Diocesan Pastoral Center Virac, Catanduanes, 4800, Philippines.
Tel: 63-052-811-1408 *Fax:* 63-052-811-1456
Email: chanceryvirac@yahoo.com

VISAKHAPATNAM—Most Rev. Mariadas Kagithapu, M.S.F.S.; Archbishop's House Maharanipeta, Visakhapatnam, A.P., 530002, India.
Tel: 91-0891-2706-428 *Fax:* 91-0891-2705-781
Email: abphvizag@rediffmail.com

Viseu—Most Rev. Ilídio Pinto Leandro; Centro Sócio-Pastoral, Quinta do Seminário, Viseu, 3500-108, Portugal.
Tel: 351-232-423-338 *Fax:* 351-232-429-547

Vitebsk—Most Rev. Wladyslaw Blin; Kuria Diecezjalna ul. Czkalowa 52/k.1 m.21, Witebsk a/R 133, 210041, Belarus.
Tel: 0212-25-31-57 *Fax:* 0212-25-31-57
Email: curia-vitebsk@mail.ru

Viterbo—Most Rev. Lino Fumagalli; Palazzo Vescovile, Piazza S. Lorenzo 9/a, Viterbo, 01100, Italy.
Tel: 39-0761-34-17-16 *Fax:* 39-0761-30-60-06
Email: giustoneri@diocesiviterbo.org

Vitoria—Most Rev. Miguel José Asurmendi Aramendía, S.D.B.; Obispado, Calle Vicente Goicoechea 7, Vitoria, 01008, Spain.
Tel: 34-945-14-81-71 *Fax:* 34-945-14-58-37
Email: secretariageneral@diocesisvitoria.org

VITÓRIA—Most Rev. Luiz Mancilha Vilela, Ss.Cc.; Cúria Metropolitana Rua Soldado Abílio dos Santos 47, C.P. 107, Vitória, ES, 29015-620, Brazil.
Tel: 55-027-3223-6711 *Fax:* 55-027-3223-1227
Email: mitra.curia@aves.org.br

VITÓRIA DA CONQUISTA—Most Rev. Luis Gonzaga Silva Pepeu, O.F.M-.Cap.; Cúria Metropolitana Praça Tancredo Neves 181, Vitória da Conquista, BA, 45045-210, Brazil.
Tel: 55-077-2101-5750 *Fax:* 55-077-2101-5754
Email: curiavdc@terra.com.br

Vittorio Veneto—Most Rev. Corrado Pizziolo; Curia Vescovile Via Lorenzo Da Ponte 116, Vittorio Veneto, Treviso, 31029, Italy.
Tel: 39-0438-9481 ***Fax:*** 39-0438-948-214
Email: curia@diocesivittorioveneto.it

Viviers—Most Rev. François Blondel; Evêché, B.P. 1, Viviers-sur-Rhône, 07220, France.
Tel: 4-7552-6412 ***Fax:*** 4-7552-8170
Email: eveche.viviers@wanadoo.fr

Volterra—Most Rev. Alberto Silvani; Via Roma 13, Volterra, Pisa, 56048, Italy.
Tel: 39-0588-86-192 ***Fax:*** 39-0588-90-133
Email: cancelleria@diocesivolterra.it

VRHBOSNA, SARAJEVO—His Eminence Cardinal Vinko Puljic; Nadbiskupski Ordinarijat, Kaptol 7, Sarajevo, BiH-71000, Bosnia-Herzegovina.
Tel: 387-033-218-823 ***Fax:*** 387-033-212-937
Email: kaptolka@bih.net.ba

W

Wa—Most Rev. Paul Bemile; Diocesan Secretariat Maria Yiri, P.O. Box 47, Wa, Upper West Region, Ghana.
Tel: 039-20-22-360 ***Fax:*** 039-20-22-597; 039-20-22-360
Email: bishopwa@gmail.com

Wabag—Most Rev. Arnold Orowae; Bishop's House P.O. Box 191, Wabag, Enga Province 291, Papua New Guinea.
Tel: 675-547-1096 ***Fax:*** 675-547-1096; 675-547-1230
Email: diocesewabag@datec.net.pg

Wagga Wagga—Most Rev. Gerard Joseph Hanna; Bishop's Office 205 Tarcutta St., P.O. Box 473, Wagga Wagga, N.S.W., 2650, Australia.
Tel: 61-02-6937-0003 ***Fax:*** 61-02-6921-5157
Email: sshaw@cso.wagga.catholic.edu.au

Wallis et Futuna—Most Rev. Ghislain de Rasilly, S.M.; Evêché de Lano, B.P. 248, Mata'utu, Iles Wallis et Futuna, 98600, Oceania.
Tel: 681-72-29-32 ***Fax:*** 681-72-27-83
Email: eveche.wallis@mail.wf

Wamba—Most Rev. Janvier Kataka Luvete; Evêché B.P. 71, Isiro, o B.P. 40, Wamba, Uele, Nepoko, Democratic Republic of Congo.
Tel: 242-099-444-7085; 242-081-302-7574
Email: diocesewamba@yahoo.fr

Wanhsíen (Wanxian)—Catholic Church 2 Anziba St., Wanxian, Sichuan, China.

Warangal—Vacant; Bishop's House Fatimanagar, Kazipet, Warangal, A.P., 506004, India.
Tel: 91-0870-2459-128 ***Fax:*** 91-0870-2459-499

WARMIA—Most Rev. Wojciech Ziemba; Kuria Metropolitalna ul. S. Pieniez-nego 22, Olsztyn, 10-006, Poland.
Tel: 48-089-524-71-71 ***Fax:*** 48-089-524-71-72
Email: kuriaol@olsztyn.opoka.org.pl

Warri—Most Rev. John 'Oke Afareha; Cathedral House 66 Warri-Sapele Rd., P.O. Box 3650, Warri, Delta State, Nigeria.
Tel: 234-053-25-12-77 ***Fax:*** 234-053-25-12-77

WARSZAWA—His Eminence Kazimierz Cardinal Nycz; Kuria Metropolitalna ul. Miodowa 17-19, Warszawa, 00-246, Poland.
Tel: 48-022-531-7200 ***Fax:*** 48-022-531-7255
Email: kanclerz@mkw.pl

Warszawa-Praga—Most Rev. Henryk Hoser, S.A.C.; Kuria Diecezjalna ul. Florianska 2/a, Warszawa, 03-707, Poland.
Tel: 48-022-518-15-00 ***Fax:*** 48-022-619-26-78
Email: kuria@wpraga.opoka.org.pl

WASHINGTON—His Eminence Donald Cardinal Wuerl (WDC); Archdiocesan Pastoral Center 5001 Eastern Ave., Hyattsville, MD, 20782.
Tel: 301-853-4520 ***Fax:*** 301-853-5346
Email: chancery@adw.org
P.O. Box 29260, Washington, DC, 20017.

Waterford and Lismore—Most Rev. William Lee; Bishop's House John's Hill, Waterford, Ireland.
Tel: 353-051-874-463 ***Fax:*** 353-051-852-703
Email: waterfordlismore@eircom.net

Wau—Most Rev. Rudolph Deng Majak; P.O. Box 29, Wau, Sudan.
Tel: 0841-8224-66; 0841-8220-39 ***Fax:*** 0841-8220-39
Email: vicargeneral.waudiocese@gmail.com

Weetebula—Most Rev. Edmund Woga, C.SS.R.; Keuskupan, Jl. Eltarí, Weetebula Radamata, Pos Waikabubak, Sumba Barat N.T.T., 87254, Indonesia.
Tel: 0387-24-064 ***Fax:*** 0387-24-064

Weíhwei (Jixian)—Catholic Mission Bishop's House, Jixian, Henan, China.

WELLINGTON—Most Rev. John Atcherley Dew; Catholic Centre 22-30 Hill St., Wellington, 6015, New Zealand.
Tel: 64-04-496-1737 ***Fax:*** 64-04-496-1754
Email: g.burns@wn.catholic.org.nz
P.O. Box 1937, Wellington, 6140, New Zealand.

WESTMINSTER—Most Rev. Vincent Gerard Nichols; Archbishop's House Ambrosden Avenue, Westminster, London, SW1P 1QJ, England.
Tel: 44-020-7798-9033 ***Fax:*** 44-020-7798-9077
Email: archbishop@rcdow.org.uk

Wewak—Most Rev. Anthony Joseph Burgess; Chancery Office P.O. Box 107, Wewak, E.S.P. 531, Papua New Guinea.
Tel: 675-456-1675 ***Fax:*** 675-456-2573

Wheeling-Charleston—Most Rev. Michael J. Bransfield; Chancery Office 1300 Byron St., P.O. Box 230, Wheeling, WV, 26003-0010.
Tel: 304-233-0880 ***Fax:*** 304-233-0890
Email: fannie@dwc.org

Whitehorse—Most Rev. Gary M. Gordon; Chancery Office 406 Steele St., Whitehorse, YT, Y1A 2C8, Canada.
Tel: 867-668-3826 ***Fax:*** 867-667-4713
Email: bishopgmg@klondiker.com

Wiawso—Most Rev. Joseph Francis Kweku Essien; Catholic Diocese, P.M.B. 77, Sefwi Wiawso, West Africa, Ghana.
Tel: 024-42-54-777

Wichita—Most Rev. Michael Owen Jackels; Chancery Office 424 N. Broadway, Wichita, KS, 67202.
Tel: 316-269-3900 ***Fax:*** 316-269-3902
Email: hembergerb@cdowk.org

Wilcannia-Forbes—Vacant; Bishop's House Johnson Str. 13, P.O. Box 28, Forbes, N.S.W., 2871, Australia.
Tel: 02-6853-9340 ***Fax:*** 02-6853-9341
Email: terrybrady@sydneycatholic.org

Willemstad—Most Rev. Luigi Antonio Secco, S.D.B.; Bisdom, Julianaplein 34, Pietermaai, Willemstad, Curaçao, Netherlands Antilles.
Tel: 59-9-462-5876 ***Fax:*** 59-9-462-7437
Email: bisdomstad@curinfo.an

Wilmington—Most Rev. William Francis Malooly (WIL); Chancery Office 1925 Delaware Ave., Wilmington, DE, 19806.
Tel: 302-573-3146 ***Fax:*** 302-573-6816
Email: pbossi@cdow.org

WINDHOEK—Most Rev. Liborius Ndumbukuti Nashenda, O.M.I.; P.O. Box 272, Windhoek, 9000, Namibia.
Tel: 061-22-83-76; 061-22-34-30 ***Fax:*** 061-22-98-36
Email: rcarch@iafrica.com.na

WINNIPEG (UKRAINIAN)—Most Rev. Lawrence Huculak, O.S.B.M.; Archeparchy Office 233 Scotia St., Winnipeg, MB, R2V 1V7, Canada.
Tel: 204-338-7801 ***Fax:*** 204-339-4006
Email: chancery@archeparchy.ca

WINNIPEG—Most Rev. James Vernon Weisgerber; Chancery Office 1495 Pembina Hwy., Winnipeg, MB, R3T 2C6, Canada.
Tel: 204-452-2227 ***Fax:*** 204-475-4409
Email: archbishop@archwinnipeg.ca

Winona—Most Rev. John M. Quinn, M.Div. (WIN); Pastoral Center 55 W. Sanborn St., P.O. Box 588, Winona, MN, 55987.
Tel: 507-454-4643 ***Fax:*** 507-454-8106
Email: dioceseofwinona@dow.org

Witbank—Most Rev. Giuseppe Sandri, M.C.C.I.; 13 Elizabeth Ave., P.O. Box 651, Witbank, Tansvaal, 1035, South Africa.
Tel: 27-013-656-68-27 ***Fax:*** 27-013-656-68-27
Email: diocesewitbank@yebo.co.za

Wloclawek—Most Rev. Wieslaw Alojzy Mering; Kuria Diecezjalna ul. Gdanska 2/4, Wloclawek, 87-800, Poland.
Tel: 48-051-801-45-00 ***Fax:*** 48-054-231-28-31
Email: kuria@diecezja.wloclawek.pl

Wollongong—Most Rev. Peter William Ingham; Catholic Church Office 86-88 Market St., P.O. Box 1239, Wollongong, N.S.W., 2500, Australia.
Tel: 02-4253-0900 ***Fax:*** 02-4253-0977
Email: bishop@woll.catholic.org.au

Wonju—Most Rev. Jacobus Kim Ji-Seok; Diocesan Office P.O. Box 11, Wonju, Kangwon-do, 220-600, Korea, South.
Tel: 82-033-765-4221 ***Fax:*** 82-033-766-1932

Worcester—Most Rev. Robert Joseph McManus (WOR); Chancery Office 49 Elm St., Worcester, MA, 01609.
Tel: 508-791-7171 ***Fax:*** 508-754-2768

Wrexham—Most Rev. Edwin Regan; Bishop's House Sontley Road, Wrexham, Clwyd, LL13 7 EW, Wales.
Tel: 44-01978-26-27-26 ***Fax:*** 44-01978-35-42-57
Email: diowxm@globalnet.co.uk

WROCLAW, BRESLAVIA—Most Rev. Marian Golebiewski; Kuria Metropolitalna, ul. Katedralna 13, Wroclaw, 50-328, Poland.
Tel: 48-071-327-1111 ***Fax:*** 48-071-322-8269
Email: kuria@archidiecezja.wroc.pl

Wroclaw-Gdansk—Most Rev. Wlodzimierz Roman Juszczak, O.S.B.M.; Kuria Biskupia Pl Biskupa Nankiera 15/a, Wroclaw, 50-140, Poland.
Tel: 071-343-9477 ***Fax:*** 071-343-9467
Email: konsystoria@wroc-gda.opoka.org.pl

Wuchang (Wuchang)—Catholic Mission, Hwayuansan, Wuchan, Hubei, China.

Wuchow (Wuzhou, Cangwu), Tsang-Wu—Catholic Mission Bishop's House, Wuzhou, Guangxi, China.

Wuhu (Wuhu)—Catholic Mission Bishop's House, Taikoo matow, Wuhu, Anhui, China.

Würzburg—Most Rev. Friedhelm Hofmann; Bischöfliches Ordinariat Domerschulstr. 2, Würzburg, D-97070, Germany.
Tel: 49-0931-386-221 ***Fax:*** 49-0931-386-334
Email: generalvikariat@bistum-wuerzburg.de

X

Xai-Xai—Most Rev. Lucio Andrice Muandula; Bispado, Av. 1 de Majo 39, C.P. 174, Xai-Xai, Mozambique.
Tel: 258-282-22-163 ***Fax:*** 258-282-22-298

Xuân Lôc—Most Rev. Dominique Nguyên Chu Trinh; Tóa Giám Muc, B.P. 11, Y-70 Hùng Vuong, Thi Trân Xuân Lôc, Long Khánh, Dông Nai, Vietnam.
Tel: 061-3877-256 ***Fax:*** 061-3781-080
Email: vptgmxuanloc@yahoo.com

Y

Yagoua—Most Rev. Barthélémy Yaouda Hourgo; Evêché, B.P. 57, Yagoua, Cameroon.

Yakima—Most Rev. Joseph J. Tyson; Pastoral Office (Chancery) 5301-A Tieton Dr., Yakima, WA, 98908-3493.
Tel: 509-965-7117 ***Fax:*** 509-966-8334

Yamoussoukro—Most Rev. Marcellin Yao Kouadio; B.P. 1555, Yamoussoukro, Ivory Coast.
Tel: 225-3064-18-84 ***Fax:*** 225-3064-18-41
Email: eveyakro@aviso.ci

Yangku (Yanggu)—Catholic Misssion Po-Li-Chwan, Yanggu, Shandong, China.

YANGON—Most Rev. Charles Maung Bo, S.D.B.; Archbishop's House 289 Theinbyu Rd., Botahtaung P.O., Yangon, 11161, Myanmar.
Tel: 01-39-25-17; 01-39-26-67 ***Fax:*** 01-37-90-59
Email: archdyangon@myanmar.com.mm

YAOUNDÉ—Most Rev. Simon-Victor Tonyé Bakot; Archevêché, B.P. 207, Yaoundé, Cameroon.
Tel: 2201-1048/9 ***Fax:*** 2221-9735
Email: archdiocesedeyaounde@hotmail.com

Yei—Most Rev. Erkolano Lodu Tombe; Diocese of Yei P.O. Box 32, Juba, Equatoria Province, Sudan.
Tel: 924-19-64-75
Email: administrator@infocom.co.ug

Yenan (Yan'an), Fu Shih—Catholic Mission Ch'iao Le-Kow, Yan'an, Shaanxi, China.

Yenchow (Yanzhou), Tze-Yang—Catholic Mission Bishop's House, Yanzhou, Shandong, China.

Yendi—Most Rev. Vincent Sowah Boi-Nai, S.V.D.; Bishop's Office P.O. Box YD 129, Yendi, NR, Ghana.
Tel: 037-24-55-201

Yenki (Yanji)—Catholic Mission Bishop's House, Yanji, Jilin, China.

Yentai (Yantai), Chefoo—Catholic Mission, Yantai, Shandong, China.

Yingkow (Yingkou)—Catholic Mission, Bishop's House, Yingkou, Liaoning, China.

Yokadouma—Most Rev. Eugeniusz Juretzko, O.M.I.; Evêché, B.P. 33, Yokadouma, La Boumba-et-Ngoko, Cameroon.
Tel: 9927-32-02

Yokohama—Most Rev. Rafael Masahiro Umemura; 44- Yamate-cho, Naka-ku, Yokohama-shi, 231-8652, Japan.
Tel: 81-045-662-5585 ***Fax:*** 81-045-641-6522

Yola—Most Rev. Stephen Dami Mamza; Bishop's House 5 Gashaka St., P.O. Box 57, Jimeta, Yola, Adamawa State, Nigeria.
Tel: 234-075-62-46-00 ***Fax:*** 234-075-62-64-88

Yopal—Most Rev. Misael Vacca Ramírez; Casa Episcopal Calle 8 N. 21-85, Yopal, Casanare, Colombia.
Tel: 8-6356-269 ***Fax:*** 8-6356-269
Email: yopaldioc@cec.or.co

Yopougon—Most Rev. Laurent Akran Mandjo; Evêché de Yopougon, 01 B.P. 2305, Abidjan, 01, Ivory Coast.
Tel: 225-2345-7439 ***Fax:*** 225-2345-3213
Email: eveyop@yahoo.com

Yoro—Most Rev. Jean-Louis Giasson, P.M.E.; Apartado 105, El Progreso, Yoro, Honduras.
Tel: 647-1198

Youngstown—Most Rev. George Vance Murry, S.J. (Y); Chancery of Office 144 W. Wood St., Youngstown, OH, 44503.
Tel: 330-744-8451 ***Fax:*** 330-742-6448
Email: chancery@doy.org

Yüanlíng (Yuanling), Shen-Chou—Catholic Mission, Bishop's House, Yuanling, Hunan, China.

YUCATÁN—Most Rev. Emilio Carlos Berlié Belaunzarán; Arzobispado, Calle 58 N. 501, Mérida, Yucatan, 97000, Mexico.
Tel: 52-999-924-7777 ***Fax:*** 52-999-923-7983
Email: aryu@prodigy.net.mx

Yükíang (Yujiang)—Catholic Mission, Bishop's House, Yujiang, Jiangxi, China.

Yungkia (Yongjia Wenzhou), Wenchow—Catholic Mission, Bishop's House, Wenzhou, Zhejiang, China.

Yüngníen (Yongnian, Weixian)—Catholic Mission, Chaokiachwang, Weixian, Hebei, China.

Yüngpíng (Yongping, Lulong), Lu Lung—Catholic Mission, Bishop's House, Yongping, Hebei, China.

Yütze (Yuci)—Catholic Mission, Bishop's House, Yuci, Shanxi, China.

Z

Zacapa y Santo Cristo de Esquípulas—Most Rev. Rosolino Bianchetti Boffelli; Casa Episcopal, 12 Calle A 0-56, Zona 1, Zacapa, 19001, Guatemala.
Tel: 502-7941-0153 ***Fax:*** 502-7491-0888Basilica de Esquipulas, Esquipulas, Depto. Chiquimula, 20007, Guatemala.
Tel: 502-7720-7050 ***Fax:*** 502-7943-1381
Email: basilicaesq@yahoo.com

Zacatecas—Most Rev. Carlos Cabrero Romero; Obispado Apartado 1, Miguel Auza 219, Zacatecas, Zac., 98000, Mexico.
Tel: 52-492-922-6537/0232 ***Fax:*** 52-492-922-2342
Email: curiadz@prodigy.net.mx

Zacatecoluca—Most Rev. Elías Samuel Bolaños Avelar, S.D.B; 4a Calle Poniente 7, Apartado 4, Zacatecoluca, El Salvador.
Tel: 2334-02-87 ***Fax:*** 2334-07-22
Email: carpiojesus@yahoo.es

ZADAR—Most Rev. Zelimir Puljic; Nadbiskupski Ordinarijat Jurja Bijankinija 2, Zadar, 23000, Croatia.
Tel: 385-023-208-650 ***Fax:*** 385-023-208-640
Email: nadbiskupija-zadarska@zd.t.com.hr

ZAGREB—His Eminence Cardinal Josip Bozanic; Nadbispupski Duhovni Stol, Kaptol 31, Zagreb, 10000, Croatia.
Tel: 385-01-48-94-808 ***Fax:*** 385-01-48-17-714
Email: kancelar@zg-nadbiskupija.hr

Zahleh—Most Rev. Mansour Hobeika; Evêché Maronite Haouch-el-Omara, Zahleh, Lebanon.
Tel: 96-08-805-111 ***Fax:*** 96-08-805-432
Email: ksaramar@hotmail.com

ZAHLEH E FURZOL—Most Rev. Issam John Darwich, B.S.; Archevêché Grec-Melkite-Catholique Saïdat Al Najat, Zahleh, Lebanon.
Tel: 96-08-800-333; 96-08-805-444 ***Fax:*** 96-08-822-406
Email: info@catholiczahle.org

Zaku, Zakho—Vacant; Evêché Catholique, Zakho, Iraq.
Tel: 733-04-72

ZAMBOANGA—Most Rev. Romulo G. Valles; Centro Pastoral, Puerto del Sol, Gov. Camins Ave., P.O. Box 1, Zamboanga City, 7000, Philippines.
Tel: 63-062-992-7668; 63-062-992-7667 *Fax:* 63-062-993-2608
Email: zambochancery-10@yahoo.com

Zamora—Most Rev. Gregorio Martinez Sacristán; Obispado Puerta del Obispo 2, Zamora, 49001, Spain.
Tel: 34-980-53-1802 *Fax:* 34-980-50-9082
Email: obzamora@planalfa.es

Zamora (in Mexico)—Most Rev. Javier Navarro Rodríguez; Obispado Apartado 18, Hidalgo 59 Sur, Zamora, Mich., 59600, Mexico.
Tel: 351-512-1208 *Fax:* 351-515-4020
Email: obispadodezamora@hotmail.com

Zamosc-Lubaczów—Most Rev. Waclaw Depo; Kuria Diecezjalna ul. Hetmana Jana Zamoyskiego 1, Zamosc, 22-400, Poland.
Tel: 48-084-627-95-21 *Fax:* 48-084-627-95-21
Email: kuria@zamosc.opoka.org.pl

Zanzibar—Most Rev. Augustine Shao, C.S.Sp.; P.O. Box 294, Zanzibar, Tanzania.
Tel: 255-024-2230-611 *Fax:* 255-024-2238-719
Email: zanzibar_diocese@yahoo.com

ZARAGOZA—Most Rev. Manuel Ureña Pastor; Arzobispado Plaza de La Seo 5, Zaragoza, 50001, Spain.
Tel: 34-976-394-800 *Fax:* 34-976-203-036
Email: vigeneral@arzobispadodezaragoza.org

Zárate-Campana—Most Rev. Oscar Domingo Sarlinga; Obispado Rivadavia 413, Campana, Buenos Aires, B2804FZE, Argentina.
Tel: 54-03489-422-817 *Fax:* 54-03489-426-606
Email: secretariado.curia.zaratecampana@gmail.com

Zaria—Most Rev. George Jonathan Dodo; Bishop's House Hospital Rd., Wusasa, P.O. Box 90, Zaria, Kaduna State, Nigeria.
Tel: 234-080-345-20-835; 234-080-545-42-201
Email: cathdiza@yahoo.co.uk

Zé-Doca—Most Rev. Carlo Ellena; Av. do Comércio 165, C.P. 05, Zé Doca, MA, 65365-000, Brazil.
Tel: 55-098-3655-3322 *Fax:* 55-098-3655-3184

Zielona Góra-Gorzów—Most Rev. Stefan Regmunt; Kuria Diecezjalna pl. Powstanców Wielkopolskich 1, Zielona Góra, 65-075, Poland.
Tel: 48-068-451-23-30 *Fax:* 48-068-451-23-31
Email: kuriazg@zgora-gorzow.opoka.org.pl

Ziguinchor—Vacant; Evêché, 64 rue du Dr. Gabriel Carvalho, B.P. 23, Ziguinchor, Senegal.
Tel: 221-33-991-26-13 *Fax:* 221-33-991-26-13
Email: diocesez@orange.sn

Zilina—Most Rev. Tomáš Galis; Biskupsky urad, Marianske nam. 23, post. schránka B-46, Zilina 1, SK-013 36, Slovenia.
Tel: 041-500-22-15 *Fax:* 041-500-22-16
Email: kuria@dcza.sk

Zipaquirá—Most Rev. Héctor Cubillos Peña; Obispado Calle 5 N. 7-20, Zipaquirá, Cundinamarca, Colombia.
Tel: 57-1-85-24-660/23-010/22-607 *Fax:* 57-1-85-22-607/24-660/23-010
Email: gmolmos@hotmail.com

Zomba—Most Rev. Thomas Msusa, S.M.M.; Bishop's House P.O. Box 115, Zomba, Malawi.
Tel: 1-51-53-24 *Fax:* 1-51-52-47
Email: zombadiocese@malawi.net

Zrenjanin—Most Rev. Ladislav Nemet, S.V.D.; Trg Slobode 8, Zrenjanin, 23001, Serbia.
Tel: 381-023-534-722 *Fax:* 381-023-528-625
Email: ordinariatus@mgnet.rs

Archdioceses & Dioceses of the World
Geographical Index

Albania
Lezhë, Lesh
Rrëshen
Sapë
SHKODRË-PULT
TIRANË-DURRËS

Algeria
ALGER
Constantine
Laghouat
Oran

Angola
Benguela
Cabinda
Caxito
Dundo
HUAMBO
Kwito-Bié
LUANDA
LUBANGO
Lwena
MALANJE
Mbanza Congo
Menongue
Namibe
Ndalatando
Ondjiva
SAURIMO
Sumbe
Uíje
Viana

Argentina
Alto Valle del Río Negro
Añatuya
Avellaneda-Lanús
Azul
BAHÍA BLANCA
BUENOS AIRES
Catamarca
Chascomús
Comodoro Rivadavia
Concepción (in Argentina)
Concordia
CÓRDOBA
CORRIENTES
Cruz del Eje
Formosa
Goya
Gregorio de Laferrere
Gualeguaychú
Jujuy
LA PLATA
La Rioja
Lomas de Zamora
Mar del Plata
MENDOZA
MERCEDES-LUJÁN
Merlo-Moreno
Morón
Neuquén
Nueve de Julio
Oberá
Orán
PARANÁ
Posadas
Puerto Iguazú
Quilmes
Rafaela
Reconquista
RESISTENCIA
Río Gallegos
ROSARIO
SALTA
San Carlos de Bariloche
San Charbel en Buenos Aires
San Francisco (Argentina)
San Gregorio de Narek en Buenos Aires
San Isidro
SAN JUAN DE CUYO
San Justo
San Luis
San Martín
San Miguel (in Argentina)
San Nicolás de los Arroyos
San Rafael
San Roque de Presidencia Roque Sáenz Peña
SANTA FE DE LA VERA CRUZ
Santa María del Patrocinio en Buenos Aires
Santa Rosa
Santiago del Estero
Santo Tomé
TUCUMÁN
Venado Tuerto
Viedma
Villa de la Concepción del Río Cuarto
Villa María
Zárate-Campana

Australia
ADELAIDE
Armidale
Ballarat
Bathurst
BRISBANE
Broken Bay
Broome
Bunbury
Cairns
CANBERRA-GOULBURN
Darwin
Geraldton
HOBART
Lismore
Maitland-Newcastle
MELBOURNE
Parramatta
PERTH
Port Pirie
Rockhampton
Saint Maron of Sydney
Saint Michael's of Sydney (Greek Melkites)
Saint Thomas the Apostle of Sydney
Saints Peter and Paul of Melbourne
Sale
Sandhurst
SYDNEY
Toowoomba
Townsville
Wagga Wagga
Wilcannia-Forbes
Wollongong

Austria
Eisenstadt
Feldkirch
Graz-Seckau
Gurk
Innsbruck
Linz
SALZBURG
Sankt Pölten
VIENNA

Bahamas
Nassau

Bangladesh
Chittagong
DHAKA
Dinajpur
Khulna
Mymensingh
Rajshahi
Sylhet

Belarus
Grodno
MINSK - MOHILEV
Pinsk
Vitebsk

Belgium
Antwerpen, Anvers
Brugge, Bruges
Gent, Gand
Hasselt
Kabinda
Liège, Luik, Lüttich
MECHELEN-BRUSSEL, MALINES-BRUXELLES
Namur, Namen
Tournai, Doornik

Belize
Belize City-Belmopan

Benin
Abomey
COTONOU
Dassa-Zoumé
Djougou
Kandi
Lokossa
N'Dali
Natitingou
PARAKOU
Porto Novo

Bermuda
Hamilton (in Bermuda)

Bolivia
COCHABAMBA
Coroico
El Alto
LA PAZ
Oruro
Potosí
San Ignacio de Velasco
SANTA CRUZ DE LA SIERRA
SUCRE
Tarija

Bosnia-Herzegovina
Banja Luka
Mostar-Duvno
VRHBOSNA, SARAJEVO

Botswana
Gaborone

Brazil
Abaetetuba
Afogados da Ingazeira
Alagoinhas
Almenara
Alto Solimes
Amargosa
Amparo
Anápolis
APARECIDA
Apucarana
ARACAJU
Araçatuba
Araçuaí
Assis
Bacabal
Bagé
Balsas
Barra
Barra do Garças
Barra do Piraí-Volta Redonda
Barreiras
Barretos
Bauru
BELÉM DO PARÁ
BELO HORIZONTE
Blumenau
Bom Jesus da Lapa
Bom Jesus do Gurguéia
Bonfim
BOTUCATU
Bragança do Pará
Bragança Paulista
BRASÍLIA
Brejo
Caçador
Cachoeira do Sul
Cachoeiro de Itapemirim
Caetité
Caicó
Cajazeiras
Camaçari
Campanha
Campina Grande
CAMPINAS
CAMPO GRANDE
Campo Limpo
Campo Maior
Campo Mourão
Campos
Caraguatatuba
Caratinga
Carolina
Caruaru
CASCAVEL
Castanhal
Catanduva
Caxias do Maranhão
Caxias do Sul
Chapecó
Colatina
Cornélio Procópio
Coroatá
Corumbá
Coxim
Crateús
Crato
Criciúma
Cruz Alta
Cruzeiro do Sul
CUIABÁ
CURITIBA
DIAMANTINA
Diamantino
Divinópolis
Dourados
Duque de Caxias
Erexim
Estância
Eunápolis
FEIRA DE SANTANA
Floresta
Floriano
FLORIANÓPOLIS
Formosa (in Brazil)
FORTALEZA
Foz do Iguaçu
Franca
Frederico Westphalen
Garanhuns
GOIÂNIA
Goiás
Governador Valadares
Grajaú
Guajará-Mirim
Guanhães
Guarabira

Guarapuava
Guarulhos
Guaxupé
Guiratinga
Humaitá
Iguatu
Ilhéus
Imperatriz
Ipameri
Irecê
Itabira-Fabriciano
Itabuna
Itaguaí
Itapetininga
Itapeva
Itapipoca
Ituiutaba
Itumbiara
Jaboticabal
Jacarezinho
Jales
Janaúba
Januária
Jardim
Jataí
Jequié
Ji-Paraná
Joaçaba
Joinville
Juazeiro
Juína
JUIZ DE FORA
Jundiaí
Lages
Leopoldina
Limeira
Limoeiro do Norte
Lins
Livramento de Nossa Senhora
LONDRINA
Lorena
Luz
Luziânia
Macapá
MACEIÓ
MANAUS
Marabá
MARIANA
Marília
MARINGÁ
Miracema do Tocantins
Mogi das Cruzes
Montenegro
Montes Claros
Mossoró
NATAL
Navirai
Nazaré
NITERÓI
Nossa Senhora do Líbano em São Paulo
Nossa Senhora do Paraíso em São Paulo
Nova Friburgo
Nova Iguaçu
Novo Hamburgo
Oeiras
OLINDA E RECIFE
Oliveira
Osasco
Osório
Ourinhos
Palmares
PALMAS
Palmas-Francisco Beltrão
Palmeira dos Índios
Paracatu
PARAÍBA
Paranaguá
Paranavaí
Parintins
Parnaíba
PASSO FUNDO
Patos
Patos de Minas
Paulo Afonso
PELOTAS
Penedo
Pesqueira
Petrolina
Petrópolis
Picos
Pinheiro
Piracicaba
Ponta de Pedras
Ponta Grossa
PORTO ALEGRE
Porto Nacional
PORTO VELHO
POUSO ALEGRE
Presidente Prudente
Propriá
Quixadá
Registro
RIBEIRÃO PRETO
Rio Branco
Rio do Sul
Rio Grande
Rondonópolis
Roraima
Rubiataba-Mozarlândia
Ruy Barbosa
Salgueiro
Santa Cruz do Sul
SANTA MARIA
Santarém (in Brazil)
Santíssima Conceição do Araguaia
Santo Amaro
Santo André
Santo Ângelo
Santos
São Carlos
São Gabriel da Cachoeira
São João Batista em Curitiba
São João da Boa Vista
São João del Rei
São José do Rio Preto
São José dos Campos
São José dos Pinhais
São Luís de Montes Belos
SÃO LUÍS DO MARANHÃO
São Luiz de Cáceres
São Mateus
São Miguel Paulista
SÃO PAULO
São Raimundo Nonato
SÃO SALVADOR DA BAHIA
SÃO SEBASTIÃO DO RIO DE JANEIRO
Serrinha
Sete Lagoas
Sinop
Sobral
SOROCABA
Taubaté
Teixeira de Freitas-Caravelas
Teófilo Otoni
TERESINA
Tianguá
Tocantinópolis
Toledo (in Brazil)
Três Lagoas
Tubarão
UBERABA
Uberlândia
Umuarama
União da Vitória
Uruaçu
Uruguaiana
Vacaria
Valença
Viana
VITÓRIA
VITÓRIA DA CONQUISTA
Zé-Doca

Bulgaria

Nicopoli
Sofia e Plovdiv

Burkina Faso

Banfora
BOBO-DIOULASSO
Dédougou
Diébougou
Dori
Fada N'Gourma
Kaya
Koudougou
KOUPÉLA
Manga
Nouna
OUAGADOUGOU
Ouahigouya

Burundi

Bubanza
BUJUMBURA
Bururi
GITEGA
Muyinga
Ngozi
Rutana
Ruyigi
Uvira

Cameroon

Bafia
Bafoussam
BAMENDA
Batouri
BERTOUA
Buéa
DOUALA
Doumé-Abong' Mbang
Ebolowa
Edéa
Eséka
GAROUA
Kribi
Kumbo
Mamfe
Maroua-Mokolo
Mbalmayo
Ngaoundéré
Nkongsamba
Obala
Sangmélima
Yagoua
YAOUNDÉ
Yokadouma

Canada

Alexandria-Cornwall
Amos
Antigonish
Baie-Comeau
Bathurst (in Canada)
Calgary
Charlottetown
Chicoutimi
Churchill-Baie d'Hudson
Corner Brook and Labrador
EDMONTON
Edmonton (Ukrainian)
Edmundston
Gaspé
GATINEAU
Grand Falls
GROUARD-MCLENNAN
HALIFAX-YARMOUTH
Hamilton
Hearst
Joliette
Kamloops
KEEWATIN-LE PAS
KINGSTON
London
Mackenzie-Fort Smith
Mar Addai of Toronto (Chaldean)
MONCTON
Mont-Laurier
MONTRÉAL
Moosonee
Nelson
New Westminster
Nicolet
OTTAWA
Pembroke
Peterborough
Prince-Albert
Prince George
QUÉBEC
REGINA
RIMOUSKI
Rouyn-Noranda
SAINT-BONIFACE
Saint Catharines
Saint-Hyacinthe
Saint-Jean - Longueuil
Saint-Jérôme
Saint John, New Brunswick
SAINT JOHN'S, NEWFOUNDLAND
Saint-Maron de Montréal
Saint Paul (in Alberta)
Saint-Sauveur de Montréal
Sainte-Anne-de-la-Pocatière
Saints Cyril and Methodius of Toronto
Saskatoon
Saskatoon (Ukrainian)
Sault Sainte Marie
SHERBROOKE
Thunder Bay
Timmins
TORONTO
Toronto (Ukrainian)
Trois-Rivières
Valleyfield
VANCOUVER
Victoria
Whitehorse
WINNIPEG (UKRAINIAN)
WINNIPEG

Cape Verde

Mindelo
Santiago de Cabo Verde

Central African Republic

Alindao
Bambari
Bangassou
BANGUI
Berbérati
Bossangoa
Bouar
Kaga-Bandoro
Mbaïki

Chad

Doba
Goré
Lai
Moundou
N'DJAMÉNA
Pala
Sarh

Chile

ANTOFAGASTA
Arica
Chillán
CONCEPCIÓN
Copiapó
Iquique
LA SERENA
Linares
Melipilla
Osorno
PUERTO MONTT
Punta Arenas
Rancagua
San Bernardo
San Carlos de Ancud
San Felipe
San Juan Bautista de Calama
Santa Maria de Los Angeles (in Chile)
SANTIAGO DE CHILE
Talca
Temuco
Valdivia
Valparaíso
Villarrica

China

ANKING (ANQING), HUAINING
Ankwo (Anguo)
CANTON (GUANGZHOU)
CHANGSHA (CHANGSHA)
Changteh (Changde)
Chaohsien (Zhaoxian)
Chengchow (Zhengzhou)
Chengting (Zhengding)
Chengtu (Chengdu)
Chihfeng (Chifeng)
Chowchich (Zhouzhi)
Chowtsun (Zhoucun)
Chumatien (Zhumadian)
CHUNGKING (CHONGQING)
Fengsiang (Fengxiang)
Fenyang (Fenyang)
FOOCHOW (FUZHOU), MINHOU
Funíng (Xiapu)
Fushun (Fushun)
Haimen (Haimen)
Hanchung (Hanzhong)
HANGCHOW (HANGZHOU)
HANKOW (HANKOU)
Hanyang (Hanyang)
Hengchow (Hengyang)
Hong Kong (Xianggang)
Hsíamen (Xiamen), Amoy
Hungtung (Hongdong)
Ichang (Yichang)
Ichow (Linyi)
Jehol (Jinzhou)
KAIFENG (KAIFENG)
Kanchow (Ganzhou)
Kangtíng (Kangding)
Kayíng (Meixian), Kíayíng
Kí-an (Jí'an)
Kíatíng (Leshan)
Kichow (Qichun)
Kinghsien (Jingxian)
Kírín (Jilin)
Kongmoon (Jiangmen)
KUNMING (KUNMING)
Kweiteh (Shangqui)
KWEYANG (GUIYANG)
LANCHOW (LANZHOU), KAO-LAN
Lanlung (Anlong)
Laohokow (Laohekou)
Lishui (Lishui)
Loyang (Luoyang)
Lu An (Changzhi)
Macau
MUKDEN (SHENYANG), FENGTIEN
NANCHANG (NANCHANG)
Nancheng (Nancheng)
NANKING (NANJING)
Nanning (Nanning)
Nanyang (Nanyang)
Níng Po (Ningbo), Ninghsien
Ningsia (Yinchuan)
Ningyüan (Xichang)
Pakhoi (Beihai)
Paotíng (Baoding), Ching-Yüan
PEKING (BEIJING)
Pengpu (Bengbu), Peng-Fou
Pingliang (Pingliang)
Puchi (Puqi)
Sanyüan (Sanyuan)
Shanghaí (Shanghai)
Shíhnan (Enshi)
Shiuchow (Shaoguan), Shao-Chou
Shohchow (Shuoxian)
Shunking (Nanchong)
Shunteh (Xingtai)
SIAN (XI'AN), CHANG-AN
Siangyang (Xiangyang)
Síenhsíen (Xianxian)
Sínyang (Xinyang)
Siwantze (Chongli-Xiwanzi)
Soochow (Suzhou), Wuhsien
Süanhwa (Xuanhua)
Süchow (Xuzhou)
Suifu (Yibin)
SUIYÜAN (HOHOT), KUEI SUI
Swatow (Shantou)
Szepíngkai (Siping), Szepingchieh
Taíchow (Linhai)
TAIYUAN (TAIYUAN)
Tali (Dali)
Taming (Daming)
Tatung (Datong)
Tientsín (Tianjin)
Tingchow (Changting)
Tsaochow (Caozhou, Heze)
TSINAN (JINAN)
Tsínchow (Tianshui)
Tsíngtao (Qingdao)
Tsíníng (Jining)
Wanhsíen (Wanxian)
Weíhwei (Jixian)
Wuchang (Wuchang)
Wuchow (Wuzhou, Cangwu), Tsang-Wu
Wuhu (Wuhu)
Yangku (Yanggu)
Yenan (Yan'an), Fu Shih
Yenchow (Yanzhou), Tze-Yang
Yenki (Yanji)
Yentai (Yantai), Chefoo
Yingkow (Yingkou)
Yüanlíng (Yuanling), Shen-Chou
Yükíang (Yujiang)
Yungkia (Yongjia Wenzhou), Wenchow
Yüngníen (Yongnian, Weixian)
Yüngpíng (Yongping, Lulong), Lu Lung
Yütze (Yuci)

Colombia

Apartadó
Arauca
Armenia
Barrancabermeja
BARRANQUILLA
BOGOTÁ
BUCARAMANGA
Buenaventura
Buga
Caldas
CALI
CARTAGENA
Cartago
Chiquinquirá
Cúcuta
Duitama-Sogamoso
El Banco
Engativá
Espinal
Facatativá
Florencia
Fontibón
Garagoa
Garzón
Girardot
Girardota
Granada (in Colombia)
IBAGUÉ
Ipiales
Istmina - Tadó
Jericó
La Dorada-Guaduas
Líbano-Honda
Magangué
Málaga-Soatá
MANIZALES
MEDELLÍN
Mocoa-Sibundoy
Montelíbano
Montería
Neiva
NUEVA PAMPLONA
Ocaña
Palmira
Pasto
Pereira
POPAYÁN
Quibdó
Riohacha
San Jose del Guaviare
SANTA FE DE ANTIOQUIA
Santa Marta
Santa Rosa de Osos
Sincelejo
Soacha
Socorro y San Gil
Sonsón-Rionegro
Tibú
Tumaco
TUNJA
Valledupar
Vélez
VILLAVICENCIO
Yopal
Zipaquirá

Cook Islands

Rarotonga

Costa Rica

Alajuela
Cartago
Ciudad Quesada
Limón
Puntarenas
San Isidro de El General
SAN JOSÉ DE COSTA RICA
Tilarán

Croatia

Bjelovar-Krizevci
Dakovo-Osijek
Dubrovnik, Ragusa
Gospic-Senj
Hvar
Krizevci, Crisio
Krk, Veglia
Porec i Pula
Pozega
RIJEKA
Šibenik
Sisak
SPLIT-MAKARSKA
Varazdin
ZADAR
ZAGREB

Cuba

CAMAGÜEY
Ciego de Avila
Cienfuegos
Guantánamo-Baracoa
Holguín
Matanzas
Pinar del Rio
SAN CRISTÓBAL DE LA HABANA
Santa Clara
SANTIAGO DE CUBA
Santísimo Salvador de Bayamo Y Manzanillo

Cyprus

CIPRO

Czech Republic

Brno
Ceské Budejovice
Hradec Králové
Litomerice
OLOMOUC
Ostrava-Opava
Plzen
PRAHA

Democratic Republic of Congo

Basankusu
Bokungu-Ikela
Boma
Bondo
Budjala
BUKAVU
Bunia
Buta
Butembo-Beni
Doruma-Dungu
Goma
Idiofa
Inongo
Isangi
Isiro-Niangara
Kabinda
Kalemie-Kirungu
Kamina
KANANGA
Kasongo
Kenge
Kikwit
Kilwa-Kasenga
Kindu
KINSHASA
KISANGANI
Kisantu
Kole
Kolwezi
Kongolo
Lisala
Lolo
LUBUMBASHI
Luebo
Luiza
Mahagi-Nioka
Manono
Matadi
MBANDAKA-BIKORO
Mbujimayi
Molegbe
Mweka
Popokabaka
Sakania-Kipushi
Tshumbe
Uvira
Wamba

Denmark

Kobenhavn, Copenhagen

Djibouti

Djibouti
Mogadiscio

Dominica

Roseau

Dominican Republic

Baní
Barahona
La Vega
Mao-Monte Cristi
Nuestra Señora de la Altagracia en Higüey
Puerto Plata
San Francisco de Macorís
San Juan de la Maguana
San Pedro de Macorís
SANTIAGO DE LOS CABALLEROS
SANTO DOMINGO

East Timor

Baucau
Díli
Maliana

Ecuador

Ambato
Azogues
Babahoyo
CUENCA
Guaranda
GUAYAQUIL
Ibarra
Latacunga
Loja
Machala
PORTOVIEJO
QUITO
Riobamba
San Jacinto de Yaguachi
Santo Domingo en Ecuador
Tulcán

Egypt
Alessandria of Copti
Assiut, Lycopolis
Guizeh
Iskanderiya, Alessandria
Ismayliah
Le Caire
Le Caire - Chaldean
Le Caire - Syrian
Luqsor, Tebe
Minya, Ermopoli Maggiore, Minieh
Sohag

El Salvador
Chalatenango
San Miguel
SAN SALVADOR
San Vicente
Santa Ana
Santiago de María
Sonsonate
Zacatecoluca

England
Arundel and Brighton
BIRMINGHAM
Brentwood
CARDIFF
Clifton
East Anglia
Hallam
Hexham and Newcastle
Lancaster
Leeds
LIVERPOOL
Menevia
Middlesbrough
Northampton
Nottingham
Plymouth
Portsmouth
Salford
Shrewsbury
SOUTHWARK
WESTMINSTER

Equatorial Guinea
Bata
Ebebiyin
MALABO

Eritrea
Asmara
Barentu
Keren

Ethiopia
ADDIS ABEBA
Adigrat
Emdeber

Fiji
SUVA

Finland
Helsinki

France
Agen
Aire et Dax
AIX
Ajaccio
ALBI
Amiens
Angers
Angoulême
Annecy
Arras
AUCH
Autun
AVIGNON
Bayeux
Bayonne
Beauvais
Belfort-Montbéliard
Belley-Ars
BESANÇON
Blois
BORDEAUX
BOURGES
Cahors
CAMBRAI
Carcassonne et Narbonne
Châlons
CHAMBÉRY
Chartres
CLERMONT
Coutances
Créteil
Digne
DIJON
Evreux
Evry-Corbeil-Essonnes
Fréjus-Toulon
Gap
Grenoble-Vienne
La Rochelle
Langres
Laval
Le Havre
Le Mans
Le Puy-en-Velay
LILLE
Limoges
Luçon
LYON
MARSEILLE
Meaux
Mende
Metz
Montauban
Montpellier
Moulins
Nancy
Nanterre
Nantes
Nevers
Nice
Nîmes
Orléans
Pamiers
PARIS
Périgueux
Perpignan-Elne
POITIERS
Pontoise
Quimper, Cornouailles
REIMS
RENNES
Rodez
ROUEN
Saint-Brieuc
Saint-Claude
Saint-Denis
Saint-Dié
Saint-Etienne
Saint-Flour
Sainte-Croix-de-Paris
Sées
SENS
Soissons
STRASBOURG
Tarbes et Lourdes
TOULOUSE
TOURS
Troyes
Tulle
Valence
Vannes
Verdun
Versailles
Viviers

French Guiana
Cayenne

French Polynesia
PAPEETE
Taiohae o Tefenuaenata

Gabon
Franceville
LIBREVILLE
Mouila
Oyem
Port-Gentil

Gambia
Banjul

Germany
Aachen
Augsburg
BAMBERG
BERLIN
Dresden-Meissen
Eichstätt
Erfurt
Essen
FREIBURG IM BREISGAU
Fulda
Görlitz
HAMBURG
Hildesheim
KÖLN
Limburg
Magdeburg
Mainz
MÜNCHEN UND FREISING
Münster
Osnabrück
PADERBORN
Passau
Regensburg
Rottenburg-Stuttgart
Speyer
Trier
Würzburg

Ghana
ACCRA
CAPE COAST
Damongo
Goaso
Ho
Jasikan
Keta-Akatsi
Koforidua
Konongo-Mampong
KUMASI
Navrongo-Bolgatanga
Obuasi
Sekondi-Takoradi
Sunyani
TAMALE
Techiman
Wa
Wiawso
Yendi

Gibraltar
Gibraltar

Greece
ATHENS
Candia, Creta, La Canea
Chios
CORFÙ - ZANTE, CEFALONIA
NAXOS, ANDROS, TINOS E MYKONOS
RHODOS
Santorini, Thira
Syros

Guadeloupe
Basse-Terre

Guatemala
Escuintla
GUATEMALA
Huehuetenango
Jalapa (in Guatemala)
LOS ALTOS, QUETZALTENANGO-TOTONICAPÁN
Quiché
San Marcos
Santa Rosa de Lima
Sololá-Chimaltenango
Suchitepéquez-Retalhuleu
Vera Paz, Cobán
Zacapa y Santo Cristo de Esquípulas

Guinea
CONAKRY, KONAKRY
Kankan
N'Zérékoré

Guinea-Bissau
Bafatá
Bissau

Guyana
Georgetown

Haiti
Anse-à-Veau et Miragoâne
CAP-HAÏTIEN
Fort-Liberté
Jacmel
Jérémie
Les Cayes
Les Gonaïves
PORT-AU-PRINCE
Port-de-Paix

Honduras
Choluteca
Comayagua
Juticalpa
San Pedro Sula
Santa Rosa de Copán
TEGUCIGALPA
Trujillo (in Honduras)
Yoro

Hungary
Debrecen-Nyíregyháza
EGER
ESZTERGOM-BUDAPEST
Györ
Hajdúdorog
KALOCSA-KECSKEMÉT
Kaposvár
Pécs
Szeged-Csanád
Székesfehérvár
Szombathely
Vác
VESZPRÉM

Iceland
Reykjavik

India
Adilabad
Agartala
AGRA
Ahmedabad
Aizawl
Ajmer
Allahabad
Alleppey
Ambikapur
Amravati
Asansol
Aurangabad
Bagdogra
Balasore
BANGALORE
Bareilly
Baroda
Baruipur
Battery (Syro-Malankaras)
Belgaum
Bellary
Belthangady
Berhampur
Bettiah
Bhadravathi
Bhagalpur
BHOPAL
Bijnor
BOMBAY
Bongaigaon
Buxar
CALCUTTA
Calicut

Chanda
CHANGANACHERRY
Chikmagalur
Chingleput
Cochin
Coimbatore
Cuddapah
CUTTACK-BHUBANESWAR
Daltonganj
Darjeeling
DELHI
Dharmapuri
Dibrugarh
Dindigul
Diphu
Dumka
Eluru
ERNAKULAM-ANGAMALY
GANDHINAGAR
GOA E DAMAO
Gorakhpur
Gulbarga
Gumla
Guntur
GUWAHATI
Gwalior
Hazaribag
HYDERABAD
Idukki
IMPHAL
Indore
Irinjalakuda
Itanagar
Jabalpur
Jagdalpur
Jaipur
Jalpaiguri
Jammu-Srinagar
Jamshedpur
Jashpur
Jhabua
Jhansi
Jowai
Jullundur
Kalyan
Kanjirapally
Kannur
Karwar
Khammam
Khandwa
Khunti
Kohima
Kothamangalam
Kottapuram
Kottar
KOTTAYAM
Krishnagar
Kumbakonam
Kurnool
Lucknow
MADRAS AND MYLAPORE (MELIAPOR)
MADURAI
Mananthavady
Mandya (Syro-Malabarese)
Mangalore
Marthandom
Mavelikara
Meerut
Miao
Muvattupuzha
Muzaffarpur
Mysore
NAGPUR
Nalgonda
Nashik
Nellore
Neyyattinkara
Nongstoin
Ootacamund
Palai
Palayamkottai
Palghat
Pathanamthitta (Malankarese)
PATNA
PONDICHERRY AND CUDDALORE
Poona
Port Blair
Punalur
Purnea
Puthur (Malankarese)
Quilon
Raiganj
Raigarh
Raipur
Rajkot
Ramanathapuram (Syro-Malabarese)
RANCHI
Rourkela
Sagar
Salem
Sambalpur
Satna
SHILLONG
Shimoga
Simdega
Simla and Chandigarh
Sindhudurg
Sivagangai
Srikakulam
Tanjore
TELLICHERRY
Tezpur
Thamarasserry (Syro-Malabar)
Thuckalay
Tiruchirapalli
Tiruvalla
TRICHUR
TRIVANDRUM
TRIVANDRUM (SIRO MALANKAR)
Tura
Tuticorin
Udaipur
Ujjain
Varanasi
Vasai
Vellore
VERAPOLY
Vijayapuram
Vijayawada
VISAKHAPATNAM
Warangal

Indonesia

Agats
Amboina
Atambua
Bandung
Banjarmasin
Bogor
Denpasar
ENDE
JAKARTA
Jayapura
Ketapang
KUPANG
Larantuka
MAKASSAR
Malang
Manado
Manokwari-Sorong
Maumere
MEDAN
MERAUKE
Padang
Palangkaraya
Palembang
Pangkal-Pinang
PONTIANAK
Purwokerto
Ruteng
Samarinda
Sanggau
SEMARANG
Sibolga
Sintang
Surabaya
Tanjung Selor
Tanjungkarang
Timika
UJUNG PANDANG (see Makassar)
Weetebula

Iran

AHWAZ
ISPAHAN
Ispahan, Esfáan
Salmas, Shahpour
TEHERAN
URMYA-URMIA, REZAYEH

Iraq

Alquoch
Amadiyah, Amadia
Aqra, Akra
ARBIL, ERBIL
BAGHDAD (BABILONIA)
BAGHDAD (BABILONIA) (ARMENIAN)
BAGHDAD (BABILONIA) (LATIN)
BAGHDAD (BABILONIA) (SYRIAN)
BASSORAH, BASRA
KERKUK
MOSSUL
MOSSUL (SYRIAN)
Sulaimaniya
Zaku, Zakho

Ireland

Achonry
Ardagh
ARMAGH
CASHEL
Clogher
Clonfert
Cloyne
Cork and Ross
Derry
Down and Connor
Dromore
DUBLIN
Elphin
Ferns
Galway and Kilmacduagh
Kerry
Kildare and Leighlin
Killala
Killaloe
Kilmore
Limerick
Meath
Ossory
Raphoe
TUAM
Waterford and Lismore

Israel

AKKA, SAN GIOVANNI D'ACRI, TOLEMAIDE
HAIFA - TERRA SANTA

Italy

ACERENZA
Acerra
Acireale
Acqui
Adria-Rovigo
AGRIGENTO
Alba
Albano
Albenga-Imperia
Ales-Terralba
Alessandria
Alghero-Bosa
Alife-Caiazzo
Altamura-Gravina-Acquaviva delle Fonti
AMALFI-CAVA DE' TIRRENI
Anagni-Alatri
ANCONA-OSIMO
Andria
Aosta
Arezzo-Cortona-Sansepolcro
Ariano Irpino-Lacedonia
Ascoli Piceno
Assisi-Nocera Umbra-Gualdo Tadino
Asti
Avellino
Aversa
Avezzano
BARI-BITONTO
Belluno-Feltre
BENEVENTO
Bergamo
Biella
BOLOGNA
Bolzano-Bressanone, Bozen-Brixen
Brescia
BRINDISI-OSTUNI
CAGLIARI
Caltagirone
Caltanissetta
CAMERINO-SAN SEVERINO MARCHE
CAMPOBASSO-BOIANO
CAPUA
Carpi
Casale Monferrato
Caserta
Cassano all'Jonio
Castellaneta
CATANIA
CATANZARO-SQUILLACE
Cefalù
Cerignola-Ascoli Satriano
Cerreto Sannita-Telese-Sant'Agata de' Goti
Cesena-Sarsina
Chiavari
CHIETI-VASTO
Chioggia
Città di Castello
Civita Castellana
Civitavecchia-Tarquinia
Como
Concordia-Pordenone
Conversano-Monopoli
COSENZA-BISIGNANO
Crema
Cremona
CROTONE-SANTA SEVERINA
Cuneo
Fabriano-Matelica
Faenza-Modigliana
Fano-Fossombrone-Cagli-Pergola
FERMO
FERRARA-COMACCHIO
Fidenza
Fiesole
FIRENZE
FOGGIA-BOVINO
Foligno
Forlì-Bertinoro
Fossano
Frascati
Frosinone-Veroli-Ferentino
GAETA
GENOVA
GORIZIA
Grosseto
Gubbio
Iglesias
Imola
Ischia
Isernia-Venafro
Ivrea
Jesi
L'AQUILA
La Spezia-Sarzana-Brugnato
Lamezia Terme
LANCIANO-ORTONA
Lanusei
Latina-Terracina-Sezze-Priverno
LECCE
Livorno
Locri-Gerace
Lodi
LUCCA
Lucera-Troia

Lungro
Macerata-Tolentino-Recanti-Cingoli-Treia
MANFREDONIA - VIESTE-SAN GIOVANNI ROTONDO
Mantova
Massa Carrara-Pontremoli
Massa Marittima-Piombino
MATERA-IRSINA
Mazara del Vallo
Melfi-Rapolla-Venosa
MESSINA-LIPARI-SANTA LUCIA DEL MELA
MILANO
Mileto-Nicotera-Tropea
MODENA-NONANTOLA
Molfetta-Ruvo-Giovinazzo-Terlizzi
Mondovi
MONREALE
Montepulciano-Chiusi-Pienza
NAPOLI
Nardó-Gallipol
Nicosia
Nocera Inferiore-Sarno
Nola
Noto
Novara
Nuoro
Oppido Mamertina-Palmi
Oria
ORISTANO
Orvieto-Todi
OTRANTO
Ozieri
Padova
PALERMO
Palestrina
Parma
Patti
Pavia
PERUGIA - CITTÁ DELLA PIEVE
PESARO
PESCARA-PENNE
Pescia
Piacenza-Bobbio
Piana degli Albanesi
Piazza Armerina
Pinerolo
PISA
Pistoia
Pitigliano-Sovana-Orbetello
Porto-Santa Rufina
POTENZA-MURO LUCANO-MARSICO NUOVO
Pozzuoli
Prato
Ragusa
RAVENNA-CERVIA
REGGIO CALABRIA-BOVA
Reggio Emilia - Guastalla
Rieti
Rimini
Roma
ROSSANO-CARIATI
Sabina-Poggio Mirteto
SALERNO-CAMPAGNA-ACERNO
Saluzzo
San Benedetto del Tronto-Ripatransone-Montalto
San Marco Argentano - Scalea
San Marino-Montefeltro
San Miniato
San Severo
SANT'ANGELO DEI LOMBARDI-CONZA-NUSCO-BISACCIA
SASSARI
Savona-Noli
Senigallia
Sessa Aurunca
SIENA-COLLE DI VAL D'ELSA-MONTALCINO
SIRACUSA
Sora-Aquino-Pontecorvo
SORRENTO-CASTELLAMMARE DI STABIA
SPOLETO-NORCIA
Sulmona-Valva
Susa
TARANTO
Teano-Calvi
Teggiano-Policastro
Tempio-Ampurias
Teramo-Atri
Termoli-Larino
Terni - Narni - Amelia
Tivoli
TORINO
Tortona
TRANI - BARLETTA - BISCEGLIE
Trapani
TRENTO
Treviso
Tricarico
Trieste
Trivento
Tursi-Lagonegro
UDINE
Ugento-Santa Maria di Leuca
URBINO-URBANIA-SANT'ANGELO (IN VADO)
Vallo della Lucania
Velletri-Segni
Ventimiglia-San Remo
VERCELLI
Verona
Vicenza
Vigevano
Viterbo
Vittorio Veneto
Volterra

Ivory Coast

Abengourou
ABIDJAN
Agboville
Bondoukou
BOUAKÉ
Cape Palmas
Daloa
GAGNOA
Grand-Bassam
Katiola
KORHOGO
Man
Odienné
San Pedro-en-Côte-d'Ivoire
Yamoussoukro
Yopougon

Jamaica

KINGSTON (IN JAMAICA)
Mandeville

Japan

Fukuoka
Hiroshima
Kagoshima
Kyoto
NAGASAKI
Nagoya
Naha
Niigata
Oita
OSAKA
Saitama
Sapporo
Sendai
Takamatsu
TOKYO
Yokohama

Jordan

PETRA E FILADELFIA

Kazakhstan

Karaganda
MARIA SANTISSIMA (IN ASTANA)
Santissima Trinità (in Almaty)

Kenya

Bungoma
Eldoret
Embu
Garissa
Homa Bay
Kakamega
Kericho
Kisii
KISUMU
Kitale
Kitui
Lodwar
Machakos
Malindi
Maralal
Marsabit
Meru
MOMBASA
Muranga
NAIROBI
Nakuru
Ngong
Nyahururu
NYERI
Rumbek
Torit

Kiribati

Tarawa and Nauru

Korea, North

Hamhung

Korea, South

Andong
Cheju
Cheongju
Ch'unch'on
DAEGU
Daejeon
Incheon
Jeonju
KWANGJU
Masan
Pusan
P'yong-yang
SEOUL
Suwon
Uijongbu
Wonju

Latvia

Jelgava
Liepaja
Rezekne-Aglona
RIGA

Lebanon

ANTÉLIAS
BAALBEK, BA'LBEK, ELIOPOLI
Baalbek - Deir El-Ahmar
Bairut, Beirut
BAIRUT, BEIRUT ARMENIAN
BAIRUT, BEIRUT-JBEIL
BAIRUT, BEIRUT (MARONITE)
Bairut, Beirut (Syrian)
BANIYAS, CESAREA DI FILIPPO, PANEADE
Batrun
Jbeil, Byblos
Joubbé, Sarba and Jounieh
SAÏDA, SAIDA, SIDONE
Saïda, Saida, Sidone (Maronite)
TRIPOLI DEL LIBANO, TARABULUS
TRIPOLI DEL LIBANO, TARABULUS (GREEK MELKITE)
TYR, TIRO, SUR
TYR, TIRO, SUR (MARONITE)
Zahleh
ZAHLEH E FURZOL

Lesotho

Leribe
MASERU
Mohale's Hoek
Qacha's Nek

Liberia

Cape Palmas
Gbarnga
MONROVIA

Liechtenstein

VADUZ

Lithuania

Kaišiadorys
KAUNAS
Panevezys
Šiauliai
Telšiai
Vilkaviškis
VILNIUS

Luxembourg

LUXEMBOURG

Macedonia

Skopje

Madagascar

Ambanja
Ambatondrazaka
Ambositra
ANTANANARIVO
Antsirabé
ANTSIRANANA
Farafangana
Fenoarivo Atsinanana
FIANARANTSOA
Ihosy
Mahajanga
Mananjary
Miarinarivo
Moramanga
Morombe
Morondava
Port-Bergé
TOAMASINA
Tôlagnaro
Toliara
Tsiroanomandidy

Malawi

BLANTYRE
Chikwawa
Dedza
Karonga
LILongwe
Mangochi
Mzuzu
Zomba

Malaysia

Keningau
KOTA KINABALU
KUALA LUMPUR
KUCHING
Melaka-Johor
Miri
Penang
Sandakan
Sibu

Mali

BAMAKO
Kayes
Mopti
San
Ségou
Sikasso

Malta

Gozo
MALTA

Martinique

FORT-DE-FRANCE

Mauritania

Nouakchott

Mauritius
Port-Louis

Mexico
ACAPULCO
Aguascalientes
ANTEQUERA, OAXACA
Apatzingán
Atlacomulco
Autlán
Campeche
Celaya
CHIHUAHUA
Chilpancingo-Chilapa
Ciudad Altamirano
Ciudad Guzmán
Ciudad Juárez
Ciudad Lázaro Cárdenas
Ciudad Obregón
Ciudad Valles
Ciudad Victoria
Coatzacoalcos
Colima
Córdoba (in Mexico)
Cuauhtémoc-Madera
Cuautitlán
Cuernavaca
Culiacán
DURANGO
Ecatepec
Ensenada
Gómez Palacio
GUADALAJARA
HERMOSILLO
Huajuapan de León
Huejutla
Irapuato
JALAPA
La Paz en la Baja California Sur
LEON (IN MEXICO)
Linares (in Mexico)
Matamoros
Matehuala
Mazatlán
Mexicali
MÉXICO
MONTERREY
MORELIA
Netzahualcóyotl
Nuestra Señora de los Mártires del Líbano en México
Nuestra Señora del Paraíso en México
Nuevo Casas Grandes
Nuevo Laredo
Orizaba
Papantla
Parral
Piedras Negras
PUEBLA DE LOS ANGELES, PUEBLA
Puerto Escondido
Querétaro
Saltillo
San Andrés Tuxtla
San Cristóbal de las Casas
San Juan de los Lagos
SAN LUIS POTOSÍ
Tabasco
Tacámbaro
Tampico
Tapachula
Tarahumara
Tehuacán
Tehuantepec
Tenancingo
Teotihuacan
Tepic
Texcoco
Tijuana
TLALNEPANTLA
Tlapa
Tlaxcala
Toluca
Torreón
Tula
TULANCINGO
Tuxpan
Tuxtepec
TUXTLA GUTIERREZ
Valle de Chalco
Veracruz
YUCATÁN
Zacatecas
Zamora (in Mexico)

Moldova
Chisinau

Monaco
MONACO

Montenegro
BAR (ANTIVARI)
Kotor

Morocco
RABAT
TANGER

Mozambique
BEIRA
Chimoio
Gurué
Inhambane
Lichinga
MAPUTO
Nacala
NAMPULA
Pemba
Quelimane
Tete
Xai-Xai

Myanmar
Banmaw
Hakha
Hpa-an
Kalay
Kengtung
Lashio
Loikaw
MANDALAY
Mawlamyine
Myitkyina
Pathein
Pekhon
Pyay
Taunggyi
Taungngu
YANGON

Namibia
Keetmanshoop
WINDHOEK

Netherlands Antilles
Willemstad

New Caledonia
NOUMÉA

New Zealand
Auckland
Christchurch
Dunedin
Hamilton (in New Zealand)
Palmerston North
WELLINGTON

Nicaragua
Estelí
Granada (in Nicaragua)
Jinotega
Juigalpa
León (in Nicaragua)
MANAGUA
Matagalpa

Niger
NIAMEY

Nigeria
Aba
Abakaliki
Abeokuta
ABUJA
Ahiara
Auchi
Awgu
Awka
Bauchi
BENIN CITY
CALABAR
Ekiti
Enugu
IBADAN
Idah
Ijebu-Ode
Ikot Ekpene
Ilorin
Issele-Uku
Jalingo
JOS
KADUNA
Kafanchan
Kano
Lafia
LAGOS
Lokoja
Maiduguri
Makurdi
Maradi
Minna
Nnewi
Nsukka
Ogoja
Okigwe
Ondo
ONITSHA
Orlu
Osogbo
Otukpo
OWERRI
Oyo
Port Harcourt
Shendam
Sokoto
Umuahia
Uromi
Uyo
Warri
Yola
Zaria

Norway
Oslo

Oceania
AGAÑA
Wallis et Futuna

Pakistan
Faisalabad
Hyderabad (in Pakistan)
Islamabad-Rawalpindi
KARACHI
LAHORE
Multan

Panama
Chitré
Colón Kuna Yala
David
PANAMÁ
Penonomé
Santiago de Veraguas

Papua New Guinea
Aitape
Alotau-Sideia
Bereina
Bougainville
Daru-Kiunga
Goroka
Kavieng
Kerema
Kimbe
Kundiawa
Lae
MADANG
Mendi
MOUNT HAGEN
PORT MORESBY
RABAUL
Vanimo
Wabag
Wewak

Paraguay
ASUNCIÓN
Benjamín Aceval
Caacupé
Carapeguá
Ciudad del Este
Concepción en Paraguay
Coronel Oviedo
Encarnación
San Juan Bautista de las Misiones
San Lorenzo
San Pedro
Villarrica del Espíritu Santo

Peru
Abancay
AREQUIPA
AYACUCHO O HUAMANGA
Cajamarca
Callao
Carabayllo
Chachapoyas
Chiclayo
Chimbote
Chosica
Chulucanas
CUZCO
Huacho
Huancavelica
HUANCAYO
Huánuco
Huaraz
Huari
Ica
LIMA
Lurín
PIURA
Puno
Tacna y Moquegua
Tarma
TRUJILLO

Philippines
Alaminos
Antipolo
Bacolod
Baguio
Balanga
Bangued
Bayombong
Boac
Borongan
Butuan
Cabanatuan
CACERES
CAGAYAN DE ORO
Calbayog
CAPIZ
Catarman
CEBU
COTABATO
Cubao
Daet
DAVAO
Digos
Dipolog
Dumaguete
Gumaca
Iba
Ilagan
Iligan
Imus
Ipil
JARO
Kabankalan
Kalibo
Kalookan
Kidapawan

Laoag
Legazpi
Libmanan
LINGAYEN-DAGUPAN
LIPA
Lucena
Maasin
Malaybalay
Malolos
MANILA
Marbel
Masbate
Mati
Naval
Novaliches
NUEVA SEGOVIA
OZAMIZ
Pagadian
PALO
Parañaque
Pasig
Romblon
San Carlos
SAN FERNANDO
San Fernando de la Union
San Jose
San Jose de Antique
San Pablo
Sorsogon
Surigao
Tagbilaran
Tagum
Talibon
Tandag
Tarlac
TUGUEGARAO
Urdaneta
Virac
ZAMBOANGA

Poland
BIALYSTOK
Bielsko-Zywiec
Bydgoszcz
CZESTOCHOWA
Drohiczyn
Elblag
Elk
GDANSK
Gliwice
GNIEZNO
Kalisz
KATOWICE
Kielce
Koszalin-Kolobrzeg
KRAKÓW
Legnica
LÓDZ
Lomza
Lowicz
LUBLIN
Opole
Pelplin
Plock
POZNAN
PRZEMYSL
PRZEMYSL-WARSZAWA
Radom
Rzeszów
Sandomierz
Siedlce
Sosnowiec
Swidnica
SZCZECIN-KAMIEN
Tarnów
Torun
WARMIA
WARSZAWA
Warszawa-Praga
Wloclawek
WROCLAW, BRESLAVIA
Wroclaw-Gdansk
Zamosc-Lubaczów
Zielona Góra-Gorzów

Portugal
Angra
Aveiro
Beja
BRAGA
Bragança-Miranda
Coimbra
ÉVORA
Faro
Funchal
Guarda
Lamego
Leiria-Fátima
Portalegre - Castelo Branco
Porto
Santarém
Setúbal
Viana do Castelo
Vila Real
Viseu

Puerto Rico
Arecibo
Caguas
Fajardo-Humacao
Mayagüez
Ponce
SAN JUAN DE PUERTO RICO

Republic of the Congo
BRAZZAVILLE
Impfondo
Kinkala
Nkayi
Ouesso
Owando
Pointe-Noire

Reunion
Saint-Denis-de-La Réunion

Romania
ALBA IULIA
BUCURESTI, BUCAREST
Cluj-Gherla, Claudiopoli-Armenopoli
FAGARAS SI ALBA IULIA
Iasi
Lugoj
Maramures
Oradea Mare Gran Varadino
Oradea Mare, Gran Varadino, Nagyvárad
Satu Mare, Szatmár
Timisoara

Russia
MADRE DI DIO A MOSCA
San Clemente a Saratov
San Giusepe a Irkutsk
Trasfigurazione a Novosibirsk

Rwanda
Butare
Byumba
Cyangugu
Gikongoro
Kabgayi
Kasongo
Kibungo
KIGALI
Nyundo
Ruhengeri

Samoa
SAMOA-APIA

Scotland
Aberdeen
Argyll and The Isles
Dunkeld
Galloway
GLASGOW
Motherwell
Paisley
SAINT ANDREWS AND EDINBURGH

Senegal
DAKAR
Kaolack
Kolda
Saint-Louis du Sénégal
Tambacounda
Thiès
Ziguinchor

Serbia
BEOGRAD
Srijem
Subotica
Zrenjanin

Seychelles
Port Victoria o Seychelles

Sierra Leone
Bo
FREETOWN
Kenema
Makeni

Singapore
SINGAPORE

Slovakia
Banská Bystrica, Neosolio
BRATISLAVA
Bratislava (Byzantine)
KOŠICE
Košice (Byzantine)
Nitra
Prešov
Rožnava
Spiš
TRNAVA

Slovenia
Celje
Koper
LJUBLJANA
Maribor
Murska Sobota
Novo Mesto
Zilina

Solomon Islands
Auki
Gizo
HONIARA

Somalia
Mogadiscio

South Africa
Aliwal
Bethlehem
BLOEMFONTEIN
CAPE TOWN, KAAPSTAD
De Aar
Dundee
DURBAN
Eshowe
JOHANNESBURG
Keimoes-Upington
Kimberley
Klerksdorp
Kokstad
Kroonstad
Mariannhill
Oudtshoorn
Pietersburg
Port Elizabeth
PRETORIA
Queenstown
Rustenburg
Tzaneen
Umtata
Umzimkulu
Witbank

Spain
Albacete
Alcalá de Henares
Almería
Astorga
Avila
Barbastro-Monzón
BARCELONA
Bilbao
BURGOS
Cádiz y Ceuta
Calahorra y La Calzada-Logroño
Cartagena (in Spain)
Ciudad Real
Ciudad Rodrigo
Córdoba (in Spain)
Coria-Cáceres
Cuenca (in Spain)
Getafe
Girona
GRANADA
Guadix
Huelva
Huesca
Ibiza
Islas Canarias
Jaca
Jaén
Jerez de la Frontera
León
Lleida
Lugo
MADRID
Málaga
Mallorca
Menorca
MÉRIDA-BADAJOZ
Mondoñedo-Ferrol
Orense
Orihuela-Alicante
Osma-Soria
OVIEDO
Palencia
PAMPLONA Y TUDELA
Plasencia
Salamanca
San Cristóbal de La Laguna, Tenerife
San Sebastián
Sant Feliu de Llobregat
Santander
SANTIAGO DE COMPOSTELA
Segorbe-Castellón de la Plana
Segovia
SEVILLA
Sigüenza-Guadalajara
Solsona
Tarazona
TARRAGONA
Terrassa
Teruel y Albarracín
TOLEDO
Tortosa
Tui-Vigo
Urgell
VALENCIA
VALLADOLID
Vic
Vitoria
Zamora
ZARAGOZA

Sri Lanka
Anuradhapura
Badulla
Chilaw
COLOMBO
Galle
Jaffna
Kandy
Kurunegala
Mannar
Ratnapura
Trincomalee-Batticaloa

Sudan
El Obeid
JUBA
KHARTOUM
Malakal
Wau
Yei

Suriname
Paramaribo

Swaziland
Manzini

Sweden
Stockholm

Switzerland
Basel, Bâle, Basilea
Chur
Lausanne, Genève et Fribourg (Freiburg)
Lugano
Sankt Gallen
Sion, Sitten

Syria
ALEP, BEROEA, HALAB
Alep, Beroea, Halab
Alep, Beroea, Halab (Armenian)
Alep, Beroea, Halab (Maronite)
Alep, Beroea, Halab (Syrian)
BOSRA E HAURAN
DAMAS, AS-SAM, DAMASCO, DIMASQ
DAMAS, AS-SAM, DAMASCO, DIMASQ - GREEK MELKITE
DAMAS, AS-SAM, DAMASCO, DIMASQ - MARONITE
HASSAKÉ-NISIBI
HOMS EMESA
HOMS EMESA - Greek Melkite
Kamichlié
LATTAQUIÉ
Lattaquié, Laodicea, Lattaqiya

São Tome and Príncipe
São Tomé e Príncipe

Taiwan
Hsinchu
Hwalien
Kaohsiung
Kiayi
Taichung
Tainan
TAIPEI

Tanzania
ARUSHA
Bukoba
Bunda
DAR-ES-SALAAM
Dodoma
Geita
Iringa
Kahama
Kayanga
Kigoma
Kondoa
Lindi
Mahenge
Mbeya
Mbinga
Mbulu
Morogoro
Moshi
Mpanda
Mtwara
Musoma
MWANZA
Njombe
Rulenge-Ngara
Same
Shinyanga
Singida
SONGEA
Sumbawanga
TABORA
Tanga
Tunduru-Masasi
Zanzibar

Thailand
BANGKOK
Chanthaburi
Chiang Mai
Nakhon Ratchasima
Nakhon Sawan
Ratchaburi
Surat Thani
THARE AND NONSENG
Ubon Ratchathani
Udon Thani

The Netherlands
Breda
Groningen-Leeuwarden
Haarlem-Amsterdam
Roermond
Rotterdam
's-Hertogenbosch, Bois-le-Duc
UTRECHT

Togo
Aného
Atakpamé
Dapaong
Kara
Kpalimé
LOMÉ
Sokodé

Tonga
Tonga

Trinidad and Tobago
PORT OF SPAIN

Tunisia
TUNIS

Turkey
DIARBEKIR, AMIDA
ISTANBUL, COSTANTINOPOLI
IZMIR

Uganda
Arua
Fort Portal
GULU
Hoima
Jinja
Kabale
KAMPALA
Kasana-Luweero
Kasese
Kiyinda-Mityana
Kotido
Lira
Lugazi
Masaka
MBARARA
Moroto
Nebbi
Soroti
Tombura-Yambio
TORORO

Ukraine
Buchach
Ivano-Frankivsk, Stanislaviv
Kamyanets-Podilskyi
Kharkiv-Zaporizhia
Kolomyia-Chernivtsi
KYIV-VYSHHOROD
Kyiv-Zhytomyr
Lutsk
LVIV
LVIV (UKRAINIAN)
Mukachevo
Mukachevo (Latin)
Odessa-Simferopol
Sambir-Drohobych
Sokal-Zhovkva
Stryj
Ternopil-Zboriv

Uruguay
Canelones
Florida
Maldonado-Punta del Este
Melo
Mercedes
Minas
MONTEVIDEO
Salto
San José de Mayo
Tacuarembó

USA
Albany
Alexandria
Allentown
Altoona-Johnstown
Amarillo
ANCHORAGE
Arlington
ATLANTA
Austin
Baker
BALTIMORE
Baton Rouge
Beaumont
Belleville
Biloxi
Birmingham (in Alabama)
Bismarck
Boise
BOSTON
Bridgeport
Brooklyn
Brownsville
Buffalo
Burlington
Camden
Caroline Islands
Chalan Kanoa
Charleston
Charlotte
Cheyenne
CHICAGO
CINCINNATI
Cleveland
Colorado Springs
Columbus
Corpus Christi
Covington
Crookston
Dallas
Davenport
DENVER
Des Moines
DETROIT
Dodge City
DUBUQUE
Duluth
El Paso
Erie
Evansville
Fairbanks
Fall River
Fargo
Fort Wayne South Bend
Fort Worth
Fresno
Gallup
GALVESTON-HOUSTON
Gary
Gaylord
Grand Island
Grand Rapids
Great Falls-Billings
Green Bay
Greensburg
Harrisburg
HARTFORD
Helena
Honolulu
Houma-Thibodaux
INDIANAPOLIS
Jackson
Jefferson City
Joliet (in Illinois)
Juneau
Kalamazoo
KANSAS CITY (IN KANSAS)
Kansas City-St. Joseph
Knoxville
La Crosse
Lafayette
Lafayette (in Indiana)
Lake Charles
Lansing
Laredo
Las Cruces
Las Vegas
Lexington
Lincoln
Little Rock
LOS ANGELES
LOUISVILLE
Lubbock
Madison
Manchester
Marquette
Memphis
Metuchen
MIAMI
Military Services, Archdiocese, U.S.A.
MILWAUKEE
MOBILE
Monterey (in California)
Nashville
NEW ORLEANS
New Ulm
NEW YORK
NEWARK
Newton (Melkite-Greek Catholic)
Norwich
Oakland
Ogdensburg
OKLAHOMA CITY
OMAHA
Orange (in California)
Orlando
Our Lady of Deliverance
Our Lady of Lebanon of Los Angeles
Our Lady of Nareg (in New York)
Owensboro
Palm Beach
Parma Byzantine
Passaic Byzantine
Paterson
Pensacola-Tallahassee
Peoria
PHILADELPHIA
PHILADELPHIA - UKRAINIAN
Phoenix
Phoenix Byzantine
Pittsburgh
PITTSBURGH - BYZANTINE
Portland (in Maine)
PORTLAND (IN OREGON)
Providence
Pueblo
Raleigh
Rapid City
Reno
Richmond
Rochester
Rockford
Rockville Centre
Sacramento
Saginaw
Saint Augustine
Saint Cloud
Saint George's in Canton (Romanian)
Saint Josaphat (Ukrainian) in Parma
SAINT LOUIS
Saint Maron of Brooklyn
Saint Nicholas (in Chicago)
SAINT PAUL AND MINNEAPOLIS
Saint Peter the Apostle of San Diego
Saint Petersburg
Saint Thomas (in the Virgin

Islands)
Saint Thomas the Apostle of Chicago
Saint Thomas the Apostle of Detroit
Salina
Salt Lake City
Samoa-Pago Pago
San Angelo
SAN ANTONIO
San Bernardino
San Diego
SAN FRANCISCO
San Jose (in California)
SANTA FE
Santa Rosa (in California)
Savannah
Scranton
SEATTLE
Shreveport
Sioux City
Sioux Falls
Spokane
Springfield-Cape Girardeau
Springfield (in Illinois)
Springfield (in Massachusetts)
Stamford (Ukrainian)
Steubenville
Stockton
Superior
Syracuse
Toledo (in Ohio)
Trenton
Tucson
Tulsa
Tyler
Venice
Victoria (in Texas)
WASHINGTON
Wheeling-Charleston
Wichita
Wilmington
Winona
Worcester
Yakima
Youngstown

Vanuatu

Port-Vila

Venezuela

Acarigua-Araure
Barcelona
Barinas
BARQUISIMETO
Cabimas
CALABOZO
CARACAS, SANTIAGO DE VENEZUELA
Carora
Carúpano
CIUDAD BOLÍVAR
Ciudad Guayana
CORO
CUMANÁ
El Vigía - San Carlos del Zulia
Guanare
Guarenas
La Guaira
Los Teques
Machiques
MARACAIBO
Maracay
Margarita
Maturín
MÉRIDA
Puerto Cabello
Punto Fijo
San Carlos de Venezuela
San Cristóbal de Venezuela
San Felipe
San Fernando de Apure
Trujillo (in Venezuela)
VALENCIA EN VENEZUELA
Valle de la Pascua

Vietnam

Ba Ria
Bac Ninh
Ban Mê Thuôt
Bùi Chu
Cân Tho
Dà Lat
Dà Nang
HÀ NÔI
Hai Phóng
HUÊ
Hung Hoá
Kontum
Lang Són et Cao Bang
Long Xuyên
My Tho
Nha Trang
Phan Thiêt
Phát Diêm
Phú Cuong
Quy Nhon
Thái Bình
Thanh Hoá
THÀNH-PHÔ HÔ CHI MINH, HÔCHIMINH VILLE
Vinh
Vinh Long
Xuân Lôc

Wales

Wrexham

West Indies

Bridgetown
CASTRIES
Hinche
Kingstown
Montego Bay
Saint George's (in Grenada)
Saint John's-Basseterre

Zambia

Chipata
KASAMA
Livingstone
LUSAKA
Mansa
Mongu
Monze
Mpika
Ndola
Solwezi

Zimbabwe

BULAWAYO
Chinhoyi
Gokwe
Gweru
HARARE
Hwange
Masvingo
Mutare

AN ALPHABETICAL LIST OF THE

Cardinals, Archbishops, Bishops, Archabbots & Abbots of the United States

CARDINALS

His Eminence Luis Aponte Martinez, Archbishop emeritus of San Juan, P.O. Box 9021967, San Juan, PR 00902-1967.

His Eminence William W. Baum, Major Penitentiary emeritus, Via Rusticucci 13, 00193 Rome, Italy.

His Eminence Anthony J. Bevilacqua, Archbishop emeritus of Philadelphia, St. Charles Borromeo Seminary, 100 E. Wynnewood Rd., Wynnewood, PA 19096.

His Eminence Daniel N. DiNardo, Archbishop of Galveston-Houston, 1700 San Jacinto St., Houston, TX 77002.

His Eminence Edward M. Egan, Archbishop emeritus of New York, 1011 First Ave., New York, NY 10022.

His Eminence Francis E. George, o.m.i., Archbishop of Chicago, 835 N. Rush St., Chicago, IL 60611-2030.

His Eminence William H. Keeler, Archbishop emeritus of Baltimore, 320 Cathedral St., Baltimore, MD 21201.

His Eminence Bernard F. Law, Archbishop emeritus of Boston, Archpriest of the Patriarchal Liberian Basilica of St. Mary Major, Patriarcale Basilica Liberiana di Santa Maria Maggiore, 00120 Vatican City.

His Eminence, William J. Levada, Prefect, Congregation for the Doctrine of the Faith, Palazzo del S. Uffizio, 00120 Vatican City State.

His Eminence Roger M. Mahony, Archbishop emeritus of Los Angeles, 3424 Wilshire Blvd., Los Angeles, CA 90010-2241.

His Eminence Adam J. Maida, Archbishop emeritus of Detroit, 1234 Washington Blvd., Detroit, MI 48226.

His Eminence Theodore E. McCarrick, Archbishop emeritus of Washington, DC, P.O. Box 29260, Washington, DC 20017.

His Eminence Sean P. O'Malley, o.f.m.cap., Archbishop of Boston, 66 Brooks Dr., Braintree, MA 02184-3839.

His Eminence Justin F. Rigali, Archbishop emeritus of Philadelphia, 222 N. 17th St., Philadelphia, PA 19103.

His Eminence J. Francis Stafford, Major Penitentiary emeritus, Piazza S. Calisto 16, Vatican City State, Europe 00120.

His Eminence Edmund C. Szoka, President emeritus Pontifical Commission, Vatican City State, Europe. 00120.

His Eminence Donald W. Wuerl, Archbishop of Washington, 5001 Eastern Ave., Hyattsville, MD 20782-3447.

ARCHBISHOPS

His Excellency,
The Most Reverend

Apuron, Anthony Sablan, o.f.m.cap., Archbishop of Agana, 196-B Cuesta San Ramon, Agana, Guam 96910.

Aymond, Gregory M., Archbishop of New Orleans, 7887 Walmsley Ave., New Orleans, LA 70125.

Beltran, Eusebius J., Archbishop emeritus of Oklahoma City, P.O. Box 32180, Oklahoma City, OK 73123.

Broglio, Timothy P., Archbishop for the Military Services, 1025 Michigan Ave., N.E., P.O. Box 4469, Washington, DC 20017-0469.

Brunett, Alexander J., Archbishop emeritus of Seattle, 710 9th Ave., Seattle, WA 98104.

Buechlein, Daniel M., o.s.b., Archbishop of Indianapolis, 1400 N. Meridian St., P.O. Box 1410, Indianapolis, IN 46206.

Carlson, Robert J., Archbishop of St. Louis, 20 Archbishop May Dr., St. Louis, MO 63119-5738.

Chaput, Charles J., o.f.m.cap., Archbishop of Philadelphia, 222 N. 17th St., Philadelphia, PA 19103-1299.

Coakley, Paul S., Archbishop of Oklahoma City, 7501 Northwest Expwy., Oklahoma City, OK 73132.

Cronin, Daniel A., Archbishop emeritus of Hartford, 469 Bloomfield Ave., Bloomfield, CT 06002.

Curtiss, Elden F., Archbishop emeritus of Omaha, 100 N. 62nd St., Omaha, NE 68132-2795.

Dimino, Joseph T., Archbishop emeritus for the Military Services, P.O. Box 4469, Washington, DC 20017.

Dolan, Timothy M., Archbishop of New York, 1011 First Ave., New York, NY 10022.

Donoghue, John F., Archbishop emeritus of Atlanta, 2401 Lake Park Dr., Smyrna, GA 30080-8862.

Favalora, John C., Archbishop emeritus of Miami, 9401 Biscayne Blvd., Miami Shores, FL 33138.

Fiorenza, Joseph A., Archbishop emeritus of Galveston-Houston, 1700 San Jacinto, Houston, TX 77002.

Flores, Patrick F., Archbishop emeritus of San Antonio, P.O. Box 28410, San Antonio, TX 78228.

Flynn, Harry J., Archbishop emeritus of St. Paul and Minneapolis, 226 Summit Ave., St. Paul, MN 55102.

His Excellency,
The Most Reverend

Garcia-Siller, Gustavo, m.sp.s., Archbishop of San Antonio, P.O. Box 28410, San Antonio, TX 78228-0410.

Gerety, Peter Leo, Archbishop emeritus of Newark, 60 Home Ave., Rutherford, NJ 07070.

Gomez, Jose H., Archbishop of Los Angeles, 3424 Wilshire Blvd., Los Angeles, CA 90010.

Gonzalez, Roberto O., o.f.m., Archbishop of San Juan, P.O. Box 9021967, San Juan, PR 00902-1967.

Gregory, Wilton D., Archbishop of Atlanta, 2401 Lake Park Dr,. Smyrna, GA 30080-8862.

Hannan, Philip M., Archbishop emeritus of New Orleans, 106 Metairie Lawn Dr., Metairie, LA 70001.

Hanus, Jerome G., o.s.b., Archbishop of Dubuque, 1229 Mt. Loretto Ave., P.O. Box 479, Dubuque, IA 52004-0479.

Hughes, Alfred C., Archbishop emeritus of New Orleans, 7887 Walmsley Ave., New Orleans, LA 70125.

Hunthausen, Raymond G., Archbishop emeritus of Seattle, 710 9th Ave., Seattle, WA 98104.

Hurley, Francis T., Archbishop emeritus of Anchorage, 225 Cordova St., Anchorage, AK 99501.

Keleher, James P., Archbishop emeritus of Kansas City in Kansas, 12615 Parallel Pkwy., Kansas City, KS 66109.

Kelly, Thomas C., o.p., Archbishop emeritus of Louisville, 212 E. College St., P.O. Box 1073, Louisville, KY 40201.

Kucera, Daniel W., o.s.b., Archbishop emeritus of Dubuque, Villa Raphael, 1155 Mt. Loretta Ave., Dubuque, IA 52003.

Kurtz, Joseph E., Archbishop of Louisville, 212 E. College St., P.O. Box 1073, Louisville, KY 40201.

Lipscomb, Oscar H., Archbishop emeritus of Mobile, 400 Government St., Mobile, AL 36602.

Listecki, Jerome E., Archbishop of Milwaukee, 3501 S. Lake Dr., P.O. Box 070912, Milwaukee, WI 53207-0912.

Lucas, George J., Archbishop of Omaha, 100 N. 62nd St., Omaha, NE 68132-2795.

Mansell, Henry J., Archbishop of Hartford, 134 Farmington Ave., Hartford, CT 06105.

His Excellency,
The Most Reverend

Myers, John Joseph, Archbishop of Newark, 171 Clifton Ave., Newark, NJ 07104-9500.

Naumann, Joseph F., Archbishop of Kansas City in Kansas, 12615 Parallel Pkwy., Kansas City, Kansas 66109.

Niederauer, George H., Archbishop of San Francisco, One Peter Yorke Way, San Francisco, CA 94109-6602.

Nienstedt, John C., Archbishop of St. Paul and Minneapolis, 226 Summit Ave., St. Paul, MN 55102.

O'Brien, Edwin F., Archbishop of Baltimore, 320 Cathedral St., Baltimore, MD 21201.

Pilarczyk, Daniel E., Archbishop emeritus of Cincinnati, 100 E. Eighth St., Cincinnati, OH 45202.

Quinn, John R., Archbishop emeritus of San Francisco, 1100 Woodside Rd., Redwood City, CA 94061.

Rodi, Thomas J., Archbishop of Mobile, 400 Government St., Mobile, AL 36602.

Sanchez, Robert F., Archbishop emeritus of Santa Fe, Catholic Center, St. Joseph's Pl., N.W., Albuquerque, NM 87120.

Sartain, James Peter, Archbishop of Seattle, 710 9th Ave., Seattle, WA 98104.

Schnurr, Dennis M., Archbishop of Cincinnati, 100 E. Eighth St., Cincinnati, OH 45202-2129.

Schulte, Francis B., Archbishop emeritus of New Orleans, 320 S. Roberts Rd., Rosemont, PA 19010.

Schwietz, Roger L., o.m.i., Archbishop of Anchorage, 225 Cordova St., Anchorage, AK 99501.

Sheehan, Michael J., Archbishop of Santa Fe, Catholic Center, 4000 St. Joseph's Pl., N.W., Albuquerque, NM 87120.

Soroka, Stefan, Archbishop of the Ukrainian Catholic Archeparchy of Philadelphia, 827 N. Franklin St., Philadelphia, PA 19123.

Sulyk, Stephen, Archbishop emeritus of the Ukrainian Catholic Archeparchy of Philadelphia, 827 N. Franklin St. Philadelphia, PA 19123.

His Excellency, The Most Reverend

Vigneron, Allen H., Archbishop of Detroit, 1234 Washington Blvd., Detroit, MI 48226.

Vlazny, John G., Archbishop of Portland in Oregon, 2838 E. Burnside St., Portland, OR 97214-1895.

Weakland, Rembert G., o.s.b. Archbishop emeritus of Milwaukee, Wilson Commons, 1400 W. Sonata Dr., #218, Milwaukee, WI 53221.

Wenski, Thomas G., Archbishop of Miami, 9401 Biscayne Blvd., Miami Shores, FL 33138.

BISHOPS

His Excellency, The Most Reverend

Adamec, Joseph V., Bishop emeritus of Altoona-Johnstown, 927 S. Logan Blvd., Hollidaysburg, PA 16648.

Allue, Emilio, s.d.b., Retired Auxiliary Bishop of Boston, St. Theresa of Avila Rectory, 10 Saint Theresa Ave., Boston, MA 02132.

Amos, Martin John, Bishop of Davenport, 780 W. Central Park Ave., Davenport, IA 52804-1901.

Anderson, Moses B., s.s.e., Retired Auxiliary Bishop of Detroit, 1234 Washington Blvd., Detroit, MI 48226.

Angadiath, Jacob, Bishop of St. Thomas Syro-Malabar Catholic Diocese of Chicago, 372 S. Prairie Ave., Elmhurst, IL 60126-4020.

Angell, Kenneth A., Bishop emeritus of Burlington, 55 Joy Dr., S. Burlington, VT 05403.

Aquila, Samuel J., Bishop of Fargo, 5201 Bishops Blvd., Ste. A, Fargo, ND 58104-7605.

Arias, David, o.a.r., Retired Auxiliary Bishop of Newark, St. Joseph of the Palisades Rectory, 6401 Palisade Ave., West New York, NJ 07093.

Baker, Robert J., Bishop of Birmingham, P.O. Box 12047, Birmingham, AL 35202.

Balke, Victor, Bishop emeritus of Crookston, 1200 Memorial Dr., Crookston, MN 56716.

Baltakis, Paul A., o.f.m., Bishop emeritus for Lithuanian Catholics Outside Lithuania, St. Anthony's Friary, P.O. Box 980, 28 Beach Ave., Kennebunkport, ME 04046.

Bambera, Joseph C., Bishop of Scranton, 300 Wyoming Ave., Scranton, PA 18503.

Banks, Robert J., Bishop emeritus of Green Bay, P.O. Box 23825, Green Bay, WI 54305-3825.

Barbarito, Gerald, Bishop of Palm Beach, 9995 N. Military Tr., Palm Beach Gardens, FL 33410.

Barnes, Gerald R., Bishop of San Bernardino, 1201 E. Highland Ave., San Bernardino, CA 92404.

Barres, John O., Bishop of Allentown, 4029 W. Tilghman St., Allentown, PA 18104

Bartchak, Mark L., Bishop of Altoona-Johnstown, 927 S. Logan Blvd., Hollidaysburg, PA 16648.

Batakian, Manuel, Eparch emeritus of Our Lady of Nareg, 167 N. 6th St., Brooklyn NY 11211-3207.

Bevard, Herbert A., Bishop of St. Thomas in the Virgin Islands, P.O. Box 301825, Charlotte Amalie, VI 00803.

Binzer, Joseph R., Auxiliary Bishop of Cincinnati, 100 E. Eighth St., Cincinnati, OH 45202-2129.

Blair, Leonard P., Bishop of Toledo, 1933 Spielbusch Ave., Toledo, OH 43604-5360.

Blaire, Stephen E., Bishop of Stockton, 212 N. San Joaquin St., Stockton, CA 95202.

Boland, J. Kevin, Bishop emeritus of Savannah, 601 E. Liberty St., Savannah, GA 31401.

Boland, Raymond J., Bishop emeritus of Kansas City-St. Joseph, 2552 Gillham Rd., Kansas City, MO 64108.

Boles, John P., Retired Auxiliary Bishop of Boston, 841 E. Broadway, Boston, MA 02127.

Bootkoski, Paul G., Bishop of Metuchen, 10 Library Pl., Metuchen, NJ 08840.

Bosco, Anthony G., Bishop emeritus of Greensburg, 723 E. Pittsburgh St., Greensburg, PA 15601.

Botean, John M., Bishop of the Romanian Catholic Eparchy of St. George's in Canton, 1325 Skyway St., N.E., Canton, OH 44721.

Boyea, Earl A., Bishop of Lansing, 228 N. Walnut St., Lansing, MI 48933.

Bradley, Paul J., Bishop of Kalamazoo, 215 N. Westnedge Ave., Kalamazoo, MI 49007-3760.

Brandt, Lawrence E., Bishop of Greensburg, 723 E. Pittsburgh St., Greensburg, PA 15601.

Bransfield, Michael J., Bishop of Wheeling-Charleston, 1300 Byron St., P.O. Box 230, Wheeling, WV 26003.

Braxton, Edward K., Bishop of Belleville, 222 S. Third St., Belleville, IL 62220-1985.

Brom, Robert H., Bishop of San Diego, P.O. Box 85728, San Diego, CA 92186-5728.

Brown, Tod D., Bishop of Orange, Marywood Center, 2811 E. Villa Real Dr., Orange, CA 92867.

Brucato, Robert A., Retired Auxiliary Bishop of New York, John Cardinal O'Connor Clergy Residence, 5655 Arlington Ave., Bronx, NY 10471.

Brungardt, John B., Bishop of Dodge City, 910 Central Ave., Dodge City, KS 67801.

Bruskewitz, Fabian W., Bishop of Lincoln, P.O. Box 80328, Lincoln, NE 68510-0328.

Buckon, Neal, Auxiliary Bishop for the Military Services, 1025 Michigan Ave., P.O. Box 4469, Washington, DC 20017-0469.

Bura, John, Auxiliary Bishop of Philadelphia for Ukrainians & Apostolic Admin. of St. Josaphat in Parma, 5720 State Rd., P.O. Box 347180, Parma, OH 44134-7180.

Burbidge, Michael F., Bishop of Raleigh, 715 Nazareth St., Raleigh, NC 27606.

Burns, Edward J., Bishop of Juneau, 415 Sixth St., #300, Juneau, AK 99801.

Byrnes, Michael J., Auxiliary Bishop of Detroit, 1234 Washington Blvd., Detroit, MI 48226.

Caggiano, Frank J., Auxiliary Bishop of Brooklyn, 310 Prospect Park W., Brooklyn, NY 11215.

Callahan, William P., o.f.m.conv., Bishop of La Crosse, 3710 East Ave., P.O. Box 4004, La Crosse, WI 54602-4004.

Calvo, Randolph R., Bishop of Reno, 290 S. Arlington Ave., Reno, NV 89501-1713.

Camacho, Tomas A., Bishop emeritus of Chalan Kanoa, Our Lady of Mt. Carmel, P.O. Box 500745 CK, Saipan, MP 96950.

Campbell, Frederick F., Bishop of Columbus, 198 E. Broad St., Columbus, OH 43215.

Cantu, Oscar, Auxiliary Bishop of San Antonio, 2718 W. Woodlawn Ave., P.O. Box 28410, San Antonio, TX 78228-0410.

Carmody, Edmond, Bishop emeritus of Corpus Christi, 620 Lipan St., P.O. Box 2620, Corpus Christi, TX 78403.

Carmon, Dominic, s.v.d., Retired Auxiliary Bishop of New Orleans, 3270 Continental Dr., Kenner LA 70065-2663.

Casiano-Vargas, Ulises, Bishop emeritus of Mayaguez, P.O. Box 2272, Mayaguez, PR 00709.

Catanello, Ignatius, Retired Auxiliary Bishop of Brooklyn, 175-20 74th Ave., Flushing, NY 11366.

Cepeda Escobedo, Jose A, Auxiliary Bishop of Detroit, 1234 Washington Blvd., Detroit, MI 48226.

Charron, Joseph L., c.pp.s., Bishop emeritus of Des Moines, 601 Grand Ave., Des Moines, IA 50309.

Chavez, Gilbert E., Retired Auxiliary Bishop of San Diego, P.O. Box 85728, San Diego, CA 92186.

Chedid, John, Bishop emeritus of Our Lady of Lebanon of Los Angeles, 333 S. San Vicente Blvd., Los Angeles, CA 90048.

Choby, David R., Bishop of Nashville, 2400 - 21st Ave., S., Nashville, TN 37212.

Chomnycky, Paul P., o.s.b.m., Eparch of Stamford Ukrainians, 14 Peveril Rd., Stamford, CT 06902-3019.

Christensen, Peter F., Bishop of Superior, 1201 Hughitt Ave., Box 969, Superior, WI 54880.

Christian, Francis J., Auxiliary Bishop of Manchester, St. Joseph Cathedral, 145 Lowell St., Manchester, NH 03104.

Cisneros, Octavio, Auxiliary Bishop of Brooklyn, Holy Child Jesus, 111-11 86th Ave., Richmond Hill, NY 11418-1613.

Cistone, Joseph R., Bishop of Saginaw, 5800 Weiss St. Saginaw, MI 48603-2762.

Clark, Edward W., Auxiliary Bishop of Los Angeles, Our Lady of the Angels Pastoral Region, 5835 W. Slauson, Culver City, CA, 90230.

Clark, Matthew H., Bishop of Rochester, 1150 Buffalo Rd., Rochester, NY 14624.

Coleman, George W., Bishop of Fall River, 47 Underwood St., Fall River, MA 02720.

Conley, James D., Auxiliary Bishop of Denver, 1300 S. Steele St., Denver, CO 80210.

Conlon, R. Daniel, Bishop of Joliet, 425 Summit St., Joliet, IL 60435.

Connolly, Thomas J., Bishop emeritus of Baker, P.O. Box 5999, Bend, OR 97708.

Cooney, Patrick R., Bishop emeritus of Gaylord, 611 W. North St., Gaylord, MI 49735-8349.

Cordileone, Salvatore J., Bishop of Oakland, 2121 Harrison St., Ste. 100, Oakland, CA 94612.

Corrada del Rio, Alvaro, s.j., Bishop of Mayaguez, P.O. Box 2272, Mayaguez, PR 00681.

Costello, Thomas J., Retired Auxiliary Bishop of Syracuse, 1515 Midland Ave, P.O. Box 511, Syracuse, NY 13205.

Cote, Michael R., Bishop of Norwich, 201 Broadway, Norwich, CT 06360.

Coyne, Christopher J., Auxiliary Bishop of Indianapolis, 1400 N. Meridian St., Indianapolis, IN 46206.

Cruz, Manuel A., Auxiliary Bishop of Newark, 171 Clifton Ave., Newark, NJ 07104.

His Excellency,
The Most Reverend

Cserhati, Ferenc, Bishop to Hungarians, Ung.Kath.Delegatur, Landwehrstr.66, D-80336, Munchen, Germany.

Cullen, Edward P., Bishop emeritus of Allentown, P.O. Box F, 4029 W. Tilghman St., Allentown, PA 18105.

Cummins, John S., Bishop emeritus of Oakland, 617 Prospect Ave., Oakland, CA 94610.

Cunningham, Robert Joseph, Bishop of Syracuse, 240 E. Onondaga St., P.O. Box 511, Syracuse, NY 13201-0511.

Cupich, Blasé J., Bishop of Spokane, 1023 Riverside Ave., P.O. Box 1453, Spokane, WA 99210-1453.

Curlin, William G., Bishop emeritus of Charlotte, 3005 Markworth Ave., Charlotte, NC 28210-6432.

Curry, Thomas J., Auxiliary Bishop of Los Angeles, Santa Barbara Pastoral Region, 3240 Calle Pinon, Santa Barbara, CA 93105.

da Cunha, Edgar M., s.d.v., Auxiliary Bishop of Newark, 171 Clifton Ave., Newark, NJ 07104-0500.

Daily, Thomas V., Bishop emeritus of Brooklyn, 7200 Douglaston Pkwy., Douglaston, NY 11362.

Daly, James J., Retired Auxiliary Bishop of Rockville Centre, P.O. Box 9023, Rockville Centre, NY 11571-9023.

Daly, Thomas A., Auxiliary Bishop of San Jose, 1150 N. First St., Ste. 100, San Jose, CA 95112.

D'Arcy, John M., Bishop emeritus of Fort Wayne-South Bend, P.O. Box 390, Fort Wayne, IN 46801.

del Riego, Rutilio J., Auxiliary Bishop of San Bernardino, 1201 E. Highland Ave., San Bernardino, CA 92404.

Dendinger, William J., Bishop of Grand Island, 2708 Old Fair Rd., Grand Island, NE, 68803.

Deshotel, J. Douglas, Auxiliary Bishop of Dallas, 3725 Blackburn, P.O. Box 190507, Dallas, TX 75219.

DeSimone, Louis A., Retired Auxiliary Bishop of Philadelphia, St. Justin Martyr Rectory, 1222 Hagysford Rd., Narberth, PA 19072.

Dewane, Frank J., Bishop of Venice, P.O. Box 2006, Venice, FL 34284-2006.

DiLorenzo, Francis X., Bishop of Richmond, 7800 Carousel Lane, Richmond, VA 23294.

DiMarzio, Nicholas A., Bishop of Brooklyn, 310 Prospect Park W., Brooklyn, NY 11215.

Dino, Gerald N., Bishop of Holy Protection of Mary Byzantine Catholic Eparchy of Phoenix, 8105 N. 16th St., Phoenix, AZ 85020.

Doherty, Timothy L., Bishop of Lafayette in Indiana, P.O. Box 260, Lafayette, IN 47902-0260.

Donato, Thomas A., Auxiliary Bishop of Newark, St. Henry's Parish, 82 W. 29th St., Bayonne, NJ 07002.

Donnelly, Robert W., Retired Auxiliary Bishop of Toledo, 4227 Bellevue Rd., Toledo, OH 43613.

Dooher, John, Auxiliary Bishop of Boston, 236 Pleasant St., Weymouth, MA 02190.

Doran, Thomas G., Bishop of Rockford, P.O. Box 7044, Rockford, IL 61125.

Dorsey, Norbert L., c.p., Bishop emeritus of Orlando, 50 E. Robinson St., Orlando, FL 32801.

His Excellency,
The Most Reverend

Doueihi, Stephen Hector, Bishop emeritus of the Maronite Eparchy of St. Maron of Brooklyn, 113 Remsen St., Brooklyn, NY 11201-4212.

Dougherty, John M., Retired Auxiliary Bishop of Scranton, 300 Wyoming Ave., Scranton, PA 18503.

Driscoll, Michael P., Bishop of Boise, 1501 Federal Way, Boise, ID 83705.

Duca, Michael G., Bishop of Shreveport, 3500 Fairfield Ave., Shreveport, LA 71104.

DuMaine, R. Pierre, Bishop emeritus of San Jose, 20 Willow Rd., Unit 43, Menlo Park, CA 94025.

Dunne, John C., Auxiliary Bishop of Rockville Centre, P.O. Box 39, Farmingdale, NY 11735-0039.

Dupre, Thomas L., Bishop emeritus of Springfield in Massachusetts, P.O. Box 1730, Springfield, MA 01101-1730.

Edyvean, Walter J., Auxiliary Bishop of Boston, St. Patrick, 44 E. Central St., Natick, MA 01760.

Elizondo, Eusebio L., Auxiliary Bishop of Seattle, 710 9th Ave., Seattle, WA 98104.

Elya, John A., b.s.o., Eparch emeritus of Newton, 126 S.E. 15th Rd., Miami, FL 33129.

Estabrook, Joseph W., Auxiliary Bishop for the Military Services, P.O. Box 4469, Washington, DC 20017-0469.

Estevez, Felipe J., Bishop of St. Augustine, 11625 Old St. Augustine Rd., Jacksonville, FL 32258.

Etienne, Paul D., Bishop of Cheyenne, P.O. Box 1468, Cheyenne, WY 82003-1468.

Evans, Robert C., Auxiliary Bishop of Providence, One Cathedral Sq., Providence, RI 02903-3695.

Fabre, Shelton J., Auxiliary Bishop of New Orleans, 7887 Walmsley Ave., New Orleans, LA 70125-3496.

Farrell, Kevin J., Bishop of Dallas, 3725 Blackburn, P.O. Box 190507, Dallas, TX 75219.

Fellhauer, David E., Bishop of Victoria, P.O. Box 4070, Victoria, TX 77903.

Fernandez, Gilberto, Retired Auxiliary Bishop of Miami, 5260 N.E. 7th Ave., Miami, FL 33137.

Fernandez Torres, Daniel, Bishop of Arecibo, 206 Dr. Salas St., P.O. Box 616, Arecibo, PR 00613.

Finn, Robert W., Bishop of Kansas City-St. Joseph, P.O. Box 419037, Kansas City, MO 64141.

Fitzgerald, Michael J., Auxiliary Bishop of Philadelphia, 222 N. 17th St., Philadelphia, PA 19103-1299.

Fitzsimons, George K., Bishop emeritus of Salina, P.O. Box 980, Salina, KS 67402-0980.

Flanagan, Thomas J., Retired Auxiliary Bishop of San Antonio, P.O. Box 28410, San Antonio, TX 78228-0410.

Flesey, John W., Auxiliary Bishop of Newark, Most Blessed Sacrament, 787 Franklin Lake Rd., Franklin Lakes, NJ 07417.

Fliss, Raphael M., Bishop emeritus of Superior, 7218 Ogden Ave., P.O. Box 3067, Superior, WI 54880.

Flores, Cirilo, Auxiliary Bishop of Orange, 2811 E. Villa Real Dr., P.O. Box 14195, Orange, CA 92863-1595.

His Excellency,
The Most Reverend

Flores, Daniel E., Bishop of Brownsville, 1910 University Blvd., P.O. Box 2279, Brownsville, TX 78522-2279.

Foley, David E., Bishop emeritus of Birmingham, 2121 Third Ave., N., Birmingham, AL 35203.

Foys, Roger J., Bishop of Covington, P.O. Box 15550, Covington, KY 41015-0550.

Franklin, William E., Bishop emeritus of Davenport, 780 W. Central Park Ave., Davenport, IA 52804-1901.

Friend, William B., Bishop emeritus of Shreveport, 3575 Broken Woods Dr. #301, Coral Springs, FL 33065.

Gainer, Ronald W., Bishop of Lexington, 1310 W. Main St., Lexington, KY 40508-2048.

Galante, Joseph A., Bishop of Camden, 631 Market St., P.O. Box 708, Camden, NJ 08101.

Galeone, Victor B., Bishop emeritus of St. Augustine, 11625 Old St. Augustine Rd., Jacksonville, FL 32258.

Garcia, Richard J., Bishop of Monterey, 425 Church St., Monterey, CA 93940.

Garland, James H., Bishop emeritus of Marquette, 300 Rock St., Marquette, MI 49855.

Gaydos, John R., Bishop of Jefferson City, P.O. Box 104900, Jefferson City, MO 65110-4900.

Gelineau, Louis E., Bishop emeritus of Providence, St. Antoine Residence, 10 Rhodes Ave., North Smithfield, RI 02896.

Gendron, Odore, Bishop emeritus of Manchester, P.O. Box 310, Manchester, NH 03105-0310.

Gerber, Eugene J., Bishop emeritus of Wichita, 424 N. Broadway, Wichita, KS 67202.

Gerry, Joseph J., o.s.b., Bishop emeritus of Portland in Maine, St. Anselm Abbey, 100 St. Anselm Dr., Manchester, NH 03102-1310.

Gettelfinger, Gerald A., Bishop emeritus of Evansville, 4200 N. Kentucky Ave., Evansville, IN 47711.

Gilmore, Ronald M., Bishop emeritus of Dodge City, 910 Central Ave., Box 137, Dodge City, KS 67801.

Goedert, Raymond E., Retired Auxiliary Bishop of Chicago, P.O. Box 1979, Chicago, IL 60690.

Gonzalez, Francisco, s.f., Auxiliary Bishop of Washington, P.O. Box 29260, Washington, DC 20017.

Gonzalez Medina, Ruben Antonio, c.m.f., Bishop of Caguas, P.O. Box 8698, Caguas, PR 00726.

Gorman, John R., Retired Auxiliary Bishop of Chicago, 10731 W. 131st. St., Orland Park, IL 60462.

Gossman, F. Joseph, Bishop emeritus of Raleigh, 2401 Crusader Dr., Raleigh, NC 27606.

Gracida, Rene H., Bishop emeritus of Corpus Christi, 620 Lipan St., P.O. Box 2620, Corpus Christi, TX 78403.

Grahmann, Charles V., Bishop emeritus of Dallas, 3725 Blackburn, P.O. Box 190507, Dallas, TX 75219.

His Excellency,
The Most Reverend

Gries, Roger W., o.s.b., Auxiliary Bishop of Cleveland, 1230 Ansel Rd., Cleveland, OH 44109.

Griffin, James A., Bishop emeritus of Columbus, 198 E. Broad St., Columbus, OH 43215.

Grosz, Edward M., Auxiliary Bishop of Buffalo, Blessed Sacrament Parish, 1035 Delaware Ave., Buffalo, NY 14209-1605.

Gruss, Robert D., Bishop of Rapid City, 606 Cathedral Dr., Rapid City, SD 57701.

Guglielmone, Robert E., Bishop of Charleston, 119 Broad St., P.O. Box 818, Charleston, SC 29402.

Guillory, Curtis J., Bishop of Beaumont, 710 Archie St., P.O. Box 3948, Beaumont, TX 77704-3948.

Gumbleton, Thomas J., Retired Auxiliary Bishop of Detroit, 1234 Washington Blvd., Detroit, MI 48226.

Habash, Yousif, Bishop of Our Lady of Deliverance, 317 Ave. E. Bayonne, NJ 07002-4678.

Hanchon, Donald F., Auxiliary Bishop of Detroit, 1234 Washington Blvd., Detroit, MI 48226.

Hanifen, Richard C., Bishop emeritus of Colorado Springs, 228 N. Cascade Ave., Colorado Springs, CO 80903.

Harrington, Bernard J., Bishop emeritus of Winona, 55 W. Sanborn St., P.O. Box 588, Winona, MN 55987.

Hart, Joseph H., Bishop emeritus of Cheyenne, Box 1468, Cheyenne, WY 82003-1468.

Hartmayer, Gregory J., Bishop of Savannah, 601 E. Liberty St., Savannah, GA 31401-5196.

Hebda, Bernard A., Bishop of Gaylord, 611 W. North St., Gaylord, MI 49735-8349.

Hennessey, Robert F., Auxiliary Bishop of Boston, 841 E. Broadway, Boston, MA 02127-2302.

Hermann, Robert J., Retired Auxiliary Bishop of St. Louis, 20 Archbishop May Dr., St. Louis, MO 63119.

Hernandez Rivera, Enrique M., Bishop emeritus of Caguas, P.O. Box 8698, Caguas, PR 00726.

Herzog, Ronald P., Bishop of Alexandria, P.O. Box 7417, Alexandria, LA 71306-0417.

Higgins, Richard B., Auxiliary Bishop for the Military Services, P.O. Box 4469, Washington, DC 20017-0469.

Higi, William L., Bishop emeritus of Lafayette in Indiana, 610 Lingle Ave., Lafayette, IN 47902.

Hoeppner, Michael J., Bishop of Crookston, 1200 Memorial Dr., Crookston, MN 56716.

Holley, Martin D., Auxiliary Bishop of Washington, P.O. Box 29260, Washington, DC 20017.

Houck, William R., Bishop emeritus of Jackson, P.O. Box 2248, Jackson, MS 39225-2248.

Howze, Joseph L., Bishop emeritus of Biloxi, P.O. Box 6067, Mobile, AL 36660-0067.

Hubbard, Howard J., Bishop of Albany, 125 Eagle St., Albany, NY 12202.

Hughes, Edward T., Bishop emeritus of Metuchen, 914 Milford-Warren Glen Rd., Milford NJ 08848-1619.

Hughes, William A., Bishop emeritus of Covington, Carmel Manor, 100 Carmel Manor Rd., Ft. Thomas, KY 41075-2395.

Hughes, William A., Bishop emeritus of Covington, Carmel Manor, 100 Carmel Manor Rd., Ft. Thomas, KY 41075-2395.

Hurley, Walter A., Bishop of Grand Rapids, Cathedral Square Center, 360 Division Ave., S., Grand Rapids, MI 49503-4539.

Hying, Donald J., Auxiliary Bishop of Milwaukee, 3501 S. Lake Dr., Milwaukee, WI 53207.

His Excellency,
The Most Reverend

Ibrahim, Ibrahim, Bishop-Eparch to St. Thomas the Apostle (Chaldean), 25603 Berg Rd., Southfield, MI 48033.

Imesch, Joseph L., Bishop emeritus of Joliet, 425 Summit St., Joliet, IL 60435.

Iriondo, Josu, Auxiliary Bishop of New York, St. Anthony Padua Parish, 832 W. 166th St., Bronx, NY 10459.

Irwin, Francis X., Retired Auxiliary Bishop of Boston, Saint Raphael Parish, 38 Boston Ave., Medford, MA 02155.

Isern, Fernando, Bishop of Pueblo, 101 N. Greenwood, Pueblo, CO 81003.

Jackels, Michael O., Bishop of Wichita, 424 N. Broadway, Wichita, KS 67202.

Jacobs, Sam, Bishop of Houma-Thibodaux, P.O. Box 505, Schriever, LA 70395.

Jakubowski, Thad J., Retired Auxiliary Bishop of Chicago, 6002 W. Berteau Ave., Chicago, IL 60634-1630.

Jammo, Sarhad Y., Bishop of St. Peter the Apostle (Chaldean), 1627 Jamacha Way, El Cajon, CA 92019.

Jarrell, Michael, Bishop of Lafayette, 1408 Carmel Dr., Lafayette, LA 70501.

Jenky, Daniel R., c.s.c., Bishop of Peoria, 419 N.E. Madison Ave., Peoria, IL 61603-3720.

Johnston, Jr., James V., Bishop of Springfield-Cape Girardeau, The Catholic Center, 601 S. Jefferson Ave., Springfield, MO 65806.

Jugis, Peter J., Bishop of Charlotte, 1123 S. Church St., Charlotte, NC 28203.

Justice, William J., Auxiliary Bishop of San Francisco, One Peter Yorke Way, San Francisco, CA 94109-6602.

Kane, Francis, Auxiliary Bishop of Chicago, 1641 W. Diversey, Chicago, IL 60614.

Kennedy, Arthur L., Auxiliary Bishop of Boston, 66 Brooks Dr., Braintree, MA 02184-3839.

Kettler, Donald J., Bishop of Fairbanks, 1316 Peger Rd., Fairbanks, AK 99709.

Kicanas, Gerald F., Bishop of Tucson, P.O. Box 31, Tucson AZ 85702.

Kinney, John F., Bishop of St. Cloud, 214 Third Ave., S., Box 1248, St. Cloud, MN 56302-1248.

Kmiec, Edward U., Bishop of Buffalo, 77 Oakland Pl., Buffalo, NY 14222-1241.

Knestout, Barry C., Auxiliary Bishop of Washington, 5001 Eastern Ave., P.O. Box 29260, Washington, DC 20017.

Kudrick, John M., Bishop of Parma, 1900 Carlton Rd., Parma, OH 44134.

Lagonegro, Dominick J., Auxiliary Bishop of New York, Sacred Heart, 301 Ann St., Newburgh, NY 12550-5467.

Latino, Joseph N., Bishop of Jackson, P.O. 2248, Jackson, MS 39225-2248.

LaValley, Terry R., Bishop of Ogdensburg, P.O. Box 369, Ogdensburg, NY 13669.

Lazaro Martinez, Felix, sch.p., Bishop of Ponce, P.O. Box 32205, Estancion 6, Ponce, PR 00732-2205.

Leibrecht, John J., Bishop emeritus of Springfield-Cape Girardeau, 1152 W. Camino Alto St., Springfield, MO 65810.

Lennon, Richard G., Bishop of Cleveland, 1404 E. Ninth St., Cleveland, OH 44114.

Lessard, Raymond W., Bishop emeritus of Savannah, St. Vincent de Paul Seminary, 10701 S. Military Tr., Boynton Beach, FL 33436-4899.

His Excellency,
The Most Reverend

LeVoir, John M., Bishop of New Ulm, 1400 6th St. N., New Ulm, MN 56073.

Libasci, Peter A., Auxiliary Bishop of Rockville Centre, Eastern Vicariate, P.O. Box 999, Riverhead, NY 11901.

Lohmuller, Martin N., Retired Auxiliary Bishop of Philadelphia, Villa Maria House of Studies, 1410 Almshouse Rd., Jamison, PA 18929.

Lori, William E., Bishop of Bridgeport, 238 Jewett Ave., Bridgeport, CT 06606-2892.

Losten, Basil, Eparch emeritus of Stamford of the Ukrainians, 122 Clovelly Rd., Stamford, CT 06902-3019.

Lotocky, Innocent, o.s.b.m., Bishop emeritus of St. Nicholas in Chicago, 2245 W. Rice St., Chicago, IL 60622.

Loverde, Paul S., Bishop of Arlington, 200 N. Glebe Rd., Arlington, VA 22203.

Lynch, Robert N., Bishop of St. Petersburg, P.O. Box 40200, St. Petersburg, FL 33743-0200.

Lyne, Timothy J., Retired Auxiliary Bishop of Chicago, Holy Name Cathedral, 730 N. Wabash, Chicago, IL 60611.

Macaluso, Christie A., Auxiliary Bishop of Hartford, 134 Farmington Ave., Hartford, CT 06105-3784.

Madden, Denis J., Auxiliary Bishop of Baltimore, 320 Cathedral St., Baltimore, MD 21201.

Madera, Joseph J., m.sp.s., Retired Auxiliary Bishop for the Military Services, P.O. Box 4469, Washington, DC 20017.

Maginnis, Robert P., Retired Auxiliary Bishop of Philadelphia, St. Edmond Home for Children, 320 S. Roberts Rd., Rosemont, PA 19010.

Maguire, Joseph F., Bishop emeritus of Springfield in Massachusetts, 76 Elliot St., P.O. Box 1730, Springfield, MA 01102-1730.

Mai Luong, Dominic, Auxiliary Bishop of Orange, 2811 E. Villa Real Dr., Orange, CA 92867.

Mallona Txertudi, Inaki, c.p. Bishop emeritus of Arecibo, Hogar Irma Fe Pol, #52 Calle Comercio, Lares, PR 00669.

Malone, Richard J., Bishop of Portland in Maine, 510 Ocean Ave., Portland, ME 04104-7559.

Malooly, William Francis, Bishop of Wilmington, P.O. Box 2030, Wilmington, DE 19899.

Mansour, Gregory J., Bishop of the Eparchy of St. Maron of Brooklyn, 109 Remsen St., Brooklyn, NY 11201.

Manz, John R., Auxiliary Bishop of Chicago, 1820 S. Leavitt St., Chicago, IL 60608.

Marconi, Dominic A., Retired Auxiliary Bishop of Newark, 71 Washington Ave., Chatham, NJ 07928.

Martino, Joseph F., Bishop emeritus of Scranton, St. Charles Borromeo Seminary, 100 E. Wynnewood Rd., Wynnewood, PA 19096.

Matano, Salvatore R., Bishop of Burlington, 55 Joy Dr., S. Burlington, VT 05403.

McCarthy, James F., Retired Auxiliary Bishop of New York, St. Elizabeth Ann Seton, 1377 N. Main St., Shrub Oak, NY 10588.

McCarthy, John E., Bishop emeritus of Austin, 6225 E. Hwy. 290 E., Austin, TX 78723.

McCormack, John B., Bishop of Manchester, 153 Ash St., P.O. Box 310, Manchester, NH 03105.

McCormack, William J., Retired Auxiliary Bishop of New York, 142 E. 29th St., New York, NY 10016.

McDonald, Andrew J., Bishop emeritus of Little Rock, St. Joseph's Home, 80 W. Northwest Hwy., Palatine, IL 60067.

*His Excellency,
The Most Reverend*

McDonnell, Charles J., Retired Auxiliary Bishop of Newark, 34 Maple Ave., Hackensack, NJ 07601.

McDonnell, Timothy A., Bishop of Springfield in Massachusetts, P.O. Box 1730, Springfield, MA 01102-1730.

McElroy, Robert W., Auxiliary Bishop of San Francisco, One Peter Yorke Way, San Francisco, CA 94109-6602.

McFadden, Joseph P., Bishop of Harrisburg, 4800 Union Deposit Rd., Harrisburg, PA 17111-3710.

McGrath, Patrick J., Bishop of San Jose, 1150 N. First St., Ste. 100, San Jose, CA 95112.

McIntyre, John J., Auxiliary Bishop of Philadelphia, 222 N. 17th St., Philadelphia, PA 19103-1299.

McLaughlin, Bernard J., Retired Auxiliary Bishop of Buffalo, 204 Knoche Rd., Tonawanda, NY 14150.

McManus, Robert J., Bishop of Worcester, 49 Elm St., Worcester, MA 01609.

McRaith, John J., Bishop emeritus of Owensboro, 529 Cedar St., Owensboro, KY 42301.

Medley, William F., Bishop of Owensboro, 600 Locust St., Owensboro, KY 42301.

Melczek, Dale J., Bishop of Gary, 9292 Broadway, Merrillville, IN 46410.

Mengeling, Carl F., Retired Bishop of Lansing, 228 N. Walnut St., Lansing, MI 48933.

Mestice, Anthony F., Retired Auxiliary Bishop of New York, Our Lady of Consolation Residence, 3103 Arlington Ave., Ste. 8, Bronx, NY 10463.

Mikloshazy, Attila, s.j., Retired Bishop for Hungarians, St. Augustine's Seminary, 2661 Kingston Rd., Scarborough, Ontario, Canada, M1M 1M3.

Milone, Anthony M., Bishop emeritus of Great Falls-Billings, 7600 S. 42nd St., Bellevue, NE 68147-1702.

Morin, Roger P., Bishop of Biloxi, 1790 Popps Ferry Rd., Biloxi, MS 39532-2118.

Morlino, Robert C., Bishop of Madison, 702 S. High Point Rd., Madison, WI 53744-4983.

Morneau, Robert F., Auxiliary Bishop of Green Bay, 333 Hilltop Dr., Green Bay, WI 54301-2713.

Moskal, Robert M., Bishop emeritus of St. Josaphat in Parma, 5720 State Rd., Parma, OH 44134.

Mouradian, Mikael Antoine, Eparch of Our Lady of Nareg, 167 N. 6th St., Brooklyn, NY 11211.

Moynihan, James M., Bishop emeritus of Syracuse, 240 E. Onondaga St., P.O. Box 511, Syracuse, NY 13201.

Muench, Robert W., Bishop of Baton Rouge, 1800 S. Acadian Thruway, P.O. Box 2028, Baton Rouge, LA 70821-2028.

Mulvee, Robert E., Bishop emeritus of Providence, 30 Fenner St., Providence, RI 02903.

Mulvey, Wm. Michael., Bishop of Corpus Christi, 620 Lipan St., P.O. Box 2620, Corpus Christi, TX, 78403-2620.

Murphy, William F., Bishop of Rockville Centre, P.O. Box 9023, Rockville Centre, NY 11571-9023.

Murray, James A., Bishop emeritus of Kalamazoo, 215 N. Westnedge Ave., Kalamazoo, MI 49007-3760.

Murry, George V., s.j., Bishop of Youngstown, 144 W. Wood St., Youngstown, OH 44503.

Naickamparambil, Thomas Mar Eusebius, Bishop of Syro-Malankara Catholic Exarchate, 950 Hillside Ave., New Hyde Park, NY 11040.

*His Excellency,
The Most Reverend*

Negron Santana, Hermin, Auxiliary Bishop of San Juan, Urb. Caparra Heights, 1562 C. Encarnacion, San Juan, PR 00920.

Nevares, Eduardo A., Auxiliary Bishop of Phoenix, 400 E. Monroe St., Phoenix, AZ 85004-2336.

Nevins, John J., Bishop emeritus of Venice, P.O. Box 2006, Venice, FL 34284-2006.

Newman, William C., Retired Auxiliary Bishop of Baltimore, 5300 N. Charles St., Baltimore, MD 21201.

Nickless, R. Walker, Bishop of Sioux City, 1821 Jackson St., P.O. Box 3379, Sioux City, IA 51102-3379.

Noonan, John G., Bishop of Orlando, 50 E. Robinson St., Orlando, FL 32801.

O'Brien, Thomas J., Bishop emeritus of Phoenix, 400 E. Monroe St., Phoenix, AZ 85004-2336.

O'Connell, Anthony J., Bishop emeritus of Palm Beach, 1098 Mepkin Abbey Rd., Moncks Corner, SC 29461-4796.

O'Connell, David M., c.m., Bishop of Trenton, 701 Lawrenceville Rd., P.O. Box 5147, Trenton, NJ 08638-0147.

O'Neill, Arthur J., Bishop emeritus of Rockford, 3330 Maria Linden Dr., Rockford, IL 61114.

Ochoa, Armando, Bishop of El Paso, 499 St. Matthews St., El Paso TX 79907.

Olivier, Leonard J., s.v.d., Retired Auxiliary Bishop of Washington, 619 Tenth St., N.W., Washington, DC 20001-4587.

Olmsted, Thomas J., Bishop of Phoenix, 400 E. Monroe St., Phoenix, AZ 85004-2336.

Ottenweller, Albert H., Bishop emeritus of Steubenville, 2544 Parkwood Ave., Toledo, OH 43610-1317.

Paprocki, Thomas J., Bishop of Springfield in Illinois, 1615 W. Washington St., P.O. Box 3187, Springfield, IL 62708-3187.

Pataki, Andrew, Bishop emeritus of Passaic of the Ruthenians, 445 Lackawanna Ave., West Paterson, NJ 07424.

Pates, Richard E., Bishop of Des Moines, 601 Grand Ave., Des Moines, IA 50309.

Pena, Raymundo J., Bishop emeritus of Brownsville, 300 N. Nebraska Ave., San Juan, TX 78589.

Pepe, Joseph A., Bishop of Las Vegas, 336 Cathedral Way, Las Vegas, NV 89109.

Perry, Joseph N., Auxiliary Bishop of Chicago, P.O. Box 733, South Holland, IL 60473-0733.

Pevec, A. Edward, Retired Auxiliary Bishop of Cleveland, 28700 Euclid Ave., Wickliffe, OH 44092.

Pfeifer, Michael D., o.m.i., Bishop of San Angelo, P.O. Box 1829, San Angelo, TX 76902.

Piche, Lee A., Auxiliary Bishop of St. Paul and Minneapolis, 226 Summit Ave., St. Paul, MN 55102.

Pilla, Anthony M., Bishop emeritus of Cleveland, 28700 Euclid Ave., Wickliffe, OH 44092.

Popp, Bernard F., Retired Auxiliary Bishop of San Antonio, Padua Place, 80 Peter Baque Rd., San Antonio, TX 78209.

Provost, Glen J., Bishop of Lake Charles, 414 Iris St., P.O. Box 3223, Lake Charles, LA 70602.

Quinn, A. James, Retired Auxiliary Bishop of Cleveland, 2345 Bassett Rd., Westlake, OH 44145.

*His Excellency,
The Most Reverend*

Quinn, Francis A., Bishop emeritus of Sacramento, 8840 E. 22nd St., Tucson, AZ 85710.

Quinn, John M., Bishop of Winona, 55 W. Sanborn St., P.O. Box 588, Winona, MN 55987.

Ramirez, Ricardo, c.s.b., Bishop of Las Cruces, 1280 Med Park Dr., Las Cruces, NM 88005.

Ramos Morales, Eusebio, Bishop of Fajardo-Humacao, Apartado 888, Fajardo, PR 00738.

Rassas, George J., Auxiliary Bishop of Chicago, 200 N. Milwaukee Ave., Ste. 200, Libertyville, IL 60048-2250.

Reilly, Daniel P., Bishop emeritus of Worcester, St. Paul Cathedral, 38 High St., Worcester, MA 01609.

Reiss, Francis R., Auxiliary Bishop of Detroit, 36800 Schoolcraft Rd., Livonia, MI 48154.

Reiss, John C., Bishop emeritus of Trenton, Villa Vianney, 2301 Lawrenceville Rd., Trenton, NJ 08648.

Rhoades, Kevin C., Bishop of Fort Wayne-South Bend, P.O. Box 390, Fort Wayne, IN 46801.

Ricard, John H., s.s.j., Bishop emeritus of Pensacola-Tallahassee, 11 N. B St., Pensacola, FL 32501.

Rice, Edward M., Auxiliary Bishop of St. Louis, 20 Archbishop May Dr., St. Louis, MO 63119-5738.

Ricken, David L., Bishop of Green Bay, 1825 Riverside Dr., Green Bay, WI 54301.

Rivera Perez, Hector M., Retired Auxiliary Bishop of San Juan, P.O. Box 31155, San Juan, PR 00929-2155.

Rizzotto, Vincent M., Retired Auxiliary Bishop of Galveston-Houston, P.O. Box 907, Houston, TX 77001-0907.

Rodimer, Frank J., Bishop emeritus of Paterson, 1082 Greenpond Rd., Newfoundland, NJ 07435.

Rodriguez, Placido, c.m.f., Bishop of Lubbock, P.O. Box 98700, Lubbock, TX 79499-8700.

Rojas, Alberto, Auxiliary Bishop of Chicago, P.O. Box 1979, Chicago, IL 60690.

Roman, Agustin A., Retired Auxiliary Bishop of Miami, 3605 S. Miami Ave., Miami, FL 33133.

Roque, Francis X., Retired Auxiliary Bishop for the Military Services, P.O. Box 4469, Washington, DC 20017.

Rosazza, Peter A., Retired Auxiliary Bishop of Hartford, 1450 Chapel St., New Haven, CT 06511.

Rose, Robert J., Bishop emeritus of Grand Rapids, 1200 104th, Apt. 4, Byron Center, MI 49315.

Rozanski, Mitchell T., Auxiliary Bishop of Baltimore, 320 Cathedral St., Baltimore, MD 21201.

Rueger, George E., Retired Auxiliary Bishop of Worcester, St. Stephen's Rectory, 16 Hamilton St., Worcester, MA 01604.

Ryan, Daniel L., Bishop emeritus of Springfield in Illinois, St. John Vianney Villa, 1464 Green Trail Dr., Naperville, IL 60540-8359.

Ryan, Sylvester D., Bishop emeritus of Monterey, 425 Church St., Monterey, CA 93940.

Salazar, Alexander, Auxiliary Bishop of Los Angeles, 3424 Wilshire Blvd., Los Angeles, CA 901010-2241.

Samo, Amando, Bishop of the Caroline Islands, P.O. Box 939, Chuuk, Caroline Islands, FM 96942.

His Excellency,
The Most Reverend

Sample, Alexander K., Bishop of Marquette, 1004 Harbor Hills Dr., Marquette, MI 49855.

Samra, Nicholas J., Eparch of Newton, 32406 Barclay Sq., Warren, MI 48093.

Sansaricq, Guy A., Retired Auxiliary Bishop of Brooklyn, St. Gregory the Great, 224 Brooklyn Ave., Brooklyn, NY 11213-2505.

Sartoris, Joseph M., Retired Auxiliary Bishop of Los Angeles, San Pedro Pastoral Region, 1988 Rolling Vista Dr., #21, Lomita, CA 90717-3761.

Schlarman, Stanley G., Bishop emeritus of Dodge City, 2620 Lebanon Ave., Belleville, IL 62221.

Schmitt, Bernard W., Bishop emeritus of Wheeling-Charleston, 1300 Byron St., Box 230, Wheeling, WV 26003.

Schmitt, Mark F., Bishop emeritus of Marquette, Grellinger Hall, Apt. 12, 224 Iroquois Ave., Green Bay, WI 54301.

Seitz, Mark J., Auxiliary Bishop of Dallas, 3725 Blackburn, P.O. Box 190507, Dallas, TX 75219.

Seminack, Richard S., Bishop of St. Nicholas in Chicago for Ukrainians, 2245 W. Rice St., Chicago, IL 60622.

Senior, Timothy C., Auxiliary Bishop of Philadelphia, 222 N. 17th St., Rm. 1200, Philadelphia, PA 19103-1299.

Serratelli, Arthur J., Bishop of Paterson, 777 Valley Rd., Clifton, NJ 07013.

Sevilla, Carlos, s.j., Bishop emeritus of Yakima, 5301-A Tieton Dr., Yakima, WA 98908.

Shaheen, Robert J., Bishop of Our Lady of Lebanon, 1021 S. 10th St., St. Louis, MO 63104.

Sheldon, Gilbert I., Bishop emeritus of Steubenville, 609 N. Seventh St., Steubenville, OH 43952.

Sheridan, Michael J., Bishop of Colorado Springs, 228 N. Cascade Ave., Colorado Springs, CO 80903.

Sheridan, Patrick J., Retired Auxiliary Bishop of New York, 5655 Arlington Ave., Bronx, NY 10471.

Siegel, Joseph M., Auxiliary Bishop of Joliet, 425 Summit St., Joliet, IL 60435.

Silva, Clarence, Bishop of Honolulu, 1184 Bishop St., Honolulu, HI 96813.

Sirba, Paul D., Bishop of Duluth, 2830 E. Fourth St., Duluth, MN 55812.

Sklba, Richard J., Retired Auxiliary Bishop of Milwaukee, 836 N. Broadway, Milwaukee, WI 53202-3608.

Skurla, William, Bishop of Passaic of the Ruthenians, 445 Lackawanna Ave., Woodland Park, NJ 07424.

Skylstad, William S., Bishop emeritus of Spokane, W. 1023 Riverside Ave., Spokane, WA 99201.

Slattery, Edward J., Bishop of Tulsa, P.O. Box 690240, Tulsa, OK 74169.

Smith, John M., Bishop emeritus of Trenton, P.O. Box 5147, 701 Lawrenceville Rd., Trenton, NJ 08638-0147.

Snyder, John J., Bishop emeritus of St. Augustine, 5 Casa San Pedro, 1714 State Rd. 13, Ste. 6, Jacksonville, FL 32259.

Soens, Lawrence D., Bishop emeritus of Sioux City, 1703 - W. 25th, Apt. 208, Sioux City, IA 51103-1700.

Solis, Oscar A., Auxiliary Bishop of Los Angeles, 3555 St. Pancratius Pl., Lakewood, CA 90712-1416.

His Excellency,
The Most Reverend

Soto, Jaime, Bishop of Sacramento, 2110 Broadway, Sacramento, CA 95818-2541.

Spencer, F. Richard, Auxiliary Bishop for the Military Services, 1025 Michigan Ave., N.E., P.O. Box 4469, Washington, DC 20017-0469.

Speyrer, Jude, Bishop emeritus of Lake Charles, 118 Marcus Dr., Carenco, LA 70502.

Steib, J. Terry, s.v.d., Bishop of Memphis, The Catholic Center, P.O. Box 341669, Memphis, TN 38184-1669.

Steiner, Kenneth D., Auxiliary Bishop of Portland in Oregon, 2838 E. Burnside St., Portland, OR 97214.

Stika, Richard F., Bishop of Knoxville, 805 Northshore Dr., S.W., Knoxville, TN 37919.

Straling, Phillip F., Bishop emeritus of Reno, 290 S. Arlington Ave., Reno, NV 89501-1713.

Sullivan, Dennis J., Auxiliary Bishop of New York, 452 Madison Ave., New York, NY 10022.

Sullivan, Joseph M., Retired Auxiliary Bishop of Brooklyn, 378 Clermont Ave., Brooklyn, NY 11238.

Sullivan, Walter F., Bishop emeritus of Richmond, 3203 Hawthorne Ave., Richmond, VA 23227.

Swain, Paul J., Bishop of Sioux Falls, 523 N. Duluth Ave., Sioux Falls, SD 57104.

Symons, J. Keith, Bishop emeritus of Palm Beach, P.O. Box 7, Alma, MI 48801-0007.

Tafoya, Arthur N., Bishop emeritus of Pueblo, 101 N. Greenwood., Pueblo, CO 81003.

Tamayo, James A., Bishop of Laredo, Chancery, 1901 Corpus Christi St., Laredo, TX 78043.

Taylor, Anthony B., Bishop of Little Rock, 2500 N. Tyler St., P.O. Box 7565, Little Rock, AR 72217.

Thomas, Daniel E., Auxiliary Bishop of Philadelphia, 222 N. 17th St., Rm. 930, Philadelphia, PA 19103.

Thomas, Elliott G., Bishop emeritus of St. Thomas, in the Virgin Islands, Natl. Shrine of Divine Mercy, 2 Prospect Hill Rd., Stockbridge, MA 01262.

Thomas, George, Bishop of Helena, 515 N. Ewing, P.O. Box 1729, Helena, MT 59624-1729.

Thompson, Charles C., Bishop of Evansville, 4200 N. Kentucky Ave., P.O. Box 4169, Evansville, IN 47724-0169.

Thompson, David B., Bishop emeritus of Charleston, 4479 Downing Pl., Mount Pleasant, SC 29466.

Timlin, James C., Bishop emeritus of Scranton, 300 Wyoming Ave., Scranton, PA 18503.

Tobin, Thomas J., Bishop of Providence, One Cathedral Sq., Providence, RI 02903-3695.

Torres Oliver, Fremiot, Bishop emeritus of Ponce, C Marques de Mondejar 24, 3B, Madrid, 28028, Spain.

Trautman, Donald W., Bishop of Erie, 205 W. 9th St., P.O. Box 10397, Erie, PA 16514.

Tyson, Joseph J., Bishop of Yakima, 5301-A Tieton Dr., Yakima, WA 98908.

Uglietto, Peter J., Auxiliary Bishop of Boston, 66 Brooks Dr., Braintree, MA 02184-3839.

Valero, Rene, Retired Auxiliary Bishop of Brooklyn, 34-43 93rd St., Jackson Heights, NY 11372.

Vann, Kevin W., Bishop of Fort Worth, 800 W. Loop 820 S., Fort Worth, TX 76108.

Vasa, Robert F., Bishop of Santa Rosa, 985 Airway Ct., Santa Rosa, CA 95403.

Vasquez, Joe S., Bishop of Austin, 6225 E. Hwy. 290 E., Austin, TX 78723.

Wall, James S., Bishop of Gallup, 711 S. Puerco Dr., P.O. Box 1338, Gallup, NM 87305.

His Excellency,
The Most Reverend

Walsh, Daniel F., Bishop emeritus of Santa Rosa, 985 Airway Ct., Ste. B, Santa Rosa, CA 95403.

Walsh, Gerald T., Auxiliary Bishop of New York, St. Joseph's Seminary, 201 Seminary Ave., Yonkers, NY 10704.

Walsh, Paul H., Auxiliary Bishop of Rockville Centre, Western Vicariate, Diocese of Rockville Centre, P.O. Box 933, Roosevelt, NY 11575-0933.

Waltersheid, William J., Auxiliary Bishop of Pittsburgh, 111 Blvd. of the Allies, Pittsburgh, PA 15222-1618.

Warfel, Michael, Bishop of Great Falls-Billings, 121 23rd St. S., Great Falls, MT 59401-3939.

Wcela, Emil A., Retired Auxiliary Bishop of Rockville Centre, Church of St. John the Evangelist, 546 St. John's Place, Riverhead, NY 11901.

Weigand, William K., Bishop emeritus of Sacramento, Pastoral Center, 2110 Broadway, Sacramento CA 95818.

Weitzel, John Quinn, m.m., Bishop of Samoa-Pago Pago, Fatuoaiga, P.O. Box 596, Pago Pago, American Samoa 96799.

Wester, John Charles, Bishop of Salt Lake City, 27 C St., Salt Lake City, UT 84103-2397.

Wilkerson, Gerald E., Auxiliary Bishop of Los Angeles, 15101 San Fernando Mission Blvd., Mission Hills, CA 91345-1109.

Williams, James K., Bishop emeritus of Lexington, 1310 W. Main St., Lexington, KY 40508.

Winter, William J., Retired Auxiliary Bishop of Pittsburgh, St. John Vianney Manor, 2600 Morange Rd., Pittsburgh, PA 15205.

Wirz, George O., Retired Auxiliary Bishop of Madison, 702 S. High Point Rd., P.O. Box 44983, Madison WI 53714.

Yanta, John W., Bishop emeritus of Amarillo, 1800 N. Spring St., P.O. Box 5644, Amarillo, TX 79117-5644.

Zarama, Luis R., Auxiliary Bishop of Atlanta, 680 W. Peachtree St., N.W., Atlanta, GA 30308.

Zavala, Gabino, Auxiliary Bishop of Los Angeles, San Gabriel Pastoral Region, 16009 E. Cypress Ave., Irwindale, CA 91706-2122.

Zipfel, Paul A., Bishop of Bismarck, 420 Raymond St., Bismarck, ND 58502-1575.

Zubik, David A., Bishop of Pittsburgh, 111 Blvd. of the Allies, Pittsburgh, PA 15222-1618.

Zurek, Patrick J., Bishop of Amarillo, 1800 N. Spring St., Amarillo, TX 79117.

U.S. HIERARCHY SERVING IN OTHER COUNTRIES

His Excellency,
The Most Reverend

Adams, Edward J., Titular Archbishop of Scala, Archbishop Apostolic Nuncio to Greece, Athenai, 154 52 Paleo Psychico, Odos Mavili, 2.

Balvo, Charles D., Titular Archbishop of Castello, Apostolic Nuncio to New Zealand, Wellington 6041, P.O. Box 14-044, 112 Queen's Dr.

Blume, Michael August, s.v.d., Titular Archbishop of Alexanum, Apostolic Nuncio in Benin and Togo, B.P. 20790, Lome, Togo.

His Excellency,
The Most Reverend

Burke, Raymond L., Prefect of the Apostolic Signatura in Rome, Palazzo della Cancelleria, 00186 Roma, Piazza della Cancelleria, 1.

Bustros, Cyril Salim, s.m.s.p., Archbishop of Beirut and Jbeil, 655 rue de Damas, B.P. 11-901 Beyrouth, Liban.

Cardone, Christopher, o.p., Bishop of Auki, Solomon Islands, P. O. Box A 13, Auki, Malaita, Solomon Islands.

Echevarria, Javier, Prelate of the Prelature of the Holy Cross and Opus Dei, Viale Bruno Buozzi 73, 00197, Rome, Italy.

Foley, John P. Cardinal, Grand Master emeritus of the Equestrian Order of the Holy Sepulchre of Jerusalem, 00120 Vatican City State, Europe.

Gilbert, Edward J., c.ss.r., Archbishop of Port of Spain, 27 Maraval Rd., St. Clair Port of Spain, Trinidad & Tobago.

Gullickson, Thomas E., Apostolic Nuncio to Ukraine, 252054 Kyiv, vul Turhenivska 40.

Harvey, James M., Titular Archbishop of Memfi, Prefect of the Papal Household, 00120 Vatican City State, Europe.

Heim, Capistrano F., o.f.m., Prelate emeritus of Itaituba, Brazil, C.P. 171, 68181-970 Itaituba, PA, Brazil.

Hermes, Heriberto, o.s.b., Bishop Prelate emeritus of Cristalandia, Brazil, C.P. 05, Praca da Catedral s/n, 77490-00, Cristalandia, TO, Brazil.

Howaniec, Henry Theophilus, o.f.m., Bishop emeritus of Holy Trinity in Almaty, Kazakhstan, Kabanbai Batyra St., 77/16, 050000 Almaty, Kazakhstan.

Kurtz, Robert, c.r., Bishop of Hamilton-in-Bermuda, P.O. Box SN629, Southhampton SNBX Bermuda.

La Fay, Michael, o.carm., Bishop Prelate of Sicuani, Peru, Apartado 46, Jiron Hipolio Unanue 236, Plaza de Armas, Sicuani, via Cuzco, Peru.

Lonchyna, Hlib, m.s.u., Titular Bishop of Bareta, Apostolic Administrator of Great Britain (Ukrainian), 22 Binney St., London, W1Y 1YN, England, Great Britain.

Manning, Elias James, o.f.m.conv., Bishop of Valenca, Brazil, C.P. 87332, 27600-000 Valenca, RJ, Brazil.

Meeking, Basil, Bishop emeritus of Christchurch, New Zealand, St. John Fisher House, 190 Brougham St., Sydenham Christchurch 8023 New Zealand.

Muldoon, Thomas A., o.f.m., Bishop of Juticalpa, Honduras, Apartado 2, Juticalpa, Olancho 16101, Honduras.

Novak, Alfred E., c.ss.r., Bishop emeritus of Paranagua, Brazil, C.P. 531, 83203-970 Paranagua, PR, Brazil.

Pelletier, Donald L., m.s., Bishop emeritus of Morondava Madagascar, Bishop's House, P.O. Box 132, Morondava 619, Madagascar.

Potocnak, Joseph J., s.c.j., Bishop emeritus of De Aar, South Africa, P.O. Box 73, 1 Van Riebeeck Str., De Aar 7000, South Africa.

Reichert, Stephen J., o.f.m.cap., Archbishop of Madang, Papua New Guinea, P. O. Box 750, Madang, Papua New Guinea.

Scarpone, Gerald, o.f.m., Bishop emeritus of Comayagua, Honduras, Obispado, Calle de la Catedral, Apartado 41, 12101 Comayagua, Honduras.

His Excellency,
The Most Reverend

Schmitz, Paul Ervin, o.f.m.cap., Vicariate Apostolic of Bluefields, Apartado Postal 8, Bluefields, R.A.A.S., Nicaragua, C.A.

Tiedemann, Neil, c.p., Bishop of Mandeville, Jamaica, P.O. Box 8, 20 Perth Rd., Mandeville, Manchester, Jamaica.

Turley, Daniel Thomas, o.s.a., Bishop of Chulucanas, Peru, Obispado, Calle Cuzco 381, Chulucanas, Depto. de Piura, Peru.

Zywiec, David Albin, o.f.m.cap., Auxiliary Bishop, Vicariate Apostolic of Bluefields, Apartado Postal 8, Bluefields, R.A.A.S., Nicaragua, C.A.

OTHER HIERARCHY RESIDING IN THE UNITED STATES

His Excellency,
The Most Reverend

Bennett, Gordon D., s.j., Bishop emeritus of Mandeville, P.O. Box 45041, Los Angeles, CA 90045.

Boland, Ernest B., o.p., Bishop emeritus of Multan, St. Thomas Aquinas Priory, Providence College, 333 Eaton St., Providence, RI 02918-0001.

McNabb, John Conway, o.s.a., Bishop emeritus of Chulucanas, Peru, St. Clare of Montefalco Parish, 1401 Whittier Rd., Grosse Point Park, MI 48230.

McNaughton, William J., m.m., Bishop emeritus of Inchon, P.O. Box 304, Maryknoll, NY 10545.

Pearce, George H., s.m., Archbishop emeritus of Suva, 10 Rhodes Ave., N. North Smithfield, RI 02896.

Sabatini, Lawrence, c.s., Bishop emeritus of Kamloops, Canada, Holy Rosary Church, 612 N. Western Ave., Chicago, IL 60612.

ARCHABBOTS

The Right Reverend

DuVall, Justin, o.s.b., St. Meinrad Archabbey, N. 100 Hill Dr., St. Meinrad IN 47577.

Knaebel, Bonaventure, o.s.b., (Resigned), St. Meinrad Archabbey, N. 100 Hill Dr., St. Meinrad, IN 47577.

Maher, Paul R., o.s.b., (Resigned) St. Vincent Archabbey, 300 Fraser Purchase Rd., Latrobe, PA 15650-2686.

Nowicki, Douglas R., o.s.b., St. Vincent Archabbey, 300 Fraser Purchase Rd., Latrobe, PA 15650-2686.

Reilly, Lambert, o.s.b., (Resigned) St. Meinrad Archabbey, N. 100 Hill Dr., St. Meinrad, IN 47577.

ABBOTS

The Right Reverend

Anderson, Hugh R., o.s.b., St. Procopius Abbey, 5601 College Rd., Lisle, IL 60532.

Anderson, Philip, o.s.b., Our Lady of the Annunciation of Clear Creek Monestery, 5804 W. Monastery Rd., Hulbert, OK 74441.

Antonucci, Richard, o.praem., Daylesford Abbey, 220 S. Valley Rd., Paoli, PA 19301.

Balsavich, Marion E., o.s.b., Retired. St. Bede Abbey, Peru, IL 61354.

The Right Reverend

Bamberger, John E., o.c.s.o., Retired. Abbey of Genesee, Piffard, NY 14533.

Barnes, Robert, o.c.s.o., Abbey of Our Lady of the Holy Cross, 901 Cool Spring Ln., Berryville, VA 22611- 2700.

Bataille, Vincent, o.s.b., Resigned. Marmion Abbey, Butterfield Rd., Aurora, IL 60504.

Benedict, Francis, o.s.b., Resigned. St. Andrew's Abbey, 31001 N. Valyermo Rd., Valyermo, CA 93563.

Benkert, Gerald, o.s.b., Resigned. Marmion Abbey, Butterfield Rd., Aurora, IL 60504.

Berndt, Alan, o.s.b., Retired. Blue Cloud Abbey, P.O. Box 98, Marvin, SD 57252.

Bock, David R., o.c.s.o., Retired. New Melleray Abbey, 6500 Melleray Circle, Peosta, IA 52068.

Boyce, Edmund J., o.s.b., St. Benedict Abbey, 12605 224th Ave., Benet Lake, WI 53102.

Boyle, Joseph, o.c.s.o., St. Benedict Monastery, 1012 Monastery Rd., Snowmass, CO 81654.

Brahill, John, o.s.b., Marmion Abbey, 850 Butterfield Rd., Aurora, IL 60502.

Brown, Justin, o.s.b., St. Joseph's Abbey, 75376 River Rd., St. Benedict, LA 70457.

Burnett, Oscar, o.s.b., Retired. Belmont Abbey, 100 Belmont-Mount Holly Rd., Belmont, NC 28012-1802.

Camacho, Isaac, o.s.b., St. Leo Abbey, Box 2350, St. Leo, FL 33574.

Carr, Christian Aidan, o.c.s.o., Retired. Our Lady of Mepkin Abbey, HC 69, Box 800, Moncks Corner, SC 29461.

Clark, Victor J., o.s.b., Retired. St. Bernard Abbey, 1600 St. Bernard Dr., Cullman, AL 35055.

Clarke, Brian H., o.s.b., Retired. St. Mary Abbey, Delbarton, Mendham Rd., Morristown, NJ 07960.

Cole, Edwin J., o.s.b., St. Anselm Church, 530 S. Mason Rd., St. Louis, MO 63141.

Connor, James, o.c.s.o., Retired. Assumption Abbey, Rte. 5, P.O. Box 1056, Ava, MO 65608.

Corpus, Roger, o.s.b., Retired. St. Bede Abbey, Peru, IL 61354.

Cyr, David J., o.s.b., Retired. Marmion Abbey, Butterfield Rd., Aurora, IL 60504.

Dagher, George, b.s.o., Retired. American Headquarters, 30 East St., Methuen, MA 01844.

Davis, Thomas X., o.c.s.o., Retired. Our Lady of New Clairvaux Abbey, P.O. Box 80, Vina, CA 96092.

De Wane, Thomas E., o.praem., Retired. St. Norbert Abbey, 1016 N. Broadway, De Pere, WI 54115-2697.

Denburger, John J., o.c.s.o., Abbey of the Genesee, Piffard, NY 14533.

Dimitrijevich, Nicholas, Our Lady of the Valley, P.O. Box 419, Gloverville, SC 29828.

Dosch, Leander, o.c.s.o., Abbey of the Holy Trinity, 1250 S. 9500 E., Huntsville, UT 84317.

Driscoll, William J., o.mar., Monastery of the Most Holy Trinity, 67 Dugway Rd., Petersham, MA 01366-9725.

Duerr, Gregory, o.s.b. Mt. Angel Abbey, St. Benedict, OR 97373.

Dzikowicz, Justin E., o.s.b., Retired. St. Paul Abbey, Newton, NJ 07860.

The Right Reverend

Eberle, Peter, o.s.b., Corpus Christi Abbey, 101 S. Vista Dr., Sandia, TX 78383.

Farkasfalvy, Denis, o.cist., Abbey of Our Lady of Dallas, 3550 Cistercian Rd., Irving, TX 75039.

Flaherty, Malachy, o.c.s.o., Abbey of Our Lady of the Holy Trinity, 1250 S. 9500 E., Huntsville, UT 84317.

Freeman, Brendan J., o.c.s.o., Abbey of Our Lady of New Melleray, 6500 Melleray Circle, Peosta, IA 52068-9736.

Frerking, Thomas, o.s.b., Abbey of St. Mary and St. Louis, 500 S. Mason Rd., St. Louis, MO 63141.

Garber, Andrew V., o.s.b., Resigned. St. Benedict Abbey, Benet Lake, WI 53102.

Geraets, David, o.s.b., Monastery of the Risen Christ, 2308 O'Connor Way, San Luis Obispo, CA 93405.

Gibbs, Gabriel, o.s.b., St. Benedict Abbey, 252 Still River Rd., Still River, MA 01467.

Gumula, Stanislaus, o.s.c.o., Mepkin Abbey, 1098 Mepkin Abbey Rd., Moncks Corner, SC 29461.

Hacker, Louis, o.s.b., Corpus Christi Abbey, HCR 2, Box 6300, Sandia, TX 78383.

Harrison, Cyprian, o.c.s.o., Retired. Assumption Abbey, Rte. 5, Box 1056, Ava, MO 65608.

Hayes, Eugene, o.praem., St. Michael Abbey, 19292 El Toro Rd., Silverado, CA 92676-9710.

Hayes, Giles, o.s.b. St. Mary's Abbey, Delbarton, Morristown, NJ 07960.

Heidgen, Warren J., o.s.b., Retired. Holy Cross Abbey, P.O. Box 1510, Canon City, CO 81215-1510.

Hein, Kenneth, o.s.b., Retired Abbot, Holy Cross Abbey, P.O. Box 1510, Canon City, CO 81215-1510.

Hillenbrand, Thomas, o.s.b., Retired. Blue Cloud Abbey, P.O. Box 98, Marvin, SD 57251.

Hinches, Augustine J., o.s.b., Resigned. St. Paul Abbey, Newton, NJ 07860.

Holmes, W. Caedmon, o.s.b., Abbey of St. Gregory, Cory's Ln., Portsmouth, RI 02871.

Homick, Joseph, Holy Transfiguration Monastery, 17001 Tomki Rd., Redwood Valley, CA 95470.

Johnson, Bernard, o.c.s.o., Retired. Our Lady of New Clairvaux Abbey, P. O. Box 80, Vina, CA 96092.

Kalcic, Dismas B., o.s.b., Retired. St. Procopius Abbey, 5601 College Rd., Lisle, IL 60532.

Keating, Thomas, o.c.s.o., St. Benedict Monastery, 1012 Monastery Rd., Snowmass, CO 81654.

Kodell, Jerome, o.s.b., New Subiaco Abbey, Subiaco, AR 72865.

Koehler, Ralph, o.s.b., Retired. St. Benedict's, Abbey, Atchison, KS 66002.

Lawrence, Philip, o.s.b., Monastery of Christ in the Desert, Abiquiu, NM 87510.

Leavy, Matthew K., o.s.b., St. Anselm Abbey, Manchester, NH 03102.

Liebl, Michael, o.s.b., Mount Michael Benedictine Abbey, 22520 Mount Michael Rd., Elkhorn, NE 68022.

Liprie, James, o.s.b., Abbot of Our Lady of Guadalupe Abbey, Pecos, NM 87552.

The Right Reverend

Logan, John M., o.praem., Daylesford Abbey, 220 S. Valley Rd., Paoli, PA 19301.

Lugo, Martin, o.s.b., Retired. St. Gregory's Abbey, Shawnee, OK 74804.

Macul, Joel P., o.s.b., St. Paul's Abbey, Newton, NJ 07860.

Massoth, Charles, o.s.b., Retired. St. Gregory Abbey, Shawnee, OK 74801.

Matter, Robert, o.c.s.o., Retired. Assumption Abbey, Rte. 5, Box 1056, Ava, MO 65608.

McCaffrey, Edmund F., Former Abbot-Ordinary Belmont Abbey, P.O. Box 70548, Myrtle Beach, SC 29572-0028.

McCarthy, Peter, o.c.s.o., The Cistercian (Trappist) Abbey of Our Lady of Guadalupe, Lafayette, OR 97127.

McCorkell, Edward, o.c.s.o., Retired. Abbey of Our Lady of the Holy Cross, Rte. 2, Box 3870, Berryville, VA 22611-9526.

McDermott, Benedict, o.s.b., Mary Mother of Church Abbey, 12829 River Rd., Richmond, VA 23221.

McGonigle, Kevin, o.s.b., Retired. Conception Abbey, Conception, MO 64433.

Meagher, Cletus D., o.s.b., St. Bernard Abbey, Cullman, AL 35055.

Moore, Patrick, o.s.b., Retired. Assumption Abbey, P.O. Box A, Richardton, ND 58652.

Morcone, Nicholas J., o.s.b., Glastonbury Abbey, 16 Hull St., Hingham, MA 02043.

Murphy, Austin, o.s.b., St. Procopius Abbey, 5601 College Rd., Lisle, IL 60532.

Neville, Gary, o.praem., Abbot St. Norbert Abbey, DePere, WI 54115-2610.

O'Connor, Philip J., o.c.s.o., Retired. New Melleray Abbey, 6500 Melleray Circle, Peosta, IA 52068.

Odenbrett, Stephen, o.s.b., Our Lady of Guadalupe Abbey, Pecos, NM 87552.

Parcher, Adrian, o.s.b., Retired. St. Martin's Abbey, 5300 Pacific Ave., S.E., Lacey, WA 98503.

Polan, Gregory, o.s.b., Abbot of Conception Abbey, Conception, MO 64433.

Purcell, Owen, o.s.b., Retired. St. Benedict's Abbey, Atchison, KS 66002.

Quinkert, Denis, o.s.b., Blue Cloud Abbey, P.O. Box 98, Marvin, SD 57251.

Rausch, Conrad, o.s.b., Retired. St. Martin's Abbey, 5300 Pacific Ave. S.E., Lacey, WA 98503.

Regan, Patrick, o.s.b., Retired. St. Joseph Abbey, St. Benedict, LA 70457.

Rigby, Luke, o.s.b., Abbey of St. Mary and St. Louis, 500 S. Mason Rd., St. Louis, MO 63141.

Rivera, Oscar, o.s.b., San Antonio Abad Abbey of the Order of St. Benedict, P.O. Box 729, Humacao, PR 00792.

Roberts, Augustine, o.c.s.o., St. Joseph Abbey, Spencer, MA 01562.

Rooney, Marcel, o.s.b., Conception Abbey, Conception, MO 64433.

Rossi, Ronald, o.praem., Retired. Daylesford Abbey, 220 S. Valley Rd., Paoli, PA 19301.

Roth, Neal G., o.s.b., St. Martin's Abbey, 5300 Pacific Ave. S.E., Lacey, WA 98503.

Ryska, Leo M., o.s.b., Retired. St. Benedict's Abbey and Retreat Center, Benet Lake, WI 53102.

Schoofs, Robert, o.s.b., Retired. St. Benedict's Abbey, Benet Lake, WI 53102.

The Right Reverend

Scott, Mark A., o.c.s.o., Retired. Assumption Abbey, Rte. 5, Box 1056, Ava, MO 65608.

Senecal, Barnabas, o.s.b., St. Benedict's Abbey, Atchison, KS 66002.

Serna, Mark, o.s.b., Retired. Abbey of St. Gregory, Cory's Ln., Portsmouth, RI 02871.

Shea, Aidan, o.s.b., St. Anselm Abbey, 4501 South Dakota Ave., N.E., Washington, DC 20017-2753.

Solari, Placid D., o.s.b., Belmont Abbey, 100 Belmont-Mount Holly Rd., Belmont, NC 28012-1802.

Stark, Matthew, o.s.b., Retired. Abbey of St. Gregory the Great, Cory's Ln., Portsmouth, RI 02871.

Stasyszen, Lawrence, o.s.b., St. Gregory's Abbey, Shawnee, OK 74804.

Thompson, Damien, o.s.c.o., Abbey of Gethsemani, Trappist, KY 40051.

Tremel, Jerome G., o.praem., Retired. Daylesford Abbey Norbertine Canonry, 220 S. Valley Rd., Paoli, PA 19301-1900.

Valvano, Melvin J., o.s.b., Retired. Newark Abbey, 528 Dr. Martin Luther King Jr. Blvd., Newark, NJ 07102.

Veilleux, Armand J., o.s.c.o., Monastery of the Holy Spirit, 2625 Hwy. 212 S.W., Conyers, GA 30094-4044.

Vollmer, Edward J., o.s.b., Retired. Holy Cross Abbey, P.O. Box 1510, Canon City, CO 81215-1510.

Vorderlandwehr, Adrian R., o.s.b., Retired. St. Gregory Abbey, Shawnee, OK 74801.

Vuong, M. John Lam Dinh, o.cist., St. Joseph Monastery, 21010 Lucerne Valley Cutoff, P.O. Box 960, Lucerne Valley, CA 92356.

Wagner, Lawrence, o.s.b., Retired. Assumption Abbey, P.O. Box A, Richardton, ND 58652.

Walsh, Raphael, o.s.b., Resigned. Mount Michael Abbey, Elkhorn, NE 68022.

Wangler, Brian, o.s.b., Assumption Abbey, P.O. Box A, Richardton, ND 58652.

Wechter, David L., o.s.c.o., Retired. New Melleray Abbey, 6500 Melleray Circle, Peosta, IA 52068.

Wiseman, James, o.s.b., Resigned. St. Anselm Abbey, 4501 South Dakota Ave., N.E., Washington, DC 20017-2753.

Wolff, Theodore, o.s.b., Resigned. Mount Michael Abbey, 22520 Mount Michael Rd., Elkhorn, NE 68022.

Wood, Joseph, o.s.b., Resigned. Mt. Angel Abbey, St. Benedict, OR 97373.

Wright, Charles, o.s.b., Prince of Peace Abbey, 650 Benet Hill Rd., Oceanside, CA 92054.

Archdioceses and Dioceses in the United States and U.S. Territories

Archdiocese of Anchorage

New Listings
Chief Operating Officer and Chief Finance Officer
Rev. Steven C. Moore '76.
**St. Catherine of Siena CUF Chapter, Inc.* P. O. Box 220106, Anchorage, AK, 99522-0106. 2928 McCollie Ave., Anchorage, AK, 99517.
Revisions
Vicar General
Very Rev. Thomas C. Lilly '03.
Chancellor
Vacant.
Office of Stewardship/Development
Ms. Julie Varee.
Tel: 907-297-7718
Diocesan Consultors
Very Rev. Thomas C. Lilly '03.
Rev. Scott Medlock '96.
Office of Finance
Rev. Steven C. Moore, CFO '76.
Ms. Monika Scott, Comptroller.
Tel: 907-297-7712
Propagation of the Faith
Ms. Julie Varee, Dir.
Superintendent of Schools
Vacant, Supt.
Tel: 907-297-7790
Victim Assistance Coordinator
Vivian Finlay, M.Ed., L.M.F.T.
Tel: 907-297-7786
Holy Family Cathedral (1915), Anchorage, AK
Rev. Antony Patalano, O.P.
Rev. Augustine Hilander, O.P.
St. Benedict
Rev. Leo Walsh, S.T.D. '94.
Holy Cross (1984)
Rev. Rafail A. Saiz '94.
Rev. Leo Walsh, S.T.D., Canonical Pastor '94.
St. Patrick (1971)
Rev. Daniel J. Hebert '79.
Holy Rosary
Rev. Nelson Marilag, Philippines '87.
Rev. Scott Garrett, J.C.L., Canonical Pastor '03.
Holy Family (1955) ***Mailing Address:*** P.O. Box 126, Glennallen, AK, 99588. *Fax:* 907-822-4208
Rev. Frank Reitter.
St. Mary's
Rev. James Classen.
St. Bernard (1970)
Rev. Scott Garrett, J.C.L., Canonical Pastor '03.
St. Francis Xavier (1908)
Rev. Frank Reitter.
Sacred Heart
Rev. Scott Garrett, J.C.L. '03.

Archdiocese of Atlanta

New Listings
Mercy Services Downtown, Inc. 424 Decatur St., Atlanta, GA, 30312.
Tel: 678-843-8500 *Fax:* 678-843-8501
Paul G. Justice Esq., Vice Pres. & Gen Counsel Sec.
Newly Ordained
St. Benedict (1987)
Rev. Charles Okeke, Parochial Vicar '11.
Church of the Transfiguration (1977)
Rev. Juan Jose Sanchez Teran, Parochial Vicar '11.
Rev. Joshua Allen '11 Pontifical North American College.
Revisions
Chancellor .
Tel: 404-920-7325 *Fax:* 404-920-7326
Deans
Rev. John Koziol, O.F.M.Conv., V.F., South Deanery '88.
Rev. James D. Duffy, S.M., M.Div., V.F., Central Deanery '79.
Rev. Terence Crone, V.F., Northeast Deanery '02.
AACCW
Rev. William M. Williams, Spiritual Moderator '96 Queen of Angels Catholic Church 1326 Washington Rd., Thomson, GA, 30824.
Tel: 706-595-2913 *Fax:* 706-595-9636
Email: ourladyqofa@comcast.net
Boy Scouts
Rev. Robert A. Frederick, Asst. Chap. '00 St. Brendan Catholic Church 4633 Shiloh Rd., Cumming, GA, 30040.
Tel: 770-205-7969 *Fax:* 770-205-5040
Email: rfrederick@stbrendansatl.com
Council of Priests
Rev. Gregory J. Hartmayer, O.F.M.Conv., Chm. '79 Saint John Vianney Catholic Church 1920 Skyview Dr., Lithia Springs, GA, 30122.
Tel: 770-941-2807 *Fax:* 770-941-5821
Email: frghartmayer@bellsouth.net
Cathedral of Christ the King (1936)
Rev. Jaime Rivera, Parochial Vicar '07.
Rev. Michael Silloway, Parochial Vicar '10.
St. Anthony of Padua (1903)
Rev. Victor A. Galier, M.Div. '98.
Holy Cross (1964)
Rev. Fausto Marquez, Parochial Vicar '97.
Holy Spirit (1964)
Rev. Nicholas G. Azar, Parochial Vicar '09.
Immaculate Heart of the Blessed Virgin Mary (1958)
Deacon Robert J. Hauert.
St. Jude (1960)
Rev. Armando Herrejon-Lopez, Parochial Vicar '07.
Our Lady of the Assumption (1951)
Deacon William H. O'Donoghue.
Mission— **San Felipe de Jesus**, Forest Park, GA
Rev. Rubens Sylvain, C.S., Parochial Vicar.
St. Thomas Aquinas (1972)
Rev. Roberto Herrera, Parochial Vicar.
Deacon Steven W. Shawcross.
St. Joseph (1873)
Rev. Omar Loggiodice, Parochial Vicar '09.
Deacon Scott E. Medine.
St. Francis of Assisi (1966)
Rev. Joseph Liem Nguyen '99.
St. Pius X (1974)
Deacon Fernando Barrueta.
St. Brendan the Navigator (2000), Cumming, GA
Rev. Robert A. Frederick '00.
Deacon Robert H. Grimaldi.
St. Luke (1960)
Rev. Neil Dhabliwala '08.
Sts. Peter and Paul (1959)
Very Rev. Kevin J. Hargaden, M.Div. '99.
Deacon Augustin Pierre-Louis.
Korean Martyrs Catholic Church (1977), Doraville, GA
Rev. Tae-su Michael Ha, S.J.
St. Monica (1994), Duluth, GA
Deacon William L. Bohn.
All Saints (1977)
Rev. Msgr. Hugh M. Marren '76.
St. Michael (1933)
Rev. Dominic Tran, Parochial Vicar '09.
Deacon Kenneth W. Lampert.
St. Brigid (1998), Johns Creek, GA
Rev. Msgr. David P. Talley, J.C.D. '89.
St. Philip Benizi (1965)
Deacon Leonard P. Chambliss Jr.
St. Peter (1936)
Rev. Theodore Book, S.L.L. '02.
St. John Neumann (1977)
Rev. John T. Howren '95.
St. Stephen the Martyr (1999)
Deacon Richard C. Kaszycki.
Our Lady of the Mount (1947)
Very Rev. Richard P. Wise, V.F. '81.
Holy Family (1973)
Rev. Armando Herrejon-Lopez, Parochial Vicar '07.
Rev. Stewart Wilber, Parochial Vicar '91.
St. Joseph (1952)
Rev. Javier Munoz, Parochial Vicar.
Deacon Norman K. Keller.
Deacon Jose T. Merlo-Quintero.
St. James the Apostle (1979), McDonough, GA
Rev. James Flanagan '08.
Rev. Mansueto P. Palang, Parochial Vicar '77.
St. Anna (1951)
Deacon Thomas J. Metzger.
Mary Our Queen Catholic Church (1994)
Deacon Joseph Ruberte.
Saint Patrick (1968)
Rev. Henry Atem, Parochial Vicar '08.
Holy Trinity (1973)
Rev. John Murphy.
Rev. Pavol Brenkus, Parochial Vicar '01.
Rev. Dairo Antonio Rico, Parochial Vicar '03.
Deacon Mark A. Sholander.
St. Andrew (1981)
Very Rev. Michael G. Kingery, V.F. '99.
Deacon Gary E. Schantz.
St. Peter Chanel (1998), Roswell, GA
Rev. Llane Briese, Parochial Vicar '10.
Deacon David J. Thomasberger.
Mission— **St. Catherine Laboure**, Jefferson, GA
Deacon Curtis D. Marsh.
St. Matthew (1999), Winder, GA
Rev. Salomon Garcia, Parochial Vicar '09.
Deacon Lawrence J. Welsh.
St. Michael the Archangel (1995)
Rev. Paul Moreau, L.C., B.A., Parochial Vicar '02.
Retired
Rev. Msgr. Leo P. Herbert '67 3131 N. Druid Hills Rd., Apt 2206, Decatur, GA, 30033-2646
Permanent Deacons
Deacon Dayle H. Geroski The Interfaith Airport Chaplaincy, Inc., Atlanta.
Deacon Mark A. Sholander The Interfaith Airport Chaplaincy, Inc., Atlanta.

Diocese of Baker

Revisions
Saint Alphonsus - Baker City, Inc. 3325 Pocahontas Rd., Baker City, OR, 97814.
Tel: 541-523-6461 (Hospital) *Fax:* 541-523-8151
Email: leanneirsik@chiwest.com
Bed Capacity 25; Nursing Home Beds 90; Patients Assisted Annually 20,114; Nursing Home 91; Staff 223
Saint Alphonsus - Ontario, Inc. 351 S.W. Ninth St., Ontario, OR, 97914.
Tel: 541-881-7000 *Fax:* 541-881-7184
Web: holyrosary-ontario.org
Bed Capacity 49; Total Staff 463; Patients Assisted Annually 73,189

Archdiocese of Baltimore

New Listings
African Conference of Catholic Clergy & Religious in the United States, Inc. 309 Cathedral St., 3rd Fl., Baltimore, MD, 21201.
Tel: 443-982-5230
Web: www.accrus.org
Rev. Martin C. Emeh, Pres.
Esperanza Center Health Services Inc. 320 Cathedral St., Baltimore, MD, 21201.
Tel: 443-825-3450 *Fax:* 443-573-6100
Mr. Timothy J. Kelly, Dir.
Friends of Ijebu-Ode Diocese, Inc. 1130 N. Calvert St., Baltimore, MD, 21202.
Tel: 410-727-3386 *Fax:* 410-727-1006
Very Rev. Nelson A. Moreira, S.S.J., Sec.-Treas. '72.

Diocese of Baton Rouge

Revisions
CHS Foundation 855 Hearthstone Dr., Baton Rouge, LA, 70806.
Tel: 225-389-0978 *Fax:* 225-389-0983

Diocese of Beaumont

Statistics Revision
Retired Priests, sick or absent 12
Extern Priests resident in your Diocese 5
Total number of Permanent Deacons in your diocese 34
Revisions
Episcopal Vicars
Southern Vicariate
Very Rev. Sinclair Oubre, J.C.L., E.V. '86 ***Mailing Address:*** St. John the Evangelist P.O. Box 123, Port Arthur, TX, 77641-0123
Presbyteral Council
Rev. Martin Lester Nelson, J.C.L. '97.
Rev. Msgr. Dan Malain, D.Min. '66.
Catholic Schools
Vacant, Supt. ***Mailing Address:*** P.O. Box 3948, Beaumont, TX, 77704-3948.
Tel: 409-924-4322 *Fax:* 409-838-4511
Diaconate, Permanent Diaconate
Deacon Steven Obernuefemann, Dir. 210 Thornridge, Bridge City, TX, 77611-2355.
Tel: 409-735-6005 *Fax:* 409-838-4511
Diaconate Formation
Very Rev. Sinclair Oubre, J.C.L., E.V., Dir. '86.
Tel: 409-924-4300, Ext. 4303 *Fax:* 409-838-4511
Office of Youth Ministry
Ailene Luistro, Interim Dir. ***Mailing Address:*** P.O. Box 3948, Beaumont, TX, 77704-3948.
Tel: 409-924-4362 *Fax:* 409-838-4511
Catholic Women, Council of
Rev. Martin Lester Nelson, J.C.L., Moderator '97 ***Mailing Address:*** Our Lady of Victory P.O. Box 1359, Sour Lake, TX, 77659-1359
St. Anne (1937)
School—, Beaumont, TX
Amy Delgado, Prin.

St. Jude Thaddeus (1978)
Rev. David A. Edwards, M.Div., Parochial Vicar '02.
Immaculate Conception (1928)
Rev. Msgr. Kenneth R. Greig '67.
St. Catherine of Siena (1954)
School—
Haidee Todora, Prin.
St. James
In Res.
Rev. R. Eathan Oakes '03.
St. Joseph (1951)
Res.: 4600 Procter St., Port Arthur, TX, 77642-1365.
Tel: 409-982-6409 ***Fax:*** 409-983-5383
Email: stjochurch@att.net
Web: www.patx.us/stjoseph
Beaumont - Federal Correctional Complex
Deacon Thomas Ewing Jr.

Diocese of Belleville

Newly Ordained
St. Stephen (1893)
Rev. Anthony O. Onyango, Parochial Vicar '11.
Holy Trinity Catholic Church (1951), Fairview Heights, IL
Rev. Anthony O. Onyango, Parochial Vicar '11.
Revisions
Diocesan Deans
Vacant, East Deanery.
Blessed Sacrament (1927)
Rev. Matthew Elie, Admin. '05.
St. Luke (1883)
Rev. Sean Palas, Parochial Vicar '10.
St. Teresa of the Child Jesus (1926)
Rev. Sean Palas, Parochial Vicar '10.
St. Bernard (1908)
Rev. John J. Joyce '89.
St. Stephen (1893)
Very Rev. C. Raymond Schultz, V.F. '91.
St. Andrew (1905)
Rev. Peter D. Balili, Philippines, Admin.
St. John Nepomucene (1893)
Rev. Slawomir Ptak, Poland, Admin. '03.
St. Damian (1861), Damiansville, IL
Rev. John J. Joyce '89.
Divine Maternity of the B.V.M. (1933)
Rev. Benjamin Stern, Admin. '07.
St. Anthony (1868)
Rev. Christian Reuter, O.F.M., Sacramental Min. '66.
St. Clement (1881)
Rev. Slawomir Ptak, Poland, Admin. '03.
St. Barbara (1867)
Rev. Steven F. Poole, Sacramental Min. '96.
St. John the Baptist (1841)
Rev. Slawomir Ptak, Poland, Admin. '03.
St. Liborius (1838)
Rev. Christian Reuter, O.F.M., Sacramental Min. '66.
St. Mary (1909)
Rev. Peter D. Balili, Philippines, Admin.
St. John the Baptist (1867)
Rev. Stan J. Konieczny '06.
St. Patrick (1850)
Very Rev. Daniel J. Jurek, V.F., Admin. Pro Tem '73.
Rev. John Kizhakedan, C.M.I., Sacramental Min.
St. Mary (1858)
Rev. Joseph C. Rascher '81.
St. Pius V
In Res.
Rev. John Kizhakedan, C.M.I.
Special Assignment
Rev. John Kizhakedan, C.M.I. Prison Ministry.
Retired
Rev. Msgr. Donald W. Eichenseer '61.
Rev. Msgr. Joseph A. Lawler, V.F. '61.
Rev. Albert E. Kreher '65.
Permanent Deacons
Deacon Omer E. DuBois, (Retired).
High School— **Althoff Catholic High School**, Belleville, IL
Rev. Sean Palas '10.

Diocese of Boise

Revisions
Vocations
Rev. Caleb Vogel, Dir. Recruitment '04.
Rev. Robert P. Cook, Dir. Seminarians '03 c/o Bishop Kelly High School 7009 Franklin Rd., Boise, ID, 83709.
Tel: 208-342-1328
Risen Christ Catholic Community (1992)
Rev. Chase R. Hasenoehrl, Parochial Vicar '10.
Sacred Heart, Boise, ID
Rev. Robert P. Cook '03.
St. Bernard's
Rev. Jose de Jesus Gonzalez, Admin. '08.
Immaculate Conception
Rev. Jorge E. Garcia.
St. Theresa
Rev. Marcos Sanchez, Admin, '09.
St. Charles Borromeo (1881)
Rev. Joseph F. McDonald III, J.C.L. '87.
Our Lady of the Lake (1916)
Rev. John Gathungu, Parochial Vicar.
Holy Apostles (1998)
Rev. Dat Vu, Parochial Vicar '04.
Our Lady of Good Counsel
Rev. Eladio Vieyra, Parochial Vicar '08.
Holy Spirit Catholic Community (2003)
Rev. Reginald Nwauzor, Parochial Vicar '80.
St. George's (1917)
Rev. Timothy M. Ritchey '85.
Chapel— **St. Joan of Arc**
Rev. Carlos S. Casavantes, F.S.S.P.
St. Mary Immaculate (1912)
Rev. Timothy M. Ritchey, Admin. '85.
Rev. Jack de Verteuil, Parochial Vicar.
St. Charles (1908)
Rev. Evarist T. Shiyo, Parochial Vicar.
Good Shepherd Catholic Community (1910)
Rev. Robert C. Irwin, Admin.
Our Lady of the Snows (1970)
Rev. Joseph F. McDonald III, J.C.L. '87.
Retired
Rev. Donald Frazier.
Saint Alphonsus Health System, Inc. 1055 N. Curtis Rd., Boise, ID, 83706.
Tel: 208-367-2000 ***Fax:*** 208-367-3966
Email: jeffcoas@sarmc.org
Saint Alphonsus Regional Medical Center, Inc. (1894) Saint Alphonsus Heal System 1055 N. Curtis Rd., Boise, ID, 83706-1370.
Tel: 208-367-2121 St. Alphonsus Regional Medical Center.St. Alphonsus Building Co., Inc.St. Alphonsus Diversified Care.
Sisters of the Holy Cross 4; Bed Capacity 387; Patients Assisted Annually 312,300
Saint Alphonsus Medical Center - Nampa Inc. Saint Alphonsus Health System 1055 N. Curtis Rd., Boise, ID, 83706.
Tel: 208-463-5000
Sisters 1; Bed Capacity 152; Patients Assisted Annually 118,857

Archdiocese of Boston

Revisions
School— **Nativity Preparatory School** Grades 5-8 39 Lamartine St., Jamaica Plain, MA, 02130.
Tel: 857-728-0031 ***Fax:*** 857-728-0037
Email: jwronskisj@nativityboston.org
Web: www.nativityboston.org
Rev. John C. Wronski, S.J., Exec. Dir. '04. Nativity Boston, Inc. A Jesuit Middle School.
Priests 1; Lay Teachers 11; Boys 60
Boston Inter-Community Ministries, Inc. 637 Cambridge St., Brighton, MA, 02135.
Tel: 617-746-2041
Sr. Ellen Powers, C.S.J., Contact Person.

Diocese of Bridgeport

Revisions
Convent— **Dominican Sisters of Our Lady of the Springs of Bridgeport** Sacred Heart Convent 21 Schuyler Ave., Stamford, CT, 06902-3759.
Tel: 203-588-0707; 203-562-9202; 203-773-4421
Sr. Melanie Hannigan, O.P., Prioress.
Tel: 203-562-9202; 203-773-4421
Total in Community 22
Magnificat, A Ministry to Catholic Women (2003) 6 W. Pine Dr., Danbury, CT, 06811-4316.
Tel: 203-744-1856
Email: magnificatbpt@sbcglobal.net
Web: www.triumphantheart.org
Frances Hood, Coord. (Triumphant Heart of Mary Immaculate)
The Pope John Paul II Center for Health Care, Inc. 33 Lincoln Ave., Danbury, CT, 06810.
Tel: 203-416-1355
Total Staff 5
St. Camillus Health Center 494 Elm St., Stamford, CT, 06902.
Tel: 203-325-0200 ***Fax:*** 203-353-0550
Web: www.stcamillushealth.org
Total Staff 4
St. Joseph's Manor 6448 Main St., Trumbull, CT, 06611.
Tel: 203-268-6204 ***Fax:*** 203-268-5271
Web: www.harborsidehealthcare.com
Capacity 297; Total Staff 6
[1125] Dominican Sisters of Our Lady of the Springs of Bridgeport O.P.

Diocese of Burlington

Revisions
Chancery Office: 55 Joy Dr., South Burlington, VT, 05403.
Tel: 802-658-6110 ***Fax:*** 802-658-0436
Web: www.vermontcatholic.org

Diocese of Camden

New Listings
St. Joachim Parish, Bellmawr, N.J. 601 W. Browning Rd., Bellmawr, NJ, 08031-1840.
Mary, Mother of Mercy Parish, Glassboro, N.J. (2011)
Res.: 500 Greentree Rd., Glassboro, NJ, 08028-1427.
Tel: 856-881-0909 ***Fax:*** 856-881-5457
Benedict's Place, Inc. 1845 Haddon Ave, Camden, NJ, 08103.
Revisions
The Church of the Annunciation BVM, Bellmawr, N.J. (1951) Closed. For inquiries for parish records please see St. Joachim Parish, Bellmawr, NJ.
St. Maurice's Church, Brooklawn, N.J. (1955) Closed. For inquiries for parish records please see St. Joachim Parish, Bellmawr, N.J.
The Church of Our Lady of Lourdes, Glassboro, N.J. (1966) Merged with Our Lady Queen of Peace R.C. Church, Pitman, N.J. to form Mary, Mother of Mercy Parish, Glassboro, N.J.
Our Lady Queen of Peace R.C. Church, Pitman N.J. (1940) Merged with The Church of Our Lady of Lourdes, Glassboro, N.J. to form Mary, Mother of Mercy Parish, Glassboro, N.J.
St. Anne's Church, Westville, N.J. (1921) Closed. For inquiries for parish records please see St. Joachim Parish, Bellmawr, N.J.

Diocese of Charleston

New Listings
Bishop's Residence and Chancery Maintenance
Donald Glover, Mgr. Bishop's Residence & Chef.
Tel: 843-327-1212
Email: dglover@catholic-doc.org
Regina Green, Housekeeper.
Tel: 843-609-6653
Wade McDaniel, Maintenance.
Tel: 843-853-2130, Ext. 232
Eddie Woods, Maintenance & Mechanical Technician.
Tel: 843-402-9115, Ext. 36
Felician Center, Inc. 908 Thorne Ave., Kingstree, SC, 29556.
Tel: 843-354-9415 ***Fax:*** 843-354-9093
Sr. Johnna Ciezobka, Pres.
Revisions
Archives
Melissa Bronheim, Asst. Archivist.
Tel: 843-724-8372
Email: mbronheim@catholic-doc.org
Charles Wujcik, Clerical Asst.
Tel: 843-724-8372
Email: cwujcik@catholic-doc.org
Office of Finance
Debby Cardenas, Financial Analyst.
Tel: 843-402-9115, Ext. 33
Email: dcardenas@catholic-doc.org
Office of Tribunal ***Mailing Address:*** P.O. Box 818, Charleston, SC, 29402.
Tel: 843-724-8363
Deacon J. Wescoat Sandlin, Esq., Procurator & Advocate.
Charles Wujcik, Ecclesiastical Notary, Sec. & Tribunal Archival Records Technician. Phone inquiries are accepted Mon.-Thurs. 10:30-11:30 am & 1:30-4 pm and Fri. 10:30-11:30 am & 1:30-3:30 pm. All petitions for a sanatio, declarations of invalidity, and other questions related to divorced persons should be sent to the Office of Tribunal. All other prenuptial matters, requests for dispensations and permissions should be sent to the: Office for Matrimonial Concerns and Dispensations, P.O. Box 818, Charleston, SC 29402. Tel: 843-853-2130, ext. 202.
Deans
Very Rev. Ronald R. Cellini, V.F., Lowcountry Deanery '79.
Tel: 843-681-6350 ***Fax:*** 843-689-5502
Email: office@stfrancishhi.org
Very Rev. C. Alexander McDonald, V.F., Midlands Deanery '91.
Tel: 803-788-0811 ***Fax:*** 803-788-1501

Email: frmcdonald@sc.twcbc.com
Very Rev. Karl J. Roesch, O.S.B., V.F., Pee Dee Deanery '60.
Tel: 843-332-7773 ***Fax:*** 843-332-2812
Family Life Services
Christy Brown, Post Abortion Ministry Coord.
Tel: 803-554-6088
Email: grace4healing@gmail.com
Vicar for African-American Catholics
Rev. Paul M. Williams, O.F.M. '86 1303 McLees Rd., Anderson, SC, 29621.
Tel: 864-225-5341
Vicar for Hispanic Ministry Please contact the Office of Ethnic Ministries.
Catholic Charities
Main Office
Caroline Weisberg, Dir.
Tel: 803-708-5146 ***Fax:*** 843-402-9071
Email: cweisberg@catholic-doc.org
Diocesan Master of Ceremonies
Rev. Bryan P. Babick, SL.L. '07.
Tel: 843-853-2130, Ext. 215
Email: frbabick@catholic-doc.org
Office of Child Protection Services
Debbie Tomak, Administrative Asst.
Tel: 843-853-2130, Ext. 206
Email: dtomak@catholic-doc.org
Vocations
Rev. Jeffrey Kirby, S.T.L., Vicar '07.
Email: frkirby@charlestonvocations.com
Deacon Joseph F. Cahill, Dir. (Chancery West).
Tel: 800-660-4102
Email: joe@catholic-doc.org
The Drexel House - Catholic Residence for Men 34 Wentworth St., Charleston, SC, 29401.
Tel: 843-727-6727 ***Fax:*** 843-723-5740
Deacon Jerome P. Remkiewicz, Admin.
Rhett Williams, Bilingual Administrative Asst.
Email: rhett@charlestonvocations.com
Cursillo Movement
Gabriel Timpano, Lay Dir. 256 Tall Pines Way, Unit 6-2B, Pawleys Island, SC, 29585.
Tel: 843-543-0138
Email: gtimpano@sc.rr.com
Web: www.southcarolinacursillo.org
Deacon Andre J.P. Guillet, Spiritual Advisor (Chancery West).
Cathedral of St. John the Baptist (1821)
Rev. Msgr. Steven L. Brovey, V.F., Rector '91.
Church: 950 Darrell Creek Tr., Mount Pleasant, SC, 29466.
Tel: 843-216-0039 ***Fax:*** 843-971-6789
Email: office@stbenedictparish.org
Web: www.stbenedictparish.org
Church of the Holy Spirit (1938) [CEM] 3871 Betsy Kerrison Pkwy., Johns Island, SC, 29455.
Tel: 843-768-0357 ***Fax:*** 843-768-0751
Email: hschrch@bellsouth.net
Web: www.holyspiritjohnsisland.com
St. John (1929)
Rev. Christopher Oranyelli, O.P.
St. Mary of the Annunciation (1789)
Rev. Msgr. Steven L. Brovey, V.F., Admin. '91.
St. Mary Help of Christians (1853), Aiken, SC
Rev. Gregory Wilson '01.
St. Joseph (1868) 1303 McLees Rd., Anderson, SC, 29621.
Tel: 864-225-5341 ***Fax:*** 864-225-6432
Rev. Paul M. Williams, O.F.M. '86.
St. Andrew (1831), Barnwell, SC
Rev. Artur Przywara, Parochial Vicar '10.
St. John of the Cross (1959)
Rev. Gustavo Corredor, Parochial Vicar.
St. Peter (1846)
Rev. Paul D. MacNeil, Admin. '89.
Deacon Edward Peitler.
St. Gregory the Great (1960), Bluffton, SC
Rev. David Nerbun, Parochial Vicar.
Transfiguration (1998), Blythewood, SC
Rev. Andrew Trapp, Admin. '07.
306 N. Pines Rd., Blythewood, SC, 29016.
St. Joseph (1948)
Rev. Matthew Gray, Parochial Vicar.
Saint Martin de Porres (1935)
Rev. Michael C. Okere, Nigeria, Admin. '91.
St. James (1945)
Rev. Timothy M. Lijewski '93.
St. Anthony (1872), Florence, SC
Rev. Richard Jackson, Parochial Vicar '10.
St. Michael (1975)
Rev. William Hearne, Parochial Vicar.
St. Mary Our Lady of Ransom (1899) [JC] (Our Lady of Ransom) ***Mailing Address:*** 317 Broad St., Georgetown, SC, 29440.
Tel: 843-546-7416 ***Fax:*** 843-546-7003
Email: smolor@sccctv.net
Web: www.stmaryourladyofransom.com

St. Anthony of Padua (1939)
Rev. David Q. Phan, Parochial Vicar.
St. Mary (1852), Greenville, SC
Rev. Ikechi Korie, O.P., Parochial Vicar.
St. Ann (1947) ***Mailing Address:*** P.O. Box 529, Kingstree, SC, 29556. 107 Hirsch St., Kingstree, SC, 29556.
Tel: 843-536-0440 ***Fax:*** 843-353-1354
Email: stannkingstree@gmail.com
St. Andrew (1946)
Rev. James L. LeBlanc '96.
Rev. Casmir Maduakor, Parochial Vicar.
Our Lady of Peace (1948)
Rev. Jacob Joseph, C.M.I. '83.
Our Lady Star of the Sea (1964)
Rev. Jose Orlando Cheverria Jimenez, Colombia, Spanish Ministry '97.
***Mission—* Catholic Church of the Resurrection** 204 Heritage Rd., Loris, Horry Co., SC, 29569.
Tel: 843-756-6168 ***Fax:*** 843-756-4197
Holy Trinity (1917)
Rev. James N. Dubrouillet '97.
Rev. Artur Przywara, Parochial Vicar '10.
St. Anthony (1963), Ridgeland, SC
Rev. Robert F. Higgins '05.
10128 S. Jacob Smart Blvd., Ridgeland, SC, 29936.
Tel: 843-726-3606 ***Fax:*** 843-726-3606
St. Mary (1946), Rock Hill, SC
Rev. Agustin Guzman, C.O., Admin.
St. Paul the Apostle (1883)
Rev. Frank Palmieri, C.R.M. '62.
Catholic Community of Sumter (1939)
Rev. Peter E. Sousa, C.Ss.R., Parochial Vicar.
Prince of Peace (1975), Taylors, SC
Rev. Richard Tomlinson, Parochial Vicar '09.
St. Theresa, Winnsboro, SC
Rev. Andrew Trapp '07.
Divine Saviour (1938), York, SC
Rev. William F. Pentis, C.O., Canonical Pastor '66.
***High School—* *St. Francis Xavier High School** (1997) 15 School St., Sumter, SC, 29150.
Tel: 803-773-0210 ***Fax:*** 803-775-0119
Email: sfxhs@sc.rr.com
Web: www.sfxhs.com
Lay Teachers 8; Students 42
**Family Honor, Inc.* (1987) 2927 Devine St., Ste. 130, Columbia, SC, 29205.
Tel: 803-929-0858 ***Fax:*** 803-771-2379
Email: famhonor@aol.com
Web: www.familyhonor.org
Healthy Learners 2749 Laurel St., Columbia, SC, 29204.
Tel: 216-696-5560 ***Fax:*** 216-696-2204
Web: www.CSAHealthSystems.org
St. Elizabeth Ann Seton High School Association 3501 N. Kings Hwy., Ste. 102, Myrtle Beach, SC, 29577.
Rev. James L. LeBlanc, Pres. '96.

Archdiocese of Chicago

New Listings
Most Reverend Andrew P. Wypych, Auxiliary Bishop of Chicago; ordained April 29, 1979; appointed Auxiliary Bishop of Chicago and Titular Bishop of Naraggara June 13, 2011; Episcopal ordination August 10, 2011.
Mailing Address: P.O. Box 1979, Chicago, IL, 60690.
Most Reverend Alberto Rojas, Auxiliary Bishop of Chicago; ordained May 24, 1997; appointed Auxiliary Bishop of Chicago and Titular Bishop of Marazanae June 13, 2011; Episcopal ordination August 10, 2011.
Mailing Address: P.O. Box 1979, Chicago, IL, 60690.
Mercy Circle 10024 S. Central Park Ave., Chicago, IL, 60655.
Tel: 219-227-6075
Web: www.mercycircle.org
Lori McLaughlin, Contact Person.
Dominican Association of Secondary Schools, Inc. 700 S. Ashland Ave., Chicago Heights, IL, 60411.
Tel: 708-755-7565 ***Fax:*** 708-756-9759
Web: www.dominicanschools.org
Sr. Kathleen Anne Tait, O.P., Contact Person.
School and Tutors on Wheels 1515 W. Ogden Ave., La Grange Park, IL, 60526.
Tel: 708-354-9200 ***Fax:*** 708-482-5036
Web: www.schoolonwheels.com

Newly Ordained
St. Barnabas
Rev. John G. Hetland '11.
St. Cajetan
Rev. Phillip T. Owen '11.
St. Mary of Celle
Rev. Orlando Flores '11.
St. Athanasius
Rev. Heman Cuevas '11.
St. Catherine Laboure
Rev. Lorenzo Gamboa Cadena '11.

Our Lady of Perpetual Help
Rev. Elliott Richard Dees '11.
St. Thomas of Villanova
Rev. Wojciech Jan Oleksy '11.
St. John of the Cross (1960)
Rev. Filbert Ngwila '11.
St. Joseph
Rev. Gosbertus Rwezahura '11.
Sacred Heart
Rev. Collins Kisaka Nyache '11.

Revisions
St. Jane de Chantal
Rev. Edward J. Cronin, Admin. '80.
Ignatian Spirituality Project 1641 S. Allport, Chicago, IL, 60608.
Tel: 312-226-9184
Email: info@ispretreats.org
Web: www.ispretreats.org
The project works with the homeless through retreats and spiritual companionship in the belief that by claiming their spiritual life they can recover from addiction and other problems associated with homelessness

Archdiocese of Cincinnati

New Listings
Hispanic Catholic Ministry, Cincinnati
Rev. Jorge Ochoa, M.C.C.J., Chap. & Moderator 115 W. Seymour Ave., Cincinnati, OH, 45216.
Tel: 513-948-1760
De Paul Cristo Rey Work Study Program Corporation 1133 Clifton Hills Ave., Cincinnati, OH, 45220.
Tel: 513-347-5201 ***Fax:*** 513-347-5228
Web: www.depaulcristorey.org
Sr. Jeanne Bessette, O.S.F., Pres.
St. Francis Seraph Ministries 1615 Vine St., Cincinnati, OH, 45202.
Tel: 513-533-2719
Web: www.sfsministry.org
Mr. Cliff Cavanaugh, Contact Person.

Newly Ordained
Immaculate Heart of Mary (Forestville) (1944)
Rev. Adam D. Puntel, Parochial Vicar '11.
Incarnation (1945)
Rev. C. Scott Wright, Parochial Vicar '11.
Holy Angels (1848)
Rev. Daniel K. Hess, Parochial Vicar '11.
***High School—* Lehman Catholic High School** (1970), Sidney, OH
Rev. Daniel K. Hess '11.

Revisions
Chancellor
Rev. Steven J. Angi, J.C.L. '85.
Office of Religious
Sr. Marilyn Kerber, S.N.D.deN., Dir.
Victim Assistance Coordinator
Sandy Keiser, L.I.S.W.
Tel: 513-263-6623
Email: skeiser@catholiccharitiesswo.org
Priests' Personnel Director
Most Rev. Joseph R. Binzer, Dir.
Archdiocesan Office of Hispanic Ministry
Rev. Louis Gasparini, M.C.C.J., Dir. '66 100 E. Eighth St., Cincinnati, OH, 45202.
Tel: 513-421-3131

Diocese of Columbus

New Listings
***High School—* Cristo Rey Columbus High School** 840 W. State St., Columbus, OH, 43222-1422.
Tel: 614-205-3958
Web: cristoreycolumbus.org
Barbara A. Brown, Dir.
Trinity Hospital Twin City Denison 819 N. First St., Dennison, OH, 44621.
Tel: 419-882-8373 ***Fax:*** 419-882-7360
James W. Pope, FACHE, Pres.
Cristo Rey Columbus High School Work Study Program 840 W. State St., Columbus, OH, 43222-1422.
Tel: 614-205-3958
Web: cristoreycolumbus.org
Barbara A. Brown, Dir.

Newly Ordained
St. Andrew (1955)
Rev. Tyron Tomson, Parochial Vicar '11.
St. Matthew (1959)
Rev. Ryan Schmit, Parochial Vicar '11.

Revisions

Christ the King (1946)
Rev. David A. Schalk '08.
Corpus Christi (1925), Columbus, OH
Rev. Donald E. Franks '79.
St. Ladislas (1908), Columbus, OH
Rev. Donald E. Franks '79.
St. Mary Church (1865)
Rev. Donald E. Franks '79.
St. Joseph (1840)
Rev. Theodore F. Machnik '91.
Our Lady of Perpetual Help (1954)
Rev. Daniel J. Millisor, M.Div. '86.
St. Mary (1818)
Rev. Craig R. Eilerman '87.
St. Peter (1877)
Rev. Stephen L. Krile '83.
St. Mary (1841)
Rev. Adam A. Streitenberger '07.
Church of the Holy Trinity (1995), Bolivar, OH
Rev. Ronald J. Aubry '81.
Hospital Ministry
Rev. Jose Souru Manickathan, C.F.I.C. '06.
Rev. Ramon Macoy Cruz, C.F.I.C. '98.
Retired
Rev. Edward Keck '73.
Rev. John L. Swickard '74.
-Congregation of the Sons of the Immaculate Conception

Diocese of Crookston

New Listings

Cathedral Campus Ministry 702 Summit Ave., Crookston, MN, 56716.
Tel: 218-281-1735
Mark Hollcraft, Campus Min.

Revisions

Finance Officer
Mr. Dan James.
Tel: 218-281-4533
Email: djames@crookston.org
Deans
Rev. William DeCrans, Northwest '08.
Pastoral Office of Administration
Mr. Dan James 1200 Memorial Dr., P.O. Box 610, Crookston, MN, 56716-0610.
Tel: 218-281-4533
Priests' Council
Rev. Msgr. Roger L. Grundhaus, J.C.L. '66.
Rev. Raul Perez-Cobo '06.
Rev. Emmanuel Sylvester '88.
Rev. Gary LaMoine, Chm. '81.
Priests' Personnel Board
Rev. Chuck Huck '06.
Very Rev. Larry Delaney '90.
Vocations
Rev. Xavier Ilango, Assoc. Dir. '88 ***Mailing Address:*** P.O. Box 610, Crookston, MN, 56716.
Tel: 218-281-4533
Safe Environment Director
James Clauson ***Mailing Address:*** P.O. Box 610, Crookston, MN, 56716.
Tel: 218-281-4533
Email: jclauson@crookston.org
St. Philip's
Rev. Donald Braukmann '86.
Rev. Craig J. Vasek '10.
Sacred Heart
Rev. Carlos Velez '00.
St. Mary Unassigned. Served by Sts. Peter & Paul, Warren. Tel: 218-281-5422. ***Mailing Address:*** P.O. Box 213, Euclid, MN, 56722.
St. Joseph, Fertile, MN
Very Rev. Msgr. David Baumgartner, V.G., J.C.L., Admin. '90.
St. Michael's Parish
Rev. Antony Fernando '85.
St. Lawrence (1920)
Very Rev. Msgr. David Baumgartner, V.G., J.C.L., Admin. '90.
St. Bernards (1896)
Rev. John Suvakeen.
St. Mary's
Rev. August Gothman '93.
Retired
Rev. Frank Kulhawik '40 516 Walsh St., Crookston, MN, 56716.
Tel: 218-784-2247
Permanent Deacons
Deacon Dennis Bivens Cathedral of the Immaculate Conception, Crookston; St. Peter's, Gentilly.
Deacon John A. Bruggeman St. Joseph's, Red Lake Falls.
Holy Spirit Newman Center, Bemidji, MN
Rev. Donald Braukmann '86.

Archdiocese of Denver

Statistics Revision

CCD High School Students 7,283
CCD Elementary School Students 23,478
Infant Baptism Total 9,701
Minor Baptism Total 484
Adult Baptism Total 380
Received into Full Communion Total 1,128
First Communions 8,934
Confirmations 6,225
Catholic Marriages 1,177
Catholic Interfaith Marriages 280
Total Marriages 1,457
Deaths 2,618
Total Catholic Population 549,325
Total Population 3,362,614

Revisions

Vacant, See.
Mercy Holly Park East 1999 Broadway, Ste. 1000, Denver, CO, 80202.
Tel: 303-830-3300 ***Fax:*** 303-830-3301 Affordable housing for singles and families.
Units 72; Residents 145; Total Staff 3; Total Assisted Annually 200

Diocese of Des Moines

New Listings

Corpus Christi
Rev. Daniel J. Kirby '94.
Rev. Kenneth Halbur, Parochial Vicar '09.
Rev. Thomas Coenen, Parochial Vicar '77.
Rev. George Komo, Parochial Vicar '09.
Deacon Darwin Kruse.
Deacon Monty Montagne.
Deacon Jean Plourde.
Res.: 3304 4th Ave., Council Bluffs, IA, 51501.
Tel: 712-323-2916 ***Fax:*** 712-323-4716
Email: queen3304@juno.com
Web: www.gapostles.org/
Worship Sites
Our Lady, Queen of Apostles 3304 4h Ave., Council Bluffs, IA, 51501.
Holy Family 2217 Ave. B, Council Bluffs, IA, 51501.
Our Lady of Carter Lake 3501 N. 9th St., Carter Lake, IA, 51510.

Newly Ordained

St. Anthony's (1905)
Rev. Guthrie Dolan, Parochial Vicar '11.

Revisions

St. Anthony's (1905)
Rev. Juan Antonio Hernandez Lozano, Hispanic Chap.
St. Augustin's (1920)
Rev. Zachary Kautzky, Parochial Vicar '10.
Rev. James Livingston, Senior Assoc.
Basilica of Saint John (1905)
Rev. Juan Antonio Hernandez Lozano, Hispanic Chap.
Christ the King (1939)
Rev. Juan Antonio Hernandez Lozano, Hispanic Chap.
St. John (1917), Adel, IA
Rev. Wayne Gubbels '71.
St. Patrick (1918)
Rev. Emmanuel S. Agwuoke, C.S.Sp., Admin.
Our Lady of Carter Lake (1970) Merged with Our Lady Queen of the Apostles, Council Bluffs and Holy Family, Council Bluffs to form Corpus Christi, Council Bluffs.
St. Patrick's (1869)
Rev. Lazarus Kirigia, Admin.
Holy Family (1908) Merged with Our Lady, Queen of Apostles, Council Bluffs and Our Lady of Carter Lake, Carter Lake to form Corpus Christi, Council Bluffs.
Our Lady, Queen of Apostles (1957) Merged with Holy Family, Council Bluffs and Our Lady of Carter Lake, Carter Lake to form Corpus Christi, Council Bluffs.
St. Patrick
Rev. Felix A. Onuora, C.S.Sp. '79.
Holy Trinity, Audubon, IA
Rev. Emmanuel S. Agwuoke, C.S.Sp., Admin.
Our Lady of the Holy Rosary (1955)
Rev. Howard E. Fitzgerald '78.
St. John (1907)
Rev. Kenneth A. Gross '71.
St. Patrick (1880)
Rev. Thomas Kunnel, T.O.R.
Holy Trinity Church of Southeast Warren County (1978)
Rev. Dean Nimerichter '92.
St. Patrick (1872)
Rev. Lazarus Kirigia, Admin.
St. Patrick (1888)
Rev. Kenneth A. Gross '71.
Holy Family (1970), Dunlap, IA
Rev. Felix A. Onuora, C.S.Sp. '79.
St. Mary (1902)
Rev. Thomas Kunnel, T.O.R.
St. Francis of Assisi (1991), West Des Moines, IA
Rev. George Komo, Parochial Vicar '09.
Sacred Heart (1892), West Des Moines, IA
Rev. Paul Cuong Hung Nguyen, S.V.D., Parochial Vicar.
Sacred Heart (1902), Dunlap, IA
Rev. Felix A. Onuora, C.S.Sp. '79.
Des Moines City Chaplaincy Program, Dexter, IA
Rev. Michael R. McLaughlin '82.
On Special Assignment
Rev. Michael Hutchins, S.V.D. Divine Word Farm, Weldon, IA.
Retired
Rev. Robert J. Aubrey '71.
Rev. Donald Bruck '68.
Rev. Albert Sherbo '87.
***High School*— Saint Albert Catholic Schools**, Council Bluffs, IA
Rev. Kenneth Halbur, Chap. '09.
City Hospital Chaplaincy Service, Des Moines, IA
Rev. Michael R. McLaughlin '82.

Diocese of Dodge City

New Listings

Office of Priestly Vocations
Rev. Wesley W. Schawe, Dir. '04.
Tel: 620-227-1533 ***Fax:*** 620-227-1545
Email: wschawe@dcdiocese.org
vocations@dcdiocese.org

Revisions

Catholic Church Offices: 910 Central Ave., P.O. Box 137, Dodge City, KS, 67801-0137.
Tel: 620-227-1500 ***Fax:*** 620-227-1545
Web: www.dcdiocese.org
Email: dcdiocese@dcdiocese.org
St. Bernard Catholic Church of Belpre, Kansas (1901)
Rev. Warren L. Stecklein '90.
St. Theresa Catholic Church of Dighton, Kansas (1927)
Rev. Bernard H. Felix '92.
St. Joan of Arc Catholic Church of Elkhart, Kansas (1921)
Rev. Francis Khoi Nguyen '90.
St. Anthony Catholic Church of Fowler, Kansas (1910)
Rev. Louis Trung Dinh Hoang, Parochial Admin. '95.
St. Dominic Catholic Church of Garden City, Kansas (1965)
Rev. Rene Labrador '91.
Rev. Peter Fernandez Jr., Parochial Vicar '95.
St. Mary Catholic Church of Garden City, Kansas (1898)
Rev. Charles F. Seiwert, J.C.L. (WCH) '99.
Prince of Peace Catholic Church of Great Bend, Kansas (2006), Great Bend, KS
Rev. Donald E. Bedore, Parochial Vicar.
St. John the Evangelist Catholic Church of Hoisington, Kansas (1892)
Rev. Francis Oroffa, M.S.P., Parochial Admin.
St. Helen Catholic Church of Hugoton, Kansas (1948)
Rev. Francis Khoi Nguyen '90.
St. Stanislaus Catholic Church of Ingalls, Kansas (1909), Ingalls, KS
Rev. Rene Labrador '91.
Rev. Peter Fernandez Jr., Parochial Vicar '95.
St. Michael Catholic Church of LaCrosse, Kansas (1911)
Rev. Pascal L. Klein '87.
Sacred Heart of Jesus Catholic Church of Larned, Kansas (1912)
Rev. Warren L. Stecklein '90.
St. Joseph Catholic Church of Liebenthal, Kansas (1876), Liebenthal, KS
Rev. Pascal L. Klein '87.
St. John the Baptist Catholic Church of Meade, Kansas (1889)
Rev. Louis Trung Dinh Hoang, Parochial Admin. '95.
St. Patrick Catholic Church of Plains, Kansas (1916), Plains, KS
Rev. Louis Trung Dinh Hoang, Parochial Admin. '95.
St. John the Apostle Catholic Church of St. John, Kansas (1949)
Rev. Floyd E. McKinney (WCH), Priest Supvr. '80.
St. Joseph Catholic Church of Scott City, Kansas (1911), Scott City, KS
Rev. Bernard H. Felix '92.
Holy Trinity Catholic Church of Timken, Kansas (1904), LaCrosse, KS
Rev. Pascal L. Klein '87.

Archdiocese of Dubuque

New Listings

Holy Spirit 2215 Windsor Ave., Dubuque, IA, 52001.
Very Rev. Dwayne J. Thoman '76.
Rev. Steven M. Garner '09.
Deacon Dave Brinkmoeller.
Deacon Stephen MacDonald.
Deacon James J. Thill.
Deacon John Stierman.

Blessed John XXIII 8100 Roncalli Dr., S.W., Cedar Rapids, IA, 52404.
Tel: 319-846-3139 ***Fax:*** 319-846-3159
Rev. Dustin L. Vu '04.
Ann Petrzelka, Pastoral Assoc.

Newly Ordained

Basilica of St. Francis Xavier (1859)
Rev. Noah J. Diehm '11.
St. Joseph (1887), Earlville, IA
Rev. Noah J. Diehm '11.
St. Joseph (1890)
Rev. Anthony J. Kruse '11.
St. Boniface (1845)
Rev. Noah J. Diehm '11.
SS. Peter and Paul (1867)
Rev. Noah J. Diehm '11.
St. Paul (1875)
Rev. Noah J. Diehm '11.

Revisions

Adult Faith
Vacant, Dir.
Archives
Vacant, Dir.
Lay Formation
Vacant, Dir.
Seminarians
Rev. G. Robert Gross, Asst. Dir. '07.
Barb Gleason, Sec. 1229 Mt. Loretta Ave., Dubuque, IA, 52003-7826.
Tel: 563-556-2580
Vocation Awareness
Associate Directors
Barb Gleason, Sec. Archdiocesan Center 1229 Mt. Loretta Ave., Dubuque, IA, 52003-7826.
Tel: 563-556-2580
Church of the Nativity (1923)
Rev. Scott E. Bullock, J.C.L. '91.
Rev. G. Robert Gross '07.
Church of the Resurrection (1857)
Rev. Gary A. Mayer '09.
Holy Ghost (1896) [JC] Merged with Holy Trinity and Sacred Heart, Dubuque to form Holy Spirit, Dubuque.
Holy Trinity (1910) [JC] Merged with Holy Ghost and Sacred Heart, Dubuque to form Holy Spirit, Dubuque.
Sacred Heart (1879) [JC] Merged with Holy Ghost and Holy Trinity, Dubuque to form Holy Spirit, Dubuque.
St. Thomas Aquinas Church (and Catholic Student Center) (1947)
Rev. James W. Dubert '98.
St. John (1914) [CEM] Closed. For sacramental records, please contact Sacred Heart parish, Maquoketa.
St. Patrick (1880)
Rev. Paul E. Lippstock, Sacramental Priest '78.
St. Patrick (1899)
Rev. Paul E. Lippstock, Sacramental Priest '78.
John XXIII (2000) [JC] Merged with John XXII, Cedar Rapids and St. Patrick, Fairfax to form Blessed John XXIII, Cedar Rapids.
St. Ludmila (1922)
Rev. Dennis D. Juhl '73.
St. Patrick (1870)
Rev. Rodney M. Allers '08.
St. Wenceslaus (1900), Garner, IA
Rev. Paul E. Lippstock, Sacramental Priest '78.
St. Patrick (1875) [CEM] Merged with John XXIII, Cedar Rapids to form Blessed John XXIII, Cedar Rapids.
St. James (1870)
Rev. Paul E. Lippstock, Sacramental Priest '78.
St. Boniface (1883)
Rev. Paul E. Lippstock, Sacramental Priest '78.
St. Boniface (1884) Closed. For sacramental records, please contact St. Patrick parish, Tama.
SS. Peter and Paul (1882), Gilbert, IA
Rev. James W. Dubert '98.
St. Ann-St. Joseph (1855)
Rev. John A. Moser '86.
St. Patrick (1870), Forest City, IA
Rev. Paul E. Lippstock, Sacramental Priest '78.
Immaculate Conception (1855)
Rev. John A. Moser '86.
Sacred Heart (1873)
Rev. Donald A. Hertges '07.
St. Joseph (1910)
Rev. John A. Moser '86.
Holy Family (1850)
Rev. Michael J. Podhajsky '03.
Sacred Heart (1878)
Rev. Jack H. McClure, C.PP.S. '76.
St. Lawrence (1854)
Rev. Donald A. Hertges '07.
St. Joseph (1881)
Rev. Donald A. Hertges '07.
Holy Name (1910)
Rev. Rodney M. Allers '08.
Sacred Heart (1878)
Rev. Rodney M. Allers '08.
St. Peter (1840) [CEM] Closed. For sacramental records, please contact St. Joseph parish, Preston.
SS. Peter and Paul (1864), Springbrook, IA
Very Rev. Phillip F. Kruse '81.
Church of the Visitation (1894), Osage, IA
Rev. Jack H. McClure, C.PP.S. '76.
Blessed Sacrament (1947)
Rev. Thomas J. McDermott '97.
Immaculate Conception (1851)
Rev. John A. Moser '86.
On Special or Other Archdiocesan Assignment
Rev. Thomas R. Zinkula, J.D., J.C.L. '90 Sabbatical, Rome.
Military Chaplains
Rev. Paul E. Lippstock '78 Iowa Army National Guard.
Retired
Rev. Msgr. Martin T. Laughlin '52 St. Francis by the Sea 45 Beach City Rd., Hilton Head, SC, 29926
Rev. James T. Chappell '67 1910 Madison St., Dubuque, IA, 52001.
Tel: 563-590-0280
Rev. Harold J. Drexler '55 Villa Raphael 1155 Mt. Loretta Ave., Dubuque, IA, 52003.
Tel: 563-556-7197
Rev. Patrick G. Geary '56 2817 Roxboro Dr., Ames, IA, 50014.
Tel: 515-451-2732
Rev. Daniel J. Knipper '67 502 Valley Dr., #24, Decorah, IA, 52101.
Tel: 563-568-7913
Rev. Mark J. McGovern '67 325 1st Ave. W., #8, Walford, IA, 52351.
Tel: 563-543-5178
Rev. David P. Remy '67 CDR, CHC, USN, 3101 Marcus Pointe Blvd., Pensacola, FL, 32505.
Tel: 850-473-9426
Rev. Louis J. Trzil '50 Thornton Manor Nursing Center 1329 Main St., P.O. Box 700, Lansing, IA, 52151
Seminary of St. Pius X, Dubuque, IA
Rev. G. Robert Gross, Vice Rector '07.
School— **Newman Catholic School System** Grades Day Care-12 Parishes served: Holy Family, St. Joseph, Mason City.
Sisters 1; Lay Teachers 43; K-12 Students 622

Diocese of El Paso

Revisions

Vicars General
Rev. Anthony C. Celino, J.C.L., V.G. '97.
Moderator of the Curia
Rev. Anthony C. Celino, J.C.L., V.G. '97.
Chancellor
Rev. Anthony C. Celino, J.C.L., V.G. '97.
Missions Office/Propagation of the Faith/Catholic Relief Services
Rev. Anthony C. Celino, J.C.L., V.G. '97 499 St. Matthews St., El Paso, TX, 79907.
Tel: 915-872-8407

Diocese of Erie

Newly Ordained

Our Lady of Peace (1955)
Rev. Jason R. Feigh, Parochial Vicar.

Diocese of Fargo

Revisions

Catholic Education and Formation
Rev. Andrew Jasinski, Dir. '98.
St. Mary's Cathedral of Fargo (1880)
Rev. Anthony Hession '99.
Sts. Anne & Joachim Church of Fargo (1995), Fargo, ND
Rev. Peter Sharpe '09.
Deacon Michael Dodge.
St. Anthony of Padua's Church of Fargo (1917)
Rev. Msgr. Gregory J. Schlesselmann '93.
Holy Spirit Church of Fargo (1951)
Rev. Jimmy Lim Tiu '00.
St. Ann (1885)
Rev. Paul Hu, S.O.L.T.
Rev. David Mumba, S.O.L.T.
St. Joseph's Church of Devils Lake (1884), Devils Lake, ND
Rev. Jason Asselin '06.
Assumption of Mary (1909), Lamoure, ND
Rev. Jerome Okafor '83.
St. Michael the Archangel Dunseith (2007), Dunseith, ND
Rev. Scott Brossart, S.O.L.T., Admin. '00.
St. Augustine's Church of Fessenden (1896), Fessenden, ND
Rev. Thomas J. Krupich '88.
St. Mary (1913), Forman, ND
Rev. William Peter Gerlach, Admin. '04.
St. Michael's Church of Grand Forks (1872), Grand Forks, ND
Rev. Neil Pfeifer.
St. Patrick's Church of Hurdsfield (1907), Fessenden, ND
Rev. Thomas J. Krupich '88.
Holy Rosary Church of La Moure (1890), La Moure, ND
Rev. Jerome Okafor '83.
Holy Family (1905), Fessenden, ND
Rev. Thomas J. Krupich '88.
Sts. Nereus & Achilleus Church of Neche (1887), Walhalla, ND
Rev. Jude Okafor, Admin. '96.
St. Charles Church of Oakes (1905), Oakes, ND
Rev. William Peter Gerlach, Admin. '04.
St. Raphael's Church of Verona (1898), Lamoure, ND
Rev. Jerome Okafor '83.
St. Boniface Church of Walhalla (1848), Walhalla, ND
Rev. Jude Okafor, Admin. '96.
Holy Cross Church of West Fargo (1981), West Fargo, ND
Rev. Andrew Jasinski '98.
Special Assignment
Rev. Joseph Christensen '97 Franciscans of Mary Immaculate.
Retired
Rev. Msgr. Robert Laliberte, Ph.D. '73.
Rev. William V. Callery '01.
Rev. John Arthur McGinnis '04.

Diocese of Fort Wayne - South Bend

New Listings

Congregation of Holy Cross, United States Province, Inc. 54515 State Rd. 933 N., P.O. Box 774, Notre Dame, IN, 46556.
Tel: 574-631-9584 ***Fax:*** 574-631-3444
Rev. David T. Tyson, C.S.C., Pres. '75.

Revisions

Blessed Pope John Paul II Center 1328 W. Dragoon Tr., Mishawaka, IN, 46544.
Tel: 574-234-0687
Judicial Vicar
Rev. Mark A. Gurtner, J.C.L. '96.
Presbyteral Council
Rev. Wilson Corzo '98.
Our Lady of Good Hope (1969)
Rev. Mark A. Gurtner, J.C.L. '96.
St. Therese (1947)
Rev. Lawrence Teteh, C.S.Sp., Nigeria '71.
St. Vincent de Paul (1846)
Rev. Polycarp Fernando, Parochial Vicar '78.
St. Anthony de Padua (1949)
Rev. David Ruppert '05.
Holy Family (1945)
Rev. Charles A. Herman '97.
Rev. Vincent Joseph, V.C., Parochial Vicar.
St. John the Baptist (1956)
Rev. Vincent Joseph, V.C., Parochial Vicar.
Our Lady of Hungary (1921)
Rev. Kevin M. Bauman '08.
St. Therese, Little Flower (1937), South Bend, IN
Rev. Jeffery A. Largent '84.
Blessed Sacrament (1875)
Rev. John Klimczyk '81.
St. Dominic (1947), Bremen, IN
Rev. Bob J. Lengerich '07.
St. Monica (1915)
Rev. Msgr. Bruce Piechocki, J.C.L. '84.
St. Rose of Lima (1868)
Rev. Lourdino Fernandes '69.

Diocese of Fresno

New Listings

Diocesan Administrator
Rev. Msgr. Myron J. Cotta, V.G. '87 appointed Dec. 7,

2010.

Revisions

Chancellor

Vacant.

Diocese of Gallup

Revisions

Life Sharing Center, Inc., St. Jude Food Bank 100 Aspen Dr., Tuba City, AZ, 86045.

Tel: 928-283-6886 ***Fax:*** 928-283-6614

Email: stjudefoodbank@frontiernet.net

-Benedictine Sisters O.S.B.

Archdiocese of Galveston-Houston

New Listings

Vietnamese Dominican Vicariate of St. Vincent Liem 12314 Old Foltin Rd., Houston, TX, 77086.

Tel: 281-999-4928 ***Fax:*** 281-820-7095

Very Rev. Liem Trung Tran, O.P., Reg. Supr.

Diocese of Gary

Revisions

Vicar General

Rev. Joseph M. Pawlowski '73.

Charities 940 Broadway, Gary, IN, 46402.

Tel: 219-886-3549 ***Fax:*** 219-886-2428

Deacon Duane W. Dedelow, Exec. Dir.

Communications Office

Debbie Bosak, Dir. 9292 Broadway, Merrillville, IN, 46410.

Tel: 219-769-9292, Ext. 286

Diaconate

Deacon Phillip L. Muvich, Dir. Diaconate Formation 508 Timber Point Dr., Valparaiso, IN, 46385.

Tel: 219-364-8338

Hispanic Diocesan Ministries

Adeline Torres 3814 Grand Blvd., East Chicago, IN, 46312.

Tel: 219-397-2125 ***Fax:*** 219-397-2168

Legal Counsel

Robert M. Schwerd 1158 Lincolnway, Ste. 2, Valparaiso, IN, 46385.

Tel: 219-841-5683

St. Patrick

In Res.

Rev. David G. Nowak '85.

St. Michael (1874)

Rev. Ted J. Mauch '10.

Permanent Deacons

Deacon Edwin J. Bodley.
Deacon Duane W. Dedelow.
Deacon Michael J. Green.
Deacon David J. Kapala.
Deacon Jim F. Knopf.
Deacon Thomas R. Kubik.
Deacon Robert W. Marben.
Deacon Jeffery L. Newburn.
Deacon Ronald L. Pyle.
Deacon William P. Sayre.

Calumet College of St. Joseph, Whiting, IN

Dr. Daniel Lowery, Pres.

Office of Hispanic Ministry (1983) 3814 Grand Blvd., East Chicago, IN, 46312.

Tel: 219-397-2125 ***Fax:*** 219-397-2168

Email: atorres@dcgary.org

Web: www.dcgary.org

Total Staff 3

Diocese of Grand Rapids

New Listings

School— **San Juan Diego Academy** 1650 Godfrey Ave., S.W., Wyoming, MI, 49509.

Newly Ordained

St. John Vianney

Rev. Luis F. Garcia, Parochial Vicar '11.

Revisions

St. Alphonsus (1888)

Rev. Patrick Grile, C.Ss.R.
Rev. Lamar Partin, C.Ss.R.

St. Alphonsus

In Res.

Rev. Thomas Danielsen, C.Ss.R.

St. James (1870)

Rev. R. Louis Stasker '65.

St. Joseph's (1894)

Rev. Philip A. Shangraw '79.

Holy Family (1970)

Rev. Dung Anton Tran '02.

St. Francis Xavier (1892)

Rev. G. Fredrick Brucker '76.

St. Mary's (1879)

Rev. Mark E. Peacock, Admin. '07.

St. Mary's (1871)

Rev. Philip A. Shangraw '79.

Our Lady of Grace (1923)

Rev. Antony Britto, S.A.C., Admin. '88.

St. Thomas the Apostle (1948)

Rev. Antony Britto, S.A.C., Admin. '88.

St. Catherine (1908)

Rev. G. Fredrick Brucker '76.

St. Joseph's (1853)

Rev. G. Fredrick Brucker '76.

On Special Assignment

Rev. Denis J. Ryan, C.Ss.R. '06 Reassigned outside of the diocese.
Rev. Andrew J. Thompson, C.Ss.R. '81 Reassigned outside the diocese.

Unassigned

Rev. Rock J. Badgerow '79.

Retired

Rev. Michael P. Olson '94.

Diocese of Great Falls - Billings

Revisions

Education

Patrick Haggarty, Ed.D., Supt. Catholic Schools ***Mailing Address:*** P.O. Box 1399, Great Falls, MT, 59403-1399.

Tel: 406-727-6683; 800-332-9998 ***Fax:*** 406-454-3480

Email: superintendent@dioceseofgfb.org

Holy Rosary (1951), Billings, MT

Rev. Stephen Zabrocki, Canonical Pastor '89.
Rev. Barton K. Stevens, Parochial Vicar.

Little Flower (1931), Billings, MT

Rev. Stephen Zabrocki, Canonical Pastor '89.
Rev. Barton K. Stevens, Parochial Vicar.

Our Lady of Guadalupe (1953), Billings, MT

Rev. Stephen Zabrocki, Canonical Pastor '89.
Rev. Barton K. Stevens, Parochial Vicar.

St. Mark the Evangelist

Rev. Wm. Paul McKane, O.S.B., Parochial Admin. '88.

St. Rose of Lima (1908), Stanford, MT

Rev. Ted F. Szudera '77.

Retired

Rev. Charles Gorman '54 2351 Solomon Ave., Apt. 157, Billings, MT, 59102
Rev. Terrence P. Regan '68 2805 3rd Ave. N., Great Falls, MT, 59401

Diocese of Green Bay

Newly Ordained

St. John

Rev. William J. Brunner, Parochial Vicar '11.

SS. Mary & Hyacinth

Rev. William J. Brunner, Parochial Vicar '11.

St. Wenceslaus, Deerbrook, WI

Rev. William J. Brunner, Parochial Vicar '11.

St. Mary

Rev. Luke A. Ferris, Sacramental Min. '11.

St. Raphael the Archangel

Rev. Luke A. Ferris, Parochial Vicar '11.

St. Mary (1884)

Rev. Luke A. Ferris, Sacramental Min. '11.

Revisions

Vicars General

Rev. Daniel J. Felton '81.

General Director of the Diocesan Curia

Deacon Timothy G. Reilly.

Tel: 920-272-8171

Annunciation of the Blessed Virgin Mary, Green Bay, WI

Rev. Callistus I. Elue, Parochial Vicar.

St. Joseph

Rev. Callistus I. Elue, Parochial Vicar.

St. Jude

Rev. Callistus I. Elue, Parochial Vicar.

St. Mary of the Angels

Rev. Patrick M. Gawrylewski, O.F.M. '76.

St. Matthew

Rev. Philip Dinh-Van-Thiep '83.

Nativity of Our Lord

Rev. John H. Harper '87.

St. Patrick, Green Bay, WI

Rev. Callistus I. Elue, Parochial Vicar.

St. Willebrord

Rev. Andrew G. Cribben, O.Praem. '94.

St. John

Rev. David R. Schmidt '81.

SS. Mary & Hyacinth

Rev. David R. Schmidt '81.

St. Bernadette

Rev. Anthony Ibekwe, Parochial Vicar.

Sacred Heart

Very Rev. Donald M. Zuleger '76.
Rev. Anthony Ibekwe, Parochial Vicar.

St. Stanislaus Kostka, Armstrong Creek, WI

Rev. Matthew W. Settle, Priest Mod. '04.

Holy Family

Rev. Timothy Brandt, Admin. '09.

St. Mary [CEM] Also serves Station at Caldron Falls.

Mailing Address: P.O. Box 159, Crivitz, WI, 54114-0159.

Tel: 715-854-2501

Email: stmarycrivitz@centurytel.net

Web: www.stmarycrivitz.net

St. Francis Xavier

Rev. Richard Getchel, J.C.L. '76.

St. Mary, De Pere, WI

Rev. Richard Getchel, J.C.L. '76.

Holy Family, Elcho, WI

Rev. David R. Schmidt, Priest Mod. '81.

Immaculate Conception

Rev. Matthew W. Settle, Priest Mod. & Sacramental Min. '04.

St. Anne

Rev. John J. Becker '72.

St. Joan of Arc

Rev. Matthew W. Settle, Priest Mod. '04.

St. Mary

Rev. Michael E. Betley '80.

Holy Cross

Deacon Bruce H. Corey.

St. Augustine, Francis Creek, WI

Rev. John J. Becker '72.

St. Mary of the Lake

Rev. Jason J. Blahnik, Admin. '09.

St. Pius Served from St. Benedict, Suamico. ***Mailing Address:*** P.O. Box 66, Suamico, WI, 54173-0066.

Tel: 920-434-2024

Email: sbsp@wi.twcbc.com

Holy Family

Deacon James Dennison.

St. Patrick

Rev. Lawrence E. Abler, O.F.M.Cap., Admin. '64.

Holy Cross

Rev. John J. Becker '72.

St. Gabriel the Archangel

Very Rev. Larry J. Seidl '75.

St. Wenceslaus, Deerbrook, WI

Rev. David R. Schmidt '81.

Holy Rosary

Joseph Zenk, Parish Dir.
Rev. Robert Kollath, Priest Mod. '97.
Rev. Harold L. Berryman, Sacramental Min. '58.
Deacon Bernard (Pat) P. Knier.

St. Joseph

Rev. David J. Hoffman, Temporary Admin. '96.

Immaculate Conception

Rev. David J. Hoffman, Temporary Admin. '96.

St. Joseph-Holy Family Parish, Phlox, WI

Rev. David R. Schmidt, Priest Mod. '81.

St. Mary, Pickerel, WI

Rev. David R. Schmidt, Priest Mod. '81.

Assumption of the Blessed Virgin Mary (1887)

Rev. Finian Andrew Zaucha, O.F.M. '68.

St. Ann (1851)

Joseph Zenk, Parish Dir.
Rev. Robert Kollath, Priest Mod. '97.
Rev. Harold L. Berryman, Sacramental Min. '58.
Deacon Bernard (Pat) P. Knier.

Res.: N188 School St., New Holstein, WI, 53061-9776.

Tel: 920-894-3147 ***Fax:*** 920-894-3147

Email: stann@bertramwireless.com

St. Gregory (1854), St. Nazianz, WI

Rev. Patrick Nelson, S.D.S., Admin.

Holy Trinity (1869)

Rev. Patrick Nelson, S.D.S., Admin.

St. John-Sacred Heart (1995)

Rev. Michael E. Betley '80.

St. Mary (1882)

Rev. Michael E. Betley '80.

Corpus Christi (1904), Sturgeon Bay, WI

Deacon Raymond G. Ambrosius Jr.

St. Benedict (1917) [CEM] Also serves St. Pius, Little Suamico. ***Mailing Address:*** P.O. Box 66, Suamico, WI, 54173-0066.

Tel: 920-434-2024 ***Fax:*** 920-662-2301

Email: sbsp@wi.twcbc.com

St. Ambrose (1905) [CEM] Served from St. Mary of the Lake, Lakewood. ***Mailing Address:*** P.O. Box 280, Wabeno, WI, 54566-0280.

Tel: 715-473-2511

Email: stambrose@centurylink.net

Rev. Jason J. Blahnik, Admin. '09.

SS. James-Stanislaus (1992), White Lake, WI

Rev. Walter P. Stumpf, Temporary Admin. '06.
Military Chaplains
Rev. Michael Dory, Lt. Cmdr. '76 16113 W. Quail Creek Ln., Surprise, AZ, 85374-4910
Rev. John W. Schuetze, Chap. U.S.A.F. '97 113 Curtiss Dr., Biloxi, MS, 39531
Retired
Rev. Msgr. John B. Dewane, M.A., S.T.L., D.Min. '62 1435 N. McCarthy Rd., Apt. 3, Appleton, WI, 54913-8285
Rev. Richard L. Allen '61 3220 E. Parkside Blvd., Apt. 82, Appleton, WI, 54915.
Tel: 920-213-0985
Rev. Harold L. Berryman '58.
Rev. Kenneth J. De Groot, O.Praem. '61.
Rev. John M. Gallagher '71 224 Iroquois Ave., #7, Green Bay, WI, 54301-1998
Rev. William Kuhr '67.
Rev. John Neuser '62 St. Mary's Home 1635 S. 21st St., Rm 327, Manitowoc, WI, 54220
Permanent Deacons
Deacon Paul J. Brulla St. Rose, Clintonville; St. Mary, Bear Creek.
Deacon Mark R. Hibbs Sr. Mary, Maplewood; St. Peter & St. Hubert, Rosiere/Lincoln.
Deacon Richard J. Matuszak St. John, Seymour; St. Sebastian, Isaar.
Deacon David G. Van Eperen St. John Nepomucene, Little Chute.
Deacon Robert Vincent, (Retired).
***Shrine*— The Chapel of Our Lady of Good Help (Diocesan Shrine)-Robinsonville**, New Franken, WI
Rev. Peter Stryker, C.P.M., Rector.
Rev. Jewel Aytona, C.P.M., Chap.
The Bridge-Between Retreat Center, Inc. 4471 Flaherty Ln., Denmark, WI, 54208.
Tel: 920-864-7230 *Fax:* 920-864-7044
Email: info@bridge-between.com
Web: www.bridge-between.org
Ecumenical Center-UWGB, Green Bay, WI
Rev. Daniel J. Schuster, Chap. '08.
The Shrine of Our Lady of Good Help, Inc., Green Bay, WI, New Franken, WI
Rev. Peter Stryker, C.P.M., Rector.
Rev. Jewel Aytona, C.P.M., Chap.

Diocese of Harrisburg

New Listings
Administrative Assistant to the Bishop and Liturgical Coordinator
Rev. Joshua R. Brommer '06 ***Mailing Address:*** 4800 Union Deposit Rd., Harrisburg, PA, 17111-3710.
Tel: 717-657-4804 *Fax:* 717-657-2453
Newly Ordained
St. Joan of Arc (1920)
Rev. Brian J. Wayne, Parochial Vicar '11.
Revisions
Secretary for Clergy and Consecrated Life
Very Rev. Philip G. Burger, V.F. '83 ***Mailing Address:*** 4800 Union Deposit Rd., Harrisburg, PA, 17111-3710.
Tel: 717-657-4804 *Fax:* 717-657-2453
Secretary for Catholic Life and Evangelization
Vacant ***Mailing Address:*** 4800 Union Deposit Rd., Harrisburg, PA, 17111-3710.
Tel: 717-657-4804 *Fax:* 717-657-4041
Buildings and Properties
Mike Ogden, Dir. 4800 Union Deposit Rd., Harrisburg, PA, 17111-3710.
Tel: 717-657-4804 *Fax:* 717-657-6208
Permanent Diaconate, Office for
Very Rev. Philip G. Burger, V.F., Dir. '83 4800 Union Deposit Rd., Harrisburg, PA, 17111-3710.
Tel: 717-657-4804 *Fax:* 717-657-2453
Prison Ministry
Vacant, Dir. 4800 Union Deposit Rd., Harrisburg, PA, 17111-3710.
Tel: 717-657-4804 *Fax:* 717-657-4041
Cathedral Parish of St. Patrick
In Res.
Rev. Michael C. Letteer '96.
St. Catherine Laboure (1948)
Rev. Joseph Howard, F.S.S.P., Parochial Vicar.
Holy Family (1958)
Rev. Robert A. Yohe Jr., V.F. '89.
Our Lady of the Blessed Sacrament (1906)
Rev. Paul C.B. Schenck, Admin.
Rev. Paul Fisher, Parochial Vicar '95.
Immaculate Heart of Mary (1809)
Rev. Kenneth G. Smith '84.
St. Columba (1882), Bloomsburg, PA
Rev. Msgr. Robert E. Lawrence, V.F. '66.
***Mission*— Christ the King**, Benton, PA
Rev. Timothy D. Marcoe, Admin. '07.
St. Ignatius Loyola (Orrtanna) (1817)
Rev. Daniel P. O'Brien '85.
Good Shepherd
In Res.
Very Rev. Philip G. Burger, V.F. '83.
St. Joseph (1850)
Rev. Caesar Belchez '95.
St. Joseph (1864)
Rev. James E. Lease, Parochial Vicar '06.
St. Vincent (1904)
Rev. Jeffrey Thoms, Admin.
St. Joan of Arc (1920)
Rev. Michael W. Rothan '04.
Iglesia Catolica San Juan Bautista, Lancaster, PA
Rev. Jose E. Mera-Vallejos, Parochial Vicar '09.
St. Benedict the Abbot (1995)
Rev. Walter F. Guzman '02.
St. Elizabeth Ann Seton (1977)
Rev. Msgr. William J. King, J.C.D., V.G. '83.
Rev. Tri M. Luong, Parochial Vicar '94.
St. Joseph (1950), Mechanicsburg, PA
Rev. David M. Hereshko, Parochial Vicar '00.
Divine Redeemer (1995)
Rev. John A. Szada Jr. '78.
St. Theresa of the Infant Jesus (1928)
Rev. Tiburtis Antony Raja, India, Parochial Vicar '96.
Immaculate Conception of the Blessed Virgin Mary (1852)
Rev. Charles L. Persing '88.
***High School*— Trinity High School**, Camp Hill, PA
Rev. David M. Hereshko, Chap. '00.
***High School*— Our Lady of Lourdes Regional School**, Coal Township, PA
Rev. Alfred P. Sceski, Chap. '91.
***High School*— York Catholic High School**, York, PA
Rev. James E. Lease, Chap. '06.
Bloomsburg University of Pennsylvania, Bloomsburg, PA
Rev. Timothy D. Marcoe, Campus Min. '07.

Archdiocese of Hartford

New Listings
***Convent*— The Community of the Dominican Daughters of Our Lady of Nazareth Corporation** 510 New Britain Ave., Hartford, CT, 06106.
Tel: 860-249-2912
Sr. Lucia Silva Cardenas, Pres.

Archdiocese of Indianapolis

Revisions
Most Reverend Christopher J. Coyne, S.L.D., Auxiliary Bishop and Vicar General of Indianapolis ordained June 7, 1986; appointed Auxiliary Bishop of the Archdiocese of Indianapolis January 14, 2011; ordained and installed as Auxiliary Bishop of Indianapolis March 2, 2011.
Moderator of the Curia
Rev. Msgr. William F. Stumpf, Ph.D. '85.
Bishop Simon Bruté College Seminary 2500 Cold Spring Rd., Indianapolis, IN, 46222.
Tel: 317-924-4100 *Fax:* 317-924-4140
Rev. Robert J. Robeson, Ph.D., Rector '03.
Rev. Patrick J. Beidelman, Vice Rector '98.
Rev. Thomas C. Widner, S.J., Dir. Spiritual Formation '69.
Rev. Jonathan Fassero, O.S.B., Spiritual Dir. '78.
Dr. Ed Mitchell, Dir. Counseling.
Seminarians 36

Diocese of Jefferson City

New Listings
Catholic Charities of Central and Northern Missouri
P.O. Box 104626, Jefferson City, MO, 65110.
Tel: 573-635-9127, Ext. 233
Web: www.cccnmo.org
Mr. Michael A. Van Gundy, Exec. Dir.
Catholic Charities of Missouri, LLC 600 Clark Ave., Jefferson City, MO, 65101.
Tel: 573-680-2038
Web: www.cc-mo.org
Janel Luck, Exec. Dir.
Revisions
St. Joseph Cathedral (1959), Jefferson City, MO
Rev. Nicholas J. Reid.
Immaculate Conception (1913)
Rev. Dylan Schrader '10.
Deacon Colin P. Franklin.
St. Boniface (1860)
Rev. Robert H. Fields, Canonical Admin. '82.
St. Anthony (1946)
Deacon Anthony J. Viviano.
Our Lady of Lourdes (1958)
Rev. Ron Kreul, O.P.
Sacred Heart (1876), Columbia, MO
Rev. Thomas Saucier, O.P. '96.
St. Peter (1875)
Rev. Frank A. Bussmann '06.
St. Bernadette (1973)
Rev. Daniel I.J. Lueckenotte, Canonical Admin. '90.
St. Raphael (1886), Brunswick, MO
Rev. Robert H. Fields, Canonical Admin. '82.
St. Patrick (1862)
Rev. P. Gregory Oligschlaeger, Canonical Pastor '93.
Immaculate Conception (1857)
Deacon William B. Tull III.
St. Joseph (1876)
Rev. Benedict Ayodi, O.F.M.Cap.
St. Brendan (1857)
Deacon Louis M. Nelen.
St. Jude Thaddeus (1900)
Rev. Frank A. Bussmann '06.
Immaculate Conception (1861)
Rev. P. Gregory Oligschlaeger '93.
Rev. Benedict Ayodi, O.F.M.Cap.
St. Joseph (1866)
Rev. Alexuis Ekka, Canonical Admin.
St. Michael (1906)
Sr. Mary Rost, S.S.N.D., Pastoral Admin.
St. Anthony (1906)
Rev. Benjamin Nwosu, Canonical Admin. '01.
St. Lawrence (1871)
Rev. Benjamin Nwosu, Canonical Admin. '01.
St. Patrick (1866)
Rev. Mark Miller, C.PP.S.
Rev. James G. Betzen, C.PP.S. '81.
Deacon Mark Yates.
Sacred Heart (1882)
Rev. Mark Miller, C.PP.S.
Rev. James G. Betzen, C.PP.S. '81.
Deacon Mark Yates.
St. Mary (1879), Shelbina, MO
Deacon John DeGraff.
Church of the Resurrection (1873)
Rev. Benedict Ayodi, O.F.M.Cap.
On Duty Outside the Diocese
Rev. Karl Barmann, O.S.B. '65.
Rev. Steven Kuhlmann, O.P. '92.
Rev. Joseph Miller, C.PP.S.
Rev. M. Christopher Smith '83.
Retired
Rev. William Miller, C.PP.S. '63.
Rev. Dean Nimerichter '92.

Diocese of Joliet in Illinois

Newly Ordained
Notre Dame (1954)
Rev. Steven Borello, Parochial Vicar '11.
Revisions
Most Reverend R. Daniel Conlon, Bishop of Joliet ordained January 15, 1977; appointed Bishop of Steubenville May 22, 2002; consecrated and installed August 6, 2002; appointed Bishop of Joliet May 17, 2011; installed July 14, 2011. ***Chancery:*** 425 Summit St., Joliet, IL, 60435.
Holy Cross (1893), Joliet, IL
Rev. Ron P. Neitzke, Admin. '89.
St. Mary Magdalene (1953)
Rev. Christopher Groh, Admin. '79.
St. Mary Nativity (1906)
Rev. Ron P. Neitzke, Admin. '89.
St. Mary (1857)
Rev. Reynaldo B. Treyes, Admin. '78.
St. Dominic (1964)
Rev. Matthew Pratscher, Parochial Vicar '08.
Immaculate Conception (1869)
Rev. Show Reddy Allam, India, Admin. '94.
St. Luke (1963)
Rev. Danilo Soriano, C.P., Admin. '78.
Our Lady of Mount Carmel (1970)
Rev. Jose Luis Torres, O.Carm., Admin.
Visitation (1953)
Rev. Jan Krutewicz, Parochial Vicar '00.
Our Lady of Lourdes (1875)
Rev. John Phan, Admin. '05.
St. Petronille (1925)
Rev. Sundar Raj Kocherla, India, Parochial Vicar '76.
St. Teresa (1949)
Rev. Santos Castillo, Admin. '04.
Sacred Heart (1912)
Rev. James Radek '89.
St. Martin (1899), Beaverville, IL
Rev. Reynaldo B. Treyes, Admin. '78.
St. Mary (1910)
Rev. Jose Kadukunnel, C.M.I., Admin.

St. Walter (1946)
Rev. Matthew Gamber, S.J., Parochial Vicar.
St. Liborius (1902)
Rev. Dennis Spies, Admin. '02.
Holy Trinity (1938)
Rev. Michael Danek, C.R., Admin.
Rev. Marion Wroblewski, C.R., Parochial Vicar.
Holy Trinity
In Res.
Rev. Gerald Watt, C.R.
St. John the Baptist (1867)
Rev. Thomas Cargo, Admin. '78.
Christ The Servant Parish (1990), Woodridge, IL
Rev. Frank Vitus, Admin. '75.
Retired
Rev. Robert J. Coleman '87.
Rev. Gerald Tivy '64.
St. Elias Carmelites, Joliet, IL
Rev. Jeffery Smialek, O.Carm.
Carmelite Provincial Office, Darien, IL
Very Rev. Carl Markelz, O.Carm., Prior Prov.
Provincial Office of Lay Carmelites and Scapular Center, Darien, IL
Very Rev. Carl Markelz, O.Carm., Prior Prov.

Diocese of La Crosse

Revisions
St. Joseph's Hospital (1888) 2661 County Hwy. I, Chippewa Falls, WI, 54729.
Tel: 715-717-7200 ***Fax:*** 715-717-7204
Web: www.stjoeschipfalls.com
Joan M. Coffman, Pres. & CEO.
Hospital Sisters of the Third Order of St. Francis.
Hospital Sisters Health System.
Total Staff 625; Bed Capacity 193; Patients Assisted Annually 58,669
Friends of St. Joseph's 2661 County Hwy. I, Chippewa Falls, WI, 54729.
Tel: 715-717-7392 ***Fax:*** 715-717-7258
Email: bgiles@sjcf.hshs.org
Web: www.stjoeschipfalls.com

Diocese of Lafayette

Newly Ordained
St. Peter (1874), Carencro, LA
Rev. Johnathan Janise '11.
Annunciation of the B.V.M. (1964)
Rev. Nathan Comeaux '11.
St. Anthony of Padua (1902), Eunice, LA
Rev. Nathan Comeaux '11.
Sts. Peter and Paul (1904), Scott, LA
Rev. David Hebert '11.
St. Joseph (1947)
Rev. Garrett McIntyre '11.
Sacred Heart of Jesus (1854)
Rev. Garrett McIntyre '11.
Revisions
Seminarians
Rev. Kevin Bordelon, Dir. '05 1408 Carmel Dr., Lafayette, LA, 70501-5298.
Tel: 337-261-5690
Vocations
Rev. Kevin Bordelon, Dir. '05 1408 Carmel Dr., Lafayette, LA, 70501-5298.
Tel: 337-261-5690
Cathedral of St. John the Evangelist (1821)
Rev. Kevin P. Bordelon '05.
Immaculate Heart of Mary
In Res.
Rev. Ryszard Kalinowski, S.V.D. '74.
St. Stephen (1950)
Rev. Msgr. J. Douglas Courville, J.C.L. '76.
St. Bernard (1847), Breaux Bridge, LA
Rev. Donald Pousson '66.
St. Francis of Assisi (1923)
Rev. Charles Moffatt, S.S.J.
St. Peter (1874), Carencro, LA
Rev. Mark Ledoux '99.
Our Lady of Lourdes (1928)
Rev. Bill Melancon '93.
St. Charles Borromeo (1819), Grand Coteau, LA
Rev. Brian Garry, S.J.
St. Anthony of Padua (1958), Krotz Springs, LA
Rev. Chanh Nguyen, Admin.
Holy Family (1953), Lawtell, LA
Rev. Justin Arockiasamy, S.V.D.
St. Nicholas (1867), Lydia, LA
Rev. Gregory Chauvin '97.
St. John the Baptist (1952), Crowley, LA
Rev. Clint James Trahan '08.
St. Ann (1856), Lawtell, LA
Rev. Justin Arockiasamy, S.V.D.
St. John the Evangelist (1882), Mermentau, LA
Rev. Neil McNeil.
Immaculate Conception (1956), Morse, LA
Rev. Clint James Trahan '08.
Holy Ghost (1920), Opelousas, LA
Rev. Bartlomiej Jasilek, S.V.D.
St. Joseph (1872), Rayne, LA
Rev. Kendal Faulk '10.
St. Leo IV (1883)
Rev. Paul Broussard '98.
St. Marcellus (1960)
Rev. Eugene R. Tremie '71.
St. Martin of Tours (1765)
Rev. Rusty P. Richard '97.
Notre Dame de Perpetuel Secours (1938)
Rev. Stanley Jawa, S.V.D.
Notre Dame de Perpetuel Secours
In Res.
Rev. Francis Damoah, S.V.D.

Diocese of Las Cruces

New Listings
On Leave for Military
Rev. Gan Nguyen, C.Ss.R. Sierra Chapel, WSMR, NM.
Revisions
Cathedral of the Immaculate Heart of Mary (1953)
Rev. William McCann, Rector '94.
Holy Cross (1970)
Deacon Francisco Gurrola.
St. Anthony's (1899)
Deacon Robert Diaz.
St. Anthony (1905)
Deacon Antonio Torrez.
St. Cecilia (1941)
Rev. Martin G. Cordero '99.
San Jose
Rev. Jose Rogelio Martinez, J.C.L. '05.
Assumption of the Blessed Virgin Mary (1963)
Rev. Joseph Pacquing, Admin. '83.
Deacon Christopher Gutierrez.
St. John the Baptist (1903)
Deacon Ernesto Martinez.
St. Peter (1903)
Deacon Frank Pitman.
St. Vincent de Paul (1874)
Deacon Joseph Arellano.
Holy Cross Retreat and Friary 600 Holy Cross Rd., Mesilla Park, CO, 80047.
Tel: 575-524-3688 ***Fax:*** 575-524-3811
Email: director@holycrossretreat.org
Web: www.holycrossretreat.org
Rev. Thomas A. Smith, O.F.M.Conv., Dir. '79.
San Patricio Retreat Center 119 La Mancha, P.O. Box 102, San Patricio, NM, 88348.
Tel: 575-653-4415
Email: sanpatricioretreat@gmail.com
Web: www.sanpatricioretreat.org
Dr. Wayne E. Pribble, Dir.
Linda Pribble, Dir.

Diocese of Lexington

Newly Ordained
Cathedral of Christ the King (1945)
Rev. Richard Watson '11.
Mary, Queen of the Holy Rosary (1960)
Rev. Jeffrey Estacio, Parochial Vicar '11.
Revisions
Secretariat for Pastoral Life
Doug Culp 1310 W. Main St., Lexington, KY, 40508-2048.
Tel: 859-253-1993, Ext. 220
Director of Religious Formation & Adult Faith Formation
Rod Stern 1310 W. Main St., Lexington, KY, 40508-2048.
Tel: 859-253-1993, Ext. 221
Director of Youth & Young Adult Ministry
Michele Faught 1310 W. Main St., Lexington, KY, 40508.
Tel: 859-253-1993, Ext. 218
Email: mfaught@cdlex.org
Coordinator of Vocation Programs
Bret Hunterbrinker 1310 W. Main St., Lexington, KY, 40508.
Tel: 859-253-1993, Ext. 248
Email: bhunterbrinker@cdlex.org
Queen of All Saints (1965), Beattyville, KY
Rev. Joseph N. Koury Jr. '07.
St. Clare (1950)
Rev. Michael Flanagan '10.
Sacred Heart (1902)
Rev. Michael Weglicki '79.
St. Boniface (1886)
Rev. Michael Weglicki '79.
St. Patrick (1868)
Rev. Frank Brawner '05.
St. Leo (1891)
Rev. Daniel P. Schwendeman '01.
St. Joseph (1872)
Rev. Frank Brawner '05.
Taylor Manor Nursing Home, Versailles, KY
Rev. Brice Bahouamio, Chap.

Diocese of Little Rock

Revisions
St. Anne (North Little Rock) (1935), North Little Rock, AR
Rev. Michael F. Walsh, C.M.
Immaculate Conception (1948), North Little Rock, AR
Rev. Thomas A. Elliott '99.
St. Theresa (1954), Little Rock, AR
Rev. Michael E. Bass '87.
St. Stephen (1989), Bentonville, AR
Rev. Jose Antonio Galvez-Orellana.
Christ the King (1928), Fort Smith, AR
Very Rev. Kevin Atunzu, V.F. '79.
Our Lady of Good Hope (1875), Hope, AR
Rev. Anthony Robbins '10.
St. John the Baptist (1907)
Rev. James P. West '86.
St. Martin Church, Nashville, AR
Rev. Anthony Robbins '10.
St. Vincent de Paul (1941)
Rev. Jose Antonio Galvez-Orellana.
Retired
Rev. Do Duy Nho '66 St. John Manor 2414 N. Tyler St., Little Rock, AR, 72207
Priestly Fraternity of St. Peter, North Little Rock, AR
Rev. Charles Ryan, F.S.S.P., Chap.

Archdiocese of Los Angeles

Revisions
Providence Health System (San Fernando Valley Service Area-Spiritual Care Dept.)
Barry Wolfman, CEO.
Sr. Colleen Settles, O.P., Chief Mission Integration Officer.
Tel: 818-847-3350
Sr. Sheila Browne, R.S.M., Mission Leader. Sponsored by Providence Ministries.
Providence Saint Joseph Medical Center 501 S. Buena Vista St., Burbank, CA, 91505.
Tel: 818-843-5111 ***Fax:*** 818-525-3444
Web: www.providence.org
Sr. Sheila Browne, R.S.M., Dir., Mission Leadership.
Tel: 818-847-3356
Rev. Mark Ciccone, S.J., Mgr., Spiritual Care '85.
Tel: 818-847-4735
Sr. Blanca Sagles, S.P., Chap.
Bed Capacity 414; Patients Assisted Annually 35,000; Total Staff 3,000
Providence Holy Cross Medical Center 15031 Rinaldi St., P.O. Box 9600, Mission Hills, CA, 91346-9600.
Tel: 818-365-8051 ***Fax:*** 818-496-4569
D.W. Donovan, Dir., Mission Leadership.
Tel: 818-496-5000
Rev. Philip Abraham, Mgr. Spiritual Care Dept.
Tel: 818-496-4355
Bed Capacity 257; Patients Assisted Annually 107,136; Total Staff 1,250
Providence St. Elizabeth Care Center 10425 Magnolia Blvd., North Hollywood, CA, 91601.
Tel: 818-980-3872 ***Fax:*** 818-980-6349
Bed Capacity 52; Patients Assisted Annually 60; Total Staff 50
Providence Little Company of Mary Medical Center San Pedro 1300 W. 7th St., San Pedro, CA, 90732.
Tel: 310-832-3311 ***Fax:*** 310-514-5314
Web: www.providence.org/sanpedro
Sr. Nancy Jurecki, O.P., Dir., Mission Leadership & Spiritual Care.
Tel: 310-514-4364 Sponsored by Providence Ministries.
Bed Capacity 210; Total Staff 889
Providence Little Company of Mary Peninsula Diagnostic Center 1360 W. 6th St., Ste. 100, San Pedro, CA, 90732.
Tel: 310-831-0371 ***Fax:*** 310-514-8920
Providence Little Company of Mary Peninsula Recovery Center 1386 W. 7th St., San Pedro, CA, 90732.
Tel: 310-832-3311 ***Fax:*** 310-514-5376
Providence Little Company of Mary San Pedro Peninsula Hospital Pavilion 1322 W. Sixth St., San Pedro, CA, 90732.
Tel: 310-832-3311 ***Fax:*** 310-514-5332 Skilled Nursing Facility.
Bed Capacity 128

Providence Tarzana Medical Center 18321 Clark St., Tarzana, CA, 91356.
Tel: 818-881-0800
Shawn Kiley, Dir. Mission Leadership Dept.
Tel: 818-757-4388
Rev. Renee Owen, Mgr. Spiritual Care Dept.
Tel: 818-757-4354

Providence Little Company of Mary Community Health Foundation 4101 Torrance Blvd., Torrance, CA, 90503.
Tel: 310-543-6900 *Fax:* 310-540-8664

Providence Little Company of Mary Medical Center Torrance 4101 W. Torrance Blvd., Torrance, CA, 90503.
Tel: 310-540-7676 *Fax:* 310-540-7659
Web: lcmhs.org
providence.org
Paul Makarewicz, Dir., Mission Leadership.
Tel: 310-303-6182
Dan Hudson, Mgr., Spiritual Care.
Tel: 310-303-6122 Sponsored by Providence Ministries.
Total Staff 3,700; Bed Capacity 250; Bassinets 35

Providence Little Company of Mary Sub-Acute Center-South Bay 3620 W. Lomita Blvd., Torrance, CA, 90505.
Tel: 310-378-8587 *Fax:* 310-791-4514 Skilled Nursing Facility.; Sponsored by Providence Ministries.
Bed Capacity 212

Diocese of Lubbock

Revisions

Chancellor
B. Marty Martin Catholic Pastoral Center P.O. Box 98700, Lubbock, TX, 79499-8700.
Tel: 806-792-3943, Ext. 212 *Fax:* 806-792-2953

Diocese of Madison

Revisions

Edgewood College, Inc. 1000 Edgewood College Dr., Madison, WI, 53711.
Tel: 608-663-2262 *Fax:* 608-663-6717
Email: dcarey@edgewood.edu
Web: www.edgewood.edu
Dominican Sisters, Sinsinawa, WI.
Sisters 9; Lay Teachers 245; Students 2,550

Diocese of Manchester

New Listings

Christ the King Parish (2011)
Very Rev. Richard A. Roberge, V.F. '85.
Rev. Marcos A. Gonzalez-Torres '06.
Deacon Winton P. DeRosia.
Office & Rectory: 135 N. State St., Concord, NH, 03301-6400.
Tel: 603-225-2131 *Fax:* 603-228-4580

Catholic Lawyers Guild of New Hampshire, Inc. 153 Ash St., Manchester, NH, 03105.

Newly Ordained

St. Joseph Cathedral (1869)
Rev. Kyle Stanton '11.

Revisions

St. John the Evangelist (1865) Merged with Sacred Heart, Concord and St. Peter, Concord to form Christ the King Parish, Concord. For sacramental records see Christ the King, Concord.

St. Peter (1946) Merged with Sacred Heart, Concord and St. John the Evangelist, Concord to form Christ the King Parish, Concord. For sacramental records see Christ the King, Concord.

Sacred Heart (1892) (French) Merged with St. John the Evangelist, Concord and St. Peter, Concord to form Christ the King Parish, Concord. For sacramental records see Christ the King, Concord.

Diocese of Memphis

Revisions

The Catholic Cafe, Inc. c/o Glankler Brown, PLLC 6000 Poplar Ave., Ste. 400, Memphis, TN, 38119.
Tel: 901-576-1714 *Fax:* 901-525-2389
Web: www.thecatholiccafe.com

Diocese of Metuchen

New Listings

***School*— Holy Savior Academy** 1 Sacred Heart Dr., P.O. Box 1179, South Plainfield, NJ, 07080-1179.
Tel: 908-822-5890 *Fax:* 908-822-5891
Melinda Hanlon, Prin.

Newly Ordained

Cathedral of St. Francis of Assisi (1871)
Rev. Lukasz Blicharski, Parochial Vicar '11.

St. Mary (1902)
Rev. Leopoldo S. Salvania, Parochial Vicar '11.

Our Lady of Fatima (1960)
Rev. Heherson Balabbo, C.M.F., Parochial Vicar '11.

Immaculate Conception (1946)
Rev. Martin Espinoza, Parochial Vicar '11.

Revisions

Cathedral of St. Francis of Assisi (1871)
Rev. Gerardo B. Paderon, Parochial Vicar '94.

Immaculate Conception (1864)
Rev. Randall J. Vashon '00.

Our Lady of Victories (1973)
Rev. Kulandairaj Madalaimuthu, Parochial Vicar '93.

Guardian Angels (1959)
Rev. Msgr. Daniel J. Herlihy '67.
Rev. Bede Kim, Parochial Vicar '07.

St. Matthew the Apostle (1952)
Rev. George Targonski '02.
Rev. Alphonsus Kariuki, I.M.C., Parochial Vicar '86.

St. Paul the Apostle (1912)
Rev. Msgr. Daniel J. Herlihy '67.
Rev. Bede Kim, Parochial Vicar '07.

Christ the King (1948)
Rev. Stanislaw Slaby, C.Ss.R. '99.

Sacred Heart of Jesus (1919)
Rev. Stanislaw Slaby, C.Ss.R. '99.

Our Lady of Mount Virgin (1943)
Rev. Matthew R. Paratore, J.C.L., Parochial Vicar '09.

St. Edward the Confessor (1944)
Rev. Krzysztof Kaczynski '93.

St. Thomas the Apostle (1921)
Rev. Thomas Myladil, O.C.D., Parochial Vicar '76.

Our Lady of the Rosary of Fatima (1981)
Rev. Waldemar Latkowski, C.Ss.R., Admin. '97.
Rev. Stanislaw Wilczek, C.Ss.R., Parochial Vicar '98.

St. Stephen (1892)
Rev. Wieslaw Bajor, C.Ss.R., Parochial Vicar '95.

St. Philip & St. James (1860)
Rev. Mark Kehoe, Parochial Vicar '99.

St. Catherine of Siena (1992)
Rev. Czeslaw Zalubski, S.D.B., Admin.

Our Lady of Victories (1885), Sayreville, NJ
Rev. Virgilio T. Tolentino, Parochial Vicar '82.

Our Lady of Mercy (1949)
Rev. Msgr. James P. Moran '72.

Sacred Heart (1906)
Rev. Juan S. Salonga, Parochial Vicar '10.

St. James (1860)
Very Rev. Charles W. Cicerale '75.

Absent on Sick Leave
Rev. Joseph L. Desmond '74.
Rev. Michael J. Bihuniak '90.

On Duty Outside the Diocese
Rev. John M. Rozembajgier '04 Pontifical College Josephinum, Columbus, OH.

Clergy Unassigned
Rev. Peter Suhaka '86.
Rev. Lauro Colen Sedlmayer '85.

Archdiocese of Milwaukee

New Listings

Blessed John Paul II Parish (2011) 3307 S. 10th St., Milwaukee, WI, 53215.
Tel: 414-744-0413
Rev. Michael A. Ignaszak '84.

***School*— All Saints Catholic School of Kenosha, Inc.** 7307 40th Ave., Kenosha, WI, 53142.
Tel: 262-694-6018
Web: www.allsaintskenosha.org
Jacqueline Lichter, Ph.D., Prin.

Revisions

St. Alexander (1926) (Polish) Merged with St. Helen & St. John Kanty, Milwaukee to form Blessed John Paul II Parish, Milwaukee.

St. Helen (1925) (Polish) Merged with St. Alexander & St. John Kanty, Milwaukee to form Blessed John Paul II Parish, Milwaukee.

St. John Kanty (1907) (Polish) Merged with St. Alexander & St. Helen, Milwaukee to form Blessed John Paul II Parish, Milwaukee.

Archdiocese of Mobile

Newly Ordained

St. Pius X (1954)
Rev. Stephen G. Vrazel, Parochial Vicar '11.

Christ the King (1896)
Rev. Travis J. Burnett, Parochial Vicar '11.

Revisions

Vicar General and Moderator of the Curia
Very Rev. Stephen E. Martin, V.G. '98 400 Government St., Mobile, AL, 36602.
Tel: 251-434-1585 *Fax:* 251-434-1588
Email: vicargeneral@mobilearchdiocese.org

Chancellor
Deacon Walter J. Crimmins.
Email: wcrimmins@mobilearchdiocese.org

Office of Religious Education
Mr. Patrick Arensberg, Dir.
Email: parensberg@mobilearchdiocese.org

Office of Religious Education Associate Directors
Ms. Jeanne C. Howard 352 Government St., P.O. Box 2405, Mobile, AL, 36652.
Tel: 251-433-6991
Email: jhoward@mobilearchdiocese.org

Censor Librorum
Very Rev. Stephen E. Martin, V.G. '98 *Mailing Address:* 400 Government St., Mobile, AL, 36602.
Tel: 251-434-1585 *Fax:* 251-434-1588

Cathedral of the Immaculate Conception (1704)
Very Rev. Stephen E. Martin, V.G., Rector '98.

St. Ignatius (Spring Hill) (1947)
Rev. W. Bry Shields '84.
St. Ignatius
In Res.
Rev. Cecil R. Spotswood '97.

St. Joseph (1857)
Very Rev. Stephen E. Martin, V.G. '98.

St. Mary (1867), Mobile, AL
Rev. Msgr. G. Warren Wall '76.

St. Pius X (1954)
Rev. Johnny S. Savoie '95.

St. Philip Neri (1908)
Rev. James F. Carlsen '00.

St. John The Evangelist (1958)
Rev. Wayne M. Youngman '10.

Christ the King (1896)
Rev. Jesu Alangaram Ronald Gajettan, Parochial Vicar.

St. Lawrence (1961)
Rev. Babu Arul Raj Jesu Raj, Parochial Vicar.

St. John Baptist (1924)
Rev. Antony Kadavil '67.

Sacred Heart (1944)
Rev. Wayne M. Youngman '10.

St. Rose of Lima (1853)
Rev. Austin Conry '65.

St. Andrew Kim Taegon (1910) *Mailing Address:* P.O. Box 241303, Montgomery, AL, 36124.
Rev. Peter Yong Mo Yeon (BIR), Parochial Admin.

Immaculate Conception
Rev. Stephen Hornat, S.S.E. '76.

St. Patrick (1974)
Rev. Patrick J. Madden '83.

Our Lady Queen of Peace (1850)
Rev. Stephen Hornat, S.S.E. '76.

St. Bridget (1864)
Rev. William Patrick Saucier '01.
St. Bridget
In Res.
Rev. Eamon Miley '73.

On Leave from the Archdiocese
Rev. Msgr. Michael L. Farmer, V.G., S.T.L. '95.

Retired
Rev. Msgr. Peter J. Cunningham '56.
Rev. Msgr. William R. James '54.
Rev. Leo Blanchet '86.
Rev. James Montini Coleman '99.
Rev. Patrick Maher '53.

Diocese of Nashville

New Listings

Executive Assistant to the Bishop
Ms. Elizabeth Clay.

Newly Ordained

Our Lady of the Lake (1969), Hendersonville, TN
Rev. Leon Gerald Strange '11.

Revisions

Accounting Systems
Mr. William J. Whalen, CFO.

Cemeteries
Mr. William J. Whalen, CFO.

Hispanic Ministry
Rev. David Ramirez, Dir.

Stewardship and Development
Mr. Ronald Szejner.

Christ the King (1937)
Rev. Joseph V. McMahon '84.
Christ the King
In Res.
Rev. Francis G. Appreh '96.

St. Ignatius of Antioch (1976)
Deacon John Downey.

Our Lady of Guadalupe, Antioch, TN

Rev. Anthony Lopez, Admin. '08.
Sacred Heart (1872), Loretto, TN
Rev. Luckas Arulappa, M.S.F.S. '96.
St. Joseph (1953)
Rev. Tomy P. Joseph, M.S.F.S. '94.
St. Joseph (1872), Loretto, TN
Rev. Luckas Arulappa, M.S.F.S. '96.
Our Lady of Lourdes (1946)
Rev. Prentice C. Dean, Admin. '10.
Permanent Deacons
Deacon Frank Bainbridge, (Retired).
Deacon William J. Dickson, (Retired).
Deacon Michael R. Kopczynski (Unassigned).
Deacon Thomas Miller (Unassigned).
Deacon James E. Stanford, (Retired).
Deacon James Walsh, (Retired).
Deacon Richard Weller, (Retired).
St. Thomas Hospital (1898), Nashville, TN
Rev. Francis G. Appreh, Chap. '96.

Archdiocese of New Orleans

New Listings
Archbishop Rummel Alumni Association Inc. *Fax:* 504-833-5796
Web: www.raiderpride.com
Dominick Impastato, Pres.
Newly Ordained
Immaculate Conception (1851)
Rev. Jeffrey C. Johnson, S.J., Parochial Vicar '11.
The Visitation of Our Lady (1963)
Rev. Bryan Howard, Parochial Vicar '11.
St. Edward the Confessor (1964)
Rev. Chris DeLerno, Parochial Vicar '11.
Revisions
Most Reverend Philip M. Hannan, D.D., J.C.D., S.T.L., Former Archbishop of New Orleans ordained December 8, 1939; appointed Titular Bishop of Hieropolis and Auxiliary Bishop of Washington June 16, 1956; consecrated August 28, 1956; promoted to Archbishop of New Orleans September 29, 1965; installed October 13, 1965; retired February 14, 1989. Chateau de Notre Dame, 2920 Burdette St., New Orleans, LA 70125-2596.
Department of Christian Formation
Executive Director
Vacant 7887 Walmsley Ave., New Orleans, LA, 70125-3496.
Tel: 504-861-6228 *Fax:* 504-861-6260
Email: cformation@archdiocese-no.org
Campus Ministry
Vacant 7887 Walmsley Ave., New Orleans, LA, 70125-3496.
Tel: 504-861-6228 *Fax:* 504-861-6260
Catholic Schools Office
Dr. Jan Lancaster, Supt. 7887 Walmsley Ave., New Orleans, LA, 70125-3496.
Tel: 504-866-7916 *Fax:* 504-861-6260
Email: superintendent@archdiocese.no.org
Office of Eucharistic Renewal
Mr. Todd Amick, Dir. 1007 Airline Park Blvd., Metairie, LA, 70003.
Tel: 504-482-8010 *Fax:* 504-836-0552
Religious Education
Mrs. Alice Hughes, Dir. 7887 Walmsley Ave., New Orleans, LA, 70125.
Tel: 504-861-6270 *Fax:* 504-861-6276
Vocation Office
Rev. Steven V. Bruno, Dir. '05 7887 Walmsley Ave., New Orleans, LA, 70125-3496.
Tel: 504-861-6298; 504-861-9521 *Fax:* 504-866-2906
Christopher Homes, Inc.
Deacon Dennis F. Adams, Dir. 1000 Howard Ave., Ste. 100, New Orleans, LA, 70113-1903.
Tel: 504-596-3460 *Fax:* 504-596-3466
Web: www.christopherhomes.org
Email: dfadams@christopherhomesinc.org
School Food and Nutrition Services of New Orleans Inc.
Ms. Janet Sanderson, COO 1000 Howard Ave., Ste. 300, New Orleans, LA, 70113-1925.
Tel: 504-596-3434 *Fax:* 504-596-3459; 504-596-6901
Email: jsanderson@schoolcafe.org
Ecumenical Officer
Rev. Donald A. Hawkins, S.J. '76 6220 LaSalle Pl., New Orleans, LA, 70118-6236.
Tel: 504-865-7420, Ext. 255 *Fax:* 504-866-3391
Email: dhawkins@hnjchurch.org
Worship Office
Rev. Msgr. Kenneth J. Hedrick, Dir. '73 7887 Walmsley Ave., New Orleans, LA, 70125-3496.
Tel: 504-861-6300; 504-861-9521 *Fax:* 504-866-2906
Email: worship@archdiocese-no.org
Liturgical Commission
Rev. Msgr. Kenneth J. Hedrick, Coord. '73 7887 Walmsley Ave., New Orleans, LA, 70125-3496.
Tel: 504-861-6300; 504-861-9521 *Fax:* 504-866-2906
Email: worship@archdiocese-no.org
***School*— Cathedral Academy**, New Orleans, LA
Sr. Mary Sheila Marksim, O.P., Prin.
St. Andrew the Apostle (1952)
Rev. Clayton "Beau" Charbonnet, Parochial Vicar '03.
St. Anthony of Padua (1915)
Rev. John G. Restrepo, O.P. '04.
Rev. Eduardo Gabriel, O.P. '92.
Rev. John M. Pitzer, O.P. '99.
Deacon Joseph M. Dardis.
St. Anthony of Padua
In Res.
Rev. Charles K. Johnson, O.P. '06.
St. Dominic (1924)
Deacon Lloyd E. Huck.
Holy Spirit (1972)
Rev. Terence Hayden, Ireland '77.
St. Mary of the Angels (1925)
Rev. Dennis Bosse, O.F.M.
Our Lady Star of The Sea (1911)
Deacon Uriel Andrew Durr.
St. Peter Claver (1920)
Deacon Lawrence C. Houston.
St. Jane de Chantal (1887)
Rev. Jeffery Jambon, Parochial Vicar.
St. Mark (1974)
Rev. Anton Ba Phan, Parochial Vicar '01.
St. Peter (1843)
Deacon Dennis F. Adams.
St. Gertrude (1955)
Rev. Edward J. Lauden, Parochial Vicar '05.
St. Charles Borromeo (1723)
Rev. Thomas M. McCann III '98.
Deacon Jeffrey R. Tully.
Our Lady of Perpetual Help (1869)
Rev. Raymond J. Guillot, Parochial Vicar '00.
***School*—**
Bro. Augustine Kozdroj, Prin.
St. John of the Cross (1984)
Deacon Steven Ferran.
St. Anthony of Padua (1961)
Rev. Anton Ba Phan, Parochial Vicar '01.
Our Lady of the Lake Roman Catholic Church (1850)
Deacon Jay C. Frantz.
Deacon Jay J. Weil III.
St. Agnes Le Thi Thanh (1995)
Rev. James Nguyen Bach, Admin. '94.
Immaculate Conception (1924)
Rev. David Nations, C.M., Parochial Vicar '97.
Deacon Gerard L. Labodot.
***School*—**, Marrero, LA
Sr. Maria Colombo, F.M.A., Prin. (Grade School).
St. Angela Merici (1964)
Deacon David P. Aaron.
St. Catherine of Siena (1921)
Rev. Kenneth Allen '04.
Rev. Alberto Villosillo, Parochial Vicar '95.
St. Clement of Rome (1965)
Rev. Peter P. Finney III, Parochial Vicar '10.
St. Edward the Confessor (1964)
Rev. Mark S. Raphael, Parochial Vicar '98.
St. Philip Neri (1960)
Rev. Msgr. Henry J. Bugler '75.
St. John the Baptist (1971)
Rev. Edward J. Lauden '05.
SS. Peter and Paul (1970)
Rev. Ray A. Hymel '87.
St. Matthew the Apostle (1959)
Deacon Jerry B. Clark Sr.
St. Matthew the Apostle
In Res.
Very Rev. Warren L. Cooper, V.F. '71.
Our Lady of Lourdes (1890) [CEM] 400 Westchester Blvd., Slidell, LA, 70458.
Our Lady of Lourdes (1916), Saint Bernard, LA
Deacon Norbert P. Billiot Jr.
Tulane Catholic Center, New Orleans, LA
Rev. Charles K. Johnson, O.P., Dir. Ministry '06.
On Special Assignment
Very Rev. Warren L. Cooper, V.F., Min. to Ill Priests; Hospital Chap. Coord. '71.
Rev. Jeffery Jambon, Northshore Hispanic Min.
Retired
Most Rev. Philip M. Hannan, D.D., J.C.D., S.T.L. 714 E. Rutland St., Covington, LA, 70433-3223
Rev. Msgr. Allen J. Roy '58 6201 Stratford Pl., New Orleans, LA, 70131
***High School*— Archbishop Rummel High School**, Metairie, LA
Mr. Michael Scalco, Pres./Prin.
***High School*— Pope John Paul II Catholic High School** (1980), Slidell, LA
Mr. Richard Berkowitz, M.Ed., Pres.
Ms. Martha M. Mundine, Prin.
***High School*— St. Augustine High School** (1951), New Orleans, LA
Rev. Charles Andrus, S.S.J., Interim Pres. '76.
***High School*— De La Salle High School** (1949), New Orleans, LA
Ms. Yvonne Gelpi, Interim Pres.
***School*— Holy Rosary High School** (1996) 3368 Esplanade Ave., New Orleans, LA, 70119-3132.
Tel: 504-482-7173 *Fax:* 504-482-7229
Email: holyrosaryaca@archdiocese-no.org
Mr. Len Enger, Prin.
Lay Teachers 18; Students 114
***High School*— St. Augustine High School**, New Orleans, LA
Rev. Charles Andrus, S.S.J., Interim Pres. '76.
***School*— De La Salle Junior High School**, New Orleans, LA
Ms. Yvonne Gelpi, Interim Pres.

Archdiocese of New York

New Listings
The Partnership for Inner-City Education 1011 First Ave., 18th Fl., New York, NY, 10022.
Tel: 646-794-3338
Email: jill.kafka@archny.org
Jill Kafka, Exec. Dir.
RDC Loaves and Fishes, Inc. 7 Market St., Dover Plains, NY, 12522.
Tel: 845-877-9076 *Fax:* 888-316-4540
Web: rdcloavesandfishes.org
Lauren McLeod, Pres.

Archdiocese of Newark

New Listings
Public Policy Committee of the New Jersey Catholic Conference
Rev. Timothy G. Graff, Social Concerns Rep. '85.
Archdiocesan Liturgies for the Archdiocese of Newark
Rev. Joseph A. Scrangella, Coord./Master of Ceremonies.
Newly Ordained
Immaculate Conception (1925)
Rev. Marco Pacciana '11.
Our Lady of Good Counsel (1902)
Rev. Marco Pacciana '11.
St. Peter's (1837)
Rev. Mayhel A. Velasquez '11.
St. Catherine of Siena (1949)
Rev. Robert P. McLaughlin '11.
Most Blessed Sacrament (1961)
Rev. John R. Job '11.
St. Aloysius (1897)
Rev. Eduardo A. Bustamante '11.
St. Paul of the Cross (1868)
Rev. Alfie A. Pangilinan '11.
St. Paul's (1861)
Rev. Juan P. Morales '11.
St. Cecilia's (1893)
Rev. Janusz Pigan '11.
St. Theresa's (1949)
Rev. Hong-Ray Peter Cho '11.
St. John the Apostle (1948)
Rev. Zbigniew Kukielka '11.
St. Francis de Sales (1854)
Rev. John C. DeSousa '11.
Sacred Heart (1902)
Rev. Pedro E. Vilchez '11.
St. Joseph's (1903)
Rev. Roy B. Regaspi '11.
St. Paul (1939)
Rev. Yeongmin Kim '11.
Our Lady of Mount Carmel (1889)
Rev. Kevin G. Waymel '11.
St. Teresa's (1863)
Rev. Rolando Rosendo DeGracia Yadao '11.
Our Lady of the Lake (1923)
Rev. Paul C. Houlis '11.
St. Helen (1968)
Rev. Frank J. Fano '11.
Revisions
Office of Archdiocesan Counsel Carella, Byrne, Cecchi, Olstein, Brody and Agnello, P.C., Archdiocesan Counsel. 5 Becker Farm Rd., Ste. 2, Roseland, NJ, 07068-1739.
Tel: 973-994-1700 *Fax:* 973-994-1744
Metropolitan Tribunal N.B. Dispensation requests or questions regarding canonical matters can be directed to Rev. Msgr. James M. Sheehan at 973-497-4148 or 171

Clifton Ave., Newark, NJ 07104.
Rev. Bryan F.J. Adamcik '96.
St. Philomena (1927)
Rev. Msgr. Kevin M. Hanbury, Ed.D., Admin. '72.
University of Medicine & Dentistry (UMDNJ), Newark, NJ
Rev. Bryan E. Page, Chap. '06.
On Duty Outside the Archdiocese
Rev. Mariano N. Dellagiovanna '07 Diocese of Gaylord 611 W. North St., Gaylord, MI, 49735-8349
Rev. Richard G. Francesco '87 Diocese of Helena P.O. Box 1729, Helena, MT, 59624-1729
Rev. Robert James Gelinas '05 Archdiocese for the Military Services United States Navy, PSC 559, Box 6092, Fpo, AP, 96377
Rev. Zeljko J. Guberovic '06 Diocese of Gaylord 611 W. North St., Gaylord, MI, 49735-8349
Rev. Manuel R. Romerde '08 Diocese of Tagilaran P.O. Box 18, Tagbilaran City, 6300, Bohol, -Philippines
Medical Leave
Rev. Fernando E. Guillen '90.
Rev. Brian F. McFadden '88.
Rev. Thomas R. McLaughlin '81.
Rev. Louis Pambello '81.
Absent on Leave
Rev. Santos B. Bertiz.
Rev. John M. Byrne.
Rev. Jian (Joseph) Cheng.
Rev. Msgr. James S. Choma '86.
Rev. Calin Cionca '00.
Rev. Nerva W. Dugue '93.
Rev. Gregory B. Hann '99.
Rev. Robert M. Hoatson.
Rev. Msgr. John J. Laferrera '73.
Rev. William A. Lusik '97.
Rev. Peter Michota.
Rev. Richard J. Mieliwocki.
Rev. James J. Reilly, S.T.L. '68.
Rev. Renzo L. Scaramella '95.
Rev. Gary C. Ward '80.
Retired
Rev. Msgr. Lawrence W. Cull '69 110 E 22nd St., Ship Bottom, NJ, 08008
Rev. Msgr. William C. Harms '65 Little Flower Parish 100 Roosevelt Ave., Berkeley Heights, NJ, 07922
Rev. Msgr. John G. Judge '69 603 Center St., Forked River, NJ, 08731
Rev. Msgr. Philip D. Morris, S.T.D. '62 St. Rose of Lima 50 Short Hills Ave., Short Hills, NJ, 07078
Rev. Msgr. William B. Naedele '49 St. John Vianney Residence 60 Home Ave., Apt. 34, Rutherford, NJ, 07070
Rev. Msgr. Ronald A. Newland '67 21 Park End Ter., Rockaway Point, NY, 11697-2303
Rev. Msgr. Joseph P. Plunkett '60 Our Lady of Czestochowa Parish 115 S. 3rd St., Harrison, NJ, 07029
Rev. Msgr. Joseph T. Slinger, Ph.D. '70 St. Anne 15-05 Saint Anne St., Fair Lawn, NJ, 07410
Rev. Msgr. Bronislaw Wielgus '62 St. Adalbert/Sts. Peter & Paul 250 E. Jersey St., Elizabeth, NJ, 07206
Rev. Robert A. Antczak, V.F. '64 Our Lady Mother of the Church 130 Apple Ridge Rd., Woodcliff Lake, NJ, 07677
Rev. Frank J. Burla '63 Immaculate Conception 30 N. Fullerton Ave., Montclair, NJ, 07042
Rev. James J. Carroll '56 3 Mary St., Warren, NJ, 07059
Rev. Donald J. Di Pasquale '62 15 Weaver Ave., Bloomfield, NJ, 07003
Rev. Joseph Fu '60 Sacred Heart 2 Welfare Rd., Wong Chuk Hang, Aberdeen, Hong Kong
Rev. Peter P. Galdon '68 c/o Ken Galdon 12 Riverside Dr., Apt. R, Cranford, NJ, 07016
Rev. John P. Holian '63 10 Overlook Rd., Apt. 4-J, Summit, NJ, 07901
Rev. Kenneth Jones '69 985 Chapel Hill Rd., Whitingham, VT, 05342
Rev. Matthew Kunnath '60 St. Mary 17 Msgr. Owens Pl., Nutley, NJ, 07110
Rev. Norbert F. Laskowski, B.A. '79 Rev. Msgr. James F. Kelley Residence 247 Bloomfield Ave., Caldwell, NJ, 07006
Rev. Rino Lavaroni '67.
Rev. Felipe Lopez '59 St. John the Baptist 239 Anderson Ave., Fairview, NJ, 07022
Rev. John P. McGovern '65 62 Tarpon Dr., Sea Girt, NJ, 08750
Rev. Ward P. Moore '72 107 Riverview Ave., #116, Neptune City, NJ, 07753
Rev. Mark A. O'Connell '79 St. Peter 155 William St., Belleville, NJ, 07109
Rev. Peter A. Oddo '61 P.O. Box 11, Swartswood, NJ, 07877
Rev. Theodore W. Osbahr, V.F. '67 P.O. Box 417, Belvidere, NJ, 07823-0417
Rev. Fernando R. Po, D.S.L. '84 Allendale Nursing Home 85 Harreton Rd., Allendale, NJ, 07401
Rev. Philip J. Rotunno '66 7004 Boulevard E., Unit 7C, Guttenberg, NJ, 07093
Rev. Jose C. Saltarin '67 c/o Antonia Sison 734 Ten Eyck Ave., Lyndhurst, NJ, 07071.
Tel: 201-636-2778
Rev. George F. Sharp '89.
Rev. Donald P. Sheehan '68 Guardian Angel 320 Franklin Tpke., Allendale, NJ, 07401
Permanent Deacons
Deacon Simplice Ahoua St. Lucy, Newark.
Deacon Wilbert Alexandre Holy Rosary & St. Michael, Elizabeth.
Deacon Justo Aliaga St. Cecilia, Kearny.
Deacon Manuel Almeida Our Lady of Fatima, Elizabeth.
Deacon Emeruwa Anyanwu Blessed Sacrament/St. Charles, Newark.
Deacon Charlie Boucher II Our Lady of Peace, New Providence.
Deacon Paul Carris Corpus Christi, Hasbrouck Heights.
Deacon Joseph Castoro St. Catherine, Glen Rock.
Deacon Arnulfo Cuesta St. Paul of the Cross, Jersey City.
Deacon James Detura St. John the Evangelist, Bergenfield.
Deacon Domenick DiBernardo Most Sacred Heart of Jesus, Wallington.
Deacon Kenneth DiPaola Our Lady of Peace, New Providence.
Deacon John J. Florio St. Joseph, Maplewood.
Deacon Angel Hernandez St. Francis of Assisi, Hackensack.
Deacon Pedro Herrera St. Mary of the Assumption, Elizabeth.
Deacon Don Hessemer St. Bartholomew, Scotch Plains.
Deacon Jose Homen Our Lady of Fatima, Elizabeth.
Deacon John J. Karal St. Ann, Jersey City.
Deacon Timothy A. Kennedy St. John the Apostle, Linden.
Deacon Tom Lagatol Our Lady of Victory, Harrington Park.
Deacon Anthony Liguori Jr. St. Elizabeth, Wyckoff.
Deacon Francis P. Materia Our Lady of the Assumption, Wood Ridge.
Deacon Robert C. Millea St. Stephen, Kearny.
Deacon Jorge A. Montalvo St. Mary of the Assumption, Elizabeth.
Deacon Brian Murphy St. Thomas the Apostle, Bloomfield.
Deacon Francis E. Noh Korean Martyrs, Saddle Brook.
Deacon Jorge E. Ochoa St. Joseph, Lodi.
Deacon Anthony Porcaro St. Therese of Lisieux, Cresskill.
Deacon Joseph S. Romano St. Anthony, Northvale.
Deacon Todd Rushing Our Lady of the Visitation, Paramus.
Deacon Louis Rusignuolo St. Valentine, Bloomfield.
Deacon Andrew E. Saunders St. Luke, Ho-Ho-Kus.
Deacon Craig Stewart Cathedral Basilica, Newark.
Deacon David Strader Our Lady of the Lake, Verona.
Deacon John Sylvester St. Mary, Dumont.
Immaculate Conception Seminary
Full-Time Faculty:
Rev. Renato J. Bautista '07.
Seton Hall University
Priest Community:
Rev. Gerald Buonopane '06.
The Newman Catholic Center at University Heights (Rutgers/Newark/NJIT), Newark, NJ
Rev. Bryan E. Page, Campus Min. '06.

Diocese of Norwich

New Listings
Diocesan Properties, Office of
Mr. Joseph M. Muscarella, Dir. 815 Boswell Ave., Norwich, CT, 06360.
Tel: 860-887-1019
Revisions
Diocesan Finance Council
Very Rev. Leszek T. Janik, J.C.L., V.G. '92.
Haiti, Diocese of Norwich Outreach to, Inc. a successor corporation of the two merged corporations, Haitian Ministries for the Diocese of Norwich and Hospice St. Joseph for the Diocese of Norwich.
Mrs. Kyn Tolson, Progs. Admin. 199 Broadway, Norwich, CT, 06360.
Tel: 860-848-2237, Ext. 206
Email: outreachtohaiti.org
Corrigan-Radgowski Correctional Institution 986 Norwich-New London Tpke., Uncasville, CT, 06382.
Tel: 860-848-5034
St. Mary
In Res.
Rev. Martin J. Jones '94.
SS. Peter and Paul (1938)
Very Rev. Leszek T. Janik, J.C.L., V.G. '92.
St. Joseph
In Res.
Rev. Charles Bak, M.S.A. '09.
St. Andrew (1860) [CEM 2] [JC 2] Yoked with St. Francis of Assisi, Lebanon.
Rev. Marek Masnicki '92.
Rev. Benjamin V. Soosaimanickam '90.
Deacon Michael L. Puscas.
Notre Dame (1955) Yoked with St. Colman, Middlefield.
Rev. Michael C. Giannitelli '91.
Rev. James Sucholet '91.
Deacon Peter L. Gill.
Our Lady of Lourdes (1960)
Rev. Brian J. Converse '91.
St. Mary (1870) (Polish) [CEM 2] Yoked with St. Catherine of Siena, Preston & St. Thomas the Apostle, Voluntown.
Very Rev. Ted F. Tumicki, S.T.L., J.C.L., J.V. '97.
Rev. Stephen S. Gulino '97.
St. Lawrence (1978)
Rev. Joseph DeCosta '90.
St. Francis of Assisi (1945) Yoked with St. Andrew, Colchester.
Rev. Marek Masnicki '92.
Rev. Benjamin V. Soosaimanickam '90.
St. Colman (1890) Yoked with Notre Dame, Durham.
Rev. Michael C. Giannitelli '91.
Rev. James Sucholet '91.
Deacon Ronald Blank.
St. Francis of Assisi
In Res.
Rev. George Busto, C.O.
St. Mary of Czestochowa (1903)
Rev. Richard Sliwinski.
St. Pius X (1957)
Very Rev. John Gallagher, O.F.M.Cap., Admin.
St. John the Evangelist (1881) [CEM] Yoked with Our Lady of Perpetual Help, Quaker Hill & Our Lady of the Lakes, Oakdale.
Rev. Joseph B. Whittel '03.
Rev. Richard D. Breton Jr. '08.
Rev. Tadeusz Zadorozny, Poland '99.
Deacon William T. Herrmann.
Deacon Ronald S. Kitlinski, Ordinary.
St. Joseph (1907)
Rev. George Mattathilanickal.
St. Mary, Star of the Sea (1870)
Rev. Robert F. Buongirno.
St. Joseph (1872)
Rev. Nicholas Mukama Mbogo, Parochial Vicar '05.
Our Lady of the Lakes (1966) Yoked with Our Lady of Perpetual Help, Quaker Hill & St. John the Evangelist Church, Montville.
Rev. Joseph B. Whittel '03.
Rev. Richard D. Breton Jr. '08.
Rev. Tadeusz Zadorozny, Poland '99.
Deacon Ronald S. Kitlinski.
St. Joseph (1878), Versailles, CT
Rev. Augustine Naduvilekoot '71.
Most Holy Trinity (1886)
Rev. David P. Choquette '98.
Rev. Anthony J. DiMarco '06.
Deacon Pierre M. Desilets.
St. Catherine of Siena (1975) Yoked with St. Mary, Jewett City & St. Thomas the Apostle, Voluntown.
Very Rev. Ted F. Tumicki, S.T.L., J.C.L., J.V. '97.
Rev. Stephen S. Gulino '97.
Deacon Paul R. Baillargeron.
Deacon Anthony Dombrowski.
St. Mary Church of the Visitation (1866)
Rev. Anthony DiMarco '06.
Deacon Jorge Escalona.
Our Lady of Perpetual Help (1904) (Polish) Yoked with St. John the Evangelist, Montville & Our Lady of the Lakes, Oakdale.
Rev. Richard D. Breton Jr. '08.
Rev. Tadeusz Zadorozny, Poland '99.
Deacon William T. Herrmann.
St. Stephen (1955) Yoked with St. Joseph, North Grosvenordale. *Mailing Address:* 12 Main St., P.O. Box 897, North Grosvenordale, CT, 06255.
St. Matthew
In Res.
Rev. William J. Olesik '72.
St, Thomas the Apostle (1892) [CEM] Yoked with St. Mary, Jewett City & St. Catherine of Siena, Preston.
Very Rev. Ted F. Tumicki, S.T.L., J.C.L., J.V. '97.
Rev. Stephen S. Gulino '97.
Deacon Paul R. Baillargeron.
Deacon Anthony Dombrowski.

St. Joseph (1859)
Rev. George J. Richards Jr., J.C.L. '95.
Rev. Luis Henry Agudelo.

Diocese of Oakland

New Listings
Exorcist
Rev. Kenneth Nobrega '08 2121 Harrison St., Ste. 100, Oakland, CA, 94612-3788.
Tel: 510-267-8345
St. Philip Neri St. Albert the Great 3101 Van Buren St., Alameda, CA, 94501-4840.
Tel: 510-373-5200, Ext. 205 ***Fax:*** 510-522-8123
Email: secretary@saspn.org
Web: www.saspn.org
Rev. Joy Kumarthusseril, M.F., India '88.
Magnificate S.O.T.I. - Walnut Creek Chapter 909 Carol Ln., Lafayette, CA, 94549.
Tel: 925-954-7205 ***Fax:*** 925-954-7205
Web: www.magnificatsoti.org
Mary L. Johnstone, Coord.
Newly Ordained
Our Lady of Guadalupe (2000)
Rev. Alexander Castillo, Parochial Vicar '11.
St. Joseph (1947)
Rev. Edilberto Castanas, Parochial Vicar '11.
St. Patrick (1923)
Rev. Rafal Duda, Parochial Vicar '11.
St. Leander (1864)
Rev. Gerald Pedrera, Parochial Vicar '11.
Revisions
The Roman Catholic Welfare Corporation of Oakland Officers
Mrs. Linda Basman, Vice Pres.
The Roman Catholic Welfare Corporation of Oakland Members of the Board - Appointed
Sr. Glenn Anne McPhee, O.P.
Mr. Joseph L. Connell, Ph.D.
Deans
Deanery #1
Rev. Raymond Sacca '79.
Deans
Deanery #2
Rev. Timothy K. Johnson '71.
Deans
Deanery #3
Rev. Jesus Nieto-Ruiz '94.
Deans
Deanery #4
Rev. James Matthews '74.
Deans
Deanery #5
Rev. Fred Riccio '77.
Deans
Deanery #6
Rev. David J. Farrugia, O.P. '60.
Deans
Deanery #7
Rev. Gary Klauer, O.F.M.Conv. '75.
Deans
Deanery #8
Rev. James J. Thottapally '71.
Deans
Deanery #9
Rev. John Kasper, O.S.F.S. '79.
Deans
Deanery #10
Rev. Leo Alban Asuncion '79.
Deans
Deanery #11
Rev. Richard Mangini.
Deans
Deanery #12
Rev. Richard J. Culver '85.
Deans
Deanery #13
Rev. Olman Solis '97.
Deans
Deanery #14
Rev. Robert Mendonca '00.
Deans
Deanery #15
Rev. John Prochaska '93.
Deans
Deanery #16
Rev. Geoffrey Baraan '97.
Deans
Deanery #18
Vacant.
Catholic Schools Office
Ms. Elizabeth Guneratne, Interim Asst. Supt.
Tel: 510-628-2157
Mrs. Margo Tanmen, Controller.
Tel: 510-628-2157
FACE (Family Aid Catholic Education, Tuition Assistance)
Chris Good, Dir. 2121 Harrison St., Ste. 100, Oakland, CA, 94612-3788.
Tel: 510-628-2169
Department for Evangelization and Catechetics
Mr. Keith Borchers, Dir. 2121 Harrison St., Ste. 100, Oakland, CA, 94612-3788.
Tel: 510-893-4711 ***Fax:*** 510-272-0738
Coordinator of Catechesis and Adult Faith Formation
Mr. Samuel Vasquez.
Vocations
Rev. Kenneth Nobrega, Priestly and Relg. & Dir. for Seminarians '08.
Tel: 510-267-8345
Cathedral Parish of Christ the Light (2008)
Rev. Joseph Nguyen, Parochial Vicar.
St. Bernard (1912)
Rev. Dominic Asare, S.V.D., Parochial Vicar.
St. Theresa of the Infant Jesus (The Little Flower) (1925)
Rev. Robert J. McCann, J.C.L. '81.
St. Albert (1976) Merged with St. Philip Neri, Alameda to form St. Philip Neri St. Albert the Great, Alameda.
St. Philip Neri (1925) Merged with St. Albert, Alameda to form St. Philip Neri St. Albert the Great, Alameda.
Most Holy Rosary (1874)
Rev. Dismas Sayre, O.P., Parochial Vicar '08.
St. Ambrose (1909)
Rev. John Gibson, S.D.B. '70.
St. Raymond (1961)
Rev. Neal Clemens, Parochial Admin. '01.
St. John the Baptist (1925)
Rev. Thuong Hoai Nguyen.
All Saints (1898)
Rev. Fernando Cortez, Parochial Vicar.
St. Clement (1951)
Rev. Giopre Prado, Parochial Vicar '09.
St. Joachim (1950)
Rev. Joseph Sebastian, S.V.D.
St. Anthony (1925)
Rev. Kenneth Sales, Parochial Vicar '04.
The Catholic Community of Pleasanton (1901)
Rev. Weerasak (Lee) Chompoochan, Parochial Vicar '06.
St. Leander (1864)
Rev. Juan Franco, Parochial Vicar '08.
Our Lady of Good Counsel (1966)
Rev. Jan Rudzewicz, Parochial Admin. '83.
St. Mary (1941)
Rev. Ruben Morales-Morfin, Parochial Vicar '04.
On Duty Outside the Diocese
Rev. Quang Minh Dong '91.
Military Chaplains
Rev. Van Dinh, Chap. '02 Barksdale AFB 111 Woodvale Cir., Bossier City, LA, 71111
On Sabbatical
Rev. Lawrence C. D'Anjou '00.

Archdiocese of Oklahoma City

New Listings
School— **Good Shepherd Catholic School** 13404 N. Meridian, Oklahoma City, OK, 73120.
Tel: 405-721-4202 ***Fax:*** 405-709-2811
Sr. Catherine Powers, C.N.D., Supt., Schools.
Mercy El Reno Hospital Corporation 2115 Parkview Dr., El Reno, OK, 73036.
Tel: 405-262-2640 ***Fax:*** 405-422-2521
Paul Foster, Contact Person.

Diocese of Orange in California

Revisions
Holy Trinity (2005) 1600 Corporate Dr., Ladera Ranch, CA, 92694.
Tel: 949-218-3131 ***Fax:*** 949-388-1311
Email: frreynold@holytrinityladera.org
Web: www.holytrinityladera.org

Diocese of Orlando

Revisions
Vicar General and Chancellor for Canonical Affairs
Very Rev. Gregory Parkes, J.C.L. '99 ***Mailing Address:*** P.O. Box 1800, Orlando, FL, 32802.
Tel: 407-246-4846
Email: gparkes@orlandodiocese.org
Presbyteral Council
President
Most Rev. John Noonan Diocese of Orlando.
Ex Officio Members
Very Rev. Esau Garcia, V.F., (South Central Dean) '87.
Very Rev. John Giel, V.F., J.C.L., (Northern Dean) '78.
Very Rev. Sean Heslin, V.F., (Southern Dean) '67.
Very Rev. Stan Murray, V.F., (Eastern Dean) '69.
Very Rev. Gregory Parkes, J.C.L., V.G., Chancellor for Canonical Affairs '99.
Very Rev. Stephen D. Parkes, V.F., (North Central Dean) '98.
Very Rev. Peter Puntal, V.F., (Western Dean) '82.
Very Rev. Richard Walsh, Vicar Gen. '68.
Very Rev. Miguel A. Gonzalez, Vicar for Priests '98.
Very Rev. Paul Henry, Vicar for Priests '68.
Representative by Age
Rev. Karl Bergin, (25-45) '04.
Rev. Richard W. Trout, (46-64) '85.
Rev. Nicholas King, (65 & over) '66.
Representative - Secular Priests Not Incardinated
Rev. Roy V. Eco '80.
Representative - Religious Priests
Rev. Benjamin A. Berinti, C.PP.S., V.F. '85.
Representative - Retired Priests
Rev. Msgr. David Page '58.
Appointed Members
Rev. Ybain F. Ramirez '96.
Rev. Jean Gaetan Boursiquot '81.
Vicar for Religious
Vacant ***Mailing Address:*** P.O. Box 1800, Orlando, FL, 32802
Secretariat for Evangelization
Daniel Hardester, Sec. ***Mailing Address:*** P.O. Box 1800, Orlando, FL, 32802.
Tel: 407-246-4895
Email: dhardester@orlandodiocese.org
Communications
Teresa Peterson, Dir. ***Mailing Address:*** P.O. Box 1800, Orlando, FL, 32802.
Tel: 407-246-4811
Email: tpeterson@orlandodiocese.org
Newspaper "The Florida Catholic"
Teresa Peterson ***Mailing Address:*** P.O. Box 1800, Orlando, FL, 32802.
Tel: 407-246-4811
Email: tpeterson@orlandodiocese.org
Secretariat for Faith Formation
Henry Fortier, Sec. & Supt. Schools ***Mailing Address:*** P.O. Box 1800, Orlando, FL, 32802.
Tel: 407-246-4904 ***Fax:*** 407-246-4940
Email: hfortier@orlandodiocese.org
Religious Education
Vacant, Sr. Dir. ***Mailing Address:*** P.O. Box 1800, Orlando, FL, 32802.
Tel: 407-246-4910 ***Fax:*** 407-246-4935
Schools
Henry Fortier, Sec. & Supt. Schools ***Mailing Address:*** P.O. Box 1800, Orlando, FL, 32802.
Tel: 407-246-4904 ***Fax:*** 407-246-4940
Email: hfortier@orlandodiocese.org
Korean Ministry
Rev. Andrea Lee.
Vocations
Rev. Jorge Torres, Dir. '05 ***Mailing Address:*** P.O. Box 1800, Orlando, FL, 32802.
Tel: 407-246-4875 ***Fax:*** 407-246-4937
Email: jtorres@orlandodiocese.org
Prison Ministry
Deacon David L. Gray, Dir. ***Mailing Address:*** P.O. Box 1800, Orlando, FL, 32802.
Tel: 407-246-4868
**Catholic Foundation of Central Florida, Inc.*
James Edwards ***Mailing Address:*** P.O. Box 4905, Orlando, FL, 32801-4905. 50 E. Robinson St., Orlando, FL, 32801.
Tel: 407-246-4841 ***Fax:*** 407-246-4939

Diocese of Paterson

New Listings
Permanent Diaconate Program
Rev. Frank P. Agresti, Spiritual Dir. '03.
NCPC, Inc. 112 Erskine Rd., Ringwood, NJ, 07456.
Tel: 973-962-7032
Most Rev. Arthur J. Serratelli, S.T.D., S.S.L., D.D., Pres.
Rev. Msgr. Patrick G. Panos, Sec. '68.
Newly Ordained
St. Anthony's (1908)
Rev. Roberto Amador, Parochial Vicar '11.
Our Lady of the Holy Angels (1883)
Rev. Ricardo Ortega, Parochial Vicar '11.
St. Joseph's (1853), Mendham, NJ
Rev. Pawel Bala, Parochial Vicar '11.
St. Margaret of Scotland (1885)
Rev. Jared J. Brogan, Parochial Vicar '11.
Rev. Michael Lee, Parochial Vicar '11.
St. Peter the Apostle (1938)

Rev. Raimundo Rivera, Parochial Vicar '11.
Assumption of the Blessed Virgin Mary (1891)
Rev. Jose Lopez, Parochial Vicar '11.
St. Nicholas (1868)
Rev. Jose Lopez, Parochial Vicar '11.
St. Cecilia's (1869)
Rev. Marcin Michalowski, Parochial Vicar '11.
Sacred Heart (1923)
Rev. Marcin Michalowski, Parochial Vicar '11.
St. Vincent de Paul (1886)
Rev. Leonardo Lopez, Parochial Vicar '11.
Revisions
Deans
Rev. Philip A. LeBeau, Northeast Morris '93.
Vacant, Paterson.
Rev. Robert J. Mitchell, Southeast Morris '85.
Rev. John DeMattia, Northern Morris '68.
Vacant, Northern Passaic.
Vice Chancellors
Rev. Kevin Corcoran.
Priest Secretary to the Bishop
Rev. Kevin Corcoran.
Diocesan Tribunal
Rev. Manuel Guevara '10.
Vocations Office 737 Valley Rd., Clifton, NJ, 07013.
Tel: 973-777-2955 ***Fax:*** 973-777-4597
Rev. Hubert Jurjewicz, Dir.
Rev. Benjamin Williams, Asst. Dir. '10.
Director of Catechesis
Rev. Derek Anderson, S.O.L.T.
Boy Scouting
Rev. Brian P. Quinn, Chap. '10.
Blessed Sacrament (1911)
Rev. Ramon Orama, Admin.
Rev. Misael Jaramillo, Parochial Vicar '01.
St. George (1897)
Rev. Robert W. Wisniefski, Admin. '80.
St. Gerard Majella (1962)
Rev. Rijo Johnson, S.D.V.
St. Michael the Archangel (1903)
Rev. Rijo Johnson, S.D.V.
Our Lady of Lourdes (1882)
Rev. Ramon Orama, Admin.
Rev. Misael Jaramillo, Parochial Vicar '01.
Our Lady of Pompei (1916)
Rev. Frank P. Agresti '03.
Rev. Sal J. Panagia, Pastor Emeritus '73.
Good Shepherd (1979)
Rev. Msgr. Martin McDonnell '68.
Rev. Msgr. Richard A. Steiger, Pastor Emeritus '67.
Our Lady of Mount Carmel (1847)
Rev. Thomas H. Fallone '02.
St. Jude (1946)
Rev. Joseph J. Orlandi '73.
St. Brendan (1945)
Rev. Robert W. Wisniefski, Admin. '80.
St. Clare (1913)
Rev. Peter VB. Wells '84.
St. Clare
In Res.
Rev. Joseph J. Garbarino '83.
St. Paul (1914)
Rev. Leonardo Jaramillo '92.
Our Lady Queen of the Most Holy Rosary (1959)
Rev. Nelson Betancur, Parochial Vicar '75.
Sacred Heart (1904)
Rev. Nelson Betancur, Parochial Vicar '75.
Holy Family (1951)
Rev. Frederick Walters '87.
St. Simon the Apostle (Rockaway Twp.) (1942)
Rev. Daniel Staniskis, Admin. '84.
St. Anthony's (1908)
Rev. Msgr. Raymond J. Kupke, Ph.D. '73.
Our Lady Queen of Peace (1921)
Rev. Michael Rodak, Admin. '07.
St. Mark the Evangelist (1986)
Rev. Abuchi Nwosu, Parochial Vicar '08.
St. Pius X (1959)
Rev. Mark Olenowski '85.
Assumption of the Blessed Virgin Mary (1848)
Rev. Philip-Michael Tangora, Parochial Vicar.
Assumption of the Blessed Virgin Mary
In Res.
Rev. Dennis J. Crowley '89.
St. Joseph (1854)
Rev. Brian Sullivan '03.
Assumption of the Blessed Virgin Mary (1891)
Rev. Edgar Ruiz, Admin. '01.
St. Nicholas (1868)
Rev. Edgar Ruiz, Admin. '01.
Rev. Msgr. Felipe N. Carvajal, Pastor Emeritus '68.
St. Cecilia's (1869)
Rev. Daniel O'Mullane, Parochial Vicar '10.
Sacred Heart (1923)
Rev. Daniel O'Mullane, Parochial Vicar '10.
Sacred Heart
In Res.
Rev. Stephen Sniscak '10.
Our Lady of the Mountain (1954)
Rev. Msgr. Joseph J. Goode, M.Ch.A. '73.
Rev. Abuchi Nwosu, Parochial Vicar '08.
Our Lady of the Lake (1935)
Rev. Gregorz Golba, Parochial Vicar '97.
St. Vincent de Paul (1886)
Rev. A. Richard Carton '93.
St. Therese (1957)
Rev. Marc A. Mancini, J.C.L. '92.
Rev. Vidal Gonzales, Parochial Vicar '09.
Rev. William Santeliz, Parochial Vicar '07.
Our Lady of Mt. Carmel (1951), Swartswood, NJ
Rev. Brian Ditullio, Admin. '06.
St. James of the Marches (1926)
Rev. J. Patrick Ryan '76.
Holy Cross (1925)
Rev. Msgr. Christopher C. DiLella, Admin. '79.
Rev. Charles J. Parr, Ph.D., Pastor Emeritus '73.
Our Lady of the Valley (1960)
Rev. Msgr. Christopher C. DiLella '79.
Rev. ST Sutton, Parochial Vicar.
Our Lady of Mercy (1854)
Rev. Janusz Rzadca, Parochial Vicar '95.
St. Clare Hospital, Denville, NJ
Rev. Stephen Sniscak, Chap. '10.
Morristown Memorial Hospital, Morristown, NJ
Rev. Dennis J. Crowley '89.
Morris County Jail
Rev. Hernan Arias, Coord. Prison Ministry '85.
Graduate Studies
Rev. Joseph J. Garbarino '83 Fordham University.
Retired
Rev. Robert K. Hooper '70.
Rev. Victor J. Mazza '70.
Domus Bartimaeus, Boonton, NJ
Rev. Hubert Jurjewicz, Dir.
St. Paul Inside The Walls: The Catholic Center for Evangelization at Bayley-Ellard
In Res.
Rev. Derek Anderson, S.O.L.T.
St. Anthony's Guild Paterson, NJ, 07509.
Tel: 973-777-1915 ***Fax:*** 973-777-5687
Email: anthonian@aol.com
Web: www.anthonian.org
Rev. David I. Convertino, O.F.M., Dir. Membership organization supports the work of The Franciscan Friars of Holy Name Province.

Diocese of Pensacola-Tallahassee

Newly Ordained
Cathedral of the Sacred Heart (1905), Pensacola, FL
Rev. Matthew Worthen, Parochial Vicar '11.
Holy Spirit (1976)
Rev. Thomas Dillon, Parochial Vicar '11.
Blessed Sacrament (1845)
Rev. Timothy Holeda, Parochial Vicar '11.
Revisions
Hispanic Ministry, Office of Co Directors
Rev. Nicholas Frank Schumm '06.
Sr. Margaret Kuntz, A.S.C.J.
Little Flower (1945)
Rev. James Thoyalil, V.C., India '91.
Sacred Heart of Jesus (1960)
Rev. Edward T. Jones, Admin. '03.
St. Rose of Lima (1957)
Rev. Msgr. Stephen C. Bosso '78.
Rev. Richard Lee Schamber, Parochial Vicar '07.
St. Thomas the Apostle (1957)
Rev. Nicholas Frank Schumm '06.
St. Stephen the Protomartyr (1979), Woodville, FL
Rev. Kurian Manikuttiyil, Admin. '90.
On Duty Outside the Diocese
Rev. Juan Pedro Hernandez '89.
Rev. Dennis J. O'Brien '81 South America.

Archdiocese of Philadelphia

New Listings
The Mercy Foundation 515 Montgomery Ave., Merion Station, PA, 19066-1297.
Tel: 610-664-6650 ***Fax:*** 610-664-3429
Sr. Christine McCann, R.S.M., Pres.
Email: cmccann@mercymidatlantic.org
Revisions
Most Reverend Charles J. Chaput, O.F.M.Cap., Archbishop of Philadelphia ordained August 29, 1970; appointed Bishop of Rapid City April 11, 1988; Episcopal ordination July 26, 1988; appointed Archbishop of Denver February 18, 1997; installed April 7, 1997; appointed Archbishop of Philadelphia July 19, 2011; installed September 8, 2011 ***Office:*** 222 N. 17th St., Philadelphia, PA, 19103-1299.
His Eminence Cardinal Justin Rigali, Archbishop Emeritus of Philadelphia ordained April 25, 1961; appointed Archbishop and President of the Pontifical Ecclesiastical Academy June 8, 1985; Episcopal ordination September 14, 1985; appointed Archbishop of St. Louis January 25, 1994; installed March 15, 1994; appointed Archbishop of Philadelphia July 15, 2003; installed October 7, 2003; created Cardinal Priest October 21, 2003; retired July 19, 2011 ***Office:*** P.O. Box 11886, Knoxville, TN 37939.

Diocese of Phoenix

New Listings
Housing for Hope, Inc. 4747 N. 7th Ave, Phoenix, AZ, 85013.
Tel: 602-650-4848
William Schultz, Principal Officer. Housing for poor & needy individuals & families.
FSL Christopher Properties 1201 E. Thomas Rd., Phoenix, AZ, 85014.

Archdiocese of Portland in Oregon

New Listings
**Fr. Bernard Youth Center, Inc.* P.O. Box 790, Mount Angel, OR, 97362-0790.
Revisions
Mount Angel Seminary, St. Benedict, OR
Very Rev. J. Richard Paperini, Pres. & Rector '77.

Diocese of Raleigh

Revisions
Stewardship and Advancement
Office of Divine Worship
Office for Peace and Justice
Vacant, Dir.
Tel: 919-821-9751
Cathedral of the Sacred Heart (1834)
Rev. Francisco Javier Garcia Gonzalez, Parochial Vicar.
Cathedral of the Sacred Heart
In Res.
Rev. Lourduraj Alapaty.
Doggett Center at Aquinas House, Raleigh, NC
Rev. Anthony De Candia, Campus Min. '07.
St. Luke the Evangelist (1985)
Rev. Msgr. John F. O'Connor, V.F. '73.
Our Lady of Lourdes
In Res.
Very Rev. Carlos Arce-Flores, V.F. '91.
St. Joseph (1908)
Rev. John Alex Gonzalez '02.
Blessed Sacrament (1929), Burlington, NC
Rev. Paul Gabriel, O.F.M.Conv. '05.
St. Michael the Archangel (1962)
Rev. Douglas Reed '71.
Rev. Jaime Perez Restrepo, Parochial Vicar.
Deacon Terry Mancuso.
St. Thomas More (1940)
Rev. Scott E. McCue '01.
Rev. James M. Labosky, Parochial Vicar '79.
Holy Infant (1970)
Rev. David J. Devlin, O.S.F.S.
Immaculate Conception (1906)
Rev. Lawrence Hayes, O.F.M., Parochial Vicar.
St. Matthew (1990)
Rev. Thanh N. Nguyen '94.
St. Anne (1858), Edenton, NC
Rev. William L. Pitts '70.
Rev. Manuel Segundo Noriega, Parochial Vicar.
St. Patrick (1824), Fayetteville, NC
Rev. Rafael A. Leon-Valencia, Parochial Vicar '04.
Shrine of the Infant of Prague, Church of the Holy Spirit (1941), Jacksonville, NC
Rev. Jeffrey Bowker, L.C., Parochial Vicar.
Holy Spirit Catholic Church (1921), Kinston, NC
Rev. Bill John Acosta-Escobar '02.
Our Lady of the Rosary (1999)
Rev. Johanes Teguh Raharjo, C.I.C.M., Admin. '06.
St. Ha-Sang Paul Jung (1988), New Hill, NC
Rev. Chul Ho Lee.
Sacred Heart (1919), Pinehurst, NC
Rev. Edward Burch '03.
Rev. Gregory Anatuanya, Parochial Vicar.
Mission— Saint Juan Diego, Robbins, NC
Rev. Rodolfo Gonzalez, Admin.
St. Elizabeth of Hungary (1959), Raeford, NC
Sr. Elizabeth Bullen, I.H.M., Pastoral Admin.

St. Catherine of Siena (1940)
Rev. Brendan K. Buckler, Parochial Vicar.
St. Eugene (1948), Wendell, NC
Rev. Ryan Z. Carnecer, C.I.C.M., Parochial Vicar.
Catholic Community of Bertie & Washington Counties (2004), Windsor, NC
Rev. Michael J. Kerin, G.H.M.
Special Assignment
Rev. Roman A. Acero '08 Cardinal Gibbons High School 1401 Edwards Mill Rd., Raleigh, NC, 27607
Absent on Leave
Rev. Walter Ospina-Briceno '02.
Rev. Michael R. Spurr '08.
Retired
Rev. Robert W. Diegelman '93.

Diocese of Rochester

Newly Ordained
Blessed Sacrament (1902)
Rev. Scott Caton, Parochial Vicar '11.
St. Boniface (1860)
Rev. Scott Caton, Parochial Vicar '11.
St. Mary (1834)
Rev. Scott Caton, Parochial Vicar '11.
Revisions
St. Boniface (1860)
Rev. Robert J. Kennedy '74.
St. Lawrence (1959)
Rev. Peter Enyan-Boadu, Parochial Vicar '84.
St. Mary (1834)
Rev. Robert J. Kennedy, Parochial Vicar '74.
Peace of Christ Roman Catholic Parish of Rochester, NY, Rochester, NY
Rev. Timothy Brown, Parochial Vicar '88.
Roman Catholic Parish of St. Francis Xavier Cabrini
Rev. William McGrath, Parochial Vicar '00.
Rev. Robert Thomas Werth, Parochial Vicar '79.
Deacon David A. Palma, Pastoral Admin.
Holy Family (1834)
Rev. John Gathenya '86.
Nativity of the Blessed Virgin Mary (1848)
Rev. Theodore J. Auble, Parochial Vicar '75.
Charlotte M. Bruney, Pastoral Admin.
St. Columba (1885)
Rev. William Endres, Parochial Vicar '69.
Rev. Steven W. Lape, Parochial Vicar '99.
Irene Goodwin, Pastoral Admin.
St. Vincent De Paul (1869)
Rev. William Endres, Parochial Vicar '69.
Rev. Steven W. Lape, Parochial Vicar '99.
Irene Goodwin, Pastoral Admin.
St. John the Evangelist (1852)
Rev. Augustine Chumo '98.
St. Jerome (1905)
Rev. William B. Leone '74.
St. Michael (1852)
Rev. Augustine Chumo '98.
Our Lady of the Lakes Catholic Community
Rev. Stanley Kacprzak '85.
St. Louis (1911), Pittsford, NY
Rev. Robert P. Ring '82.
St. Mary of the Assumption (1853)
Rev. William Endres, Parochial Vicar '69.
Rev. Steven W. Lape, Parochial Vicar '99.
Irene Goodwin, Pastoral Admin.
Holy Trinity (1861)
Rev. Timothy E. Horan '79.
St. Paul (1967)
Rev. Paul Gitau '94.
Our Lady of the Snow (2005), Weedsport, NY
Rev. William G. Darling '73.
Mercy Community Services, Inc. (1980) 198 Oriole St., Rochester, NY, 14613-1923.
Tel: 585-254-2175 ***Fax:*** 585-254-2229
Email: info@mercyresidential.org
Web: www.mercyresidential.org
Supportive Housing for Single Mothers and their Children.
Total Staff 17; Families Assisted 90

Archdiocese of St. Louis

New Listings
School Sisters of Notre Dame Central Pacific Province, Inc. 320 E. Ripa, Saint Louis, MO, 63125.
Sr. Mary Anne Owens, S.S.N.D., Prov. Supr.
Revisions
Alexian Court Apartments 2636 Chippewa St., Saint Louis, MO, 63118.
Tel: 314-771-5604 ***Fax:*** 314-771-7629
Web: www.alexianbrothers.net
Alexian Brothers Services, Inc. Sponsored by Alexian Brothers Senior Ministries. Managed by National Church Residence.
Mercy Hospital St. Louis formerly: St. John's Mercy Medical Center 615 S. New Ballas Rd., Creve Coeur, MO, 63141.
Tel: 314-251-6000 ***Fax:*** 314-251-4168
Web: www.stjohnsmercy.org
Conducted by the Sisters of Mercy of the Americas-St. Louis Region.
(See Branch Unit under Washington, MO).
Sisters 3; Nurses 2,000; Bed Capacity 979; Skilled Nursing 120; Total Staff 5,800
Mercy Hospital Washington formerly: St. John's Mercy Hospital (1926) 901 E. 5th St., Washington, MO, 63090.
Tel: 636-239-8000 ***Fax:*** 636-569-6733
Web: www.stjohnsmercy.org/sjmh
(See Listing Under Creve Coeur, MO).
Bed Capacity 187; Total Staff 790; Total Assisted Annually 18,990
St. Francis de Sales Association (Paris 1872) (St. Louis 1950) 9328 Pine Ave., St. Louis, MO, 63144.
Tel: 314-963-9603
Email: ann.wiedl@sbcglobal.net
A call to the laity to live their individual vocation in the spirit of Jesus, using the writings of St. Francis de Sales as a means to see and do God's will and grow in holiness.; Private Universal Association of the Faithful.
Room at the Inn formerly: Providence Ministry Corporation (1998) 3415 Bridgeland Dr., Bridgeton, MO, 63044.
Tel: 314-209-9181 ***Fax:*** 314-209-9207
Web: www.divineprovidenceweb.org
Mercy Health formerly: Sisters of Mercy Health System 14528 S. Outer Forty, Ste. 100, Chesterfield, MO, 63017.
Tel: 314-579-6100 ***Fax:*** 314-628-3732
Email: michele.giunta@mercy.net
Web: www.mercy.net

Archdiocese of St. Paul and Minneapolis

New Listings
Regional Vicars
Rev. Michael C. Skluzacek, Vicar Region 1 (Northeast) '80.
Rev. Charles Lachowitzer, Vicar Region 2 (South).
Rev. Robert M. Schwartz, Vicar Region 3 (Northwest) '67.
Newly Ordained
St. Joseph (1942), West St. Paul, MN
Rev. James Lannan '11.
St. John Neumann (1977)
Rev. Anthony O'Neill '11.
St. Stephen (1856)
Rev. Nathan LaLiberte '11.
St. Elizabeth Ann Seton (1987)
Rev. Cole Kracke '11.
All Saints (1877), Lakeville, MN
Rev. Jonathan Kelly '11.
High School— **Hill-Murray School**, Maplewood, MN
Rev. James Lannan, Chap. '11.
High School— **Convent of the Visitation School** (1873), Mendota Heights, MN
Rev. Anthony O'Neill, Chap. '11.
Revisions
Catholic Charities
Tim Marx, CEO 1200 2nd Ave. S., Minneapolis, MN, 55403.
Tel: 612-664-8527
Web: www.cctwincities.org
Judicial Vicar
Very Rev. Timothy Cloutier, J.C.L. '83 328 Kellogg Blvd. W., St. Paul, MN, 55102-1997.
Tel: 651-291-4466 ***Fax:*** 651-291-4467
Email: tribunal@archspm.org
Web: www.archspm.org/tribunal
Vicar for Latinos
Rev. Kevin T. Kenney '94 Our Lady of Guadalupe 401 Concord St., Saint Paul, MN, 55107-2475
Office of Indian Ministry
Rev. Michael Tegeder '78 The Church of Gichitwaa Kateri 3045 Park Ave. S., Minneapolis, MN, 55407.
Tel: 612-824-7606
Worship Site: St. Thomas the Apostle 2119 Stillwater Ave., St. Paul, MN, 55119.
St. Thomas The Apostle (1954) Merged with Blessed Sacrament, St. Paul.
Church of St. Rita (1966), Cottage Grove, MN
Rev. Richard A. Banker '88.
St. Jude of the Lake (1939)
Rev. Kevin P. Magner '03.
St. Peter (1888), North Saint Paul, MN
Rev. William Deziel, O.S.C. '97.
Guardian Angels (1885), Oakdale, MN
Rev. Rodger Bauman '82.
St. Michael (1868)
Rev. Michael L. Rudolph '05.
St. Mary of the Lake (1881)
Rev. Ralph W. Talbot '04.
All Saints (1916)
Rev. Nels H. Gjengdahl, Parochial Admin. '07.
Church of St. Anne - St. Joseph Hien (1884/1987)
Rev. Ignatius Nguyen Dai Kinh, C.M.C.
Rev. Hilary M. Nhuan Tran, C.M.C. (SPC) '10.
St. Frances Cabrini (1946)
Rev. Michael Tegeder, Parochial Admin. '78.
St. Philip (1906), Minneapolis, MN
Rev. Michael O'Connell '67.
St. Edward (1967), Bloomington, MN
Rev. Daniel F. Griffith, Parochial Admin. '02.
Nativity of the Blessed Virgin Mary (1949)
Rev. Abraham Kochupurackal, C.M.I.
St. Vincent de Paul (1855)
Rev. Jon Bennet Tran '08.
Church of the Risen Savior (1970)
Rev. Thomas Krenik '77.
Immaculate Conception (1923)
Rev. Eugene W. Tiffany '72.
St. Raphael (1951)
Rev. James Hermann, Parochial Admin.
St. Thomas Becket (1989)
Rev. Timothy Wozniak '74.
Pax Christi (1981)
Rev. William A. Murtaugh '72.
Our Lady of Grace (1946)
Rev. Allan Paul Eilen '09.
St. Patrick (1857)
Rev. Timothy C. Rudolphi '89.
St. Joseph (1858)
Rev. Terrence Rassmussen, Parochial Admin. '79.
St. Peter (1943), Richfield, MN
Rev. Gerald Dvorak '79.
St. Richard (1952)
Rev. William F. Martin '78.
St. Charles (1943), Bayport, MN
Rev. Mark R. Juettner '79.
St. Hubert (1865)
Rev. Rolf R. Tollefson '01.
Rev. Paul Basil Kubista '10.
Guardian Angels (1858)
Rev. Douglas Ebert '09.
St. Thomas the Apostle (1896)
Rev. John Gallas '05.
St. Joseph (1902), Delano, MN
Rev. Paul A. Kammen '07.
St. Peter (1865)
Rev. Paul A. Kammen '07.
The Church of Saint Francis Xavier of Franconia, Franconia, MN
Rev. Frank J. Wampach '84.
St. Joseph's (1922), Hopkins, MN
Rev. James C. Liekhus '05.
Immaculate Conception (1903), Lonsdale, MN
Rev. Thomas E. McCabe '92.
St. Mary of the Purification (1855), Shakopee, MN
Rev. Thomas Boedy, S.J. '70.
Holy Name of Jesus (1865)
Rev. Stephen D. Ulrick '82.
St. Henry (1904)
Rev. Tony VanderLoop '03.
Our Lady of the Lake (1909)
Rev. Timothy E. Dolan '83.
St. Michael (1878), Pine Island, MN
Rev. Randal J. Kasel '05.
St. Joseph (1865), Rosemount, MN
Rev. Paul Jarvis '04.
Church of St. Mary (1865)
Rev. Thomas Boedy, S.J. '70.
St. Mark (1856)
Rev. Peter C. Wittman '75.
Rev. Thomas Boedy, S.J. '70.
St. Augustine (1896) Merged with Holy Trinity, South St. Paul.
Worship Site: St. Augustine 408 Third St., N., South St Paul, MN, 55075.
St. Joseph's (1873)
Rev. Frank J. Wampach '84.
Immaculate Conception (1863)
Rev. Joseph Fink '83.
St. Mary (1884)
Rev. Kenneth L. O'Hotto '80.
St. Paul (1900), Zumbrota, MN
Rev. Randal J. Kasel '05.
St. Therese Care Center & Residence 8000 Bass Lake Rd., New Hope, MN, 55428.
Rev. Matthew Ehmke, Chap. '70.
Special Assignment
Rev. James Gorman '81.
Rev. Timothy Morin '77.
Rev. Jules Omba Omalanga '93.

Rev. Leo J. Tibesar '68.
On Duty Outside the Archdiocese
Rev. Shane A. Campbell '08 Serving in Diocese of Bismarck.
Rev. Timothy L. Norris '94 Venezuelan Mission, Diocese of Ciudad Guayana.
Graduate Studies
Rev. Daniel J. Bodin '05. Catholic University of America.
Retired
Rev. Albert P. Backmann '00 1304 Medicine Lake Dr. W. #222, Plymouth, MN, 55441
Rev. Gregory T. Welch '67 181 Edgecumbe Rd., #1402, St. Paul, MN, 55105
***High School*— DeLaSalle High School**, Minneapolis, MN
Rev. Patrick Thomas Barnes, Chap. '10.
***School*— Holy Cross Catholic School**, Webster, MN
Rev. Thomas E. McCabe, Canonical Admin. '92.

Diocese of St. Petersburg

Revisions

Vicar General
Rev. Msgr. Robert F. Morris, V.G. '91.
Moderator of the Curia
Rev. Msgr. Robert F. Morris, V.G. '91.
Promoters of Justice
Very Rev. Joseph L. Waters, V.F., J.C.L. '87.
Department of Christian Formation
Rev. Msgr. Robert F. Morris, V.G. '91.
Cursillo, English
Jay Taylor, Lay Dir.
Email: jct1013@verizon.net
Ecumenical and Inter-Religious Affairs
Rev. Robert J. Schneider, Dir. '81 Espiritu Santo Church 2405 Philippe Pkwy., Safety Harbor, FL, 34695.
Tel: 727-726-8477
Deacon James Grevenites, Asst. Dir. St. Raphael Church 1376 Snell Isle Blvd., N.E., Saint Petersburg, FL, 33704.
Tel: 727-821-7989
Lay Pastoral Ministry Institute .
Tel: 727-344-1611
Dale Brown, Dir.
Multicultural Ministry
Mrs. Angelina Karpinski, Assoc. Dir.
Ms. Anyely Garcia, Sec.
Catholic Schools Office
Mrs. Helen S. Marston, M.S., Deputy Supt.
Mrs. Kay Rizzo, MAT, CAS, District Supt.-Northern.
Mr. Christopher Wiand, M.Ed., District Supt.-Pinellas.
Mr. Adam Jenkins, Asst. Supt. Educ. Programs.
Dr. Kristy Swol, Ed.D., District Supt.-Hillsborough.
Catholic Schools Office Secretaries
Mrs. Debra Kleinberger.
Presbyteral Council
Executive Committee
Rev. Msgr. Robert C. Gibbons, J.C.L., Chm. '81.
Catholic Daughters of America
Ms. Delia Sunnell, State Regent.
Tel: 813-714-9685
Email: dlsunn@verizon.net
National Office .
Tel: 212-877-3041
Cathedral of St. Jude the Apostle (1950)
School—
Mrs. Kelly Wiand, Interim Prin.
Transfiguration (1959)
Rev. Edward Wal '79.
Our Lady of Grace (1966)
Rev. Msgr. Avelino R. Garcia '68.
Church of the Nativity (1960)
Rev. Carlos Rojas '06.
All Saints (1987)
Deacon Thomas Shiel.
St. Catherine of Siena (1976)
Rev. Msgr. Robert Morris, V.G. '91.
Rev. John J. Marino, O.F.M. '88.
Our Lady of Lourdes (1958)
Rev. Jose Colina '89.
Most Holy Name of Jesus (1960)
Rev. James Ruhlin, Parochial Admin. '02.
St. Michael the Archangel (1971)
Rev. Jose Tejada '92.
St. Jerome (1956), Indian Rocks Beach, FL
Rev. Frans Berkhout.
Our Lady of the Rosary (1952), Land O'Lakes, FL
Rev. Rene Tapel.
St. Timothy (1985)
Rev. Kenneth Malley '97.
St. Clement (1912)
Rev. Paul Mizener '64.
Resurrection (1983), Riverview, FL
Rev. Eugeniusz Gancarz '71.
St. John Vianney (1939)
***School*—**, St. Pete Beach, FL
Jillian Hudson, Prin.
Espiritu Santo (1960)
Rev. Joseph Musco '06.
St. Francis of Assisi (1987)
Rev. Martin Madavana, I.C.
Rev. Christopher Fitzgerald, I.C., Pastor Emeritus '58.
Incarnation (1962)
Rev. Philip Dac Clement '08.
St. Joseph (1896), Tampa, FL
Rev. Vladimir Dziadek '82.
***School*— St. Joseph Catholic School**
Brenda Budd, Prin.
Mary Help of Christians (1966)
Rev. Joseph Chong, S.D.B.
St. Paul (1963), Tampa, FL
Rev. J. Glenn Diaz '87.
Rev. Timothy Cummings '08.
Sacred Heart (1860), Tampa, FL
Rev. Zachary Elliott, O.F.M.
***School*—**, Tampa, FL
Mr. Kenneth Hitchcock, Prin.
St. Stephen (1987)
Rev. Jose George '77.
Rev. Emery Longanga.
***School*—** Grades PreK-8 10424 St. Stephen Cir., Riverview, FL, 33569.
Tel: 813-741-9203 ***Fax:*** 813-741-9622
Ms. Therese Jackson, Prin.
Lay Teachers 52; Students 346
Retired
Rev. Msgr. Antonio Diez '59.
Rev. Msgr. Austin Mullen '65.
Rev. Patrick Kennedy '59.
Rev. Vincent Morton '86.
Rev. Felix Sanchez '65.
***High School*— Jesuit High School**, Tampa, FL
Barry Neuburger, Prin.
***School*— Most Holy Redeemer Interparochial School** (1954), Tampa, FL
Mr. Thom Laux, Prin.
***School*— Academy of the Holy Names** (1881), Tampa, FL
Bridgid Fishman, Interim Prin. Elementary School.
***School*— Villa Madonna School**, Tampa, FL
Sr. Danielle Gonzalez, F.M.A., Prin.
St Paul Children's Center, St. Petersburg, FL
Ms. Toni Johnston, Dir.
St. Paul Child Enrichment (1981), Tampa, FL
Mrs. Martha Aguiar, Dir.
***School*— Morning Star Catholic School - Pinellas Park, Inc.** (1969), Pinellas Park, FL
Mrs. Susan Conza, Prin.
St. Peter Nolasco Residence (1984), St. Petersburg, FL
Rev. Kenneth Breen, O.de.M., Local Supr. '85.
**Help Brings Hope for Haiti, Inc.* 3816 Morrison Ave., Tampa, FL, 33629.
Tel: 813-832-4244
Email: hbhh123@gmail.com
Web: www.hbhh.org
Patricia M. Eddy, Board Chair & Founder.

Diocese of Salina

New Listings

Diocesan Administrator
Rev. Barry Brinkman, J.C.L. '91.

Newly Ordained

St. John the Baptist Parish (1869)
Rev. Charles Awotwi, Parochial Vicar '11.

Revisions

St. Joseph Parish (1902), Wilson, KS
Rev. Jarett Konrade, Parochial Admin. '05.
St. Joseph Parish (1876)
Rev. Michael Scully, O.F.M.Cap. '65.
Rev. Barnabas Eichor, O.F.M.Cap., Parochial Vicar.
Rev. Felix Petrovsky, O.F.M.Cap. '55.
St. Mary Parish (1886), Wilson, KS
Rev. Jarett Konrade, Parochial Admin. '05.
St. Fidelis Parish (1876)
Rev. Jeff Ernst, O.F.M.Cap., Parochial Admin.
Rev. Earl Meyer, O.F.M.Cap. '60.
Rev. Myron Flax, O.F.M.Cap. '64.
St. Boniface Parish (1904), Victoria, KS
Rev. Jeff Ernst, O.F.M.Cap., Parochial Admin.
St. Ann Parish (1904), Victoria, KS
Rev. Jeff Ernst, O.F.M.Cap., Parochial Admin.
St. Wenceslaus Parish (1882)
Rev. Jarett Konrade, Parochial Admin. '05.
St. Fidelis Friary, Victoria, KS
Rev. Jeff Ernst, O.F.M.Cap., Guardian.
Capuchin Center for Spiritual Life, Victoria, KS
Rev. Earl Meyer, O.F.M.Cap., Dir. '60.
Nazareth Convent & Academy Corporation, Concordia, KS
Rev. James Hoover, Chap. '60.

Diocese of San Angelo

Revisions

St. Francis of Assisi (1906)
Rev. Bhaskar Morugui.
St. Mary's (1896)
Rev. Francis Njoku, Africa '97.
St. Stephen's (1982)
Rev. Joseph Prem Thumma.
St. Anthony (1948), Odessa, TX
Rev. Patrick Akpanobong.
St. Joseph (1948)
Rev. Patrick Akpanobong.
St. Lawrence (1948)
Rev. Arockiaraj Gali.

Archdiocese of San Antonio

New Listings

Future Evangelization Program for the Missions with Archbishop Gustavo Garcia Siller
Rev. David Garcia, Dir. '75.
Christus Santa Rosa Hospital - Alamo Heights 403 Treeline Park Dr., San Antonio, TX, 78209.

Revisions

Office of the Archbishop
Rev. Jonathan W. Felux, Personal Sec. to Archbishop '09.
Vocation Office
Rev. Alex Pereida, Dir. '08.
Cathedral of San Fernando (1731)
Rev. Edvin Rodriguez, Parochial Vicar '07.
St. Agnes (1923)
Rev. Jaime Renteria Torres, M.N.M.
St. Alphonsus (1925)
Rev. Horacio Florez Coicedo, Admin.
St. Ann (1912)
Rev. N. James Rutkowski, S.T.L., Admin. '77.
St. Bonaventure (1959)
Rev. Celso Tabalanza, C.I.C.M.
***Mission*— Purisima Concepcion**, San Antonio, TX
Rev. David Garcia, Admin. '75.
Holy Trinity (1987)
Rev. Martin Garcia Avila, Parochial Vicar.
St. John The Evangelist
In Res.
Rev. Raymond Schuster '93.
St. Lawrence (1959)
Rev. Tu T. Nguyen '07.
Our Lady of Perpetual Help (1913)
Rev. Daniel Cisneros '03.
St. Patrick (1895)
Rev. Andre Kazadi, C.I.C.M. '03.
St. Philip of Jesus (1914)
Rev. Steven A. Gamez '08.
St. Rose of Lima (1981)
Rev. Gonzalo Meza Razo, Parochial Vicar.
St. Stanislaus (1855)
Rev. Gabriel Kamienski, S.D.S., Parochical Vicar '82.
St. Monica (1959)
Rev. Alejandro del Bosque, L.C. '87.
St. Joseph's (1927)
Rev. Henry Clay Hunt III '09.
St. Joseph's (1897)
Rev. Robert Ploch, Poland '92.
St. Joseph's (1899)
Rev. Jose Antonio Villanueva '63.
St. Anthony's (1908), Harper, TX
Rev. Michael Peinemann, Admin.
St. Philip Benizi (1897)
Rev. Albert Lelo, C.I.C.M.
Sacred Heart of Mary (1900)
Rev. Sady Nelson Santana, Admin. '93.
Church of the Good Shepherd (1972)
Rev. Edward A. Pavlicek Jr. '83.
St. Mary's (1920), Somerset, TX
Rev. Rolando Rivera, Admin.
Purisima Concepcion, San Antonio, TX
Rev. David Garcia, Admin. '75.
Permanent Deacons
Deacon Raul Adam.
Deacon Juan A. Bosquez.
Deacon David Burkart.
Deacon Richard T. Coronado.
Deacon Leonard T. Cortinez.
Deacon Edward T. Ferguson.
Deacon Apolonio Eduardo Garcia.
Deacon Francisco D. Garcia II.

Deacon Victor Garcia.
Deacon Robert Paiz Ibarra.
Deacon Edward G. Jimenez.
Deacon John Klapuch.
Deacon Timothy Duane McCarthy.
Deacon John Patrick McGarrity.
Deacon Daniel T. McShane.
Deacon Pedro G. Nanez.
Deacon Michael Portele.
Deacon David R. Seguin.

Assumption Seminary aka Assumption-St. John's Seminary, San Antonio, TX
Rev. Jeffrey Pehl, Interim Rector '95.
Rev. Alex Pereida, Vocation Dir. '08.
Rev. Jonathan W. Felux, Dir. '09.

***Convent*— Seraphic Sisters of Our Lady of Sorrows Convent**, San Antonio, TX
Rev. Stanislaw Pieczara, S.D.S, Chap. '76.

Diocese of San Diego

New Listings

The Bellesini Foundation Funding for the education of members of the Order of St. Augustine. 1605 28th St., San Diego, CA, 92104.
Tel: 619-235-0247 ***Fax:*** 619-231-2814
Rev. Gregory Heidenblut, O.S.A., Contact Person '04.

The Tagaste Foundation Funding for the support, care and maintenance of the Order of St. Augustine. 1605 28th St., San Diego, CA, 92104.
Tel: 619-235-0247 ***Fax:*** 619-231-2814
Rev. Gregory Heidenblut, O.S.A., Contact Person '04.

The Genesis Initiative Supports development movie, television and education iniatives. P.O. Box 612, Poway, CA, 92074.
Tel: 858-748-3348
Martha Lyles, Contact Person.
Dick Lyles, Contact Person.

Revisions

Blessed Sacrament Catholic Parish (1938)
Rev. Agustin Opalalic '77.
Immaculate Conception Catholic Parish (1849)
Rev. Justin Langille '80.
Our Lady of the Rosary Catholic Parish (1925)
Rev. Joseph Tabigue, C.R.S.P. '05.
Our Mother of Confidence Catholic Parish (1964)
Rev. Msgr. Mark A. Campbell '71.
Saint Charles Catholic Parish (1946)
Rev. James Bahash '99.
Saint Therese Catholic Parish (1956)
Very Rev. Bruce J. Orsborn '81.
Saint Richard Catholic Parish (1954)
Rev. Nemesio Sungcad '76.
Sacred Heart Catholic Parish Brawley (1908)
Rev. Alexander Aquino '74.
Saint Margaret Mary Catholic Parish (1934)
Rev. Alexander Aquino '74.
Holy Trinity Catholic Parish (1903)
Rev. Alfredo Heyrosa.
Our Lady of Grace Catholic Parish (1954)
Rev. Enrique Fuentes, O.C.D.
Saint Louise de Marillac Catholic Parish (1944)
Rev. Scott A. Burnia '88.
Saint Anthony of Padua Catholic Parish Imperial (1948)
Rev. Reynaldo Roque.
Saint Pius X Catholic Parish Jamul (1956)
Rev. Victor Maristela '87.
Saint Mark Catholic Parish (1963)
Rev. Julio Castillo, C.J.M.
Rev. Dickens Remy, C.I.C.M.
Guardian Angels Catholic Parish (1962)
Rev. Kevin P. Casey, S.J. '72.
Saint Francis of Assisi Catholic Parish (1941)
Rev. Efrain Bautista '10.
On Duty Outside the Diocese
Rev. Giles Conwill '73 Xavier University, LA.
Retired
Rev. Msgr. Frederick J. Florek '64.
Rev. Msgr. Donal C. Sheehan '60.
Rev. Michael A. Cunnane '61.

Diocese of Santa Rosa in California

Revisions

Most Reverend Robert Francis Vasa, Bishop of Santa Rosa in California ordained May 22, 1976; appointed Bishop of Baker November 19, 1999; consecrated and installed January 26, 2000; appointed Coadjutor Bishop of Santa Rosa in California January 24, 2011; installed March 6, 2011; succeeded June 30, 2011.

Most Reverend Daniel F. Walsh, D.D., Retired Bishop of Santa Rosa in California ordained March 30, 1963; appointed Titular Bishop of Tigia and Auxiliary of San Francisco September 24, 1981; appointed Bishop of Reno-Las Vegas June 9, 1987; installed August 6, 1987; appointed Bishop of Las Vegas March 21, 1995; installed June 28, 1995; appointed Bishop of Santa Rosa in California on April 4, 2000; installed May 22, 2000; retired June 30, 2011.

Diocese of Savannah

Revisions

Most Reverend Gregory J. Hartmayer, O.F.M.Conv., Bishop of Savannah Catholic Pastoral Center 601 E. Liberty St., Savannah, GA, 31401-5196. ordained May 5, 1979; appointed Bishop of Savannah July 19, 2011.

Most Reverend J. Kevin Boland, D.D., Bishop Emeritus of Savannah ordained June 14, 1959; appointed Bishop of Savannah February 7, 1995; ordained and installed April 18, 1995; retired July 19, 2011.

Diocese of Shreveport

New Listings

On Sabbatical
Rev. Zacharias Prakuzhy, C.M.I., India '68.

Revisions

Vicars Forane
Very Rev. Frank Coens, O.F.M., Eastern Deanery '73.
St. Benedict the Black (1966)
Rev. Patrick J. Madden, Ph.D. '74.
St. Lucy (1935)
Rev. Patrick J. Madden, Ph.D. '74.
St. Patrick (1870)
Rev. Mark A. Watson '96.
Jesus the Good Shepherd (1958)
Rev. David T. Richter, J.C.L. '86.
Sacred Heart (1947)
Rev. Mark A. Watson '96.

Diocese of Sioux City

Revisions

Nativity of Our Lord Jesus Christ (1966)
Rev. Steven J. McLoud '94.
St. Patrick (1888)
Rev. Roger J. Linnan '62.
St. Mary's (1892)
Rev. Paul D. Bormann '85.
Sacred Heart (1868)
Rev. Randy L. Schon '88.
St. Boniface (1883)
Rev. Paul Kelly '83.
Rev. Timothy A. Friedrichsen, Parochial Vicar '84.
St. Columbkille (1886)
Rev. Donald C. Ries '59.
Annunciation (1891)
Rev. Andrew W. Hoffmann '74.
St. Joseph's (1892)
Rev. Andrew W. Hoffmann '74.
St. Marys (1947)
Rev. Paul Kelly '83.
Rev. Timothy A. Friedrichsen, Parochial Vicar '84.
St. Patrick's (1891)
Rev. Msgr. Michael D. Sernett, J.C.D., V.G. '70.
St. Augustine's (1904)
Rev. Steven W. Brodersen '85.
Sacred Heart (1881)
Rev. James J. Tigges '71.
Church of the Resurrection (1973)
Rev. Andrew Bao Vo '07.
St. Margaret's (1895)
Rev. Andrew Bao Vo '07.
Holy Angels (1874)
Rev. Steven W. Brodersen '85.
St. Louis (1923)
Rev. John J. Gerald, India '82.
Sacred Heart (1888)
Rev. Clement W. Currans '74.
St. Benedict's (1877)
Rev. Peter Duc Hung Nguyen '97.
St. Paul's (1926), Scranton, IA
Rev. Donald C. Ries '59.
St. Mary's (1914)
Rev. Brian C. Hughes '81.
Sacred Heart (1882)
Rev. Steven W. Brodersen '85.
St. Joseph's (1891)
Rev. Peter Duc Hung Nguyen '97.
Retired
Rev. Msgr. Richard E. Zenk, J.C.D. '54.
Rev. Robert P. Brown, S.T.L. '63.
Rev. Gerald F. Feierfeil '67.
Rev. Anthony Pick '67.
Rev. Dale E. Reiff '67.
Rev. James R. Smith '67.

Diocese of Spokane

Newly Ordained

Cathedral of Our Lady of Lourdes (1881)
Rev. Jeffrey Lewis, Parochial Vicar '11.
St. Thomas More (1957)
Rev. Jason Hiner, Parochial Vicar '11.
Assumption of the Blessed Virgin Mary (1953)
Rev. Jeffrey Core, Parochial Vicar '11.
Rev. Tyler Smedley, Parochial Vicar '11.
St. Francis of Assisi (1915)
Rev. Jeffrey Core, Parochial Vicar '11.
Rev. Tyler Smedley, Parochial Vicar '11.
St. Patrick (1859)
Rev. Jeffrey Core, Parochial Vicar '11.
Rev. Tyler Smedley, Parochial Vicar '11.

Revisions

Moderator of the Curia
Rev. Michael Savelesky, Ph.D. '73 ***Mailing Address:*** P.O. Box 1453, Spokane, WA, 99210-1453.
Tel: 509-358-7303
Bishop White Seminary
Rev. Steven L. Dublinski, V.G., Rector & Dir. Seminarians '85 429 E. Sharp Ave., Spokane, WA, 99202.
Tel: 509-326-3255
Web: bishopwhiteseminary.org
Detention Ministry
Rev. Miguel Mejia, Coord. '00 ***Mailing Address:*** P.O. Box 1453, Spokane, WA, 99210-1453.
Tel: 509-358-7315
Cathedral of Our Lady of Lourdes (1881)
Rev. Darrin Connall '92.
St. Ann (1902)
Rev. Patrick Baraza '82.
Assumption of the Blessed Virgin Mary (1958)
Rev. Sean Raftis, S.J., Parochial Vicar.
Sacred Heart (1958)
Rev. Matthew Nicks '08.
St. Rose of Lima (1881)
Rev. Miguel Mejia '00.
St. Joseph (1910)
Rev. Timothy Hays '96.
St. Gall (1893)
Rev. Joseph Sullivan '03.
Immaculate Conception (1861)
Rev. Kevin Oiland, Parochial Vicar '09.
Our Lady of Sorrows
Rev. Edward Marier '88.
St. Bernard, Ione, WA
Rev. Steven Werner.
Rev. Kevin Oiland, Parochial Vicar '09.
Sacred Heart of Jesus (1906), Colville, WA
Rev. Kevin Oiland, Parochial Vicar '09.
St. Joseph (1950), Metaline Falls, WA
Rev. Steven Werner.
Rev. Kevin Oiland, Parochial Vicar '09.
St. Anthony (1908)
Rev. Edward Marier '88.
Pure Heart of Mary (1898), Colville, WA, Northport, WA
Rev. Kevin Oiland, Parochial Vicar '09.
St. Catherine of Alexandria
Rev. Jose Luis Hernandez '99.
St. Patrick (1909)
Rev. Lutakome Nsubga, Parochial Vicar.
Holy Rosary (1892)
Rev. Jose Luis Hernandez '99.
Our Lady of Perpetual Help (1960), Saint John, WA
Rev. Jose Luis Hernandez '99.
Sacred Heart (1893)
Rev. Jose Luis Hernandez '99.
St. Genevieve (1907)
Rev. Matthew Nicks '08.
St. Boniface (1882)
Rev. Joseph Sullivan '03.
St. Jude (1941)
Rev. Edward Marier '88.
Assumption of the Blessed Virgin Mary (1953)
Rev. Patrick Kerst '90.
Rev. Miguel Angel Gusatvo Ruiz Juarez, Parochial Vicar '06.
St. Francis of Assisi (1915)
Rev. Miguel Angel Gusatvo Ruiz Juarez, Parochial Vicar '06.
St. Patrick (1859)
Rev. Miguel Angel Gusatvo Ruiz Juarez, Parochial Vicar '06.

Diocese of Springfield in Illinois

New Listings

Blessed Pope John Paul II
Rev. Larry Anschutz '82.

Res.: 705 E. Main St., Mount Olive, IL, 62069.
Tel: 217-999-4981 *Fax:* 217-999-4036

Revisions

Vicars Forane
Effingham Deanery
Very Rev. David J. Hoefler, V.F. '02.
Springfield Deanery
Very Rev. John Nolan, V.F. '77.
Office for Finances
Patrick Ketchum, Assoc. Dir. Insurance Fire, Extended Coverage, Vandalism, Multi-Peril Liability, Workers Compensation, Unemployment, Lay Employee Pension Plan, Priests' Personal Property, Seminarians' Medical Care and Coordinator for Diocesan Health Insurance Program.
Michael Kelly, Insurance Assoc.
Office for Finances
Clerk, Annual Catholic Svcs. Appeal
Vacant.
Blessed Sacrament (1924)
Rev. Jeffery A. Grant '82.
St. Katharine Drexel
In Res.
Rev. Paul Habing, Area Hispanic Min. '80.
St. Mary's (1858), Alton, IL
Rev. Thomas Canon, O.M.V.
St. Mary's
In Res.
Rev. David Beauregard, O.M.V.
Holy Family (1903), Petersburg, IL
Rev. James Palkudy, S.A.C.
Saints James and Patrick Parish (2007), Decatur, IL
Rev. Robert Spriggs, Parochial Admin. '65.
St. Anthony of Padua (1858)
Very Rev. David J. Hoefler, V.F. '02.
Rev. Brian C. Alford, Parochial Vicar.
Rev. Sunder Ery, Parochial Vicar.
Deacon Joseph A. Emmerich.
Sacred Heart (1892)
Very Rev. David J. Hoefler, V.F. '02.
Rev. Brian C. Alford, Parochial Vicar.
Rev. Sunder Ery, Parochial Vicar.
Deacon Joseph A. Emmerich.
St. Mary and St. Mark (2002)
Rev. William Jeffrey Holtman.
St. Elizabeth (1856)
Rev. Carlos M. Bohorquez '99.
Ascension (1886) (Croatian) [CEM] Consolidated with Holy Trinity to form Blessed Pope John Paul II, Mount Olive.
Holy Trinity (1912) (Slovak) [CEM] Consolidated with Ascension to form Blessed Pope John Paul II, Mount Olive.
St. Peter (1868)
Rev. James Palakudy, S.A.C. '78.
Immaculate Conception (1892)
Rev. Jeffrey D. Long '06.
St. Nicholas (1871)
Rev. Jeffrey D. Long '06.
St. James (1894), Troy, IL
Rev. Carlos M. Bohorquez '99.
St. John Vianney (1931)
Deacon James Guy Bollman.
Annunciation (1879)
Very Rev. David J. Hoefler, V.F. '02.
Rev. Brian C. Alford, Parochial Vicar.
Rev. Sunder Ery, Parochial Vicar.
Deacon Joseph A. Emmerich.
Illinois College Newman Catholic Community, Jacksonville, IL
Rev. Thomas C. Meyer, Chap. '98.
MacMurray College Newman Catholic Community, Jacksonville, IL
Rev. Thomas C. Meyer, Chap. '98.

Diocese of Springfield in Massachusetts

New Listings

Our Lady of the Cross 23 Sycamore St., Holyoke, MA, 01040.
Rev. Alexander B. Cymerman, O.F.M.Conv., B.A., M.Th. '65.
Rev. Stanley Sobiech, O.F.M.Conv., Parochial Vicar '62.
Res.: Blessed John Paul II Friary 71 Maple St., Holyoke, MA, 01041-4698.
Tel: 413-532-8272
Offices
Tel: 413-532-7889 *Fax:* 413-538-6754
School— **Mater Dolorosa School** Grades K-8 25 Maple St., Holyoke, MA, 01040.
Tel: 413-532-2831 *Fax:* 413-532-8588
Email: sunnyc515@aol.com
Web: www.mater-dolorosa.com
Franciscan Sisters of St. Joseph 1; Lay Teachers 19; Students 256
Catechesis/Religious Program— .
Tel: 413-532-8272
Students 115
Genesis Spiritual Life and Conference Center, Inc. 53 Mill St., Westfield, MA, 01085.
Tel: 413-536-7511
Email: kpopko@sisofprov.org
Sr. Kathleen Popko, S.P., Contact Person.

Newly Ordained

St. Jerome (1854)
Rev. Raymond Cordani, Parochial Vicar '11.
Our Lady of Guadalupe (2001)
Rev. Raymond Cordani, Parochial Vicar '11.
St. Mary's (1862)
Rev. Ryan Rooney, Parochial Vicar '11.

Revisions

St. Michael's Cathedral
In Res.
Rev. Daniel R. Foley, J.C.D. '60.
Blessed Sacrament (1953)
Rev. Jose Siesquen Flores, Peru, Parochial Vicar '88.
St. Catherine of Siena (1961)
Rev. Mark Glover, Admin. '08.
Holy Cross (1949)
Rev. Anthony F. Cullen '75.
Holy Cross
In Res.
Rev. Robert W. Thrasher, J.C.D. '62.
Our Lady of the Sacred Heart
In Res.
Rev. Robert H. Riel '80.
Sacred Heart
In Res.
Rev. Howard W. McCormick '57.
St. John the Evangelist
In Res.
Rev. John S. Lis '73.
Holy Cross (1905) Merged with Mater Dolorosa, Holyoke to form Our Lady of the Cross, Holyoke. Parish records are located at Our Lady of the Cross.
St. Jerome (1854)
Rev. William H. Lunney '94.
Mater Dolorosa (1896) (Polish) [CEM] Merged with Holy Cross Holyoke to form Our Lady of the Cross, Holyoke. Parish records are located at Our Lady of the Cross.
Our Lady of Guadalupe (2001)
Rev. William H. Lunney '94.
Our Lady of Guadalupe
In Res.
Rev. John G. Lessard-Thibodeau '92.
St. Mary's (1857)
Rev. John K. Sheaffer '93.
St. Mary's (1936)
Rev. James Longe, Parochial Vicar '07.
St. Mary (1903)
Rev. Jose Bermudez, Admin. '80.
Absent on Leave
Rev. John G. Lessard-Thibodeau '92.
Retired
Rev. Daniel R. Foley, J.C.D. '60 St. Michael's Cathedral Rectory 260 State St., Springfield, MA, 01105
Rev. Roland J. Galipeau '64 Pinevalley Plantation Belchertown, MA, 01007
Rev. Charles F. Gonet '58 Mont Marie Health Care Center 36 Lower Westfield Rd., Holyoke, MA, 01040
University of Massachusetts, Amherst, MA
Rev. Michael J. Twohig, Asst. Dir. '83.
University of Massachusetts
In Res.
Rev. John Gawienowski '00.

Diocese of Springfield-Cape Girardeau

Revisions

Social Ministry
Mr. Nicholas C. Lund-Molfese, Dir.
**Catholic Charities of Southern Missouri, Inc.* 601 S. Jefferson Ave., Springfield, MO, 65806.
Tel: 417-866-0841 *Fax:* 417-866-1140
Email: ccsomo@ccsomo.org
Mrs Maura A. Taylor, Exec. Dir.
Missionary Apostolate - Society for the Propagation of the Faith
Rev. Mark G. Boyer '76.
Tel: 417-887-4811
Cathedral of St. Agnes (1908)
Rev. James Long Hai Do, C.M.C. '10.
Cathedral of St. Agnes
In Res.
Rev. Msgr. Mark C. Ernstmann, S.T.L., M.Ed. '51.
St. Elizabeth Ann Seton (1981)
Rev. John Barasa Khaemba, Kenya, Sacramental Priest.
Holy Trinity (1906)
Rev. Thomas A. McGann, C.M.F., Sacramental Priest '76.
St. William (1946)
Rev. David L. Miller '81.
Rev. Vincent E. Bertrand, J.C.L., Sacramental Priest '87.
St. Edward, Cassville, MO
Rev. Paul J. McLoughlin '71.
Rev. John S. Braun, Sacramental Priest '87.
Sacred Heart (1908)
Rev. Scott M. Sunnenberg '02.
Rev. Vincent E. Bertrand, J.C.L., Sacramental Priest '87.
St. Mary (1938) [JC] *Mailing Address:* P.O. Box 106, Joplin, MO, 64802.
St. Peter The Apostle (1877)
Rev. Shoby Mathew Chettiyath.
St. Mary (1904)
Rev. John (J.) F. Friedel, M.A., M.Div. '86.
Rev. Shoby Mathew Chettiyath.
St. Francis De Sales (1870)
Rev. David L. Miller '81.
Rev. Vincent E. Bertrand, J.C.L., Sacramental Priest '87.
St. Lawrence (1891)
Rev. John S. Braun, Sacramental Priest '87.
St. Francis of Assisi (2004), Nixa, MO
Rev. Msgr. Thomas E. Reidy, V.G. '67.
Rev. John Barasa Khaemba, Kenya, Sacramental Priest.
St. Joseph the Worker (1961)
Rev. Saviour Nundwe '08.
SS. Peter and Paul (1892)
Rev. Peter J. Morciniec '70.
Holy Family (1978)
Rev. Mark G. Boyer, Parochial Admin. '76.
Sacred Heart (1874), Aurora, MO
Rev. Paul J. McLoughlin, Canonical Pastor '71.
Rev. John S. Braun, Sacramental Priest '87.
High School— **Springfield Catholic High School**, Springfield, MO
Rev. Mark Clarke, C.M.F.
Catholic Campus Ministry O'Reilly Catholic Student Center, Missouri State University, Drury University, Ozarks Technical Community College 847 S. Holland, Springfield, MO, 65806-3513.
Tel: 417-865-0802 *Fax:* 417-865-0895
Web: www.ccm847.org
Rev. Mark Clarke, C.M.F.

Diocese of Steubenville

Newly Ordained

St. Mary's
Rev. Michael Gossett '11.

Revisions

Diocesan Administrator
Rev. Msgr. Kurt H. Kemo, J.C.L., M.Div. '83.
Vicar General
Vacant 422 Washington St., P.O. Box 969, Steubenville, OH, 43952-5969.
Tel: 740-282-3631
Episcopal Vicar for Pastoral Planning & Personnel
Vacant 422 Washington St., P.O. Box 969, Steubenville, OH, 43952-5969.
Tel: 740-282-3631
Email: tchillog@diosteub.org
Diocesan Finance Office
Mr. James Piazza, Finance Officer (pro tem).
Triumph of the Cross, Steubenville, OH
Rev. Bradley Greer '09.
Christ the King University Parish
Rev. Msgr. Patrick Gaughan, V.F. '68.
Rev. Mark Moore, Parochial Vicar '03.
St. Paul's
Rev. Mark Moore, Parochial Vicar '03.
Corpus Christi
Rev. Chester J. Pabin '92.
St. Stephen
Rev. Chester J. Pabin '92.
St. Michael [CEM] *Mailing Address:* P.O. Box 286, Caldwell, OH, 43724.
Rev. Wayne Morris '01.
Rev. Chester J. Pabin '92.
Immaculate Conception [CEM] P.O. Box 286, Caldwell, OH, 43724.
Rev. Wayne Morris '01.
Rev. Chester J. Pabin '92.
St. Louis
Rev. Thomas F. Hamm Jr. '00.

St. Joseph
Rev. Mark Purcell.
St. Lawrence
Rev. Mark Purcell.
Sacred Heart
Rev. Timothy J. Kozak '04.
Retired
Rev. Msgr. William R. Myers '69.
Rev. Walter E. Heinz '62.
Rev. Martin J. Holler '66.

Diocese of Stockton

Revisions
Chancery Office 212 N. San Joaquin St., Stockton, CA, 95202.
Tel: 209-466-0636 ***Fax:*** 209-941-9722
Web: www.stocktondiocese.org

Diocese of Syracuse

Newly Ordained
Sacred Heart (1888)
Rev. James A. Schultz, Parochial Vicar '11.
Revisions
Asian Apostolate
Rev. John Bosco Pham Trung Thuc, Chap.
Formation for Ministry and Liturgy
Rev. Charles S. Vavonese, Dir. '73 ***Mailing Address:*** P.O. Box 511, Syracuse, NY, 13202.
Tel: 315-470-1420 ***Fax:*** 315-579-3564
Public Policy
Rev. Charles S. Vavonese, Dir. '73 240 E. Onondaga St., Syracuse, NY, 13202
Basilica of the Sacred Heart (1892)
Rev. Andrew E. Baranski, Rector '92.
Rev. Stanislaw Kardas, Poland, Parochial Vicar.
St. Brigid and St. Joseph (1926 and 1869)
Rev. John P. Fenlon '70.
St. James (1925)
Rev. John D. Manno '01.
Our Lady of Pompei/St. Peter (1924)
Rev. Daniel J. Caruso '94.
St. Mary of the Assumption (1852)
Rev. Joseph E. Scardella '81.
St. Mary of the Assumption (1887; 1913)
Rev. Thomas I. Ward '97.
St. Paul (1896)
Rev. Thomas I. Ward '97.
St. Agnes (1958)
Rev. Christopher Celentano, Admin. '08.
St. Joseph (1852)
Rev. James P. Lang, Temporary Admin. '75.
St. Agatha (1883)
Rev. Kevin Maloney '05.
St. James (1847)
Rev. Kevin J. Corcoran.
St. Michael (1928)
Rev. Christopher Celentano, Admin. '08.
St. Patrick-St. Anthony (1907)
Rev. Abraham L. Esper '85.
St. Anthony of Padua (1917)
Rev. Lucian Urbaniak '85.
St. Mary (1855)
Rev. Lucian Urbaniak '85.
Our Lady of Good Counsel (1941)
Rev. Michael Galuppi '07.
Immaculate Conception (1889)
Rev. Lukasz Kozlowski, Admin. '09.
St. Mary (1869)
Rev. Richard B. Dunn '80.
Our Lady of the Rosary (1954)
Rev. John F. Hogan Jr. '88.
St. Margaret (1908)
Rev. Paul J. Alciati, Admin. '77.
Our Lady of Peace (1935)
Rev. Amedeo G. Guida '85.
St. Joseph the Worker (1890)
Rev. Daniel J. O'Hara '87.
St. Francis Xavier (1873)
Rev. Daniel C. Muscalino, Admin. '78.
Church of Sacred Heart and St. Mary (1909)
Rev. Artur Krawczenko, Poland '03.
St. Joseph (1870)
Rev. Paul V. Carey '71.
St. Joseph (1915), Oswego, NY
Rev. Gregory J. Kreinheder, Admin. '07.
St. Mary (1848)
Rev. John F. Hogan Jr. '88.
St. Stephen the King (1908)
Rev. Gregory J. Kreinheder, Admin. '07.
St. Joseph (1849)
Rev. Lukasz Kozlowski, Admin. '09.
St. Stephen (1880)
Rev. Philip C. Brockmyre '02.
St. John the Baptist (1909)
Rev. Paul F. Angelicchio '77.
Transfiguration (1909)
Rev. Paul F. Angelicchio '77.
Retired
Rev. Msgr. John R. Madden '59.
Rev. Michael J. Carmola '64.
Rev. R. Daniel DeLorme '57.
Rev. J. Michael Donovan '65.
Rev. Stanley Dudkiewicz, Poland '52.
Rev. John E. Fetcho '64.
Rev. Vincent J. Kelly '57.
Rev. Laurence W. Kennedy '57.
Rev. Charles M. Major '59.
Rev. Richard P. Morisette '61.
Rev. James F. Quinn '58.
Rev. John J. Smegelsky '66.
Rev. Frank Young '70.
Our Lady of Lourdes Memorial Inc. 169 Riverside Dr., Binghamton, NY, 13905.
Tel: 607-798-5111 ***Fax:*** 607-798-7681
Web: lourdes.com
Daughters of Charity of St. Vincent de Paul 9; Bed Capacity 267; Patients Assisted Annually 400,000; Total Staff 1,300
Christ the King Retreat House, Syracuse, NY
Rev. Mark P. Kaminski, Ph.D., D.Min., Dir. '01.

Diocese of Trenton

New Listings
Diocese of Trenton Endowment Trust for Catholic Charities 701 Lawrenceville Rd., Trenton, NJ, 08648.

Diocese of Tulsa

New Listings
Monastery of Our Lady of the Cenacle (2010) 1132 E. 21st St. S., Tulsa, OK, 74114.
Tel: 918-749-0995
Email: cenacle@sbcglobal.net
Rev. Mark Kirby, O.S.B., Prior '86.
Priests 1; Brothers 2
Convent— **Daughters of Mary, Mother of Israel's Hope** P.O. Box 2976, Broken Arrow, OK, 74013.
St. John Auxiliary, Inc. 1923 S. Utica Ave., Tulsa, OK, 74104.
Gwen Humphrey, Pres.
Newly Ordained
Special Assignment
Rev. Jorge Gomez, Hispanic Ministry '11.
On Duty Outside the Diocese
Rev. Michael Pratt '11 Pontificio Istituto Di Spiritualita, Rome.
Revisions
Permanent Deacons
Deacon Peter Byrne.
Deacon Peter J. Faber.
Deacon Ernesto Fernandez.
Deacon Craig Gunter.
Deacon Larry E. McFadden.
Deacon Thomas Moyes.
Deacon Kevin Sartorius.
Deacon John L. Sommer.
Deacon Nelson M. Sousa.
Deacon Greg Stice.
Deacon Rick Stookey.
Deacon Dean Wersal.
Deacon Robert Wilson.
School— **San Miguel School of Tulsa, Inc.* (2004) Grades 6-8 2444 E. Admiral Blvd., Tulsa, OK, 74110.
Tel: 918-728-7337 ***Fax:*** 918-660-2040
Lay Teachers 10; Students 71
St. John Health System Foundation, Inc. (1981) 1923 S. Utica, Tulsa, OK, 74104.
Tel: 918-749-3553 ***Fax:*** 918-744-2716

Diocese of Tyler

Revisions
Office of Bishop
Vacant 1015 ESE Loop 323, Tyler, TX, 75701-9663.
Tel: 903-534-1077 ***Fax:*** 903-534-1370
Email: bishopoffice@dioceseoftyler.org
Diocesan Administrator (Not named until after Sept. 12, 2011).
Vicar General
Mrs. Terry Bolton, Admin. Asst.
Tel: 903-534-1077, Ext. 137
Email: tbolton@dioceseoftyler.org
Vice Chancellor
Rev. Robert H. (Hank) Lanik.
Cathedral of the Immaculate Conception (1987)
Rev. Brandon Bernhard, Parochial Vicar.
Cathedral of the Immaculate Conception
In Res.
Deacon Dwight (Sam) Hall.
Mission— **St. Boniface** (1997), Chandler, TX
Rev. Rafael Angel Rodriguez, Admin.
St. Boniface
In Res.
Rev. Octavio Suarez '64.
St. Francis of the Tejas (1931)
Mission— **St. Leo the Great**, Centerville, TX
Rev. Nolan Lowry, S.T.L., Admin. '10.
Station— **St. Thomas More** Hilltop Lake Chapel Fellowship Hall P.O. Box 1400, Hilltop Lakes, TX.
Tel: 936-855-2640 ***Fax:*** 936-855-2935
Rev. Nolan Lowry, S.T.L. '10.
St. Jude (1975)
Rev. Daniel L. Daugherty '94.
Mission— **St. Augustin Mission** San Augustine, TX, 75972.
Rev. James Rowland '09.
Our Lady of Guadalupe
In Res.
Rev. Jose Cortez '73.
Christ the King (1936)
Rev. Daniel Dower, Parochial Vicar '84.
Christ the King
In Res.
Rev. Matias Rodriguez '66.
St. Mary
In Res.
Rev. Mark Dunne '02.
St. Andrew (1998)
Deacon Jesus Reyes.
St. Michael (1917), Mount Pleasant, TX
Rev. Patrick Hartnett, Parochial Vicar.
Sacred Heart (1716)
Rev. James Rowland, Parochial Vicar '09.
Mission— **Our Lady of Guadalupe**, Nacogdoches, TX
Rev. Luis Alphonse Roncancio, Colombia '95.
St. Mary of the Cenacle (1918), New Boston, TX
Rev. Michael Snider, Admin.
Our Lady of Victory (1880)
Rev. Guillermo Gabriel-Maisonet, Parochial Vicar.
Holy Cross (1987), Pittsburg, TX
Rev. Christians Zelaya, Admin.
St. James (1880), Sulphur Springs, TX
Deacon Joe Ibarra Moreno.
Deacon William Flores.
Sacred Heart (1874)
Rev. Juan Carlos Rivera, Parochial Vicar.
Most Holy Trinity (1972)
Rev. Patrick Fenton, Admin. '08.
St. Theresa of the Infant Jesus (1945), Gladewater, TX
Rev. Robert H. (Hank) Lanik, Admin.
Prince of Peace (1995), Whitehouse, TX
Rev. Ariel Cortes '96.
On Duty Outside the Diocese
Rev. Thomas Edelen '01.
Hermitage (1968), Palestine, TX
Rev. Ronald G. Demski '69.
Convent— **Monastery of the Infant Jesus**, Lufkin, TX
Rev. Paul Philibert, O.P., Chap.

Diocese of Venice

Revisions
Hope for Haiti, Inc. 1021 Fifth Ave N., Naples, FL, 34102.
Tel: 239-434-7183
Email: info@hopeforhaiti.com
Web: www.hopeforhaiti.com
JoAnne Kuehner, Founder & Chair.

Diocese of Victoria in Texas

Revisions
Vicar General
Rev. Msgr. Thomas C. McLaughlin, V.G. '56 ***Mailing Address:*** P.O. Box 4070, Victoria, TX, 77903.
Tel: 361-573-0760 ***Fax:*** 361-572-8204
Diocesan Consultors
Rev. Charles Dwomoh, V.F. '86.
Vicars Forane
Cuero Deanery
Vacant St. Michael Church 302 E. Church St., Cuero, TX, 77954-2906.
Tel: 361-275-3554

Vicars Forane
Edna Deanery
Rev. Charles Dwomoh, V.F. '86.
Diocesan Tribunal 1505 E. Mesquite Ln., Victoria, TX, 77901.
Tel: 361-573-0760 ***Fax:*** 361-827-7176
Judicial Vicar
Rev. Matthew H. Huehlefeld, J.C.L.
Tel: 361-573-0760
Notaries
Irene Martinez Marler.
Priests' Personnel Board
Most Rev. David Eugene Fellhauer.
Rev. Charles Dwomoh, V.F. '86.
School Board
Mr. John Quary, Supt. Schools.
Catholic Youth Ministry
Ms. Wendy Eggert, Assoc. Youth Min. 1505 E. Mesquite Ln., P.O. Box 4070, Victoria, TX, 77901.
Tel: 361-573-0828
Respect Life-Pro Life
Rev. Tommy Chen '08 Sacred Heart P.O. Box H, Hallettsville, TX, 77964.
Tel: 361-798-5888
Scouting
Mr. Dave Kouba, District Chm. Eagle Court 202 Ruidosa, Victoria, TX, 77904.
Tel: 361-575-6693
Vietnamese Apostolate
Rev. Dominic Nguyen, C.SS.R. St. Anthony Church P.O. Box 900, Palacios, TX, 77465
Our Lady of Victory Cathedral (1957)
Deacon Lawrence Rossow.
Holy Family of Joseph, Mary & Jesus (1981)
Rev. Robert E. Knippenberg '00.
Our Lady of Lourdes (1875)
Rev. John Kollannur.
Holy Cross (1909), Bay City, TX
Rev. Gregory E. Korenek '93.
Holy Cross
In Res.
Rev. Casimir Jarzombek '60.
St. Anthony's (1930)
Rev. Augustine N. Asante '98.
St. Michael (1875), Cuero, TX
Rev. David Berger '06.
Rev. Joseph Kariuki, Parochial Vicar.
Our Lady of Guadalupe (1923)
Rev. David Berger '06.
Rev. Joseph Kariuki, Parochial Vicar.
Holy Rosary (1856)
Rev. Daniel P. Kahlich '66.
SS. Peter & Paul (1858)
Rev. David Berger, Parochial Admin. '06.
Rev. Joseph Kariuki, Sacramental Min.
SS. Peter and Paul (1897)
Rev. Daniel P. Kahlich '66.
Our Lady of the Gulf (1865)
Rev. Paul Kadamkuzhy, S.J., Parochial Vicar.
St. Rose of Lima (1889)
Rev. Edward J. Winkler '86.
SS. Cyril and Methodius
Rev. Kirby Hlavaty '99.

Archdiocese of Washington

Revisions
Equestrian Order of the Holy Sepulchre of Jerusalem - Middle Atlantic Lieutenancy U.S.A. ***Mailing Address:*** P.O. Box 5150, Arlington, VA, 22205. Franciscan Monastery of the Holy Land 1400 Quincy St., N.E., Washington, DC, 20017.
Tel: 202-526-4217 ***Fax:*** 202-526-4218
His Eminence William Cardinal Keeler, D.D., J.C.D., Grand Prior.
H.E. Ronald G. Precup, Lieutenant.

Diocese of Wheeling-Charleston

New Listings
Heralds of the Good News Missionary Society Inc. 51 Madison Ave., Madison, WV, 25130-2714.

Diocese of Wichita

Newly Ordained
Church of the Magdalen (1950)
Rev. John P. Fogliasso '11.
St. Elizabeth Ann Seton (1982)
Rev. Marco A. de Loera '11.
St. Francis of Assisi (1959)
Rev. Jeremy S. Huser '11.
St. Thomas Aquinas (1957)
Rev. Daniel J. Duling '11.

Revisions
Chancellor
Rev. John P. Lanzrath, S.T.L. '88.
Presbyteral Council/College of Consultors
Rev. John P. Lanzrath, S.T.L. '88.
Ongoing Formation of the Clergy Committee
Rev. Kenneth S. Van Haverbeke '91.
Stewardship Office
Rev. Kenneth S. Van Haverbeke, Dir. '91.
Office of Faith Formation
Rev. C. Jarrod Lies, Dir. '01 424 N. Broadway, Wichita, KS, 67202.
Tel: 316-269-3946
Youth and Young Adult Ministry
Ms. Christine Edmonds, Prog. Coord. 424 N. Broadway, Wichita, KS, 67202.
Tel: 316-269-3930
Religious Education Office
Ms. Shelly Bole, Prog. Coord. Catechist Formation & Special Projects 424 N. Broadway, Wichita, KS, 67202.
Tel: 316-269-3940 ***Fax:*** 316-269-3967
Mission Office
Sr. Ursula Fotovich, C.S.J., Prog. Coord. 424 N. Broadway, Wichita, KS, 67202.
Tel: 316-269-3946
Totus Tuus and College Outreach
Lisa Sharp, Prog. Coord. 424 N. Broadway, Wichita, KS, 67202.
Tel: 316-440-1732
Retreats
Rev. Kenneth S. Van Haverbeke, Dir. '91 Spiritual Life Center 7100 E. 45th St. N., Wichita, KS, 67226.
Tel: 316-744-0167
Cathedral of the Immaculate Conception (1887)
Res.: 442 N. Emporia, Wichita, KS, 67202.
Tel: 316-263-6574 ***Fax:*** 316-201-1306
Email: stmarys@cathedral.kscoxmail.com
Web: www.wichitacathedral.com
St. Anne
In Res.
Rev. Michael M. Simone, S.T.L. '03.
Christ the King
In Res.
Rev. Benjamin S. Sawyer '09.
Church of the Resurrection (1965)
Rev. James F. Weldon '98.
St. Elizabeth Ann Seton (1982)
Rev. Sherman A. Orr '91.
St. Vincent de Paul (1955)
Rev. Kent A. Hemberger '88.
Sacred Heart (1886)
Rev. Ruben Ortiz-Montelongo '07.
St. Joseph (1934)
Rev. Roger S. Lumbre '86.
Holy Name of Jesus (1878)
Rev. Robert K. Spencer '85.
St. Francis Xavier's (1871)
Rev. Andrew Heiman '05.
St. Mary (1954)
Rev. David J. Lies '98.
Sacred Heart (1891)
Rev. Thomas J. Stroot, Admin. '70.
St. Michael (1925)
Rev. Roger S. Lumbre '86.
St. Andrew (1869)
Rev. Andrew Heiman '05.
St. Patrick (1885)
Rev. John P. Lanzrath, S.T.L., Admin. '88.
St. Bridget of Sweden (1985)
Rev. Dwight J. Birket '72.
Holy Trinity (1885)
Rev. Robert K. Spencer '85.
St. Paul (1927)
Rev. Robert K. Spencer '85.
St. Joseph (1880)
Rev. Dwight J. Birket '72.
Our Lady of Lourdes (1881)
Rev. Michael E. Baldwin '83.
St. Anthony/St. Rose, Wellington, KS
Rev. Lawrence D. Carney III '07.
On Duty Outside the Diocese
Rev. Daniel S. Lorimer '04.
Rev. Charles F. Seiwert, J.C.L. '99.
Temporary Leave of Absence
Rev. Benjamin D. Shockey '04.
Retired
Rev. Wayne L. Schmid '68 1408 S. Gasaway Dr., Derby, KS, 67037
Newman University, Wichita, KS
Rev. Michael Linnebur, Chap. '08.
High School— **Bishop Carroll Catholic High School** (1964), Wichita, KS
Rev. Benjamin S. Sawyer, Chap. '09.
Via Christi Hospital on North St. Francis, Wichita, KS
Rev. Yancey O. Burgess, Chap. '10.
Via Christi Hospital on Harry Street, Wichita, KS
Rev. Douglas L. Campbell, J.C.L., Chap. '76.
Spiritual Life Center, Wichita, KS
Rev. Kenneth S. Van Haverbeke, Dir. '91.

Diocese of Winona

Revisions
Vicar General
Very Rev. Richard M. Colletti '78 ***Mailing Address:*** 55 W. Sanborn St., P.O. Box 588, Winona, MN, 55987.
Tel: 507-454-4643 ***Fax:*** 507-454-8106
Email: rcolletti@dow.org

Diocese of Youngstown

New Listings
Office of Parish Planning Reconfiguration
Rev. Nicholas R. Shori, Dir. '74.
Holy Trinity Parish (2011)
Rev. Peter Haladej, Admin. '02.
Office & Mailing Address: 512 Monroe St., East Liverpool, OH, 43920.
Tel: 330-385-7131 ***Fax:*** 330-385-3025
Email: immconc01@comcast.net
School— Grades PreK-8 335 W. 5th St., East Liverpool, OH, 43920.
Tel: 330-385-5963 ***Fax:*** 330-385-6455
Email: ygnaloysius@doy.org
Web: www.staloysius.k12.oh.us
Donna Hall, Librarian.
Lay Teachers 10; Students 86
Catechesis/Religious Program— .
Tel: 330-385-6455
Mr. Robert Barto, D.R.E. (H.S. refer to Immaculate Conception Church, Wellsville).
Students 68
Worship Sites
St. Aloysius Church (1838) 235 W. 5th St., East Liverpool, OH, 43920.
Immaculate Conception Church (1842) 1021 Riverside Ave., Wellsville, OH, 43968.
Holy Family Parish (2011)
Rev. Michael D. Seifert '84.
Rev. Edward L. Beneleit '74.
Church: 216 Wooster St. E., Navarre, OH, 44662.
Catechesis/Religious Program—
Students 49
Worship Sites
St. Clement Church (1832)
St. Therese Church (1928) 456 Wabash Ave., S., Brewster, OH, 44613.
Christ Our Savior Parish (2011)
Rev. Bernard R. Bonnot '67.
Rev. Bernard N. Gaeta '73.
Deacon John Terranova.
Res.: 250 N. Bridge St., Struthers, OH, 44471.
Tel: 330-755-2115
Parish Office 764 5th St., Struthers, OH, 44471-1704.
Tel: 330-755-9819 ***Fax:*** 330-755-9949
School— Grades K-8 762 5th St., Struthers, OH, 44471-1702.
Tel: 330-755-2128
Lay Teachers 15; Students 151
Catechesis/Religious Program— .
Tel: 330-755-6245
Miss Stephanie Tarajcak, D.R.E.
Students 371
Worship Sites
St. Nicholas Church
Holy Trinity Church 250 N. Bridge St., Struthers, OH, 44471.

Newly Ordained
St. Joseph (1862)
Rev. Ernesto Rodriguez '11.
Mother of Sorrows (1890), Ashtabula, OH
Rev. Ernesto Rodriguez '11.
Our Lady of Mt. Carmel (1897)
Rev. Ernesto Rodriguez '11.
St. Charles Borromeo (1926)
Rev. Michael Marcelli '11.
St. Paul (1845)
Rev. Stephen Zeigler '11.
SS. Cyril and Methodius (1928)
Rev. Jeffrey Stealey '11.
St. James (1947)
Rev. Jeffrey Stealey '11.

Revisions
Tribunal
Staff
Rev. Martin Celuch '03.
Office of Catholic Schools
Dr. Nicholas Wolsonovich, Acting Supt.

Mary Fiala, Asst. Supt. Curriculum, Accreditation & Personnel.
Mr. Randal Rair, Asst. Supt. Govt. Progs., Athletics & Institutional Advancement.
Dr. Michael Skube, Asst. to Bishop for Regl. School Planning & High School Bd. Devel.
University Parish Newman Center (Kent State)
Rev. Steven J. Agostino, S.J., Pastor '93.
St. Christine (1953)
Rev. Christopher Cicero '10.
SS. Cyril and Methodius (1896)
Rev. Msgr. Peter M. Polando, J.C.L. '80.
St. Stephen of Hungary (1905)
Rev. Joseph Rudjak '00.
St. Joseph (1854)
Rev. Maciej Mankowski '01.
Regina Coeli (1958)
Rev. Howard Ziemba '79.
St. Joseph (1862)
Rev. Raymond J. Thomas '72.
Mother of Sorrows (1890), Ashtabula, OH
Rev. Raymond J. Thomas '72.
Our Lady of Mt. Carmel (1897)
Rev. Raymond J. Thomas '72.
St. Therese (1928) [JC] Merged with St. Clement, Navarre to form Holy Family Parish, Navarre.
St. John the Baptist (1919)
Rev. Joseph Ruggieri '95.
Rev. Shawn Conoboy '06.
St. Joseph the Provider (1919)
Rev. Joseph Ruggieri '95.
Rev. Shawn Conoboy '06.
School—
Rev. Michael Swierz, Pres. '85.
St. Lucy (1937)
Rev. Joseph Ruggieri '95.
Rev. Shawn Conoboy '06.
St. Rose of Lima (1961), Campbell, OH
Rev. Joseph Ruggieri '95.
Rev. Shawn Conoboy '06.
St. Peter (1845)
Rev. Edward L. Beneleit '74.
Rev. John Sheridan '10.
Saint Mary/Saint Frances Cabrini (2008)
Rev. Philip Miller '77.
St. Aloysius (1838) (Irish) [CEM] Merged with Immaculate Conception, Wellsville to form Holy Trinity Parish, East Liverpool.
St. Joseph Calasanctius (1858)
Rev. Charles Poore '89.
University Parish Newman Center (1953)
Rev. Steven J. Agostino, S.J. '93.
St. Andrew Bobola (1936)
Rev. Charles Poore '89.
Sacred Heart of Mary (1833)
Rev. Nicholas Mancini '75.
Our Lady of the Holy Rosary (1867)
Rev. John Jerek, Admin. '88.
St. Joseph (1850)
Rev. Howard Ziemba '79.
St. Mary (1870)
Rev. Thomas P. Kraszewski '97.
St. Clement (1832) [CEM] Merged with St. Therese, Brewster to form Holy Family Parish, Navarre.
St. Mary and St. Joseph Parish (1923)
Rev. Donald L. Feicht, Admin. '70.
Rev. Thomas Ungashick '76.
Holy Family (1956)
Rev. Martin Celuch '03.
St. Ann (1908)
Rev. Maciej Mankowski '01.
Holy Trinity (1907) (Slovak) Merged with St. Nicholas, Struthers to form Christ Our Savior Parish, Struthers.
St. Nicholas (1865) Merged with Holy Trinity, Struthers to form Christ Our Savior Parish, Struthers.
St. James (1947)
Rev. James P. Walker '77.
Immaculate Conception (1842) [CEM] Merged with St. Aloysius, East Liverpool to form Holy Trinity Parish, East Liverpool.
***High School*— Cardinal Mooney High School** (1956), Youngstown, OH
Rev. Gerald DeLucia, Chap. '78.

Eparchy of Newton (Melkite-Greek Catholic)

Revisions

Most Reverend Nicholas James Samra, D.D., Bishop of Newton; ordained May 10, 1970; appointed Auxiliary Bishop of Newton June 29, 1989; appointed fifth Bishop of Newton June 15, 2011; enthroned August 23, 2011. ***Mailing Address:*** 32406 Barclay Square, Warren, MI 48093.

Metropolitan Archeparchy of Philadelphia Ukrainian

Revisions

Protopresbyters (Deans)
Very Rev. Robert Hitchens, Washington '94.
St. Nicholas
Rev. Oleksandr Dumenko, Ukraine '01.
Assumption of B.V.M. (1908)
Rev. Ivan Turyk '03.
St. Stephen's, Toms River, NJ
Rev. Oleksandr Dumenko, Ukraine '01.
SS. Peter and Paul (1920), Cherry Hill, NJ
Rev. Ruslan Romanyuk, Admin. '09.
Assumption of B.V.M., Mount Carmel, PA
Rev. Archpriest Michael Hutsko, Admin. '84.
Patronage of the Mother of God (1911), Shamokin, PA
Rev. Stepan Bilyk, Admin. '01.
SS. Peter and Paul (1891)
Rev. Archpriest Michael Hutsko '84.
St. Nicholas, Shenandoah, PA
Rev. Msgr. Myron Grabowsky, Admin. '67.
St. Michael's (1884)
Rev. Msgr. Myron Grabowsky '67.
SS. Peter and Paul (1905), Scranton, PA
Rev. Paul Wolensky, Admin. '94.
Annunciation of the Blessed Virgin Mary (1925), Silver Spring, MD
Rev. Volodymyr Baran, Admin.
St. John the Baptist (1966), Silver Spring, MD
Rev. Volodymyr Baran, Admin.
Retired
Rev. Roman Dubitsky '65.
***Convent*— Provincial Motherhouse of the Sisters of St. Basil the Great**, Fox Chase Manor, PA
Very Rev. Archpriest Daniel Troyan, Chap. '82.

Eparchy of St. Maron of Brooklyn

New Listings

Heart of Jesus Catholic Church 1800 N.E. 6th Ct., Fort Lauderdale, FL, 33304.
Chorbishop Michael G. Thomas, J.C.D., Admin. '83.

Revisions

Mission—
Rev. Naji Kiwan, Admin.
St. Joseph (1919)
Rev. Anthony J. Salim.
St. Ann (1905)
Rev. Georges Bouchaaya, M.L.M.
Our Lady of Lebanon (1975), Waterbury, CT
Rev. Danny Abi-Akar, Admin. '10.
Mary Mother of Light Maronite Mission
Rev. Jorge Perales, Admin. '78.
St. Theresa (1932), Brockton, MA
Rev. Tony Mouannes, Admin. '05.
Our Lady of Victory (1902)
Rev. Simon Elhajj, Parochial Vicar.
St. Maron (1862)
Rev. Vincent Farhat, Admin. '10.
St. George (1927)
Rev. Nadim Helou, M.L.M.
St. Anthony + St. George (1911)
Rev. Hanna Karam '01.
On Sabbatical
Rev. Msgr. Ronald Beshara '71.
Rev. Joseph G. Akiki '87.

Diocese of Mayaguez, Puerto Rico

Revisions

Most Reverend Alvaro Corrada del Rio, S.J., Bishop of Mayaguez ordained July 6, 1974; appointed Auxiliary Bishop of Washington DC May 30, 1985; consecrated August 4, 1985; on assignment, as Apostolic Administrator, Diocese of Caguas; appointed Bishop of Tyler December 5, 2000; installed January 30, 2001; appointed Bishop of Mayaguez, Puerto Rico July 6, 2011. ***Mailing Address:*** P.O. Box 2272, Mayaguez, PR, 00681.
Most Reverend Ulises Aurelio Casiano Vargas, D.D., Bishop Emeritus of Mayaguez ***Res.:*** P.O. Box 2272, Mayaguez, PR, 00681.
Tel: 787-831-2942; 787-833-5411 (Office) ordained May 30, 1967; appointed Bishop March 4, 1976; ordained April 30, 1976; retired July 6, 2011.

Religious Institutes of Men

New Listings

Brothers of the Holy Spirit - Cleveland
General Motherhouse: Holy Spirit Monastery 4150 Rabbit Run Dr., Brooklyn, OH, 44144.
Tel: 216-741-3653
Email: brotherdale@catholicweb.com
Bro. Dale Sefcik, B.H.S., Supr.
Bro. David Robert, B.H.S., Community Councilor.
Brothers of the Holy Spirit Cleveland. Represented in the Ukrainian Catholic Diocese of St. Josaphat in Parma.
Institute of the Incarnate Word
General Motherhouse: Province of the Immaculate Conception of the Institute of the Incarnate Word 113 E. 117th St., New York, NY, 10035.
Rev. Gustavo Javier Nieto, I.V.E., Provincial Supr.
Represented in the Archdiocese of New York.

Revisions

Franciscan Missionary Brothers of the Sacred Heart of Jesus
(1927) ***Motherhouse:*** Our Lady of Angels Monastery 265 Saint Joseph Hills Rd., Pacific, MO, 63069.
Tel: 636-587-3661
Mailing Address: Box 550, Eureka, MO, 63025.
Bro. John A. Spila, O.S.F., Dir. Gen. Legal Holdings or Titles: The Black Madonna Shrine and Grottos (Our Lady of Czestochowa); St. Joseph Hill Infirmary, Inc.; Price Memorial, Eureka, MO; Merkle-Knipprath Nursing Home and Apartment Community, Clifton, MO.; Represented in the Archdiocese of St. Louis and in the Diocese of Joliet.
Brothers 8
Priests of the Congregation of Holy Cross
Res.: Provincial House 1304 E. Jefferson Blvd., South Bend, IN, 46617.
Rev. David T. Tyson, C.S.C., Prov. Supr. '75.
Rev. Kenneth M. Molinaro, C.S.C., First Asst. Prov. & Vicar '76.
Rev. Anthony V. Szakaly, C.S.C., Second Asst. Prov. '92.
Rev. Edwin H. Obermiller, C.S.C., Third Asst. Prov. '96.
Priests of Holy Cross, Indiana Province, Inc.
Properties owned, sponsored or staffed: College Seminary; Theological Seminary; Novitiate; Mission Center; Provincial House; Postulate; Universities 2; High Schools 1; Parishes 12; Chaplaincies 17; Publishing House; Retreat House.
Represented in the Archdioceses of Anchorage, Baltimore, Chicago, Detroit, Los Angeles, Military Service, USA, New Orleans, New York, Portland in Oregon, San Antonio, San Francisco and Washington and in the Dioceses of Bridgeport, Cleveland, Colorado Springs, Erie, Fall River, Fort Wayne-South Bend, Gary, Kalamazoo, Monterey, Oakland, Phoenix, San Bernardino and San Jose.
Fathers 287; Professed Clerics 4; Temporary Professed Clerics 32; Novices 20; Candidates 47; Professed Brothers 14 **Provincial Councilors:** Rev. William Beauchamp, C.S.C. '82; Rev. Thomas E. Blantz, C.S.C. '60; Rev. Peter A. Jarret, C.S.C. '92; Rev. Charles W. Kohlerman, C.S.C. '73; Rev. William M. Lies, C.S.C. '94; Rev. Michael C. Mathews, C.S.C. '99; Rev. James E. McDonald, C.S.C. '84; Rev. Francis J. Murphy, C.S.C. '86; Rev. Neil F. Wack, C.S.C. '04
(1987) ***Puerto Rico Province - Society of Jesus:*** Urb. Santa Maria 1940 Calle Sauco, San Juan, PR, 00927-6718.
Tel: 787-765-3814 ***Fax:*** 787-758-4145
Rev. Mario A. Torres, S.J., Reg. Supr. '01.
Rev. John F. Talbot, S.J., Exec. Asst. to Reg. Supr. '59.
Rev. Baudillo Guzman, S.J., Exec. Treas. '91.
Rev. Alvaro Velez, S.J., Auditor '71.
Properties owned, sponsored or staffed: Parishes 3; High Schools 1; Residences 2; Campus Ministry Centers 1.
Represented in the Archdiocese of San Juan and in the Dioceses of Fajardo-Humacao, Mayaguez, and Palm Beach.
Fathers 17; Scholastics 7
Atlantic Province: Society of the Precious Blood, Atlantic Province 1261 Highland Ave., Rochester, NY, 14620.
Tel: 585-461-0318
Provincial House 13313 Niagara Pkwy., Niagara Falls, ON, L2E 6S6, Canada.
Tel: 905-382-1118
Very Rev. Jeffrey Finley, C.PP.S., Provincial Dir. '90.
Rev. James Reposkey, C.PP.S., Vice Provincial.
Rev. Peter Nobili, C.PP.S., Treas.
Rev. Ronald Wiecek, C.PP.S., Sec. '71.
Rev. John A. Colacino, C.PP.S., Council Member '80.
Rev. Brendan Doherty, C.PP.S., Council Member.
Represented in the Archdioceses of Boston and Miami and in the Dioceses of Albany and Rochester. Also in Canada.
Priests in the U.S. 4

United States Conference of Catholic Bishops

Revisions

Diocesan Fiscal Management Conference ***National Office:*** P.O. Box 60210, San Angelo, TX, 76906.
716 S. Koenigheim St., San Angelo, TX, 76903-6709.
Tel: 877-709-3362 ***Fax:*** 800-455-9859
Email: lesmaiman@dfmconf.org
Mindful of their special ministry in the Roman Catholic Church as the extension of the Diocesan Bishop in fiscal matters, the members of the DFMC unite to be of service to the Church in the ministry of fiscal management.; In particular, this organization promotes the spiritual growth of its members; promotes financial and administrative knowledge and expertise in service to the local and national Church; facilitates the free exchange of ideas and information, and serves as a liaison among the fiscal managers of the Dioceses and Archdioceses of the Church.

Catholic Library Association 205 W. Monroe St., Ste. 314, Chicago, IL, 60606-5061.
Email: cla@cathla.org
Web: www.cathla.org
Malachy R. McCarthy, Pres.

National Service Committee of the Catholic Charismatic Renewal of the United States, Inc., Locust Grove, VA
Rev. Robert E. Hogan, B.B.D., Chm. '83.

Religious Institutes of Women

Revisions

Dominican Sisters of Our Lady of the Springs of Bridgeport Founded April 2, 2009 in Bridgeport CT.
Ministry in education at all levels; nursing home pastoral care.; Represented in the Archdioceses of Hartford and New York and the Dioceses of Bridgeport and Pittsburgh. ***Motherhouse:*** Sacred Heart Convent 21 Schuyler Ave., Stamford, CT, 06902-3759.
Tel: 203-588-0707; 203-562-9202; 203-773-4421
Sr. Melanie Hannigan, O.P., Prioress. Dominican Sisters of Our Lady of the Springs of Bridgeport, Inc.
Total in Congregation 22

St. Lucy Filippini Province: Villa Walsh, Morristown, NJ, 07960-4928.
Tel: 973-538-2886 Ministry in the field of Religious and Academic Education in elementary and secondary schools; Child Care Centers; Parish Ministry; Pastoral Care; Foreign Mission Work; House of Prayer; Retreat House.; Properties owned and sponsored: Villa Walsh, Morristown, NJ; Villa Victoria, Trenton, NJ; St. Joseph by The Sea, South Mantoloking, NJ.; Represented in the Archdioceses of Hartford, Newark, Philadelphia and Santa Fe, and in the Dioceses of Brooklyn, Cleveland, Camden, Metuchen, Orlando, Paterson, Pittsburgh, Providence, Scranton and Trenton.
Total in Community 220